HOW TO GET
EQUIPMENT
FOR
DISABILITY

The Disabled Living Foundation would like to acknowledge the generous
sponsorship of the Nuffield Provincial Hospitals Trust.

Legal responsibility. The Disabled Living Foundation takes no legal responsibility for information contained in this book. Every effort has been made to ensure that legislation is cited correctly, and interpreted reasonably. However, users of the book are advised to consult source legislation themselves.

Practice. In a number of areas of equipment provision, local practice varies. The book intends to provide a useful outline, within which local details can be supplied by the local user of the book.

Currency. Rapidly changing legislation and practice always presents a problem for a publication of this nature. The book attempts to anticipate future change. It should be noted:

– the NHS and Community Care Bill is now the NHS and Community Care Act 1990: the sections (clauses in the Bill), referred to, are not yet (July 1990) in force, nor is it known exactly when they will be;

– the two draft Housing (England and Wales) Circulars referred to, on renovation and disabled facilities grants, are now Circulars DoE 12/90 (renovation) and joint Circular DoE 10/90, LAC(90)7 (disabled facilities) and are in force;

– family practitioner committees (England/Wales) are replaced by family health services authorities in September 1990 (SI 1990/1330);

– the Children Act 1989 (s.17, not yet in force), not referred to in the text, will affect the legislative basis for welfare duties of social services departments (England and Wales) in relation to children with disabilities;

– the sections (4(a) and (c), 5 and 6) of the Disabled Persons (Northern Ireland Act 1989, referred to in the text, as yet not in force, may come into force in April 1991, resources permitting.

July, 1990

HOW TO GET
EQUIPMENT
FOR
DISABILITY

COMPILED BY MICHAEL MANDELSTAM

foreword by Professor Lord McColl

Jessica Kingsley Publishers and Kogan Page

for

The Disabled Living Foundation

First published in 1990 by
Jessica Kingsley Publishers Ltd
118 Pentonville Road
London N1 9JN
and
Kogan Page Ltd
120 Pentonville Road
London N1 9JN
for
The Disabled Living Foundation
380–384 Harrow Road
London W9 2HU

ISBN 1 85302 095 8

British Library Cataloguing in Publication Data
Mandelstam, Michael 1956—
    How to get equipment for disability
    1. Great Britain. Equipment for physically
    handicapped persons
    I. Title

    ISBN 1 85302 095 8

Typeset by Invicta, Folkestone, Kent
Printed and bound by
Biddles Ltd, Guildford and Kings Lynn.

Contents

The freedom to look after your own financial affairs -FREE from NatWest
See for yourself

Large print correspondence, specialist inform-ation, Rapid Cash Till and Servicetill details.

Large cheque book and writing template. Tape service. Many services to personal customers also available in Braille.

The Service is FREE through over 3000 Branches.
For more details call in at your local NatWest Branch, telephone 071-480 2285

or write to: General Administration Services National Westminster Bank PLC 1 Prescot Street, London E1 8RN

Our booklet 'Make NatWest Work For You', will tell you all we can do for you.

Bank with NatWest and bank on a better service.

☢ NatWest The Action Bank

Foreword

If people with disabilities are to have the same chance as the rest of us, solutions must be found to the many daily living problems which they have to face.

Equipment and home adaptations can solve many of these problems. However, the system of provision is very confusing, and, on the horizon, are radical reforms relating to community care, hospital trusts, GP contracts, housing renovation grants, and the wheelchair service.

How to get equipment for disability is the first book to attempt to give an overview of this area of provision, in order to guide prescribers, policy makers and consumers through a complicated maze of diverse legislation and practice. Such an overview also allows, for example, professionals in one field to become aware of how others in different fields work. This is vital if efficient and appropriate referral between services is to take place.

The book will also help policy makers to plan and target services, supplies officers to rationalise ordering procedures and suppliers and manufacturers to identify the market and to ensure that people with disabilities receive the equipment which they need.

The short introductions and flow charts which precede each chapter will make it easy for these different groups to find the information they need.

Most of us will be disabled to a greater or lesser extent before we die. This may goad people on to help if they find altruism alone does not motivate them.

McColl of Dulwich

The Rt Hon Lord McColl of Dulwich,
Professor of Surgery and Chairman of the United Medical and Dental Schools of Guy's and St Thomas's Hospitals, London.

The Disabled Living Foundation

The Disabled Living Foundation (DLF) is a national charity providing practical, up-to-date advice and information on all aspects of living with disability for disabled people and their carers. It offers information via: a telephone/letter enquiry service staffed by professional advisers; a subscription service to statutory and voluntary organisations and to individuals working with disabled people; and DLF-DATA, the computerised information system of the DLF, to which organisations dealing with enquiries from the general public can subscribe for on-line access. Two specialist services provide advice on clothing and footwear and on incontinence. The equipment centre of the DLF's London headquarters, which is staffed by a team of professional advisers, displays a comprehensive range of equipment for disabled people of all ages. The Foundation also has a reference library, publishes books and resource papers, and offers conferences and training for both professional and voluntary sector workers.

Acknowledgements

This book is essentially a compilation of information. In order to effect this compilation, it has been necessary to request extensive information in various forms from a large number of people and organisations. I am most grateful to all of these. All errors and other infelicities are mine.

Without the generous support of the Nuffield Provincial Hospitals Trust, which has funded the work, the book would not have been possible.

From the outset, a number of people have variously and generously supplied general advice, help with specific problems, comment on parts of the text, and encouragement. They have functioned as an advisory core: Virginia Beardshaw (health policy analyst, King's Fund Institute); Diana de Deney (DLF editor); Lady Hamilton (DLF Trustee, former chairman of the board of trustees); Mrs Sheila Holden (retired Department of Health principal officer); Dr John Hunter (consultant in rehabilitation medicine, Edinburgh); Mr Brian Jones (assistant under-secretary of social services, Association of Metropolitan Authorities); Dr Monnica Stewart (vice-chairman, DLF board of trustees, retired community physician); PHS2 Division: Department of Health.

Sheila Holden and Diana de Deney have, in particular, given sustained and detailed help with the text.

All the DLF information advisers (past and present) (particularly Tina Stevens, Sue Clements, Ann Silvester, Wendy Prince), and special advisers at the DLF (Ginny Jenkins, Dorothy Mandelstam, Christine Norton (ACA)) have patiently made available their wide subject knowledge and experience; whilst Philippa Lane and Jayne Parkin in the DLF library have provided an exemplary service. The DLF company secretary, Richard Paget, has supported administratively; and a number of other staff have done so generally.

Both the Northern Ireland Council on Disability and Joanna Clark (Disabled Living Centre, Musgrave Park Hospital) organised contact with various professionals and policy makers in Northern Ireland; as did Disability Scotland in Scotland.

Many organisations contributed in different ways by providing information, documents, and by reading draft chapters of the book. This has often involved time-consuming and detailed work, which, given the number of organisations involved, cannot be itemised here. I can only re-iterate my thanks in general.

Advisory Centre for Education
Aids to Communication in Education Centre (Oxford)
Artificial Limb and Appliance Centre, Aberdeen Royal Infirmary
Association of British Dispensing Opticians
Association of Continence Advisers
Association of County Councils

Association of Directors of Social Services
Association of Metropolitan Authorities
Avon County Council (education, social services)
Belfast Education and Library Board (special education)
Borders Regional Council (social work)
British Colostomy Association
British Diabetic Association
British Medical Association
British Paediatric Association
British Red Cross Society
Buckinghamshire County Council (social services)
CALL project (Scotland)
Cancer Relief Macmillan Fund
Central Regional Council (social work)
Chailey Heritage Hospital
Chartered Society of Physiotherapy (various groups)
Cheyne Centre for Children with Cerebral Palsy
City of Birmingham Metropolitan District Council (social services)
City of Liverpool (social services)
Cleveland County Council (social services)
College of Occupational Therapists (community, paediatric groups)
College of Speech Therapists
Common Services Agency
Communication Aids (Advice) Centres (various)
Convention of Scottish Local Authorities
Cumbria County Council (social services)
Department of Education Northern Ireland
Department of Education and Science (Special Education, and Inspectorate)
Department of Environment
Department of Health (various divisions including library)
Department of Health and Social Services Northern Ireland (various divisions
    including library and in particular the Elderly Care and Physically
    Handicapped Branch)
Department of Medical Physics and Bio-Engineering, Raigmore Hospital,
    Highland Health Board
Disabled Living Centres Council
Disablement Services Authority (DSA) (Russell Square, London)
DSA, Oxfordshire Region
DSA, South East Thames Region
DSA, Trent Region
DSA West Midland
DSA, Yorkshire Region
Disability Scotland (formerly Scottish Council on Disability)
Dorset County Council (social services)
Dudley Metropolitan Borough Council (social services)
Dumfries and Galloway Regional Council (social work)
Dundee Limb Fitting Centre
Durham County Council (social services)
East Dyfed Health Authority (community services)
East Sussex County Council (social services)
Eastern Health and Social Services Board (health and social services)
Employment Service

English National Board for Nursing, Midwifery and Health Visiting (Education officer, district nursing)
Grampian Health Board (Limb and Appliance Centre)
Grampian Regional Council (social work)
Grimsby Health Authority
Habinteg Housing Association (London)
Habinteg Housing Association (Ulster) Ltd
Hampshire County Council (social services)
Hampstead DHA (various professionals)
Health Visitors' Association
Hertfordshire County Council (social services)
Highland Regional Council (education, social services)
HMSO Books
Huntingdonshire District Council
Ileostomy Association
Independent Schools Information Service
Institution of Environmental Health Officers
King's Fund Institute (library, and other staff)
Kirklees Metropolitan Council (social services)
Leeds County Council (social services)
Leicestershire City Council (housing department)
Leicestershire County Council (social services)
Leonard Cheshire Foundation
London Borough of Barnet (social services)
London Borough of Camden (social services)
London Borough of Hammersmith and Fulham (social services, housing services)
London Borough of Harrow (social services)
London Borough of Islington (social services)
London Borough of Merton (social services)
London Borough of Newham (social services)
London Borough of Richmond upon Thames (social services)
London Borough of Tower Hamlets (social services)
London Borough Waltham Forest (education)
London Borough of Wandsworth (social services)
Lothian Health Board (various professionals, including consultant in rehabilitation medicine at Astley Ainslie Hospital)
Lothian Regional Council (social work)
Margaret Blackwood Association
Marie Curie Memorial Foundation
Mary Marlborough Lodge, Nuffield Orthopaedic Centre, Oxford
Medical Aid Department (Red Cross), Leicester
Mersey Regional Health Authority
Musgrave Park Hospital (Northern Ireland) (Regional Disablement Services, including, in particular, Disabled Living Centre)
National Association of Health Authorities
National Deaf Children's Society
National Federation of Kidney Patients' Associations
National Information Forum
National Pharmaceutical Association
National Toy Libraries Association
North Eastern Education and Library Board (special education)

North West Thames Regional Health Authority
Northallerton Health Authority (HAS report)
Northern Health and Social Services Board
Northern Ireland Central Services Agency
Northern Ireland Council on Disability
Northern Ireland Housing Executive
Northern Regional Health Authority
Optical Information Council
Orkney Islands Council
Oxfordshire County Council (social services)
Oxfordshire Health Authority (community occupational therapy)
Possum Controls Limited
Powys Health Authority (community nursing)
Registered Nursing Home Association
Rotherham Metropolitan Borough Council (social services)
Royal College of General Practitioners
Royal College of Nursing (various specialist advisers)
Royal College of Physicians
Royal Hospital and Home, Putney
Royal Marsden Hospital
Royal National Institute for the Blind
Royal National Institute for the Deaf
Sandwell Metropolitan District Council (social services)
Scottish Development Department (SDD)
Scottish Education Department
Scottish Home and Health Department (various divisions, including library)
Shetland Islands Council (social work)
Shropshire County Council (social services)
Social Work Services Group (Scottish Office)
Society of Chiropodists
Society of Family Practitioner Committees
Somerset County Council (social services)
South Eastern Education and Library Board (special education)
South West Thames Regional Health Authority
South Western Regional Health Authority
Southampton General Hospital (Professor in Rehabilitation Medicine)
Southern Education and Library Board (special education)
Southern Health and Social Services Board
Spastics Society
Strathclyde Regional Council (education, social work)
Surrey County Council (social services)
Tayside Regional Council (education, social work)
Warwickshire County Council (social services)
Welsh Office (various divisions including library)
West Sussex County Council (social services)
Western Education and Library Board (special education)
Western Health and Social Services Board
Western Isles Council (social work)
Wigan Health Authority (community nursing)
Wiltshire County Council (social services)
Winchester Health Authority (various professionals)
Wirral Metropolitan Borough Council (social services)
Wolverhampton Metropolitan Borough Council (social services)

Glossary

ACA	Association of Continence Advisers
ACC	Association of County Councils
ADSS	Association of Directors of Social Services
ALAC	Artificial Limb and Appliance Centre (Wales, Scotland)
BPRO	Blind Persons' Resettlement Officer (employment)
BPTO	Blind Persons' Technical Officer (Employment Service)
CAC	Child Assessment Centre
CAC	Communication Aids (Advice) Centre
CAMO	Chief Administrative Medical Officer (Scotland, Northern Ireland)
CANO	Chief Administrative Nursing Officer (Scotland, Northern Ireland)
CMHN	Community Mental handicap Nurse
CMO	Clinical Medical Officer
CDS	Community Dental Service
COSLA	Convention of Scottish Local Authorities
CSA	Common Services Agency (Scotland)
CSDPA	Chronically Sick and Disabled Persons Act
CSDP(NI)A	Chronically Sick and Disabled Persons (Northern Ireland) Act
DA	Disablement Adviser (Employment Service)
DAS	Disablement Advisory Service (Employment Service)
DED	Department of Economic Development (Northern Ireland)
DENI	Department of Education Northern Ireland
DES	Department of Education and Science
DH	Department of health (England)
DHA	District Health Authority (England and Wales)
DHSS	Department of Health and Social Services (Northern Ireland)
DHT	District Handicap Team (England, Wales)
DLC	Disabled Living Centre
DN	District Nurse
DMO	District Medical Officer (England, Wales)
DoE	Department of environment (England, Wales, Northern Ireland)
DO	Dispensing Optician
DP(SCR)A	Disabled Persons (Service, Consultation and Representation) Act
DRO	Disablement Resettlement Officer (Employment Service)
DSA	Disablement Services Authority
DSC	Disablement Services Centre (England)
DSS	Department of Social Security
EHO	Environmental Health Officer

ELB	Education and Library Board (Northern Ireland)
FHSA	Family Health Services Authority
FOC	Family Practitioner Committee
GDP	General Dental Practitioner
GDS	General Dental Services
GMS	General Medical Services
GOS	General Ophthalmic Services
GP	General Practitioners
HB	Health Board (Scotland)
HC	Health Circular (England)
HDS	Hospital Dental Service
HES	Hospital Eye Service
HIO	Housing Improvement Officer
HN	Health Notice (England)
HPSS(NI)O	Health and Personal Social Services (Northern Ireland) Order
HSSB	Health and Social Services Board (Northern Ireland)
HV	Health Visitor
LAC	Local Authority Circular (England)
LASSL	Local Authority Social Services Letter
LEA	Local Education Authority (LEA)
MCSP	Member of the Chartered Society of Physiotherapy
MO	Medical Officer (England, Wales)
MTO	Medical Technical Officer
NICSA	Northern Ireland Central Services Agency
NIHE	Northern Ireland Housing Executive
NIOS	Northern Ireland Orthopaedic Service
OMP	Ophthalmic Medical Practitioner
OO	Ophthalmic Optician
OT	Occupational Therapist
RMO	Regional Medical Officer (England)
SCMO	Senior Clinical Medical Officer
SDD	Scottish Development Department
SED	Scottish Education Department
SEN	Special Education Needs
SHHD	Scottish Home and Health Department
SAB	Safety Action Bulletin
SI	Statutory Instrument
SIB	Safety Information Bulletin
SR	Statutory Rule (Northern ireland)
SRCh	State Registered Chiropodist
SRP	State Registered Physiotherapist
SSD	Social Services Department (England, Wales)
SWD	Social Work Department (Scotland)
SWSG	Social Work Services Group (Scotland)
TC	Technical Consultant (Employment Service)
TO	Technical Officer
WHC	Welsh Health Circular
WHCSA	Welsh Health Common Services Authority
WO	Welsh Office
WOC	Welsh Office Circular

1 | Introduction

2 *How to Get Equipment for Disability*

Equipment in general

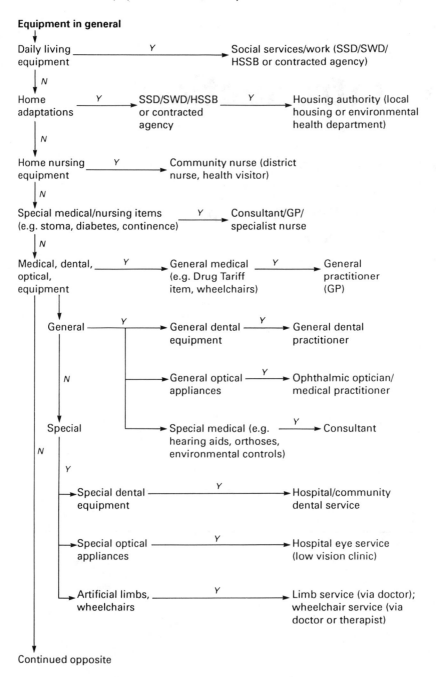

Daily living equipment ——— Y ——→ Social services/work (SSD/SWD/HSSB or contracted agency)

N

Home adaptations —— Y ——→ SSD/SWD/HSSB or contracted agency —— Y ——→ Housing authority (local housing or environmental health department)

N

Home nursing equipment —— Y ——→ Community nurse (district nurse, health visitor)

N

Special medical/nursing items (e.g. stoma, diabetes, continence) —— Y ——→ Consultant/GP/specialist nurse

N

Medical, dental, optical, equipment —— Y ——→ General medical (e.g. Drug Tariff item, wheelchairs) —— Y ——→ General practitioner (GP)

General —— Y ——→ General dental equipment —— Y ——→ General dental practitioner

N

—→ General optical appliances —— Y ——→ Ophthalmic optician/medical practitioner

Special ——→ Special medical (e.g. hearing aids, orthoses, environmental controls) —— Y ——→ Consultant

N

Y

→ Special dental equipment —— Y ——→ Hospital/community dental service

→ Special optical appliances —— Y ——→ Hospital eye service (low vision clinic)

→ Artificial limbs, wheelchairs —— Y ——→ Limb service (via doctor); wheelchair service (via doctor or therapist)

Continued opposite

Equipment need (continued)

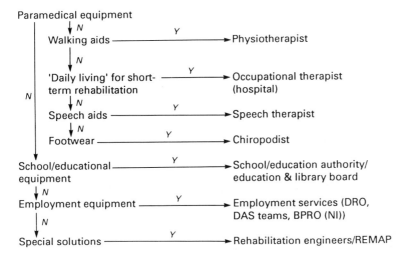

Paramedical equipment
Walking aids ——————Y——————→ Physiotherapist
'Daily living' for short- ——————Y——————→ Occupational therapist
term rehabilitation (hospital)
Speech aids ——————Y——————→ Speech therapist
Footwear ——————Y——————→ Chiropodist

School/educational ——————Y——————→ School/education authority/
equipment education & library board

Employment equipment ——————Y——————→ Employment services (DRO,
DAS teams, BPRO (NI))

Special solutions ——————Y——————→ Rehabilitation engineers/REMAP

1.1. The aim of the book

This book describes how equipment is provided for people with disabilities in the United Kingdom. It explains the statutory framework and how the system works in practice.

Intended to be a practical handbook, it aims to give a simple account of the subject – given that provision of equipment is made through a variety of channels and is recognised to be complicated.

In particular, the book is designed to assist a number of groups:

- central government policy makers;
- local statutory authority policy makers;
- local authority associations and professional associations;
- medical and other prescribers of equipment;
- professional staff who refer to prescribers;
- staff concerned with purchasing and supplying equipment;
- voluntary bodies concerned with disability;
- manufacturers and suppliers of equipment.

If the book succeeds in giving these groups an overview of the system, they will have a clearer understanding of its totality and their role within it. Better understanding, in turn, should lead to more efficient referral, prescribing, planning, targeting and supply practices. Any improved standard of equipment provision will help secure the due role of equipment in the process of rehabilitation, which is so important to people with disabilities.

Note: the term equipment is used very widely, ranging from artificial limbs to long-handled shoe horns, and from computers in special education to home adaptations.

1.2. How to use it

The needs of the above groups differ. They may require different levels of detail, and have varying amounts of time to spend consulting a book of this type. Each chapter therefore consists of four elements. There are appendices at the end of the book, together with a comprehensive index. A glossary is also included.

1.2.1. Flowchart: flowcharts, at the beginning of each chapter, illustrate the provision pattern of each type of equipment.

1.2.2. Introduction: the introductions, amounting in total to some 20 or 30 pages, can be used alone, almost as a separate booklet.

1.2.3. Main text: this expands the introduction, and is divided into short, numbered paragraphs to enable the reader to quickly locate and read particular points.

1.2.4. Boxes contain more detailed (background) information and are interspersed in the main text.

1.2.5. Appendices at the end of the book contain a number of examples of local authority practices.

1.2.6. Index. The comprehensive index is designed to allow quick and detailed reference to particular points.

1.2.7. Glossary. The glossary, very necessary in a work of this nature, contains a list of acronyms.

1.3. How the system of provision is analysed

Each chapter is organised, with some variation, in the following way:

- flowchart;
- introduction;
- type of equipment;
- legislative basis for provision;
- referral;
- assessment;
- prescription;
- supply;
- follow-up;
- maintenance;
- recall.

1.4. The scope of the book

1.4.1. Statutory services. The book covers equipment provided by the following types of statutory services:

- health services;
- social services (work);

- housing authorities;
- education services;
- employment services.

1.4.2. Geographical scope. Since the book covers the whole of the United Kingdom, reference to legislation is given in triplicate (England/Wales, Scotland, and Northern Ireland), and the accounts of practice cover all four countries.

Circular guidance is given three-fold (where equivalent Circulars for England, Scotland, Northern Ireland have been identified), and sometimes four-fold (where separate Welsh Circular guidance has been identified).

1.4.3. Description. The book is descriptive, and not prescriptive: the system of equipment provision is described as it is, and not as it could, or should, be.

However, prescriptive statements contained in legislation, circulars, guidelines are of course included.

1.4.4. Basis of information. The content of the book is based on the following sources:
- Acts of Parliament;
- statutory instruments/rules;
- circulars and other government guidance;
- government papers and reports;
- local written guidelines and policies;
- journal articles;
- books;
- written questionnaires;
- interviews (telephone and face-to-face).

1.4.5. Status of information. Because of the wide scope of the book, and the variable nature of information available, the book can give a broad picture only of equipment provision.

To detail, statistically, the extent of the many practices mentioned, would be an enormous task, even supposing it were possible. Therefore, extensive (almost tedious) use of terms, such as 'might', 'for example' and 'sometimes' have been employed.

Information has been used from many sources, ranging from government report to verbal communication. All sources are given.

1.4.6. Currency of information. 'Time of writing' is April 1990. The book looks forward to, and tries to anticipate, imminent changes. These include, for example, the integration of the wheelchair service (England) into the NHS and the introduction of community care policies.

The book details the new home adaptation grant system in England and Wales, but refers to a draft Circular, rather than the final version.

1.4.6.1. Currency of terminology. Terminology is continually changing, and, in this respect, it is recognised that the book is unlikely to be completely up-to-date, even on publication.

However, efforts have been made to achieve currency. For example, the bodies known as family practitioner committees (FPCs) at the time of writing, will shortly become family health services authorities (FHSAs). Both are included in the glossary, although FPCs, rather than, FHSAs are referred to in the text.

1.4.6.2. Proper names have been kept to a minimum, since the book attempts to describe a system, rather than local or particular services or equipment types.

1.4.6.3. Anonymity of sources. Information on practice, derived, for example, from questionnaires, local authority document 'trawls', written communications and verbal communications, has been used anonymously.

The reasons for this are that:

- the book attempts to give an overall picture only;
- in any case, the book could not possibly attempt to systematically detail individual local practices and variations;
- some ·of the information gathered is essentially confidential, and supplied, on the understanding that it be used anonymously.

1.4.6.4. Interpretation of legislation. The interpretation of legislation is always difficult, and readers are advised to always refer to source legislation.

For health service legislation, duties and powers have been taken to refer to delegated functions (for example, health authorities, rather than the Secretary of State), except where central responsibility is explicitly retained (for example, environmental controls in England).

1.5. Background to the book

1.5.1. Significance of equipment. Equipment helps people with disabilities to carry out ordinary daily living activities. It cannot fully replace body function or fully compensate for disability, but it can make the difference between independence (full or part) and dependence.

For example, the recent survey on disability by the Office of Population, Censuses and Surveys (OPCS) commented that its methods of identifying disability meant that people who used equipment effectively to carry out daily living activities were not identified as disabled.

The survey identified disability primarily by questions relating to daily living activities, rather than by medical diagnosis of impairment. Spectacles and cardiac pacemakers were cited as examples of equipment which compensated for

impairment to such an extent that its users did not show up at all in the survey (*Martin J., Meltzer H., Elliot D. OPCS surveys of disability in Great Britain. Report 1. OPCS. Social Survey Division. HMSO 1988 pp. 8–10.*).

1.5.2. Complexity of the system of equipment provision

1.5.2.1. A King's Fund report (1988) on community services for people with physical disabilities stated that: 'Aids and equipment supply is the single most confused area of service provision for disabled people'.

According to this report contributory factors to this situation include, for example, multiple sources of supply for some equipment, but non-supply of other equipment; policy, and consequent supply, variations between areas; confusion of professionals, disabled people and their carers; resulting inability of professionals to gain a comprehensive knowledge of the system (*Beardshaw, V. Last on the List. Research Report. King's Fund Institute 1988 pp. 27–8*).

1.5.2.2. The system of equipment provision in Northern Ireland in general, seems to be less complicated than in the rest of the UK. This may be because of:
• integrated health and social services;
• a single housing authority;
• a small population (c. 1.5 million), and greater contact between professionals and policy makers, as a result (this point seems to hold true, to some extent, in Scotland and Wales also).

1.5.2.3. Right to equipment. Equipment provision by the statutory services is not a 'right'. Ultimately it depends on professional judgement. Thus, the initiation of the many procedures and practices detailed is for the most part dependent on professional assessment.

Professionals will be aware that equipment is only one part of a range of possible services; indeed it is not always the solution to an individual problem and can sometimes positively hinder the process of rehabilitation.

1.5.2.4. 'Duty' in legislation. The term 'duty' in legislation must be interpreted with caution, since it is generally surrounded by qualifying factors.

1.5.2.4.1. Duty in the health service. For example, the duty (delegated by the Secretary of State) of DHAs to provide 'medical services' is qualified in two main ways.

Firstly, this duty binds only 'to such extent as he [the Secretary of State] considers necessary to meet all reasonable requirements' (*eg NHS Act 1977 s.3*).

Secondly, within this general duty, the DHA has discretion to organise its resources so as to determine which services to offer, and at what standard. Therefore, DHA duty to provide medical services may in practice 'become' discretion to provide any one service or standard of service.

1.5.2.4.2. Social services/work duties. Similarly, although social services and social work departments, for example, have a duty, where an individual need has been identified, to help disabled people with equipment ('facilities' is the legislative term), circular guidance has stated that criteria of need are to be determined in the light of resources.

1.5.2.5. Definition of equipment. Equipment is often classified according to the purpose for which it is intended, rather than in relation to the inherent properties of the item itself.

On this basis the main types of equipment are:

- general medical equipment (prescribed by family GPs);
- special medical equipment (prescribed by hospital consultants);
- home nursing equipment (prescribed by community nurses);
- specialist nursing equipment (eg. specialist nurses involved in supply of equipment for diabetes, incontinence, stoma care);
- paramedical equipment (supplied by therapists as part of active rehabilitation treatment);
- daily living equipment (supplied by therapists for longer term compensation, rather than active treatment, of a stable condition);
- educational equipment (supplied by education authorities or boards);
- employment equipment (supplied by employment services).

This is a broad categorisation and ignores awkward detail.

1.5.2.5.1. Example of difficulty of definition. Wheelchairs, depending on the purpose for which they are loaned and on which particular professional prescribes or supplies them, can be defined as medical (general or special), home nursing, paramedical, daily living, employment or educational equipment.

1.5.2.5.2. Consumer definition of equipment. It is worth pointing out that to the disabled person, this equipment serves a single purpose: daily living function. The fragmented world of statutory service definitions is not useful to him or her.

Surveys carried out amongst people with disabilities sometimes find that the source of equipment provision is unknown (*Verbal communication: OPCS office, in relation to Martin J. et al. OPCS surveys of disability in Great Britain. Report 4. Disabled adults: services, transport and employment. HMSO, 1989; Marie Curie Cancer Care. A Study of the Marie Curie Community Nursing Service. Marie Curie Foundation, 1989 pp. 144–55*).

1.5.2.6. Equipment and the medical profession. There is a considered opinion, that while many doctors have an excellent knowledge of equipment, others may not.

Doctors in general have a very different relationship to equipment than to drugs. Whilst all doctors have easy access to the British National Formulary, for example, which contains a vast amount of drug information, they do not have similar access to information about the vast range of equipment which their patients might need.

(It has been pointed out that failure by a doctor to consider drug therapy, ensure compliance and provide medication is considered bad practice. But while medical training gives a sound pharmacological basis, it does not encourge doctors to 'think of aids, appliances and adaptations that can help overcome or compensate for disability' (*Mulley G.P. Provision of aids. BMJ 1988: 296, 1317–1318*).)

1.5.2.7. Costs of equipment provision. The total cost to statutory services of equipment and adaptation provision for disability is unknown.

However, large sums of public money are involved, as the following few examples indicate.

Example 1. Orthotic service. In England the orthotic service costs annually about £40 million (*NHS Management Consultancy Services. Study of the Orthotic Service. Crown Copyright, 1988 p. 7*).

Example 2. Wheelchair service. In England, the wheelchair service (permanent loan) costs annually over £31.5 million (*DSA Annual Report 1988/89*); in Scotland, over £1.7 million (*Verbal communication: Scottish Office, 1990*).

Example 3. Artificial limb service. In England, the artificial limb service annually costs over £42.7 million (*DSA Annual Report, 1988/89*).

In Scotland, the upper limb service annually costs over £1.4 million; the lower limb service, over £3.9 million (*Verbal communication: Scottish Office, 1990*).

Example 4. Environmental controls. In Scotland, environmental controls, supplied on medical prescription, cost over £281,520 (*Verbal communication: Scottish Office, 1990*).

Example 5. Stoma care. In 1986, the cost of the stoma care service in England was estimated to be approaching £50 million (*Physical Disability and Beyond. Royal College of Physicians, 1986 p. 27*).

Example 6. Local joint equipment store. One joint store document (1985) includes annual costs:

- daily living equipment (including stairlifts): £169,000;
- home nursing equipment: £4,300;
- disposable materials (eg incontinence pads): £60,000 (*North of England joint store document, 1985*).

Example 7. Local authority costs for daily living equipment and home adaptations. A comparison between four authorities found budgets ranging from about £440,000 to over £2 million, the lowest overall sum, however, representing the highest sum per capita (*Local authority document, 1989*).

Example 8. Local joint equipment store. One joint store document (1989) states that annual expenditure (1988/89) in relation to the occupational therapy service entailed:

- equipment: over £273,000;
- adaptations: over £340,000;
- lift repair and maintenance: over £43,000 (*Midlands Joint store document, 1989*).

2 Daily Living Equipment

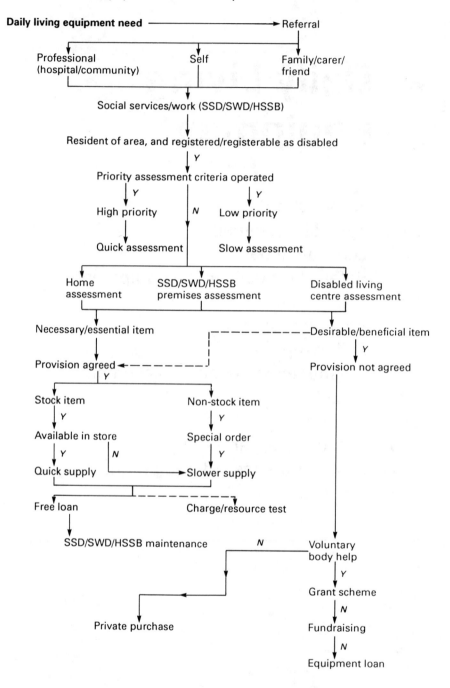

Introduction

Type of equipment
Daily living equipment is difficult to define, other than to say that it is equipment which helps people with disabilities in their everyday life; and that it is not seen to meet a medical or home nursing need. It includes, for example, bath, toilet, feeding, seating, household, kitchen and telephone aids.

Responsibility for provision falls on:
- social services departments (SSDs, England and Wales);
- social work departments (SWDs, Scotland);
- health and social services boards (HSSBs, Northern Ireland).

These authorities have a duty, where an individual need has been identified, 'to make arrangements for . . . the provision of additional facilities for . . . greater safety, comfort or convenience'.

The word 'equipment' is not included or defined in legislation, and authorities tend to make their own definitions according to their interpretation of legislation and according to whatever resources they have available.

Referral
Referral to the SSD/SWD/HSSB is open, although a letter of support from another professional such as a general practitioner is often useful.

Assessment
In order to receive services, clients must normally be resident in the area of the SSD/SWD/HSSB and either be registered disabled, or be judged at least 'registerable'.

Assessment is often carried out by community occupational therapists (OTs); but sometimes by other community SSD/SWD/HSSB staff. Depending on local arrangements, hospital (health service) OTs sometimes carry out assessment more or less formally on behalf of the SSD/SWD or HSSB (under social services functions).

Assessment is usually made at a client's own home, but can take place elsewhere, at, for example, SSD/SWD/HSSB community OT premises, a hospital OT department, or a disabled living centre (DLC).

There are sometimes waiting times for assessment and in some areas clients are seen according to a priority system, which is sometimes operated according to local, written guidelines.

Assessment outcome
The outcome of assessment depends on either the recognition or non-recognition of a particular individual's need for equipment. Equipment is only one from a number of options in relation to the needs of an individual.

SSD/SWD/HSSBs sometimes operate local guidelines on assessment. These vary: they may not exist at all, may document general principles, or may carry specific and extensive details.

Provision

Local circumstances often mean that most provision is centred around a stock range of items. Requests for non-stock items often entail special authorisation and ordering procedures, which can delay provision.

Equipment tends to be loaned from a local SSD/SWD or HSSB (social services) store; or from a joint (funded) equipment store (carrying both daily living and home nursing equipment). Sometimes a voluntary organisation runs the store on behalf of the SSD/SWD/HSSB.

Charges

SSD/SWD/HSSBs have the power to make charges for equipment, but this power is rarely used. However, increasing numbers of SSD/SWD/HSSBs do now suggest that clients buy cheaper, commonly available items themselves.

Voluntary organisation help and private purchase

Voluntary organisations sometimes help with the provision of equipment which the SSD/SWD/HSSB is unable to supply. Such help is usually in the form of either loan from a central bank of equipment, or grant/fundraising aid.

Facilities for the viewing and purchasing of daily living equipment are increasing, in the form of centres, such as disabled living centres, for viewing (and occasionally buying) equipment, mail order firms, or larger high street pharmacies which sell equipment.

Follow-up

Follow-up and review procedures vary, but are often affected by staff shortages. The SSD/SWD/HSSB generally has responsibility for maintenance; there may be an agreement with the manufacturer or a private contractor in the case of larger equipment.

Recall procedures

Recall procedures are likely to vary. They might barely exist, might be 'passive', or might be 'active'.

Note: this chapter deals, in general, with daily living equipment for people with physical disabilities. Some other equipment, dealt with specifically in other chapters, is also supplied as daily living equipment: and so the procedures described in this chapter apply also, in general, to this other equipment, which includes:

- environmental daily living equipment for people with hearing impairment;
- environmental daily living equipment for people with visual impairment;
- simpler (ie not medically prescribed) environmental controls;
- walking aids supplied as daily living equipment;
- wheelchairs supplied as daily living equipment.

2.1. Type of equipment

2.1.1. Definition of daily living equipment. The definition of daily living equipment is very wide. Depending on one's view of daily living, there is virtually no limit to what people in different environments, of different ages, cultures, living style, abilities or disabilities need.

Central government definitions are few and vague: they include:

- 'facilities . . . for greater safety, comfort and convenience' (legislation) (*Chronically Sick and Disabled Persons' Act 1970 s.2; Chronically Sick and Disabled Persons' (Northern Ireland) Act 1978 s.2*);
- 'greater independence in the home' through equipment 'predominantly of a domestic character' (*Circular guidance) (NHS Memorandum 1976(GEN)90*);
- 'help with long term effects of disability' (*public information booklet: HB2. DHSS (NI) 1988 p. 19*).

Local authorities sometimes also produce their own definitions, depending on local interpretation of legislation and local circumstances and resources.

2.1.2. Examples of daily living equipment. Daily living equipment typically includes bath, toilet, feeding, kitchen, household, telephone/television, reading, leisure equipment etc.

For examples, given by central government in legislation, Circular guidance, and public information booklets, see Box 2.1. Only Circular guidance (Scotland, 1976) attempts to give an extensive list of examples (*NHS Memorandum 1976 GEN(90)*).

Box 2.1: Examples of daily living equipment

B2.1.1. Primary legislation. Legislation does not mention daily living equipment in general other than by reference to 'additional facilities designed to secure . . . greater safety, comfort or convenience' (*Chronically Sick and Disabled Persons Act 1970 s.2(1)(e); Chronically Sick and Disabled Persons (Northern Ireland) Act 1978 s.2(e)*). Specifically mentioned however are telephones (and aids to use the telephone), television and radio:

- 'the provision for that person in obtaining, wireless, television, library or similar recreational facilities' (*Chronically Sick and Disabled Persons Act 1970 s.2(1)(b); Chronically Sick and Disabled Persons (Northern Ireland) Act 1978 s.2(b)*);
- 'the provision for that person of, or assistance to that person in obtaining, a telephone and any special equipment necessary to enable him to use a telephone' (*Chronically Sick and Disabled Persons Act 1970 s.2(1)(h); Chronically Sick and Disabled Persons (Northern Ireland) Act 1978 s.2(h)*).

B2.1.2. Circular guidance

B2.1.2.1. England/Wales and Northern Ireland. Circular guidance, detailing examples of daily living equipment, has not been issued. One reason given for this is that lists can both act restrictively in practice and become rapidly obsolescent.

B2.1.2.2. Scotland. Circular guidance (1976) contains a detailed list of daily living equipment. Stressed to be in no way comprehensive, it lists items which are 'no more than examples of aids that may be provided and are a small percentage of the total aids available':
- toilet aids:
  - raised toilet seats;
  - toilet support rails – free standing;
- bath aids:
  - bath rails;

- bath seats;
- bath boards;
- bath mats;
- bath tap fitting shower;
- bed aids:
  - bed over-tables;
- sitting aids:
  - special chairs;
  - foot stools;
  - self-lift chairs;
- dressing aids:
  - stocking aids;
  - long-handled shoehorns;
- feeding aids:
  - special cutlery;
  - special tableware;
  - plate guards;
  - non-slip materials;
- general personal aids:
  - helping hands;
- walking aids:
  - ferrules for crutches and walking sticks;
- lifting aids other than nursing;
- personal hygiene;
  - washing aids;
- household aids:
  - stair climbers;
  - telephone aids;
  - tables;
  - stools;
  - trolleys;
  - lighted switches;
  - plugs with handles;
- kitchen aids:
  - tin and screw top openers;
  - kitchen utensils;
  - left-handed utensils;
  - taps and tap-turners;
  - gas and electric cookers;
  - laundry equipment;
  - cleaning equipment;
- aids to leisure:
  - reading aids;
  - magnifiers;
  - page turners;
  - book rests and stands;
  - books on tape;
  - books on film;
  - adaptations to sport and leisure equipment;
  - projectors;
  - car seats;
  - car safety belts;
  - car hoists (*Scotland, NHS Memorandum 1976 (GEN)90*).

B2.1.3. Public information booklets. A DHSS (NI) information booklet notes that daily living equipment includes 'aids to toileting, washing and dressing, to sitting and walking, and to food preparation, eating and recreation'. There are also some fairly simple environmental control systems which allow household equipment, eg a door lock, an electric light or heater or a radio/TV, to be controlled by those who are moderately disabled and could not otherwise easily reach or operate them' (*HB2 DHSS (NI) 1988 p. 19*).

A DH information booklet (1990) includes reference to 'equipment for use in the kitchen, and equipment which helps with personal care, getting about the house, doing the garden, etc.' (*HB6 1990*).

2.1.3. Uncertainty over the definition of daily living equipment sometimes arises; for example, when it is unclear whether an item of equipment is for daily living or home nursing. The uncertainty can relate to the definition of a type of equipment in general, or its definition in a case of particular individual need.

The definition can determine the source of statutory supply. In many areas, effective local agreements are reached between authorities and professionals. Sometimes, however, uncertainty, exacerbated by financial contraints, can cause delay in provision. For details, see Box 2.2.

Box 2.2: Definition of daily living equipment and statutory responsibilities

B2.2.1. Acknowledgement of possible uncertainty is made in Circular guidance (Scotland, 1976), for example. It states that 'it would be unrealistic to expect that there will not be a grey area which will give rise to difficulty in determining responsibility for supply' (*NHS Memorandum 1976(GEN)90*).

Uncertainty can arise typically between the health services (DHA/HB/HSSBs) and social services/work departments (SSD/SWD/HSSBs), in relation to, for example, the distinction between daily living equipment and home nursing equipment.

B2.2.2. Co-operation

B2.2.2.1. General duty to co-operate. There is anyway a general (not specific to equipment provision) legislative duty on authorities to co-operate in England, Wales and Scotland (*eg NHS Act 1977 s.22; NHS (Scotland) Act 1978 s.13*): in Northern Ireland the health and social services are already integrated, thus reducing the likelihood of difficulty.

B2.2.2.2. Specific duty to co-operate in relation to daily living equipment. Circular guidance (Scotland, 1976) states that: 'It is suggested that to facilitate the supply of an aid – and the aim of all concerned will be to provide the disabled person with the aid that he needs as quickly as possible – health boards and local authorities should enter into early discussions to work out local procedures' (*NHS Memorandum 1976 (GEN)90*).

Circular guidance (Scotland, 1985) contains similar advice, stating that the disabled client should not be subjected to unnecessary inconvenience caused by delay in provision; that co-operation between responsible authorities is of the 'utmost importance'; and that occasionally authorities may have to depart from normal arrangements (*Joint Circular: SDD 40/1985 – NHS 1985(GEN)33 – SWSG 17/1985*).

B2.2.2.3. Local co-operation. Agreements are often made at local level between authorities. For example (England), SSDs and DHAs within the area of a regional health authority might try and make an agreement to establish 'common policies and practice throughout the area of the RHA'. Such an agreement would include division of responsibility, between DHAs and SSDs, for various types of equipment (*SSD (19) guidelines received 1989*).

B2.2.2.4. Northern Ireland. The combined nature of the health and social services system in Northern Ireland, means that while professional responsibilities must still be defined, problems are unlikely to arise on the same scale as they sometimes do in England.

For example, there is general agreement that community nurses take responsibility for all equipment relating to the bed and portable hoists; community OTs for other daily living equipment including bath and toilet equipment and fixed hoists.

B2.2.3. Examples of uncertainty over provision responsibility

B2.2.3.1. Earlier hospital discharge policies, for example, have increased pressure on both providers of home nursing and daily living equipment: and the SSD or SWD could be asked to provide items which it considers are for treatment of illness rather than everyday living – even if the person is not receiving any nursing care (eg trolleys for oxygen cylinders, equipment for postural drainage, pressure relief beds) (*London SSD (19) guidelines received 1989*).

B2.2.3.2. Community nurses and daily living equipment. In some areas where provision of daily living equipment is tardy (for example, because of a shortage of community OTs employed by the SSD/SWD/HSSB), community nurses might be under pressure to authorise and provide equipment which they do not consider an aid to nursing.

In some areas provision (eg of bath aids) by community nurses might be by formal agreement and arrangement with community OTs. For example, district nurses in rural districts might be issued (by the SSD/SWD) with a small stock of bath and toilet aids; the CNS store might be issued with a small stock of SSD/SWD equipment; SSD/SWD elderly resource centres, holding basic equipment might be accessible to community nurses (*eg Scotland SWD OT questionnaire 1988; Southwest England SSD (40) guidelines 1989*).

B2.2.3.3. General pressures in terms of increasing demand for equipment and financial pressures sometimes create problems.

For example, a report (1985), concerned with the respective responsibilities of SSDs and DHAs, arising from a working group (of SSD and DHA members) within the area of an RHA noted that:

- very little central guidance on relevant legislation existed;
- consequently different practices and policies within the region had developed;
- some of these practices had never been satisfactory;
- others (previously satisfactory) had not kept pace with changing trends in community care;
- demand for the provision of aids and adaptations had increased;
- consequent demand on limited resources had led to more rigid attitudes being adopted;
- there was duplication of time and effort;
- confusion for both staff and consumers;
- unacceptable delays in making provision;
- this all reflected badly on the authorities concerned and impaired staff morale (*SSD guidelines (19) received 1989*).

B2.2.3.4. Examples of equipment falling within grey areas can include equipment for postural drainage (eg reclining chairs, footstools, bed raising blocks); beds; hoists; commodes; bath aids.

Use of language can be the determining factor: a paediatric OT, for example, making exactly the same request to a SSD, may succeed if she couches it in 'daily living language' (ie in simple functional language), but fail if it is in the language of physiology (*Verbal communication, paediatric OT, London teaching hospital 1989*).

2.2. Legislative basis in law for the provision of daily living equipment

Equipment (other than telephone and television) is not mentioned by name in legislation, but is implied by the term 'facilities'. The provision of daily living equipment rests on three main 'sets' of legislation, and one impending.

2.2.1. Duty to provide facilities for safety, comfort or convenience: the Chronically Sick and Disabled Persons Acts.

The primary basis for the provision of daily living equipment lies in the Chronically Sick and Disabled Persons Acts of 1970 (England and Wales), 1972 (amending the 1970 Act so as to extend the relevant section to Scotland), and 1978 (Northern Ireland) (*Chronically Sick and Disabled Persons Act 1970 s.2(1(e); Chronically Sick and Disabled Persons (Scotland) Act 1972; Chronically Sick and Disabled Persons (Northern Ireland) Act 1978 s.2(b)*).

2.2.1.1. Basis for provision of daily living equipment in general. SSD/SWD/HSSBs have a duty, where an individual need has been identified, to 'make arrangements for . . . the provision of additional facilities for his greater safety, comfort or convenience' (*Chronically Sick and Disabled Persons Act 1970 s.2(1(e); Chronically Sick and Disabled Persons (Northern Ireland) Act 1978 s.2(b)*).

Note: 'facilities' in practice are interpreted as including equipment.

2.2.1.2. Basis for provision of television or radio. SSD/SWD/HSSBs have a duty, where an individual need has been identified, to 'make arrangements for . . . the provision for that person of, or assistance to that person in obtaining, wireless, television, library or similar recreations' (*Chronically Sick and Disabled Persons Act 1970 s.2(1)(b); Chronically Sick and Disabled Persons' (Northern Ireland) Act 1978 s.2(b)*).

2.2.1.3. Basis for provision of telephone (and equipment to use the telephone). SSD/SWD/HSSBs have a duty, where an individual need has been identified, to 'make arrangements . . . for the provision for that person of, or assistance to that person in obtaining, a telephone and any special equipment necessary to enable him to use a telephone' (*Chronically Sick and Disabled Persons Act 1970 s.2(1)(h); Chronically Sick and Disabled Persons (Northern Ireland) Act 1978 s.2(h)*).

2.2.2. Basis for provision in general welfare legislation. The Chronically Sick and Disabled Persons Acts reinforce previous general welfare legislation which give SSDs powers, and HB/HSSBs duties, to meet the needs of people with disabilities. This legislation consists of the:

- National Assistance Act 1948 (England/Wales);
- Social Work (Scotland) Act 1968;
- Health and Personal Social Services (Northern Ireland) Order 1972 (*SI 1972/1265*).

For details of these powers and duties, and definitions of disability, see Box 2.3.

2.2.3. Basis for request for assessment. More recent legislation places a duty on SSD/SWD/HSSBs to carry out assessment, when requested to do so by a disabled person or his/her carer (relevant section 4 not yet in force in Northern Ireland).

This legislation consists of the Disabled Persons (Services, Consultation and Representation) Act 1986 (England, Wales, Scotland) and the Disabled Persons (Northern Ireland) 1989 (not yet in force).

Part of this legislation, not yet in force anywhere in the UK, requires the SSD/SWD/HSSB to respond to a request for assessment by the disabled person's authorised representative, and to provide a written account of the assessment and decision, if requested to do so by the disabled person or his or her representative. For details of this legislation see Box 2.3.

2.2.4. Basis for community care assessment. Legislation (England, Wales, Scotland) (NHS and Community Care Bill 1989) is currently passing through Parliament and is expected to come into force by April 1991.

It places a duty on SSD/SWDs to decide whether a person requires services in their own home, or residential accomodation with or without nursing care. Also required will be that, when assessing people with a disability, duties under the Disabled Persons (Services, Consultation and Representation) Act 1986 (2.2.3.), concerning assessment, be carried out. Details of this impending legislation are given in Box 2.3.

2.2.4.1. Northern Ireland. Similar legislation for Northern Ireland is expected.

Box 2.3: Legislation

B2.3.1. General welfare powers and duties

B2.3.1.1. England and Wales. General welfare provision by SSDs is covered by the 'power to make arrangements for promoting the welfare of persons . . . who are blind, deaf or dumb, and other persons who are substantially and permanently handicapped by illness, injury or congenital deformity or such other disabilities as may be prescribed by the Minister' (*National Assistance Act 1948, s.29*).

B2.3.1.2. Scotland. In Scotland, general welfare provision is covered by the 'duty of every local authority to promote social welfare by making available advice, guidance and assistance on such a scale as may be appropriate for their area, and in that behalf to make arangements and to provide or secure the provision of such facilities . . . as they may consider suitable and adequate . . .' (*Social Work (Scotland) Act 1968 s.12*).

B2.3.1.3. Northern Ireland. General welfare provision is covered by the duty of HSSBs 'to provide or secure the provision of personal social services in Northern Ireland designed to promote the social welfare of the people of Northern Ireland'. This includes the provision of 'advice, guidance and assistance, to such extent as it considers necessary, and for that purpose shall make such arrangements and provide or secure the provision of such facilities . . . as it considers suitable and adequate' (*SI 1972/1269 HPSS(NI)O 1972 a.4,15*).

B2.3.2. Assessment on request. Recent legislation places a duty on SSD/SWD/HSSBs to 'assess on request' (not yet in force in Northern Ireland).

B2.3.2.1. England, Wales, Scotland. The SSD/SWD has a duty, if requested by a disabled individual or his/her carer, to assess a person who is eligible under general welfare legislation (*ie the National Assistance Act 1948 s.29 or the Social Work (Scotland) Act 1968 s.12*).
'When requested to do so by . . . a disabled person . . . or . . . any person who provides care for him as mentioned in Section 8, a local authority shall decide whether the needs of the disabled person call for the provision by the authority of any services in accordance with section 2(1) of the 1970 Act (provision of welfare services)' (*Disabled Persons (Services Consultation and Representation) Act 1986 s.4*).

B2.3.2.2. Northern Ireland (not yet in force). 'A Board shall, when requested to do by . . . a disabled person . . . or . . . any person who provides care for him in the circumstances mentioned in Section 8, decide whether the needs of the disabled person call for the provision by the Board of any services in accordance with section 2 of the 1978 Act (provision of welfare services)' (*Disabled Persons (Northern Ireland) Act 1989 s.4, not yet in force*).

B2.3.2.3. Written account of assessment. The same legislation (Disabled Persons (Services Consultation and Representation) Act 1986; Disabled Persons (Northern Ireland) Act 1989) also contains a legal requirement (not yet in force anywhere in the UK) which obliges a SSD/SWD/HSSB to provide in writing, if so requested, details of what needs it has identified; what services it either intends to provide; or why it does not intend to provide services (*Disabled Persons (Services Consultation and Representation) Act 1986 s.3; Disabled Persons (Northern Ireland) Act 1989 s.3*).
This is not yet in force anywhere in the United Kingdom.

B2.3.3. Assessment under community care arrangements. Impending legislation (expected to come into force in 1991) gives SSD/SWDs new and additional duties to assess people to decide what form of community care is most appropriate. Their duty will be to assess whether a person should receive care in their own home, or in residential accomodation with or without nursing care (*NHS and Community Care Bill cl. 37, 42, 49, 50; Caring for People. HMSO 1989 pp. 18–19, 80*).

In order to facilitate such a system of assessment, the government proposes to publish 'a detailed code of guidance for local authorities, copied to health authorities, to advise on the workings of the new assessment system' (*Caring for People, HMSO 1989 20*). This may include reference to assessment for equipment provision, which is a key element in community care.

B2.3.3.1. General assessment duties for community care (based on contents of the NHS and Community Care Bill 1989 (England, Scotland, Northern Ireland))

B2.3.3.1.1. England/Wales 'Where it appears to a local authority that any person for whom they may provide or arrange for the provision of community care services may be in need of any such services, the authority . . . shall carry out an assessment of his needs for those services; and, having regard to the results of the assessment, shall then decide whether his needs call for the provision by them of any such services' (*NHS and Community Care Bill 1989 cl.42*).

B2.3.3.1.2. Scotland. 'Where it appears to a local authority that any person for whom they are under a duty of have a power to provide community care services may be in need of any such services, the authority shall make an assessment of the needs of that person for those services; and, having regard to the results of that assessment, shall then decide whether the needs of that person call for the provision of any such services' (*NHS and Community Care Bill 1989 cl.49*).

2.3.3.2. Assessment duties specific to disability. If the above general assessment discloses that a person has a disability, the SSD/SWD 'shall proceed to make such a decision as to the services he requires as is mentioned in section 4 of the Disabled Persons (Services, Consultation and Representation) Act 1986 without his requesting them to do so under that section; and shall inform him that they will be doing so and of his rights under that Act' (*NHS and Community Care Bill 1989 cl.42 and 49*).

2.3. Referral for daily living equipment

2.3.1. Referral to the SSD/SWD/HSSB is open. It might be:

- self-referral;
- referral by carer/family/friends;
- referral by professionals, such as GPs, health visitors, district nurses, therapists (occupational, physio-, speech), consultants, ward sisters, medical social workers, DROs etc.

Although not strictly necessary, a supportive letter from professionals, such as a GP or therapist, can ensure that the individual is seen more quickly. This might be especially so where there is overdemand for services, and waiting lists exist. Local SSD guidelines might state, for example, that requests will only be given priority if there are medical reasons (*London SSD (24) 1989*).

2.3.2. Registration and registerability. Legislation states that in order to receive services from a SSD/SWD/HSSB the client must be eligible for those services (*Chronically Sick and Disabled Persons' Act 1970 1970 s.2; Chronically Sick and Disabled Persons' (Northern Ireland) Act 1978 s.2*). In practice this means that clients must either be actually registered as disabled with the SSD/SWD/HSSB; or be 'registerable' (ie be eligible for registration).

Box 2.4: Waiting time and priorities

B2.4.1. Length of waiting time

B2.4.1.1. Variation between areas. Great differences can exist side-by-side within one geographical area. For example, London boroughs, barely a few miles apart, can display great differences: from a well-organised OT service assessing extensively for equipment and adaptations with short waiting times, to a virtually non-existent service carrying out few assessments.

B2.4.1.2. Waiting time depending on circumstances. For example, one London borough's public information booklet notes that it is low priority cases which are slow to be dealt with, and that it is from such people (rather than high priority) that complaints emanate.

'In relation to minor items of equipment, it takes some 8/9 months to provide items such as bath boards and rails. Provision is often delayed following hospital discharge, due to pressure of work' (*London borough public information booklet, 1987*).

B2.4.1.3. Legal 'reasonableness' in waiting time. There seems to be no agreement as to what a reasonable waiting time is. A recently produced code of practice for seven SSDs in England notes that there 'is no specific and absolute time limit regarding waiting list delays. Therefore the matter legally rests on a test of "reasonableness". Local authorities must demonstrate an early response to referral even when visits are not possible' (*Disabled Persons (Services, Consultation and Representation) Act 1986 Code of Practice. Dorset Social Services 1989 p. 2*).

Comment is also made that it 'is not clear when a delay in waiting time assessment becomes a refusal to assess. Professional advice is that a delay in excess of 6 months is unacceptable and that most Local Authorities should be working to a 3 month limit.' (*Disabled Persons (Services, Consultation and Representation) Act 1986 Code of Practice. Dorset Social Services 1989 p.2*).

During 1989, an SSD was criticised by the local Ombudsman over its failure for almost a year to carry out an assessment of a person with multiple sclerosis who had requested a groundfloor lavatory. The SSD argued that earlier assessment was not possible due to a shortage of qualified OTs (*Community Care 1989*).

B2.4.2. Priorities for assessment. Some local authorities deal with overdemand by operating (written) guidance, which establishes priority categories for equipment (and home adaptations) assessment.

Such guidance may or may not exist, and varies in its form and content. It might operate permanently, or perhaps in time of financial restriction. Alternatively, there may be a deliberate policy not to prioritise (*SWD guidelines received 1989; Scottish SWD OT questionnaire 1988*).

Such priority criteria can be quite controversial and elicit letters from MPs and councillors: even though it may be the same councillors who may have voted the policy in. The principal OT may maintain that 'threats of letters to MPs make no difference as far as she is concerned because the councillors know why the OTs have to prioritise their work (*Assessment Criteria for House Adaptations. CEH, 1987 p. 13*).

B2.4.2.1. Examples of priority assessment (of equipment and home adaptations).
Example 1. 'Risk to life and those who are terminally ill' followed by 'those who are at severe or quantifiable risk of damaging themselves' (*CEH. Assessment Criteria for House Adaptations, 1987 p. 7*).
Example 2.
First priority is given to people with acute and chronic conditions. Acute would 'indicate that without immediate action the client's health could be seriously impaired, for example hospital discharges'; chronic 'indicate that action is required in order to prevent the client's circumstances rapidly deteriorating with the possibility of hospital admission'.

Second priority would 'indicate that the client is unable to sustain independence without further support or that informal carers can no longer cope'.

Third priority would 'indicate that the client is unable to sustain independence without further assistance but where support systems are available via informal carers and/or support services which can at least hold the situation in the short term' (*Example given in: Assessment Criteria for House Adaptations. Centre on Environment for the Handicapped, 1987*).

Example 3. Priority groups are: elderly people living at home following hip replacement, arthritis (affecting the femur), people with rapidly deteriorating (and terminal) conditions such as motor neurone disease, Parkinson's disease, provision of seating for children (*Scotland SWD OT questionnaire 1988*).

Example 4. Priority categories include terminal conditions, rheumatoid arthritis, traumatic injuries, osteo-arthritis, hip replacement (*Scotland SWD OT questionnaire 1988*).

Example 5.

High priority:

- living alone and at risk of injury as determined by content of referral;
- living alone and elderly where risk of injury in ADL is highlighted, determined by content of referral;
- living alone – replacement of essential aids;
- terminal illness where patient/family encountering functional management problems;
- mobility where urgent;
- urgent intervention regarding housing adaptations/allocation required to:
  - enable disabled person to be discharged from hospital as quickly as possible;
  - facilitate urgent housing allocation;
  - where the content of referral indicates toiletting problems being encountered.

Medium priority:

- physically/mentally handicapped or elderly with mobility problems and experiencing difficulties with activities of daily living;
- replacement of essential aids;
- assessment for housing adaptations/rehousing on grounds of disability;
- assessment and advice on problems related to the provision of wheelchairs, disabled driving and access.

Routine:

- advice and support to carers;
- counselling;
- ambulant patients requiring assessment for, or advice, regarding minor aids or adaptations;
- ambulant patients where problems of self care skills are being highlighted;
- advice and help with social, leisure and sporting activities (*Northern Ireland questionnaire to community OTs, 1988*).

Example 6. *High priority* includes personal care needs (eg eating, toileting, mobility). Equipment supplied might be bathing aids, chairs, stairlifts, self-lift/recliner chairs.

Medium priority includes prevention of institutionalised care (ie avoid residential care or enable hospital discharge). Stairlifts might be supplied under this category, but to enable the client to leave the home each day, rather than to meet personal daily living needs within the home.

Low priority might include maintenance of near normal functioning of family unit. Equipment might include bathing aids, high seat raisers, gardening equipment, and leisure equipment. This equipment might only be supplied at the end of the financial year if there is any money left (*Southwest England SSD (13) guidance received 1989/1990*).

Example 7.
Priority 1:

- instant response from someone in the SSD (eg to enable client to sleep, transfer, eat, go to the toilet, communicate in an emergency; terminal illness; at risk because of no support network; sudden onset or deterioration of disability which leads to hospital admission or puts the carer at risk; breakdown of essential equipment).
- high priority requiring qualified intervention (eg incapacity for self-care with danger of client becoming 'at risk'; recently diagnosed condition which will lead to disability; decline in capabilities of client with longstanding condition and intervention required to aid carer).

Priority 2:

- information given indicates that involvement is needed within one month of referral (eg for daily living activities other than contained in Priority 1; mobility assessment where immobility is causing practical problems; assessment for adaptations; assessment of environmental control systems; family crisis/relationship problems).

Priority 3:

- work which may be placed on a waiting list with the referrer notified and given information on any alternative avenues of help in the interim (maintenance or obtaining of independence; post hospital discharge problems; younger people who wish to achieve a different lifestyle; bathing assessment where there is no medical requirement; access to facilities normally available to someone at home and enabling him or her to participate fully in family life; people with cognitive problems).

Priority 4:

- needs unlikely to be met (clients who require assistance and support to fill full potential role in society – including advice on leisure time activities employment preparation; clients whose quality of life could be improved to 'care, comfort and convenience' standards' – eg adaptations to allow access to hobby areas etc.) (*South of England SSD (16) guidance received 1989/1990*).

This basic criterion for service provision cannot always include assessment services, since 'registerability' might sometimes only be established following assessment. However, in many cases, registerability is probably decided on the basis of information conveyed by a written or verbal referral.

In the case of people with visual impairment, registration is advisable, but in relation to other statutory benefits (15.4.3.).

Box 2.5: Definitions of need in assessment for daily living equipment

B2.5.1. General legislative requirement in relation to eligibility for assistance.

B2.5.1.1. England and Wales. People in need include those who are 'blind, deaf or dumb, and other persons who are substantially and permanently handicapped by illness, injury, or congenital deformity or such other disabilities as may be prescribed by the Minister' (*National Assistance Act 1948, s.29*).

B2.5.1.2. Scotland. The definition of 'persons in need' includes being 'in need of care and attention arising out of infirmity, youth or age; or suffer from illness or mental disorder or are substantially handicapped by any deformity or disability' (*Social Work (Scotland) Act 1968, s.94*).

B2.5.1.3. Northern Ireland. The definition includes a person who is in 'need of care and attention arising out of infirmity or age' or who suffers 'from illness or is substantially handicapped by any deformity or disability' (*SI 1972/1265 HPSS(NI)O 1972 a.2*).

B2.5.1.4. Definition of 'substantially and permanently handicapped'. Circular guidance (England, Wales, Northern Ireland) states that it has not been possible to give precise guidance on the interpretation of this phrase. However, authorities (SSDs and HSSBs) are asked to interpret the term 'substantially' broadly; and to interpret the term 'permanent' flexibly enough to avoid non-provision in individual cases, where the duration of the disability is uncertain (*LAC 17/74; WOC (74)93?; HSS(OS5A)4/78*).

B2.5.1.5. Disability categories. Circular guidance suggests a three-fold categorisation of disability (*LAC 17/74; WOC 93/74; HSS(OS5A)4/78*).

B2.5.1.5.1. Very severe handicap:

- people who need help going to or using the WC practically every night. In addition, most of those in this group need to be fed and dressed or, if they can feed and/or dress themselves, they need a lot of help during the day with washing and WC, or are incontinent;
- people who need help with the WC during the night but not quite so much help with feeding, washing, dressing; or, while not needing night-time help with the WC need a great deal of day-time help with feeding and/or washing and the WC;
- people who are permanently bedfast or confined to a chair and need help to get in and out, or are senile or mentally impaired, or are not able to care for themselves as far as normal everyday functions are concerned (but who do not need as much help as the above two categories) (*LAC 17/74; WOC 93/74; HSS(OS5A)4/78*).

B2.5.1.5.2. Severe or appreciable handicap:

- people who either have difficulty doing everything, or find most things difficult and some impossible;
- people who find most things difficult, or three or four items difficult and some impossible;
- people who can do a fair amount for themselves but have difficulty with some items, or have help with one or two minor items (*LAC 17/74; WOC 93/74; HSS(OS5A)4/78*).

B2.5.2. Need determined by local resources

B2.5.2.1. Circular guidance. Circular guidance (England and Scotland) states: 'Criteria of need are matters for the authorities to determine in the light of resources' (*DHSS 12/70; SW12/1972*). (Note: this guidance would seem to imply that the fewer resources an authority has, the higher the threshold need should be set. This would make it theoretically impossible for a SSD/SWD/HSSB to identify a need which it cannot afford to meet.)

B2.5.2.2. Shortfall between assessment and provision. However, a recent code of practice developed by, and for, 7 SSDs in Southwest England, states that assessment 'should be needs-based, not resource-based'.

It goes on: 'The local authority has an opportunity within the written statement to acknowledge that there may be a difference between assessed need and actual service provision. This represents the shortfall or 'unmet need' that is a reality of Social Services. This issue should not be masked or hidden from the disabled person or Department' (*Disabled Persons (Services, Consultation and Representation) Act 1986 Code of Practice. Dorset Social Services 1989 p. 5*). (Note: this is not in line with determining need with reference to resources. The validity of this approach depends on whether lack of resources can be pleaded as a valid excuse for non-provision. Legislation would appear to suggest that if a need is recognised, then there is a duty to meet the need, irrespective of lack of resources (*Chronically Sick and Disabled Persons Act 1970 s.2; Chronically Sick and Disabled Persons (Northern Ireland) Act 1978 s.2*).

B2.5.3. Need against want or desirability. Some SSD/SWD/HSSBs make a distinction between equipment which is necessary, and that which the client wants but which is not assessed as necessary as well.

For example, one set of guidelines states: 'All aids will be provided free of charge on loan and it is imperative to distinguish between those who desire aids and those who need them' (*HSSB guidelines received 1989*).

Nevertheless, although good communication between client and assessor can often prevent disagreements arising, the distinction between 'necessary' and 'desirable' seems to persist.

2.3.2.1. General definition of eligibility for SSD/SWD/HSSB services. Legislation includes terms, such as illness, handicap, deformity, disability and permanence of handicap (England, Wales), to define people who are eligible for assistance under general welfare legislation (*see variously in: National Assistance Act 1948 s.29; Social Work (Scotland) Act 1968 s.94; SI 1972/1265 HPSS(NI)O a.2*). See Box 2.5 for details.

2.3.2.2. Registers of people with disabilities

2.3.2.2.1. Registers, England and Wales. SSDs have the power to compile and maintain classified registers of people with disabilities (*National Assistance Act s.29(4)(g)*).

However, the actual provision of services is not dependent on registration; people sometimes wish to register and sometimes not. But if they are 'registerable', then they are eligible for services. Circular guidance (England, Wales, Scotland) stresses that registration is not necessary for access to services (*LAC 17/74; WOC(74)93*).

2.3.2.2.2. Registers, Scotland and Northern Ireland. The compilation and maintenance or registers of people with disabilities is not a duty.

However, Circular guidance (Northern Ireland) suggested that Boards continue to keep registers for planning purposes (*HSS(OS5A)4/78*), and in Scotland SWDs, in practice, keep registers (*see eg Joint circular NHS 1986(PCS)35 -SWSG 8/1986; SHHD. Management of ENT Services in Scotland. HMSO, 1989 p. 51*), especially for blind and partially-sighted people (15.4.2.). (As in England and Wales, registration does still take place for people with visual impairment because of other benefits dependent on registration (15.4.2.).)

2.3.2.2.3. Categories of disability. Circular guidance (England, Wales, Northern Ireland) gives guidance on categories of disability, for the purpose of establishing eligibility of an individual for services (for details see Box 2.5).

2.3.2.3. Registration practice

2.3.2.3.1. Registration and letter of support. Although eligibility for services does not depend on registration, some people may wish to register. If they do, SSD/SWD/HSSBs might suggest that initial applications for registration be accompanied by a letter from the person's GP or from a hospital doctor (*London Borough of Hammersmith and Fulham. A Directory of Resources for People with Disabilities. 1989*).

2.3.2.3.2. Occasional necessity for registration in practice. In some areas however, registration is still cited as necessary by internal SSD guidelines for some services such as assessment for certain adaptations (*eg Midlands SSD (3) 1990. London SSD (2) 1990*).

Other areas might distinguish between the keeping of a formal register, and the keeping of a more informal 'listing' of people with disabilities, but require one or the other as an eligibility criterion (*London borough SSD (10) guidelines received 1990*).

Occasionally other criteria are used in place of registration/registerability: for example, in one area, people over 65 years qualify 'automatically' for equipment assessment because of their age (*London borough SSD (10) guidance received 1990*).

2.3.3. Residency requirement. Legislation states that services can only be provided by the SSD/SWD/HSSB to a client who is normally resident within the area covered by the SSD/SWD/HSSB.

Sometimes, however, consideration might be given to a temporary resident, who is being cared for by a family established and resident in the area (*eg London borough SSD (17) guidelines received 1990*).

2.4. Assessment

2.4.1. Professionals involved in assessment

2.4.1.1. Community occupational therapist (OT) assessment

2.4.1.1.1. Community OTs are the experts on daily living equipment. Central government guidance does not prescribe which professionals should carry out assessment for daily living equipment; although Circular guidance (Scotland, 1976) does suggest that OTs are the most appropriate staff (*eg Joint Circular SDD 40/1985 – NHS 1985(GEN)33 – SWSG 17/1985*).

2.4.1.1.2. Shortage of community OTs. In many areas community OTs employed by the SSD/SWD or HSSB (under social services functions) assess for daily living equipment. Because of a national shortage of OTs (*see eg NHS Handbook, NAHA 1989 p.191; Report of a Commission of Enquiry (Louis Blom-Cooper). Duckworth 1989 p.30*), other areas either have too few OTs or do not employ any.

In such circumstances, assessment is sometimes undertaken by other SSD/SWD/HSSB staff including, for example, specialist social workers, generic social workers, OT assistants or technical officers.

2.4.1.1.3. Title and organisation of community OTs. Community OTs go by various names (England, Wales, Scotland). For example, aids and adaptation officer, adviser to the disabled, social rehabilitation officer or consultant practitioner.

Organisation can vary: in England and Wales, for example, SSD area OT teams might be responsible to a principal OT, or there might be no principal OT for the authority. Whereas in England, Wales and Scotland, SSD/SWD community OTs are organised separately from the health service, in Northern Ireland both community and hospital OTs are professionally responsible to one area OT.

2.4.1.2. OT assistant/helper assessment. The activities of OT assistants/helpers are likely to vary as much as their backgrounds and experience (*see eg Report of a Commission of Enquiry (Louis Blom-Cooper). Duckworth 1989 p. 30*). For example, they might:

- carry out initial assessments (following OT vetting of cases): in order to try and contain waiting times for OT assessment (*Midlands SSD (21) 1990*);
- formally and routinely take responsibility for minor equipment (eg bath aids) and minor adaptations, referring only more complex (eg hoists, mobile and ceiling) (*Northeast England SSD (25) 1989*) cases to the OTs;
- mainly be involved with delivery and recall only (*Scotland SWD OT questionnaire 1988*).

2.4.1.2.1. Assistant/helper titles. OT assistants/helpers or other staff (other than OTs), undertaking such responsibilities might be known as, for example, helpers, helper technical instructors, technical instructors, (*Report of a Commission of Enquiry (Louis Blom-Cooper). Duckworth 1989 p. 30*), disability fieldworkers, welfare assistants, community care officers (*SSD guidelines received 1989*).

2.4.1.3. Assessment by staff other than SSD/SWD or HSSB (under social services functions) staff. In some areas formal or informal arrangements between hospital and community OTs (or other SSD/SWD/HSSB staff), results in assessment by hospital OTs.

Community physiotherapists or district nurses sometimes become involved in assessment, and more rarely in provision, 'on behalf' of the SSD/SWD/HSSB community OTs.

2.4.1.3.1 Hospital-based OT assessment

2.4.1.3.1.1. Hospital-based OT assessment: England, Wales, Scotland. Sometimes health service (DHA/HB) OTs are seconded from a DHA/HB to carry out assessments. Alternatively, the DHA/HB might place OTs within the community, or at least halfway between community and hospital, to facilitate the rehabilitation of people leaving hospital.

Where the SSD/SWD is under strain, hospital OTs might informally help out; for example, hospital-based paediatric OTs might undertake community assessment of children, and then make recommendations to the SSD/SWD.

In some areas the position can be quite confusing; within one SSD area, for example, part of the community occupational therapy service could be SSD-based; and part DHA-based (*Midlands SSD (3) guidelines received 1990*).

2.4.1.3.1.2. Hospital-based OT assessment: Northern Ireland. In one Northern Ireland HSSB, for example, hospital OTs overlap with community OTs when they attend day hospitals or day centres, but otherwise there is generally a dividing line between hospital and community OT responsibilities (*Verbal communication: area OT, 1990*).

2.4.1.3.2. Assessment by other health professionals

2.4.1.3.2.1. Referral to community OTs by other professionals. Professionals such as GPs, community physiotherapists, community nurses (district nurses, health visitors) sometimes identify daily living equipment needs, which they then bring to the attention of the SSD/SWD/HSSB. Community OTs might then carry out a full assessment; or they (or other SSD/SWD staff) sometimes accept the original assessment (eg of a community physiotherapist for a handrail), especially where there is good local co-operation and a shortage of OTs.

2.4.2. Assessment location

2.4.2.1. Home assessment. An individual is normally assessed in his or her own home. This is usually necessary because the suitability and effectiveness of even the simplest equipment depends on circumstances in the home environment.

The first visit might be made by, for example, a generic social worker, an OT, an OT helper or a specialist social worker. A generic social worker might visit initially to deal with a range of other problems which the person might have, and which the occupational therapist may have neither the time nor the expertise to deal with.

Assessment of people with relatively minor problems might be delegated to OT assistants. Equally, it might be thought most important that initial assessment be carried out by an experienced OT.

2.4.2.1.1. Demonstration and trial of daily living equipment. Sometimes the supplier/manufacturer visits the home with the OT (eg for assessment of a special chair), (*London SSD Guidelines 1987*)) or by OT arrangement (to see about a stairlift for example). Sometimes the supplier/manufacturer agrees to a period of trial use.

Alternatively the SSD/SWD/HSSB might have the item in stock anyway, or purposely keep an assessment stock.

Local SSD/SWD/HSSB written guidelines might stress the importance of the client's actually demonstrating, to the assessor, the difficulties which he or she is experiencing in the home.

2.4.2.2. Disabled living centres (DLCs) (where they exist), variously funded and organised, are concerned with equipment demonstration and information in relation to the practical aspects of daily living (*Verbal communication: DLCC, 1990*).

They sometimes carry out, for the SSD/SWD/HSSB, formal assessments, which are built into a financial funding agreement. Equally they might carry out informal assessments which are, nevertheless, utilised by the SSD/SWD/HSSB.

Although DLCs are open to anybody to visit, OTs are probably the most important source of referral (*see eg Gallop JF, Chamberlain MA. Use of Disabled Living Centres by Disabled People. British Journal of Occupational Therapy. 1989:52;12, 469–71*).

2.4.2.3. SSD/SWD/HSSB assessment centres. Some SSD/SWD/HSSBs directly fund a DLC and use it as a formal assessment centre; or have their own centre which includes a range of equipment for demonstration.

Although home assessment is often thought to be necessary for most equipment assessment, this is a subject which is debated (2.4.2.1.). For example, one SWD aims to carry out 70% of its assessments at such a centre; 30% only requiring home visits (*Disability Resource Centres – A Humane Occupation. Paper at College of Occupational Therapists Annual Conference, Glasgow 29.6.89*).

The SSD/SWD/HSSB might also have access to an assessment flat (eg run by a local voluntary organisation) in which a person can stay for 2 weeks and try out various equipment (*Midlands SSD (21) guidelines received 1989*).

2.4.2.4. Hospital assessment.

2.4.2.4.1. Occupational therapy department. Hospital OTs often assess daily living equipment needs, sometimes making home visits with other staff, before a person leaves hospital. Circular guidance (England, Wales) on hospital discharge specifically mentions the importance of collaboration between hospital OTs and community OTs, or other community staff, in relation to the provision of disability equipment (*HC(89)5 and Discharge of Patients from Hospital. DH, 1989; WHC(90)1*).

2.4.2.4.2. Physiotherapy departments or OT departments for children or people with learning difficulties (mental handicap) sometimes also hold a range of daily living equipment for assessment, and sometimes for loan (2.5.5.3.).

2.4.2.5. Rehabilitation centre assessment. Specific rehabilitation units/centres (29.) (where they exist) include assessment of daily living equipment in the assessment of a person's total needs. Where such equipment is necessary, specific and formal recommendation is usually made to the individual's own SSD/SWD/HSSB.

2.4.3. Assessment of school leavers. SSD/SWD/HSSB duties to assess school leavers are discussed in detail elsewhere (27.2.5.6.). These include close co-operation between SSD/SWD/HSSBs and education authorities (LEA/ELBs), to ensure that children/young persons, who are leaving school, have their needs adequately assessed, and met, by SSD/SWD/HSSBs.

2.4.4. Assessment of people with a mental handicap. The community mental handicap teams (CMHTs), which exist in many areas, often include hospital (health service) OTs. Where this is the case, these teams form an alternative avenue for referral, and assessment.

2.4.5. Assessment of carers. The assessment of carers is integral to the assessment of the client: it might take account, for example, of the effect of equipment supplied, the carer's ability to cope or the effect on the carer's health. Local guidelines often refer to the importance of carer assessment (*SSD/SWD/HSSB guidelines received 1989/1990*).

2.4.6. Waiting times and priorities for assessment. In some areas the waiting time for assessment is short. In others it can be as long as one year or more (*see eg Smart W. et al. Referrals to an occupational therapy division: a descriptive survey. Occupational Therapy 1983: 46;3, 83–6;*). Lack of staff (*see eg Northern Ireland questionnaire, SSD* *guidelines rec. 1989/1990*), and over-demand (higher referral rates) (*SWD question-naire 1988*) is often the reason for waiting times.

2.4.6.1. 'Reasonable' response time. It is uncertain, given the duty which SSD/SWDs currently have to 'assess on request' (2.2.3.), and which HSSBs will have in the future (2.2.3.), what constitutes a reasonable response time (*see eg Disabled Persons (Services, Consultation & Representation) Act 1986. Code of Practice. Devon Social Services, 1989*).

2.4.6.2. Assessment 'priority' categories. Where waiting times exist, the SSD/ SWD/HSSB sometimes operates written guidelines which detail 'priority' categor-ies. These are generally designed to ensure that people at risk are seen within a few days, while those thought to be at less risk might have to wait much longer (*SSD guidelines received 1989/1990. Scotland SWD OT questionnaire, 1988; Northern Ireland community OT questionnaire 1988*).

Some authorities cite the disability categories of disability given in Circular guidance (2.3.2.2.3.), as a basis for priority categories.

Sometimes these priority categories apply not only to assessment waiting times, but also to provision practice. Clearly, high or low priority may not be established until after assessment, when it may be decided, given existing resources (2.4.7.1.), that provision of certain equipment is low priority, and not strictly necessary (2.4.7.2.).

2.4.6.2.1. Examples of high priorities for assessment. Factors considered include, for example, terminal illness, high risk incurred in daily living activities, physical or psychological collapse of client or carer, hospital discharge (*Midlands SSD guidelines received 1990*).

Medical diagnosis is not always a guide to need, since clients with identical impairment might have different needs in both type and urgency: depending on individual circumstances (*eg SWD/HSSB OT questionnaire 1988*).

Local examples of guidelines on priority are given in Box 2.4.

2.4.6.2.2. 'Safety' as opposed to 'comfort' or 'convenience'. Local guidelines on the operation of priorities often seem to relate, in particular, to safety and risk: the other two terms in legislation (2.2.1.), 'comfort' and 'convenience' are not so evident, or are explicitly relegated to a low priority category.

Circular guidance (Scotland, 1972) recognises that authorities might need to consider priority in relation to services intended to help overcome the effects of disability 'as against . . . services for purely recreational or leisure purposes' (*Joint circular SWSG SW5/1972, SHHD 16/1972, SDD 36/1972, LHAS 5/1972*).

In some guidelines, it is clearly stated that leisure equipment will only be supplied if there is money and time left at the end of the financial year (which is unlikely) (*eg London SSD guidelines (10) received 1990*). In one case, SSD guidelines state (in apparent contradiction of legislation) that items 'needed to promote comfort or safety . . . do not fall within Social Services responsibility' (*London borough SSD (18) guidelines received 1989/1990*).

2.4.6.2.3. Policy of no priority categories. Alternatively, some SSD/SWD/HSSBs (*eg SWD guidelines received 1989*) do not, by policy, create priorities; decisions are left to professional judgement and time and money pressures monitored and resolved centrally (*Southwest England SSD (26) 1989*).

2.4.7. Assessment outcome. SSD/SWD/HSSBs only have a duty in relation to the provision of daily living equipment if they identify an individual need during the assessment; thus eligibility for provision depends on recognition or non-recognition of individual need.

2.4.7.1. Resource limitations and generosity in assessment

2.4.7.1.1. Need defined in relation to local resources. Circular guidance (England, Scotland) states that criteria of need are to be determined in the light of local resources (*see eg Joint Circular DHSS 12/70 – DES 13/70; SWSG Circular SW12/1972*). Resources includes both financial and staff resources (*eg Joint circular SWSG SW5/1972 – SHHD 16/1972 – SDD 36/1972 – LHAS 5/1972 Services for the Handicapped Living in the Community*). (Note: yet at the same time, once a need is recognised, lack of resources might be no legal defence for non-provision (see Box 2.5 for details).

This question is relevant given that some SSD/SWD/HSSB internal guidelines do suggest that threshold of need be varied according to available resources (*SSD guidelines received 1989/1990*), while other guidelines appear to maintain that assessment should be based on need, and not on the services currently available (*Northwest England SSD (12) 1990; Disabled Persons' (Services, Consultation and Representation) Act 1986. Code of Practice. Dorset Social Services, 1989, p. 5*). This latter approach does not appear to be consistent with the Circular guidance.

2.4.7.1.2. Generosity in assessment. Circular guidance (Scotland, 1972) requests that local SWDs 'be as generous as possible within the resources available in their provision of services' (*SWSG 12/1972*); and that, despite other priorities, they be as 'generous as possible as well as imaginative in their provision of services' to people with disabilities (*Joint Circular SWSG SW5/1972, SHHD 16/1972, SDD 36/1972, LHAS 5/1972*).

Circular guidance (England, 1970) states that the government, although recognising resource constraints, expects SSDs to keep in mind the purposes of the relevant legislation (which includes, 'when priorities are settled' the giving of full weight to finding solutions to the problems of people with disabilities)' (*Joint circular DHSS 12/70 -DES 13/70*).

2.4.7.2. Distinction between necessity and want/desirability. Many SSD/SWD/HSSBs make a distinction between equipment which the client wants (entailing no duty in relation to provision), and that which is necessary or essential (entailing duty in relation to provision). Terms used in this connection by SSD/SWD/HSSBs include, for example, 'necessary', 'desirable', 'essential', 'beneficial' (*SSD guidelines received 1989/1990*).

2.4.7.3. Assessment guidelines and criteria. Central government has produced little guidance on assessment. However, what central guidance there is relates to:

- telephone provision: local authority association guidance (ACC/AMA, England and Wales); Circular guidance (Scotland, Northern Ireland);
- television provision: Circular guidance (Northern Ireland). For details, see Appendix 1.

In some areas, SSD/SWD/HSSBs produce their own internal written guidelines and criteria in relation to assessment. Such guidelines sometimes include both general principles and specific eligibility criteria, in relation to the provision of particular types of equipment. For details, see Appendix 2.

2.4.7.4. Purpose of local assessment guidelines and criteria. Although local SSD/SWD/HSSB guidelines are sometimes intended to ensure consistency of assessment and provision, and establish thresholds of need (2.4.7.1.1.) according to local resources, this is not always achieved.

For example, one SSD has found that such written guidelines did not ensure consistency, or a high standard of prescription; they were abandoned in favour of frequent staff meetings and 'ad hoc' guidance documents (*North of England SSD (14) guidance received 1989/1990*). It is sometimes considered generally impracticable to produce detailed guidelines on different equipment types (*SSD guidelines received 1990*). For details of all these assessment criteria and guidelines, central or local, see Appendix 1.

2.4.8. Assessment checklists. Apart from producing criteria to determine whether provision is justified, SSD/SWD/HSSBs sometimes produce detailed documents which 'guide' an OT (or other professional) through a series of questions and points to consider during assessment. These questions are likely to deal with all aspects of the client's (and carer's) situation. Such guidance exists to aid efficient and consistent assessment (*SSD/SWD/HSSB guidelines received 1989/ 1990*).

2.4.9. Equipment assessment and provision as part of a package of care. Equipment assessment is likely to be only part of full functional assessment. For example, equipment assessment and provision might be part of a planned package of support which includes home care, meals on wheels and day care, as well as equipment such as a walking frame, high backed chair, raised toilet seat and a bath aid (*London SSD (18) guidelines received 1990*).

2.5. Provision/supply

2.5.1. Stock and non-stock items. Local SSD/SWD/HSSBs generally base provision on a stock range of items, relatively easily available from a local equipment store.

Where non-stock (expensive) items are requested by the assessing OTs, special authorisation may be necessary. This might involve, for example, the senior or principal occupational therapist, or even the director of social services/work in some cases (*SSD/SWD/HSSB guidance received 1989/1990*). Special authorisation and ordering procedures, for non-stock items, can sometimes cause delay in provision.

2.5.2. Making and adaptation of equipment. Sometimes SSD/SWD/HSSB OTs and technical staff make or adapt simple equipment: for example; changing plinths for use after bathing, or adapted toilet aids for children, (*West Sussex County Council. Services for People in West Sussex with Physical Disabilities 1989*) or dressing aids (*Northern Ireland community OT questionnaire, 1988*).

2.5.3. Local resources affecting provision. Where provision and planning are adequate, or demand is not too great, cost might normally be a relatively minor factor in assessment (*eg SWD guidelines received 1989*).

However, sometimes local SSD/SWD/HSSB equipment budgets are unable to cope with demand. This could be for longer or shorter periods within each financial year. Provision sometimes ceases altogether, is limited, or can become highly uneven and unpredictable, depending on what time of year application and assessment take place (*Scotland SWD OT questionnaire 1988. Verbal communications: community OTs*).

2.5.3.1. Local solutions to lack of resources. Internal SSD/SWD and HSSB (under social services functions) guidelines sometimes explicitly recognise the need to impose constraints as demand increases but budgets do not (*eg Northwest England SSD (11), guidelines received 1990*).

They might recognise that hardship to people with disabilities is likely to result, but that there is little choice.

Proposed solutions might include:

- careful assessment;
- the making of charges;
- agreed non-provision of either high or low cost items (2.9.5.);
- short-term loan only of certain equipment (*North of England SSD (14) 1990*), until the client can buy the equipment themselves (*Northern Ireland questionnaire 1988*);
- 'stringent assessments' might be recommended to prevent budgets 'drying up', especially where there is no addition possible to local budgets towards the end of the financial year (*London SSD (18) guidelines received 1990*);
- identification of equipment, such as geriatric/high seat chairs, (*SWD OT questionnaire 1988, SSD guidelines received 1989/1990*);

2.5.4. Equipment stores

2.5.4.1. Type of equipment store Supply can be from one of the following types of store, for example:

- an SSD/SWD or HSSB (under social services functions);
- a joint (funded) store containing both daily living (social services/work) equipment and home nursing (health service) equipment;
- a voluntary organisation running either a daily living equipment store or a joint store (Box 2.6.2). In such circumstances the voluntary organisation acts as an agent for the SSD/SWD/HSSB, and acts in accordance with agreed standards.

A voluntary organisation running the store might keep and loan simple equipment, other than that recommended by the SSD/SWD/HSSB. In such circumstances, formal assessment and approval may not be necessary; there might also be a charge in this case. For details of equipment stores, see Box 2.6.

2.5.4.2. Delivery, installation and initial instruction in use. Clients can expect to have equipment delivered and installed, although friends and relatives are sometimes encouraged to collect items which do not require special installation or instructions for use. Delivery time can depend on whether the item is in stock and

Box 2.6: Stores

B2.6.1. Type of equipment store

B2.6.1.1. SSD/SWD/HSSB daily living equipment stores. SSD/SWDs and HSSBs (social services) often have their own stores of equipment.

Even in Northern Ireland, where there might be a joint store at Board level, there may still be 'social services' unit or sub stores.

B2.6.1.2. Joint (funded) equipment stores. Alternatively, both daily living equipment and home nursing equipment are kept in a joint (funded) store (B6.2.) by the SSD/DHA, SWD/HB or HSSB.

B2.6.1.3. Remit of equipment stores. Various procedures have to be operated by equipment stores: these include for example ordering, storing (including storage space and effect on stock items held), authorisation and issuing procedures, delivery, recall, computerisation, hazard notice procedures, cleaning and refurbishment (including sterilisation procedures), date coding (both for product liability and for monitoring of 'active' life of certain types of equipment).

Joint equipment stores (see below) are one attempt to rationalise these sorts of procedures.

B2.6.2. Joint equipment stores usually refer to equipment stores which hold both daily living and home nursing equipment and are joint funded by DHA/HB and SSD/SWD equipment. In a Northern Ireland HSSB, this means that the Board's daily living and nursing equipment is housed together. Occasionally a voluntary body (eg the Red Cross) may run such a joint store on an 'agency' agreement basis.

In England and Wales, for example, the creation of joint stores can be difficult where DHA/SSD and HB/SWD boundaries are not co-terminous.

B2.6.2.1. Joint store purpose. Joint stores can contribute to efficient ordering, provision, assessment for, storage, recall, cleaning etc of equipment.

B2.6.2.2. Flexibility. A certain amount of flexibility may be agreed, allowing professionals to recommend some equipment which they would not normally recommend. The store usually has a list of equipment with codes marked against each item – indicating which professionals can authorise its supply.

Some lists still show many items as strictly segregated between home nursing and daily living; in other lists the majority of the items are seen as common, with a minority remaining segregated (*eg Northeast England SSD (25) guidance 1989*).
Example 1. For example, certain home nursing equipment items may be authorised not only by district nurses and health visitors, but also by GPs, OTs and physiotherapists (*North of England (1) Joint store catalogue 1985*). In another store, cot sides can be authorised by an occupational therapist, an OT assistant, a physiotherapist, community nursing staff, or a GP (*Joint store catalogue, Midlands received 1988*).
Example 2. Equally bathing aids, helping hands, reachers, non-slip pads etc. (often regarded as OT responsibility) might be issued by community physiotherapists and district nurses (*Joint store catalogue, Midlands, received 1988*).

B2.6.2.2.1. Example. The aim of the Red Cross Leicestershire joint store (see below) is to achieve:

- a cost effective service;
- standardisation of service across the area;
- standardisation of a recording and issue system;
- introduction of a better recall system;
- suitable cleansing of reusable equipment;
- standardisation of equipment available;
- reduction of referrals due to a problems being dealt with by a 'primary worker' undertaking total assessment;
- avoidance of staff and equipment duplication;

- reduction of waiting times/list;
- reduction of delays in equipment supply;
- reduction in the under-use of equipment (*Notes from talks given in 1988-89 on The Supply, Distribution and Retrieval of Nursing Aids and Aids to Daily Living. Brian Wilson, Director Medical Aid Dept., Leicester*).

B2.6.2.3. Budgets. In England/Wales/Scotland, one of the purposes is to overcome the problems of equipment 'grey areas' in relation to provision (2.1.3.).

However, because of separate budgets, (eg SSD/SWD on the one hand, the DHA/HB Community Nursing Services on the other), (*Keeble P. Dual key health aids. Health and Social Service Journal 1984: 94; 4882, 140-142. Numerous internal SSD documents received 1989–1990*) this purpose is not always realised.

For example, one joint store policy document states: 'It is recognised that the variation in budget levels, which remain clearly distinct from each other at agency level will tend to limit joint store philosophy' (*Joint store catalogue, North of England, received 1989/1990*).

B2.6.2.3.1. Northern Ireland. However, in Northern Ireland this problem does not arise. Thus, whether a board joint store is funded centrally and in block at board level, or through individual unit contributions, the community services budget is unified at either level, and there is no division between daily living and home nursing equipment budgets.

Even where there is ultimate division of the budget at very local level, difficulties are not likely to arise to the extent that they can in the rest of the UK.

B2.6.2.4. Choice of equipment. Regular meetings might take place between the manager of the store, and the statutory bodies to review the type and quantities of equipment kept within the store (*Midlands joint store guidelines received 1989*).

B2.6.2.5. Topping-up of other sites. A large joint equipment store is likely to keep various sites topped up with certain equipment. For example, health centres may be kept stocked with bed pans, urinals, rubber rings; OT depts with daily living aids (*North of England joint store guidelines (1) received 1985*).

Hospital wards not covered by OTs might, for example, be kept stocked with simple toilet aids; a children's assessment centre may also be stocked with a few specialist items (*North of England joint store guidelines (1) received 1989*).

B2.6.2.6. Demonstration area. The joint store may have a demonstration area (or even a DLC) attached or as part of the store.

---

the frequency and organisation of 'delivery runs' to any one area (*eg Northeast England SSD (25) guidelines received 1989*).

2.5.4.2.1. OT and OTA delivery. Special arrangements are sometimes made by the OT, OT assistant, or other specialist staff, to be present on delivery (or to themselves deliver), in order to demonstrate, as well as sometimes install, the equipment.

Local guidelines sometimes clearly state that the OT (or OTA) has responsibility for education in the use (*Northwest England SSD (11) guidelines received 1990*), correct fitting and adjustment, of equipment provided (*Northeast England SSD (25) received 1989*).

Some SSD/SWD/HSSBs might supply leaflets to clients, which explain how to use certain items of equipment, such as hoists, adjustable height chairs or self-lift chairs (*eg West Midlands SSD (44) received 1989/1990*).

2.5.4.2.2. SSD/SWD/HSSB delivery drivers are sometimes specially trained to install equipment (with OT instructions), such as toilet frames, bath seats/boards, bath rails, bed and chair raisers, raised toilet seats in òne area (*South of England SSD (16) guidelines received 1990*); or, in another, perhaps, to install only tap-fixed rails (*Northeast England SSD (25) guidelines received 1989*).

2.5.4.2.3. SSD/SWD/HSSB technical officer installation. These staff, either specifically concerned with aids and adaptations, or otherwise employed within the SSD/SWD/HSSB, sometimes install certain equipment.

2.5.4.2.4. Private contractor delivery and installation. Where the SSD/SWD/HSSB does not stock the item, a private contractor might supply it by agreement with the SSD/SWD/HSSB. For example, chemical toilets authorised by the SSD/SWD/HSSB, might be supplied, delivered and emptied by a private firm (*London SSD guidance, received 1989*).

More complex (electrical) equipment is likely to be installed by the supplier/manufacturer.

2.5.5. Health service provision

2.5.5.1. Hospital OT provision

2.5.5.1.1. Hospital OT department loan on its own account. Hospital OT departments sometimes have a small stock of daily living equipment for short-term loan.

Sometimes there is a formal agreement between the hospital (health service) OTs and the SSD/SWD or HSSB (under social services functions), that the hospital take responsibility (including financial) for equipment needed for short-term loan (*London borough SSD (10) guidelines received 1990*); for example, up to 3 months (*Midlands SSD (23) guidelines received 1990*).

There is sometimes a hospital-based OT technician who can install minor aids and adaptations where necessary.

2.5.5.1.2. Hospital OT loan on behalf of the SSD/SWD or HSSB (under social services functions). Often, where equipment loan is made by hospital OTs, it is on behalf of the SSD/SWD or HSSB (under social services functions).

2.5.5.1.2.1. Arrangements between hospital and community for hospital OT provision of equipment. Where such a system operates, the SSD/SWD or HSSB (community budget) reimburses the hospital, or directly supplies the hospital with stocks of equipment -or both (*eg London SSD (24) guidance received 1989*). Equipment loaned in this way usually includes simpler items only, and might be limited financially both per item (eg £50) and on an annual budget basis.

For provision of other and more expensive equipment, in areas where such arrangements exist, hospital OTs normally place an order through community OTs or other SSD/SWD and HSSB (social services) staff responsible for daily living equipment.

Such equipment loan by hospital OTs is often intended to meet short-term need only: in principle, referral to community OTs is still necessary in case of longer term need (*Northwest England SSD (11) guidelines received 1989*).

2.5.5.1.2.2. Examples of equipment loaned by the hospital on behalf of the SSD/SWD or HSSB (under social services functions) include:

- bath and toilet equipment;
- chair raisers;
- helping hands;
- cutlery and dressing equipment (*London SSD (19) guidelines received 1989*);
- a 'package', following a hip operation, which might include a raised toilet seat, a dressing aid, a walking aid and a bath board (*Verbal communication: Area OT, Northern Ireland, 1989; SSD guidelines received 1989/1990*).

2.5.5.1.2.3. Prevalence of arrangements for hospital OT loan of equipment. It seems that, in England, for example, hospital OTs increasingly loan equipment on behalf of the SSD. One reason given is the saving of time for both patient/client and staff, especially where there is a shortage of community OTs (2.4.1.1.2.).

In some areas, however, this practice is discouraged, because it is felt that not even simpler equipment should be provided without a home visit and assessment by a community OT. Reasons given for this can refer both to the welfare of the client, and to questions of litigation (in relation to negligence and product liability). For example, the suitability of bath boards, seats or rails can depend on the size of the bath, the material from which it is made or the type of taps (*Verbal communication: Area OT, Northern Ireland, 1989*).

2.5.5.1.2.4. Principle of hospital OT provision. The distinction between hospital and community OT provision is a little difficult to understand, but, in theory, hospital OTs might be expected to loan equipment for short-term active rehabilitation; while community OTs might be expected to loan equipment for longer term daily living need, caused by a more stable condition.

In some areas, this distinction is recognised to the extent that hospital OTs can only loan for short-term need; and also to the extent that the hospital finances such short-term loan (rather than be reimbursed by the SSD) (*SSD guidelines received 1989/1990*).

2.5.5.2. Hospital ward sister provision

2.5.5.2.1. Ward sister loan for individual use. Ward sisters sometimes loan daily living equipment. This can happen informally when ward stock is loaned to people who are going home from hospital, and for whom other arrangements have not been made.

Such provision might be more formal: in one area for example, a joint equipment store keeps some hospital wards (not covered by OTs) supplied with toilet aids for home loan (*Joint store catalogue received 1989/1990*).

2.5.5.2.2. Equipment for common use on the ward. Ward sisters on orthopaedic wards, for example, are sometimes responsible, with more or less advice from therapists, for the ordering of a variety of daily living equipment, as general ward stock. For example, walking sticks, crutches, walking frames, helping hands, long shoe horns, wheelchairs, bath seats, bath mats, shower chairs, non-slip table mats and plate surrounds etc. (*Woolliscroft A. Orthopaedic Working Party. Nursing Standards – Equipment. 1988*).

2.5.5.3. Physiotherapy department or OT department provision for children or people with learning difficulties (mental handicap). Physiotherapy departments for children (26.4.1.2.), or for people with learning difficulties, sometimes have a

certain amount of daily living equipment for loan, overlapping in this respect with OT departments. Arrangements vary locally (*Verbal communication: physiotherapists, occupational therapists*).

2.5.5.4. Community physiotherapists sometimes identify daily living equipment problems in the course of their work. Sometimes their assessment for minor daily living equipment might be accepted by the SSD/SWD/HSSB without further (duplicate) assessment.

Less commonly, community physiotherapists, with direct access to a (joint equipment) store, can authorise the provision of daily living equipment themselves. They may be able to authorise the loan of, for example, bath boards/seats/mats, dressing aids, non-slip table mats, hoists/slings, bed/chair raisers, cot sides, raised toilet seats, chairs, trolleys, transfer boards (*eg Midlands SSD Joint store catalogue received 1989*).

2.5.5.5. GP and community nurse provision. Community nurses and, less commonly GPs, have access to some daily living equipment by local arrangement; this might include bath aids (district nurse only), commodes, temporary loan wheelchairs (*SWD questionnaire 1988. Southwest England SSD (40) 1989*), chairs, footrests, V-shaped cushions/pillows, dressing aids, feeding cups, bed table, helping hands, standard walking aids, commodes (*2 Midlands joint store catalogue, received 1988, 1989*).

Special arrangements might be made with the community nurse when, for example, an OT is unable to assess a client within a month of referral; or in sparsely populated areas where OTs cannot easily or frequently visit (*Scotland SWD guidelines received 1990; SWD OT questionnaire 1988*).

2.5.6. Provision for people with learning difficulties (mental handicap). When people with learning difficulties return to the community, they might stay in what are sometimes termed 'half-way homes'.

These homes may be classified as 'hospital' premises where nursing care is required, or social services/work premises where less nursing care is needed.

In the former case, a special budget (eg from the institution/hospital) from which the residents have been discharged, is used to run the home, and to provide equipment. Hospital OTs are likely to be involved, and community OTs would not normally loan equipment on what are, in effect, hospital/health services premises.

In the latter case (social services/work premises), community OTs are involved, as necessary.

2.5.6.1. Northern Ireland. This division of responsibility for such units does not arise to the same extent in Northern Ireland where health and social services are integrated.

2.5.7. Provision of daily living equipment in residential homes

2.5.7.1. Circular guidance on residential home provision of equipment states that people in residential homes (public sector or private) are entitled to the same SSD/SWD/HSSB services, for individual need, as they would be entitled to receive in their own home (24.4.4.1.).

2.5.7.2. Local SSD/SWD/HSSB guidelines on residential home equipment provision sometimes state that responsibility for equipment for common use (eg furniture) lies with the home owner, but that equipment for individual need is the SSD/SWD/HSSB responsibility (*SSD/SWD/HSSB guidelines received 1989/1990 London SSD (17) 1990; North of England SSD (15) 1990*).

For example, personal equipment such as eating aids, long-handled shoe-horns are provided by the SSD/SWD/HSSB: but hoists, handrails, stairlifts, grab rails would generally be seen as the responsibility of the home.

Occasionally, however, local SSD/SWD/HSSB guidelines state that no equipment, for either common or individual use, is to be provided to private residential homes, although assessment and advice can be provided (*London SSD (24) guidelines received 1989*).

In practice it seems that residents are sometimes placed in a low priority category for SSD/SWD/HSSB assessment and provision because they are already in care and not perceived to be at immediate risk.

2.5.7.3. Equipment for common use in statutory residential homes. In the case of statutory homes, the SSD/SWD/HSSB has responsibility, as home owner, for equipment both for common and individual use. However, authorisation procedures and budgets are likely to differ in relation to the provision of equipment for these two different purposes.

2.5.8. Delays in provision of daily living equipment Apart from assessment waiting times, there are sometimes provision waiting times (*see eg Chamberlain MA, Gallop J. The disabled living centre: What does it do? BMJ 1988:297, 1523-1526*).

Authorisation procedures and budget factors (see above) are sometimes the cause of such delays. They can also be caused by uncertainty over responsibility and possible disagreement over funding (*see eg Mulley GP. Provision of aids. BMJ 1988:296;6632, 1317–1318. London SSD (19) guidelines 1989*).

2.5.9. Inappropriate provision, non-use of daily living equipment. There is various evidence as to the extent of inappropriate provision.

Some evidence suggests that equipment sometimes remains unused because inappropriately supplied (*eg Keeble P. Provision of Aids by Health and Social Services: Examples of Good and Bad Practice. Contact, Spring 1984, 36–38. Thomas A. et al. Health and Social Needs of Physically Handicapped Adults: are they being met by the Statutory Services. Developmental Medicine and Child Neurology. Supplement No. 50. 1985 p. 3. George J. Aids and Adaptation for the elderly at home: underprovided, underused, and undermaintained. BMJ 1988:296, 1365–1366. Penn ND. Old and unwashed: bathing problems in the over 70s. BMJ 1989; 298, 1158–1159. Mulley GP. Provision of aids. BMJ 1988:296;6632, 1317–1318*).

Reasons for non-use can include, for example:

- poor design (complicated, uncomfortable, unattractive, socially unacceptable, ineffective);
- ill-fit or lack of safety (eg loose or slippery bath rails and mats, worn or defective walking aids);
- little or no instruction given to client and family;
- change in client's condition (amelioration or deterioration);

- equipment is an inappropriate solution (*Mulley GP. Provision of aids. BMJ 1988: 296;6632, 1317–1318*).

Other evidence suggests much greater and more satisfactory use of equipment: a 1989 survey of over 300 people with multiple sclerosis found that there was 'a high level of use and satisfaction with the aids and equipment' (daily living and home nursing) which had been supplied (*Southampton MS Survey Research Team. Multiple Sclerosis in the Southampton District. Rehabilitation Unit and Dept. of Sociology and Social Policy. 1989 pp. 124–5*).

2.5.10. Loan periods. Daily living equipment is usually loaned for as long as it is needed.

There are sometimes local guidelines to limit loan periods; for example, chairs, bath aids and raised toilet seats are sometimes issued for six to eight weeks to clients who have just had a total hip replacement (*North of England. Joint store document 1985. Northern Ireland community OT questionnaire 1988*).

2.5.11. Information and advice. Where it is decided that there is no duty to supply the equipment, information on how to obtain the equipment by other means (eg statutory or voluntary) is often given. Local guidelines sometimes stress that it is important to provide such information (*Northwest England SSD (12)*).

Legislation places a duty on SSD/SWD/HSSBs to provide information to people with disabilities in relation to other services available, from whatever source (*Chronically Sick and Disabled Persons Act 1970 s.1 as amended by Disabled Persons (Services, Consultation and Representation) Act 1986 s.9; Chronically Sick and Disabled Persons (Northern Ireland) Act 1978 s.1*).

2.6. Follow-up

Follow-up of the client ensures that he or she is using and benefiting from the equipment. SSD/SWD/HSSB guidelines sometimes clearly state the importance of this (*eg London borough SSD (10) received 1990*).

It is often recognised locally that good follow-up practice cannot be adhered to, because of staff shortages (*Scotland SWD OT questionnaire 1988, Northern Ireland community OT questionnaire 1988; SSD/SWD/HPSSB guidelines rec. 1989-1990*). Follow-up (of equipment), and review (of the client's condition) procedures can overlap.

Apart from the client's welfare and cost savings, follow-up is also important, given concern over product liability and litigation (*Northern Ireland community OT questionnaire 1988*).

Both policy and actual practice vary in relation to equipment follow-up and client review; examples are given in Box 2.7.

2.7. Maintenance, repair, replacement of equipment

(This section can be read generally to apply to other equipment, such as home nursing equipment, wheelchairs, walking aids.)

In general the SSD/SWD/HSSB maintains, repairs and replaces its equipment: for example, re-upholstery of chairs is carried out in its workshops (*Northern Ireland community OT questionnaire 1988*).

It might also maintain more complex and expensive equipment. For example,

---

> **Box 2.7: Examples of equipment follow-up and client review procedures**
>
> - one further visit;
> - an annual review visit (*eg Southwest England SSD (26) 1989*);
> - two initial follow-up visits followed by annual reviews (*SWD OT questionnaire 1988*);
> - annual review for all equipment; after a certain time, certain equipment might cease to be liable for this review, and the client is advised to inspect it regularly (*Southwest England (40) guidelines received 1989*);
> - more regular review of people with severe problems and/or more complex equipment (*see eg North of England Joint Store Document (1), 1985; London SSD (18,19) 1990; SWD OT questionnaire 1988; Northern Ireland community OT questionnaire 1988*);
> - more regular and specific review of people with more expensive equipment such as geriatric chairs, wheelchairs, self-lift chairs, some commodes, chemical toilets and hoists (*London SSD guidelines 1989 (19)*);
> - use of OT assistants (or other staff) to carry out frequent reviews in between longer term reviews by OTs (*SWD Guidance, received 1989*);
> - use in some areas of hospital OTs with special remit to 'bridge the gap' between hospital and community and to follow up patients discharged from hospital (*see eg Newman D. Bridging the Gap: an Evaluation of the Joint-Funded Occupational Therapy Approach. Occupational Therapy 1987:50; 6, 191–194. Sutton J et al. Primary Care Occupational Therapy Service, Bromley Health Authority: Bridging the Gap. Occupational Therapy 1985: 48;10, 311–313*);
> - general responsibility in some areas of hospital OTs to follow up equipment loaned on behalf of the SSD/SWD or HSSB (social services) (*Northwest England SSD (11) guidelines 1990*);
> - clients suffering from severely degenerative conditions or totally wheelchair dependent and severely handicapped children: case to be brought up every 6 months and reviewed by the OT probably involving a home visit (*Midlands SSD (23) guidance received 1989)/1989*);
> - clients suffering from conditions which are likely to deteriorate: cases to be brought up on an annual basis and reviewed by the OT probably by means of a telephone call (*Midlands SSD (23) guidance received 1989)/1990*);
> - clients suffering from relatively stable disabilities where circumstances are unlikely to change except from aging or trauma: cases to be brought up on an annual basis and client sent a standard letter (*Midlands SSD (23) 1989*).

one joint equipment store has identified large financial savings by repairing and servicing its own bath lifts, and its own special beds (*Midlands joint store catalogue (2) 1989*). Many common stock small items require minimal servicing and maintenance anyway (*Southwest England (40) guidelines received 1989*).

There is some evidence that equipment, in general, is not satisfactorily maintained, and that significant quantities on loan are in need of repair or are worn out (*see eg Thomas A. et al. Health and Social Needs of Physically Handicapped Adults: are they being met by the Statutory Services? Developmental Medicine and Child Neurology. Supplement No. 50. 1985 p. 3. George J. Aids and Adaptation for the elderly at home: underprovided, underused, and undermaintained. BMJ 1988: 296, 1365–1366*).

2.7.1. Government safety bulletins on equipment. The DH/SHHD/WO/ DHSS(NI) circulates safety action bulletins concerning equipment such as, hoist slings, harnesses, straps (*eg SAB(89)14, March 1989*).

2.7.2. Manufacturer/supplier maintenance. More complex equipment such as electric hoists or stairlifts is likely to be maintained by means of contracts with the supplier/manufacturer. Chemical toilets, for example, are sometimes maintained, filled and emptied by a commercial contractor. Such contracts might also cover repair and replacement.

A single maintenance contract for all hoists or stairlifts on loan might be operated SSD/SWD/HSSB-wide (*eg Southwest England SSD (40) guidelines 1989*).

2.8. Recall

(This section can be read to apply generally to other equipment, such as home nursing equipment, wheelchairs, walking aids.)

There seems to be general awareness that a great deal of equipment sooner or later is unused, but does not find its way back to the SSD/SWD/HSSB. Recall procedures are likely to vary from organised and effective, to virtually non-effective: from active to passive (*see eg Brett T., Only on loan. Health and Social Service Journal 1983:93;4826, 24; Anonymous. Remedial Therapist 1984:7; 23, p.1; Argus. Finding Ways of retrieving aids. Remedial Therapist 1984: 7; 23, p. 4; Manthorpe J. Therapy Weekly 1986: 12; 47, 6); Mulley GP. Provision of aids. BMJ 1988: 296; 6632, 1317-1318*).

Reasons for non-retrieval of equipment can include:

- clients, patients, carers do not know where to return it;
- confusion as to (statutory body) ownership of the equipment);
- insufficiently trained staff to operate effective recall;
- lack of resources for retrieval;
- problems arising from the need to refurbish, check and sterilise new aids (*NAHA News 1986:97, p. 4*);
- lack of effective policy on recall.

Factors affecting recall are listed in Box 2.8. It should also be pointed out that improved recall systems are seen to be one of the potential benefits of joint (funded) equipment stores (Box 2.6.2.).

Box 2.8: Factors affecting recall of equipment

2.8.1. Active recall of equipment might include, for example:

- regular follow-up letters and visits;
- publicity campaigns in the local media;
- clear labelling;
- client signature for expensive equipment;
- use of selected volunteers by SSD/SWD/HSSB to collect equipment to be returned (*Southwest England SSD (26) 1989*);
- limited loan period 'enforced' for some equipment loan such as raised toilet seats and dressing aids loaned for a period of 8 weeks following hip replacement operations (*SWD OT questionnaire 1988*);
- other professionals (such as district nurses, health visitors, GPs, home helps) might be encouraged to look out for unused equipment (*SWD questionnaire 1988*);
- joint equipment store allows rationalisation of recall system for both daily living equipment (SSD/SWD/HSSB) and home nursing equipment (DHA/HB/HPSSB) (*see variously Ward PR. Recovery and reuse of aids for disabled people: the costs and value. Health Trends 1980: 12;1,14-15; Brett T. Only on loan. Health and Social Service Journal 1983:93;4826, 24; Anonymous. Remedial Therapist 1984: 7; 23, p. 1; Finding Ways of*

retrieving aids. Remedial Therapist 1984: 7; 23, p. 4. Manthorpe J; Please . . . can we have our aid back? Therapy Weekly 1986:12; 47, 6.).

Thus, one 'active' scheme, for example:

- recalls 90-95% of equipment successfully;
- operates from a joint equipment store run by a voluntary organisation on behalf of the local SSD and DHA;
- requires renewal of the loan every six months: after two reminders, a storeman visits the person to see whether the equipment is still used, and recover it, if appropriate (*Leicestershire Red Cross, written and verbal, 1989*).

B2.8.2. Passive recall of equipment. A more 'passive' recall system means that responsibility for initiating return/recall procedures rests with the client, family or carers (*eg Northern Ireland, Scotland questionnaires 1988*). This arrangement is probably quite common, but may only recover 30%-50% of equipment (*Ward PR. Recovery and reuse of aids for disabled people: the costs and value. Health Trends 1980: 12;1, 14–15*).

Clients (and family) might also be encouraged to both initiate the return and also deliver the equipment back to the SSD/SWD/HSSB (*see eg Midlands SSD (23) 1989. Northeast England SSD (25) 1989*).

B2.8.3. Small community: equipment recall. In a small (eg island) community, recall is likely to be more effective, since there is a likelihood that many professionals and clients alike know where to return equipment (*eg Scotland SWD OT questionnaire 1988*).

B2.8.4. Other professional help in relation to recall of equipment. Community nurses or home helps, for example, sometimes inform the SSD/SWD/HSSB that equipment should be collected when it is no longer needed (*Scotland SWD OT questionnaire 1988*), and are sometimes actually encouraged to do so (*Northern Ireland community OT questionnaire 1988; Scotland SWD OT questionnaire 1988*).

B2.8.5. Deposit system in relation to equipment recall. Deposits on equipment are generally not taken by statutory services: reasons which have been cited against so doing include: difficulty in setting up a separate accounting system, and the large number of exemptions which might be accorded to old people and children (*Ward PR. Recovery and reuse of aids for disabled people: the costs and value. Health Trends 1980: 12;1, 14–15*).

However, the Red Cross, for example, does sometimes make deposit charges for equipment loaned (though not when it is acting in its capacity of formal agent for a statutory service).

B2.8.6. Cost effectiveness of recall. Lack of recall procedures is sometimes accounted for in terms of cost-effectiveness.

For example, factors which have been cited in relation to cost-effectiveness of recall are given in Box 2.9.

Box 2.9: Cost effectiveness factors relevant to recall include:

- lack of hygienic cleansing facilities (and staff);
- sparse population in geographically large areas;
- automatic writing off:
  - bath and toilet aids at initial issue because of the soiled or poor condition in which they are usually returned (eg plastic urinals, pressure relief rings and plastic sheeting) (*Northwest England SSD (12) 1990. Scotland and OT questionnaire 1988. Keeble P. Provision of Aids by Health and Social Services: Examples of Good and Bad Practice. Contact, Spring 1984, 36–38*);

> – feeding and dressing equipment, grab rails and equipment known to deteriorate, such as plastic coated grip rails (*Midlands SSD (23) 1989*);
> - automatic writing off of certain types of equipment is undertaken in accordance with a loan general principle: that the item be recoverable, re-useable and generally worth the cost of recovery, cleaning, storage and reissue (*Southwest England SSD (40) guidelines 1989*);
> - existence, in relation to any writing-off procedure, of formal recording procedures involving the authority's treasurer, for example (*Southwest England SSD (13) 1990*);
> - cost-effectiveness of procedures required to ensure the re-use of equipment including inspection for mechanical and electrical function and safety, cleaning and disinfection (*Ward PR. Recovery and reuse of aids for disabled people: the costs and value. Health Trends 1980: 12;1,14–15*);
> - efficient store management;
> - use of volunteers, adult training centres or sheltered industrial groups to help with the ordering, checking, labelling, return, cleaning, refurbishment of equipment (*eg Scotland SWD OT questionnaire 1988*).
> - review of expensive items on a regular basis eg 6 weekly, 6 monthly or yearly (*eg Northwest England SSD (12) 1990*); especially where it is expected that the need for the equipment is only short-term (*Northeast England SSD (25) 1989*).

2.8.1. Cleaning and decontamination procedures. Recent concern over infectious disease has led to greater concern over cleaning and decontamination procedures. Effective organisation of such procedures is important if recall is to be cost-effective, adequate cleaning is to be possible, and professional staff's (eg community OTs) time is not to be wasted. Large, joint equipment stores are seen as one way of rationalising such procedures (*2.5.3.1./B2.6.2.*).

Circular guidance (England, Scotland, 1987), in relation to 'all health care equipment which comes into contact with patients or their body fluids', makes reference to various decontamination methods including steam sterilisation, low temperature steam, dry heat, chemical methods and swabbing with warm water. These are given as examples only, and the different methods are appropriate to different levels of contamination.

The guidance states that the health service has a duty to both its own employees, and to other people, to ensure (as far as possible) that they are not exposed to risks.

The guidance is aimed at general managers, regional scientific officers, supplies officers, sterile supply managers, medical, dental, nursing, pharmacy, medical physics, operating theatre, engineering, maintenance and domestic staff, infection control personnel, general medical and dental practitioners, nominated safety officers and all laboratory staff (*Joint circular HN(87)22,HN(FP)(87)35; SHHD/DGM(1987)66*).

2.9. Charges

2.9.1. Power to charge. SSD/SWD/HSSBs have the power to charge for equipment (30.2), but this power is rarely used.

SSD/SWD/HSSB internal guidelines sometimes emphasise this by stating quite clearly that equipment is loaned at no cost to the client (*SSD/SWD/HSSB guidelines received 1989/1990*).

Occasionally, a test of resources might be made for more major and expensive items of equipment (eg SWD OT questionnaire 1988). However, if a client cannot afford to buy the equipment, and a need has been identified, the SSD/SWD/HSSB remains under a duty to provide it, since the need remains.

Occasionally, an SSD, for example, might make a hire charge for special equipment such as chairs (*Midlands SSD (21) guidelines received 1990*).

2.9.2. Maintenance of equipment. The SSD/SWD/HSSB normally remains responsible for the maintenance and repair of equipment. Where the client has equipment such as a stairlift through a housing authority grant (3.8), the SSD/SWD/HSSB might help with maintenance costs. Otherwise the responsibility rests with the client (3.8).

2.9.3. Voluntary organisation store provision of 'beneficial' equipment. Voluntary organisations (such as the British Red Cross) running an equipment store on behalf of the SSD/SWD/HSSB, might make hire and deposit charges for equipment supplied, which is deemed, for example, 'beneficial' or 'desirable' but not 'essential' or necessary; which does not fall under the remit of the SSD at all (eg glideabout chairs, baby buggies); or which is deemed 'de-luxe' equipment (*Midlands SSD (21) 1990*).

2.9.4. Donations. Some SSDs, for example, while providing equipment at no charge, might suggest that clients either buy the equipment from the SSD, or at least make a donation towards it.

Sometimes clients wish to pay the SSD/SWD/HSSB anyway for any equipment provided.

2.9.5. Private purchase suggested. Some SSD/SWD/HSSBs may suggest private purchase if the equipment is either cheap (eg under a threshold such as £10, £20, £30), or the sort of common equipment which is required by everybody.

For example, local SSD guidelines might state that 'allowing people to achieve for themselves, where they are able , the purchase of small items of equipment, is a natural extension of . . . independence' (*London borough SSD (18) 1990*).

2.9.5.1. Examples of equipment suggested for private purchase include rubber bathmats, kitchen utensils, high stools, foot-stools, milk bottle holders, velcro tape, plugs with handles (*London SSD (18) 1990*), potato peelers, electric can openers and bath mats (*Northern Ireland community OT questionnaire 1988*).

However, adaptations to small aids might still be provided (eg tap turners, large handles for cutlery) (*Northern Ireland questionnaire 1988*).

While restricting the range of such smaller, common items which it supplies, an SSD/SWD/HSSB might retain a set of these items for demonstration and trial purposes (*Southwest England SSD (20) 1990*).

2.9.5.2. Client's means in relation to suggested private purchase of equipment. If the client receives income support, for example, and cannot afford the recommended equipment, the SSD/SWD/HSSB is likely to provide the equipment: and is under a legislative duty to do so if a need for the equipment has been identified (2.2.1.).

There is sometimes difficulty in asking people to actually purchase small items themselves. For example, sometimes those most in need might be the least able to cope with catalogue purchase; there may also be no stockist in the area (*Northern Ireland community OT questionnaire 1988*).

2.10. Voluntary organisation help with equipment

When provision of equipment has not taken place through statutory channels, voluntary organisations are sometimes able to help. Such help is normally in the form of either a loan from a central bank of equipment, or a grant.

The SSD/SWD/HSSB sometimes suggests that the client approach voluntary organisations, either when it cannot supply certain equipment in principle, or when there is likely to be assessment or provision delay (*see eg London borough SSD (18) 1990. Northern Ireland questionnaire 1988*).

Occasionally, there is local agreement with a voluntary organisation, by means of which the SSD?SWD/HSSB has potential access to a charity fund for special expensive equipment: it might operate specific criteria for referral to the fund (*London SSD (24) guidelines received 1989*).

2.10.1. Rehabilitation engineering movement advisory panels (REMAP) can help with special, custom-made, 'one-off' equipment, when there is no statutory or commercial solution. REMAP consists of local teams of, for example, engineers (rehabilitation or otherwise), doctors, therapists and social workers, who devise and make equipment free of charge (except occasional charges for materials) (29.3).

2.10.2. Family Fund. The Family Fund is government-supported and administered by the Joseph Rowntree Memorial Trust. Help can be given to families with a very severely disabled child under sixteen years of age, and whose social and economic circumstances are such as to meet the Trust's criteria.

Depending on these individual circumstances, and the non-provision by statutory services, help can be given with, for example, laundry equipment (including washing machines), equipment and adaptations, heating, bedding, clothing, telephone, and unusual requests.

Following application (by a standard form), one of the Fund's 'visiting social workers' makes a home visit. Sometimes further medical information needs to be obtained by the Fund.

2.11. Private purchase of daily living equipment

2.11.1. Increased opportunities for private purchase. Opportunities for private purchase have increased in recent years:

- high street chemists are starting to stock more and more daily living equipment;
- commercial versions of DLCs (2.4.2.2.), both displaying and selling equipment, are beginning to appear;
- mail order schemes offer all sorts of equipment by post;

- disabled living centres (DLCs) provide information and demonstration facilities for private consumers, before they actually decide to purchase equipment.

2.11.2. Postal purchase of equipment. There are now a number of firms offering mail order daily living equipment.

Some voluntary organisations offer a mail order facility. A 1980 study, for example, found that people with arthritis buying in this fashion did so because:

- of lack of mobility;
- they wished to remain independent and not rely on social services;
- they were unaware of the possibility of help from the social services;
- because the equipment was cheap.

The drawback was that some people would have preferred to assess and try out the equipment before purchase. It was thought that the problem could be remedied by a prior visit to a DLC (2.4.2.2.) (*Stowe J. Chamberlain MA. Aids for Arthritics. Occupational Therapy Weekly 1980: 43;3, 80–84*).

2.11.3. Insurance claims. Claims for personal injury now often include assessment for equipment and adaptations needed both immediately and foreseeably in the future (as the disability predictably progresses with age).

Awards can include money for items such as cars, washing machines, wheelchairs, ramps, rails, environmental control equipment, special WCs, electric hoists, user controlled outdoor powered wheelchairs, special baths and special clothing (*Smith ME. Insurance Compensation for Severe Injury – What Happens after Settlement. Rehabilitation Studies Unit, University of Edinburgh 1987 p. 10*).

There is some uncertainty as to how the claim is decided, in terms of equipment which might be available through statutory services. The person's own local authorities might have to be approached and asked whether they can guarantee provision of certain items (*Verbal communication: Personal Injuries Compensation Claims Service, 1989*).

2.12. Balance between statutory provision, voluntary provision, voluntary body provision and private purchase

All three channels of provision complement each other, not just in relation to daily living equipment, but also to, for example, home nursing equipment, communication aids, wheelchairs. See Box 2.10 for examples.

> **Box 2.10: Examples of studies demonstrating source (statutory body/ voluntary body/private purchase) of equipment provision**
>
> **Example 1.** A study of people with motor neurone disease showed that:
>
> - charities supplied 21 % of the equipment (eg electric armchairs, electric beds and a Possum word processor system);
> - statutory services 62% (eg manual wheelchairs [orthotic], appliances and most of the mobility and communication aids);
> - private purchase accounted for 21% including ramps, grab rails and smaller items such as adapted drinking straws; (*Harper J. Therapy Weekly, 17.8.99*).

Example 2. A study of people with multiple sclerosis found that in the case of:

- bath aids:
  - 78% were funded by statutory services;
  - most of the remainder were privately purchased;
  - 7% were funded from a 'mixture' of sources;
- toilet aids:
  - 84% were funded by statutory services;
  - nearly all the rest were privately purchased;
- communication aids (including portable telephones, alarm systems;
- environmental control systems):
  - 48% were funded by statutory services;
  - 43% privately purchased;
  - 9% were funded by charities;
- bedroom equipment:
  - 74% were funded by statutory services;
- mobility aids (including walking aids and wheelchairs):
  - 71% were funded by statutory services;
  - 24% were privately purchased (*Southampton MS Survey Research Team. Multiple Sclerosis in the Southampton District. Rehabilitation Unit and Dept. of Sociology and Social Policy. 1989 pp. 124–5*).

Example 3. A study of home nursing equipment in relation to terminal care. Results included information on:

- nutritional equipment: a large number of feeding cups and blenders (expensive items), used as necessary items, were supplied by the family;
- mobility equipment:
  - wheelchairs: supplied mostly by health service, voluntary bodies, social services, in that order. Occasionally, social services had provided an electric wheelchair;
  - walking aids: supplied mostly by health service, voluntary bodies, social services in that order (some walking sticks privately purchased);
- bed/bed equipment and related equipment:
  - most large items (eg special beds, mattresses, sheepskins) were provided by the health service;
  - some items such as backrests and sorbo rings were also significantly provided through voluntary bodies or family purchase as well as through the health service;
  - v-shaped pillows, duvets, extra bed linen, bed tables were mostly family purchased;
- sanitary aids:
  - mostly supplied by the health service, although over 40% of commodes were supplied through a voluntary organisation;
- miscellaneous equipment:
  - more expensive equipment, perhaps regarded as luxury rather than necessity (although improving care facilities for both patient and carer), such as alarms/ intercoms, telephones/telephone equipment, electric fans, heating; were generally privately purchased (*Marie Curie Cancer Care. Study of the Marie Curie Community Nursing Service. Marie Curie Memorial Foundation, 1989, pp. 144–55*).

Example 4. A survey (*OPCS, 1989*) of source (statutory supply or private purchase) of equipment used by adults, in private households included the following results (ratios given in brackets):

(The figures given below relate to questions asked of people with the most relevant disability in the case of each type of equipment (eg locomotor disability, seeing disability, incontinence).)

- walking aids:
  - walking frames: most (9:1) frames were provided by statutory services;
  - walking sticks: most (30:19) were privately purchased;

- surgical corset/other brace or support: most (7:3) were provided by statutory services;
- wheelchairs: most (9:2) were provided by statutory services;
- equipment for visual impairment:
  - magnifying glass/low vision aids: most (31:6) were bought privately;
  - aids to mobility:
    - white canes: most (7:1) were provided by statutory services;
    - ordinary sticks: most (5:2) were privately purchased;
- equipment for hearing impairment:
  - personal hearing aids: most (26:6) were provided by statutory services;
  - adaptors (telephone, television, radio): most (6:2) were privately purchased;
  - flashing lights: evenly supplied (1:1);
- equipment for the assessment of incontinence:
  - ileostomy/colostomy bag: all (6:0) provided by statutory services;
  - catheter/bag for urine: most (8:1) provided by statutory services;
  - incontinence pads: most (30:12) provided by statutory services;
  - rubber sheet, mattress, other protective bedding: statutory services provide slightly (12:11) more;
- small aids and gadgets:
  - special crockery/cutlery/utensils: most (25:14) were privately purchased;
  - special taps: most (8:5) were provided by statutory services;
  - pick-up aid or long-handled aid: most (18:6) were provided by statutory services;
  - dressing aids/electric toothbrush: most (4:2) were provided by statutory services;
- special furniture and aids to personal care:
  - special beds or bedding
    - bed hoist/bed poles/bed ladders: most (2:0) provided statutory services;
    - bed cradles: even (1:1) provision;
- aids to toileting:
  - commode/sanichair: more (10:8) provided by statutory services;
  - toilet hoist/raised seat: most (6:1) were provided by statutory services;
- aids to bathing:
  - bath seat/bath hoist/other aids for getting in and out of bath: most (23:4) provided by statutory services;
  - non-slip mat: most (25:6) privately purchased;
- aids to sitting:
  - special chair: more (7:6) privately purchased (*Martin J.* et al. *Disabled adults: services, transport and employment. OPCS surveys of disability in Great Britain. Report 4. OPCS, Social Survey Division. HMSO, 1989, pp. 46–59*).

3 Home adaptations

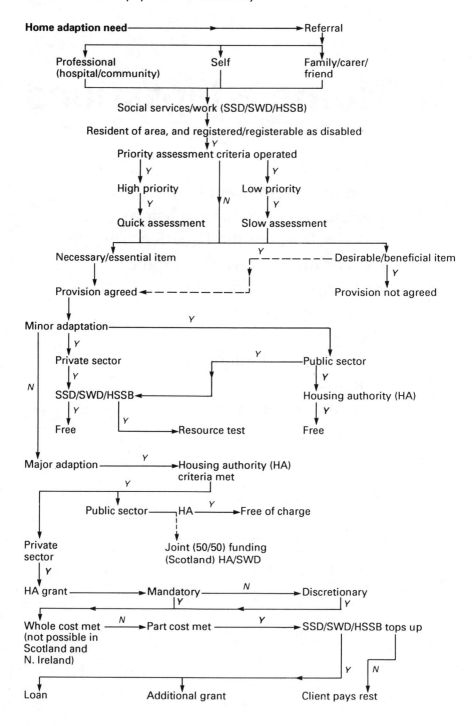

Introduction

Type of equipment

Home adaptations include both non-structural (minor) adaptations such as removeable rails or temporary, removeable ramps; and structural (major) adaptations such as permanent ramps, lifts, extra ground floor facilities.

Responsibility for provision

Home adaptations form probably the most complicated area of provision dealt with in this book. Powers and duties lie with both social services and housing authorities:

- social services departments (SSDs, England/Wales);
- social work departments (SWDs, Scotland);
- health and social services boards (HSSBs, Northern Ireland);
- district, borough, city, metropolitan borough councils (England and Wales);
- district councils (Scotland);
- Northern Ireland Housing Executive (NIHE).

These powers and duties relate respectively to the individual needs of people with disabilities and to considerations of the renovation or improvement of housing stock. They overlap – this means that the different authorities involved need to work closely together at local level.

Referral, assessment and provision.

SSD/SWD/HSSBs normally assess the needs of a disabled person thought to need a home adaptation, and if a need is identified, they have a duty to make arrangements for the provision of the adaptation. SSD/SWDs also have a duty to make an assessment in response to a request from the disabled person, or his/her carer. Referral to the SSD/SWD/HSSB for assessment of home adaptations is open, although it is often made by professionals.

SSD/SWD/HSSBs themselves take reponsibility for the carrying out of minor adaptations in both private, and sometimes public sector, housing. Charges for such minor adaptations can be made, although this is not usual; however, sometimes a test of resources is made, to decide what level of assistance should be given.

More rarely, SSD/SWD/HSSBs undertake the arrangements for a major adaptation if, for example, the client fails to obtain a housing authority grant and cannot afford to pay for the work privately.

They sometimes give financial assistance, known as 'topping up', extra to any grant already received from a housing authority. A test of resources is often employed when determining the level of such assistance.

Housing authorities have both powers and duties to give grants for the renovation and improvement of the homes of people with disabilities. Under certain conditions such grants are mandatory; otherwise they are discretionary.

Following assessment of a disabled person by the SSD/SWD/HSSB, the housing authority assesses the technical feasibility of the recommended adaptation, as well as the general eligibility of the applicant and dwelling. The planning and work stages of major adaptations can be long and complicated.

Various grants are available from housing authorities. The grant systems in Scotland and Northern Ireland are similar to one another, while a new system is now in operation in England and Wales since July 1990. The amount of grant does not cover the total cost of the work in Scotland and Northern Ireland; in England and Wales it can do so, in some cases, under the new grant system.

Sometimes the SSD/SWD/HSSB gives financial assistance of some sort, additional to housing authority grant received.

Housing authorities also have powers to carry out major and minor adaptations free of charge to their own housing stock, without using the grant system; such work falls under 'duties to own stock'. The degree to which they use these powers varies from area to area.

3.1. Type of home adaptation

3.1.1. Definition of structural adaptations and non-structural adaptations. Home adaptations are normally divided into two main categories: 'structural' major adaptations; and 'non-structural' (minor adaptations).

3.1.1.1. Non-structural adaptations. Circular and other guidance has characterised non-structural adaptations as:

- removable *(eg Draft joint circular DoE X/90, WO Y/90, DH Z/90 para 21; Joint circular SDD 40/1985 – NHS 1985(GEN)33 – SWSG 17/1985)*;
- portable *(England: Joint circular DoE 59/78, LAC(78)14, WO 104/78)*; or
- re-useable *(Draft joint circular DoE X/90, WO Y/90, DH Z/90 para 21)*.

NIHE Guidance has referred to non-structural adaptations as 'minor works' *(Joint Code of Guidance. Housing the Disabled. NIHE, 1987 p. 4)*.

3.1.1.2. Structural adaptations. Circular and other guidance has characterised structural adaptations as:

- 'permanent in nature' *(Joint circular SDD 40/1985 – NHS 1985(GEN)33 – SWSG 17/1985)*;
- non-removable *(Draft joint circular DoE X/90, WO Y/90, DH Z/90 para 21; Joint circular SDD 40/1985 – NHS 1985(GEN)33 – SWSG 17/1985)*;
- non-portable *(Draft joint circular DoE X/90, WO Y/90, DH Z/90 para 21: Joint circular DoE 59/78, LAC(78)14, WO 104/78)*; or
- non-re-useable *(Draft joint circular DoE X/90, WO Y/90, DH Z/90 para 21)*.

3.1.1.3. Division of responsibility. Broadly speaking, the distinction between structural and non-structural adaptations is used to divide responsibility (finance and arrangements) for adaptations between SSD/SWD/HSSBs and housing authorities.

Such a division is referred to in Circular and other guidance *(see eg Joint circular DoE 59/78, LAC(78)14, WO 104/78; Draft joint circular DoE X/90, WO Y/90, DH Z/90 para 21; Joint circular SDD 40/1985 – NHS 1985(GEN)33 – SWSG 17/1985; Joint Code of Guidance. Housing the Disabled. NIHE, 1987 pp. 4, 5)*, but is not always hard and fast. Stairlifts for example are sometimes classed as structural *(eg Joint circular DoE 59/78, LAC(78)14, WO 104/78; Joint Code of Guidance. Housing the Disabled. NIHE 1987 p. 4)* or as non-structural *(eg Scotland Joint circular SDD 40/1985 – NHS*

1985(GEN)33 – SWSG 17/1985; Joint Code of Guidance. Housing the Disabled. NIHE 1987 p. 5).

Recognising that the powers and duties of the different authorities overlap and are dependent on one another, Circular guidance recommends close co-operation (3.6.7.).

3.1.2. Examples. Typical examples of non-structural adaptations include temporary ramps, portable heaters, environmental hearing equipment and re-usable rails. Structural adaptations include bathrooms, permanent ramps, permanent rails, shower units or kitchen units.

For a detailed listing of examples of structural and non-structural adaptations, as given by Circular (England, Wales, Scotland) and NIHE guidance, see Box 3.1.

Box 3.1: Examples of home adaptations

B3.1.1. Non-structural adaptations

B3.1.1.1. Scotland. Examples given in Circular guidance (1985) are:

- additional internal grab rails;
- temporary ramps;
- door answering intercoms;
- individual emergency call facilities;
- removable stair lifts;
- laundry and cleaning equipment.

Community alarm schemes are also mentioned as being subject to joint Social Work and housing authority schemes (*Joint Circular SDD 40/1985, NHS 1985(GEN)33, SWSG 17/1985*).

B3.1.1.2. England and Wales. Circular guidance (1978) lists examples (stressed to be only examples):

- portable or re-usable ramps (eg timber or metal);
- environmental controls;
- hearing induction loops;
- telephone installations;
- portable heaters;
- portable lamps/dimmer switches (for people with visual impairment), portable hoists;
- suspended hoists including ceiling track;
- tap turners;
- special kitchen utensils or cooking equipment;
- portable WC seat raisers;
- portable or re-usable support rails or support frames (*Joint circular DoE 59/78 – LAC(78)14 – WO 104/78*).

B3.1.2. Structural adaptations

B3.1.2.1. Circular guidance (Scotland). Examples given in Circular guidance (Scotland) include:

- accessible bathrooms;
- bedrooms;
- permanent concrete ramps, wooden ramps;
- fixed track and electric hoists;
- internal and external handrails;

- floor fixed support rails;
- toilet grab rails;
- bath grab rails;
- widening doors;
- fitting special doors and windows;
- special kitchen units (eg raised or lowered);
- lever taps;
- special bath or shower units;
- raised or lower plugs/points;
- electric immersion heater installation;
- front door and telephone aids for the deaf;
- automatic garage doors;
- emergency call and intercom systems;
- other adaptations to the building fabric (*Joint Circular SDD 40/1985 – NHS 1985(GEN)33 – SWSG 17/1985. And SW 19/1976 with NHS Memorandum 1976 (GEN)90*).

B3.1.2.2. Circular guidance (England) and Northern Ireland Housing Executive guidance give a fuller list structural adaptation examples.

1. *General alterations:* extension or alterations to provide bathrooms, WCs, or bedrooms with level or suitably ramped access.

2. *Garaging and external facilities:*

- widening of garden paths hardstanding;
- carport and/or undercover access to dwelling if possible.

3. *Approaches to entrance doors:*

- fixed ramp in place of steps;
- handrails or balustrading to ramps or steps (also other parts of the dwelling where necessary).

4. *Doors and windows:*

- widening or rehanging of doors to permit wheelchair manoeuvre;
- suitable ironmongery, for example pull handles and rail handles to doors, kicking plate and protective edging to door frames and hanging stiles.

5. *Staircases and vertical circulation:*

- additional handrail to staircase;
- gate at head and/or foot of stairs.

6. *Water services:*

- substitution of lever for screwdown taps;
- refixing of taps at convenient level;
- thermostatic control for shower;
- relocation of control valve for mains water supply.

7. *Electrical and heating services:*

- change of heating;
- refixing of socket outlets at convenient level;
- additional socket outlets;
- rocker light switches;
- alarm call (private sector only);
- loud bell for hard of hearing people;
- relocation of pre-payment meters;
- relocation of thermostat, or heating controls;
- relocation of main switches for gas or electricity;

- fluorescent lights in kitchen, bathroom and working areas for visually impaired people;
- warning systems for people who are hard of hearing eg flashing lights.

8. Provision for lifting aids:

- reinforcement of ceilings for provision of trace for personal hoist;
- vertical or stair lift.

9. Acoustic insulation:

- acoustic insulation (for example, for households in which there is an exceptionally noisy and disruptive child).

10. Entrance halls:

- letter cages;
- delivery shelf;
- relocation of clothes hanging rails (also in bedrooms).

11. Kitchens:

- alterations to provide fixed storage units, worktops and sink;
- units at convenient levels;
- waste disposal unit to sink.

12. Bathroom and WCs:

- shower unit in place of or to supplement bath;
- shower cubicle;
- suitable proprietary bath;
- suitable proprietary WC fixture;
- suitable wash basin;
- bidet/closomat;
- raising of WC fixture;
- support rails to walls by bath and WC and/or other supports;
- platform at head of bath.

13. Storage:
- storage provision for wheelchair;
- rearrangement of existing storage provision.

3.2. Legislative basis for provision

3.2.1. Basis for SSD/SWD/HSSB assessment and provision

3.2.1.1. The Chronically Sick and Disabled Persons Acts (*CSDPAs, 1970 and 1978*) place specific powers and duties on SSD/SWDs and HSSBs (under social services functions) in relation to home adaptations.

3.2.1.1.1. Basis for structural adaptations in relation to SSD/SWD/HSSBs. SSD/SWD/HSSBs have a duty, where an individual need is identified, to 'make arrangements . . . for the provision of assistance . . . in arranging for the carrying out of any works of adaptation in his home' (*CSDPA 1979 s.2(1)(e), CSDP(NI)A 1978 s.2(e)*).

(This duty includes, in practice, the assessment for home adaptations (3.6.); provision of 'topping up' help additional to housing authority grants (3.9.7.); joint-funding arrangements (3.9.2.); and the arranging and funding of minor adaptations and, more exceptionally, of major structural adaptations (3.9.8.)).

3.2.1.1.2. Basis for non-structural adaptations in relation to SSD/SWD/HSSBs. SSD/SWD/HSSBs have a duty, where an individual need is identified, to 'make arrangements . . . for the provision of any additional facilities designed to secure . . . greater safety, comfort or convenience' (*CSDPA 1970 s.2(1)(e), CSDP(NI)A 1978 s.2(e)*).

(In practice, the term 'facilities' is taken to include daily living equipment, which in turn might be taken to include non-structural adaptations such as removeable ramps or rails.)

3.2.1.2. Basis in general welfare powers and duties for SSD/SWD/HSSB assessment and provision. The specific CSDPA duties outlined immediately above (3.2.1.1.) reinforce previous general welfare legislation embodied in the:

- National Assistance Act 1948 (England and Wales);
- Social Work (Scotland) Act 1968;
- Health and Personal Social Services (Northern Ireland) Order 1972.

This legislation involves general powers (England and Wales) and duties (Scotland and Northern Ireland) towards people with disabilities (2.2.2.).

3.2.1.3. Basis for request for assessment by the SSD/SWD/HSSB. The CSDPA duty has itself been reinforced by recent legislation (not yet in force in Northern Ireland), which places a duty on the SSD/SWD/HSSB, to carry out an assessment, when requested to do so by a disabled person, or his/her carer (*Disabled Persons (Services, Consultation, Representation) Act 1986 s.4; Disabled Persons (Northern Ireland) Act 1989) (2.2.3.)*).

This legislation also places a duty (not yet in force anywhere in the UK) on SSD/SWDs to give an account, if requested to do so, of the assessment, and of services it either intends to provide or not provide (2.2.3.).

3.2.1.4. Basis for community care assessment. Community care legislation not yet in force, entails new assessment duties for SSD/SWD/HSSBs. These duties will be to determine whether the best form of care for a person can be provided in their own home or in a residential home (with or without nursing) (2.2.4.) (*NHS and Community Care Bill 1989*).

Draft Circular guidance (England/Wales) emphasises that SSD recommendation of a disabled facilities grant, for example, should be the outcome of a careful assessment of a community care plan for an individual elderly or disabled person (*Draft joint circular DoE X/90, WO Y/90, DH Z/90 para 30*).

3.2.1.5. Basis for SSD/SWD/HSSB power to charge. SSD/SWD/HSSBs have the power to charge for any services provided, although they can only do so if the client can afford to pay (30.2.).

3.2.2. Legislative basis for housing authority assessment and provision

3.2.2.1. Legislative basis for housing authority assessment and provision: England and Wales

3.2.2.1.1. Basis for provision by renovation grant: these grants were introduced in July 1990 as part of a new grant system in England and Wales.

For the purpose of bringing a dwelling up to a defined level of fitness for habitation, they are mandatory. Beyond that level, they are discretionary for the repair or improvement of a dwelling (*Local Government and Housing Act 1989 Part 8*).

The amount of either mandatory or discretionary grant available is determined by a test of resources with a special premium given for disability (*DoE Consultation Paper 6.3.90: Local Government and Housing Act 1989. Disabled Facilities Grants: Test of Resources*).

These grants are normally available to private owners and owner occupiers: not normally to tenants (except for private tenants where there is a repairing obligation) (*Joint draft circular DoE X/90; WO Y/90 House Renovation Grants para 2.22*).

3.2.2.1.2. Basis for disabled facilities grants: these grants are an integral part of the renovation grant scheme, but extend the normal definition of fitness for habitation, applicable to standard renovation grants, to take account of a person's disability.

They are mandatory if awarded on the basis of this extended definition of fitness for habitation, and otherwise discretionary.

The amount of either mandatory or discretionary grant available is determined by the same test of resources as for renovation grants (including a special premium for disability).

They are available to both private sector owner-occupiers and tenants, and public sector tenants (*Local Government and Housing Act 1989 Part 8*).

3.2.2.1.3. Basis for minor works assistance. This is part of the new renovation grant system, and in certain circumstances is available in the form of grant or materials for minor works. These circumstances include repair, home insulation, improvement or adaptation to benefit elderly people.

Assistance is discretionary, determined by a test of resources (in practice receipt of income support, family credit, housing benefit or community charge benefit), and anyway limited to a maximum of £1000 per application, and £3000 in a three year period.

It is available to private sector owner-occupiers and tenants, but not to public sector tenants or absentee landlords (*Local Government and Housing Act 1989 s.131; SI 1990/388 Assistance for Minor Works to Dwellings Regulations 1990*).

3.2.2.2. Scotland

3.2.2.2.1. Improvement grants (mandatory) are available to provide a dwelling with standard amenities (3.6.2), which it lacks.

They are also available to disabled people if the standard amenities already exist, but additional amenities are essential to meet the special needs of that person.

Financial assistance is determined by both a standard maximum amount, and by a fixed percentage of that maximum amount.

These grants are available to both private sector owners and tenants; and to public sector tenants (*Housing (Scotland) Act 1987 Part 13*).

3.2.2.2.2. Improvement grants (discretionary) are available to alter, enlarge and carry out works of repair (so that the house is in a good state of repair).

The purpose is extended, in the case of disabled people, to make the dwelling suitable for accommodation, welfare or employment.

Financial assistance is determined by both a standard maximum amount, and by a fixed percentage of that maximum amount.

These grants are available to both private sector owners and tenants, and public sector tenants (*Housing (Scotland) Act 1987 Part 13*).

3.2.2.3. Northern Ireland

3.2.2.3.1. Intermediate grants (mandatory) are available to provide standard amenities which are lacking. They are also available to disabled people, if such standard amenities already exist, but are not accessible to the person because of disability.

Financial assistance is determined by both a standard maximum amount, and by a fixed percentage of that maximum amount.

The grants are available to both private sector owners and tenants, and public sector tenants (*SI 1983/1118 (NI 15) Housing (Northern Ireland) Order 1983, Part 3*).

3.2.2.3.2. Improvement grants (discretionary). These discretionary grants are available to alter, enlarge and carry out works of repair (so that the house is in a good state of repair).

The purpose is extended, in the case of disabled people, to make the dwelling suitable for accommodation, welfare or employment.

Financial assistance is determined by both a standard maximum amount, and by a fixed percentage of that maximum amount.

The grants are available to both private sector owners and tenants, and public sector tenants (*SI 1983/1118 (NI 15) Housing (Northern Ireland) Order 1983, Part 3*).

3.2.2.4. Duties to own stock (UK wide). Housing authorities have duties to their own housing stock, which can include the power to alter, enlarge, repair and improve (*Housing Act 1985 s.9; Housing (Scotland) Act 1987 s.2; SI 1981/156 (NI 3) Housing (Northern Ireland) Order r.27*).

Circular guidance (England, Wales) also recommends that wide use be made of powers in the CSDPA 1970 concerning new housing, so as to include the carrying out of adaptations for people with disabilities within these powers (*see eg Draft joint circular DoE X/90, WO Y/90, DH Z/90 para 23; DoE 59/1978*).

3.3. Initial referral to the SSD/SWD/HSSB

3.3.1. Referral to the SSD/SWD/HSSB is open: it can be self-referral, referral by carers, friends, relatives, or from one of any number of professionals, such as hospital consultants, general practitioners (GPs), occupational therapists (OTs), physiotherapists or district nurses. Letters of support from professionals such as GPs can be very helpful both in relaying information to the SSD/SWD/HSSB: and sometimes in receiving a prompt assessment (2.3.1.).

Referral is sometimes made by the hospital, when a person is going to be discharged – or some time before, if possible, in order to allow time for an adaptation to be carried out. Referral sometimes comes from the wheelchair service (6.), for example, for adaptation required inside or outside the home for wheelchair use.

3.3.2. If an initial approach is made to the housing authority, it is likely to refer the person to the SSD/SWD/HSSB for assessment of individual need (in England and Wales it is under an explicit duty to do so (*Local Government and Housing Act 1989 s.114*). This is because the assessment in many areas will be carried out by OTs, or other SSD/SWD/HSSB staff.

(However, in some cases, the housing authority does carry out certain adaptations to its own stock (3.2.2.4.) as a matter of course (eg rails, ramps, central heating), without initial referral and assessment through the SSD/SWD/HSSB.

3.4. Registration and registerability

In order to qualify for SSD/SWD/HSSB services, it is not necessary to be registered disabled: 'registerability' is sufficient (2.3.2.). If a client is not already known to the SSD/SWD/HSSB, the assessment can establish whether the client is eligible to receive services; alternatively, eligibility of the client might already be known.

There seems to be occasional local variation in this respect. For example, one London borough's internal guidelines state that a client must be registered disabled to receive a home improvement grant (*London SSD (2) guidance received 1989/1990*). This is apparently inconsistent with government guidance (2.3.2.3.2.).

3.5. Residential qualification

Legislation states that in order to receive services from the SSD/SWD/HSSB, the disabled person must normally be resident in the area (*CSDPA 1970 s.2; CSDP(NI) A 1978 s.2*).

3.6. Assessment procedures

The normal pattern of assessment is that the SSD/SWD/HSSB assesses for individual need and proposes a solution involving, where appropriate, home adaptation.

If the proposed adaptation is structural (major) in nature, the housing authority then makes an assessment of the technical feasibility of the proposed adaptation.

Both the SSD/SWD/HSSB, and especially the housing authority (as grant maker), explain the mechanics of, and eligibility for, grant aid; early explanation ensures that grant application is appropriate, and that the client knows what to expect.

Box 3.2: Assessment criteria: 'necessary and appropriate', 'reasonable and practicable' (England and Wales, disabled facilities grant)

Note: Circular guidance referred to in this box is draft guidance only.

B3.2.1. Legislation states that housing authorities have a duty in England and Wales to consult SSDs about whether a proposed adaptation (to be arranged through a disabled facilities grant) is 'necessary and appropriate' (*Local Government and Housing Act 1989 s.114*).

The legislation also states that housing authorities cannot approve a disabled facilities grant unless they believe that it is 'reasonable and practicable' (*Local Government Housing Act 1989 s.114*).

B3.2.2. 'Necessary and appropriate'

B3.2.2.1. Necessity. Draft Circular guidance makes the difference between 'need' (necessity) and 'want'. The first word must apply in application for a mandatory disabled facilities grant. The second word 'want' is more appropriate for application for a discretionary disabled facilities grant (*Draft joint circular DoE X/90, WO Y/90, DH Z/90 House adaptations for disabled people, para 32*).

It is accepted that strict boundaries cannot be imposed to decide what is necessary, and that individual circumstances will often determine them.

Broadly speaking an adaptation is necessary:

- 'in order to enable that disabled person to remain in the dwelling with as great a degree of independence as possible'
- 'in order to enable their carer to care for them' (*Draft joint circular DoE X/90, WO Y/90, DH Z/90 House adaptations for disabled people para 33*).

B3.2.2.2. Appropriate

B3.2.2.2.1. Medical and physical needs of individual and carers. Draft Circular guidance states that to be appropriate, the adaptation should 'cater for the needs of the individual and their carers and should take into account both medical and physical needs' (*Draft joint circular DoE X/90, WO Y/90, DH Z/90 House adaptations for disabled people para 34*).

B3.2.2.2.2. Psychological needs and personal relationships. Draft Circular guidance states that psychological needs and personal relationships within the home should also be considered (*Draft joint circular DoE X/90, WO Y/90, DH Z/90 House adaptations for disabled people, para 35*).

B3.2.2.2.3. Future needs. Draft Circular guidance states that adaptations should be assessed bearing in mind the future course of eg a degenerative disease, the psychological effect of the adaptation on the individual and family/carers, and the individual's ability to benefit from the adaptation (*Draft joint circular DoE X/90, WO Y/90, DH Z/90 House adaptations for disabled people, para 37,38*).

B3.2.2.2.4. Terminal illness. Draft Circular guidance states that adaptations may be justified in cases of terminal illness, so as to allow 'the disabled person to come home from hospital or hospice care for the remainder of their life' (*Draft joint circular DoE X/90, WO Y/90, DH Z/90 House adaptations for disabled people, para 38*).

B3.2.2.3. Balance between 'necessary and appropriate'. Draft Circular guidance recognises that there may be difficult and sensitive decisions in deciding what is 'necessary and appropriate', especially when the disabled person knows what he or she wants.

By way of illustration the guidance goes on: 'Adaptations enabling a severely disabled person to live independently may involve disproportionate cost in comparison with a more modest scheme of adaptations with care services. By contrast, where the only alternative to major adaptation is for the disabled person to live in long-term institutional care, the welfare authority may deem the adaptation scheme to be a more appropriate solution of that person's needs' (*Draft joint circular DoE X/90, WO Y/90, DH Z/90 House adaptations for disabled people, para 39*).

B3.2.3. 'Reasonable and practicable'. Legislation states that the housing authority must believe that an adaptation, proposed for funding by a disabled facilities grant (mandatory or discretionary), is 'reasonable or practicable' (*Local Government and Housing Act s.114*).

The factors which determine the decision are as follows.

B3.2.3.1. Age and condition of the building. Legislation states that the age and condition of the building must be taken into account (*Local Government and Housing Act 1989 s.114*).

Draft Circular guidance states that the age itself is not relevant, but rather architectural styles associated with age which might make adaptation difficult (eg narrow doorways, narrow passages, small rooms) (*Draft joint circular DoE X/90, WO Y/90, DH Z/90 House adaptations for disabled people, paras 45,46,47*).

B3.2.3.2. Condition of the building. Draft Circular guidance states that if a home is unfit for habitation in the normal sense of the word (3.6.2.2.1.1.), then a Renovation Grant may be necessary, either before or simultaneously with, a Disabled Facilities Grant (*Draft joint circular DoE X/90, WO Y/90, DH Z/90 House adaptations for disabled people, para 46,47*).

But renovation grant, with or without a disabled facilities grant, cannot be given for properties under 10 years old (*Draft joint circular DoE X/90, WO Y/90, DH Z/90 House adaptations for disabled people, para 48*).

B3.2.3.3. Impact on other residents. Draft Circular guidance lists impact on other resident as an important consideration (*Draft joint circular DoE X/90, WO Y/90, DH Z/90 House adaptations for disabled people, para 49*).

B3.2.3.4. Value for money. Draft Circular guidance states that if the proposed adaptation reduces the value of the property extensively, it may not be in the interests of the client to proceed, and authorities may suggest alternative solutions (*Draft joint circular DoE X/90, WO Y/90, DH Z/90 House adaptations for disabled people, para 50*).

3.6.1. SSD/SWD/HSSB assessment of need

3.6.1.1. SSD/SWD/HSSBs' general role as assessors of need. Circular and other guidance states that assessment for home adaptations should be undertaken by the SSD/SWD/HSSB (*Joint circular DoE 59/78, LAC(78)14, WO 104/78 para 5 and Draft joint circular DoE X/90, WO Y/90, DH Z/90 para 16; Joint circular SDD 40/1985 – NHS 1985(GEN)33 – SWSG 17/1985 para 4; Joint Code of Guidance. Housing the Disabled. NIHE 1987 p. 3*).

Legislation (England and Wales) explicitly places a duty on the housing authority to consult the SSD about the necessity for, and appropriateness of, a disabled facilities grant (*Local Government and Housing Act 1989 s.114*) (see Box 3.2 for details). This formally recognises the co-operation between authorities, which has been practised for years.

3.6.1.2. SSD/SWD/HSSB professionals involved

3.6.1.2.1. OT assessment of need. Assessment of individual need, and of possible solutions, is often by community OTs employed by the SSD/SWD/HSSB (2.4.1.1.).

3.6.1.2.2. Other SSD/SWD/HSSB staff assessment. OT assessment does not always take place: other SSD/SWD/HSSB staff may undertake assessment, such as experienced social workers, or technical officers, OT assistants.

For example, OT assistants, social workers or social work assistants might be able to authorise (with OT advice as appropriate) minor adaptations; while OTs remain responsible for assessment of major adaptations (*London borough SSD guidelines received 1989*).

Neither legislation nor Circular guidance stipulates that OTs must be the professionals to assess, but the latter (England, Wales, Scotland) does suggest that OTs are the most appropriate professionals to do so (*see eg Joint circular DoE 59 78 – LAC(78)14 – WO 104/78; Joint circular SDD 40/1985 – NHS 1985(GEN)33 – SWSG 19/1985*).

3.6.1.3. Hospital OT assessment on behalf of the SSD/SWD/HSSB. Alternatively, OTs working in hospitals might sometimes undertake assessment on behalf of the SSD/SWD or HSSB (under social services functions), especially when there is a shortage of SSD/SWD/HSSB community OTs, in any one area.

3.6.1.4. Waiting times for SSD/SWD/HSSB assessment. Heavy demand on OTs sometimes leads to assessment waiting times (2.4.6.). When this occurs, a system of priority groups is sometimes operated. People at risk are then seen quickly, but other people, who are judged to be at rather less risk, can wait some time for assessment (2.4.6.2.).

3.6.1.5. SSD/SWD/HSSB assessment (of need) involving adaptation grants: criteria

3.6.1.5.1. England and Wales: disabled facilities grants

3.6.1.5.1.1. Necessity and appropriateness: disabled facilities grants. Legislation (England and Wales) states clearly that housing authority assessment for adaptations (in relation to a disabled facilities grant) must establish whether the proposed adaptations are 'necessary and appropriate to meet the needs of the disabled occupant' (*Local Government and Housing Act 1989 s.114*). See Box 3.2.

In establishing this, the housing authority has a duty to consult the SSD. Thus, it is the SSD which in practice assesses for necessity and appropriateness, although the final decision rests with the housing authority.

3.6.1.5.1.2. Needs of carers: disabled facilities grants. Draft Circular guidance (England, Wales: disabled facilities grants), for example, specifically mentions that assessment should take account of carers: eg impact of adaptations on caring tasks (*Draft joint circular DoE X/90, WO Y/90, DH Z/90 para 41*).

3.6.1.5.2. Access criteria (UK): housing authority grants. In relation to housing authority grants for people with disabilities, the adaptation is generally required for access: and housing authorities must be satisfied that access criteria are met. Such criteria are listed in considerable detail in some legislation (England, Wales); and more broadly in other legislation (Scotland, Northern Ireland).

Although it is the housing authority which must make the final decision about whether these criteria are met, SSD/SWD/HSSBs need to consider these criteria when carrying out an assessment, and when consulted by a housing authority. For details of these access criteria see Box 3.3.

Box 3.3: Access criteria to be met for home adaptation grants

B3.3.1. England and Wales

B3.3.1.1. Disabled facilities grant (mandatory). Legislation states that a mandatory disabled facilities grant cannot be given unless at least one of the following access criteria (constituting 'fitness for habitation' in the case of disability) is met:

- facilitating access by the disabled occupant to and from the dwelling or the building in which the dwelling, or as the case may be, flat is situated;
- facilitating access by the disabled occupant to a room used or usable as the principal family room;
- facilitating access by the disabled occupant to a room used or usable for sleeping;
- facilitating access by the disabled occupant to, or providing for the disabled occupant, a room in which there is a lavatory, bath, shower or washhand basin or facilitating the use by the disabled occupant of such a facility;
- facilitating the preparation and cooking of food by the disabled occupant;
- improving any heating system in the dwelling to meet the needs of the disabled occupant or, if there is no existing heating system in the dwelling or any such system is unsuitable for use by the disabled occupant, providing a heating system suitable to meet his needs;
- facilitating the use by the disabled occupant of a source of power, light or heat by altering the position of one or more means of access to or control of that source or by providing additional means of control;
- facilitating access and movement by the disabled occupant around the dwelling in order to enable him to care for a person who is normally resident in the dwelling and is in need of such care' (*Local Government and Housing Act 1989 s.114*).

B3.3.1.2. Disabled facilities grants (discretionary). Legislation states that a discretionary disabled facilities grant cannot be given unless one of the following access criteria is met: suitability for the disabled person's welfare, accomodation or employment (*Local Government and Housing Act 1989 s.114*).

B3.3.2. Scotland

B3.3.2.1. Improvement grants (mandatory): criteria. Legislation states that housing authorities cannot give mandatory improvement grants in case of disability unless either standard amenities are missing, or are inaccessible to a disabled person and are essential for his or her needs (*Housing (Scotland) Act 1987 s.244*).
    Standard amenities are defined as 'fixed bath or shower, hot and cold water supply at a fixed bath or shower, wash-hand basin, hot and cold water supply at a wash-hand basin, sink, hot and cold water supply at a sink, water closet' (*Housing (Scotland) Act 1987 Sched. 18*).

B3.3.2.2. Improvement grants (discretionary): criteria. Legislation states that housing authorities can give discretionary improvement grants for disability if the adaptation is to make the home suitable for welfare, accomodation or employment of a disabled person (*Housing (Scotland) Act 1987, s.236*).

B3.3.3. Northern Ireland

B3.3.3.1. Intermediate grants (mandatory): criteria. Legislation states that housing authorities cannot give intermediate grants unless either standard amenities are missing, or are inaccessible to a disabled person (*SI 1983/1118 (NI 15) Housing (Northern Ireland) Order 1983 r.58*).
    Standard amenities are defined as 'fixed bath or shower, hot and cold water supply at a fixed bath or shower, wash-hand basin, hot and cold water supply at a wash-hand basin, sink, hot and cold water supply at a sink, water closet' (*SI 1983/1118 (NI 15) Housing (Northern Ireland) Order 1983 Sched. 4*).

B3.3.3.2. Improvement grants (discretionary): criteria. Legislation states that housing authorities can give discretionary improvement grants for disability if the adaptation is to make the home suitable for the welfare, accomodation or employment of a disabled person. (*SI 1983/1118 (NI 15) Housing (Northern Ireland) Order 1983 r.48*).

3.6.1.5.3. SSD/SWD/HSSB assessment (not involving housing authority grants)

3.6.1.5.3.1. Non-structural adaptation assessment. SSD/SWD/HSSB assessment for non-structural adaptations employs the criteria described in legislation of: 'any additional facilities designed to secure . . . greater safety, comfort or convenience' (*CSDPA 1970 s.2(1)(e); CSDP(NI)A 1978 s.2(e)*).

Draft Circular guidance (England, Wales) here suggests that non-structural adaptations be classed as equipment under the word 'facilities' (*implication of Draft joint circular DoE X/90, WO Y/90, DH Z/90 para 21*).

3.6.1.5.3.2. Structural adaptation assessment. SSD/SWD/HSSB assessment for structural adaptations, with a view to itself carrying out the adaptation, is not covered by any specific criteria described in legislation.

However, draft Circular guidance (England and Wales, 1990), for example, states clearly that there may be occasions when an SSD chooses to operate different criteria to those operated by a housing authority. Using such criteria, the SSD has the power to fund a major adaptation (with the power to charge), which it considers necessary, but which does not attract an housing authority grant (*Draft joint circular DoE X/90, WO Y/90, DH Z/90 para 17,18*).

3.6.1.5.4. Local SSD/SWD/HSSB criteria and guidelines on assessment sometimes exist. These can relate to both guidance and advice on the assessment of adaptations, and to criteria for adaptations.

The very existence of such guidelines and, where in existence, their form and content, varies greatly from area to area.

Such local guidelines have been developed, amongst other possible reasons, to try and ensure consistency and fairness of assessment. The future duty to provide accounts of assessments in writing (2.2.3.) has also lent some urgency to their development.

For example, the London Boroughs Occupational Therapy Managers Group (LBOTMG) has developed and published 'Occupational Therapists' Criteria for the Provision of Adaptations in the Homes of People with Disabilities' (1988). It seems that this document is being used as a basis, by a number of SSDs and SWDs in England and Scotland. For examples of such local guidelines, see Appendix 3.

3.6.2. Housing authority assessment of technical feasibility

3.6.2.1. Housing authority professionals involved. Housing authority officers who assess for home adaptations are known as environmental health officers (EHOs), housing improvement officers (HIOs), grants officers, regional welfare officers: and various other names.

3.6.2.1.1. Housing authorities: England/Wales, Scotland. Housing authorities in England, Wales and Scotland vary in organisation and name. Responsibility for assessment (technical feasibility) of adaptations, and for the making of grants, rests sometimes with EHOs and sometimes with HIOs (who may go under other names). The relevant department is either the housing department or the environmental health department; they may be one and the same.

In some areas there may be different officers and departments responsible for adaptations depending on whether they are private or public sector adaptations.

EHOs, for example, are specialists in public health matters, and have a wide range of duties, including in many areas special responsibility for home adaptations.

3.6.2.1.2. Housing authorities: Northern Ireland. The Northern Ireland Housing Executive (NIHE) has responsibility for adaptations and grants. It is divided into regions, which in turn contain district offices.

Responsibility in the public sector is usually held by regional welfare officers; in the private sector by grants officers.

3.6.2.2. *Housing authority grants: England and Wales*

3.6.2.2.1. Renovation and disabled facilities grants: England and Wales

3.6.2.2.1.1. Fitness for habitation. Legislation states that these grants are mandatory if the housing authority is satisfied that they are necessary to bring a dwelling up to a fit level of habitation (which includes factors such as repair, stability, freedom from damp, internal arrangement, natural lighting, ventilation, water supply, drainage and sanitary conveniences; cooking/food preparation/waste water disposal facilities (*Housing Act 1985 s.604*).

In case of disability, fitness of habitation is extended to include a number of comprehensive access criteria (3.6.2.2.1.5.).

In some instances, a disabled person might be eligible for both a renovation and disabled facilities grant, when the application satisfies both the basic criteria for 'fitness for habitation', and the extended criteria specific to disability.

3.6.2.2.1.2. Accommodation, welfare, employment criteria (England and Wales). A housing authority can approve a discretionary disabled facilities grant if it does not meet specific access criteria (see Box 3.3), but is 'for the purpose of making the dwelling or building suitable for the accommodation, welfare or employment of the disabled occupant' (*Local Government and Housing Act 1989 s.114*).

3.6.2.2.1.3. Housing authority assessment: 'necessary and appropriate' (England and Wales). Legislation states that the housing authority cannot approve an application for a disabled facilities grant unless it believes that 'the relevant works are necessary and appropriate to meet the needs of the disabled occupant'.

To establish this belief, the housing authority has a duty to consult the SSD (*Local Government and Housing Act s.114*).

Draft Circular guidance discusses the meaning of these words (see Box 3.2).

3.6.2.2.1.4. Housing authority assessment: 'reasonable and practicable' (England and Wales). Legislation states that the housing authority must also be satisfied in the case of a disabled facilities grant that 'it is reasonable and practicable to carry out the relevant works, having regard to the age and condition of the dwelling or building' (*Local Government and Housing Act 1989 s.114*).

Draft Circular guidance discusses at some length, the terms 'reasonable' and 'practicable' (see Box 3.2).

3.6.2.2.1.5. Housing authority assessment: access criteria (England and Wales). The housing authority must approve an application for a disabled facilities grant if certain access criteria are met.

These are listed comprehensively in legislation (Local Government and Housing Act 1990 s.114) (for details see Box 3.3). Circular guidance explains that these access criteria are what establish the extended definition of 'fitness for habitation' (3.6.2.2.1.1.) in the case of disability (*Draft joint Circular DoE X/90/, WO Y/90 House Renovation Grants para 3.31*).

3.6.2.2.2. Housing authority assessment: minor works assistance: elderly people (England and Wales). Housing authorities have powers to give such assistance in the case of elderly people to help them repair, improve or adapt their home.

Legislation states that the housing authority has the discretion to give assistance in certain cases, including the following:

- 'the repair, improvement or
- adaptation of any dwelling'; or
  'the adaptation of any dwelling to enable a person who is 60 years of age or over who is not an owner or tenant of the dwelling but is or proposes to be resident in the dwelling to be cared for';
- the provision or improvement of thermal insulation in any dwelling (*Local Government and Housing Act 1989 s.131*).

3.6.2.3. Housing authority grants: Scotland and Northern Ireland assessment of technical feasibility: improvement and intermediate grants

3.6.2.3.1. Age and condition of the building (Scotland, Northern Ireland). General criteria such as age and condition of the building normally have to be satisfied (*see eg Housing (Scotland) Act 1987 s.240,244; SI 1983/1118 Housing (NI) Order r.55, 60*); although these criteria can be waived sometimes (*see eg Housing (Scotland) Act 1987 s.240, s.244; SI 1983/1118 Housing (NI) Order r.55, r.60*).

In Scotland criteria concerning the age of the building are waived if the client has a disability (Housing (Percentage of Approved Expense for Improvement Grants) (Disabled Occupants) (Scotland) Order 1982 and SDD 36/1982).

3.6.2.3.2. Need for standard amenities because of disability: mandatory improvement grant (Scotland), intermediate grant (Northern Ireland).

These mandatory grants are available if the housing authority believes that they are necessary either to provide missing standard amenities (for anyone, disabled or otherwise); or to provide additional standard amenities because existing ones are inaccessible to a a disabled person because of his or her disability (*Housing (Scotland) Act 1987 s.244; SI 1983/1118 (Housing (NI) Order) r.58*).

Standard amenities are defined as:

- fixed bath or shower with hot and cold water supply;
- wash-hand basin with hot and cold water supply;
- sink with hot and cold water supply;
- WC (*Housing (Scotland) Act 1987 Sched. 18; SI 1983/1118Housing (NI) Order 1983 Sched.4*).

3.6.2.3.3. Improvement grants for accommodation, welfare, employment (Scotland and Northern Ireland).

Discretionary grants are generally for the purpose of alteration, enlargement and for works of repair to bring the dwelling up to a good state of repair.

The purpose is extended in the case of people with disabilities to make the dwelling suitable for that person's accommodation, welfare or employment (*Housing (Scotland) Act 1987 s.236; SI 1983/1118 Housing (NI) Order a.48*).

3.6.3. Housing authority assessment of general eligibility for grants

3.6.3.1. Certificates of future occupation

3.6.3.1.1. England, Wales, Northern Ireland. Certificates of future occupation are required for renovation, improvement and intermediate grants (*Local Government Housing Act 1989 s. 106; SI 1983/1118 Housing (NI) Order r.51,53*).

3.6.3.1.2. Scotland. In Scotland, no such certificates exist (*Written communication: SDD, 1990*).

3.6.3.2. Status of applicant re: ownership/tenancy/sector

3.6.3.2.1. Status of applicant for housing authority grant (England and Wales)

3.6.3.2.1.1. Renovation grants are open to private sector owners and owner-occupiers, but not normally to private sector tenants (except to those with repairing obligations). They are not open to public sector tenants.

3.6.3.2.1.2. Disabled facilities grants are available to private sector owner-occupiers and tenants; and to public sector tenants.

3.6.3.2.1.3. Minor works assistance is open to private sector owner-occupiers and tenants (including housing association tenants) but not to public sector tenants or private sector landlords (*DoE 4/90 para 8*).

3.6.3.2.2. Status of applicant for housing authority grant (Scotland, Northern Ireland).

3.6.3.2.2.1. Improvement grants and intermediate grants. These are open to private sector owner-occupiers and tenants, and to public sector tenants.

3.6.3.3. Status of applicant re: disability. For the purposes of housing authorities, disability is defined in accordance with general welfare legislation (2.3.2.1.).

3.6.3.3.1. Disability eligibility (England and Wales). A person who is registered or registerable under welfare legislation (2.3.2.1.) (*Local Government and Housing Act 1989 s.114*).

3.6.3.3.2. Disability eligibility (Scotland). A person who is 'substantially handicapped by illness, injury or congenital deformity' (2.3.2.1.) (*Housing (Scotland) Act 1987 s.236*).

3.6.3.3.3. Disability eligibility (Northern Ireland). A person who is registered or registerable under 'arrangements made by a Health and Social Services Board under Article 15(1) of the Health and Personal Social Services (Northern Ireland) Order 1972' (2.3.2.1.) (SI 1983/1118(NI.15) Housing (Northern Ireland) Order 1973 r.48).

3.6.4. Assessment for new housing. Adaptation is not always the best, or even a possible solution.

It can be that, when new housing is being built, foreseeable needs of people with disabilities can be taken into account.

Legislation (England/Wales, Northern Ireland) places a duty on housing authorities to consider the needs of people with disabilities when planning new housing (*CSDPA 1970 s.3, CSDP(NI)A 1978, s.3*).

NIHE guidance (Northern Ireland), for example, states that when new housing is being planned, mobility and wheelchair accomodation must be considered. General disability needs should be discussed with the HSSB, as well as the needs of any individual known to the NIHE (*Joint Code of Guidance. Housing the Disabled. NIHE 1987 p. 1*).

Sometimes cost is inevitably considered. For example, in one SSD, local guidelines state that rehousing should be considered very carefully, if a home lift adaptation is likely to cost over a certain threshold (eg £7000) (*Southwest England (40) guidelines received 1989/1990*).

3.6.5. Assessment for transfer of home. Especially where major adaptations are being considered, the question of transfer to other suitable property can arise. This can happen, where, for example, the present property is unsuitable for adaptation. Such transfer to public sector property (or housing association property) can take place either from a present private or public sector property.

Often, however, such transfer does not take place either because there is no suitable property available, or because the disruption to the life of the person is excessive (eg in terms of friends'/neighbours' support). Circular guidance (England, 1978) points out the advantage of enabling 'people to go on living in familiar surroundings and near to friends and relatives' (*Joint circular DoE 59/78, LAC(78)14, WO 104/78*).

A housing authority may have a priority transfer scheme in operation: for an example (the Northern Ireland scheme), see Box 3.4.

Box 3.4: Transfer scheme example

For example, the NIHE Joint Code of Guidance addresses the question of transfer when there is a housing need and adaptation is not the proposed solution.

Where there is a housing need, there is a priority group for transfer to another property. The priority group includes 'those who are suffering from exceptional hardship or severe stress caused or aggravated by their housing.

The group includes those handicapped persons:
(a) who suffer from:

- blindness;
- serious illness;
- injury;
- congenital deformity;
- disablement of a nature likely to be permanent or long-standing and to an extent which requires special care and attention. If on the recommendation of the appropriate officer(s) of the Health and Social Services Boards, the accomodation occupied is, because of its condition, its design or its location causing extensive hardship, or may lead to the breakdown in the health of the applicant or a member of his family.

(b) those who could be discharged from hospital or residential care if suitable accomodation were made available.'

It is noted that admission to the priority group 'cannot be awarded solely because of the handicap or the condition, design, or location of the property. It is the combination of the person's condition together with the condition, design or location of the property which will determine whether or not priority housing is required' (*Joint Code of Guidance. Housing the Disabled. NIHE, 1987. p.2*).

3.6.6. Assessment of equipment as an alternative to adaptations. SSD/SWD/HSSBs might, rarely, consider, as policy, suitable equipment alternatives to adaptations which are difficult and expensive to carry out. This is believed to result in cost-saving, and eventual re-use of the equipment as opposed to the lost investment of an adaptation, when the original client no longer needs it or has moved away (*SWD guidelines received 1989*).

3.6.7. Co-operation between SSD/SWD/HSSBs and housing authorities is required, given the fact that powers and duties, in relation to home adaptations, overlap and depend on each other.

Co-operation in many cases seems to be good, with detailed arrangements agreed and adhered to (*SSD guidelines received 1989/1990; Scotland SWD OT questionnaire 1988; Northern Ireland community OT questionnaire 1988*), despite the complications of the system. In Northern Ireland, for example, the NIHE has issued a joint code of guidance, which operates province wide.

Nevertheless, in some areas the achievement of common policies by authorities can be difficult. For example, an SSD area might contain several district councils (housing authorities) with different policies: the picture can become even more confused if a DHA, for example, is also involved, in the same area, with assessment of minor adaptations, and their fitting, by arrangement with the SSD (*London SSD (19) guidelines 1989*). The geographical boundaries of the SSD, housing authorities, health authority(ies) may all be non co-terminous.

3.6.7.1. Circular guidance (England and Scotland) states the importance of co-operation and that flexibility in arrangements may be required (*Joint circular SDD 40/1985 – NHS 1985(GEN)33 – SWSG 17/1985*) since powers overlap (*Joint circular DoE 59/78, LAC(78)14, WO 104/78*). It, together with NIHE guidance, also states that good co-operation is required to prevent delay and consequent inconvenience to the client (*Joint circular DoE 59/78, LAC(78)14, WO 104/78; Joint circular SDD 40/1985 – NHS 1985(GEN)33 – SWSG 17/1985; Joint Code of Guidance. Housing the Disabled. NIHE 1987 p. 3*).

Recent draft Circular guidance (England) not only stresses the importance of co-operation, but also consistency of provision between authorities. It advises that SSD/SWD/HSSBs and housing authorities should consult neighbouring authorities to try and ensure consistency across wider areas (*Draft joint circular DoE X/90, WO Y/90, DH Z/90 para 29*).

3.6.8. Final decision on grants for home adaptations. Although housing authorities consult SSD/SWD/HSSBs, the final decision on the giving of grants rests with the housing authority.

For example, Circular guidance (England) stresses that while housing author-ities are normally expected to take account of SSD views, they are not under a duty to follow those views (*Draft joint circular DoE X/90, WO Y/90, DH Z/90 para 44*).

3.6.9. SSD/SWD/HSSB assessment unit. Where there is an assessment unit for daily living equipment, there may also be adequate facilities to help the client plan an adaptation. For example, there might be a centre with fully equipped kitchen, bathroom, WC, bedroom (*London SSD (2) guidelines received 1989/1990*).

DLCs, hospital-based centres (*eg Manthorpe J. Extraordinary solutions to ordinary house problems. Therapy Weekly 1988:14; 35, p. 6*), or even assessment flats (allowing short trial occupancy period) (*Midlands SSD (21) guidelines 1989*) are all used to help plan adaptations.

3.7. Provision

3.7.1. Provision of non-structural adaptations. Following assessment, non-structural or minor adaptations are supplied and installed, usually on free loan by SSD/SWD/HSSBs, in both private and public sector. Alternatively, the housing authority sometimes supplies and fits such adaptations in public sector housing.

3.7.1.1. SSD/SWD/HSSB provision of non-structural adaptation

3.7.1.1.1. Authorisation. Depending on the cost of the adaptation, authorisation at different levels is likely to be required ranging, for example, from an OT who carries out the assessment, to a principal OT, to an area/division director to the director of the social services/work or to a management level committee etc. (*SSD guidelines received 1989/1990; Housing Adapations Conference, SCD, 1986*).

3.7.1.1.2. Fitting. SSD/SWD/HSSB technical officers, or 'handymen', sometimes fit small items, such as rails, on instructions from the assessing OT.

Sometimes hospital OTs carry out assessment for minor adaptations (eg grab rails, stair rails, toilet aids) prior to hospital disharge. Some hospitals employ a hospital OT technician to fit such items on behalf of the SSD/SWD or HPSSB (under social services functions) (*London SSD (19) guidelines 1989*).

3.7.1.1.3. Waiting times for SSD/SWD/HSSB provision. As in the case of daily living equipment, provision waiting times (2.5.7.) can exist.

For example, financial pressures can sometimes force an SSD to work with existing stairlifts and hoists rather than buy new ones; this can result in a waiting list for re-allocation. In practice this could mean waiting until a client dies (*Southwest England SSD (20) guidelines received 1989/1990*).

There can be a waiting list of several months for non-urgent minor adaptations such as grab rails, ramps, stair rails, rehanging doors, lever taps (*eg London SSD (24) guidelines received 1989*).

3.7.1.2. Housing authority provision of non-structural adaptations. Housing authorities sometimes install (and finance) some minor or non-structural adapta-tions, as part of duties to their own housing stock, but do not consider the same adaptations for grant aid in private housing, unless they are part of a larger scheme involving major adaptation (*see eg Joint Code of Guidance. Housing the Disabled. NIHE 1987 p. 4*).

3.7.2. Provision of structural adaptations. Structural adaptations are sometimes arranged (free of charge) as part of a housing authority's duty to its own stock; otherwise generally by means of grants, which are available for both private and public sector housing.

SSD/SWD/HSSBs have the power (3.2.1.1.1.) to arrange and finance structural adaptations, although this power is rarely used (except, perhaps, in some areas of Scotland). (3.9.3.1.)

3.7.2.1. Grant procedures for structural adaptations following assessment. The carrying out of major adaptation work can be a long, complicated and disruptive process. Housing officers try and involve the client as much as possible from the outset so as to avoid misunderstandings and difficulties.

Assessment is undertaken by architects and builders to prepare plans and quotes. Some of the elements involved include full site survey, drawings, specifications, OT and other professional consultations, tendering, costings, specifications, supervision of building, architects' fees, VAT and so on. During this process, the EHO or HIO, and OT may need to be heavily involved in advising the client.

Problems such as long delays by architects, contractors' declining small jobs, delays in estimates, planning and building regulations' difficulties can occur (*see eg Housing Adaptations Conference SCD 1986 p. 13*).

3.7.2.2. Procedures following assessment of adaptation to housing authority's own stock (without use of grant). The complications of major adaptation work as described above can apply to adaptations of public sector stock, carried out as duties to own stock by a housing authority. However, the client is not ultimately responsible for organising the adaptation, as he or she is in the case of adaptation by means of grant. The relevant housing officer takes responsibility for co-ordinating the various services and operations (*see eg Joint Code of Guidance. Housing the Disabled. NIHE 1987 p. 3*).

3.7.2.3. Waiting times for provision. Delay can occur, if a housing authority's budget is under strain, or overspent, toward the end of the financial year.

There may be other causes of delay such as a shortage of housing authority surveyors, for example (*eg Community Care 27.10.1988*).

3.7.2.4. Housing authority 'consultancy/agency' services. Housing authorities sometimes offer help to clients to arrange adaptations in the form of a consultancy or 'agency'. For a certain fee (eg percentage of the cost, or up to a maximum figure such as £500) the housing authority might undertake all the adaptation arrangements, following initial (OT) assessment. The fee might be included in the grant.

3.8. Follow-up and maintenance

Once a structural adaptation has been carried out, it is part of the dwelling and the responsibility of the owner (an individual or a housing authority, for example). In the case of lifts and fixed hoists, provided by means of grants, there might be various arrangements and responsibilities (see Box 3.5).

3.9. Finance

The finances of adaptations are quite complicated.

Box 3.5: Stairlifts

Stairlifts are often provided according to a variety of different arrangements from area to area. This is in part due to the fact that they can be viewed as either structural or non-structural adaptations.

The following examples indicate possible arrangements for provision and maintenance of lifts and stairlifts.

B3.5.1. Public sector property

Example 1. Northern Ireland Housing Executive guidelines state 'A lift may be one of the agreed options to assist a disabled person. The responsibility for the provision, installation, maintenance and insurance of lifts in the public sector rests with the Northern Ireland Housing Executive.

'Where an NIHE property is sold to a tenant, the ownership of the stair, vertical or home lift which has already been installed by the Housing Executive will transfer to the ownership of the Board. It is the responsibility of the NIHE to advise the appropriate assistant director of social services (unit of management) of all the relevant information' (*Joint Code of Guidance. Housing the Disabled. NIHE, 1987, p.4*).

Example 2. Funding for the item itself and the surrounding work (public sector housing). In some areas items such as overhead hoists, household lifts, baths (Parker), showers (Chiltern) might be paid for by the SSD/SWD/HSSB: while the surrounding structural work is undertaken by the housing authority as part of duties to own stock.

B3.5.2. Private sector

Example 1. Installation as equipment. NIHE guidelines state that, on the other hand, responsibility for the installation of lifts in the private sector is generally that of the HSSB, and when the lift is 'installed by the board in the private sector, the lift will remain the property of the board which is also responsible for the installation, maintenance and insurance of the lift' (*Joint Code of Guidance. Housing the Disabled. NIHE, 1987, p.4*).

Example 2. Lift installed as equipment. The SSD might have a stock of secondhand lifts, or sometimes order new lifts, to install as equipment in a property. The SSD then retains ownership and responsibility for maintenance (*London SSD (19) guidelines received 1989; Midlands SSD (3) guidance received 1990*).

Example 3. Lift installed as (part of a) home adaptation with grant aid: various arrangements for maintenance. If the SSD has provided 'topping up' (3.9.7.) help additional to the grant, it might also retain responsibility for maintenance, although the lift is the property of the client. This would be on the basis that the client is unable to afford the maintenance charges.

Alternatively clients might have to take out a maintenance contract privately since the lift is their property (*London Borough SSD (19) guidelines received 1990. South of England SSD (16) guidelines received 1989/1990*).

If the client agrees that, despite grant aid, the stairlift should remain the property of the SSD, then the latter might service and repair the lift until the lift is no longer needed (*Midlands SSD (3) guidelines received 1989/1990*).

The SSD/SWD/HSSB might arrange an authority-wide servicing agreement for stairlifts (*Scotland SWD OT questionnaire 1988*).

Example 4. Variability of arrrangements. Even within the area of one SSD, for example, improvement grants are available for stairlifts in some areas but not in others depending on the policy of local housing authorities (district councils) (*Southwest England SSD (20) guidelines received 1990*).

It is even possible in some areas for the SSD to fund the cost of the lift and receive any direct improvement grant from the housing authority (*Midlands SSD (3) guidelines received 1990*).

3.9.1. Non-structural adaptations provided by SSD/SWD/HSSBs are usually free of charge, although the power to charge does exist (30.2.). A test of resources might be employed in some areas to determine whether clients can afford to pay for the adaptation themselves.

Housing authorities sometimes carry out non-structural adaptations to their own housing stock, free of charge, as part of their duties to their own stock.

3.9.2. Adaptation defined by a financial threshold. In some areas of England and Wales (at least up to April 1990), and in some areas of Scotland, local arrangements and divisions of responsibility depend on financial thresholds.

The financial threshold (anything from £200 to £1000 and more) is generally used to determine the definition of minor and major adaptation. Arrangements vary, but the SSD/SWD generally funds an adaptation falling under the threshold; and housing authority grants are used over the threshold.

In some areas of Scotland, the SWD seems to play a larger role in the funding of public sector housing adaptations (3.9.3.1.).

3.9.3. Public sector adaptations (structural or non-structural), as duties to own stock, are sometimes carried out by a housing authority free of charge.

3.9.3.1. Scotland: the COSLA agreement. The position in some areas of Scotland seems to vary in this respect, where an agreement known as COSLA operates. Generally, this places all responsibility for adaptations under a certain financial threshold (eg £1000) with the SWD. Over the threshold, costs are shared by the

SWD and housing authority: either the whole cost is shared, or just the excess over the threshold (*SWD OT questionnaire 1988*).

3.9.4. Disabled facilities grants (and renovation grants) are either mandatory or discretionary. In either case, a test of resources is applied to establish the amount of financial help the applicant is entitled to.

Help with the cost is worked out on a sliding scale: from 100% help where the income falls below a certain threshold, to 0% help where the income is above a certain threshold.

This income assessment is used for all applicants, with disabilities or otherwise. There is, however, a disability 'premium' to raise the threshold, and thereby increase the amount of financial help available. The income of the whole (dependent) household is taken into account, not just that of the disabled person (*DoE Consultation letter, 6.3.90. Local Government and Housng Act 1989. Disabled Facilities Grants: test of resources*).

3.9.5. Mandatory improvement grants (Scotland) and intermediate grants (Northern Ireland) are given by the housing authority according to:
- firstly, a total maximum amount determined by the number and type of standard amenities needed (Box 3.6.1.1.);

Box 3.6: Details of financial arrangements for housing authority grants in Scotland and Northern Ireland

B3.6.1. Mandatory improvement grants (Scotland), intermediate grants (Northern Ireland)

B3.6.1.1. Total amount. Legislation states that improvement grants for standard amenities in Scotland, or intermediate grants in Northern Ireland are subject to two limitations.

Each item has a 'maximum eligible amount' (eg £450 for fixed bath or shower), and the total grant is limited at most to the sum of £3010 (*Housing (Scotland) Act 1987 Sched. 18; SI 1983/1118 (NI 15) Housing (Northern Ireland) Order 1983 Sched.4 amended by SR 1988/354*). Such figures are subject to alteration and are only valid at the time of writing.

1. Fixed bath and shower	£450
2. Hot and cold water supply at fixed bath or shower	£570
3. Wash hand basin	£170
4. Hot and cold water supply at wash hand basin	£305
5. Sink	£450
6. Hot and cold water supply at sink	£385
7. Water closet.	£680

If the housing authority feels that extra expense is needed above the itemised amounts, this can be authorised (*Housing (Scotland) Act 1987, Sched. 18; SI 1983/118 (NI 15) Housing (Northern Ireland) Order 1983, s.62*).

B3.6.1.2. Additional amounts for repairs and replacment. Legislation states that with repairs and replacement needed as a result of installation or adaptation of standard amenities, additional amounts of grant are available (*SI 1987/2269 (S.153)r.53) Schedule; SR 1988/354 Schedule*).

B3.6.1.3. Percentage of total amount available. The housing authority has a duty to contribute a certain percentage toward the cost of the grant.

B3.6.1.3.1. Scotland. The normal percentage in Scotland is 50% (*Housing (Scotland) Act 1987 s.244*); it can rise to 75% in case of disability only when associated with a discretionary improvment grant (*Written communication, Scottish Office 1990*).

B3.6.1.3.2. Northern Ireland. The amount is normally specified as 50% but is 75% if 'the application is in respect of a house for a disabled occupant and the relevant works consist of or include works needed to meet a requirement arising from the particular disability from which that person suffers' (*SI 1983/1118 (NI 15) Housing (Northern Ireland) Order 1983, r.52*).

In cases of hardship, this percentage can rise to 90% (*SI 1983/1118 (NI 15) Housing (Northern Ireland) Order 1983, r.52(8)(b)*).

B3.6.2. Discretionary improvement grants (Scotland and Northern Ireland)

B3.6.2.1. Total amount of grant. Discretionary improvement grants are subject (at the time of writing 2.90) to a maximum of £12,600 pounds (*SI 1987/2269 (S.153); SR 1988/354*).

B3.6.2.2. Percentage of total amount available

B3.6.2.2.1. Scotland. The normal contribution of 50% (*Housing (Scotland) Act 1987 s.242 (1)*) is increased to 75% in case of disability (*Housing (Percentage of Approved Expense for Improvment Grants) (Disabled Occupants) (Scotland) Order 1982; SDD 36/1982*), and to 90% in a Housing Action Area in cases of hardship (not necessarily connected with disability) (*Housing (Scotland) Act 1987 s.250*).

B3.6.2.2.2. Northern Ireland. The amount is normally specified as 50% but is 75% if 'the application is in respect of a house for a disabled occupant and the relevant works consist of or include works needed to meet a requirement arising from the particular disability from which that person suffers' (*(NI 15) Housing (Northern Ireland) Order 1983, s.52*).

This can rise to 90% if the person 'would not without undue hardship be able to finance so much of the cost of the relevant works as is not met by the grant...' (*SI 1983/1118 Housing (Northern Ireland) Order 1983, s. 52(6)*)

- secondly, according to a percentage of that total maximum amount. In Scotland this is normally 50% unless it is associated with a discretionary improvement grant: in which case it is 75% (*Written communication: SDD 1989*). If the house happens to be in a housing action area, this can raise the percentage available (Box 3.6.1.3.2.).

In Northern Ireland, the amount available is normally 75% (*SI 1983/1118 (NI 15) Housing (NI) Order 1983 r.52*) (Box 3.6.1.3.2.).

3.9.6. Discretionary improvement grants (Scotland and Northern Ireland) are awarded by the housing authority according to both a total amount (subject to a ceiling) and a percentage of that amount (Box 3.6.1.2.1.)

This amount is normally 75% in the case of people with a disability (*Housing (Percentage of Approved Expense for Improvement Grants) Disabled Occupants (Scotland) Order 1982; SDD 36/1982; SI 1983/1118 (NI 15) Housing (NI) Order 1983) r.52*) (Box 3.6.2.2.).

3.9.7. 'Topping up'. SSD/SWD/HSSBs retain a duty (3.2.1.1.1.), where there is continuing need (referred to in draft Circular (England, Wales) guidance (*Draft joint circular DoE X/90, WO Y/90, DH Z/90 para 19*)), to 'top up' any grant given by a housing authority .

Box 3.7: 'Topping up' arrangements by SSD/SWD/HSSB

B3.7.1. England and Wales (the following is based mostly on draft Circular guidance only). The practical working of the new renovation grant (including disabled facilities grant) system (introduced July 1990) in England and Wales is not yet known.

Draft Circular guidance states that if a person cannot afford the difference between the total cost of an adaptation and the amount of housing authority grant received, then the SSD has a 'continuing duty to provide assistance' (*Draft joint circular DoE X/90, WO Y/90, DH Z/90 House adaptations for disabled people, para 19*).

B3.7.1.1. Test of resources for assistance. The complication arises that in order to determine whether to give such assistance, the SSD needs to carry out a test of resources. If help is to result, the test of resources must of course be more generous than that operated by a housing authority to determine the level of grant awarded in the first place.

B3.7.1.2. Test of resources for repayment. Draft Circular guidance goes on to say that in deciding to charge for any such assistance given, a test of resources should be applied 'to determine ability to pay'; this test might be the same as that used by the housing authority in the first place (*Draft joint circular DoE X/90, WO Y/90, DH Z/90 House adaptations for disabled people, para 19*). This suggests possible confusion and circularity.

B3.7.1.3. Waiver of part or full repayment. Legislation states that SSDs can only 'recover charges', if the individual can afford such charges (*HASSASSA 1983 s.17*).

Draft Circular guidance (1990) suggests that in certain circumstances repayment (part or full) can be waived if:

- 'the applicant is undertaking the care of a disabled person on behalf of the welfare authority and where this care generates the need for an adaptation, for which the applicant is assessed as having a requirement to contribute';
- 'such unreasonable hardship would be suffered by the disabled person or the applicant as a result of the contribution repayments, that the application for grant is likely to be withdrawn, and the welfare authority required to purchase residential care facilities which they deem are not in the best interests of the disabled person' (*Draft joint circular DoE X/90, WO Y/90, DH Z/90 House adaptations for disabled people, para 20*).

B3.7.1.4. Form of assistance. Such topping up assistance is likely to be either free or in the form of a repayable (in part or full) loan; depending on circumstances.

B3.7.2. Scotland and Northern Ireland. SWD/HSSB duties to help with home adaptations (*Chronically Sick and Disabled Persons' Act 1970 s.2; Chronically Sick and Disabled Persons' (Northern Ireland) Act s.2*) include the duty to help with the remaining cost of adaptations where there is continuing need. This is where the individual cannot afford the outstanding costs (after receipt of the improvement grant).

SWD/HSSBs have the power to ask for full or part repayment of a loan if the person can afford such repayment (30.2.).

Topping up can cover the percentage of the approved full cost of the work not covered by the housing authority grant (eg 25%). Tests of resources are often applied, and such topping up is by no means standard or automatic (*Scotland SWD OT questionnaire 1988; Northern Ireland community OT questionnaire 1988*).

This involves meeting some or all of the shortfall between the total amount of the cost of the work and the size of the grant given, and is known as 'topping up'.

In practice, such, 'topping up' can take the form of outright financial help or a repayable loan for example. The loan might be a deferred interest loan (*Midlands SSD (3) guidelines, received 1989/1990*) or some housing authorities might help to bridge the gap with a further maturity loan (*Midlands SSD guidelines received 1989/1990*).

The position now in England and Wales is not quite so clear, since in theory there are now (from July 1990) 100% disabled facilities grants available, subject to a test of resources. The issue is discussed by recent draft Circular guidance (Box 3.7.1.).

Topping up is likely to be determined by a test of the client's resources, but this is not always so (*SWD OT questionnaire 1988; SSD guidelines rec. 1989*) there might be a policy to accept voluntary contributions, but to not make charges (*SWD (1) guidelines received 1990*).

3.9.8. SSD/SWD/HSSB funding of structural adaptations. Where SSD/SWD/ HSSBs have a continuing duty (*see eg Draft joint circular DoE X/90, WO Y/90, DH Z/90 para 17*) towards someone who has been assessed as needing an adaptation, but who has not received a grant, and who cannot afford to pay for the adaptation: then they have a duty to make arrangements and fund the adaptation.

SSD/SWD/HSSBs have the power to charge for such assistance. Such help would normally be a loan which might either be free, or repayable (in part or full) depending on the person's ability to make such repayment (30.2.).

In areas of Scotland, where the COSLA agreement operates, the SWD might be significantly funding, or greatly contributing to, structural adaptations in the public sector (3.9.3.1.). There might be a test of resources: there might also be a policy not to charge, but to accept voluntary contributions (*Scotland SWD OT questionnaire 1988*).

3.9.9. Minor works assistance (3.2.2.1.3.) (England and Wales) in the form of grant or materials is available up to £1000 per application and a maximum of £3000 in three years.

It is restricted (in financial terms) to owner occupiers and private sector tenants (or their spouses, or the person they live with as husband or wife) who receive housing benefit, community charge benefit, income support or family credit (*SI 1990/388 Assistance for Minor Works to Dwellings Regulations 1990*).

3.9.10 War pensioners, apart from being eligible for assistance with adaptations, in the same way as other people with disabilities, are able to benefit from additional help.

A sum of £250, subject to certain conditions, is available. It is based on a general clause in legislation, allowing extra provision for war pensioners where statutory services have not supplied what is necessary (*The Naval, Military and Air Forces etc. (Disablement and Death) Service Pensions Order 1983/883, Reg. 26*)).

This scheme was introduced before the existence of legislation (*eg Chronically Sick and Disabled Persons Acts, and Housing Acts of the 1970s*), which clarifies the powers of local authorities to carry out home adaptations. Hence the figure of £250 is 'frozen' and somewhat inadequate by modern adaptation costs.

3.9.11. Payment of grant. Grants are generally paid either following completion of the work, or in instalments as work progresses (*Local Government and Housing Act 1989 s.117; Housing (Scotland) Act 1987 s.243; SI 1983/1118 (NI15), Housing (Northern Ireland) Order 1983, s.72*)).

3.10. Housing associations

SSD/SWD/HSSB assessment procedures apply to housing associations (*see eg Joint circular DoE 59/78, LAC(78)14, WO 104/78 p. 3*). However the grant system differs: special grants are available through the Housing Corporation (England and Wales), Housing for Wales, Scottish Homes, and the DoE (Northern Ireland).

3.10.1. England/Wales. Following OT assessment, grants are available to housing associations via the Housing Corporation (*Housing Corporation Procedure Guide 5.6.1*). The grant is known as 'housing association grant' (HAG).

3.10.2. Scotland. Grants may be payable to housing associations in Scotland by Scottish Homes (a new body, which has taken on the functions of the Scottish Special Housing Association and the Housing Corporation in Scotland, but with additional powers relating to the provision of housing in Scotland). The grant is known as housing association grant (HAG) (*Written communication: SDD 1990*).

Hitherto, the Housing Corporation Procedure Guide has been used as in England for guidance on adaptations; a new rule book might be developed by Scottish Homes.

3.10.3. Northern Ireland. There is no intermediate body as in England, Wales and Scotland, and grants for housing associations come directly from the Department of Environment, Northern Ireland. Grants can be made for the improvement of accomodation. A DoE (NI) Housing Association Manual is used to provide criteria and guidance.

3.10.4. OT assessment. For many adaptations, OT assessment is required as a pre-condition, for the making of any grant to a housing association.

4 Home nursing equipment

Introduction

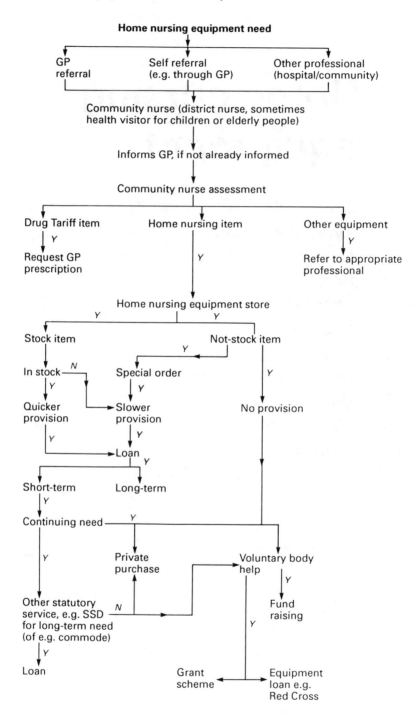

Introduction

Type of equipment

Home nursing equipment is generally any equipment which a community nurse considers necessary to enable her to fulfill her nursing duties. It includes:

- bed accessories;
- urinals;
- commodes;
- hoists;
- incontinence pads;
- suction apparatus.

Responsibility for provision

rests with the health service:

- district health authorities (DHAs, England and Wales);
- health boards (HBs, Scotland);
- health and social services boards (HSSBs, Northern Ireland).

Provision by these authorities is based on legislative duties to provide nursing services in general; and in particular services to prevent illness and to care for people who are ill or who have been ill. Local level and type of service is discretionary and depends on local policies in respect of use of resources.

Referral

Referral is often by the GP to a community nurse (usually district nurse but sometimes health visitor), who is often attached to a GP practice. Other professionals might also make a referral to the community nurse. Health visitors have particular responsibilities for children and, increasingly, for elderly people; there is also an increasing number of paediatric district nurses.

Community nurses are employed by DHA/HB/HSSBs within the community nursing services (CNS).

Prescription items

The community nurse sometimes requests the GP to prescribe items for nursing care which are listed on the Drug Tariff. In the future, it is expected that both district nurses and health visitors will themselves be able to prescribe some of these items (to be listed in a nurses' formulary).

Charges, and exemptions as appropriate, apply to items such as incontinence equipment and dressings.

Provision of home nursing equipment

Community nurses have access to equipment stores from which they can authorise the loan, free of charge, of home nursing equipment. In England and Wales such loan might, in principle but not always in practice, be short-term only. In Scotland and Northern Ireland, there appears to be no such short-term principle; home nursing equipment is loaned for as long as it is needed (except in the case of wheelchairs).

The dividing line between home nursing equipment and daily living equipment is not always clear, but local agreements between the CNS and community occupational therapists usually resolve any difficulties. Nevertheless, confusion sometimes does arise, and in such cases there can be some delay in provision.

Ordering, storing, maintenance, recall and cleaning

Procedures are likely to vary in type and quality. Joint (funded) equipment stores, holding both home nursing and daily living equipment are seen as one way of rationalising such procedures.

Sometimes a voluntary body, such as the Red Cross, runs an equipment store on behalf of the health service by formal agreement, or it runs a loan service independently, informally supplementing local CNS provision.

Voluntary bodies

Sometimes help with the provision of home nursing equipment, by means of loan from a central bank of equipment; or by means of a grant scheme. There can be reluctance to help with equipment, which is thought to be the responsibility of the health service.

4.1. Type of equipment

4.1.1. Definition of home nursing equipment. Home nursing equipment is any equipment which a community nurse (usually district nurse, but sometimes health visitor) considers necessary to fulfil his or her nursing duties effectively.

Sometimes there is uncertainty over the difference between home nursing equipment and daily living equipment. Local agreements between different authorities and professionals often resolve such uncertainty; but sometimes confusion persists and, aggravated by financial pressures, can cause delay in provision (2.1.3.).

4.1.2. Examples of home nursing equipment. Circular guidance (Scotland, 1976) gives examples of home nursing equipment, which are listed in Box 4.1.

Box 4.1: Examples of equipment to be supplied by a community nurse

Equipment required on medical and nursing grounds (the list is stated to be 'in no way comprehensive or exhaustive'):

- **bed equipment:**
  - air ring cushions and covers;
  - anti-pressure equipment;
  - bed backrests;
  - bed cradles;
  - bed tables;
  - bed blocks;
  - bed rails (normal bed);
  - pillows;
  - bed linen;
  - plastic sheets;
  - sputum mugs;
- **beds and patient support surfaces:**
  - air beds;
  - water beds;

– ripple beds;
– nursing beds and mattresses;
● **toileting equipment:**
– bedpans;
– urinals;
– commodes;
– sanichairs;
● **feeding equipment:**
– feeding cups;
– tubes;
– straws;
– bibs;
– protective clothing;
● **transfer and support equipment:**
– fracture boards;
– transfer boards (*NHS Memorandum 1976 (GEN)90*).

One Scottish health board has added an addendum to this list adding the following items:
– bed boards;
– bed cages;
– rubber sheets;
– one way sheets;
– bedsteads;
– incontinence pads (including Kanga pads);
– leg rests;
– liquidisers;
– monkey poles;
– nurse-operated hoists;
– oxygen trolleys;
– special commodes (*Scottish health board addendum (1978) to NHS Memorandum 1976 (GEN)90*).

4.2. Legislative basis for home nursing equipment provision

4.2.1. Basis: community nursing provision is covered by the DHA/HB/HSSB duty to provide 'nursing services' (*NHS Act 1977 s.3; NHS (Scotland) Act 1978 s.36; SI 1972/1265 HPSS(NI)O a.5*).

It is also covered more specifically by the DHA/HB/HSSB duty which includes 'the prevention of illness, the care of persons suffering from illness' and the after-care of such people (*NHS 1977, s.3; NHS 1978, s.37; SI 1972/1265 HPSS(NI)O 1972, a.7*).

4.2.2. Basis for voluntary body provision, by formal agreement. Where a voluntary body undertakes home nursing equipment loan by formal agreement with a DHA/HB/HHSB, then the agreement is covered by specific legislation allowing such discretionary arrangements with voluntary bodies (*NHS Act 1977 s.23; NHS (Scotland) Act 1978 s.16; SI 1972/1265 HPSS(NI)O a.71*).

4.3. Referral for home nursing equipment

The experts on, and main providers of, home nursing equipment are community nurses. Primarily district nurses have traditionally been involved; but health visitors, depending on local arrangements, are also involved (in relation to young children and elderly people).

4.3.1. Referral to the community nursing services (CNS) is frequently through the GP, but also through professionals and staff, such as consultants, ward sisters, therapists, home care assistants, social workers, practice nurses.

The GP should normally be informed, and become involved anyway, whatever the initial referral source.

4.3.2. Community nurse base. Many district nurses and health visitors are attached to GP practices (although they are usually employed by the DHA/HB/HSSB as part of the community nursing services): alternatively they sometimes cover a 'patch' without being specifically attached to one practice.

Where there is attachment, its nature can vary; the nurse might cover, for example:

- only those GP patients who live within a certain geographical area;
- all the GP's patients;
- additional areas or patches outside the one GP surgery's area (which she anyway covers all, or part of) (*Nurses Working in the Community. OPCS. HMSO, 1982 p.68*).

4.3.3. Referral from a community nurse. The district nurse or health visitor might equally make a referral to, for example, community therapists, the GP or chiropodist, if he or she identifies equipment needs other than home nursing.

4.4. Assessment and provision of home nursing equipment

4.4.1. Community nurse assessment and provision

4.4.1.1. Assessment and provision: district nurses. District nurses are the main professionals and experts in relation to home nursing equipment (they also supply home nursing care, administer drugs, change dressings and help people with personal care).

They often advise GPs on what to prescribe, in terms of home nursing equipment listed on the Drug Tariff (eg incontinence and stoma appliances, dressings). In the future it is expected that district nurses will be able to prescribe certain items from a nurses' formulary (*Report of the Advisory Group on Nurse Prescribing. DH, 1989, p.25 -*).

4.4.1.2. Assessment and provision: health visitors (HVs). Health visitors have traditionally worked with children (under-five), but increasingly work also with elderly people.

When HVs identify a need for home nursing equipment, they might either make a referral to the district nurse, or authorise the loan of the equipment themselves. Local arrangements seem to vary as to whether or not a health visitor has access to home nursing equipment. In the future it is expected that health visitors, like district nurses, will be able to prescribe certain items from a nurses' formulary (*Report of the Advisory Group on Nurse Prescribing. DH, 1989, p.25 -*).

4.4.2. Terminal care home nursing equipment. The provision of home nursing equipment for people with a terminal illness might be arranged, for example, by a hospital community liaison nursing team in co-operation with the community nursing services, hospice home care teams, and specialist nurses (eg Cancer Relief Macmillan Fund or Marie Curie Memorial Foundation nurses, who work with the health service) (*Written communication: hospital (specialising in terminal care) superintendent physiotherapist, 1990*).

4.4.2.1. Help with home nursing equipment for terminal care. Of the voluntary organisations which can help with home nursing equipment in general (4.6.3.), some are concerned with equipment for terminal care in particular. Help can be by means of patient grant schemes, or loan from a bank of equipment; depends on individual circumstances; and, in principle, might extend only to equipment which the health service is not expected to provide.

Help might be given for items such as bedding, nightwear, liquidisers, electric fans, fuel bills, clothing; and occasionally special mattresses, reclining chairs and telephone installation (*based on Written communication: Marie Curie Memorial Foundation; Verbal communication: Cancer Relief Macmillan Fund*). It should be stressed that any application is assessed on individual circumstances.

4.4.2.2. Other specialist terminal care services: eg paediatric oncology unit community service. A home terminal care team for children might be run by a hospital: the team might consist of, for example, a family support nurse, a social worker, a clinical assistant, a consultant paediatric oncologist and a GP.

Care and provision by such a team might include, for example, home nursing equipment such as pressure relief mattresses, mouthcare packs, incontinence

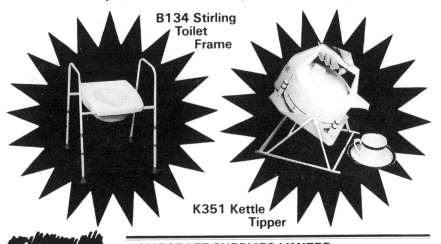

pads, buggies, syringe drivers, suction apparatus. This equipment is provided by the hospital and CNS, with the family support nurse supervising much of the provision of the equipment (*Chambers EJ* et al. *Terminal care at home for children with cancer. BMJ 1989: 298; pp. 937–940*).

4.4.3. Doctors and home nursing equipment

4.4.3.1. GPs and home nursing equipment

4.4.3.1.1. Drug tariff items. A GP can prescribe any item on the Drug Tariff (5.1.1.), some of which might be considered to be home nursing equipment, for example, incontinence appliances or dressings.

Initially the GP might assess for this equipment: or the community nurse might request the GP to prescribe a particular item.

4.4.3.1.2. GPs and other home nursing equipment. GPs either make a referral to a community nurse (4.4.1.); or in some areas (and more rarely), they have direct access to CNS equipment stores (4.6.1.) and can authorise the loan of some home nursing equipment, such as beds and bed accessories (*eg Midlands Joint Store Catalogue, received 1988*).

4.4.3.1.3. Hospital doctor request to the community nursing services. Earlier hospital discharge policies can result in more requests to the CNS, by hospital consultants, to loan equipment not previously requested with such frequency.

Such equipment can include, for example, suction apparatus, special beds (*Written communication: Welsh DHA*) or nebuliser units (21.) (*Verbal communication: London DHA CNS manager and district physiotherapist; London SSD (19) guidelines including joint DHA/SSD report, received 1989/1990*).

4.4.4. Therapists and home nursing equipment. The CNS often accepts requests and recommendations from other professionals, such as therapists (eg occupational therapists, physiotherapists), although further assessment by a nurse is usually necessary to confirm such requests.

However, sometimes flexibility, afforded by joint (funded) equipment stores (4.6.1.1.), for example, enables therapists to directly authorise the loan of some home nursing equipment. For example, community therapists might be able to loan some beds, bed raisers, divan bed cot sides, pillows, bed cradles, bed tables, backrests, commodes, rubber rings, bed pads (heel/elbow), sheepskin pads (full length), mattress covers, lifting poles, standard mattresses, male/female urinals etc. (*taken from 3 SSD joint store catalogues, received 1988/89/90*).

4.4.5. Community mental handicap nurses (CMHNs) and home nursing equipment. CMHNs, working in health service 'halfway homes' for people with learning difficulties (mental handicap), often have access to a separate budget and channel of supply for home nursing equipment needed. More rarely do they have formal access to a CNS equipment store; where they do not, occasional special requests might still be made, for example, for short-term loan of specialist equipment (*Verbal communications: DHA CMHNs 1989, DHA CNS Manager 1990*).

4.4.6. Nursing auxiliaries do not authorise equipment loan, but make regular home visits to people to undertake basic nursing care; they can identify equipment needs and alert the district nurse as appropriate (*Verbal communication: English National Board for Nursing, Midwifery and Health Visiting, 1990*).

4.4.7. Practice nurses employed by GPs and working on the GP's premises, sometimes become aware of a home nursing need and refer to a community nurse.

4.4.8. Hospital discharge and community nurses. Circular guidance (England, Wales) on hospital discharge states that community nurses can:

- make arrangements for continuing care at home;
- provide useful information about the patient's home circumstances;
- visit the patient before he/she leaves hospital. A discussion at this stage with the ward sister and the patient may avoid possible later problems (*HC(89)5 with Discharge of Patients from Hospital DH, 1989; WHC(90)1*).

4.4.9. Rehabilitation unit assessment for home nursing equipment. Where special rehabilitation units (29.) undertake assessment of a person's total needs (including home nursing equipment), special recommendations are likely to be made to the individual's own DHA/HB/HSSB, before hospital discharge.

4.4.10. Home nursing equipment for war pensioners. Traditionally, war pensioners (30.3.) have been able to receive special services from wheelchair and limb service centres (DSC/ALACs or the Regional Disablement Services (Northern Ireland)).

In theory, such services still include certain items of home nursing equipment such as catheters, supra-pubic appliances, urinals, bed linen, lifting hoists, special toilet (with 'self-washing' facilities), mechanical respirators (exceptionally), beds.

Such provision has, in the past, been made on the basis that it is for the 'management or alleviation of an accepted disability and is not available from local Health authorities or Local Authority Social Services Departments' (*ALAC manual, DHSS (as it was then), now obsolete. See also SI 1983/883. Naval, Military and Air Forces Etc. (Disablement and Death) Service Pensions Order 1983 r.26*).

Provision in this way is now rare, but is possible if the local DHA/HB/HSSB community nursing services are unable to loan an item which is needed.

4.5. Loan conditions

4.5.1. Length of loan

4.5.1.1. Loan (England and Wales). In some areas it has been the custom for home nursing equipment to be loaned for short-term periods, perhaps for a maximum of three to six months. In other areas there is no such limit.

Where the short-term loan principle is operated, longer term needs are sometimes regarded as daily living needs and therefore the responsibility of the SSD. For example, a commode might be supplied by a district nurse for up to 6 months, after which time the local SSD should supply a substitute. In practice such an arrangement does not always work, and the home nursing loan becomes long term (*Verbal communication: London DHA CNS 1989; Verbal communication: English National Board for Nursing, Midwifery and Health Visiting, 1990*).

However, CNS loan of wheelchairs is nearly always restricted to a period of three months or less, since permanent needs are met by the wheelchair service.

4.5.1.2. Loan (Scotland and Northern Ireland). In Scotland and Northern Ireland, home nursing equipment is loaned for both long and short-term periods as required (except wheelchairs, restricted to short-term).

Circular guidance (Scotland, 1976), for example, defines health board (community nursing) responsibilities as 'directly related to the management of an illness, especially to facilitate the patient domiciliary nursing care...' (*NHS Memorandum No 1976 (GEN)90*). The definition makes no reference to short-term need.

4.5.2. Residential homes and home nursing equipment. People in residential homes, both private or statutory, should have the same rights to home nursing equipment as people living in their own homes (24.4.3.).

4.5.3. Private nursing homes and home nursing equipment. Private nursing homes are expected to provide, as an integral part of their services, nursing equipment. DHA/HB/HSSB CNS might give general (including equipment) advice to such homes on a consultative basis, but do not normally loan equipment to individuals (25.4.3.).

4.6. Supply of home nursing equipment

4.6.1. Equipment stores. Home nursing equipment is loaned from various types of equipment store. The store might be referred to, for example, as the home equipment loan service or medical loan department. It might be run by the CNS, by a hospital supplies department, or by a voluntary organisation on behalf of the DHA/HB/HSSB.

4.6.1.1. Joint equipment store (2.5.4.1./Box 2.6). The store might be a joint (funded) equipment store, containing both daily living and home nursing equipment: run by the DHA/SWD, HB/SWD, HSSB or by a voluntary organisation on behalf of these authorities.

Where joint DHA/SSD, HB/SWD and HSSB stores operate, there is sometimes increased flexibility, itself variable, as to which equipment particular professsionals can authorise for loan (2.5.4.1./Box 2.6.2.2.).

4.6.2. Supply of stock and non-stock equipment. Most CNS equipment loan is based on stock items, which are subject to relatively straightforward supply; non-stock items might require special authorisation, and if approved, take longer to be supplied.

4.6.2.1. Supply of home nursing equipment, other than through the CNS. The CNS might sometimes, depending on local arrangements, rely, to a greater or lesser degree, on outside bodies for the loan of special equipment. For example:

- some special equipment might not be available in CNS stock: available in principle, or because of a shortage of funds;

- it might be in stock but in such a quantity as to be unable to meet demand;
- it might be required for a period greater than normally allowed.

The CNS might advise the client which voluntary bodies (4.6.3.) to approach for help with either purchase or loan of the required equipment (*eg Verbal communications: CNS manager southwest England; 3 national voluntary bodies*).

4.6.3. Voluntary body provision of home nursing equipment

4.6.3.1. Agency agreement with a voluntary body in relation to home nursing equipment. In some areas a voluntary body might formally run an equipment store on behalf of the DHA/HB/HSSB.

The British Red Cross, for example, runs a major joint equipment store in Leicester (2.5.4.1./Box 2.6.2.2.1.).

Even when acting as an agent for the local DHA/HB/HSSB, Red Cross branches might loan certain equipment (with or without hire charges) on its own account, without the necessity of professional recommendation. For example, bed backrests, bed blocks, bed cradle, bed pan, ferrules, polythene sheets, urinals (male and female) (*Red Cross Branch guidelines, South of England*), 1989).

4.6.3.2. Informal help with home nursing equipment. Voluntary organisations might informally help with the provision of home nursing equipment.

For example, the Red Cross has many medical loan branches which informally supplement local CNS provision. These branches generally loan smaller items of equipment rather than more major items such as hoists and special beds (*SWD OT questionnaire 1988. Red Cross HQ verbal communication*). Smaller branches tend to hold small stocks of equipment such as wheelchairs, commodes, bath seats, bed pans, simple bed accessories and the occasional bed or hoist (*Verbal communication: British Red Cross, 1989*).

Other (national) voluntary organisations might either hold a stock of special equipment for loan, or alternatively run grant schemes, which tend to operate on the principle of not subsidising statutory services.

Voluntary organisations also help with, and undertake fundraising, for which they are often pleased to receive requests.

4.6.4. Private purchase of home nursing equipment. Some high street shops, chemists for example, increasingly stock home nursing equipment such as incontinence pads, bed cradles, bed backrests and walking frames.

4.7. Home nursing equipment charges

Home nursing equipment is loaned free of charge by community nursing services.

4.8. Delivery of home nursing equipment

Community nurses sometimes pick up equipment from stores themselves to deliver, and sometimes keep small stocks of equipment in their own home. Friends and relatives are sometimes encouraged to pick up the equipment themselves. Alternatively, an organised store delivery system, with drivers, would be used.

Delivery, in general, of various (including home nursing) equipment is discussed elsewhere (2.5.4.2.).

4.9. Follow-up of home nursing equipment

Continual evaluation of a person's needs means that successful use of equipment can be monitored, and equipment adjusted or replaced as necessary.

However, unless a person continues to require other home nursing services, there is a danger that equipment use is not monitored. For example, a person's condition (or environment) can change, and the equipment become inappropriate: or it can be that the person (or carer) never fully understands the equipment (eg hoist) or uses it to full advantage.

Sometimes nursing auxiliaries, regularly continuing to visit a person, to assist, for example, with bathing, are able to monitor the use of any equipment in the home (*Verbal communication: English National Board for Nursing, Midwifery and Health Visiting, 1990*).

4.10. Maintenance of home nursing equipment

Maintenance of equipment is the responsibility of the DHA/HB/HSSB; larger items of equipment, such as hoists, might be maintained by contract with the manufacturer or supplier of the item.

4.11. Recall of home nursing equipment

Recall, in general, of various types of equipment (including home nursing equipment) is discussed elsewhere (2.8.).

4.12. Disposal of home nursing equipment

Some home nursing equipment must be specially disposed of: for example, used needles, dirty dressings, used incontinence pads. DHA/HB/HSSBs have special collection services for such items.

4.13. Cleaning and refurbishment of home nursing equipment

Such procedures, in general, are discussed elsewhere (2.8.1.).

5 | Medical equipment in general

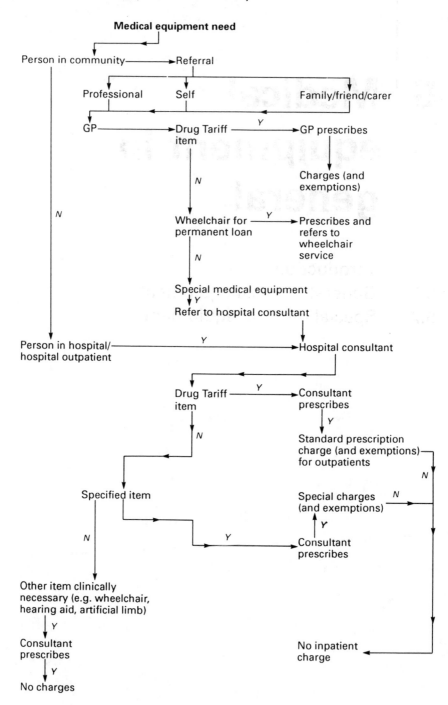

Introduction

Type of equipment
Medical equipment includes any equipment which a doctor considers clinically necessary for the treatment of his or her patient. Such equipment can be divided into:

- 'general medical' equipment, prescribed by general practitioners (GPs), and including incontinence, stoma, diabetes equipment, trusses, elastic hosiery;
- 'special medical' equipment, prescribed by a hospital consultant, and including orthotic appliances, hearing aids, low vision aids, communication aids.

General practitioners
General practitioners are in a key position, if not 'the' key position, in relation to the supply of not only medical equipment, but of all the equipment dealt with in this book. This is because nearly everybody has a GP, whom they see on a regular or semi-regular basis, thus affording GPs access to virtually the whole population. GPs can themselves prescribe:

- items listed on the Drug Tariff (including equipment for the management of incontinence, stoma, diabetes; support and wound dressings; respiratory equipment);
- wheelchairs for permanent use.

Otherwise, they can refer their patients for the following types of equipment:

- 'special medical' equipment (eg orthotic appliances, hearing aids, low vision aids): to hospital consultants;
- paramedical equipment (eg walking aids, speech aids, footwear appliances): to physiotherapists, speech therapists, chiropodists either by direct referral, or via a consultant;
- home nursing equipment (eg bed aids, incontinence pads): to the community nursing services (CNS);
- daily living equipment and home adaptations: to community OTs;
- educational equipment: to education authorities or boards;
- employment equipment: to employment services.

Consultants
Consultants have very wide powers to prescribe whatever is clinically necessary. In practice such wide powers are limited by the availability of local financial resources. They are also, for example, ultimately reponsible for hospital admissions and discharges of all inpatients and most outpatients.

Consultants can prescribe (in common with GPs) any item in the Drug Tariff, and wheelchairs for permanent use. They can also prescribe orthotic appliances, hearing aids, low vision aids, speeech aids and any other equipment clinically necessary. Like GPs, consultants are also in a key position to refer patients to other services (listed above) as appropriate.

There is a considered view that, while there are some excellent examples of good practice, not all hospital consultants give sufficient attention to the rehabilitation, and to the followup care, of people with medical conditions which cause disabilities. It is hoped that, in the future, consultants in rehabilitation medicine (a relatively new specialism) will bring about more integrated services for people with disabilities.

Note on terminology. 'General medical' equipment is taken, for the purpose of this book, to mean equipment prescribed by a GP; 'special medical' equipment is taken to mean equipment prescribed by a hospital consultant.

5.1. General medical equipment

5.1.1. Type of equipment. General medical services are provided by general practitioners (GPs); general medical equipment is equipment that can be prescribed by GPs.

Equipment prescribed by GPs includes:

- items listed in the Drug Tariff (see Box 5.1);
- wheelchairs for permanent loan (prescription and referral to the wheelchair service);
- orthotic appliances (not on the Drug Tariff) (more rarely, when, for example, the GP has had special training and has direct access to an orthotist's clinic (10.3.2.2.));
- home nursing equipment (more rarely, when, for example, the GP has access to a DHA/HB/HSSB home nursing equipment store; or if a small supply is kept at the GP's premises).

Box 5.1: Examples of Drug Tariff equipment prescribed by GPs (and hospital consultants)

B5.1.1. Equipment for stoma care (Box 18.1).

B5.1.2. Equipment for the management of incontinence (17.3.1.5.).

B5.1.3. Equipment for people with diabetes (20.1.).

B5.1.4. Elastic hosiery (graduated compression): light, medium or strong support. Thigh stocking, below knee stocking, suspender belts, anklet support, kneecap support.

B5.1.5. Miscellaneous: breast relievers, breast shields, nipple shields, throat brushes, droppers (for eye/ear/nose drops), eye baths, finger cots, finger stalls, gauzes, adhesive latex foam (for use with cervical collars), lint, plasters, suprapubic belts (replacement only).

B5.1.6. For support/compression: stockinettes for compression, retention of dressings, as protective dressings. Trusses: single side or double side, inguinal or scrotal, spring truss or elastic band truss.

B5.1.7. Respiratory equipment: throat and nasal sprays, nebulisers (21.), inhalers, insufflators, oxygen concentrators (21.), oxygen cylinders (21.).

B5.1.8. Chiropody appliances: adhesive zinc oxide felt, all-wool felt, animal wool for chiropody, bunion rings, corn plasters, corn rings, metatarsal pads, sponge rubber.

B5.1.9. Dressings: boil, multiple pack dressing, perforated film absorbent dressing

---

> sterile, povidone iodine fabric dressing sterile, knitted viscose primary dressing impregnated, semipermeable adhesive film, semipermeable waterproof plastic wound, standard dressings, sterile dressing packs, sterile knitted viscose, wound management (calcium alginate, hydrocolloid) dressings.
>
> **B5.1.10. Bandages:** cotton conforming bandage, cotton elastic heavy, cotton crepe, elastic adhesive bandage, elastic diachylon (ventilated), elastic web bandage with or without foot loop, heavy cotton and rubber elastic, hydrocortisone and silicone, polyamide and cellulose contour, open wove bandage, plaster of paris, porous flexible adhesive, suspensory bandage (cotton net bag with draw tapes/elastic edge), triangular calico bandage, tubular bandage, zinc paste bandages.

5.1.2. Legislative basis for provision of general medical equipment

5.1.2.1. GP prescription is covered by the DHA (through FPC)/HB/HSSB duty to make arrangements with medical practitioners to provide 'personal medical services' (known as 'general medical services') for people 'who wish to take advantage of them' (*NHS Act 1977 s.15, s.29; NHS (Scotland) Act 1978 s.19; SI 1972/1265 HPSS(NI)O a.56*).

More specifically, the terms of service of GPs are specified in principal regulations, made in the 1970s and recently extensively amended (*SI 1974/160; SI 1974/506 (S.41); SR&O 1973/421*).

5.1.3. Referral to GPs

5.1.3.1. Open referral to GPs. Referral to GPs is open. People need to register with GPs who will normally accept requests for registration unless their list is full. Lists of local GPs are held by FPC/HB/HSSBs, public libraries and post offices for example.

Many other professionals may also suggest, in the course of their work, that a person consult their GP.

5.1.3.2. Temporary resident eligibility. Legislation states that the GP can also see somebody who is visiting or living temporarily in another district – such a 'temporary resident' is defined if he or she is staying more than 24 hours but less than 3 months (*SI 1974/160 r.21; SI 1974/506 (S.41) r.22; SR&O 1973/421 r.21*).

5.1.3.3. GP domiciliary visits. Legislation states that the GP has a duty to make domiciliary visits 'if the condition of the patient so requires' (*SI 1974/160 Sched. 1 para 13A as inserted by SI 1989/1897; SI 1974/506 (S.41) Sched.1 para 10 as amended by SI 1990 (S.139); SR&O 1973/421 (NI) Sched. 1 para 8A as inserted by SR 1989/454*).

5.1.3.4. GP advice on local social services. Legislation states that the GP has a duty to give advice, 'as appropriate', to their patients on how to benefit from 'social services', 'social work services' or 'personal social services' provided by the SSD, SWD, HSSB respectively (*SI 1974/160 Sched. 1 para 13 as amended by SI 1989/1897; SI 1974/506 (S.41) Sched.1 para 9 as amended by SI 1990 (S.139); SR&O 1973/421 Sched.1 para 8 as amended by SR 1989/454*).

Apart from social services, GPs are very well placed to refer people for all sorts of other services, such as employment, housing or education services.

5.1.3.5. GP location. GPs might be based in their own premises or health centres, and be organised into group, partnership or single-handed practices.

Health centres can afford easy GP access to a number, depending on the centre's size and organisation, of different professionals. For example, chiropodists, speech therapists, community physiotherapists, district nurses and health visitors might be based at a health centre.

5.1.3.6. GP attached/employed professionals. Other professionals are sometimes found at GP premises. For example, GPs sometimes employ practice nurses (4.4.7.); often have community nurses (district nurses and health visitors) (4.4.1.) attached; and sometimes have community physiotherapists attached.

5.1.3.7. Remit of GPs. GPs have been identified in recent government reports and White Papers as key professionals in community care. They 'are unique in having near universal contact with the whole population' (*Community Care: Agenda for Action. A Report to the Secretary of State for Social Services by Sir Roy Griffiths, 1988, p.9*); are usually the 'first point of contact with the NHS' (*Promoting Better Health. HMSO 1987 p.11*); and 'can bring together physical, psychological and social factors when considering health and illness' (*Caring for Patients. HMSO 1989, p. 34*).

5.1.4. Assessment and provision

5.1.4.1. Prescription of Drug Tariff equipment by GPs. A GP can prescribe appliances and equipment listed in the Drug Tariff, which is compiled and published under regulations (*SI 1974/160 r.28 as amended; SI 1974/506 (S.41) r. 32 as amended; SR&O 1973/421 r.40 as amended*).

5.1.4.2. Special medical equipment.

5.1.4.2.1.Referral, by GPs, for other special medical equipment. If the GP thinks that other special medical equipment is needed, he or she refers the patient to a hospital consultant.

5.1.4.2.2. Exceptional GP prescription of special medical equipment. Exceptionally, if a GP is appointed to the staff of a hospital and receives consultant sanction, he or she can prescribe a wider range of appliances on behalf of the consultant (*MHM 50 NWTRHA p. 2; MHM 50 SHHD p. 6*).

Sometimes GPs, with direct access to an orthotist's clinic, can prescribe simple orthotic appliances (in addition to the Drug Tariff trusses and elastic hosiery) (10.3.2.2.).

5.1.4.3. Home nursing equipment and paramedical equipment

5.1.4.3.1. Referral by GPs for home nursing and paramedical equipment. The GP can make a direct referral to, for example:
- community nurses (district nurses or sometimes health visitors) for home nursing equipment;
- community physiotherapists or chiropodists for mobility equipment and foot appliances;
- speech therapists for communication (speech) aids.

These professionals are sometimes attached to the GP practice, or health centre at which the GP works (5.1.3.5./6.).

5.1.4.3.2. Exceptional GP supply of home nursing equipment. More rarely, the GP has access to a local DHA/HB/HSSB home nursing equipment store, from which he or she can directly authorise the loan of simple home nursing equipment (4.4.3.1.2.).

5.1.4.4. GP wheelchair prescription. If a wheelchair is needed, the GP can prescribe (through the wheelchair service) a wheelchair for permanent loan (6.4.3.1.); or, for temporary loan refer to the CNS (6.3.2.), refer to a voluntary organisation (such as the Red Cross) (6.3.3.), or (more rarely) directly authorise the loan (6.3.5.).

Sometimes the GP directly authorises temporary loan of a wheelchair if he or she has access to a local DHA/HB/HSSB home nursing equipment store (*Midlands joint store catalogue, received 1988*).

5.1.4.5. GP assessment and referral for environmental controls. The GP can make a referral to a DHA/HB/HSSB medical officer or administrative 'co-ordinator', if sophisticated environmental controls, requiring medical prescription, are needed (16.4.2.1.2.).

Referral for simpler environmental controls, not requiring medical prescription, can be made to the SSD/SWD or HSSB (under social services functions) (16.4.1.).

5.1.4.6. GP assessment of elderly people. A recent White Paper (for England, Wales and Scotland) stresses that GPs have a great contribution to make to the care of elderly people (*Caring for People. HMSO 1989 p. 35*).

5.1.4.6.1. New GP contract. The new GP contract (operative from 1.4.90) contains special reference to people who are over 75 years old. The GP has a duty every year to 'invite each patient on his list who has attained the age of 75 years to participate in a consultation, and offer to make a domiciliary visit to each such patient, for the purpose of assessing whether he needs to render personal medical services to that patient'.

The assessment should include consideration of sensory functions, mobility, mental condition, physical condition including continence, social environment and use of medicines (*SI 1974/160 Sched 1. para 13D (inserted by 1989/1897); SI 1974/506 (S.41) Sched. 1 para 10C (inserted by 1989/1990 (S.13)); SR&O 1973/421 Sched 1 para 8D (inserted by SR 1989/454)*).

5.1.4.7. GP surveillance of children. From April 1990, FPC/HB/HSSBs hold lists of GPs providing 'restricted services'. One of these services is child surveillance (26.4.2.1.).

5.1.4.8. GP hospital links. Good links between GPs and hospital are important for patient care, as noted by a report, for example (*see eg Primary Care Review, DHSS (NI) July 1988, para 20*).

Both recent Circular guidance (England), and British Geriatrics Society guidelines, outline GP responsibilities in relation to discharge of patients from hospital and state the importance of:

- continuing medical care on return home (so the GP must be informed of discharge as early as possible, as well as of diagnosis, treatment, medication) (*Discharge of Patients From Hospital. DH, 1989, issued with HC(89)5*);
- the takeover of care must be immediate (*Joint Statement of Professional Associations. Discharge to the Community of Elderly Patients in Hospital. British Geriatrics Society 1989 p. 3*).
- the GP may need to visit the patient in hospital to give advice on the patient's home circumstances to doctors, ward sisters, other members of the multi-disciplinary (*Discharge of Patients From Hospital. DH, 1989, issued with HC(89)5*);
- GP's initial referral letters should give details of problems likely to be encountered on discharge (*Discharge of Patients From Hospital. DH, 1989, issued with HC(89)5*).

Similar guidance has been issued for Wales (WHC(90)1).

5.1.4.9. GP assessment of carers. GPs need to assess carers and their social, environmental and housing problems as well as any medical problems. GPs can offer consultation to the carer about the person who is disabled; can organise respite care; and can respond to requests for home visits (*Davies, Mary A. Doctors, Carers and General Practice. MSD Foundation 1989*).

5.1.4.10. Dispensing. The GP prescription is normally taken to a pharmacist for dispensing. However, in certain circumstances, the GP dispenses drugs or appliances.

There are also a number of dispensing appliance centres to which prescriptions for certain appliances can be taken.

5.1.4.10.1. Pharmacist dispensing. Regulations place certain duties on pharmacists in relation to the dispensing of prescriptions for drugs and appliances (*SI 1974/160; SI 1974/506 (S.41); SR&O 1973/421*).

In particular, regulations (England, Wales), for example, place a duty on the pharmacist to 'make all necessary arrangements . . . for measuring a person who presents a prescription for a truss or other appliance of a type requiring measurement and fitting by a chemist, and . . . for fitting the appliance' (*SI 1974/160 Sched.4 para 4*).

5.1.4.10.2. GP dispensing sometimes occurs if the patient has a 'serious difficulty in obtaining any necessary drugs or appliances from a chemist by reason of distance or inadequacy of means of communication, or is resident in an area which . . . is rural in character, at a distance of more than one mile from the premises of any chemist'.

Permission to dispense is subject to the approval of the FPC, and the Local Medical or Local Pharmaceutical Committee (*SI 1974/160 r.30; SI 1974/506 (S.41) r.30; SR&O 1973/421 r.41*).

5.1.4.10.3. Dispensing appliance centres are run by private contractors and offer a fitting and dispensing service for (Drug Tariff) prescribed appliances such as incontinence and stoma care appliances, trusses and elastic hosiery.

Some of the companies, members of the British Surgical Trades Association (BSTA), adhere to a code of practice which includes home visits; provision of suitable facilities and access at the centre; use of appropriately qualified staff; an emergency service; and putting patients' needs before commercial considerations when giving advice (*BSTA Code of Practice for Dispensing Appliance Contractors*).

5.2. Special medical equipment

*Note.*This term is used, for the purposes of this book, to refer to equipment prescribed by hospital consultants.

5.2.1. Type of equipment. Consultants have the power to prescribe whatever they consider clinically necessary.

Other sections of this book deal with certain types of equipment prescribed by consultants: for example orthotic appliances, renal dialysis equipment, prostheses, hearing aids, low vision aids etc.

Some equipment is prescribed by both consultants and GPs; for example, wheelchairs, and items listed in the Drug Tariff (5.1.1./Box 5.1).

5.2.2. Legislative basis for the provision of special medical equipemnt. Legislation makes little reference to special medical equipment provision, except in relation to procedures for charges. DH (generally but informally applying to Northern Ireland) and SHHD guidelines do make reference, however, to 'medical and surgical appliances'; these guidelines are referred to, as appropriate, below.

5.2.2.1.Consultant prescription is covered by the DHA/HB/HSSB duty to provide 'medical services' (NHS Act 1977 s.3; NHS (*Scotland) Act 1978 s.36; SI 1972/1265 SI 1972/R65HPSS (NI) O a.5*).

5.2.3. Referral for special medical equipment

5.2.3.1. Inpatient referral to a consultant. Referral to a consultant for hospital admission is normally through a GP ('cold' or emergency); through the consultant (or members of the consultant's duty team) following a domiciliary visit; or through the accident and emergency department of a hospital (*NHS Handbook. NAHA 1989 p. 180*); or through another consultant already treating the patient.

5.2.3.2. Outpatient referral to a consultant. Referral to a consultant for outpatient admission normally takes place through a GP. Occasionally it is through other channels (eg referral by a doctor at a child health clinic), but the GP is informed anyway. Another consultant can refer a patient, whom he or she is already treating.

5.2.3.3. Types of hospital doctor. Hospital doctors include consultants or junior hospital doctors (including senior registrars, registrars, senior house officers, house officers) (*NHS Handbook, NAHA 1989. p. 181*).

5.2.3.3.1. Consultant specialisms. There are many specialisms within medicine, and many types of consultant prescribe equipment and appliances.

Examples of consultants who prescribe the sort of equipment discussed in this book are: consultants in rehabilitation medicine, geriatricians, paediatricians, rheumatologists, neurologists, urologists, ophthalmologists, otologists, ENT surgeons, orthopaedic surgeons, diabetic consultants.

5.2.3.3.2. Distribution of consultants. Consultants involved with rehabilitation, such as rheumatologists, neurologists and consultants in rehabilitation medicine are distributed very unevenly around the UK (*see eg Physical Disability and Beyond. Royal College of Physicians, 1986 p. 7; Hunter J, Walker J. Role of a Rehabilitation Medicine Service. Rehabilitation Studies Unit, University of Edinburgh. 1989 p. 2*).

5.2.3.3.3. Consultants in rehabilitation medicine are a new specialism with interest in chronically disabled people, mainly in the 16-64 year age group. They provide special services for this group, much as geriatricians and paediatricians do for elderly people and children.

Physical, psychological and social factors are all likely to be taken into account by consultants in rehabilitation medicine (*Hunter J, Walker J. Role of a Rehabilitation Medicine Service. Rehabilitation Studies Unit, University of Edinburgh. 1989 p. 2*), as part of the assessment of the total needs of the patient.

5.2.4. Assessment and prescription of special medical equipment

5.2.4.1. Wide consultant powers to prescribe equipment. DH (applying informally to Northern Ireland) and SHHD guidelines, and a Northern Ireland public information booklet state that consultants have the power to prescribe whatever is medically or clinically necessary. For example:

- 'it is for the consultant dealing with the patient to prescribe whatever appliance is considered necessary for the patient's condition' (*MHM 50. NWTRHA, p. 2*);
- 'a consultant may prescribe the appliance necessary to meet the clinical needs of the patient including those prescribable by a general practitioner' (*MHM 50. SHHD, p. 7*);
- 'a consultant may prescribe on free loan any piece of equipment which he considers necessary as part of his patient's treatment' (*Equipment for Disabled People. HB2 Leaflet. DHSS (NI) 1988*).

In practice, local resources restrict these powers. Where special (costly) equipment is prescribed (eg electronic speech aids), consultants in some areas might need, for each item of equipment, to make a special case with hospital administrators – without any guarantee of success. In other areas, local arrangements between consultants and administrators facilitates such special prescription (Verbal communication: hospital consultant 1989).

5.2.4.2. Prescription 'under the direction' of the consultant. DH (informally applying to Northern Ireland) guidelines state that equipment can be prescribed 'under the direction' of a consultant (*MHM 50 NWTRHA, p. 2*). This could, for example, cover prescription by junior doctors or hospital GP practitioners as well as provision of equipment (eg walking aids) by paramedical staff, following delegation by the consultant.

5.2.4.3. Consultant responsibility for the supply and fitting of equipment. DH (informally applying to Northern Ireland) and SHHD guidelines state that the prescribing consultant is responsible for seeing that equipment is successfully used. For example:

- 'the consultant is responsible for ensuring that each completed appliance

conforms to the prescription and is satisfactory in manufacture, fit and function when fitted on the patient' (*MHM 50 NWTRHA p. 7*);
- it 'is the consultant's responsibility to ensure that the appliance prescribed is provided, that it continues to meet the needs of the patient and that it is adjusted, modified or replaced as appropriate' (*MHM 50 SHHD p. 7*).

5.2.4.4. Hospital discharge: consultant responsibility. Circular guidance (England, Wales 1989/1990) emphasises the responsibility of consultants for hospital discharge of patients, for example:

- the consultant is responsible for admission and discharge of patients; discharge responsibility may be delegated but only where such delegation is clearly understood (*HC(89)5; WHC(90)1*);
- patients must not be discharged until the consultant (or doctor to whom responsibility is delegated), or other member of staff (eg a ward sister) to whom responsibility is delegated, is satisfied that adequate arrangements have been made (*HC(89)5; WHC(90)1*);
- consultants should play an important role in reviewing discharge procedures (*HC(89)5*).

5.2.4.5. Follow-up by consultants, in general, for people with disabilities. There is a considered opinion that, while there are many examples of good practice, consultants do not always follow up patients sufficiently (following an operation, for example), to ensure full rehabilitation (*see eg Physical Disability and Beyond. Royal College of Physicians 1986 p. 5*).

6 | Wheelchairs

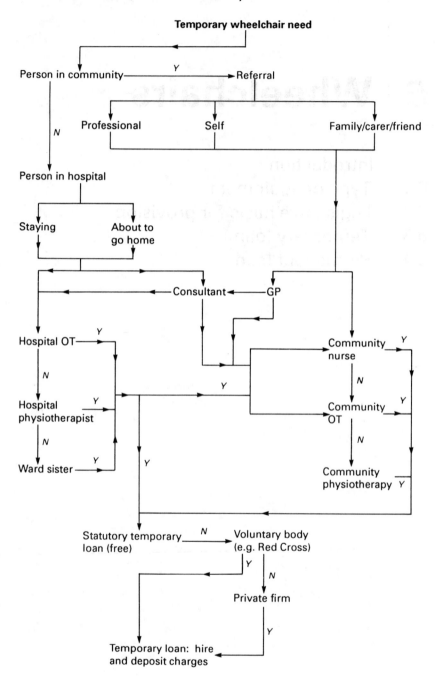

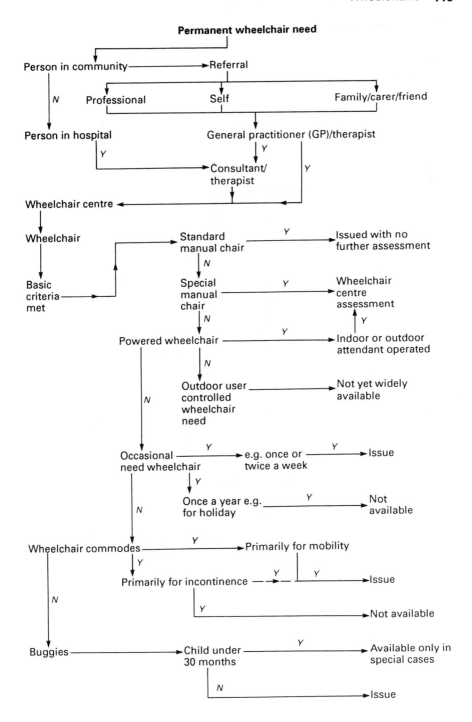

Wheelchair need (continued)

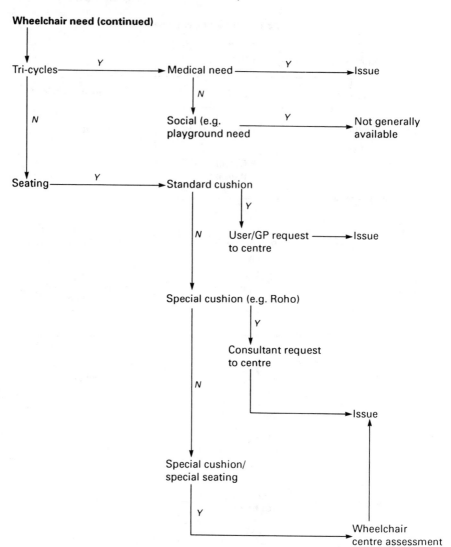

Introduction

The loan (free of charge) of wheelchairs is undertaken mainly by the health service and special health authorities, and sometimes by social services, education services and employment services, depending on the type of need which the wheelchair will meet. Wheelchair loan also falls into two other main categories, temporary and permanent.

Temporary loan (usually up to 3 months)

Temporary loan of wheelchairs is generally made in the following ways:

- hospital loan of wheelchairs;
- the community nursing services (CNS) which are part of:
  - district health authorities (DHAs, England/Wales);
  - health boards (HBs, Scotland);
  - health and social services boards (HSSBs, Northern Ireland);
- a voluntary organisation acting either on behalf of, or independently of, the CNS (in which case a hire charge may be made);
- social services:
  - social services departments (SSDs, England, Wales);
  - social work departments (SWDs, Scotland)
  - health and social services boards (HSSBs, Northern Ireland);
- other health service (DHA/HB/HSSB) professionals such as physiotherapists, occupational therapists, ward sisters;
- private firms which loan wheeelchairs on the basis of deposit and hire charges.

Permanent loan

Permanent loan of wheelchairs, free of charge, is administered through the following channels:

- Disablement Services Authority (DSA, England: until 31.3.91);
- Welsh Health Common Services Authority (WHCSA, Wales);
- health boards (HBs, Scotland);
- Regional Disablement Services (RDS, Northern Ireland).

Referral to the wheelchair service requires prescription (in Scotland, recommendation) by a GP or consultant. In practice therapists often assess and fill out most of the details of the prescription form.

In a minority of cases, depending on individual special needs and the type of wheelchair required, the wheelchair service undertakes further assessment. This sometimes involves multi-disciplinary assessment by, for example, doctors, therapists, rehabilitation engineers, nurses and social workers.

A wide range of standard wheelchairs is available, obtained by wheelchair service central contract. If there is a special need, commercial models, adaptations and, exceptionally, bespoke wheelchairs can be provided. Similarly, standard cushions, special cushions and special seating are available, requiring varying degrees of assessment and authorisation.

Outdoor, powered user controlled wheelchairs have not, in the past, been provided by the wheelchair service. This situation might change in the near future.

Basic maintenance and repair is carried out by a national network of approved repairers.

The loan of wheelchairs for education and employment purposes is discussed elsewhere (27. and 28.).

6.1. Type of equipment

Wheelchairs include push chairs (attendant propelled wheelchairs), user propelled (self-propelled) wheelchairs, electric wheelchairs, various parts and accessories.

Buggies, trolleys, cycles and tricycles are also provided by the wheelchair service. This equipment is detailed in Box 6.1.

Box 6.1: Examples of wheelchairs, accessories and other carriages (not all of these are available through the wheelchair service: those that are, are marked with an asterisk)

B6.1.1. Push chairs (ie attendant propelled chairs) include:

- folding/transit chairs;*
- hospital-type pushchairs;
- spinal carriages* (rarely supplied now).

B6.1.2. Self-propelled wheelchairs include:

- folding;*
- high performance;*

- sports;
- one-side drive;*
- amputee;*
- reclining;*
- with commode seats;*
- hospital-type wheelchairs.

B6.1.3. Electric wheelchairs include:

- dual speed (for both pavement use at 4mph and road use at 8mph);
- indoor;*
- indoor/outdoor;
- outdoor/indoor;
- scooters;
- standup;
- with elevating seat;
- stair climbing;
- attendant controlled powered outdoor wheelchairs.*

B6.1.4. Buggies,* self-propelled trolleys*, tricycles/cycles*

B6.1.5. Parts and accessories

B6.1.5.1. A variety of alternative (to standard) parts and accessories include:

- backrest extensions;*
- commode facilities;*
- foam cushions;*
- trays;*
- folding backrests;*
- detachable armrests;*
- footrest extensions;*
- elevating legrests;*
- one arm drive attachments;*
- single side brake levers;*
- solid tyres;*
- adjustable angle backrests;*
- angled backrests;*
- various wheel sizes;*
- rigid seat and backrests.*

B6.1.5.2. Other accessories/parts (less commonly needed) include:

- toe straps;*
- footboxes;*
- special desk armrests;*
- special trays;*
- capstan handrims;*
- harnesses/belts* for chest, shoulder, thigh, groin, leg;
- mobile arm support* (*list of alternative parts and accessories is taken from Wheelchair Prescription. North Western Region DSA.*).

6.2. Legislative basis for provision of wheelchairs

6.2.1. Basis for temporary loan of wheelchairs

6.2.1.1. The basis for hospital temporary loan of wheelchairs, for either use within the hospital or home use, lies in the duty of the DHA/HB/HSS to provide 'medical services', 'nursing services' or 'other services' depending on whether the member of staff responsible for the loan of the chair is respectively a doctor, a nurse, or a therapist (*NHS Act 1977 s.3; NHS(Scotland) Act 1978 s.36; HPSS(NI)O 1972 a.5*).

6.2.1.2. The basis for community nursing service (CNS) temporary loan of wheelchairs lies in the DHA/HB/HSSB duty to provide 'nursing services' and, more specifically, by the duty to prevent illness, to care for people who are ill, and to provide after-care for such people (*NHS Act 1977 s.3, NHS (Scotland) Act 1978 s.36, 37; HPSS(NI)O 1972 a.5, 7*).

6.2.1.3. Basis for voluntary body temporary wheelchair loan, by formal agreement. Where a voluntary body undertakes temporary wheelchair loan by formal agreement with either a DHA, HB, SSD, SWD, HSSB, then the agreement is covered by specific legislation allowing such discretionary arrangements with voluntary bodies (*NHS Act 1977 s.23; NHS (Scotland) Act 1978 s.16; National Assistance Act 1948 s.30; Social Work (Scotland) Act 1968 s. 10; SI 1972/1265 HPSS(NI)O a.71,*).

6.2.1.4. The basis for SSD/SWD/HSSB (social services) temporary wheelchair loan lies in the same legislation as applies to the provision of daily living equipment in general (2.) (*Chronically Sick and Disabled Persons Act 1970 s.2(1)(e); CSDP(NI)A 1978 s.2(e) and other legislation*).

Such loan is likely to be short-term only, perhaps up to three months for example (*London SSD (19) guidelines 1989*).

6.2.1.5. Basis for other health professional temporary wheelchair loan. Where, for example, other professionals have formal access to a joint community equipment store and can loan wheelchairs, such provision is covered by, in the case of:

- a ward sister: DHA/HB/HSSB duty to provide 'nursing services' and to prevent illness, to care for people who are ill, and to provide after-care for such people (*NHS Act 1977 s.3; NHS (Scotland) Act 1978 s.36,37; HPSS(NI)O 1972 a.5,7*);
- a community physiotherapist: the DHA/HB/HSSB duty to provide 'other services' (*NHS Act 1977 s.3; NHS (Scotland) Act 1978 s.36; SI 1972/1265 HPSS(NI)O 1972 a.5*).
- a GP: the DHA (through the FPC)/HB/HSSB duty to provide 'general medical services' (*NHS Act 1977 s.29; NHS (Scotland) Act 1978 s.19; SI 1972/1265 HPSS(NI)O 1972 a.56*).

6.2.2. Basis for permanent loan

6.2.2.1. The basis for consultant or GP prescription of wheelchairs for permanent loan lies in the DHA/HB/HSSB duty to provide 'medical services' (consultants) and duty (in the case of DHAs through FPCs) to provide 'general medical services' (GPs) (*NHS Act 1977 s.3,29; NHS (Scotland) Act 1978 s.19,36; SI 1972/1265 HPSS(NI)O 1972 a.5,56*)

6.2.2.2. The basis for therapist assessment for (and more rarely prescription of) of wheelchairs for permanent loan lies in the DHA/HB/HSSB duty to provide 'other services' (*NHS Act 1977 s.3; NHS (Scotland) Act 1978 s.36; SI 1972/1265 HPSS(NI)O a.5*).

6.2.3. The basis for education and employment services' provision of wheelchairs on loan is discussed elsewhere (27. and 28.).

6.3. Temporary loan

Where the need for a wheelchair is seen as temporary, the wheelchair can be supplied through a number of channels. Manual wheelchairs only are supplied on temporary loan. Three months is probably the average maximum loan period.

6.3.1. Hospital loan

6.3.1.1. Hospital inpatient loan. Wheelchairs, for temporary use by inpatients, are generally recommended and supplied by doctors, occupational therapists, physiotherapists and ward sisters.

6.3.1.2. Hospital discharge wheelchair loan. An inpatient about to go home, with a temporary wheelchair need, might have wheelchair loan arranged through the CNS or through a local voluntary organisation such as the Red Cross. Some SSD/SWDs or HSSBs (social services) hold a small stock of wheelchairs for loan, but this is less common.

Alternatively, some people go home with a hospital wheelchair, either intentionally – there may be an informal loan pool of hospital wheelchairs (*Scottish ALAC questionnaire 1988*); or unintentionally. This latter case can occur, for example, in the confusion of of a sudden weekend discharge, when it is unclear what arrangements (if any) have been made, or to whom (eg the individual, the wheelchair service, or hospital department) the wheelchair in question actually belongs.

6.3.1.3. Hospital wheelchair pools. Within the hospital there is a pool of wheelchairs, which it is often difficult to effectively organise and maintain. Some hospitals are now drawing up 'wheelchair policy' documents in an attempt to rectify what has long been recognised as a major problem.

Such a policy might recognise, for example, various hospital pools of wheelchairs including portering, ward, individual department/clinic, physiotherapy assessment, physiotherapy loan, occupational therapy loan and occupational therapy assessment wheelchairs; as well as patients' personal wheelchairs (including wheelchairs issued by the wheelchair service).

A variety of procedures and responsibilities are needed for effective organisation and maintenance of these wheelchairs (*Stoke Mandeville Wheelchair Policy. Final Draft. January 1989*).

6.3.1.4. *Ownership of hospital wheelchairs.* Without clear procedures, the ownership of and responsibility for wheelchairs can become very confused: for example one study (1985) showed that 60% of wheelchairs in hospitals did not actually belong to the hospital (*Anonymous. OTs vital to combat wheelchair danger. Therapy Weekly 1985:12;21, 1-2*).

6.3.1.5. *Maintenance of hospital wheelchairs.* Hospital wheelchairs seem to be ill-maintained. A 1985 government Safety Information Bulletin noted that reports were continuing to be received of wheelchair incidents, which included patient and staff injury. Aspects of wheelchair maintenance mentioned included frame structure, wheels and castors, brakes, foot/leg rests and upholstery (*SIB(85)18*).

Recent correspondence in the BMJ noted that the 'problem of inadequate, poorly maintained, and incomplete wheelchairs in hospitals is well known, and fewer than a quarter of hospital wheelchairs are safe and in good working order...' (*Crewe R. Letter. BMJ 299 a1.7.89 p.53-54; Mulley G.P Standards of Wheelchairs. Awful: can only get better.BMJ 298 6.5.89 pp. 1198–99*).

6.3.1.5.1. Product liability in relation to hospital wheelchairs. Poor maintenance not only threatens the welfare of wheelchair users, but also raises questions, for professionals, of product liability (31.), and health and safety at work (*see eg Crewe R. Standards of wheelchairs. BMJ 1989:299,53-54*).

6.3.2. Community nursing services (CNS) temporary loan of wheelchairs is sometimes made to people at home (or leaving hospital to go home). The maximum loan period is usually about 3 months, although it might be up to six months in some circumstances. The loan might equally be for a short holiday period of a week or two, if that is all that is required. It is free of charge.

6.3.3. Voluntary body temporary loan of wheelchairs is sometimes made by organisations such as the Red Cross. Such provision might be independent of any statutory provision, might informally supplement statutory provision, or might be on formal behalf of the DHA/HB/HSSB.

Where the voluntary organisation makes such provision by contract to the DHA/HB/HSSB, no charge is likely to be made. However, where such provision is made by the voluntary body independently, it might make deposit and hire charges which can can vary in amount. For example, loan at a busy seaside resort might include both definite deposit and hire charges; in a small rural market town there might be little or no charge (*Verbal communication: British Red Cross, 1989*).

6.3.4. SSD/SWD/HSSB temporary loan of wheelchairs. SSD/SWDs and HSSBs (under social services functions) sometimes hold, for short-term loan, a small stock of wheelchairs, which are loaned by community OTs.

This is likely to vary from area to area; however, where there is a joint equipment store (2.5.4.1./Box 2.6.) then community OTs are likely to have routine access to standard short-term loan wheelchairs.

6.3.5. Other health professional temporary loan of wheelchairs. Other health professionals sometimes have formal access to short-term loan wheelchairs held in home nursing or community equipment stores, particularly in the case of joint equipment stores (2.5.4.1./Box 2.6.).

Professionals, with such access, can include ward sisters, district nurses, occupational therapists and sometimes GPs (both hospital and community), physiotherapists (both hospital and community) (*variously: Equipment store catalogues: 3 Midlands stores. Received 1988/1989*).

6.3.6. Private hire. A number of private hire firms exist, making daily/weekly hire and deposit charges which vary in amount and conditions attached.

6.4. Permanent loan

6.4.1. Wheelchair service organisation. The term 'wheelchair service' is used in this book to refer to the variously organised and named statutory agencies which are responsible for permanent wheelchair loan in the United Kingdom.

Similarly the term 'wheelchair centre' is used to refer to the variously named centres of the wheelchair service.

6.4.1.1. Wheelchair service organisation: England. The wheelchair service is currently administered by a special health authority known as the Disablement Services Authority (DSA). The DSA will cease to exist on 31.3.1991 when the wheelchair service will become part of the NHS.

The wheelchair service is currently based at centres known as disablement services centres (DSCs), formerly known as artificial limb and appliance centres (ALACs). There is an average of two DSCs per regional health authority. In some areas, DHAs have already taken over the service, and it would appear that, in the future, the wheelchair service will be based mainly at DHA level.

6.4.1.2. Wheelchair service organisation: Wales. The wheelchair service in Wales is administered by a special health authority called the Welsh Health Common Services Authority (WHCSA). Wheelchair centres are known as artificial limb and appliance centres (ALACS).

6.4.1.3. Wheelchair service organisation: Scotland. The wheelchair service is adminstered by health boards (HBs). Wheelchair centres in Scotland are known as artificial limb and appliance centres (ALACs) or limb fitting centres, and are part of the NHS.

There are centres in Aberdeen, Dundee, Edinburgh, Glasgow, Inverness, which between them cover the 15 Scottish health boards.

6.4.1.4. Wheelchair service organisation: Northern Ireland. The wheelchair service for Northern Ireland is administered as part of Regional Disablement Services (RDS) at Musgrave Park Hospital. The RDS is run by the Eastern Health and Social Services Board (EHSSB) on behalf of the other three HSSBs.

6.4.2. Professionals involved in the assessment and prescription of wheelchairs for permanent loan include:

- GP or consultant (initial prescription to the service);

- therapist (initial recommendation assessment and sometimes prescription; participation in wheelchair service assessment);
- wheelchair service consultant or medical officer (assessment/authorisation);
- rehabilitation engineer (assessment, and carrying out of special adaptation work; and occasionally the building of bespoke wheelchairs);
- technical officer (technical assessment and carrying out, or arranging, of adaptations).

Staff involved vary from area to area, and the position is slightly confused in England during the transition process between the DSA and the NHS (6.4.1.1.). The degree and organisation of multi-disciplinary assessment varies, depending on local arrangement. For details see Box 6.2.

6.4.3. Referral

6.4.3.1. Medical prescription. Referral to the wheelchair service is normally made by a GP or consultant, who prescribes (or in Scotland, recommends) the wheelchair. In England, Wales and Northern Ireland, a form known as AOF 5G is used; this must be signed by a doctor. In England, this form has been revised by the DSA to include greater detail.

In Scotland, each centre uses its own (simpler) form, and the referring doctor recommends a wheelchair (as opposed to prescribes). Official prescription is actually made by the wheelchair service doctor (*Verbal communication: consultant in rehabilitation medicine, 1990*).

6.4.3.2. Therapist assessment and prescription.

6.4.3.2.1. Assessment. Although prescription forms have to be signed by a doctor, the details of the form are often filled in by occupational therapists, physiotherapists and sometimes by nurses (eg ward sisters).

6.4.3.2.2. Prescription of wheelchairs on permanent loan.

6.4.3.2.2.1. Wheelchair prescription: England. In England both policy and practice seems to be slowly changing; the pivotal role of therapists is increasingly recognised and in some areas they are now able to officially prescribe wheelchairs (ie sign the prescription form,) as well as continue to fill out the details of the form.

For example, within one DHA already running its own wheelchair service, the AOF 5G (6.4.3.1.) form has been abandoned. The new form can be signed by either a doctor or a therapist: but a doctor's signature is no longer a requirement (*Verbal communication: DHA wheelchair service: open day, 1989*).

(In the past, therapists have sometimes signed prescription forms, and the wheelchair service has quietly and unofficially accepted them; doctors have sometimes signed blank prescription forms, and therapists have sometimes been able to authorise subsequent prescription following initial prescription by a doctor).

6.4.3.2.2.2. Wheelchair prescription: Wales, Scotland, Northern Ireland do not appear to be changing in respect of therapist prescription, a doctor's signature is still formally required.

Box 6.2: Wheelchair service staff

B6.2.1. Wheelchair service doctors

B6.2.1.1. Wheelchair service doctors: England. Medical officers (MOs) (civil service post) will will be replaced by health service consultants after 31.3.1991.

This change has occurred where DHAs already run the service. For example, in one such DHA, a consultant rheumatologist provides the medical input (part-time), as backup to assessment by therapists and rehabilitation engineers (*DHA wheelchair service open day, 1989*). Other consultants who typically provide such input are consultants in rehabilitation medicine (where they exist), orthopaedic surgeons.

B6.2.1.2. Wheelchair service doctors: Wales. WHCSA employs one doctor known as a medical officer (a former surgeon), and uses two health service consultants on a sessional basis (*Written communication: WHCSA 1989*).

B6.2.1.3. Wheelchair service doctors: Scotland. NHS employed consultants supply medical input to the service (which is within the health service, anyway).

B6.2.1.4. Wheelchair service doctors: Northern Ireland. A HSSB orthopaedic consultant works within the Regional Disablement Services (RDS) (part of the EHSSB) and supplies medical input to the wheelchair service.

B6.2.2. Technical officers

B6.2.2.1. Technical officers: England. The post of technical officer (civil service post) will cease to exist after 31.3.91. Suggestions that they will be renamed rehabilitation engineers are the cause of some confusion, since there are rehabilitation engineers already working at specialist (rehabilitation) centres, who possess higher qualifications than the present DSC technicians (*see eg SHHD. Wheelchair Service in Scotland. HMSO,1983, p. 12; McColl I. Review of Artificial Limb and Appliance Centres. DHSS, 1986, Vol. 1, p. 43*).

B6.2.2.2. Technical officers: Wales. Technical officers (to be differentiated from rehabilitation engineers) are employed by WHCSA.

B6.2.2.3. Technical officers: Scotland. The post of medical technical officer (NHS post) has been retained.

B6.2.3. Rehabilitation engineers (29.2.) are not normally employed by the wheelchair service, but generally work within a specialist rehabilitation unit (eg at a hospital or university). They give special assistance in assessment for, and provision of, adaptations and specialist seating systems.

B6.2.4. Therapists. Occupational therapists and physiotherapists are key professionals in wheelchair assessment. They often fill out the details of wheelchair prescription forms, even though the prescription is signed by a doctor.

The McColl (1986) report, for example, recognised their importance and recommended their employment by the wheelchair service (*McColl I. Review of Artificial Limb and Appliance Centres. DHSS, 1986, Vol. 1, p. 44*); and some present RHA/DSA integration plans in England recognise the importance of therapists to the service.

Therapists (from the health service) normally contribute to the wheelchair service on a sessional basis.

B6.2.5. Other staff. Various other professionals such as nurses and social workers may work within the wheelchair service on a part-time or sessional basis.

Although initial prescription forms have to be authorised by a doctor, subsequent prescription (recommendation) can sometimes be made by therapists.

6.4.4. Wheelchair service assessment and provision

6.4.4.1. Standard prescription: no further assessment. For most wheelchair provision, no further assessment takes place once a doctor and therapist have completed the prescription form.

However, practice occasionally varies in this respect. In one DHA (already running its own wheelchair service), for example, all wheelchair applicants (except for standard attendant propelled wheelchairs) are assessed by therapists within the DHA.

6.4.4.2. Further assessment by the wheelchair service is made when there is need of, for example, a powered chair; adaptations to a wheelchair, special seating, or special models.

In the case of attendant controlled powered wheelchairs (now rarely issued), the attendant is also assessed.

6.4.4.2.1. Assessment location. Wheelchair service asssessment might be at the wheelchair centre, at a hospital, special school, or at the person's home.

Sometimes special rehabilitation centres (29.) undertake assessment and adaptations on behalf of the wheelchair centre (see below).

6.4.4.2.1.1. *Rehabilitation centre assessment and provision of wheelchairs.* Recommendations by rehabilitation centres (29.), either within the health service or independent of it, for special chairs, chair adaptations, special seating might be accepted by the wheelchair service according to local arrangements.

Sometimes the rehabilitation centre carries out adaptations to wheelchairs itself, on behalf of, and financed by, the wheelchair service.

6.4.4.2.2. Staff involved in wheelchair service further assessment. Any one or combination of, for example: therapist; rehabilitation engineer; consultant or medical officer; technical officer; nurse or social worker may participate in (multi-disciplinary) wheelchair service assessment.

6.4.4.2.2.1. *Multi-disciplinary assessment* involving various staff (see immediately above) takes place to greater or lesser or extent depending on the level of integration and organisation of services.

The importance of such assessment was pointed out by a 1983 SHHD report (Scotland), and the McColl report for example (*SHHD. Wheelchair Service in Scotland. HMSO, 1983, p. 13; McColl I. Review of Artificial Limb and Appliance Centres. DHSS, 1986, Vol. 1, p. 42*).

6.4.4.3. Wheelchair assessment guidelines, criteria, range of provision. Wheelchair assessment and provision are guided both by centrally produced criteria on assessment, and by the availability of a standard range of wheelchairs.

Criteria and guidelines determine eligibilty and also exclude certain types of wheelchair from wheelchair service provision (see Box 6.3 for details). Different types of cushions and seating require varying degrees of authorisation and assessment.

A variety of alternative parts and accessories are ordinarily available (6.1./Box 6.1.5.1.). Others (6.1./Box 6.1.5.2.) might require special request and medical authorisation by the wheelchair service.

6.4.4.3.1. DSA directives on wheelchair provision. These guidelines and criteria are based on DSA directives (themselves of varying force) for England. The wheelchair services in Wales, Scotland and Northern Ireland follow the DSA lead at their discretion.

The directives have, in effect, replaced the old ALAC Manual (containing guidance and criteria), which was used by the wheelchair service throughout the United Kingdom as a guide to provision.

6.4.4.3.2. Main criterion for permanent wheelchair loan. The main criterion for wheelchair service provision is that a person's walking ability be permanently limited (for details see Box 6.3).

Box 6.3: Criteria and guidelines for wheelchair assessment

(The following consists mainly of information taken from DSA statements and from DH guidelines, and some comments on practice.)

B6.3.1. Main criterion; permanent limited walking ability

B6.3.1.1. Limited walking ability. DH guidelines state that a wheelchair can be supplied to: 'A disabled person who has limited walking ability and whose need for a wheelchair etc. is permanent may be supplied with one by the Department [DSA] on the recommendation of any National Health Service doctor' (*MHM 50 NWTRHA p. 14*)

A DSA statement is similar: 'The broad aim of the service is to provide help with short range mobility to those people with very limited walking ability whose need for a wheelchair is permanent. There is a wide range of wheelchairs available for users of all ages suitable for use both within and around the home, comprising three broad types: non-powered wheelchairs ... electric indoor wheelchairs ... attendant controlled powered wheelchair for outdoor use...' (*Written communication: DSA 1989*).

B6.3.1.1.1. Chairs not primarily aids to mobility. Wheelchairs supplied by the wheelchair service are meant to be primarily for mobility. If the chair has wheels, but is primarily an 'easy chair' for elderly people, or is primarily a commode, then the wheelchair service would not expect to supply it (*MHM 50 NWTRHA p. 14*).

B6.3.1.2. Permanent need in practice. In practice, although permanence of need is necessary, the wheelchair service is likely to loan wheelchairs, where a medical condition necessitates wheelchair use for a period of 6 months or a year, for example. This period is longer than temporary loan schemes usually allow. Conditions, necessitating such a loan, might include a wait for a hip operation or recovery from a severe fracture.

If a person has only a few days to live, and needs a wheelchair, he or she has permanent need of it.

B6.3.1.2.1. Permanent need, but not everyday use. The definition of permanent as opposed to temporary use has been under discussion recently. A letter from the DSA to GPs, concerning wheelchair prescription, stated 'that large numbers of the wheelchairs that are supplied for one reason or another are very seldom used'. It went on to suggest that people whose needs 'are not so serious should perhaps not be prescribed wheelchairs' (*DSA letter to Family Doctors 1.89*).

An interpretation of occasional use means, for example, the need once a year for a holiday wheelchair; it is then reasonable that the wheelchair should be borrowed from elsewhere, rather than supplied by the wheelchair service. However, not regarded as occasional use, is the need of a wheelchair once a week for shopping; this is permanent essential use (*Verbal communication: DSA 1989*).

Nevertheless one recent RHA/DSC consultation document suggested that the existence of temporary loan schemes including 'Shopmobility' could allow DHAs to 'feel more confident in limiting the permanent supply of a wheelchair to an individual, referring them instead to the appropriate loan scheme' (*SETRHA Joint Consultation Document. Integrating Services. 1989, p. 10*).

B6.3.2. Specific criteria

B6.3.2.1. Indoor user controlled powered wheelchairs. Criteria to be met include the person being:

- to all intents and purposes permanently unable to walk;
- unable to self-propel a non-powered wheelchair;
- able to derive some measure of independence in the home from using such a chair;
- eligible on the basis of home environment only (*Written communication DSA, 1988. See also MHM 50. SHHD p. 24*).

B6.3.2.2. Ineligibility for a powered chair. 'Clients who are ineligible for a powered chair because it is required at work or school rather than at home are referred to their local Disablement Resettlement Officer or Education Authority as appropriate' (*Written communication: DSA 1988*).

B6.3.2.3. Outdoor attendant controlled powered wheelchairs. An 'attendant operated powered wheelchair is available for the user who needs a pushchair and whose attendant is unable to push a non-powered wheelchair' (*Written communication: DSA, 1989*).

(*Note:* this model (known as the 28B) is clumsy and difficult to manoeuvre up and down kerbs, and may often be unsuitable for a person's home environment. It is often returned within a short time; if possible, home visits/assessments before supply can at least identify practical difficulties. It is increasingly rarely issued).

B6.3.2.4. Outdoor (indoor/outdoor) user controlled powered wheelchairs have not, in the past, been supplied by the wheelchair service. The position might, however, be changing; for example, two pilot schemes, involving the loan of indoor/outdoor user controlled powered wheelchairs, operated in 1989 (6.4.4.4./Box 6.4.7).

B6.3.2.5. Custom-made (bespoke) wheelchairs and adaptations to wheelchairs. The wheelchair service stresses that every case is individual: if there is a medical need, a wheelchair can be 'built around' a person.

Similarly, extensive adaptations can be carried out to wheelchairs, if necessary.

B6.3.2.6. More than one wheelchair

B6.3.2.6.1. Indoor and outdoor (manual wheelchairs). 'Where clearly an indoor wheelchair is on issue and an outdoor one is requested it may be supplied and vice versa'(*Written communication: DSA 1988*).

B6.3.2.6.2. Work or school. 'Where a wheelchair is requested for work or school in addition to the wheelchair used at home, it should be ascertained whether one lightweight model could be used for all purposes and, if not, a second chair may be supplied' (*Written communication: DSA 1988*). This applies to non-powered chairs. (*Note:* however, wheelchair services vary their approach; some might say that is up to the LEA/ELB authority to provide transport, or for employment services to supply an additional wheelchair at work; others may take each case on its merits.)

B6.3.2.6.3. Transportation of powered chair. As long as conditions for a supply of a powered wheelchair are met, 'clients may transport their powered wheelchairs to other locations such as work or school, to facilitate transportation and may be issued with a second set of batteries and a second battery charger. Under no circumstances can clients be issued with a second powered chair' (*Written communication: DSA 1988*).

(*Note:* the wheelchair centre will check that there are no specific environmental hazards which would make use of the chair at work or at school inadvisable. The wheelchair user should inform the centre if he or she intends to transport the chair in this way).

B6.3.2.6.4. Upstairs and downstairs. 'If a client needs a wheelchair for upstairs home use and downstairs, a second chair may be supplied. It is expected that the downstairs chair would be used for outdoor and transit purposes also' (*Written communication: DSA 1988*).

B6.3.2.6.5. Indoor powered and outdoor non-powered. If an electric indoor chair is on issue, a non-powered chair may be issued for outdoor and transit purposes (*Written communication: DSA 1988*).

B6.3.2.6.6. Dirt. 'Requests for an additional chair on the grounds that one all purpose chair brings dirt into the home will normally be rejected. Clients who live or work in exceptionally dirty surroundings, ie farm labourers, could be considered for a second chair' (*Written communication: DSA 1988*).

B6.3.2.6.7. More than two wheelchairs for children. 3 models may be available for children:
- eg for school, home, public transport
- eg for school, home, cycle (on medical grounds only)
  4 models may be available in special individual circumstances.
  However, such supply is likely to vary (*Written communication: DSA 1988*).

B6.3.2.6.8. Cycles. 'A non-powered cycle can be supplied in addition to a wheelchair providing that there is a definite clinical need, the item is of a kind which is properly the concern of the service and that it will give an element of extra mobility' (*Written communication: DSA 1989*). (*Note:* in the past, tricycles were supplied to children for not only 'medical' but also 'social' (eg playground mobility) reasons. The DSA now emphasise that there must be a medical need).

B6.3.2.6.9. Buggies are not issued to children under 30 months except in special clinical circumstances (*eg Wheelchair Prescription. Northwest Region DSA; Verbal communication, DSA 1989*). This guidance is based on the premise that all parents anyway need buggies for children up to that age: so there is no justification for routine supply.
  Special seating is considered, though, for fitting in a standard buggy; and a whole buggy can be considered where the special seating is built in to the buggy (*eg Wheelchair Prescription. Northwestern Region of the DSA*).

B6.3.2.6.10. Wheelchairs with commode facilities. Wheelchairs with commode facilities are available if a person is permanently incontinent and disabled.
  The DSA has ruled that chairs should not be issued if the prime need is not one of mobility. Thus 'proper' wheelchairs with a commode facility are still issued: the wheelchair is prescribed in the first instance for a permanent mobility need (*Verbal communication: DSA, 1989*). (*Note:* castor chairs ('glideabouts') with a commode facility will no longer be issued at all by some DSCs. Others, however, will still issue them, if the prime need is one of mobility. Practice in Wales, Scotland and Northern Ireland is likely to vary.)

B6.3.2.6.11. Priority supply, for example, will be accorded to those who have a short time to live or whose hospital discharge is prevented for want of a wheelchair. The wheelchair service always attempts to get a wheelchair out within twenty four hours for a person with only a few days to live (*Written communication: Scotland ALAC, 1988*).

B6.3.2.6.12. Wheelchair centre and privately acquired wheelchairs. The wheelchair centre is sometimes prepared to maintain a privately acquired wheelchair, if the person is eligible for supply from the wheelchair service, and the model is one which the wheelchair service normally maintains.
  However, practice is likely to vary in this respect, especially in the light of product liability concerns, in relation to maintenance of equipment (31.).

6.4.4.3.3. Specific criteria for permanent wheelchair loan exist, concerning the provision (or non-provision) of, for example:

- powered wheelchairs (indoor);
- outdoor attendant controlled powered wheelchairs;
- more than one wheelchair;
- buggies;
- wheelchairs with commode facilities;
- cycles;
- priority supply of wheelchairs;
- powered user controlled outdoor wheelchairs etc. (for details see Box 6.3).

6.4.4.4. Range of wheelchairs, other carriages and available through the wheelchair service. The range of wheelchairs is detailed, in Box 6.4, in various aspects including those aspects relating to:
- wheelchair service handbook;
- uncertainty over what is available;
- potential of range available;
- strength of request;
- general discretion of wheelchair centres;
- adaptations and custom-made wheelchairs;
- outdoor, powered user controlled wheelchairs;
- wheelchairs for occasional use;
- modular wheelchairs;
- children's wheelchairs;
- high performance wheelchairs;
- cushions and special seating.

The range of wheelchairs available is also affected by various criteria (6.4.4.3.).

6.4.4.4.1. Pattern of provision. Most wheelchairs provided by the wheelchair service are part of a standard wheelchair range available to the service through central contracts.

Wheelchair provision can be seen to adhere to the following pattern:
- basic standard models;
- 'semi-standard' models (available as part of the wheelchair service main range, but subject to certain specific criteria, and less commonly supplied than standard models);
- commercial models (available when standard range wheelchairs cannot meet a particular individual need);
- adaptations and custom-made wheelchairs (6.4.4.3.3./B3.2.5.).

For examples of wheelchair service models, see Box 6.1 (examples with asterisk).

6.4.5. Standard of wheelchair provision. Wheelchair service wheelchairs have been criticised, to some extent, in the past. Powered wheelchairs have been criticised for their 'size, weight, jerky power drive, lack of manoeuvrability'. A number of other criticisms relating to manual wheelchairs (both wheelchair service and hospital) have been made (*see eg Mulley G.P. Awful: can only get better BMJ, 1989 vol. 298 pp. 1198–99.*)

Box 6.4: Range of wheelchairs available through the wheelchair service

B6.4.1. Wheelchair service handbook. The standard range of wheelchairs available through the wheelchair service has been defined by the contents of a DHSS Handbook of Wheelchairs and Bicycles and Tricycles produced in 1982. This book is still used as a guide, although it is recognised to be out of date.

(However, Northwest region of the DSA has recently produced a new updated looseleaf book on wheelchair prescription (*Wheelchair Prescription. Northwestern Region of the DSA*)).

B6.4.2. Uncertainty over range available. There has been some confusion as to which chairs, exactly, the wheelchair service does provide. This is because, for example:
- obsolete models are still listed in the old handbook;
- new models are not included in it;
- special (commercial) models are sometimes listed, and supply might depend on various criteria and strength of request (see below).

B6.4.3. Potential extent of available wheelchairs. For example, the McColl report noted that there were:
- 70 separate models of non-powered wheelchairs in the wheelchair service (then DHSS) range;
- that these were available from stock with 144 variants of the basic models;
- in addition, 655 models of proprietary chairs could be supplied to meet particular needs;
- if all else failed, bespoke chairs could be manufactured;
- there were 12 models of indoor powered chairs with 13 variations . . .' (*McColl I. Review of Artificial Limb and Appliance Centres. DHSS, 1986, Vol. 1, p. 47*).

B6.4.4. Strength of request. Requests by prescribing doctors and by therapists for special wheelchairs or seating are more likely to be acceded to by the wheelchair service if supported by strong reasoning (*Verbal communications: consultant in rehabilitation medicine, 1989; occupational therapists, physiotherapists 1989*).

B6.4.5. General discretion of wheelchair centres in relation to range available. When the wheelchair service is devolved to local (DHA) level in England (6.4.1.1.), for example, DHAs will have some discretion to make decisions on which types of wheelchair are supplied. This discretion already exists to some extent in Scotland, where health boards run the wheelchair service and can buy small numbers of non-standard wheelchairs. However, most wheelchairs supplied are likely to still be obtained through central contracts (offering cost-savings).

B6.4.5.1. Limits to discretion. If, as seems likely, therapists in England, for example, formally play a greater role in such devolved services, there could be difficult decisions concerning local guidelines and use of resources. Therapists have, in the past, joined with criticisms of the range of chairs available through the wheelchair service (*eg SHHD. Wheelchair Service in Scotland. HMSO, 1983 Appendix E*), which in the past has acted as a brake on prescribing (*see eg McColl I. Review of Artificial Limb and Appliance Centres. DHSS, 1986, Vol. 1, p. 43*). There will in theory be a 'carte blanche' after March 1991, when existing DSA guidance will cease to be valid; however, there will still be the problem of limited resources.

B6.4.6. Adaptations and custom-made wheelchairs. The wheelchair service, however, stresses that every case is individual; if necessary, adaptations are carried out; and, if necessary, a wheelchair can be 'built around' a person.

B6.4.6.1. Adaptations are carried out where needed:

- relatively minor adaptations by technical officers (6.4.2.1/Box 6.2.2.) or approved repairers (6.4.8.) (under instructions from the wheelchair centre);
- more complex adaptations by rehabilitation engineers attached to a special (rehabilitation) centre (eg hospital or university based).

For example, perceived need for adaptations is increasing in the light of the trend toward community living. Some wheelchair services are adapting chairs or supplying special seating on a greatly increased scale, for people with learning difficulties (mental handicap), for example (*Verbal communication: DSC manager, 1989*).

B6.4.6.2. Custom-made wheelchairs. Policy/criteria, employed to determine whether or not to make a wheelchair vary from wheelchair centre to centre. The obvious advantages are sometimes offset by the disadvantage of the time taken to build the wheelchair (*Verbal communication: consultant in rehabilitation medicine, 1990*).

B6.4.7. User controlled, powered outdoor wheelchairs are not currently provided, although two DSA pilot schemes (1989), providing indoor/outdoor powered wheelchairs in England (*DSA Annual Report1988/89 p. 9*), are signs of possible change.

Eligibility criteria for these pilot schemes consisted of mobility allowance eligibility, inability to propel a wheelchair indoors and inability to walk effectively indoors.

B6.4.7.1. SSD/SWD and HSSB (under social services functions). In theory SSD/SWDs and HSSBs (under social services functions) have the power (6.2.1.4.) to provide such powered wheelchairs on loan as daily living equipment.

In practice such provision does not generally take place. However, the SSD/SWD/HSSB might still give extensive help in the form of OT assessment and advice, and social worker assistance to aid the client obtain funding (*eg London SSD (42) guidelines received 1989*).

B6.4.7.2. Special schools sometimes have a stock of wheelchair types not provided by the wheelchair service, and these might include user controlled powered wheelchairs suitable for outdoor use.

B6.4.8. Wheelchairs for occasional users have been considered by the DSA, on the recommendation of the McColl report, with a view to saving money; but the issue has not been pursued because such savings were thought to not be possible (*DSA Annual Report 1988/89 p. 8*).

B6.4.9. Modular wheelchair. Lothian health board is currently involved in trying to make standardly available a 'multi-purpose' wheelchair' constructed out of many modular parts and therefore capable of many variations, and of meeting many needs from occasional to specialised (*Verbal communication: consultant in rehabilitation medicine*).

B6.4.10. New children's wheelchair. The DSA has commissioned Salford University to produce a performance specification (as opposed to a prescriptive design) of a new wheelchair for children with slight to moderate disabilities. The results of a field trial are awaited. This development has taken place as a result of criticism contained in the McColl report (*DSA Annual Report 1988/89 p. 7*).

Lothian health board also is involved in the development of a children's wheelchair.

B6.4.11. High performance wheelchairs. A new breed of wheelchairs is known as active or high performance wheelchairs. The DSA has been criticised for not keeping up with the times. As a result, it has recently agreed to add a commercially produced model to its range (*DSA Annual Report 1988/89*).

B6.4.12. Cushions and special seating. The wheelchair service increasingly emphasises the importance of good seating, and holds special seating clinics, which include multi-disciplinary assessment of seating support systems and special cushions. Therapists and rehabilitation engineers often attend.

B6.4.12.1. Standard cushions. Ordinary foam cushions are probably available on request by the person or by their GP. The more specialised and expensive the cushion, so the more authorisation is required for clinical and financial reasons.

B6.4.12.2. Special cushions and special seating systems. Consultant (or medical officer) approval is often necessary for gel-type cushions, latex foam cushions, Roho cushions and sheepskin cushions. Moulded seat inserts and body support systems would in any case require special assessment.

B6.4.12.3. Seating clinic examples.
Example 1. One DHA, running its own wheelchair service, holds regular seating clinics which are attended by a therapist, a rehabilitation engineer, and a commercial orthotist (for moulded seat inserts). A consultant rheumatologist is available to provide medical support where necessary (*Verbal communication: Grimsby DHA wheelchair service: open day 1989.*)
Example 2. Pressure clinics, for people with spinal injuries, exist in some areas; they might be run by nurses, together with a multi-disciplinary team, to assess for the correct cushion, which will prevent the development of pressure sores. A community liaison nurse might follow people up when they have returned home, and make sure (amongst other things) that wheelchair and cushion are performing adequately (*Sadler C. Wheelchair Comfort. Community Outlook. Nov. 1989 p. 4–8*).

Evidence given in connection with the McColl report (1986) by a voluntary organisation was to the effect that 90% of young people with spina bifida were in unsuitable wheelchairs, requiring adjustment or repair. A specialist health service rehabilitation centre also said that 10% of severely disabled people had unsafe or unsuitable wheelchairs (*McColl I. Review of Artificial Limb and Appliance Centres. DHSS, 1986, Vol. 1, p. 41*).

People with learning difficulties and a physical disability might, in particular, end up with ill-fitting wheelchairs, in terms of seating, which in turn cause further physical disability (*see eg Eve L, Kinnear EML. Does the Wheelchair Fit? A Study of seating for Adults with Mental Handicap. Physiotherapy 1989: 75; 2, pp. 72–6*).

6.4.6. Delivery of wheelchairs

6.4.6.1. Approved repairer delivery of wheelchairs. Stock wheelchairs are often held in the garages of, and delivered by, approved repairers.

6.4.6.2. Speed of wheelchair delivery. One of the purposes of devolution of wheelchair services (England) to district (DHA) level is to improve local service including supply times (*Verbal communication: DHA wheelchair service, open day*

1989; Ham R. Wheelchair Provision in a London Health Authority. Physiotherapy 1987: 72;10,576–578). One DHA, for example, running its own wheelchair service, is achieving same day delivery for some standard wheelchairs.

Special (non-standard) wheelchairs, required by about 20% of users, have often taken longer for delivery, and this has been a cause of concern (*see eg SHHD. Wheelchair Service in Scotland. HMSO, 1983, p. 22*). Even stock chairs (used by about 80% of users) have in the past been subject to delays in delivery (*McColl I. Review of Artificial Limb and Appliance Centres. DHSS, 1986, Vol. 1, p. 53; Ham R. Wheelchair Provision in a London Health Authority. Physiotherapy 1987: 72;10,576–578).*

6.4.7. Wheelchair follow-up. The degree and type of follow-up is likely to vary. In general, follow-up and case review tends to be responsive to requests for further assessment.

A letter, for example, might be sent after 6 months to enquire if the chair is satisfactory. In special cases (such as children or people with a rapidly deteriorating condition) a visit might be made anyway. Regular visits/clinics might be held at institutions, such as special schools or residential homes, where there are a number of wheelchair users.

Powered wheelchair users might receive an annual visit from wheelchair service staff to check the continuing efficiency and use of the wheelchair (*see eg SHHD. Wheelchair Service in Scotland. HMSO, 1983 p. 24*).

6.4.8. Wheelchair maintenance and repair. The maintenance of wheelchairs is carried out by approved repairers, either at the user's own home, or at a workshop. In the latter case, a temporary loan wheelchair can be supplied, if same day repair is not possible (*Written communication: DSA 1989*).

The contract to approved repairers (England) now includes, for example, the following elements:

- it is put out to tender;
- it is capitation based;
- it includes emergency callout from 7am to 11pm (including to 10.59 pm) 365 days per year);
- repairer premises must have adequate waiting area and faciliites;
- it includes a delivery and collection service (*Verbal communication; DSA regional manager, 1989; DSA Contract to repairers*).

These new contract conditions are intended to improve the service; in the past, the standard of repair and maintenance of whelchairs has been criticised (*see eg McColl I. Review of Artificial Limb and Appliance Centres. DHSS, 1986, Vol. 1, p.52; Physical Disability and Beyond. A report of the College of Physicians. RCP 1986 p. 24; Hunter J. Surveys of Problems in Wheelchair Patients. Rehabilitation Newsletter 1980:19,28–31).*

6.4.9. Charges. The wheelchair service loans, maintains, repairs and replaces wheelchairs and accessories free of charge.

6.4.10. Private purchase. Not all wheelchairs and specialist seating needed are provided through the wheelchair service; at one hospital for people with severe disabilities the main sources of funding are:

- the wheelchair service (where possible);
- insurance claims;
- personal funding (*Written communication: hospital director of medical and research Services, 1990*).

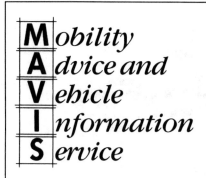

WHO ARE WE?

The Mobility Advice and Vehicle Information Service was set up by the Department of Transport to provide practical advice on driving, car adaptations and car choice, both for disabled drivers and passengers.

WHAT CAN WE OFFER?

- Assessment and advice on driving ability and car adaptation.
- Consultation and advice on car adaptations.
- The opportunity to try out one or more of the wide range of adapted vehicles at the Centre.
- Information on all aspects of transport and outdoor mobility for people with disabilities.

For more information please write to:

MAVIS

Department of Transport
Transport and Road Research Laboratory
Crowthorne, Berkshire RG11 6AU
or telephone: (0344) 770456

MOBILITY ADVICE AND VEHICLE INFORMATION SERVICE

Being able to drive is probably the biggest single factor in determining the level of freedom and independence which a severely disabled person can enjoy. And yet many disabled people have never been given the opportunity either to find out if they have the potential to learn to drive or to discover what kind of car or adaptations they may need. There is now a small but growing number of centres around the country which offer advice and assessment to disabled people on driving and car choice.

The largest of these is the Department of Transport's Mobility Advice and Vehicle Information Service (MAVIS).

Central to the service that MAVIS offers is its extensive fleet of adapted cars including the latest models from most of the manufacturers currently selling in the UK. Every car is fitted with adaptations to the controls (again representing the full range of currently available adaptations). Disabled people who visit the centre for assessment or advice can test drive as many of the vehicles as they want either on private road system (and for learner drivers each car is fitted with dual controls) or on the public roads.

A range of other equipment including wheelchair hoists, swivel seats, back supports, additional wing mirrors and so on are also available to look at and test. Advice on of low cost modifications to help elderly drivers overcome problems of stiffness and arthritic joints is also available.

For further information about MAVIS or to make an appointment telephone: (0344) 770456 or write to MAVIS, TRRL, Old Wokingham Road, Crowthorne, Berkshire RG11 6AU.

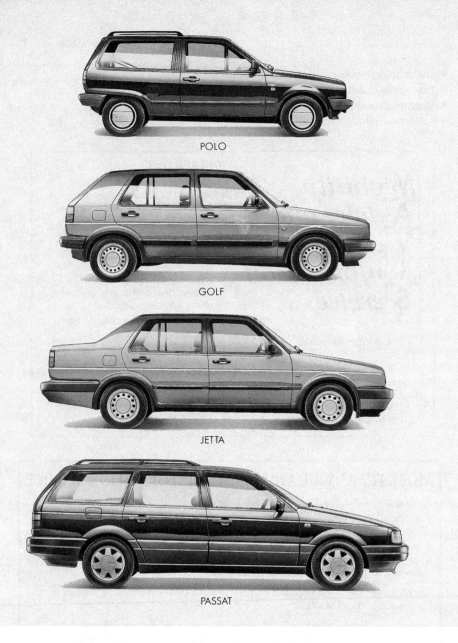

POLO

GOLF

JETTA

PASSAT

With a mobility allowance, they're all convertibles.

Naturally, we are proud that Volkswagen have been chosen to take part in the Government's Mota-bility scheme.

But then it's hardly surprising.

Few cars are designed to make driving less of a hassle.

They're frugal, for one thing. So visits to the pump are far from regular.

Servicing is scarcely an every-day event, either. It'll be all of twenty thousand miles before you need a major one.

Rare, too, are those occasions when a Volkswagen lets you down.

If it should happen, though, our free 6-year recovery service will re pair to the rescue.*

A puncture, flat battery, lost car keys, the same applies.

Call in at your local Volkswagen dealer. Or contact us at the address below. You'll soon be converted.

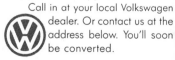

FLEET SALES DEPT., VAG (UK) LTD., JENNA WAY, INTERCHANGE PARK, NEWPORT PAGNALL MK16 9QB. TEL: (0908) 211616.
*Applies to vehicles serviced at recommended intervals at a registered VW dealer.

7 | Cars

Introduction

Cars

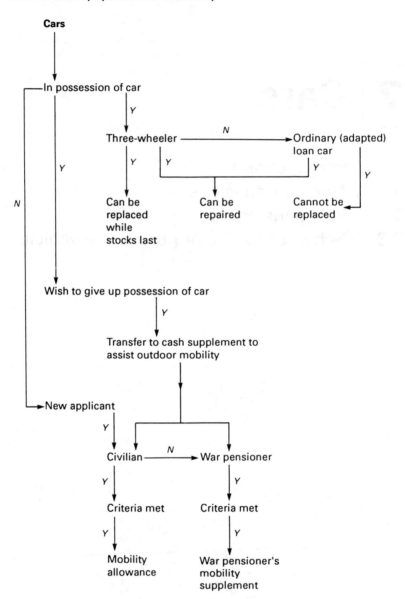

Introduction

Under services provided by limb and wheelchair centres (6.and 11.), special vehicles were, in the past, issued to eligible applicants. Such vehicle provision has been replaced, for some time, by mobility allowances (for both civilians and war pensioners), although some of these vehicles can still be repaired and replaced.

7.1. Non-war pensioners

7.1.1. Repair/replacement of vehicles. Invalid 3-wheelers and loan cars can be repaired, and replaced while stocks last. Loan cars (commercial, adapted models) can no longer be replaced.

7.1.2. Mobility allowance has replaced the vehicle scheme, and can be claimed by a person who no longer wishes to benefit from a vehicle under the old scheme, or by new applicants. This weekly sum of money is intended to assist outdoor mobility and might be used on, for example, car and outdoor wheelchair hire/purchase or taxi fares. However, the way in which the allowance is used is not circumscribed.

Certain conditions, relating to medical condition, age, potential benefit from receipt, must be met. There is an appeal procedure laid down.

7.2. War pensioners (30.3.)

7.2.1. Repair/replacement or vehicles. The situation is the same as for civilians.

7.2.2. War pensioners' mobility supplement has replaced the vehicle scheme and can be claimed by a war pensioner, who no longer wishes to retain a vehicle under the old scheme, or by a 'new' war pensioner.

It takes the form of a weekly sum of money, for the same purposes as mobility allowance (7.1.2.).

In order to qualify for the supplement, the lack of mobility must be due to disablement incurred during service in the armed forces, and certain medical criteria must be met. A formal appeal procedure is laid down.

7.3. Schemes to aid hire or purchase of vehicle

A government-backed organisation called Motability helps people use their mobility allowance or war pensioners'·mobility supplement to hire or purchase a car. There also other organisations offering similar help. Adaptations to the car may or may not be included in the 'package' of help offered.

8 | Walking aids

Walking aid need

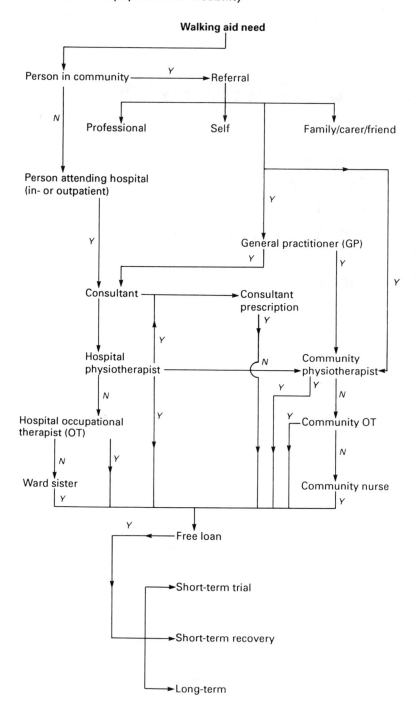

Introduction

Type of equipment

Walking aids include walking frames, crutches and walking sticks.

There are a number of different channels for walking aid provision depending on the complexity of need, the circumstances and location of the client, or the level and organisation of local services. These channels include the health service and social services.

Responsiblity for provision of walking aids rests mainly with the health service, and sometimes with social services: health service:

- district health authorities (DHAs, England and Wales);
- health boards (HBs, Scotland);
- health and social services boards (HSSBs, Northern Ireland).

social services:

- social services departments (SSDs, England and Wales);
- social work departments (SWDs, Scotland);
- HSSBs (Northern Ireland).

Assessment for, and provision of, walking aids

Physiotherapists are the experts on mobility and walking aids. Employed by the health service in hospital or the community, they assess for, and provide walking aids on free loan, both short- and long-term.

Hospital consultants can prescribe walking aids, but more usually delegate responsibility for detailed assessment and provision to physiotherapists.

Physiotherapy assessment is not always possible and standard walking aids are sometimes assessed for and loaned by:

- hospital occupational therapists (at hospital discharge);
- ward sisters (at hospital discharge);
- community occupational therapists (SSD/SWD/HSSB);
- community nurses;
- general practitioners.

Follow-up and recall of walking aids.

It is generally recognised that, despite examples of good practice, both follow-up and recall systems vary and can be inadequate.

8.1. Type of equipment

There are various types of walking aid, including walking frames, crutches and walking sticks (including tripod and quadrupod sticks). Examples are given in Box 8.1.

Box 8.1: Examples of walking aids

B8.1.1. Walking frames

Walking frames include the following types (not necessarily exclusive of one another):

- various height (high or low);
- adjustable height;
- fixed height;
- foldable;
- with seat;
- with basket;
- with high forearm supports;
- triangular shaped;
- reciprocal (hinged, allowing one side of the frame to move in advance of the other);
- mobile frames (two or four castors/wheels);
- with flexible gait attachments.

B8.1.2. Crutches

Crutches are of two main types, elbow and axilla.

B8.1.2.1. Elbow crutches are usually metal with a handgrip and an armband through which the lower arm fits. They are either:

- single (handgrip to ground) adjustable;
- double adjustable (handgrip to ground, and handgrip to armband adjustable) in height.

B8.1.2.2. Axilla crutches (metal or wooden) are full-length, the top fitting under the armpit. Special crutches include:

- crutches with trough armrests (forearm supports);
- with tripod or quadrupod base;
- 'Canadian' crutches which combine axilla and elbow crutch features (*Equipment for the Disabled. Walking Aids. Oxfordshire Health Authority, Nuffield Orthopaedic Centre. 1985*).

B8.1.3. Walking sticks

Walking sticks include the following types:

- metal/wooden;
- lightweight/middleweight/heavyweight;
- adjustable height;
- swan-neck handle;
- crook shape handle;
- right-angled handle;
- D-shape handle;
- moulded handle;
- straight handle;
- curved handle;
- with tripod or quadrupod base;
- with built-in reflectors;
- with seat;
- with built-in alarm.

B8.1.4. Accessories

Ferrules, usually rubber tips, are fitted on to walking sticks and crutches to reduce the possibility of slipping. They are crucial safety accessories. Ice spikes, hand pads and axilla pads are also available.

8.2. Legislative basis for walking aid provision

Walking aids are not mentioned specifically in legislation; nor are there detailed central government guidelines on the provision of walking aids, as there are for orthotic appliances, for example (10.2.).

8.2.1. The basis for consultant provision of walking aids lies in the DHA/HB/HSSB duty to provide 'medical services' (*NHS Act 1977 s.3; NHS (Scotland) Act 1978 s.36; SI 1972/1265 HPSS(NI)O a.5*).

8.2.2. Basis for therapist prescription/loan of walking aids

8.2.2.1. Basis for physiotherapist/occupational therapist (health service) provision of walking aids. Provision (without formal medical prescription), by DHA/HB or HSSB (under health service functions) physiotherapists or occupational therapists, is covered by the DHA/HB/HSSB duty to provide 'other services' (*NHS Act 1977 s.3; NHS(S)Act 1978 s.36; SI 1972/1265 HPSS(NI)O 1972 a.5*).

8.2.2.2. The basis for occupational therapist (social services, SSD/SWD/HSSB) provision lies in SSD/SWD/HSSB duty (where an individual need is identified) to 'make arrangements for . . . the provision of any additional facilities designed to secure his greater safety, comfort or convenience' (*CSDPA 1970 s.2(1)(e); CSDP(NI) A 1978 s.2(e)*).

Details of this legislation, background welfare legislation and legislation concerning assessment requests, are given elsewhere (2.2.2.1.).

8.2.3. Basis for nurse provision of walking aids. District nurse, ward sister, or other specialist nurse provision of walking aids is generally covered by the DHA/HB/HSSB duty to provide 'nursing services' (*NHS Act 1977 s.3; NHS (Scotland)Act 1978 s.36; SI 1972/1265 HPSS(NI)O 1972 a.5*).

More specifically, provision of walking aids, as home nursing equipment, is covered by the DHA/HB/HSSB duty to prevent illness, care for people suffering from illness and provide after-care for people who have been ill (*NHS Act 1977 s.3; NHS Act (Scotland) 1978 s.37; SI 1972/1265 HPSS(NI)O 1972 a.7*).

8.3. Referral, assessment, provision

8.3.1. GP referral and assessment in relation to walking aids. GPs can refer patients to hospital for an outpatient appointment with a consultant.

They sometimes also make outpatient referrals direct, to a hospital physiotherapy department or community physiotherapist, rather than via the consultant. This can save time, in the case of more routine conditions and treatments. Known as 'open access', it is approved in Circular guidance (England 1981, Northern Ireland 1985) (*JM/2 Physiotherapy in the Community and Open Access to Physiotherapy Departments for General Practitioners August 1981; HSS(PH)1/85*).

In any areas where they have access to a (joint) equipment store (2.5.4.1.1./Box 2.6.2.), GPs themselves assess for, and provide on free loan, simple walking aids such as walking sticks or standard walking frames (*eg Midlands joint store catalogue, received 1988*).

8.3.2. Consultant referral, assessment and provision in relation to walking aids. Special walking aids are sometimes prescribed, explicitly, on free loan by a consultant; more usually he or she may delegate responsibility for assessment and provision to a physiotherapist.

8.3.2.1. Consultant referral to a physiotherapist for walking aid provision. Inpatient referral to physiotherapists can be specific, when a consultant refers an individual (on a general medical ward for example); or open, when the physiotherapist screens all patients on an elderly ward, for example.

Consultants, typically involved in referral to physiotherapists (for walking aid provision) include orthopaedic surgeons, rheumatologists, geriatricians, neurologists, consultants in rehabilitation medicine (where they exist).

8.3.3. Physiotherapist assessment for, and provision of, walking aids. Physiotherapists are the professional experts on questions of mobility. They are employed by DHAs, HBs, and HSSBs, and are either hospital-or community-based.

For example, Circular guidance (Scotland, 1976) states that health board responsibility exists where the 'skills of a particular discipline within the health service are more appropriate to the prescription and use of aids required on medical or nursing grounds, eg the provision of walking aids by physiotherapists' (*NHS Memorandum No 1976 (GEN) 90*).

8.3.3.1. Remit of physiotherapy re: walking aids. In some areas the ideal is that all people with mobility problems be assessed by physiotherapists. Since this is not always possible, various other professionals also assess for, and provide, walking aids, in practice (*eg Verbal communication: consultant in rehabilitation medicine 1990; London SSD (19) guidelines 1989; Verbal communication: Chartered Society of Physiotherapy, 1990*).

8.3.3.1.1. Referral to hospital physiotherapists for walking aids. Hospital-based physiotherapists normally take referrals from hospital consultants and sometimes, directly, from GPs.

8.3.3.1.2. Hospital physiotherapists' assessment for, and provision of, walking aids. Physiotherapy departments normally hold stocks of the more common walking aids. Other non-stock items can be specially ordered. Short-term loan is for a recovery period or a trial period; longer-term loan for a more permanent and stable condition. Loan is free, unless to private patients (30.1.8.).

If a special walking aid is needed, the physiotherapist might request that the consultant prescribe (8.3.2.) the walking aid, in the light of budgetary considerations, for example. Loan is free of charge.

8.3.3.1.3. Hospital discharge and walking aids. Recent Circular guidance (England, Wales) (HC(89)5; WHC(90)1) emphasises the importance of adequate discharge procedures. Physiotherapists should (where appropriate), for example:

- undertake any necessary pre-discharge assessments;
- liaise with other services;
- make a home visit (with other professionals);
- assess for eg wheelchair service provision;

- refer to the Employment Service (*see variously HC(89)5 with Discharge of Patients from Hospital. DH 1989; WHC(90)1*).

These procedures can all include, where appropriate, assessment and provision of walking aids.

8.3.3.2. Community physiotherapist referral, assessment, provision, in relation to walking aids. Circular guidance (England, Northern Ireland) has recognised the potential importance of community physiotherapy, since 'the patient's home environmental conditions crucially affect the type of treatment and cannot be reproduced in the hospital' (*JM/2 1981; HSS(PH)1/85*).

In recognition of the role which a community physiotherapist plays, some DHA/HB/HSSBs might try to channel long-term loan walking frame requests via the community service; through hospital physiotherapists, district nurses and social services/work staff (*see eg Wood, M. Therapy Weekly, 1985 Vol.11; 37, p. 4*).

Such a policy recognises the difference between short-term 'paramedical' (active rehabilitation) loan by hospital therapists; and longer term 'daily living' loan by therapists in the community (2.5.5.1.2.4.).

8.3.3.2.1. Referral to community physiotherapists. Community physiotherapists sometimes operate an open referral service, accepting, where this is the case, referrals from, for example, disabled people; their friends, relatives, carers; consultants; GPs; community nurses;occupational therapists; social workers; and home helps.

Nevertheless, the community physiotherapist needs to contact the person's GP, both to find out medical history, and out of courtesy (*Gibson A. Physiotherapy in the Community. Woodhead Faulkner, 1988, p. 21*).

The different medical specialisms, referring to community physiotherapists, can include (in order of frequency), for example, orthopaedics, paediatrics, geriatrics, general medicine, rheumatology, neurology, general surgery, obstetrics. (*Partridge C.J. Community Physiotherapy and Direct Access to Physiotherapy Services by General Practitioners within the National Health Service. King's College, London 1984*).

8.3.3.2.2. Community physiotherapist location.

8.3.3.2.2.1. Community physiotherapist treatment location. Community physiotherapists might see people at the following locations, for example: individual home, health centre, residential home, special school, day centre for the physically handicapped, GP premises, ordinary school, child assessment centres, day centre, adult training centres and hostels, stroke club, GP community hospital, nursery play group, day hospital (*Partridge C.J. Community Physiotherapy and Direct Access to Physiotherapy Services by General Practitioners within the National Health Service. King's College, London 1984*).

8.3.3.2.2.2. Community physiotherapists' base. The community physiotherapy service can, for example, be based at a GP practice; be hospital-based; be part of an existing general community service run either by the DHA/HB or the SSD/SWD or the HSSB; or be based at health centres (*Burnard S. Development of a Community Physiotherapy Service. Physiotherapy 1988, vol.74, no.1, pp. 4–8*).

Where the service is part-funded by an SSD, for example, it could be SSD-based (rather than DHA-based) and function in very close collaboration with the SSD community OT service (*London SSD (2) guidelines received 1989/90*). In Northern Ireland, where the health and social services are integrated, fairly close working arrangements could be expected anyway.

8.3.3.2.3. Community physiotherapists' assessment for walking aids. Community physiotherapists (in contact with the person's GP) can assess for walking aids: if there are special problems, referral to a hospital consultant and hospital physiotherapy department is made.

8.3.3.2.4. Community physiotherapy advice. Apart from direct loan, a community physiotherapy service may offer extensive advice on the use of and need for equipment, in general.

For example, a community physiotherapy service for people with learning difficulties (mental handicap) might include advice on physical management/use of equipment in 54% of its assessments; referral to an orthopaedic clinic for advice and monitoring of orthoses in 27%; and identification of seating adaptation need in 24% of assessments (*Rushfirth S. Community Physiotherapy Services for People with Mental Handicap. Physiotherapy, 1985, vol.71, no.3 pp. 119–23*).

8.3.3.2.5. Community physiotherapist walking aids stores. Walking aids, loaned by a community physiotherapist, are variously stored, for example, in the physiotherapist's own garage, in a health centre, at a hospital or in a joint equipment store (2.5.4.1./Box 2.6.2.) etc.

8.3.3.3. Private physiotherapists. There are a number of physiotherapists in private practice (for example, as an individual, in a private physiotherapy service, in private hospitals). Physiotherapists are sometimes employed by special schools, by residential and nursing homes for people with disabilities or by industry (The letters SRP or MCSP are evidence that the private physiotherapist is adequately qualified).

8.3.3.3.1. Private loan of walking aids

8.3.3.3.1.1. Private hospital loan of walking aids. Walking aids are sometimes loaned for short-term use, by the physiotherapy department of a private hospital, to a person going home following an operation. A returnable deposit is normally charged (*Verbal communication: Private hospital chain*).

8.3.3.3.1.2. Private community physiotherapists loan of walking aids. Private patients are treated under private health insurance schemes, or just simply seek one-off private treatment. Referral is likely to be by GPs and consultants.

Private (self-employed) physiotherapists are not so involved with chronic disability itself, though they sometimes treat a person with such disability if a different, additional problem arises. The majority treat people with orthopaedic problems, although there are those specialising in neurology, for example.

Private physiotherapy services do however provide both general (eg exercise classes) and specific (individual) treatment to both private residential and nursing homes.

Equipment, such as walking sticks or crutches, might be loaned by private physiotherapists, on a deposit or rental basis, or simply privately purchased by the person receiving treatment.

8.3.4. Ward sister, and other hospital specialist nurse assessment, referral, provision, in relation to walking aids

8.3.4.1. Referral by hospital nurses for walking aids. Hospital nurses are well placed to refer people to physiotherapists for possible supply of a walking aid, if they become aware of mobility problems. Ward sisters have greater contact with patients than physiotherapists, and so are in a good position to identify such problems.

8.3.4.2. Assessment by hospital nurses for walking aids. Although it is thought that hospital nurses do not generally officially assess and authorise the issue of walking aids, this is not always strictly true.

For example, ward sisters and other specialist nurses on elderly or orthopaedic wards can gain great knowledge of equipment. Where they develop such expertise, they can make recommendations to physiotherapists, and in effect participate in the assessment process.

8.3.4.3. Provision by ward sisters of walking aids

8.3.4.3.1 Ward sister provision of walking aids for common ward use. Hospital wards (eg orthopaedic) require stocks of equipment for common use; the ward sister is usually responsible for ordering (with or without physiotherapist advice) walking sticks, zimmer frames, elbow crutches, axillary crutches (*Woolliscroft D.*

Orthopaedic Working Party. Nursing Standards – Equipment. 1989?). Such ward stock is not usually officially for home loan.

8.3.4.3.2. Ward sister provision for individual use. Hospital nurses do not normally loan walking aids for a particular individual; though they might well advise physiotherapists (8.3.4.2.).

In some areas, ward sisters have formal access to a (joint-funded) home nursing equipment store (4.6.1.), in which case they can authorise the issue of standard walking frames, or walking sticks to a patient who is leaving hospital (*eg Midlands Joint Store Catalogue, received 1988*).

Sometimes a person going home from hospital takes with them one of the walking aids belonging to the ward; this might be for convenience because of sudden hospital discharge; by mistake, or in the absence (for whatever reason) of physiotherapy assessment and provision.

Such loan is free of charge.

8.3.5. Community nurse, referral, assessment, provision, in relation to walking frames

8.3.5.1 Referral by community nurses for walking aid provision. District nurses (and health visitors) are much more numerous than community physiotherapists and are well placed to identify mobility problems in people's own homes. They can make referrals to physiotherapists or the GP when they identify problems.

Equally, they sometimes receive a referral from a GP or other professional, for supply of a simple walking aid.

8.3.5.2 Community nurse assessment for, and provision of, walking aids. District nurses (and sometimes health visitors), in some areas, have access to simple walking aids in a home nursing equipment store, or a joint (funded) equipment store (4.6.1.). Where this is the case, the loan (in England and Wales) is likely, in principle, to be for short-term loan only (4.5.1.).

In Scotland and Northern Ireland, no such principle appears to operate, although, as pointed out, physiotherapists ideally assess for, and provide, walking aids, especially for long-term need (8.3.3.1.).

Loan is free of charge.

8.3.6. Occupational therapist referral, assessment, provision, in relation to walking aids

8.3.6.1. Hospital occupational therapist referral, assessment, provision, in relation to walking aids. Hospital OTs often refer people to physiotherapists in case of walking aid need.

Alternatively, they sometimes informally loan an aid from their own stock, or loan the simpler types of walking aid to people going home, on behalf of the SSD/SWD or HSSB (under social services functions). In the latter case, the SSD/SWD or HSSB (under social services functions) normally reimburses the hospital (2.5.4.1.2.).

8.3.6.2 Community occupational therapist referral, assessment, provision, in relation to walking aids. Community OTs might refer clients to physiotherapists for walking aid provision; alternatively they sometimes, themselves, loan simple walking aids, either from their own store or from a joint (funded) equipment store (2.5.3.1.).

Walking aids loaned in this manner are categorised as daily living equipment, and are subject to the various procedures associated with the provision of such equipment (2.).

Loan is free of charge.

8.3.7. Provision of walking aids for children, through special services for children, is covered elsewhere (26.).

8.3.8. Provision of walking aids in residential homes and private nursing homes is covered elsewhere (24. and 25.).

8.4. Follow-up of walking aids

8.4.1. Continuing treatment and follow-up of walking aids. Where physiotherapy inpatient or outpatient treatment continues, follow-up of walking aids, to monitor successful use, is facilitated. Where both in-and outpatient treatment ceases, follow-up of the equipment becomes more difficult. If community physiotherapy services exist, contact between the hospital-based and the community physiotherapist helps in this respect.

Otherwise a community nurse, GP, community occupational therapist or other professional sometimes becomes aware of problems relating to the use of walking aids, and can make a referral. Sometimes there are special schemes to ensure adequate follow-up (8.4.3.).

8.4.2. Non-use of walking aids. It is generally recognised that many walking aids loaned in the community are not used at all, or not used properly. Reasons for this can include initial inappropriate supply, inadequate instruction in use of the equipment, changing condition and needs of the person.

8.4.3. Example of follow-up scheme using 'health auxiliaries'. For example, a special community care plan involving both DHA and SSD might include the training by physiotherapists (and occupational therapists) of home care assistants; including in relation to wheelchairs and walking frames. The home care assistants are able to advise on the use of these and identify problems as they care for (and follow-up) elderly people (*Stone M. Physiotherapy Support to a Domiciliary Care Scheme for Physically Handicapped Elderly People. Physiotherapy, 1987: 73, 5, pp. 227N9*).

8.5. Recall of walking aids

Recall procedures are likely to vary from area to area; it is generally known that such procedures are somewhat arbitrary and very variable; stories of health service crutches for sale in markets, and walking frames used for washing are legion: the solutions apparently not so (*Verbal communication: Chartered Society of Physiotherapy, 1989*).

Recall of equipment in general is discussed elsewhere (2.8.).

8.6. Product liability

Product liability, in general, is discussed elswhere (31.). Examples of advice, given to physiotherapists in particular, are also given (Box 31.1.).

9 Footwear

Introduction

Footwear need

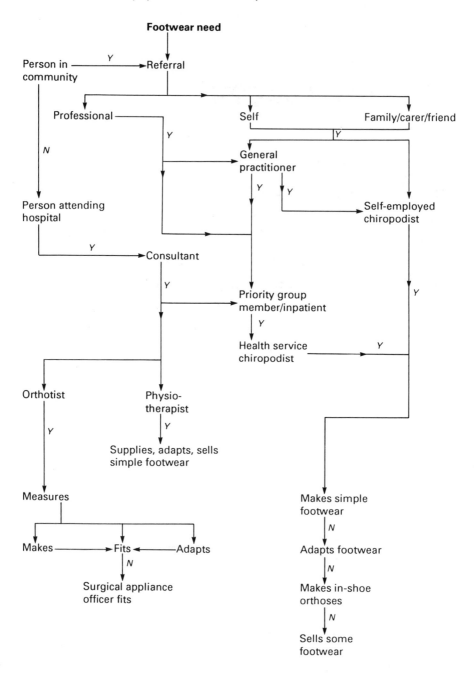

Introduction

Type of equipment

Footwear, defined as surgical or orthopaedic, is provided within the orthotic service (described, in general, elsewhere). Surgical footwear can include custom-made shoes, readymade shoes, in-shoe orthoses and adaptations to footwear.

In-shoe orthoses, adaptations to footwear, protective pads and simple footwear are also provided by chiropodists and to some extent, by therapists.

General practitioners prescribe some protective items, such as dressings or plasters.

Reponsibility for provision lies with the health service:

- district health authorities (DHAs, England and Wales);
- health boards (HBs, Scotland);
- health and personal social services boards (HSSBs, Northern Ireland).

Referral, assessment, provision

Consultants and orthotists. GP referral to a hospital consultant is the usual channel of referral. Consultant prescription of surgical footwear is normally followed by referral to an orthotist (usually a private contractor who attends hospital premises) to make and/or fit the footwear.

Provision is free of charge, except that in the case of adaptation to ordinary footwear, the patient must provide his or her own footwear; the actual adaptation is free of charge.

Chiropodists are experts on conditions of the foot and lower limb. The consultant might refer to a chiropodist (rather than to an orthotist) for some orthoses; sometimes GPs refer patients directly to chiropodists. Referral to chiropodists is in general open, though in practice it is often made by other professionals.

There is a national shortage of health service chiropodists (who are all state-registered), and in many areas only priority groups of people can be treated. GPs and other professionals sometimes advise people to seek chiropody privately. Many chiropodists in private practice are not state registered.

Provision by health service chiropodists is normally free of charge, except where the disabled person provides their own shoes for adaptation, or where the chiropodist recommends GP prescription of protective plasters or dressings (to which charges, and exemptions as appropriate, apply). Sometimes health service chiropodists sell special footwear.

Physiotherapists sometimes provide simple footwear (for example, temporary footwear) and carry out simple adaptations. They sometimes sell slippers to elderly patients in hospital, who do not have suitable footwear to cope with swollen feet for example.

9.1. Type of equipment

Equipment for the feet includes orthopaedic (surgical) footwear, 'rehabilitation footwear', temporary footwear, minor orthoses, minor prostheses, adaptations and protective materials. Examples are given in Box 9.1.

9.2. Legislative basis for provision of footwear

Legislation does not make explicit reference to footwear. Surgical footwear, however, is covered by DH (applying informally to Northern Ireland) and SHHD guidelines, and chiropody services by various Circular guidance. This guidance is referred to, as appropriate, throughout this chapter.

9.2.1. Consultant prescription of footwear is covered by the DHA/HB/HSSB duty to provide 'medical services' (*NHS Act 1977 s.3; NHS (Scotland) Act 1978 s.36; SI 1972/1265 HPSS(NI)O 1972 a.5*).

9.2.2. Chiropodist or physiotherapist provision of footwear is covered by the DHA/HB/HSSB duty to provide 'other services' (ie paramedical services) (*NHS Act 1977 s.3; NHS (Scotland) Act 1978 s.36; SI 1972/1265 HPSS(NI)O a.5*).

9.3. Referral

9.3.1. General practitioner (GPs) referral for footwear. GPs refer patients to both chiropodists and consultants.

A report (England,1986) found, however, that some elderly people do not consult their GP about foot problems; and that GPs themselves are sometimes discouraged, in relation to referral, by the delays and inadequacies in NHS chiropody services (*Cartwright A., Henderson G. More Trouble with Feet. DHSS 1986 p. 39*).

The same report found that GPs should discuss foot problems with more of their elderly patients especially those with diabetes; also with those who are disabled and/or have difficulty going out of the home (*Cartwright A., Henderson G. More Trouble with Feet. DHSS 1986 p. 39*).

9.3.2. Community nurse referral for footwear. District nurses might anyway be giving help with feet in terms of washing and cutting toe nails, application of ointments, dressing or padding (*Cartwright A. Henderson G. More Trouble with Feet. DHSS, 1986 p. 39*). They are well placed, in such circumstances, to identify other foot problems and make referrals, if necessary.

Health visitors sometimes identify foot problems of children, and elderly people, and make a referral to the GP or chiropodist.

9.3.3. Referral to chiropodists. Chiropodists are experts on conditions affecting the foot and lower limb. Their work includes assessment for, and provision of, appliances 'to compensate for structural imbalances affecting the function of the feet and legs' (*The Chiropodist: a Specialist in the Medical Team. Society of Chiropodists, 1988*); and they 'aim to prevent immobility by the treatment of corns and

---

Box 9.1: Footwear: examples

B9.1.1. Orthopaedic footwear
Includes readymade footwear made on extra deep or wide lasts, and made-to-measure footwear. Readymade footwear includes:

- extra wide and deep shoes with removable insoles;
- shoes with standard depth but range of widths;
- plastazote shoes (can be moulded by spot heating);
- readymade boots giving ankle support;
- soft boots made on deep lasts (for example, for people with bulky dressings following surgery).

B9.1.2. 'Rehabilitation footwear'
Includes footwear with rigid sole (immediately following operation) or with semi-rigid sole (for later rehabilitation stage); footwear of this sort may be a clog with laces to tie over a bulky bandage.

B9.1.3. Temporary footwear
For an elderly person with a bandaged foot; includes stretch slippers, plastazote slippers.

B9.1.4. Minor orthoses
Inshoe orthoses are either removable or permanently fixed in the shoe. They can fix to the foot with a loop or strap; the padding is often covered in leather. The orthoses are sometimes moulded out of latex rubber, or silicone rubber for orthoses to fit between the toes (eg to straighten toes in danger of becoming hammer toes).

Insoles might be made-to-measure or readymade. Made-to-measure insoles can be moulded directly on the foot (eg plastazote); moulded insoles on a plaster-of-Paris cast of the foot (eg laminations of plastazote, rubber-like materials, leather, cork). Insoles can be emulated by padding and strapping.

Inserts are similar to insoles but do not extend the whole length of the foot. They include pads under different parts of the foot.

B1.9.5. Minor prostheses
Where part of the foot has been amputated, a toe filler can be used

B9.1.6. Adaptations
Adaptations to footwear include sole and heel raises, wedged soles, floated heels (wide base), elongated heels (part of heel has wide base and is extended forward toward the instep); rocker sole, sockets and stops (to receive an orthosis at the heel of the shoe); valgus inserts (support along inside of long arch of foot to compensate for 'rolled-in' ankle), shoe upper stiffening, shoe stretching, slit release (cuts made in upper to allow leather stretching), lacing adaptations, balloon patches.

B9.1.7. Protective materials
Include foam squares, tubigrip, corn plasters, lambswool (*whole section derived from Hughes J. Footwear and Footcare for Adults. DLF, 1983*).

---

callosities, foot problems in children, wart and fungal infections, ingrowing toenails and toenails damaged by trauma or by disease' (*NHS Handbook. NAHA, 1989 p. 192*).

9.3.3.1. Health service chiropodists, who are always state registered (SRCh), operate a system of open referral, although in practice they are likely to receive many referrals from health service colleagues (*Society of Chiropodists. The Chiropod-*

ist: Specialist in the Medical Team. 1988). Once a person is receiving routine care, future appointments are often on a self-referral basis, when the person feels the need for treatment.

Within a hospital, chiropodists are likely to work in diabetic, antenatal, orthopaedic, neurological and rheumatology wards as well as the outpatients department (*Society of Chiropodists. The Chiropodist: a Specialist in the Medical Team. 1988*).

However, it should be pointed out that only 15% of NHS hospitals provide a chiropody service on a consultant referred basis (*Society of Chiropodists. The Chiropodist: a Specialist in the Medical Team. 1988*).

9.3.3.1.1. Health service priority groups for chiropody services. A national shortage of health service chiropodists means that chiropody services are often restricted to priority groups. Circular guidance (England) has referred to these groups as including elderly people; young adults (16-64) with physical or mental disabilities; expectant mothers, and school children (*see eg HRC(74)33; HC(77)9;*).

A report (Scotland, 1987) stated that such a situation is not desirable, and recommended that health boards make their services available to all groups in need of them (*SHHD. Five Health Professions: Guidance to Health Boards HMSO, 1987. p. 36*).

9.3.3.2. Self-employed chiropodists operate a system of open referral: they also receive direct referrals from medical colleagues (also working privately).

Health service professionals would not formally recommend a particular self-employed chiropodist, but a GP for example would normally have a list of local private chiropodists. About 50% of state registered chiropodists are self-employed.

Some self-employed chiropodists work for the health service on a sessional basis, rather than as full-time employees. Circular guidance (England,1977) has not encouraged this practice (*see eg HC(77)9*), which has been pointed to in Parliament as possibly very expensive (*Weekly Hansard No.1352, 17-21 June 1985. Oral answers 18 June 1985, Columns 160–61*).

Many self-employed chiropodists, working in private practice, are not state-registered.

9.3.4. Referral to consultants in relation to foot care. The main source of referral to consultants is the GP. Depending on the problem, consultants involved in foot care include orthopaedic surgeons, vascular surgeons, diabetic consultants, dermatologists (*Cartwright A., Henderson G. More Trouble with Feet. DHSS 1986 p. 35*), rheumatologists, obstetricians, neurologists (*Society of Chiropodists. The Chiropodist: a Specialist in the Medical Team. 1988*).

Consultant prescription of orthotic appliances, in general, is discussed elsewhere (10.3.1.).

9.3.5. Referral to orthotists and therapists for footwear operates similarly to referral for orthotic appliances, in general (10.3.1.).

9.4. Assessment for footwear

9.4.1. Chiropodist assessment.

9.4.1.1. Chiropodist assessment of children Screening of schoolchildren by health service chiropody services varies. For example, a 1987 Report (Scotland) stated the importance of comprehensive school chiropody services, but noted that they had not been developed in some health boards (*SHHD. Five Health Professions: Guidance to Health Boards HMSO, 1987. p. 36*).

Children might be screened, for example, on starting and on leaving school. It is also thought that if one screening only is possible, nine years of age might be the optimum age of the child at the time of such screening (*Wessex Feet: A regional foot health survey. Chiropodist, August 1988, p. 163*).

9.4.1.2. Chiropodist assessment of people with diabetes. Foot care is vital to many people with diabetes (20.) because of the dangers of ulceration, infection and gangrene. Problems of personal foot inspection are exacerbated when the person is also suffering from poor vision.

Chiropodists work closely with specialist diabetes consultants and sometimes regularly attend their clinics for screening purposes.

9.4.1.3. Waiting times for chiropody services. In some areas people outside the priority groups are treated by the health service; in others there might be waiting lists even for the priority groups (9.3.3.1.1.).

Waiting times are likely to vary: for 'full' treatment on initial referral, or for subsequent 'repeat' treatment. Waiting times for initial treatment can vary from a week to a year (*Collyer M. Hanson-Kahn C. Feet First. A re-appraisal of footcare services in London. Age Concern, 1989 p. 2*). Some districts have a maximum number of treatments allowed per year eg 2,3,4,5: others have no limit (*Cartwright A., Henderson G. More Trouble with Feet. DHSS 1986 p. 70*).

Waiting lists for home visits can be much longer (eg 2 years) and hence the tendency to transport people to clinics instead (9.4.1.5.) (*Collyer M. Hanson-Kahn C. Feet First. A reappraisal of footcare services in London. Age Concern, 1989 p. 3*).

9.4.1.4. Chiropodist assessment location. Chiropodists attend various clinics within a hospital, complementing other specialisms. They might, for example, attend outpatient, diabetic, antenatal, orthopaedic, neurology, rheumatology wards and clinics (*Society of Chiropodists. The Chiropodist: a Specialist in the Medical Team. 1988*).

Whether based at a hospital or health centre, for example, the chiropodist is likely to hold clinics in the community. Locations include schools/school clinics, health centres, day centres, residential homes and people's own homes (*Society of Chiropodists. The Chiropodist: a Specialist in the Medical Team. 1988*).

Mobile clinics are sometimes operated in rural districts (*Society of Chiropodists. The Chiropodist: a Specialist in the Medical Team. 1988*). However, for reasons such as hygiene and sterilisation of equipment, the days of treatment in the village hall are over (*Verbal communication: Society of Chiropodists, 1989*).

9.4.1.5. Home visits. Chiropodist home visits particularly benefit groups, such as elderly people and people with disabilities, but equally consume time which can be ill-afforded by a service, which is understaffed.

In the light of this, Circular guidance (England, 1977) suggests that, where a person in need of chiropody services is not housebound, transport arrangements in the form of ambulance, hospital car service, sharing of transport with social services or voluntary organisation transport be made (*HC(77)9*).

Chiropody services sometimes have their own vehicle, but in general transport can be a problem: it can happen that people are classed as domiciliary patients simply because of unreliable transport (*Collyer M. Hanson-Kahn C. Feet First. A re-appraisal of footcare services in London. Age Concern 1989, p. 4*).

9.4.1.6. Chiropody services to residential and private nursing homes. Circular guidance (England, 1974, 1978) clearly states that NHS chiropody services should be available to residents, who belong to priority groups (9.3.3.1.1.), of both residential and private nursing homes (*HRC(74)16; HC(78)16*).

Circular guidance (England, 1977) also recommends that routine footcare in residential homes for the elderly can be carried out by the home staff, suitably instructed and advised by health service chiropodists (*HC(77)9*).

Recent Circular guidance (Scotland, 1989) emphasises that residents of private nursing homes should have full access (through their GP) to health services (including chiropody) (with the exception of nursing services, which should be supplied through the home) (*NHS 1989(GEN)39*).

Nevertheless a 1989 Age Concern Report found that 'some state-funded elderly patients living in private longstay establishments are being denied access to chiropody services'. The inconsistencies of provision were highlighted by a list of variations found in ten nursing homes in Bromley (see Box 9.2).

Box 9.2: Examples of variation in provision of chiropody services to elderly people in private nursing homes *(taken from an Age Concern report)*

1. Some residents receive free care, others pay privately. Limited amount of free care provided.
2. DSS residents receive free care, private residents pay.
3. No free care provided.
4. Private patients pay in full; DSS patients included in fee.
5. All pay privately.
6. Provided free to all by health service.
7. Provided by health service to some; others pay privately.
8. Those in need receive free treatment; others pay.
9. All receive free treatment.
10. Provided free for all by health service, though some choose to pay.

(*Collyer M. Hanson-Kahn C. Feet First. A re-appraisal of footcare services in London. Age Concern, 1989 p. 5*).

9.4.2. Assessment for orthopaedic (surgical) footwear as part of the orthotic service follows, in general, the same procedures as the orthotic service as a whole, which is discussed elsewhere (10.).

There are, however, a number of DH (applying informally to Northern Ireland) and SHHD guidelines and criteria specific to orthopaedic footwear. These include reference to footwear duplication, provision of adaptations, odd-sized or unusual feet, provision of bootees (see Box 9.3 for details).

Box 9.3: Guidelines (DH, informally applying to Northern Ireland, and SHHD) on surgical footwear provision

B9.3.1. Adaptations
People are asked to provide their own footwear; the actual adaptation to the shoes is supplied free of charge by the health service. Advice should be given by the hospital on the type of footwear considered most suitable (*MHM 50 NWTRHA p. 3; MHM 50 SHHD p. 3*).

B9.3.2. Odd-sized or unusual feet
People with unusual or odd-sized feet do not qualify for help from the health service, unless built-in surgical features are required, or the footwear is required for an allergic condition (*MHM 50 NWTRHA p. 3; MHM 50 SHHD, p. 3*).
   Scottish guidelines note that this guidance might not apply to children. For example, if the child is undergoing surgical treatment for foot problems and required odd-sized shoes, the shoes would in this case be regarded as surgical footwear and could be supplied by the health service (*MHM 50 SHHD p. 4*).

B9.3.3. Footwear duplication
Footwear does need to be duplicated, particularly in the case of children and adults who make heavy demands on their footwear due to their condition or occupation. For example, 3 or 4 pairs may be adapted initially, a new pair then being adapted each year (*MHM 50 NWTHRA p. 3; MHM 50 SHHD p. 4*).
   (*Note:* the Northern Ireland Orthopaedic Service (NIOS) seems to take the view that because of the rapid growth of children, it is better to make single pairs frequently, than to extensively duplicate footwear for them (*Verbal communication: NIOS, 1989*)).

B9.3.4. Bootees
For children suffering from spina bifida and 'other diseases or disorders causing gross sensory disturbance of the feet' special 'lace to toe' bootees can be supplied (*MHM 50 NWTRHA p. 3; MHM 50 SHHD p. 4*).

9.5. Provision of footwear

9.5.1. Surgical footwear provision

9.5.1.1. Consultant prescription of footwear, or of surgical adaptation to existing footwear, is free of charge; although in the case of adaptations, a person must buy their own shoes. The adaptation is then free of charge (30.1.1.).

9.5.1.2. Orthotists (10.3.6.) generally measure and fit surgical footwear: surgical shoe makers (who may be also qualified orthotists) make the footwear (*Hughes J, Footwear and Footcare for Adults. 1983 p. 174*).
   Surgical appliance officers (SAOs) (10.3.7.) can be involved with the fitting of footwear to greater or lesser extent.

9.5.1.3. Rehabilitation engineer or health service orthotist. Where there is an accessible specialist centre with rehabilitation engineering facilities (29.2.), footwear might be made on site by rehabilitation engineers or health service employed orthotists (there are very few of these).

9.5.1.4 Readymade shoes, custom-made shoes. The trend is toward increased prescription of readymade shoes, as they improve in quality (*Klenerman L, Hughes J. Surgical Footwear: an assessment of the place of ready-made extra-depth shoes. Health Trends 1986; 18,45-46; Lord M, Foulston J Surgical Footwear: a survey of prescribing consultants. BMJ 1989. 299 p. 657*). They are supplied more cheaply and quickly than bespoke shoes, and tend to have a better cosmetic appearance.

9.5.1.5. Choice, cosmetic appearance, delivery etc. Sometimes deficiencies exist in the orthopaedic footwear service. Problems can include speed of delivery, lack of choice, inadequate relationships between consultant/orthotist/patient/ chiropodist, discomfort, cosmetic appearance, fastenings on the shoe (*see eg NHS Management Consultancy Services. Study of the Orthotic Service. Crown Copyright 1988; Costigan PS et al. Are surgical shoes providing value for money? BMJ 1989:299, p.950; Lord M, Foulston J Surgical Footwear: a survey of prescribing consultants. BMJ 1989. 299 p. 657*).

9.5.1.6. Charges. The service is free of charge (for adaptations to ordinary shoes, the person must first buy their own shoes). It is a costly service (about £12 million for the United Kingdom in 1986), and there have been suggestions that small charges be made (*see eg Lord M, Foulston J Surgical Footwear: a survey of prescribing consultants. BMJ 1989. 299 p. 657; SHHD. Orthopaedic Footwear Service in Scotland. HMSO, 1983 p. 16*).

9.5.2. Provision of (in-shoe) orthoses, supports, pads, protective materials, dressings, alterations/adaptations

9.5.2.1 Chiropodist provision of footwear. Chiropodists often have access to a workshop in which appliances and orthoses can be made, and footwear adapted.

A DHA/HB/HSSB sometimes has a central 'prescription service' for items, which chiropodists do not make locally (*Wessex Feet: A regional foot health survey. Chiropodist, August 1988, p. 167*).

Circular guidance (England) recommends a well-equipped central laboratory, as opposed to a number of laboratories dotted around (*HC(77)9*).

There might be, for example, a 'bio-mechanics' clinic and centre for children, where shoes and insoles can be made or adapted, and fastenings altered, for example (*Verbal communication: chiropodist, London DHA 1988*).

9.5.2.1.1. Variation in arrangements. Local facilities and organisation in this respect is likely to vary. A 1986 survey (of 10 DHAs) found that in relation to appliances and orthoses:

- one did not prescribe them;
- six designed and made them;
- one district designed and made some of them;
- one had them all supplied by another district;
- one made some of its own, and had some supplied by another district (*Cartwright A., Henderson G. More Trouble with Feet. DHSS 1986 p. 68*).

9.5.2.1.2. Adaptations. Chiropodists carry out many adaptations: a 1983 Scottish Office report noted that out of a total 3,500 surgical appliances supplied annually by a school of chiropody, many were adaptations to all sorts of shoes (*SHHD Orthopaedic Footwear Service in Scotland. HMSO, 1983*).

9.5.2.1.3. Chiropodist provision of protective materials. Chiropodists sometimes provide foam squares and a protective material called tubigrip (not available on prescription) as part of treatment: but if, for example, the chiropody budget is hard-pressed, the person might have to buy it from a pharmacy.

Creams for callosities, fissures, dry skin, and dressings and plasters are available on prescription (5.1.4.1.) from GPs (though perhaps recommended by chiropodists). Items prescribable by GPs are sometimes initially supplied by a chiropodist free of charge: they are then subsequently and regularly supplied through GP prescription.

9.5.2.1.4. Chiropodist sale of footwear. In some areas, health service chiropodists sell special footwear, such as odd/shaped or unusual-size shoes. Such sales might be part of an health service 'income generation' scheme.

9.5.2.2. Therapist provision of footwear. Orthopaedic physiotherapists, in particular, sometimes provide simple footwear (such as plastazote temporary footwear), provide or make minor orthoses and carry out minor adaptations.

They also sometimes sell comfortable slippers to elderly people.

9.5.3. Chiropodist advice. Chiropodists and foot care assistants give advice on, for example:

- shoes with gusset substitute for buckle or laces when a person has difficulty putting the shoes on;
- slippers for the elderly with zip or velcro fastenings;
- shoes in general with broad heels and suitable support and balance;
- the parents of toddlers and young children on well-fitting shoes and socks and on how to judge when shoes still fit (*Society of Chiropodists. The Chiropodist: a Specialist in the Medical Team. 1988*);
- teenagers and young adults: the age when the majority of foot deformities come to light (*Society of Chiropodists. The Chiropodist: a Specialist in the Medical Team. 1988*).

Chiropodists sometimes recommend ordinary shoes rather than surgical footwear; problems encountered with surgical footwear can include weight, dexterity required for laces, and appearance (*Verbal communication: chiropodist London DHA, 1988*).

9.5.4. Footcare assistants. Some DHA/HB/HSSBs employ footcare assistants who might, for example, cut nails, give advice, or carry out home visits following prior assessment by the chiropodist (*Cartwright A., Henderson G. More Trouble with Feet. DHSS 1986 p. 67*).

Circular guidance (England) has encouraged the use of footcare assistants (*see eg HC(77)9*).

9.5.5. Shoe fitters. People working as shoe fitters (in shops) are not required to hold qualifications. However, they might have a certificate from the Society of Shoe Fitters, have attended a manufacturer or trade association course, or have received inhouse training (*Hughes J. Footwear and Footcare for Adults. DLF, 1983 p. 172*).

9.5.6. War pensioners (30.3.), can benefit from special arrangements, if their need for footwear is due to the condition for which they receive a war pension. They have traditionally been able to obtain surgical footwear through services provided at wheelchair and artificial limb services, as opposed to ordinary hospital services.

If they need private chiropody treatment, because health service chiropody treatment is not available, the cost of the treatment can be paid for (by the War Pensions Branch of the DSS, Blackpool).

9.6. Follow-up of footwear

9.6.1. Surgical footwear. Follow-up, maintenance and repair procedures for surgical footwear are similar to those for orthotic appliances in general (10.6. and 10.7.).

9.6.2. Chiropody equipment. Follow-up and continuing care by health service chiropodists depends, at least partly, on local waiting times and policies (9.4.1.3.).

10 Orthotic appliances

Orthotic appliance need

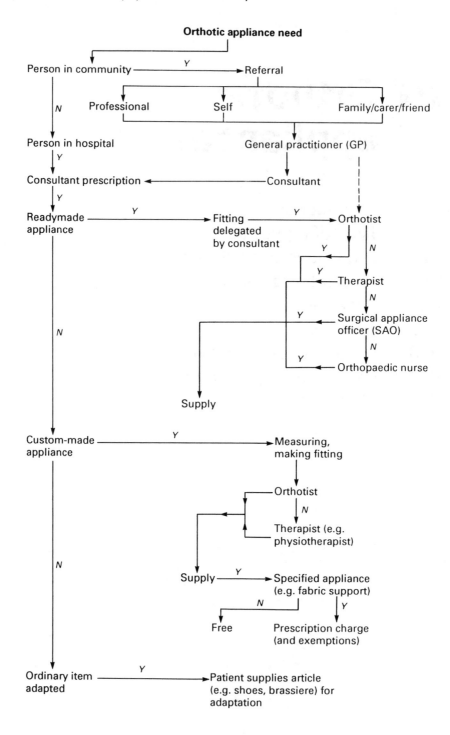

Introduction

Type of equipment

Orthotic appliances are also known as orthoses or surgical appliances. An orthosis is defined by the International Standards Organisation (ISO) as 'an externally applied device used to modify structural and functional characteristics of the neuro-muscular skeletal system' (*ISO quoted in Study of the Orthotic Service. A report by NHS Management Consultancy Services. Crown Copyright, 1988 p. 9*).

A major part of the orthotic service is concerned with the provision of surgical footwear. The procedures described in this chapter apply to orthotic appliances, in general (including surgical footwear); surgical footwear is also discussed specifically elsewhere (9.).

Responsibility for provision of orthotic appliances
rests with the health service:

- district health authorities and family practitioner committees (DHAs and FPCs, England and Wales);
- health boards (HBs, Scotland);
- health and social services boards (HSSBs, Northern Ireland);

Assessment and provision of orthotic appliances

Orthotic appliances are normally prescribed by a consultant, following general practitioner (GP) referral. Sometimes GPs (with suitable training) refer directly to orthotists for the provision of simple orthotic appliances, thus bypassing the consultant. GPs can also prescribe standard trusses and elastic hosiery, which are listed on the Drug Tariff.

Orthotists measure, make and fit custom-made appliances; readymade items are fitted, at the consultant's discretion, by a number of different staff such as orthotists, orthopaedic physiotherapists, orthopaedic nurses and hospital surgical appliance officers (SAOs).

Sometimes the consultant delegates responsibility for assessment, and provision (including the making) of simple appliances, to orthopaedic physiotherapists, orthopaedic nurses or chiropodists, for example.

Delivery and follow-up of orthotic appliances

Following delivery of the appliance (from the orthotist), the prescribing consultant should check that the appliance conforms to the prescription, and that it fits the patient. Follow-up and review procedures are necessary to ensure effective use of the appliance. There is evidence that the quality of such checking and follow-up procedures varies.

Charges for orthotic appliances.

Orthotic appliances are provided by the health service free of charge, except for trusses and elastic hosiery which attract the standard prescription charge; and surgical brassieres and abdominal spinal supports which attract special prescription charges. Prescription charges are made, subject to various exemptions, as appropriate.

10.1. Type of equipment

10.1.1. Definition of orthotic appliances. Orthotic appliances are also known as orthoses or surgical appliances. The ISO definition is:

'An orthosis is an externally applied device used to modify structural and functional characteristics of the neuro-muscular-skeletal system' (*ISO quoted in Study of the Orthotic Service. A report by NHS Management Consultancy Services. Crown Copyright, 1988 p. 9*).

10.1.2. Orthotic appliances. Include foot/leg orthoses, support frames and swivel walkers, trunk/neck orthoses, arm orthoses, other miscellaneous orthoses and adaptations to items of clothing or footwear. Examples are given in Box 10.1.

10.2. Legislative basis for orthotic appliance provision.

Orthotic appliances are not mentioned in legislation (except for the few items which attract prescription charges).

However, DH/WO (applying informally to Northern Ireland) and SHHD guidelines do detail various procedures and criteria, concerning the provision of orthotic appliances. These are referred to, as appropriate, in this chapter.

10.2.1. The basis for consultant provision of orthotic appliances lies in the DHA/HB/HSSB duty to provide 'medical services' (*NHS Act 1977 s.3; NHS (Scotland) Act 1978 s.36; SI 1972/1265 HPSS(NI)O 1972 a.5*).

10.2.2. The basis for therapist provision (of simple stock items or manufacture) lies in the DHA/HB/HSSB duty to provide 'other services' (*NHS Act 1977 s.3; NHS (Scotland) Act 1978 s.36; SI 1972/1265 HPSS(NI)O 1972 a.5*).

10.2.3. The basis for nurse (eg orthopaedic nurse) recommendation, measuring, fitting, supply (of simple stock item) or advice lies in the DHA/HB/HSSB duty to provide 'nursing services' (*NHS Act 1977 s.3; NHS (Scotland) Act 1978 s.36; SI 1972/1265 HPSS(NI)O 1972 a.5*).

10.2.4. The basis for GP prescription of orthotic appliances lies in the DHA (through FPC)/HB/HSSB duty to provide 'general medical services' (*NHS Act 1977 s.29; NHS (Scotland) Act 1978 s.19; SI 1972/1265 HPSS(NI)O 1972 a.56*).

10.3. Referral, assessment and prescription

10.3.1. Consultant referral, assessment and prescription of orthotic appliances

10.3.1.1. Consultant referral. Most orthotic appliances are prescribed by a hospital consultant, often an orthopaedic surgeon.

Box 10.1: Examples of orthotic appliancese

B10.1.1. Foot/Leg orthoses:

- special footwear;
- foot orthoses (eg insoles, heel cups, foot cradles);
- ankle foot orthoses;
- knee orthoses (eg fabric/elastic, hinged metal/plastic);
- knee-ankle-foot orthoses;
- hip orthoses (CDH rings, special splints).

B10.1.2. Support frames and 'swivel walkers':

- hip-knee-ankle-foot orthoses (eg standing frames, swivel walkers).

B10.1.3. Trunk/neck orthoses:

- spinal orthoses (fabric corsets, plastic jackets, metal/leather braces);
- cervical orthoses (soft collars, moulded collars, 4 poster/SOMI braces).

B10.1.4. Arm orthoses:

- shoulder-elbow orthoses (fabric/elastic, plastic);
- wrist-hand orthoses (fabric/plastic);
- hand orthoses (plastic, metal/leather);
- finger orthoses (plastic, metal/leather).

B10.1.5. Miscellaneous:

- helmets;
- harnesses and restraints;
- gloves and other miscellaneous items meeting special needs (*above list taken from: Murdoch G, Condie D, Carus DA, Lamb J. 'A Model Orthotic Service'. Report to the Advisory Group on New Developments in Health Care, Scottish Home and Health Department. Tayside Rehabilitation Engineering Services. Tayside Health Board, Dundee District, 1984*).

B10.1.6. Adaptations are carried out to ordinary items such as shoes and brassieres.

B10.1.7. Wigs are often thought of as part of the orthotic service: they are in fact prostheses and are discussed elsewhere (12.).

Referral to the consultant normally takes place through a GP, who refers a person as an outpatient to a clinic, or as an inpatient.

10.3.1.2. Type of consultant. A number of different specialist consultants assess for, and prescribe, orthotic appliances.

Although orthopaedic surgeons are the major source of prescription, other specialisms involved are, for example, neurology, plastic surgery, general medical, neurosurgery, rheumatology, urology, general rehabilitation (*Murdoch G, Condie D, Carus DA, Lamb J. 'A Model Orthotic Service'. Report to the Advisory Group on New Developments in Health Care, Scottish Home and Health Department. Tayside Rehabilitation Engineering Services. Tayside Health Board, Dundee District 1984. Table 2*).

10.3.1.3. Assessment location. Consultants normally see inpatients and outpatients at the hospital, but sometimes hold clinics at, for example, health centres, community hospitals or special schools. DH/WO (applying informally to Northern Ireland) guidelines state that consultants might make home visits to assess the need for an orthotic appliance (*MHM 50 NWTRHA para 12*).

A report (Scotland, 1987) stated that clinics, held at health centres by consultants, can improve collaboration between consultants and GPs (*SHHD. Management of the Orthopaedic Service in Scotland. HMSO, 1987 p. 16*).

10.3.1.4. Staff present at assessment. Assessment is normally by a consultant or by another doctor authorised by the consultant (5.2.4.2.). An orthopaedic nurse is likely to be present, and sometimes an orthotist (*Study of the Orthotic Service. A report by NHS Management Consultancy Services. Crown Copyright, 1988 p. 30*). Where there is an organised system of multi-disciplinary assessment, other professionals such as therapists might regularly participate (10.3.5.).

10.3.1.5. Consultant prescription. The prescribing consultant determines, to greater or lesser extent, the precise specification of an appliance. He or she might explicitly specify a particular type or instead delegate the specification decision to an orthotist.

10.3.1.6. Consultant delegation. DH/WO (applying informally to Northern Ireland) guidelines state that, for example, it is 'for prescribing consultants to decide when ready made stock sized articles may be supplied, which hospital staff are qualified to fit them and when the services of a contractor's orthotist are not necessary' (*MHM 50 NWTRHA p. 5*).

Thus, in practice, for example, a therapist, chiropodist, orthopaedic nurse, or surgical appliance officer might fit a stock item (*Study of the Orthotic Service. A report by NHS Management Consultancy Services. Crown Copyright, 1988 p. 18*), an orthotist a bespoke item such as calipers or footwear.

10.3.1.7. Variations in practice of assessment. Although consultant assessment is the model, this does not always happen. In some cases, assessment might be carried out with no doctor present and sometimes prescription forms are pre-signed by a consultant or signed by a therapist (*Study of the Orthotic Service. A report by NHS Management Consultancy Services. Crown Copyright, 1988 p. 28*).

10.3.2. GP referral, assessment and prescription. GPs often refer patients to hospital consultants for orthotic appliances.

10.3.2.1. Prescription of elastic hosiery and trusses. GPs are empowered to prescribe elastic hosiery and trusses, which are items listed in the Drug Tariff (5.1.1./Box 5.1.).

10.3.2.2. Prescription of simple orthotic appliances. Sometimes GPs have open access to orthotists' clinics (not Northern Ireland), and can assess for, and prescribe simple appliances (not on the Drug Tariff) such as collars, insoles, wrist splints, lumbosacral supports (*Study of the Orthotic Service. A report by NHS Management Consultancy Services. Crown Copyright, 1988 p. 30*).

A report (SHHD, 1987) recommended that in order to reduce outpatient referrals, GPs might prescribe stock sizes of surgical corsets, callipers and insoles for shoes: and that in such cases repeat prescription should be authorised by senior paramedical staff (*SHHD. Management of Orthopaedic Services in Scotland. HMSO, 1987 p. 16*).

10.3.2.3. Hospital therapy departments (physiotherapy and occupational therapy) might supply, or make, simple orthotic appliances (10.3.4.), and be open to GP referral.

10.3.3. Orthopaedic nurses. Orthopaedic clinics are often held by orthopaedic nurses who, with consultant support, might undertake a certain amount of assessment and recommendation (though not prescription) of appliances. They sometimes measure, supply and fit stock appliances (*Study of the Orthotic Service. A report by NHS Management Consultancy Services. Crown Copyright, 1988 p. 36*).

These regular clinics might be the first point of contact for people with any problems, concerning their orthotic appliances.

In Northern Ireland, for example, the Northern Ireland Orthotic Service (NIOS) operates 27 clinics throughout the province, with 10 orthopaedic nurse sisters and two consultants involved (*Verbal communication: NIOS, 1989*).

10.3.4. Therapists and other departments. Appliances such as collars, simple splints, hosiery and belts are sometimes supplied, made and fitted by, for example, physiotherapists in particular; but also by occupational therapists, chiropodists, orthopaedic nurses (outpatient and ward-based), speech therapists, dieticians, the plaster room and casualty (accident and emergency) department.

Activities can include seeing patients, measuring and taking casts, ordering,

making appliances, keeping stock (*Study of the Orthotic Service. A report by NHS Management Consultancy Services. Crown Copyright, 1988 p. 18, and Table*).

Advantages in therapy involvement may be seen as 'speed and cost effectiveness', a person being able to have supplied, modified and repaired appliances without direct consultant and orthotist referral (*Study of the Orthotic Service. A report by NHS Management Consultancy Services. Crown Copyright, 1988 p. 18*).

10.3.5. Rehabilitation centres. Some special (rehabilitation) centres (29.) offer regular and organised multi-disciplinary assessment involving for example, consultants, therapists, rehabilitation engineers, nurses and orthotists; with workshop facilities to hand.

These centres assess the total needs of a person, including the need for an orthotic appliance.

Reports (England, Scotland) have recommended respectively the systematic development of regional orthotic centres, and fully integrated rehabilitation engineering centres (see eg (*Study of the Orthotic Service. A report by NHS Management Consultancy Services. Crown Copyright, 1988 p. 40; SHHD. Prostheses, Orthoses and Aids for the Disabled. HMSO, 1983, p. 40*).

10.3.5.1. Specialist centres, offering specialist multi-disciplinary assessment of disabled people (including orthotics needs) include, for example: Mary Marlborough Lodge (Department of Orthotics) (Oxford), Rookwood Hospital (Cardiff), Musgrave Park Hospital (Belfast), the Dundee Orthotic Service.

10.3.5.2. Specialist orthotic service referral system: example. Two levels of initial referral are operated by one special centre.

Simple referral involves the referring doctor prescribing the necessary appliance: eg for definitive dynamic finger orthoses for traumatic injury and repair surgery, for example. The request for the making and supply of the appliance goes through the District Orthotic Department.

The other type of referral involves a complete multi-disciplinary assessment of the person at the orthotic department involving doctors, therapists, technicians and rehabilitation engineers, as appropriate (*Murdoch G, Condie D, Carus DA, Lamb J. 'A Model Orthotic Service'. Report to the Advisory Group on New Developments in Health Care, Scottish Home and Health Department. Tayside Rehabilitation Engineering Services. Tayside Health Board, Dundee District, 1984*).

10.3.5.3. Northern Ireland. The Northern Ireland Orthotic Service (NIOS) is based at Musgrave Park Hospital, Belfast. It runs 27 orthopaedic clinics throughout Northern Ireland, but at Musgrave Park Hospital, is able to use the services of the rehabilitation engineering unit (part of Regional Disablement Services) to assess for special problems. Consultant, rehabilitation engineer, therapist and orthotist assess people with more difficult problems.

10.3.6. Orthotists. Orthotists are responsible for the measuring, making and fitting of orthotic appliances. They take referrals from prescribing consultants, and sometimes from GPs.

10.3.6.1 Status. Most orthotists work for private companies and work under contract to health service hospitals. They often rent facilities on health service property, as well as working from their own premises. There are a few health service employed orthotists in England and Wales (*Study of the Orthotic Service. A report by NHS Management Consultancy Services. Crown Copyright, 1988 p. 41*).

10.3.6.2. Qualifications. Since 1982, there have been two main four-year courses for orthotists. However, there are still a number of older orthotists practising who have not undergone formal training. A report (England, 1988) recommended that all orthotists should undergo formal training (offered by the two courses) – although there would still be for the foreseeable future, 'unqualified fitters' practising (*Study of the Orthotic Service. A report by NHS Management Consultancy Services. Crown Copyright, 1988 pp. 13,16*).

10.3.6.3. Orthotist clinics. Commercial orthotists normally hold regular hospital clinics, at which they measure and fit appliances. They sometimes make home visits, though DH/WO (applying informally to Northern Ireland) and SHHD guidelines suggest that 'such visits should be kept to a minimum and in every case the appliance order must indicate that the consultant has authorised domiciliary visits to be made' (*MHM 50, NWTRHA p. 7; MHM 50 SHHD p. 7*).

Sometimes hospital surgical appliance officers (see below) accompany orthotists on home visits. In so doing they can provide 'help and reassurance' to the person to whom they may be already known (*Study of the Orthotic Service. A report by NHS Management Consultancy Services. Crown Copyright, 1988 p. 26*).

An orthotist might typically need to see the person three times; for measuring, initial fitting and final fitting.

10.3.7. Surgical appliance officers (SAOs) are usually clerically graded offficers, responsible for arrangements for the ordering, supply and stocking of orthotic appliances.

They are involved, to greater or lesser extent, with the fitting of appliances, for which activity they may or may not be suitably qualified (*Study of the Orthotic Service. A report by NHS Management Consultancy Services. Crown Copyright, 1988*).

10.3.8. Adaptations to appliances. DH/WO (applying informally to Northern Ireland) and SHHD guidelines, state that if the consultant feels that the patient's need can be met by use of a standard article, adapted in a certain way, then the patient is expected to buy the original article.

Examples of items adapted include footwear, corsets, brassieres. The guidelines state that advice should be given by the hospital on the purchase of the original item (*MHM 50 NWRTHA p. 3; MHM 50 SHHD p. 3*).

10.3.9. Stock or non-stock orthotic appliances. DH/WO (applying informally to Northern Ireland) and SHHD guidelines state that it is for the consultant to decide whether to prescribe a stock (readymade) item, or non-stock item (*MHM 50 NWTRHA p. 5,7; MHM 50 SHHD p. 8*).

In practice, depending on local arrangements, an hospital might more or less rely on stock items. There are both advantages and disadvantages of stock item bulk orders. Cost-saving and quick supply to a patient are obvious benefits, while unsuitability for a significant proportion of patients is a disadvantage. Typical readymade stock items, held at the hospital, can include surgical collars, simple splints, hosiery and belts (*Study of the Orthotic Service. A report by NHS Management Consultancy Services. Crown Copyright, 1988 p. 36*).

10.3.10. Choice of appliance

10.3.10.1. Range available. Hospitals are often served by one commercial orthotist, or more than one. There is concern that the commercial interest limits the range of appliances available (*Study of the Orthotic Service. A report by NHS Management Consultancy Services. Crown Copyright, 1988 p. 14*).

10.3.10.2. Consultant responsibility for choice of contractor. SHHD guidelines state that, for example, the 'consultant, in selecting the contractor to supply the appliance, should be guided by his own and his colleagues' experience of the quality of work and service provided by the contractors who have undertaken to supply hospitals in the area together with their respective costs' (*MHM 50 SHHD p. 7*).

10.3.10.3. Patient choice is referred to in DH/WO (applying informally to Northern Ireland) and SHHD guidelines, which state that, though it is the hospital's choice, nevertheless, 'it may sometimes be advantageous to place the order with the firm with which the patient has dealt with in the past as the firm may have the necessary measurements and knowledge of the patient's disability . . .'(*MHM 50 NWTRHA p. 6; MHM 50 SHHD p. 7*).

10.3.10.4. War pensioners (30.3.) have traditionally been able to benefit from the special supply of orthotic appliances, through services provided at wheelchair/ artifical limb centres, as opposed to normal health service channels.

10.4. Ordering

Following prescription, it is the hospital SAO who then sees to the supply of the appliance. He or she raises an order (either straightaway or following orthotist assessment).

The order is usually placed through an orthotist working for a private contractor, or rarely through a health service employed orthotist.

The Dundee orthotic service, for example, has in the past had all orders processed by a health service orthotist, checking them to see that 'the orthosis described is practical and realistic', before the order is actually placed (*Murdoch G, Condie D, Carus DA, Lamb J. 'A Model Orthotic Service'. Report to the Advisory Group on New Developments in Health Care, Scottish Home and Health Department. Tayside Rehabilitation Engineering Services. Tayside Health Board, Dundee District 1984*).

10.5. Delivery of appliance

DH/WO (applying informally to Northern Ireland) and SHHD guidelines state that the consultant is responsible for ensuring that the appliance is satisfactory in manufacture, fit and function.

The guidelines also state that appliances should normally be delivered to the hospital where the consultant, SAO and any other staff can ensure that the appliance is satisfactory. Only exceptionally, in the case of minor appliances, should the appliance be delivered direct to the person without inspection at the hospital (*MHM 50 NWTRHA p. 7; MHM 50 SHHD pp. 7–8*).

In practice, it seems, in England and Wales at least, that this does not always happen: consultants rarely check the appliance and SAOs carry out a post-delivery inspection, for which they might not be qualified (*Study of the Orthotic Service. A report by NHS Management Consultancy Services. Crown Copyright, 1988 p. 35*).

In practice, in Northern Ireland, the NIOS inspects all appliances (without the patient at this stage) ordered for quality, soundness etc. before the appliance is 'placed on the shelf' for fitting at a local clinic.

10.6. Follow-up and review

10.6.1. Guidelines. SHHD guidelines state, for example, that the consultant is responsible for ensuring that the 'appliance prescribed is provided, that it continues to meet the needs of the patient and that it is adjusted, modified or replaced as appropriate' (*MHM 50, Scotland p. 7*).

10.6.2. Practice. In practice, in England and Wales at least, a report has found that follow-up appointments, to check the effectiveness of the appliance, are arbitrary and depend on the judgement and wishes of the clinician. This can result in a lack of systematic follow-up and assessment (*Study of the Orthotic Service. A report by NHS Management Consultancy Services. Crown Copyright, 1988 p. 16*).

10.6.3. Specialist centre follow-up and review is likely to be more active. Systematic review of the finished product, the effect on the patient's condition, achievement of satisfactory supply and fiting, inhouse workshop for minor repairs and modifications – can all be elements of a specialist centre's follow-up procedures (*Study of the Orthotic Service. A report by NHS Management Consultancy Services. Crown Copyright, 1988 p. 35*).

10.6.3.1. Specialist centre follow-up example. Patient review is seen as 'in many ways, the most important element of the comprehensive system of orthotic care'. See Box 10.2 for details.

Box 10.2: Example of specialist centre's orthotic appliance follow-up procedures

B10.2.1. Multi-disciplinary review. For people who initially had multi-disciplinary assessment, appointments are made for that patient to undergo review by the same assessment team, either to assess the success of the appliance and/or to reassess where the person's condition is changing.

B10.2.2. Stability of condition and appliance. Where the person's condition is stable, but the appliance is likely to wear out, routine 'technical' reviews are carried out by an orthotist.

Where both the person's condition and appliance are stable, a letter of enquiry is sent out to the person.

B10.2.3. Training in the use of the appliance. People might need help, in the form of training, to use an appliance. The district orthotic service, for example, has physiotherapy and occupational therapy staff; they can advise therapist colleagues in 'referring' clinics, as well as themselves provide special training for patients with complex equipment (*(Murdoch G, Condie D, Carus DA, Lamb J. 'A Model Orthotic Service'. Report to the Advisory Group on New Developments in Health Care, Scottish Home and Health Department. Tayside Rehabilitation Engineering Services. Tayside Health Board, Dundee District 1984, p. 15*).

10.6.4. Hospital inpatients. Therapists sometimes ensure, daily, that inpatients wear their orthotic appliances correctly. Suitably trained physiotherapy helpers, for example, sometimes systematically check that they are properly applied when patients get up in the morning (*Sweetlove F. Therapy Weekly 1982. 9:15; p. 5*).

10.7. Repair and replacement

10.7.1. Repeat prescription. DH/WO (applying informally to Northern Ireland) and SHHD guidelines state that the consultant can authorise repeat prescription of appliances without reassessment for a period of up to five years, if the person's condition is stable. If, however, doubts arise during re-measuring and re-fitting, referral by the orthotist to the consultant for re-assessment should take place (*MHM 50 NWTRHA Introduction; MHM 50 SHHD*).

10.7.2. Repairs to surgical appliances in general. DH/WO (applying informally to Northern Ireland) and SHHD guidelines state that repairs are carried out free of charge, subject only to the general proviso that a charge can be made if the person is blame-worthy through an 'act or omission' (30.1.6.2.). Where the repair is straightforward, there will normally be no need to see the consultant (*NHS Act 1977 s.82 and MHM 50 NWTRHA p. 9; NHS (Scotland) Act 1978 s.74 and MHM 50 SHHD p. 14; SI 1972/1265 Health and Personal Social Services (Northern Ireland) Order 1972 Schedule 15*).

10.7.3. Repair to an adapted article. DH/WO (applying informally to Northern Ireland) and SHHD guidelines state that repair to an adapted article, which is not concerned with the surgical features, 'should be carried out privately at the patient's own expense'. If the feature to be repaired is the surgical feature then repair is free of charge (*MHM 50 NWTRHA Introduction; MHM 50 SHHD*).

10.7.4. Replacement criteria. DH/WO (applying informally to Northern Ireland) and SHHD guidelines stress that the criteria for replacement are 'serviceability of the appliance and continued clinical needs'(*MHM 50 NWTRHA Introduction; MHM 50 SHHD*).
   DH/WO (applying informally to Northern Ireland) guidelines note that 'the frequency at which replacement will be necessary cannot be arbitrarily determined and will depend upon the individual circumstances and disability ...'(*MHM 50 NWTRHA pp. 8–9*).

10.7.5. Duplication of appliances. DH/WO (applying informally to Northern Ireland) and SHHD guidelines state that appliances can be supplied in duplicate, if otherwise the person's employment would be interfered with, or the person would suffer hardship. 'Medical or hygienic' grounds also justify duplication.

Examples given, where duplication might be appropriate are calipers, surgical boots and shoes, surgical supports (*MHM 50 NWTRHA p. 3; MHM 50 SHHD p. 4*).

10.8. Charges

There are charges for certain orthotic appliances, which are either listed on the Drug Tariff, or are specified elsewhere.

Elastic hosiery and trusses are listed on the Drug tariff and attract (at the time of writing) the standard prescription charge of £3.05 whether prescribed by a GP or a consultant (*SI 1989/419 as amended; SI 1989/326 (S.36) as amended; SR&O 1973/419 as amended*).

Other items specified elsewhere in regulations are surgical brassieres (£13.00) and abdominal or spinal supports (£17.00) (*SI 1989/419 as amended; SR&O 1989/326 (S.36) as amended; SR&O 1973/419 as amended*).

These charges are subject to exemption and partial exemption, depending on invididual circumstances (30.1.1./Box 30.1.).

11 Prostheses 1: artificial limbs

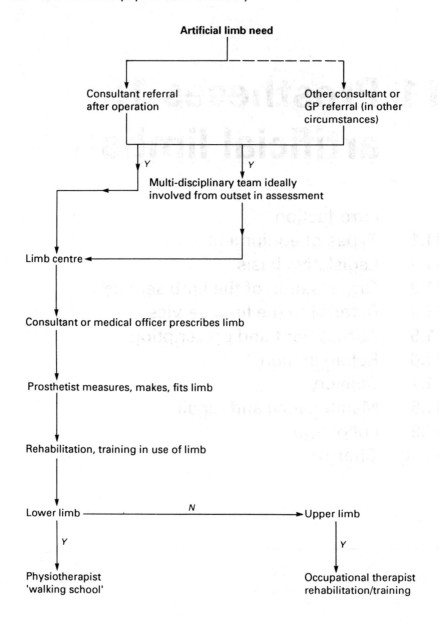

Introduction

Type of equipment

Artificial limbs include, for example, old-style metal/tin limbs, modern modular moulded limbs, 'electric hands', and a wide range of accessories.

Responsibility for provision

Lies with the limb service which is administered by:

- the Disablement Services Authority (DSA, England), a special health authority which will administer the service until 1991, when the service becomes part of the NHS;
- the Welsh Health Common Services Authority (WHCSA, Wales), a special health authority;
- health boards (HBs, Scotland);
- health and social services boards (HSSBs, Northern Ireland); the eastern HSSB administers the service on behalf of the other three boards.

Limb service centres go by different names:

- disablement services centres (DSCs, England). Formerly known as artificial limb and appliance centres (ALACs);
- artificial limb and appliance centres (ALACs, Wales);
- artificial limb and appliance centres (ALACs) or limb fitting centres (Scotland);
- regional disablement services (RDS, Northern Ireland). The limb service is part of the RDS, which is run by the eastern HSSB.

Referral, assessment and provision

Referral to the limb service is usually made by a hospital consultant, following an operation, but sometimes by a general practitioner (GP) in other circumstances.

Referring consultants sometimes recommend a specific type of limb; but it is the limb service doctor (consultant or medical officer) who formally prescribes.

Multi-disciplinary assessment (including doctors, therapists, rehabilitation engineers), undertaken from the period prior to the operation, to the rehabilitation period following fitting, can ensure effective prescription and use of the limb.

Rehabilitation and training in the use of upper and lower limbs is routinely undertaken by occupational therapists and physiotherapists respectively.

The limb service retains responsibility for the maintenance, repair and replacement of the limb.

Note on terminology. For the purposes of this book, the term 'limb service' is used to include the various arrangements for artificial limb provision in the United Kingdom. The term 'limb centre' is used to cover the various names of limb service centres.

11.1. Type of equipment

Artificial limbs include for example old-style metal/tin limbs, modern modular moulded limbs, 'electric hands' and a wide range of accessories. For details see Box 11.1.

Box 11.1: Type of equipment: artificial limbs

B11.1.1. Metal/tin limbs. The older range of rigid metal limbs are still maintained (and occasionally supplied) for (older) people who prefer them to the newer moulded (foam padded) limbs.

B11.1.2. Modern limbs. Lower limbs are modular, moulded plastic (padded with foam) and can be locked or flexible at the knee.

An example of an upper limb prosthesis is the myo-electric hand. This is connected to nerve endings on the arm stump, and responds to muscle movements in the arm. Young children learn to use such a hand by stages (for example, by starting with a cosmetic prosthesis, which is then replaced by a working hand). As the child grows, the myo-electric hand is available in a number of sizes.

Alternatively, cosmetic arms with 'give' in the fingers are supplied.

B11.1.3. Pylons. In the past temporary 'pylon' limbs have often been provided on a temporary basis (preferably made by the same limb contractor who made the proper limb).

This is rarer now, a definitive leg often being supplied straightaway, even where there is still some stump fluctuation expected. The modular limb system allows a new leg to be supplied quickly, the casting for the socket being the only major bespoke operation involved.

B11.1.4. Short prostheses. For a person with a double amputation, temporary short prostheses are sometimes supplied for habituation purposes before full-size limbs are supplied.

B11.1.5. Accessories. A number of accessories are used with artificial limbs.

For example: elastic thigh stockings (alternative suspension to leather cuff), special belts (eg for high amputation, fluctuating stump), woollen stump socks (issued in some quantity to patient), anti-perspirant lotion (where excessive stump sweating), suspender belts, rubber protection covers (if limb used in wet conditions), arm mittens, gloves (leather, fabric, string) with artificial arm, stout glove (where partial amputation of hand), special cutlery (can be specially recommended by consultant/ MO).

11.2. Legislative basis for artificial limb provision

11.2.1. Basis for artificial limb provision: England. Provision is covered by the Secretary of State's duty to provide 'medical services' (*NHS Act 1977 s.3*) delegated to the Disablement Services Authority (DSA) until 31.3.91 (*SI 1987/808,809*).

After March 31st 1991, responsibility for provision will be covered by the DHA duty to provide 'medical services' (*NHS Act 1977 s.3*).

11.2.2. Basis for artificial limb provision: Wales. Provision is covered by the Secretary of State's duty to provide 'medical services' (*NHS Act 1977 s.3*) delegated to the Welsh Health Common Services Authority (WHCSA) (*see eg SI 1985/996*).

11.2.3. Basis for artificial limb provision: Scotland. Provision is covered by the health board duty to provide 'medical services' (NHS (Scotland) Act 1978 s.36).

11.2.4. Basis for artificial limb provision: Northern Ireland. Provision is covered by the HSSB duty of to provide 'medical services' (*SI 1972/1265 HPSS (NI) O a.5*).

11.3. Organisation of the limb service.

The limb service in the United Kingdom is organised variously.

In England (until 1991), and Wales, it is administered by special health authorities, the DSA and WHCSA respectively; in Scotland by health boards; and in Northern Ireland by the Regional Disablement Services (run by the EHSSB on behalf of the other HSSBs).

Central contract arrangements also vary, as do staffing arrangements and titles. Staff involved in the limb service include medical officers, consultants, prosthetists, technical officers, rehabilitation engineers and therapists. For details see Box 11.2

Box 11.2: Limb service organisation, contracts, staff

B11.2.1. England. In England, the limb service is in a state of transition, following a 1987 report on the artificial limb and wheelchair service (*McColl I. Review of Artificial Limb and Appliance Centre Services. DHSS, 1986*).

B11.2.1.1. Disablement services authority (DSA). Until April 1991 limbs will be supplied through disablement services centres (DSCs), of which there are on average two within each RHA (though there may only be one, or as many as three). These are administered by a discrete health authority known as the Disablement Services Authority (DSA).

B11.2.1.2. 1991 formal transfer of service to the NHS. The DSA remains in overall control of the limb service until 31.3.91 when the limb service will become the responsiblity of the NHS.

It appears at the time of writing that limb services within each RHA will in many cases remain at the premises they already occupy. Thus unlike the wheelchair service (6.4.1.1.), the limb service will generally be organised at 'supra-district' rather than DHA level.

B11.2.2. Wales. In Wales, limb centres are still known as artificial limb and appliance centres (ALACS), and are administered by the Welsh Health Common Services Authority (WHCSA), on behalf of the Welsh Office.

Artificial limbs are assessed for and supplied at Rookwood Hospital, Cardiff and at Swansea. There are plans for a new ALAC at Wrexham to include artificial limb provision as well, and a new ALAC at Bryn-y-Neuadd, Llanfairfechan, near Bangor.

B11.2.3. Scotland. Limb centres in Scotland are known still as ALACs or limb fitting centres and are part of the NHS, and therefore run by health boards.

There are centres in Aberdeen, Dundee, Edinburgh, Glasgow, and Inverness, which between them cover the fifteen health boards.

B11.2.4. Northern Ireland. The limb service for Northern Ireland is part of Regional Disablement Services at Musgrave Park Hospital. This is is run by the EHSSB on behalf of the other three boards, thus covering the whole province.

B11.2.5. Staff. A general explanation of limb service staff other than prosthetists (including consultants, medical officers, technical officers, rehabilitation engineers, therapists:) is given elsewhere in connection with the wheelchair service (6.4.2.).

B11.2.5.1. Prosthetists. Prosthetists are experts in measuring, casting and fitting artificial limbs. They work mainly for commercial companies, often renting space (for measuring, fitting) from the health service or DSA.

The McColl report (1986) found that prosthetists were inadequately trained in England and Wales compared for example with prosthetists trained at Strathclyde University and abroad. The standard of prosthetic care in England and Wales was found to be low (*McColl I. Review of Artificial Limb and Appliance Centre Services. DHSS, 1986. Vol.1, p. 20*).

B11.2.5.2. Medical officers. As described elsewhere (6.4.2./B6.2.1.), the post of medical officer in England will no longer exist after 31.3.90: the 1986 McColl report found that they were inadequately trained to effectively supply limbs (*McColl I. Review of Artificial Limb and Appliance Centre Services. DHSS, 1986. Vol.1, p. 18*).

B11.2.6. Range of limbs available through the limb service

B11.2.6.1. England. A central approval system, and a monopoly on services by two or three companies have meant that in the past, the range of limbs available in England was limited (see eg McColl I. Review of Artificial Limb and Appliance Centre Services. DHSS, 1986. Vol.1, p. 25).

This situation has been changing; the English limb service should now be able to supply the whole range of approved limbs. The DSA has broken the monopoly previously held by two or three companies by separating the hardware and fitting contracts, and twelve firms now hold fitting contracts (*DSA Annual Report 1988/89 p. 12*).

A move away 'from centralised liability for safety standards and control towards manufacturers's product liability' will also allow a greater range of limbs to be supplied by limb centres (*Galasko, Lipkin. Competing for the Disabled. IEA Health Unit Paper No.7 1989, p. 40*)

B11.2.6.2. Wales, Scotland, Northern Ireland. Limb centres have been more easily able to introduce European limb systems, for example, than has been possible in England (*see eg Galasko, Lipkin. Competing for the Disabled. IEA Health Unit Paper No.7 1989, p.40*).

11.4. Referral to the limb service

Amputees and people with congenital deformities (involving limblessness) can be referred to the limb service by a consultant (following an operation), or by another consultant or GP in other circumstances.

11.5. Assessment and prescription

11.5.1. Link between hospital consultant and limb service. A consultant (surgeon, for example) can recommend a particular limb: but it is the limb service medical officer or consultant who formally prescribes it.

Assessment by the limb service involves at least the consultant or medical officer, a prosthetist and a nurse. Following prescription, the prosthetist measures, takes a casting and fits the limb.

Sometimes, depending on local arrangements, routine multi-disciplinary assessment takes place; this can include assessment by rehabilitation engineers and therapists.

Limbs might be made by rehabilitation engineers in difficult or complex cases (29.2.).

11.5.2. Criteria for prescription of artificial limbs. As in the case of the wheelchair service (6.), the DSA (England) has issued directives (6.4.4.3.1.) containing guidelines and criteria for provision. These have superseded the old ALAC manual, on the basis of which the limb service throughout the UK formerly operated.

The directives themselves have varying force in England; they do not formally apply to the limb services in Wales, Scotland or Northern Ireland, but are generally followed, nevertheless. On 31 March 1991, the directives will cease to be valid when the DSA itself ceases to exist (11.3.).

Therefore, the criteria, based on DSA policy and outlined below apply more or less to the whole of the United Kingdom.

11.5.2.1. Main criterion for prescription of artificial limbs. The DSA has stated: 'All amputees resident in the United Kingdom are eligible for the supply, repair and renewal of artificial limbs under the National Health Service' (*Written communication: DSA, 1989*).

(*Note:* in practice, not all people who are eligible, are supplied with an artificial limb. They might not wish to have it, or may be unable to use it.

A 1989 DSA letter to vascular, orthopaedic and general surgeons pointed out that some 70% of lower limb amputees receive artificial legs in the UK, but that many do not use them. The letter urged surgeons to only prescribe limbs following careful assessment.)

11.5.2.2. Duplication of limb. Duplicate limbs in the past have been supplied almost as a matter of course. DSA directive guidance in 1989 was to the effect that DSCs should cease to supply automatically the second limb. One of the reasons given was that modern modular limbs could be repaired quickly (eg on-the-spot) at the DSC (*Written communication: DSA 1989*), thereby removing the need for duplicate limbs.

11.5.2.2.1. Automatic supply. Certain categories of people, automatically eligible for supply of a duplicate limb, include: 'war pensioners, children, people in employment, those who are very active, those who are overweight or subject to

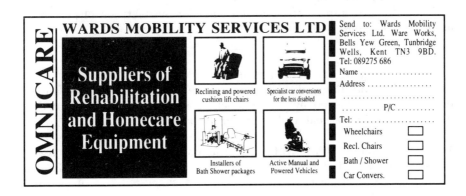

breakages and those subject to intermittent stump fluctuations' (*Written communication: DSA, 1989*).

11.5.2.2.2. Consultant and medical officer discretion to prescribe duplicate limb. Nevertheless DSA directive guidance states that the final decision on whether to supply a duplicate limb or not rests with the consultant or MO.

There is discretion to prescribe a duplicate limb for other categories of person 'where they are satisfied that clinical reasons show such a need exists. They will always take account of an individual's particular requirements, especially when the old-style conventional limb system is prescribed' (*Written communication: DSA, 1989*).

11.5.2.3. Range of artificial limbs available. This is discussed in Box 11.1.

11.5.2.4. Private supply of artificial limbs. Private supply of limbs through the limb service is not possible. The private supplier/manufacturer is responsible for assessment of medical aspects; but walking and training facilities might be available from the limb service, or from the hospital where the amputation was performed (eg private hospital).

Prosthetists often rent certain areas of the limb centre premises, and private patients can attend those areas within the limb centre.

11.6. Rehabilitation in relation to artificial limb use

11.6.1. Rehabilitation planning before amputation of a limb. The 1986 report on the limb and wheelchair service in England recommended that rehabilitation plans start at the amputation stage when a multi-disciplinary team can support the surgeon performing the operation.

Assessment of the expected degree of rehabilitation can be made and advice given on home conditions, functional re-education and walking training (*McColl I. Review of Artificial Limb and Appliance Centre Services. DHSS, 1986. Vol.1, pp. 6–7*).

The degree to which this takes place is likely to depend on local arrangements.

11.6.2. Rehabilitation following amputation and fitting. Walking training is carried out by physiotherapists, often at a 'walking school' attached to the limb centre. Where the limb centre does not have such a school, or the centre is distant from the person's home, then the training is likely to be carried out by a suitably experienced physiotherapist at a local hospital.

Occupational therapists are involved with the rehabilitation of people with artificial upper limbs

11.7. Delivery of artificial limbs

The McColl report (England, 1986), for example, found serious shortcomings in delivery times, achieved by the prosthetic commercial companies (*McColl I. Review of Artificial Limb and Appliance Centre Services. DHSS, 1986. Vol.1, p. 23*).

11.7.1. Transport to limb centres. The ambulance service is often used to transport people to and from the limb centre; the McColl report (1986, England) found serious deficiencies in the system and suggested use of alternative transport (for example, the hospital car service), as well as satellite centres and mobile workshops (*McColl I. Review of Artificial Limb and Appliance Centre Services. DHSS, 1986. Vol.1, p. 26*).

11.8. Maintenance and repair of artificial limbs

Maintenance advice is given by the limb centre, which is is responsible for maintenance, repair and replacement of the limb, as needed; the modern modular limb systems can be repaired much more quickly and easily than older style limbs. Same-day repair is possible.

11.9. Follow-up

People with artificial limbs are reviewed regularly, though precise frequency and arrangements vary from centre to centre.

Children are followed up more actively. Apart from close contact with a child's paediatrician and therapists, the limb centre might, for example, arrange therapy/play sessions in holiday periods (*Verbal communication: DSA Regional manager 1989*).

11.10. Charges

Artificial limbs and their accessories are supplied, mantained, repaired and replaced free of charge by the limb service.

Jessica Kingsley Publishers

118 Pentonville Road, London N1 9JN Tel 071-833 2307 Fax 071-837 2917

Dramatherapy with Families, Groups and Individuals

Waiting in the Wings

Sue Jennings

1990 ISBN 1 85302 014 1 160 pages, illus hardback £18.95

This book - by one of the leaders in this exciting and relatively new field - is the first to present a working framework for dramatherapists, social workers, family and marital therapists, and others conducting groups.

Storymaking in Education and Therapy

Alida Gersie and Nancy King

1990 ISBN 1 85302 519 4 416 pages hardback £29.50

ISBN 1 85302 520 8 paperback £18.95

'This is an essential and wonderful book for anyone interested in working with stories in education or therapy... It is a true discovery'
- Dr Ofra Ayalon, Haifa University

Storymaking in Bereavement

Alida Gersie

1990 208 pages ISBN 1 85302 065 6 hardback £17.95

This book is about a specific way of helping people work through their losses, even though such losses may have occurred many years before. It contains a unique collection of stories from around the world.

Drama and Healing: The Roots of Drama Therapy

Roger Grainger

1990 ISBN 1 85302 048 6 144 pages hardback £18.95

Roger Grainger shows how drama therapy draws on both drama and ritual. He examines the specific relationship between ratonal thought and artistic experience which allows the second to act as the mediator of the first in therapy.

Art Therapy and Dramatherapy: Their Relation and Practice

Sue Jennings and Ase Minde

1991   ISBN 1 85302 027 3 176 pages, illustrated £24.50

This is the first book to explore the relationship and differences between art therapy and dramatherapy. The book is based on eight years of research and practice of art therapy and dramatherapy, in training, clinical practice and theory.

Art Therapy in Practice

Edited by Marian Liebmann

1990 192 pages ISBN 1 85302 057 5 hardback £24.50

ISBN 1 85302 058 3 paper £9.95

This book describe what actually happens in art therapy in a variety of contexts, as practised by particular art therapists.

Please send for information about other JKP titles in the arts therapies

12 Prostheses 2: breast, hair (wig) and eye prostheses

Jessica Kingsley Publishers

118 Pentonville Road, London N1 9JN Tel 071-833 2307 Fax 071-837 2917

Approaches to Case Management for People with Disabilities

Doria Pilling

1991 ISBN 1 85302 099 0 hb £22.50
Disability and Rehabilitation series 1
Published with the Rehabilitation Resource Centre, City University

Is there a need for case management? What is case management? Why is it on the map? The author answers these questions and provides an in depth survey of current and recent case-management and co-ordination projects and services in Britain describing their main features and the differences between them and what is known so far about their successes and failures.

Contents: Part I: Case management in Britain today. 1. Is there a need for case management? 2. A British experience of case management. Part II: Evaluation of the Camden and Islington Case Manager Project for people with physical disabilities. 1. The design of the evaluation. 2. The clients' views of the Case Manager Project. 3. Case Manager roles and achievements: a review of the client records. 4. Service Providers' view of the Case Manager Project. 5. Summary and conclusions. Part III. Evaluation of the Disability Team in Westminster and Kensington and Chelsea. 1. Introduction. 2. The objectives of the project. 3. The clients' views. 4. The service providers' views. 5. Overview and conclusions.

Psychosocial Interventions with Physically Disabled Persons

Edited by Bruce W Heller, PhD, Louis M Flohr, MD, Leonard S Zegans, MD

1990 ISBN 1 85302 050 8 hb £25.00
ISBN 1 85302 051 6 paper £14.95

This book addresses a range of concerns about the psychosocial assessment, counselling, rehabilitation, and adaptations of people with physical disabilities. It offers theoretical, research-based, and clinical information useful for professionals in rehabilitation, nursing, mental health, and medicine, who, in partnership with disabled persons and their families, compose the treatment/rehabilitation team. Each chapter is written by an expert in the field, most of whom are pioneers in their respective specialities.

Social Work: Disabled People and Disabling Environments

Edited by Mike Oliver

1990 ISBN 1 85302 042 7 hb £16.95
Research Highlights in Social Work 21

The contributors cover a wide range of concerns in working with a variety of client groups. Separate chapters cover such topics as disability and new technology, the OPCS report, independent living, and working with disabled children.

Please send for a complete catalogue of publications

12.1. Breast prostheses

12.1.1. Type of equipment. There are about 13 main types of breast prosthesis available in th UK (*see eg NHS Management Consultancy Services, Study of the Orthotic Service. Crown Copyright, 1988, p. 38*).

12.1.2. Basis for provision of breast prostheses. Provision is by the health service and covered by the DHA/HB/HSSB duty to provide 'medical services' (*NHS Act 1977 s.3; NHS (Scotland) Act 1978 s.36; SI 1972/1265 HPSS(NI)O a.5*).

12.1.3. Assessment and prescription of breast prostheses is by a hospital consultant.

12.1.4. Fitting of breast prostheses might be carried out by a commercial company representative (who is male), by the hospital surgical appliance officer (SAO) (10.4.7.) or by a clinical nurse specialist.

A report (England, 1988) recommended that fitting should preferably be by a clinical nurse specialist, and failing that, by a female commercial fitter. Lack of suitable privacy and facilities was also seen to be a problem (*NHS Management Consultancy Services, Study of the Orthotic Service. Crown Copyright, 1988, pp. 37–38*).

12.1.5. Choice of breast prosthesis. The report also found that there has in the past been insufficient choice from among the 13 main types of breast prosthesis available; it criticised this aspect of the service (*NHS Management Consultancy Services, Study of the Orthotic Service. Crown Copyright, 1988, p. 38*).

12.1.6. Charges. Breast prostheses are supplied free of charge.

12.2. Wigs

12.2.1. Type of equipment. Wigs are of three main types: artificial modacrylic, part human hair and full human hair.

12.2.2. Legislative basis for provision. Provision is covered by the DHA/HB/HSSB duty to provide 'medical services' (*NHS Act 1977 s.3; NHS (Scotland) Act 1978 s.36; SI 1972/1265 HPSS(NI)O a.5*).

12.2.3. Assessment and presription. Assessment and prescription is by a hospital consultant, usually a dermatologist, neuro-surgeon, radiotherapist or oncologist (*Cheesbrough MJ. Wigs. BMJ 1989; 299 pp. 1455–56*).

12.2.3.1. Criteria for provision. There a number of conditions and criteria laid down in guidance (DH/WO – applying informally to Northern Ireland, and SHHD) for the provision of wigs:

12.2.3.1.1. Conditions justifying provision. 'Wigs may be provided only in cases where a consultant considers a wig to be necessary and where the baldness is due to any of the following conditions':

- congenital dystrophy of the skin;
- alopecia totalis;
- alopecia areata, severe and of long standing;
- extensive scarring following trauma, X-ray application or an inflammatory condition;
- illness or treatment of illness where baldness, though not permanent, is likely to be prolonged (eg after inter-cranial operation or radiotherapy);
- prolonged administration of cytotoxic drugs (*MHM 50 NWTRHA p. 3; similar criteria in MHM 50 SHHD p. 20*).

12.2.3.1.2. Normal baldness. 'It is not the intention that normal male baldness should itself justify the provision of a wig under the National Health Service nor that elderly female patients whose hair is thinning due to age should qualify under b. and c. in previous paragraph' (*MHM 50 NWTRHA p. 3; similarly MHM 50 SHHD p. 20*).

12.2.4. Type of wig prescribed. Acrylic wigs are now of a high standard and easier to look after; because of this consultants do not prescribe many human hair wigs (*Cheesbrough MJ. Wigs. BMJ 1989; 299 pp. 1455–6*).

12.2.4.1. Guidelines on wig type (DH/WO, informally applying to Northern Ireland).

12.2.4.1.1. Stock wigs: ready made stock size wigs should be supplied in all cases where, in the opinion of the consultant, they will adequately meet the patient's requirements (*MHM 50 NWTRHA, p. 4*);

12.2.4.1.2. Human hair wigs can be supplied:

- to patients for whom a stock wig would be unsuitable should be provided with a made to measure hair wig;
- when stock wigs, because of their construction and the difficulty in obtaining a match with residual hair, are not suitable as semi-transformations. In such cases made to measure transformations in human hair should be ordered (*MHM 50. NWTRHA, p. 4*).

12.2.4.1.3. Personal preference: 'if in order to meet a personal preference for which there is no medical justification, a patient requires a wig to incorporate special features, the effect of which will render the wig or its maintenance more expensive, the patient must make his or own arrangements and meet the whole cost. When wigs are supplied by hospitals the aim should be to restore the patient's natural appearance' (*MHM 50 NWTRHA, p. 4*).

12.2.5. Supply. Following prescription, the hospital surgical appliance officer (SAO) (10.4.7.) normally organises the supply. A 'wig agent' (usually a hairdresser) helps the person choose a wig, and is responsible for checking that the finished article fits, and for instructing the person in its maintenance (*Cheesbrough MJ. Wigs. BMJ 1989; 299 pp. 1455–6*).

12.2.5.1. Supply of acrylic wig. Acrylic wigs come in stock sizes, can be adjusted to any head, and are usually delivered within a few days (*Cheesbrough MJ. Wigs. BMJ 1989; 299 pp. 1455–6*).

12.2.5.2. Supply of human hair wig. Human hair wigs have to be made to order, and may take 8 to 12 weeks to be delivered (*Cheesbrough MJ. Wigs. BMJ 1989; 299, pp. 1455–6*).

12.2.5.3 Voucher scheme. Some DHAs, for example, issue vouchers which can be used at selected hairdressers or department stores (*Cheesbrough MJ. Wigs. BMJ 1989; 299, pp. 1455–6*).

12.2.6. Replacement. Two wigs are usually supplied; they are replaced at consultant discretion, though an average rate might be one per year (acrylic wig) or two every three years (human hair) (*Cheesbrough MJ. Wigs. BMJ 1989; 299 pp. 1455–6*).

12.2.7. Charges. There are special charges for wigs, to which various exemption categories apply (30.1./Box 30.1.). The charges are, at the time of writing:

- stock modacrylic wig, £26.00;
- partial human hair wig, £67.00;
- full bespoke human hair wig, £97.00.

12.3. Artificial eyes

12.3.1. Type of equipment. Guidelines (*DH/WO, informally applying to Northern Ireland; SHHD*) state that plastic artificial eyes are available, to give the 'closest possible match with the natural eye'. Special eyes can also be made for sockets into which magnetic or other implants have been inserted (*MHM 50. NWTRHA, p. 16; MHM 50. SHHD, p. 25*).

Orbital prostheses are also available; these facial prostheses include lid and socket reconstruction and attempt to match the eye and surrounding tissue as closely as possible.

12.3.2. Legislative basis for provision. Provision is covered by the Secretary of State's (England and Wales) and HB/HSSBs' (Scotland and Northern Ireland) duty to provide 'medical services' (*NHS Act 1977 s.3; NHS (Scotland) Act 1978 s.36; SI 1972/1265 HPSS(NI)O a.5*).

(In England the Department of Health (DH), and in Wales the Welsh Office (WO), retain responsibility for the artificial eye service).

12.3.3. Assessment, and prescription of artificial eyes is normally carried out by a consultant ophthalmologist. Referral is then made to the eye fitting service/ artificial eye service (*MHM 50 NWTRHA p. 16; MHM 50. SHHD, p. 25; Equipment for Disabled People HB2. DHSS (NI) 1988 p. 16*).

12.3.4. Eye fitting service/artificial eye service

12.3.4.1. England. The eye fitting service in England is based at DSCs (6.4.1.1.), although it is still administered by the DH. However, the orbital prosthetists working within the eye fitting service may also hold clinics in NHS hospitals.
    The service is due to be integrated with the NHS by 31st March 1991.

12.3.4.2. Wales. The eye fitting service remains the responsibility of the Welsh Office.

12.3.4.3. Scotland. Artificial eyes are supplied through the NHS; orbital prosthetists work at the Glasgow Eye Infirmary or the Eye Pavilion, Edinburgh. Orbital prostheses are fitted and made in association with plastic surgery units.

12.3.4.4. Northern Ireland. Eyes and orbital prostheses are individually made and are fitted by HSSB staff working within the artificial eye service at the Royal Victoria Hospital, Belfast.

12.3.5. Replacement is made on the recommendation of a consultant ophthalmologist.

12.3.6. Polishing. Polishing can be undertaken on the spot, or via a postal service, by the eye fitting service.

12.3.7. Charges. Artificial eyes are provided, maintained and replaced free of charge.

13 Communication (speech) equipment

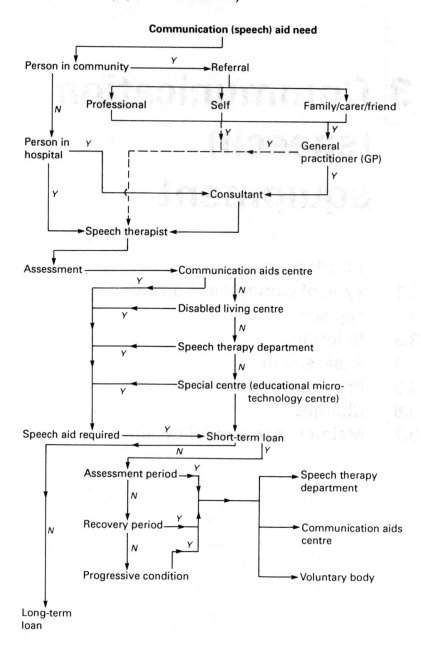

Speech aid required (continued)

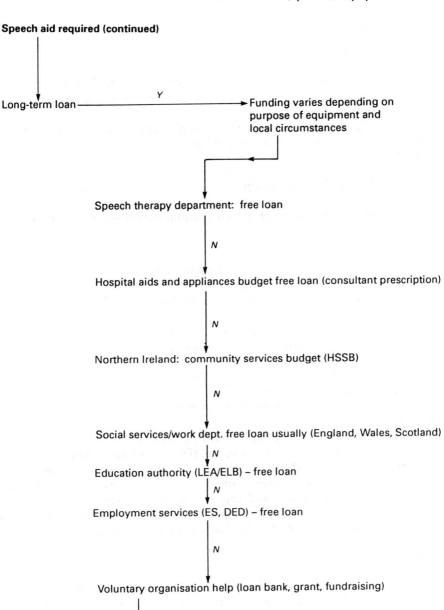

Long-term loan ——————— Y —————→ Funding varies depending on
purpose of equipment and
local circumstances

Speech therapy department: free loan

N

Hospital aids and appliances budget free loan (consultant prescription)

N

Northern Ireland: community services budget (HSSB)

N

Social services/work dept. free loan usually (England, Wales, Scotland)

N

Education authority (LEA/ELB) – free loan

N

Employment services (ES, DED) – free loan

N

Voluntary organisation help (loan bank, grant, fundraising)

N

Private purchase

Introduction

Type of equipment

Communication equipment for speech assistance and replacement includes communication boards and charts, speech synthesizer units, artificial larynxes, speech amplifiers and electronic communicators.

It is available, normally on free loan, through a number of different channels, depending on how the primary purpose of the equipment is perceived in any individual case.

Responsibility for provision

The different channels through which communication equipment is supplied include:

- health services:
  - district health authorities (DHAs, England/Wales);
  - health boards (HBs, Scotland);
  - health and social services boards (HSSBs, Northern Ireland);
- social services:
  - social services departments (SSDs, England/Wales);
  - social work departments (SWDs, Scotland);
  - HSSBs (Northern Ireland);
- education services:
  - local education authorities (LEAs, England/Wales, Scotland);
  - education and library boards (ELBs, Northern Ireland);
- employment services:
  - employment service (ES, England/Wales, Scotland);
  - department of economic development (DED, Northern Ireland).

It is not always clear which statutory service should take responsibility for provision; the expense of some communication equipment can sometimes exacerbate such uncertainty and cause delay in provision. Assistance from voluntary bodies, in the form of equipment loan or financial assistance, is sometimes available; private purchase is sometimes necessary.

Assessment

The experts on speech aids are speech therapists, who are generally employed by the health service, but who work a great deal in the community (including schools). It is generally recognised that there is a national shortage of speech therapists, however, and the level of speech therapy services is perceived to be inadequate.

There are a number of communication aids (or advice) centres (CACs) in the UK which act as major assessment centres for communication equipment. Staffed by speech therapists and usually attached to a hospital, they display equipment for demonstration purposes and for short-term trial home loan.

Provision

Can be through any of the above mentioned channels including joint funding arrangements. Short-term trial loan is often made, before a decision concerning purchase of an expensive item of equipment is reached.

13.1. Type of communication aids

13.1.1. Scope. For the purposes of this chapter, communication aids are taken to include equipment for speech assistance and replacement.

13.1.2. Examples. Speech assistance and replacement aids take, for example, the following forms:

13.1.2.1. Communication boards and charts. Communication boards or charts with letters, words, symbols. These range from the (Blis-symbolics) charts with 160 to 400 symbols, much used by children – to eye transfer frames ('E-Tran') for people who can only communicate by eye movement.

13.1.2.2. Speech synthesizer units can be used with electronic equipment (computers, typewriters) to produce 'unnatural' speech: either built in to such equipment or attached.

13.1.2.3. Artificial larynxes are small electronic pieces of equipment producing a constant sound which can be modified by mouth and throat movements. They can be neck-used, pressed against the neck or cheek – or they can be 'intra-oral' – the sound is introduced through a tube into the mouth. Both types are handheld (*Equipment for the Disabled. Communication. Compiled at Mary Marlborough Lodge. Oxfordshire Health Authority, 1987*).

13.1.2.4. Speech amplifiers. A bodyworn speech amplifier system typically consists of a microphone and amplifier.

13.1.2.5. Electronic communicators range from heavy electronic communication boards with light-scan facility to small portable units with a display panel and a few keys, which can be used in multiple combination. Such units are attachable, for example, to a VDU, a printer or speech synthesizer.

13.2. Legislative basis for the provision of communication aids.
Communication aids are not referred to directly in legislation.

13.2.1. Basis for speech therapist provision of communication aids lies in the DHA/HB/HSSB duty to provide 'other services'(*NHS Act 1977 s.3; NHS (Scotland) Act 1978 s.36; SI 1972/1265 HPSS(NI)O 1972 a.5*).

(*Note:* a Parliamentary answer explained that the level of speech therapy services is for health authorities (DHAs) to determine 'in the light of local circumstances, their assessment of priorities and the available resources' (*Weekly Hansard No. 1400, 8-12 December 1986 cols. 209–210*).

13.2.2. The basis for consultant provision of communication aids lies in the DHA/HB/HSSB duty to provide 'medical services' (*NHS Act 1977 s.3; NHS (Scotland) Act 1978 s.36; SI 1972/1265 HPSS(NI)O 1972 a.5*).

13.2.3. SSD/SWD and HPSSB (under social services function) provision of communication aids is covered specifically by the duty to make arrangements (where an individual need has been identified) for 'the provision of additional facilities to secure ... greater safety, comfort or convenience (*CSDPA 1970 s.2(1)(e), CSDP(NI)A 1978 s.2(e)*).

Such provision is also covered by general welfare legislation, and legislation concerning requests for assessment, all of which is detailed elsewhere (2.2.).

13.2.4. LEA/ELB provision of equipment (including communication aids) for educational need is discussed elsewhere (27.2.).

13.2.5. ES/DED provision of equipment (including communication aids) for employment need is discussed elsewhere (28.2.).

13.3. Referral

13.3.1. Speech therapists are the experts on communication (speech) aids. They are normally employed by DHA/HB/HSSBs, and spend a lot of their time working in the community, especially with children with special (educational) needs.

There is generally considered, in the light of demands on speech therapy services, to be a national shortage of speech therapists, although this is not recognised by central government (*see eg NHS Handbook. NAHA 1989 p. 193*); and speech therapy services are distributed unevenly (*see eg Weekly Hansard, No.1411, 16-20 March 1987, Written answers 18.3.87, cols. 513–5*).

Recent Circular guidance (England, 1988) recommends that authorities should consider 'the availability of . . . speech therapy to disabled people living in the community' (*HN (88)26*).

13.3.2. Referral to DHA/HB/HSSB speech therapy dept. In theory, speech therapists run an open referral system.

13.3.2.1. GP referral. In practice, referral is often through professional channels; for example, GPs, consultants, occupational therapists, ward nurses, teachers and educational psychologists.

It would seem, however, that relatively few referrals come from GPs (*7th Annual Report of the Assistive Communication Aids Centre, Frenchay Hospital, Bristol. For 1988; Rowley C. Stowe J.* et al. *Communication Aids Provision. Rheumatology and Rehabilitation Research Unit, University of Leeds, 1986 p. 42*); although Circular guidance (England, 1988) states that DHAs should consider open access for GPs to speech therapists (*HN (88)26*).

13.3.3. Referral to communication aids centre (CAC). There are a number of communication aids centres within the UK (usually attached to a hospital), which hold stocks of communication aids for assessment (including short-term loan) purposes. Speech therapists work in these centres, with more or less formal input from rehabilitation engineers, technicians and occupational therapists. Main centres exist in London, Cardiff, Glasgow, Belfast as well as in other towns and cities.

13.3.3.1. Open referral to CACs. Referral is open, in that anyone can contact a CAC directly. However, CAC advice at this stage is often that the person should contact their local speech therapist first. The speech therapist then contacts the CAC to discuss whether a visit would be appropriate. Most referrals are from speech therapists anyway (*see eg Scottish Centre of Technology for the Communication Impaired. 2nd annual report 1989 p. 3*).

If it is agreed that a visit is appropriate, the person, and ideally their own speech therapist, both attend the CAC assessment.

13.3.3.2. Question of funding at the CAC referral stage. Most CACs are only able to loan equipment on a short-term trial basis: even those which are able to loan for longer periods would usually not do so for people outside the area of the DHA/HB/HSSB in which they are situated.

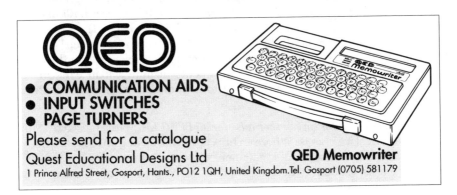

Given disappointed expectations following assessment, some CACs now strongly urge that funding arrangements be made before assessment (*CAC leaflet; Verbal communication CAC 1989*).

Difficulties are not always easy to resolve in relation to funding undertakings at this stage. A consultant's signing of a referral form, noting the possible financial implications of CAC referral, might facilitate health service provision at a later stage (*Easton J., Bennett J. Assistive Communication Aids Centre. Frenchay Hospital, Bristol. 1988*). On the other hand costs involved are often not known until assessment is complete (*Verbal communication, CAC 1989*), thus making prior funding commitments difficult.

13.4. Assessment

13.4.1. Speech therapist assessment

13.4.1.1. Location. Speech therapists carry out a great deal of their work in the community. Much of this work is with children with special educational needs (27.2.1.).

Speech therapists visit and treat, for example, at hospitals, health centres, schools, adult training centres, child assessment centres (26.4.7.1.), day nurseries, toy libraries, partial hearing units, residential homes or a person's own home.

13.4.1.2. Joint assessments. It is sometimes useful if other professionals, such as occupational therapists (OTs), attend the CAC assessment. Such joint assessment is facilitated if there is either an OT employed (eg part-time) at the centre, or if the centre is based at a hospital where therapists are easily accessible.

Technicians are sometimes employed by the centre, and there is sometimes more or less formal/informal input from rehabilitation engineers; both can assist assessment and carry out various adaptations (*Wardle J. Aids to Communication. Where do I go? ACE Centre 1988; Verbal communications: CACs, 1989*).

13.4.1.3. Equipment banks. Communication equipment is becoming increasingly complex and diverse, as well as more expensive, and careful assessment is required. In order to facilitate this, access to an equipment display is often needed.

CACs hold relatively larger displays; disabled living centres (DLCs) (2.4.2.2.) sometimes carry some communication equipment; and local hospital speech therapy departments often have equipment stock/displays, although these may be small (*see eg Rowley C. Stowe J. et al. Communication Aids Provision. Rheumatology and Rehabilitation Research Unit, University of Leeds, 1986 pp. 39–41*).

Circular guidance (England, 1988) states that joint planning between DHAs and SSDs 'might also consider the provision of communication aids with the District speech therapy services; possible arrangements include a loan bank of communication aids and linking a therapist to a Communication Aids Centre . . .' (*HN(88)26*).

13.4.1.4. Assessment by speech therapist for an LEA/ELB. Many speech therapists work a great deal in schools. Where an LEA or ELB is making an assessment (with or without a view to making a statement or record of needs), DHA/HB/HSSB speech therapists submit, where appropriate, assessment details concerned with communication aids.

Independent special schools sometimes employ their own speech therapists.

Provision of equipment (including communication aids) for special educational needs is discussed elsewhere (27.).

13.4.2. Consultants. The types of consultant with whom speech therapists typically work and take referrals include: ear nose throat (ENT), neurology, general medicine, oncology, orthodontics, paediatric, plastic surgery (eg for cleft palate) and so on.

13.4.3. Occupational therapists (OTs) and physiotherapists. Occupational therapists sometimes assist speech therapists to assess for communication aids.

For example, OTs and physiotherapists can advise on dexterity, support (eg arm supports for keyboard use) and posture, as they affect use of communication aids. An OT can also assess and categorise computer software relating to motor, visual and perceptual skills (7th Annual Report of the Assistive Communication Aids Centre, Frenchay Hospital, Bristol. For 1988, p. 8).

Multi-disciplinary assessment of this nature is not always possible due to the general workload of therapists (especially community OTs).

13.4.4. Assessment by a specialist centre for educational micro-technology. Two specialist centres, for example, which assess for both speech and writing aids, in relation to education are the ACE Centre (children) in Oxford and Oldham, and the CALL Centre (children and adults) in Edinburgh (13.5.9.).

Other specialist, rehabilitation centres (29.), include communication needs within the assessment of a disabled person's total needs.

13.4.5. SSD/SWD assessment for communication aids, cannot usually be carried out in any detail, since SSD/SWDs do not employ speech therapists.

However, community OTs might sometimes select and authorise equipment (*see eg Rowley C* et al. *Communication Aids Provision. Rheumatology and Rehabilitation, University of Leeds, 1986 p. 42*), refer to speech therapists and might assist a speech therapist with assessment (13.4.3.).

13.4.6. Assessment for cleft palate. Speech therapists might see children born with cleft palate, for example, as part of a special team including surgeon,

orthodontist, paediatrician and ENT specialist. Speech therapists give advice, for example, on feeding with a spring-loaded feeding plate made by the orthodontist (*Remedial Therapist 1985. Vol. 8 No.13, p. 12*).

13.5. Provision and funding of communication aids

Takes place through a number of different channels depending on local arrangements. The expense of many electronic communication aids can sometimes result in funding difficulties and delay in provision (*Verbal communications: CACs. Verbal communication: speech therapists*).

13.5.1. Sophisticated and expensive communication aids. In the last few years communication aids have become more sophisticated and expensive. As a result of this trend, less 'low-technology' equipment might be loaned by a CAC: most equipment costs between £100–£500, but an increasing amount of equipment is costing £500–£1000 (*7th Annual Report of the Assistive Communication Aids Centre, Frenchay Hospital, Bristol. For 1988*).

13.5.2. Continuing need for communication aids. A funding authority might not always recognise that the supply of one item of equipment is not necessarily the 'end of the story'. An individual's needs change for all sorts of reasons: a child grows, a condition alters or equipment wears out, for example. Equipment is often part of a continuing service, not a 'one-off', isolated solution (*Verbal communications: CACs 1989*).

13.5.3. Communication aids centre (CAC) loan

13.5.3.1. CAC short-term trial loan of communication aids. CACs are usually able to loan equipment for short-term use. This could be for a trial period of 4 to 6 weeks, for example. However, the increasing complexity and expense of equipment sometimes demands longer trial periods in order to establish suitability (*7th Annual Report of the Assistive Communication Aids Centre, Frenchay Hospital, Bristol. For 1988*).

13.5.3.1.1. Example of CAC loan service. The range and depth of stock, and therefore the power to loan even on a short term basis, varies from centre to centre.

For example, a CAC in Scotland loans a stock of 142 items all over Scotland: picked up/delivered personally or sent by registered post/courier. The loan period is very short, necessarily so, since there is strain on the centre's resources given that the equipment is also needed for further assessments, display, in-service training etc (*Scottish Centre of Technology for the Communication Impaired. 2nd annual report 1989*).

13.5.3.2. Difficulty of long-term loan. Alternatively, equipment is sometimes loaned for longer periods to patients with rapidly progressive disorders (eg motor-neurone disease): the aid is changed as the condition changes (*7th Annual Report of the Assistive Communication Aids Centre, Frenchay Hospital, Bristol. For 1988; Verbal communication: CAC, 1989*).

Long term loan is not normally possible through a CAC, except sometimes to residents of the DHA/HB/HSSB in which the CAC is situated. The CAC might have tried to establish a funding source (such as a consultant, speech therapy dept, SSD/SWD, voluntary body) before assessment; otherwise it might refer a person to various possible sources following assessment.

13.5.4. DHA/HB/HSSB loan. The level of provision by DHA/HB/HSSBs is likely to vary: for example, one CAC in Scotland has found that the health boards fund about 50% of the recommended communication systems (although usually the boards are approached for the cheaper less sophisticated equipment) (*Scottish Centre of Technology for the Communication Impaired. 2nd annual report 1989 p. 4*).

A 1986 study (UK wide) found, however, that DHA/HB/HSSBs funded a rather smaller proportion (about 33%) of communication equipment (*Rowley C. et al. Communication Aids Provision. Rheumatology and Rehabilitation, University of Leeds 1986 p. 42*).

13.5.4.1. Speech therapy department loan. Speech therapy departments sometimes have their own budgets with which to buy and then loan equipment (*see eg 7th Annual Report of the Assistive Communication Aids Centre, Frenchay Hospital, Bristol. For 1988, p. 8*).

Where a successful trial loan from a CAC or from the department's own small stock of equipment has taken place, the equipment is sometimes bought by the speech therapy department for more permanent loan.

Circular guidance (England, 1988) recommends that DHAs consider 'the provision of communication aids within the District speech therapy services' (*HN(88)26*).

13.5.4.2. Consultant prescription. Consultants have the power to prescribe any item of equipment which is clinically necessary (5.2.4.1.).

Circular guidance (England, 1984) states that, when a patient is referred to a CAC, the health authority of the referring consultant is expected to provide the aids that may be recommended by the centre. 'It will be the responsibility of the patient's own consultant to prescribe such aids' (*HN(84)12*).

CACs sometimes prefer consultants to undertake to fund any equipment needed, before their patient visits the centre (13.3.3.2.). Even where a consultant makes such an undertaking in good faith, he or she may be unable to persuade the health authority or board to buy the equipment (*see eg 6th Annual Report of the Assistive Communication Aids Centre, Frenchay Hospital, Bristol. For 1987, p. 4*).

13.5.5. Social services/social work dept. SSD/SWDs sometimes fund communication aids (eg following assessment at a CAC.)

However costs can seem prohibitive, and there is evidence that SSD/SWD provision lags behind DHA/HB, voluntary organisation funding and private purchase (*see eg Rowley C. et al. Communication Aids Provision. Rheumatology and Rehabilitation, University of Leeds 1986 p. 42*).

13.5.6. Northern Ireland HSSB loan. Following assessment by a speech therapist and/or the communication advice centre (CAC) in Belfast, recommendation is made to the person's own HSSB unit of management for funding (*Verbal communication: CAC, 1989*).

13.5.7. Voluntary organisations. Where statutory provision fails for whatever reason, alternative funding is often sought through voluntary organisations, some of which include, for example, SEQUAL, Spastics Society (local branches), Round Table, Rotary Clubs, the Possum Trust, League of Friends, AFASIC, Electronic Aids Loan Service (R. Jefcoate).

Some voluntary bodies have banks of equipment for loan, which include communication aids (*see eg Easton J. BMJ 1988, vol. 296, No. 6616, pp. 193–5*).

13.5.8. Joint funding of communication aids. Sometimes communication aids are provided by means of joint-funding. Such funding might be by statutory authorities (eg health and education), a statutory authority and voluntary organisation, or two or more voluntary organisations.

Local SSD/SWD/HSSB guidelines might be established with respect to joint funding, for example:

- communication aids for children of school age are equally and jointly funded by the SSD, DHA and LEA;
- for other people they are equally and joint funded by the SSD and DHA.
- if any one of the statutory bodies cannot meet its share of the expenditure, the shortfall is sought from charities. It is agreed that assessment be carried out by the DHA speech therapy dept., and that the DHA store, re-issue and repair the equipment (*Midlands SSD (3) 1990*).

13.5.9. Specialist educational micro-technology centre provision. Centres such as the ACE Centre or CALL project (27.3.2./Box 27.2.) are not designed to loan equipment on a long-term basis: although they do so, to some extent, on a short-term trial basis. Otherwise they make recommendations and referral, as appropriate, to education authorities, for example.

Special rehabilitation centres (29.) are likely, following assessment, to make recommendations, where appropriate, for the provision of communication aids to the relevant local authority of the person.

13.5.10. Manufacturer/supplier loan. Some manufacturers/suppliers loan equipment, although the loan might be only for a week or two (which may not be long enough for assessment/trial purposes), and a rental might be charged (*Information on the ACE Centre. ACE Centre 1989*).

13.5.11. Waiting times. The different sources of possible responsibilty for funding can lead to waiting times, while responsibility is agreed.

Even if responsibility is clear there may be waiting times. A Parliamentary answer on the subject of laryngectomy aids explained that they are normally prescribed by consultants, but that the provision of the aid, 'is dependent on the ability of individual health authorities to meet the cost and this can cause delay in provision' (*Weekly Hansard no.1361, 11-15 Nov. 1985 Written answers 11 Nov. 1985, Col. 88*).

13.5.12. Private purchase. People sometimes buy communication aids out of personal choice; because they are unable to obtain the equipment through statutory channels; or because they do not know about statutory provision.

Prior (sometimes multi-disciplinary) assessment helps appropriate choice of equipment, and CACs and DLCs can be used in this respect by people, who intend to privately purchase equipment (*see eg, Stowe, J* et al. *Acquisition and Use of Communication Aids by Those Buying Aids Directly from the Supplier. British Journal of Occupational Therapy. 1988: 51; 3, 97–100*).

Private purchase is probably a significant method of obtaining speech aids (*see eg Rowley C.* et al. *Communication Aids Provision. Rheumatology and Rehabilitation, University of Leeds 1986 p. 42*).

13.5.13. REMAP is a special organisation consisting of panels of engineers and other professionals who can undertake to make 'one-off' solutions to equipment problems (29.3.).

13.6. Charges

Loan of communication aids is usually free, as undertaken by the DHA/HB/HSSB, the CAC or SSD/SWD. SSD/SWDs and HSSBs (under social services functions) do have the power to charge, but this power is rarely used (30.2.).

13.7. Maintenance and repair

Maintenance and repair of electronic communication aids might be undertaken by the manufacturer/supplier, either in direct contact with the user or via the loan source.

14 Equipment for people with hearing impairment

Personal hearing aid

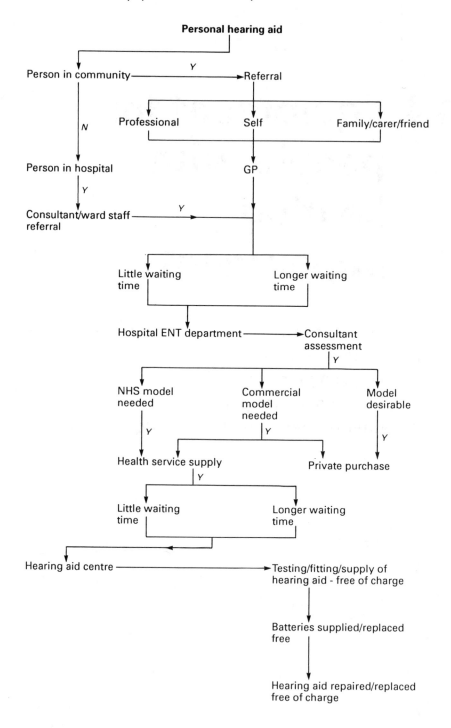

Environmental daily living equipment need for people with hearing impairment

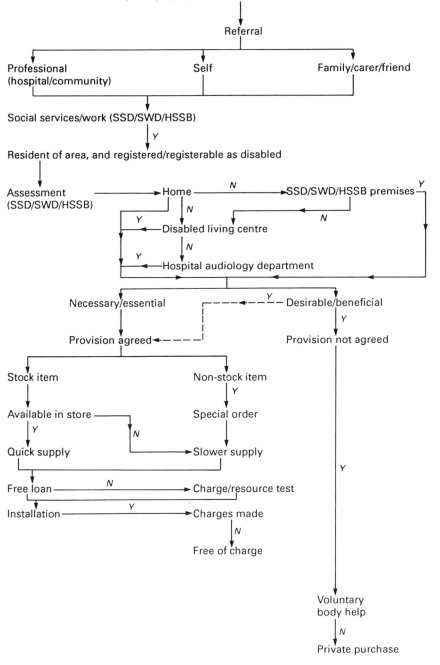

Introduction

Type of equipment

Equipment for people with hearing impairment includes both personal hearing aids and environmental equipment. Personal hearing aids include:

- in-the-ear hearing aids;
- behind-the-ear hearing aids;
- spectacle and bodyworn hearing aids;

Enviromental daily living equipment includes for example:

- visual doorbells;
- visual alarm systems;
- listening and text aids for television and telephone.

Responsibility for provision

Personal (body/head worn) hearing aids (including batteries) are available, free of charge, through the health service:

- district health authorities (DHAs, England and Wales);
- health boards (HBs, England and Wales);
- health and social services boards (HSSBs, Northern Ireland).

Environmental equipment for people with hearing impairment is available through different channels depending on how the primary purpose of the equipment is perceived. It can be provided by social services, education services, or employment services:

- social services:
  - social services departments (SSDs, England and Wales);
  - social work departments (SWDs, Scotland);
  - HSSBs (Northern Ireland);
- education services:
  - local education authorities (LEAs, England/Wales, Scotland);
  - education and library boards (ELBs, Northern Ireland);
- employment services:
  - Employment Service (ES, England/Wales, Scotland);
  - Department of Economic Development (DED, Northern Ireland).

Personal hearing aids

Referral for personal hearing aids is normally through the general practitioner (GP) to a hospital consultant in an ear, nose and throat (ENT) department (sometimes called an audiology department); and from there, following assessment, to a hearing aid centre (which may or may not be attached to the hospital ENT/audiology department).

Occasionally, GP referral is direct to a hearing aid centre. Audiology technicians sometimes make visits to housebound people, to carry out evaluation, testing, fitting.

Waiting times for both hospital ENT department and hearing aid centre appointments vary from area to area.

Provision. At least two visits to the hearing aid centre are usually necessary for initial testing and taking of a mould; and then for fitting of the hearing aid and permanent mould. The centre can be based, for example, at a hospital, sometimes at a health centre, or sometimes it is mobile.

Follow-up and rehabilitation. Hearing therapists (of whom there is a shortage), and sometimes audiology technicians, provide follow-up services to ensure that the hearing aid is appropriate and being used effectively. Such follow-up activities tend to be exceptional, and rehabilitation services for people with hearing impairment are perceived to be poor.

Private purchase. About 20% of people with a hearing aid buy it themselves privately; a wider range of aids and quicker service are amongst the advantages of private supply. Quality of service in the private sector varies.

Environmental daily living equipment for people with hearing impairment

Referral. Referral to the SSD/SWD/HSSB for environmental equipment is open; it can be self, family, carer, friend or professional referral. There are specialist social workers for the deaf who undertake assessment; sometimes occupational therapists or other SSD/SWD/HSSB staff also assess.

Assessment might take place at the client's own home, or at SSD/SWD/HSSB, voluntary body, disabled living centre (DLC) or hospital audiology clinic premises, all of which might have a demonstration display of equipment.

Provision is usually made free of charge by the SSD/SWD/HSSB, although the power to charge does exist and the client is sometimes asked to meet installation costs.

Sometimes a voluntary body undertakes assessment and provision by agreement, on behalf of the SSD/SWD/HSSB.

Maintenance and technical support are normally provided either by the SSD/SWD/HSSB or by the manufacturer/supplier of the equipment.

Environmental equipment for people with hearing impairment and an educational or employment need is discussed elsewhere (27., 28.).

14.1. Type of equipment

Examples of both personal hearing aids, and environmental daily living equipment for people with hearing impairment, are given in Box 14.1.

14.2. Legislative basis for provision of equipment with hearing impairment

Hearing aids are not mentioned specifically in legislation; but various government guidelines, concerning health service provision of personal hearing aids, exist and are referred to, as appropriate, in this chapter.

14.2.1. Legislative basis for provision of personal hearing aids. The provision of personal hearing aids by the health service is covered by the DHA/HB/HSSB duty to provide 'medical services' *(NHS Act 1977 s.3; NHS(Scotland) Act 1978 s.36; SI 1972/1265 HPSS(NI) Order 1972 a.5)*.

14.2.2. Basis for the provision of environmental daily living equipment for people with hearing impairment. Other than explicit mention of telephone and television, such equipment is not mentioned in legislation specifically, but is covered by the term 'facilities'.

14.2.2.1. Basis for provision of environmental daily living equipment in general. The provision of environmental daily living equipment in general is covered by the SSD/SWD/HSSB duty to make arrangements (where the need is identified) for 'the provision of any additional facilities designed to secure ... greater safety, comfort or convenience' *(CSDPA 1970 s.2(1)(e); CSDP(NI)A 1978 s.2(e))*.

14.2.2.1.1. The basis for provision of telephone (and equipment to use the telephone) lies in the SSD/SWD/HSSB duty concerning: 'the provision for that person of, or assistance to that person in obtaining, a telephone and any special equipment necessary to enable him to use a telephone' *(CSDPA 1970 s.2(1)(h); CSDP(NI)A 1978 s.2(h)*.

14.2.2.1.2. The basis for the provision of television lies in the SSD/SWD/HSSB duty concerning: 'the provision for that person of, or assistance to that person in obtaining ... television ...' *(CSDPA 1970 s.2(1)(b); CSDP(NI)A 1978 s.2(b))*.

14.2.2.2. General welfare legislation. The above relatively specific legislation reinforces welfare legislation which covers provision of services to people with disabilities, more generally (2.2.2.).

14.2.2.3. Request for assessment. More recent legislation places a duty on SWD/HB/HSSBs to assess a person with a disability, if requested by the disabled person, or the carer of the disabled person (not yet in force in Northern Ireland) (2.2.3.).

Box 14.1: Examples of equipment for people with hearing impairment

B14.1.1. Personal hearing aids

B14.1.1.1. In-the-ear hearing aids (not normally supplied by the health service), moulded individually to the ear, are of two main types:
- all-in-the ear aids: fit into the bowl of the ear;
- canal aids (for mild hearing loss) which are smaller and fit into the canal of the ear (*RNID leaflet. Hearing aids – Questions and Answers*).

B14.1.1.2. Behind-the-ear aids (there is a health service standard range) consist of a mould worn in the ear and a plastic unit worn behind the ear (*RNID Questions and Answers leaflet*).

The mould worn in the ear is usually transparent and the unit behind the ear usually pink; dark brown units are also available to blend with other skin or hair colour (*RNID leaflet. NHS Hearing aids*).

B14.1.1.3. Spectacle hearing aids have the hearing aid mould fitted to the frame arm(s).

B14.1.1.4. Bodyworn aids (health service models available) consist of an amplifier box worn on the chest for example, connected to an earphone and mould in the ear (*RNID leaflet. Hearing Aids – Questions and Answers*). Controls allow 'alteration of maximum gain, maximum output and tone', and can be either user-or technician-adjustable (*RNID NHS Hearing aids leaflet*).

B14.1.1.5. Non-electric hearing (prescribable through health service) aids include ear trumpets and conversation tubes.

B14.1.2. Environmental hearing aids include:

- loud doorbells;
- visual doorbell systems;
- flashing or vibrating bedside alarms (eg clocks, baby alarms);
- fire alarms (eg visual or vibrating);
- smoke detectors (eg with vibrating pad);
- listening devices for television, including microphone or plug-in listening aids, amplified headphones, loop systems and infra-red systems;
- televisions or television adaptors to enable subtitling reception;
- telephone aids including:
  - amplifiers or inductive couplers for use with personal hearing aids;
  - keyboard and visual display communication sytems;
  - loud telephone bells, vibrating and visual signals are available (*see RNID Aids to Daily Living leaflet*).

14.2.3. Provision of environmental equipment for an employment or education need is discussed elsewhere (27. and 28.).

14.3. Personal hearing aids

14.3.1. Referral, assessment and provision

14.3.1.1. General practitioners (GPs) are the main 'entry' point to hospital assessment of a hearing problem, by outpatient referral to an ENT department. GPs are likely to treat minor ear infections or an accumulation of wax themselves.

Circular guidance (Scotland, 1982), for example, states that it is important that domciliary health and social work personnel should be alert, when visiting housebound elderly and disabled people, to hearing impairment, with a view to

GP referral (*Joint circular NHS 1982(GEN)7, SWSG 1982/2. Care of the Eyesight and Hearing of Elderly and Disabled People*).

14.3.1.1.1. Factors affecting referral. There are sometimes various obstacles to effective identification of hearing loss and referral by GPs (see Box 14.2 for examples).

Box 14.2: Factors affecting effective identification of hearing loss and referral by GPs include:

- elderly people might not seek help in the first place (*Hearing aids. The case for change. RNID 1988 p. 6*);
- people might not be aware of the hearing loss, which onsets slowly, and which family members imperceptibly compensate for (*Pedley K.M. Earlier referral of adult patients with hearing loss. Update. 1988, 36(15) 1837–43*);
- a stigma might be felt in relation to the disability of hearing loss, and to the wearing of a hearing aid;
- people might be inhibited by the inaccessibility of the health service system in terms of geography and complexity (*Stephens SDG. Journal of the Royal Society of Medicine 1982. 75; 137*).
- the GP might not become aware of the problem (eg the GP's surgery is often quiet and the conversation of limited context) (*Pedley K.M. Earlier referral of adult patients with hearing loss. Update. 1988, 36(15) 1837–43*);
- the GP might be aware of long hospital waiting lists and either not refer or delay referral (*SHHD. Management of ENT Services in Scotland. HMSO 1989 p. 44*);
- GP involvement and interest can vary (for example, in relation to children) according to local historical factors and the GP's own interests (*SHHD. Management of ENT Services in Scotland. SHHD 1989 p. 18*);
- there is sometimes a lack of 'positive' attitude by the GP to hearing loss in the case of elderly people who might be told that 'it is to be expected at their age' (*Written communication: RNID, 1990; Hearing aids. The case for change. RNID, 1988 p. 6*).

14.3.1.1.2. Direct GP referral to a hearing aid centre. GPs sometimes directly refer people to hearing aid centres. (Very rarely, a GP holds a regular special clinic for people with hearing problems).

Benefits of such direct referral (or 'open access') are time-saving (*eg HAS/SSI(88) 1988 E.496, p. 34; The case for change. RNID 1988 p. 8*), given long hospital waiting lists, although this has been disputed (*see eg Watson C. Provision of hearing aids: Does specialist assessment cause delay? BMJ 1989;299,437–9*).

14.3.1.2. Referral of children. Apart from GPs, other professionals might identify hearing problems in children.

14.3.1.2.1. (Senior) Clinical medical officers (SCMO/CMOs) in the community child health services might refer children to consultants and themselves monitor the use of hearing aids.

14.3.1.2.2. Health visitors carry out a great deal of screening of very young children, and a report (Scotland, 1989) on the ENT service recommends that 'all such staff should be encouraged by Health Boards to develop their skills and knowledge of this work' (*SHHD. The Management of ENT Services in Scotland. HMSO 1989 p. 18*).

14.3.1.2.3. Audiology technicians carry out screening of children in some areas;

school nurses are sometimes involved in various hearing screening programmes; and educational audiologists, employed by education departments, are teachers of the deaf with other qualifications to assess hearing loss and compensatory aids and equipment (*SHHD. The Management of ENT Services in Scotland HMSO 1989 p. 19–20*).

14.3.1.2.4. Paedo-audiology clinics. Children are sometimes referred to paedo-audiology clinics; specialist child hearing clinics (*Written communication. RNID, 1990*).

14.3.1.3. Hospital consultant assessment and prescription. Initially people are usually referred to an ear, nose, throat (ENT) clinic by their GP where they are normally seen by an ENT consultant, an audiology physician or an otologist.

If a hearing aid is required, the consultant prescribes it and refers the person to a hearing aid centre for audiometric testing and hearing aid provision.

14.3.1.3.1. Community audiology physicians carry out specific audiology work with children (*Written communication: RNID*).

14.3.1.3.2. Hospital inpatients. Circular guidance (Scotland, 1982), for example, states that hospital staff should be watchful, and should refer inpatients who appear to have an hearing impairment to a specialist consultant (*Joint circular NHS 1982(GEN)7, SWSG 1982/2 Care of the Eyesight and Hearing of Elderly and Disabled People*).

14.3.1.4. Waiting times. Waiting times vary from none to weeks and months, for both hospital consultant and hearing aid centre appointments (*Hearing Aids. The case for change. RNID 1988 p. 7*).

14.3.1.4.1. Quicker appointments. Referral is sometimes speeded up by the following methods, for example:
- direct GP referral system (14.3.1.1.2.);
- 'special' hearing aid clinics or priority appointments (eg for people with multiple disability, whose employment is at risk, who have medical priority, expectant women or mothers with young children or those who have already used (private) aids successfully) (*Grover BC. Johnson JA. Survey of some procedures employed in the National Health Service to accelerate the provision of hearing aids. RNID 1986*).

14.3.1.5. Guidelines on hearing aid prescription. Government guidance exists, concerning the provision of personal hearing aids through the health service.

These include reference to, for example, the range of health service hearing aids as including headworn, bodyworn, electric, non-electric aids; the provision of

---

Box 14.3: Government guidelines on hearing aid provision through the health service

B14.3.1. Standard health service aids. DH/WO (informally apply to Northern Ireland) guidelines state:

'An extensive range of electronic hearing aids, covering both head worn and body worn types, is available to patients under the National Health Service. Some non-electric types are also available. Most patients in need of a hearing aid will be able to benefit from the models now available in the NHS range' (*MHM 50 NWTRHA p. 18*).

B14.3.2. Commercial hearing aids through the health services. DH/DHSS/(NI) guidance states that a health authority (board) has discretion to 'make its own arrangements for the supply of appropriate commercial models of hearing aid to patients of any age' if there is 'exceptional medical need' which a health service hearing aid cannot meet (*Services for Hearing Impaired People. Information sheet. DHSS/DHSS (NI), 1985*).

Other DH/WO (informally apply to Northern Ireland) guidelines also note the discretion of the consultant to prescribe exceptionally when he or she 'considers that an adult, young person, or child requires an aid outside the NHS range' (*MHM 50 NWTRHA p. 18*).

SHHD guidance seems to restrict this consultant discretion to children and young persons in full-time education (*MHM 50 SHHD p. 26*). (*Note:* it has been pointed out that in Scotland the supply of special non-NHS hearing aids to adults is not common and is made only in cases of severe deafness. Most such supply is to children (see below). However, it is also pointed out that most of these children 'who need the more sophisticated non-NHS appliances, will continue to require them for the duration of their lives' (*SHHD. Management of ENT services in Scotland. HMSO 1989, p. 44*).

B14.3.3. Children: radio microphone hearing aids. DH/DHSS(NI) guidance states:

'In addition, in respect of children, there may be occasions when normal development could be enhanced by the use of a radio microphone hearing aid, issued on the recommendation of a consultant. These aids were originally developed to assist partially hearing children receiving education in ordinary schools. It is now recognised that children can also benefit from the use of these aids in the home environment. Assessment of the hearing aid needs of young children is commonly made on a multi-disciplinary basis so that the child's needs both in and out of school may be considered. Therefore Health Authorities will need to liaise closely with their corresponding Education Authorities.' (*Services for Hearing Impaired People. Information sheet. DHSS/DHSS (NI), 1985*) (*Note:* this statement does not really seem to clarify whether the responsibility for such radio microphone hearing aids rests with health or education).

B14.3.4. Spare aid – duplication. DH/DHSS(NI) guidance states: 'With the exception of patients with a severe impairment of hearing and vision, spare aids should not be provided to individual patients. However, it will be helpful if a pool of spare aids can be maintained in battery issuing centres for urgent replacements' (*Services for Hearing Impaired People. Information sheet. DHSS/DHSS(NI) 1985*).

B14.3.5. Ear moulds. DH/DHSS(NI) guidance states: 'The use of high quality ear moulds is essential for high power aids'. (*Services for Hearing Impaired People. Information sheet. DHSS/DHSS(NI) 1985*).

commercial hearing aids to anyone if there is a medical need; the provision of radio microphone aids for pupil and teacher (for details see Box 14.3).

14.3.1.6. Radio microphone hearing aids are special hearing aids which include a radio transmitter microphone used by teacher and a receiver by the pupil. They are generally supplied either by a DHA/HB or HSSB (under health service functions) or by a LEA or ELB (as part of education services).

A report (Scotland, 1989) suggests that responsibility should be health rather than educational since they are personal hearing aids, and the person will continue to need the aid after leaving school (*SHHD. Management of ENT Services. HMSO, 1989 p. 25*).

DH/DHSS(NI) guidance is unclear, but possibly suggests health responsibilty by mentioning consultant recommendation, and the fact that the aid is useful in the home, as well as in the school environment (*Services for Hearing Impaired People. DH/DHSS(NI), 1985*) (Box 14.3.3.).

14.3.1.7. Hearing aid centre assessment and provision. Referral from the hospital ENT department to the hearing aid centre can be quick, on the same day, for example, or take up to 8 weeks (*Hearing aids. The case for change. RNID, 1988 p. 7*).

At the hearing aid centre audiometric testing is carried out and a mould-impression taken (sometimes a temporary mould and hearing aid is provided at this first visit).

Provision and fitting of the hearing aid and permanent mould usually takes place on a second visit (*Hearing aids. The case for change. RNID, 1988, p. 7*).

14.3.1.7.1. Mobile hearing aid centres. Where there is no local hearing aid centre, a mobile hearing aid unit sometimes operates to supplement the nearest hospital facilities (*eg HAS/SSI(89) E.512 p. 27*).

14.3.1.7.2. Home visits by audiology technicians. Home visits to both individuals' and residential homes are sometimes made by audiology technicians to house-bound patients, but this is not an extensive service (*Hearing aids. The case for change. RNID, 1988, p. 8*).

14.3.1.7.3. Audiological scientists are often in charge of hearing aid centres and audiological clinics (*Written communication: RNID, 1990*).

14.3.1.7.4. Alternative to an audiology clinic or hearing aid centre. The distribu-tion of audiology clinics and hearing aid centres is uneven. Apart from mobile hearing aid centres (14.3.1.7.1.) there are other possibilities. The example in Box 14.4 is deliberately atypical to illustrate the possible diversity:

> ### Box 14.4: Example: 'open hearing clinic' for children
>
> Referral is made by school doctors, community physicians, head and class teachers, general practitioners, speech therapists, health visitors and parents. Appointments are arranged at health centres in three towns, and assessments made at the health centres, schools or individual homes.
>
> The testing is carried out by special teachers for the deaf. Referral to ENT departments is suggested as appropriate. GPs seem to be happy with a system which compensates for the lack of an audiological physician in the area (*Allen TJ., Richardson T. Providing Open Hearing Clinics in a Rural Area of Cambridgeshire. Health Visitor 1988,61;2:52-55*).

14.3.2. Repair and replacement. Audiology clinics and hearing aid centres carry out a great deal of work on hearing aids.

Thus, for example, one hospital centre in 1987 undertook the fitting of 1,500 hearing aids and the repair of 15,000 (not including battery replacement) (*HAS/SSI(88)E.496 1988*).

Some hearing aid centres recommend that hearing aids be routinely checked every 6 months. Replacements are available free of charge, although, in theory, a charge can be made if the replacement is needed due to an act or omission of the patient (30.1.6.2.)

14.3.2.1. Battery replacement. Replacement batteries are available from hearing aid centres, and sometimes from health centres.

DH/WO (informally applying to Northern Ireland) and SHHD guidelines state that batteries should be supplied free of charge through the health service (*MHM 50 NWTRHA p. 18; MHM 50 SHHD p. 26*).

14.3.2.1.1. Batteries for commercial hearing aids

14.3.2.1.1.1. England, Wales, Northern Ireland. DH/WO (informally apply to Northern Ireland) guidelines also state, concerning commercial hearing aids batteries that:

- they should be provided free to patients who have been issued with commercial aids through the health service;
- they can also be provided free to patients who have purchased aids privately, in cases where consultants are satisfied that the aid is suitable;
- where commercial aids require batteries not purchased through central contracts, health authorities should make local arrangements for their supply (*Services for Hearing Impaired People, Information Sheet, DHSS/DHSS(NI) 1985*).

14.3.2.1.1.2. Scotland. The above applies, except that people who have bought commercial hearing aids, have, in any case, to purchase their own batteries (*Verbal and written communication. SHHD, 1990*).

14.3.2.2. Special hearing aid maintenance and replacement. DH guidelines state that: 'Health Authorities will remain responsible for servicing and replacing special hearing aids purchased for individual patients through the NHS' (*Services for Hearing Impaired People, Information Sheet, DHSS/DHSS(NI) 1985*).

14.3.2.3. Earmould replacement. DH/WO (informally apply to Northern Ireland) guidelines state: 'Young children with high power aids will usually need to have their earmoulds replaced frequently. If feedback occurs, or the earmould causes discomfort, then a replacement is likely to be necessary.' (*Services for Hearing Impaired People. Information Sheet, DH/DHSS(NI), 1985.*)

14.3.3. Follow-up

14.3.3.1. Level of follow-up. Follow-up and rehabilitation services are perceived to be generally poor (*see eg Hearing aids. The case for change. RNID, 1988 p. 13*).

A report (*SHHD, 1989*) found that 'rehabilitation provision for the deaf is poor, fragmented and inadequately organised' (*SHHD. Management of the ENT Services in Scotland. HMSO 1989, p. 43*). Inadequate time for fitting, counselling, and a shortage of technicians and hearing therapists may affect follow-up after initial provision (*Hearing aids. The case for change. RNID 1988, p. 13*).

14.3.3.2. New equipment developments. Because of continued development in the field of hearing aids, more powerful aids can be supplied to 'keep up' with further deterioration. Thus follow-up, re-testing and re-referral are required. Hearing therapists, and in their absence sometimes audiology technicians, can carry this out (*SHHD. Management of ENT Services in Scotland. HMSO 1989 p. 44*).

14.3.3.3. Educational audiologists. For children at school, educational audiologists may be the best equipped to provide monitoring of hearing aid use and technical supervision (*SHHD. Management of ENT Services in Scotland. HMSO, 1989 p. 25*)).

14.3.3.4. Level of use of hearing aids. There is evidence that many people do not use their hearing aids (*Abstracts. British Journal of Audiology, 1985, 19, 291-292; Corrado OJ. Hearing aids. BMJ,296,2.1.88:33-35; Hearing aids. The case for change. RNID, 1988 p. 7*), and that people (in residential homes for example) possess hearing aids which do not function (due, for example, to flat batteries or wax blockage) (*Anand JK, Court I. Hearing loss leading to impaired ability to communicate in residents of homes for the elderly. BMJ 1989. 298 1429-1430*).

14.3.3.5. Follow-up: hearing therapists. Hearing therapists are experts in helping people to manage hearing difficulties, by instructing 'a patient in communication skills including the use of hearing aids, environmental aids, lipreading and auditory training in hospital, community and domiciliary situations'(HC(78)11).

14.3.3.5.1. Shortage of hearing therapists. There are, however, very few hearing therapists in existence: in 1987 there were only 60 within the NHS in England; and in 1989 only one in Scotland (*Weekly Hansard No. 1411 16-20 March 1987: written answers 19th March cols. 495-496; SHHD. Management of ENT services in Scotland. HMSO 1989, p. 46*).

Circular guidance (England, 1988) states the importance of hearing therapists in providing audiological rehabilitation services within DHAs (*HN(88)26*). A report recommended the establishment of hearing therapist posts in Scotland (*SHHD. Management of ENT Services in Scotland. HMSO 1989 p. 43*).

14.3.3.6. Private purchase. 20% of people obtain hearing aids privately (*Hearing aids. The case for change. RNID, 1988 p. 9*). The private sector can offer a wider range of hearing aids than the health service, inner ear hearing aids, for example. It can also sometimes offer a quicker service.

Some parts of the private sector provide high standards of service, while there is also evidence, despite the Hearing Aid Council (under the regulation of which, the private sector operates), that private advertising, sales techniques and effectiveness of provision sometimes leave much to be desired (*Hearing aids. The case for change. RNID 1988 pp. 9–11*).

14.4. Environmental daily living equipment for people with hearing impairment

14.4.1. Referral

14.4.1.1. Self or professional referral. Referral to the SSD/SWD/HSSB, or any voluntary organisation undertaking services on its behalf, can be open, allowing self-referral or referral by friends, family and carers.

Alternatively, prior attendance at an audiology clinic or hearing aid centre, or referral from another professional, is sometimes required (*So little for so many. A survey of provision to hearing impaired people by social services departments. RNID research report No. 1 (1987) p. 7,12,17*).

Professionals and services, referring people for assessment for environmental equipment, include, for example, education departments, housing departments, hospital day centres, hearing aid (audiology) clinics, consultant geriatricians, consultant otologists, speech therapists, hearing therapists, occupational therapists, health visitors district nurses and GPs (*So little for so many. A survey of provision to hearing impaired people by social services departments. RNID research report No. 1 (1987) p. 8,13,18*).

14.4.1.2. Registration. Questions of registration as a disabled person are detailed elsewhere (2.3.2.). Registration is not compulsory. All that is required is 'registerability' (that is, eligibility for registration).

However, it would appear that (1987), despite government emphasis that actual registration is not necessary, some SSDs and HSSBs do require formal registration, before providing services in the form of environmental equipment (*So little for so many. A survey of provision to hearing impaired people by social services departments. RNID research report No. 1 (1987) pp. 12, 17*).

14.4.1.2.1. Circular guidance (England, Wales, Northern Ireland), states that formal procedures, to determine the eligibility of hearing impaired people to receive services, do not exist (*LAC 17/74; WOC(74)93; HSS(OS5A)4/78*).

14.4.2. Assessment and provision services

14.4.2.1. Personnel

14.4.2.1.1. Social workers for the deaf. SSD/SWD/HSSBs often employ specialist social workers to provide services to people with hearing impairment. They are variously qualified, holding, for example, the CQSW/Home Office Letter of Recognition, Certificate in Social Service, Deaf Welfare Examination Board or Approved for mental health work (*SSI. Say it Again. DHSS, 1988 p. 35*).

Equally, many staff working with the deaf have no special qualification (*SSI. Say it again, 1988 p. 1; SHHD. Management of ENT Services in Scotland. HMSO, 1989 p. 47*).

Sometimes occupational therapists (OTs) assess for environmental equipment for people with hearing impairment (*SSI. Say it again. DHSS 1988 p. 16*).

14.4.2.1.2. Organisation. A specialist team sometimes provides services, including the assessment of equipment, for people with hearing impairment.

The existence of such teams, and their organisation, is likely to vary. There can, for example, be a single sensory handicap team, or one or more separate specialist teams for hearing impairment, within one SSD (*SSI. Say it again. DHSS, 1988 p. 7*).

Specific members of staff might be formally or informally responsible for the provision and delivery of environmental equipment.

14.4.2.2. Voluntary organisations. In some areas, social workers for the deaf might work for a voluntary organisation, which is in receipt of a grant from the local SSD/SWD/HSSB, according to an 'agency agreement' (*see eg SHHD. Management of ENT Services in Scotland. HMSO 1988 p. 46*).

Voluntary organisations undertaking such 'agency' work have different responsibilities depending on the nature of the agreement: responsibilities sometimes include assessment for, and provision of, equipment (*eg Midlands SSD (21) guidance received 1989/1990*).

14.4.2.3. Assessment location can be:

- at the person's home;
- on SSD/SWD/HSSB premises;
- at a hearing aid centre or audiology clinic which holds appropriate equipment for demonstration purposes;
- at local voluntary organisation premises, where there is a demonstration display of equipment (*So little for so many. A survey of provision to hearing impaired people by social services departments. RNID research report No. 1 (1987) pp. 9, 14, 19*).

14.4.2.4. Local guidelines on environmental equipment assessment and provision.

SSD/SWD/HSSBs sometimes operate according to written guidance on the assessment and provision of environmental equipment for people with hearing impairment. The guidance might contain general advice for staff on the nature of hearing impairment and assessment for equipment, as well as detail both general and specific (to particular equipment) provision criteria.

The existence of such guidance, and its form and content, varies from area to area (see Box 14.5 for examples).

Box 14.5: Local SSD/SWD/HSSB guidelines on the provision of environmental daily living equipment for people with hearing impairment

B14.5.1. General guidelines.
Example 1.

- user has a moderate, moderate/severe, severe or profound hearing loss;
- provision of equipment would reduce their dependence on carers/outside agencies;
- provision would greatly increase the user's quality of life (*London SSD (45) guidelines 1989*).

Example 2. Equipment can be supplied if, in addition to general conditions (applicable to daily living equipment in general), the following specific conditions are met:

- the client has moderate/severe, severe or profound hearing loss;
- provision would mean reduction of dependence on carers; great improvement in quality of life (*London SSD guidelines received 1989*).

Example 3. Equipment is available to people who have no hearing or impaired hearing. The service is not age or means dependent. The equipment is not to be used for employment or business use. The equipment is on loan only. The main daily living needs to be met by equipment are listening, warning, telephone (*Southwest England SSD guidelines received 1989*).

Example 4. General criteria. Equipment is available to people who are resident within the SSD area and in approved cases to people on an SSD placement outside the area. The service is available with hearing impairment irrespective of age. Equipment is not dependent on ability to pay, but must be used for personal rather than business purposes. Main areas of provision include listening, warning telephone equipment (*West of England SSD (40) guidelines received 1989*).

B14.5.2. Guidelines specific to equipment types (the following specific criteria are normally operative once general criteria have been met).

Example 1. Equipment such as telephone couplers, hearing cushions, induction loop systems must be technically assessed for by an audiologist before the equipment can be supplied by the HSSB (*HSSB guidelines received. 1989*).

Example 2. Flashing doorbells can be assessed for by specialist social workers.

Before supplying a flashing doorbell certain points should be checked including (correct) use of a personal hearing aid, considering a different type (ie louder or different ringing tone or pattern) of ordinary doorbell, repositioning of present bell (*HSSB guidelines received 1989*).

Example 3. Television and telephone aids. Certain factors should be checked including:

- extent and social effect of hearing loss;
- details of personal hearing aid;
- carrying out of a recent demonstration and assessment of the proposed aid at the audiology department;
- client's attitude to proposed aid;
- possibility of private purchase (*HSSB guidelines received 1989*).

Example 4. Telephone text terminals. Assessment includes factors such as degree of hearing loss, degree of isolation, ability or potential to use the terminal and registration.

The SSD provides a flashing telephone light, if necessary, and maintains the terminal. The client is responsible for the installation (payment and arrangements) of the telephone line and appropriate sockets; and also for the ordering of an appropriate telephone handset.

The client also pays for the telephone line, handset (and rental charges), and the cost of the telephone calls. The terminal is on loan and must be returned when no longer needed (*Southwest England SSD guidelines received 1989*).

Example 5. Telephone text terminal. A telephone must already be in place (unless the client also meets the criteria for telephone provision). The person would be isolated without it, wants it, and would use it at least 2 or 3 times a week, and would be seriously disadvantaged without it (*SSD guidelines received 1989*).

Example 6. Telephone amplifiers and visual indicators. Criteria include:

- prior possession of telephone (or eligibility for telephone installation);
- inability to use the telephone without additional aid;
- ability to use the phone;
- likelihood of frequent use and of serious disadvantage without use of the telephone (*Midlands Metropolitan Borough SSD guidelines received 1989*).

Example 7. Telephone text terminal. Assessment includes consideration of:

- level of hearing loss;
- degree of isolation;
- ability/potential to use terminal;
- registration of disability with the SSD.

Conditions for provision are that:

- the terminal be provided free of charge including if necessary flashing telephone light;
- the SSD maintains it;
- the terminal be for personal and not business use.

The client is responsible for the installation of a telephone line, appropriate sockets and the ordering of a suitable handset, and the cost of calls (*West of England (40) SSD 1989*).

14.4.2.4.1. Need and want/desirability. As is the case with daily living equipment in general (2.4.7.2.), SSD/SWD/HSSBs sometimes apply the distinction between necessity and desirability to environmental equipment for hearing impaired people.

Recent examples (1988) of this distinction in practice occurred when two SSDs refused to provide a telephone deaf communicating terminal on the grounds that they were not necessary but only desirable. Following a three year-long appeal (to the DH, DHSS as it was then) procedures, provision by one SSD, but not the other, eventually took place (*Disability Now 1988*).

14.4.2.5. Resources for provision of environmental daily living equipment for people with hearing impairment

14.4.2.5.1. Variable local budgets. A study (*voluntary organisation, 1989*) found that allocated money varied enormously, from 0.3 pence per head in an English northern county, to 6.7 pence in a Scottish county. Likewise, three areas of similar population numbers had budgets respectively of £13,000, £55,000 and 'no limit'.

Demand on budgets sometimes results in extra money being added to the budget towards the end of the financial year; the carrying over of a waiting list to the next financial year; or the seeking of charitable help (*A good deal for deaf children? National Deaf Childrens's Society, 1989*).

14.4.2.5.2. Installation costs. It seems to be unknown to what extent local budgets include installation charges (*A good deal for deaf children? National Deaf Childrens's Society 1989*). These can be quite high, running into several hundred pounds. For example, installation (including wiring) in some SSD/SWD/HSSBs carried out by technicians and charged to a different budget; in others it might be included within the equipment budget, whether a technician or outside contractor undertakes the work (*Verbal communication, national voluntary organisation, 1989*).

14.4.2.6. Voluntary organisations. Voluntary organisations can sometimes help people on an individual basis to obtain environmental equipment which they have failed to obtain through statutory sources.

Sometimes the SSD/SWD/HSSB suggests that the client should approach a voluntary organisation for help with equipment, when it cannot provide it, either in principle, or because of lack of local resources at the time.

14.4.3. Delivery. Arrangements for the actual delivery and installation of equipment might be undertaken by specialist social workers, by occupational therapists or by specially appointed staff with technical knowledge (*SSI. Say it Again. DHSS, 1988 pp. 16–18*).

Delivery times, following assessment, can vary from from less than one month to several months. Shortage of staff, or lack of financial resources, can account for this (*So little for so many. A survey of provision to hearing impaired people by social services departments. RNID research report No. 1 (1987) pp. 9, 14, 19*).

Installation and re-wiring is likely to be carried out either by SSD/SWD/HSSB technicians or by a contracted electrician.

14.4.4. Follow-up. Monitoring of the use of environmental equipment can be an integral part of SSD provision (*see eg SSI. Say it again DHSS, 1988, p. 18*).

Where hearing therapists (health service) exist, and make home visits, they are able to check on the correct use of environmental equipment as well as personal hearing aids.

Audiology technicians (health service) sometimes also monitor environmental equipment, as well as personal hearing aids, when making home visits.

14.4.4.1. Examples of follow-up. HSSB (Northern Ireland) local guidelines state that the audiology technician should visit a residential unit once every six months to check up on equipment (in general) and assess the hearing of the residents (*HSSB guidelines, received 1989*).

In one area of England, the DHA and SSD have collaborated to train volunteers to supply a visiting service to housebound people 'to ensure that they were utilising both personal hearing aids and environmental equipment to their full potential' (*SSI. Say it again. DHSS, 1988 p. 17*).

14.4.4.2. Technical support services can, for example, be provided by a technical services branch of the SSD/SWD or by the manufacturer/supplier of the equipment (*So little for so many. A survey of provision to hearing impaired people by social services departments. RNID research report No. 1 (1987) pp. 9, 18*).

In Northern Ireland, both the Northern Ireland Housing Executive (in relation to public sector housing) and the works department of a local hospital might provide such support (*So little for so many. A survey of provision to hearing impaired people by social services departments. RNID research report No. 1 (1987) p. 13*).

14.4.5. Charges. SSD/SWD/HSSBs have the power to charge for equipment (30.2.), though this is probably rarely used.

A report (*voluntary organisation, 1987*) found that, in Northern Ireland and Scotland, charges were not generally being made. In England and Wales, there did seem to be more financial transactions involving, for example, part payment and 'donations' (*So little for so many. A survey of provision to hearing impaired people by social services departments. RNID research report No. 1 (1987) pp. 8, 14, 18*).

14.4.5.1. Installation charges. Charges are sometimes made for electrical installation, if not for the equipment itself. Following installation and wiring by the SSD/SWD/HSSB technician or by a private contractor, the client is sometimes asked to contribute. A test of resources might be applied to determine whether the client can afford to pay for such installation charges.

Installation of telephone lines and points, for example, in connection with telephone equipment supplied by the SSD/SWD/HSSB, might be payable by the client.

14.4.6. Private purchase. Environmental equipment for people with hearing impairment is available direct from manufacturers/suppliers. British Telecom, for example, offers a wide range of telephones and telephone aids which can help people with hearing impairment.

15 Equipment for people with visual impairment

Spectacles, contact lenses, low vision aids need

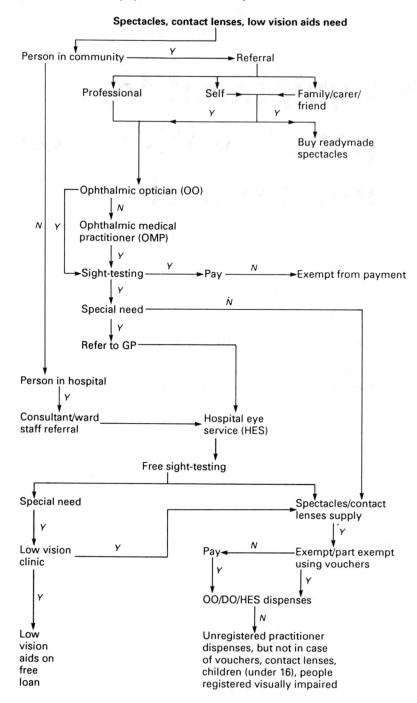

Environmental daily living equipment for people with visual impairment

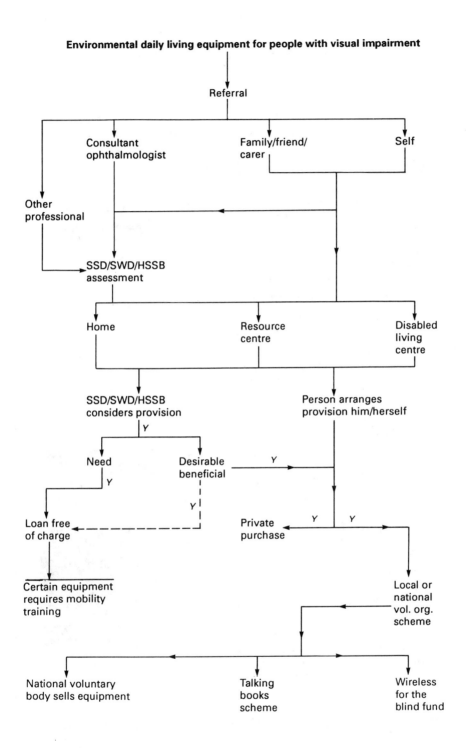

Introduction

Type of equipment. Equipment for people with visual impairment includes personal equipment, such as spectacles, contact lenses and special low vision aids; and environmental daily living equipment such as equipment with braille markings, talking books, speaking clocks, writing guides, contoured maps.

Personal equipment for visual impairment is provided in a number of ways.

Hospital eye service (HES) (including low vision clinics): assessment and prescription of spectacles, contact lenses and low vision aids.

Sight-testing is free of charge. Spectacles and contact lenses are subject to charges (full or part help with the cost is available through a health service voucher scheme). Low vision aids are prescribed on free loan(Hospital inpatients are exempt from charges anyway.)

Ophthalmic opticians (OOs) and ophthalmic medical practitioners (OMPs): assessment, prescription and dispensing (OOs only) of spectacles and contact lenses and, occasionally, low vision aids on behalf of the HES.

Sight-testing is subject to charges which are waived if a person falls into certain exemption categories, which depend on factors such as age, medical condition and financial circumstances.

Spectacles and contact lenses are subject to charges. Help with the whole or part of the cost of spectacles is available in the form of a health service voucher scheme to people who fall into certain categories (dependent on factors, such as age, medical condition, financial circumstances). The voucher scheme allows part, or all, of the cost of the appliance to be met.

Vouchers can be issued by OOs and OMPs (and accepted by OOs), who by agreement participate in the voucher scheme.

Dispensing opticians (DOs): dispensing of spectacles and contact lenses. By agreement DOs accept health service vouchers issued with the prescription.

Unregistered practitioners and spectacle shops. Unregistered practitioners dispense prescriptions for spectacles, though cannot accept health service vouchers; both unregistered practitioners and spectacle shops can sell ready-made spectacles and magnifiers.

Unregistered practitioners cannot, by law, dispense contact lenses, nor dispense at all to children under the age of 16, or to people who are registered blind or partially-sighted.

Environmental equipment for visual impairment can be provided through a number of different channels depending on how the primary purpose of the equipment is perceived. The purpose could be to meet a daily living, employment, or educational need. Statutory agencies responsible are:

- social services departments (SSDs, England and Wales);
- social work departments (SWDs, Scotland);

- health and social services boards (HSSBs, Northern Ireland);
- employment service (England, Wales, Scotland);
- department of economic development (DED, Northern Ireland);
- local education authorities (LEAs, England, Wales, Scotland);
- education and library boards (ELBs, Northern Ireland).

SSD/SWD/HSSB assessment and provision for daily living. The SSD/SWD/ HSSB has a duty to make arrangements, where it has identified an individual need, for the provision of daily living equipment in general, and, in particular, the provision of radio and telephone (and aids to use the telephone). Where appropriate, this duty applies to the provision of environmental daily living equipment for people with visual impairment.

When requested by a disabled person or his/her carer, the SSD/SWD/HSSB also has a duty to make an assessment (not yet in force in Northern Ireland). Provision is usually made in one of the following ways:

- SSD/SWD/HSSB assessment and loan of equipment (usually free of charge);
- private purchase of small items of equipment from local resource centres at reduced cost;
- direct purchase from a national voluntary organisation;
- national voluntary organisation-run-schemes including, for example, the loan of radios and talking books.

    (Local resource centres, run either by a voluntary body or by the SSD/ SWD/HPSSB hold displays of equipment for trial and assessment purposes; and act as sales points for equipment.)

Provision for employment or educational need is dealt with elsewhere (27. and 28.).

15.1. Type of equipment

Equipment for visual impairment can be divided into personal headworn appliances, low vision aids and environmental equipment for visual impairment.
    Examples are given in Box 15.1.

Box 15.1: Examples of equipment for visual impairment

B15.1.1. Personal head worn equipment includes spectacles, contact lenses, and some low vision aids.

B15.1.2. Low vision aids include:

- hand magnifiers;
- stand magnifiers (adjustable and illuminated);
- loupes (eg 'watchmaker's eye glass');
- headband magnifiers;
- spectacle magnifiers (microscopes for near vision which can be glazed or clipped on to existing spectacles);
- telescopes (distance aids: monocular, binocular, mounted on spectacle frames, handheld);
- closed circuit television (reading, writing, typing use).

B15.1.3. Environmental equipment for visual impairment includes:

- equipment with braille markings of all sorts (eg clocks, timers, thermometers);
- medicine dispensers;
- liquid level indicators;
- canes and sticks;
- braille writers;
- moon script writers;
- braille frames;
- writing guide frames;
- mobility homing devices;
- learning educational equipment (eg geometry equipment);
- contoured maps;
- speech synthesizers;
- laptop computers;
- talking books and newspapers;
- games;
- kitchen/cooking aids;
- sewing aids;
  etc.

(Many of these items of environmental equipment are included in the RNIB catalogue of equipment and games (*Equipment and Games Catalogue. RNIB, 1988).*)

15.2. Legislative basis for the provision of equipment for people with visual impairment

15.2.1. The basis for hospital eye service provision of sight-testing and optical appliances lies in the DHA/HB/HSSB duty to provide 'medical services' (*NHS Act 1977, s.3; NHS (Scotland) Act 1978, s.36; SI 1972/1265 HPSS(NI)O 1972 a.5*).

15.2.2. The basis for ophthalmic optician, and ophthalmic medical practitioner provision of health service sight testing and health service vouchers toward the cost of equipment lies in the DHA (through FPC), HB and HSSB duty to provide 'general ophthalmic services' (*GOS*) (*NHS Act 1977 s.38; NHS (Scotland) Act s.26; SI 1972/1265 HPSS(NI)O 1972 a.62*).

15.2.3. The basis for provision of environmental daily living equipment. Other than telephones and radios, environmental equipment for people with visual impairment is not mentioned specifically in legislation, but is referred to as 'facilities'.

15.2.3.1. The basis for provision of environmental daily living equipment, in general, lies in the SSD/SWD/HSSB duty, where an individual need has been identified, to 'make arrangements for . . . the provision of additional facilities for . . . greater safety, comfort or convenience' (*CSDPA 1970 s.2(1)(e); CSDP(NI)A 1978 s.2(e)*).

15.2.3.2. The basis for provision of radios lies in the duty, where an individual need has been identified, to 'make arrangements for...the provision for that person of, or assistance to that person in obtaining, wireless, television, library or similar recreational facilities' (*CSDPA 1970 s.2(1)(b); CSDP(NI)A 1978 s.2(b)*).

15.2.3.3. The basis for provision of telephone and equipment to use the telephone lies in the duty, where an individual need has been identified, to 'make arrangements for . . . the provision for that person of, or assistance to that person in obtaining, a telephone and any special equipment necessary to enable him to use a telephone' (*CSDPA 1970 s.2(1)(h); CSDP(NI)A 1978 s.2(h)*).

15.2.3.4. General welfare legislation. Provision is also covered by general welfare legislation (2.2.2.).

15.2.3.5. Legislation concerning duty to assess. Recent legislation places a duty on the SSD/SWD/HSSB (but not yet in force in Northern Ireland) to carry out an assessment if requested by a disabled person or by his/her carer (2.2.3.).

15.2.4. The basis for provision of environmental equipment for education or employment is covered elsewhere (27.2. and 28.2.).

15.3. Personal head-worn optical appliances (spectacles and contact lenses) and low vision aids: referral, assessment, provision

15.3.1. Referral for personal optical appliances

15.3.1.1. Referral to ophthalmic opticians (OOs) (also known as optometrists). There is open referral to registered ophthalmic opticians or ophthalmic medical practitioners. GPs often recommend that people go to an OO for sight-testing.

5.3.1.1.1. Remit. OOs are registered practitioners, who can test for, prescribe and make up spectacles, contact lenses and some magnifiers.

15.3.1.1.2. OO referral to the GP. If, on testing, certain problems appear, the ophthalmic optician has a duty to refer a person to their GP (*SI 1986/975 Sched.1 para 10; SI 1986/965 (S.82) Sched. 1 para 10; SR 1986/163 Sched. 1 para 10*). The GP can then refer the person on to a hospital consultant in the HES.

15.3.1.2. Referral to ophthalmic medical practitioners (OMPs). There is open referral to registered ophthalmic opticians or ophthalmic medical practitioners. GPs often recommend that people go to an OMP for sight-testing.

15.3.1.2.1. Remit. OMPs are fully qualified doctors, with special qualifications to detect eye abnormalities and disease (*Optics at a Glance, 1988 ed. FODO*). They can test for sight and prescribe spectacles, contact lenses and some magnifiers, and issue health service vouchers (Box 15.2.2.3.), for help with payment, with the prescription.

Under contract to FPC/HB/HSSBs, they are usually based in medical eye centres or in their own consulting rooms. They do not usually make up and dispense appliances, but often work with a dispensing optician.

15.3.1.2.2. OMP referral to the GP. If, on testing, certain problems appear, the OMP has a duty to refer a person to their GP (*SI 1986/975 Sched.1 para 10; SI 1986/965 (S.82) Sched. 1 para 10; SR 1986/163 Sched. 1 para 10*). The GP can then refer the person to a hospital consultant in the HES.

(As qualified specialist doctors, OMPs, in theory, have the power to refer a person direct to a hospital department to see a consultant ophthalmologist: but they would inform the person's GP in any case).

15.3.1.3. Referral to dispensing opticians (DOs). People can take prescriptions, and vouchers (for help with payment) (Box 15.2.2.3.) to any DO, who will accept them.

DOs make up, fit and supply spectacles, contact lenses and some magnifiers. They interpret a person's individual visual and fitting requirements and translate the prescription into specifications and instructions for the optical manufacturer (*Optics at a Glance FODO 1988*).

15.3.1.4. Unregistered practitioners and spectacle shops function just as any other highstreet shop; there is open access, although certain categories of person cannot be dispensed to (see below).

Readymade spectacles and magnifiers can also be found in 'non-specialist' premises (spectacle shop); for example, in a chemist's shop, a public library or large department store.

15.3.1.4.1. Remit. Unregistered practitioners can sell ready made spectacles and magnifiers. They can also dispense prescriptions.

15.3.1.4.2. Restrictions. They cannot by law dispense contact lenses, nor can they dispense spectacles to children under 16 or to registered blind or partially-sighted people. Unregistered practitioners cannot undertake formal sight-testing (*see: Opticians Act 1989 s.24); and Circular guidance: HC(89)12 Append. 1 para 24; NHS 1986(GEN)17 Memo. para 15; HSS(GHS)1/89 para 24*).

Unregistered practitioners cannot deal with prescriptions, if health service vouchers (15.3.3.1.3.) are involved.

15.3.1.5. Referral to the hospital eye service (HES). Consultant ophthalmologists work in the HES.

Low vision clinics are part of the HES and provide special services, including the free loan of low vision aids, recommended by a consultant.

15.3.1.5.1. Referral to the HES can be through a:

- general practitioner (GP);
- ophthalmic optician (via the GP);
- ophthalmic medical practitioner (via GP or with GP's knowledge);
- SSD/SWD or HSSB (social services) (for the purposes of certification by a consultant of person's blindness or partial-sight as part of the registration (15.5.) process).

15.3.1.5.2. Low vision clinics, part of the HES, treat people with more complex problems. A person is sometimes instead referred to an ophthalmic medical practitioner or ophthalmic optician (outside the hospital), who specialises in low vision work, if there is no low vision clinic easily accessible.

Low vision clinics also carry out closed circuit television assessments in relation to the provision of equipment for employment purposes (28.4.3.4).

15.3.1.5.3. Referral of hospital inpatients. Circular guidance (Scotland, 1982) states that hospital medical and nursing staff should be aware of the activities of the HES, and refer patients who appear to have a visual impairment (*Joint Circular*

NHS(GEN)7,SWSG 1982/2. Care of the Eyesight and Hearing of Elderly and Disabled People).

15.3.1.6. Domiciliary and social work personnel, are urged, by Circular guidance (Scotland, 1982), for example, to be alert to visual impairment, when they visit housbound elderly or disabled people *(Joint Circular NHS(GEN)7,SWSG 1982/2. Care of the Eyesight and Hearing of Elderly and Disabled People).*

15.3.2. Sight-testing.

15.3.2.1. OO and OMP sight-testing is free under the health service to certain categories of people. It is also free, if the testing is carried out on behalf of the HES, since HES sight-tests are anyway free of charge.

In other cases, a charge is made.

15.3.2.1.1. Free sight tests by OOs and OMPs. Registered OOs and OMPs can carry out free health service sight tests to eligible groups of people (Box 15.2.). Such health service tests are either under the general ophthalmic services (GOS), or on behalf of the hospital eye service (HES).

Practitioners who can carry out health service sight tests are under contract to the FPC/HB/HSSB (and display an approved notice to that effect) *(HC(89)12, Appendix 6 para 2; NHS 1986(GEN)17,Memo para. 1-3; HSS(GHS)1/89 para. 3).*

15.3.2.1.2. Charges for OO and OMP sight tests are made, except in the case of people who are exempt from such charges (see Box 15.2.).

Box 15.2: Charges: health service sight-testing; health service appliances

B15.2.1. Sight-testing charges

B15.2.1.1. Hospital eye service (HES). Sight tests carried out by, or on behalf of, the hospital eye service are free of charge. This is so, even if the test has to be carried out off hospital premises on behalf of the HES.

Where the test is carried out off the hospital premises, the person is given a special form by a consultant: the test can be carried out by a practitioner who displays the fact that health service sight-tests are available there.

B15.2.1.2. General ophthalmic services (GOS). Some groups are eligible, anyway, for a free GOS (health service test), even though it is not carried out under the HES:

- children under 16;
- full-time students under age of 19 at a recognised educational establishment;
- people or their partners who are receiving Income Support or Family Credit;
- those whose resources are less than or equal to their requirements and who have a DSS prescription exemption certificate;
- the registered blind or partially sighted;
- those prescribed complex lenses;
- diagnosed diabetic and glaucoma sufferers;
- close relatives (parents, brothers, sisters and children) age 40 and over of glaucoma sufferers *(Regulations: SI 1986/975 r.13 amended by SI 1985/395 r.4; SI 1986/965 r.14 amended by SI 1989/387 (S.41) r.4; SR 1986/163 r.15 as amended by SR 1989/113 r.4. Circulars: HC(89)12; NHS 1986(GEN)17; HSS(GHS)1/89).*

(Under the HES, the consultant should check whether patients fall in any of these eligible groups. If they do not, but are still being tested under the HES, they receive a

---

free sight test, but require a different form to be presented to the GOS practitioner, the OO or OMP, if the test is being carried out off hospital premises).

B15.2.2. Charges for appliances

B15.2.2.1. HES inpatients receive free glasses or contact lenses, so long as they receive the cheapest clinically necessary appliances (30.1.2.1.).

B15.2.2.2. HES outpatients

B15.2.2.2.1. HES maximum charges

B15.2.2.2.1.1.Lenses. People are liable to pay charges for spectacles or contact lenses dispensed under the HES. There are maximum charge arrangements under the HES; people should be informed of this fact. The purpose of this HES maximum charge is to protect people who need (for clinical reasons) very expensive lenses (*HC(89)12; NHS 1986(GEN)17; HSS(GHS)1/89*).

B15.2.2.2.1.2. Frames. A maximum charge for frames applies only to patients who require more expensive frames on clinical grounds. They are then charged the cost of the cheapest frame normally supplied by the DHA/HB/HSSB (*HC(89)12; NHS 1986(GEN)17; HSS(GHS)1/89*).

B15.2.2.2.1.3 Vouchers. These maximum charges operate in the context of the health service voucher scheme).

B15.2.2.3. Health service vouchers: HES and GOS. Depending on various eligibility conditions, vouchers are available corresponding to the full value of the prescription. People are then eligible for help for the full or part value of the voucher.
Vouchers can be issued by the HES, and by OOs and OMPs.
Contact lenses can only be prescribed for clinical reasons by the HES; although vouchers for spectacles can be used to contribute toward the cost of contact lenses.

B15.2.2.3.1. General conditions which must be met (other than where there is technical non-tolerance) for the issue of health service vouchers, are that:

- the person is being prescribed spectacles or contact lenses for the first time;
- the prescription has altered;
- the person's existing spectacles are no longer useable through general wear and tear (*SI 1989/396 r.8; SI 1989/392(S.46) r.8; SR 1989/114 r.8*).

B15.2.2.3.2. Specific conditions.

B15.2.2.3.2.1. Full cost. The full cost of the spectacles or contact lenses is met for:

- patients who are under 16;
- full-time students under 19;
- people (or their spouse or partner) getting Income Support or Family Credit;
- those whose resources are less than, or equal to, their requirements and who have a DSS exemption certificate AG2 (*SI 1989/396 r.8; SI 1989/392(S.46) r.8; SR 1989/114 r.8*).

B15.2.2.3.2.2. Partial cost. Part of the cost is met for:

- people who hold a prescription partial-exemption certificate on the basis of low income;
- people who require complex lenses (ie the lens has a power in any meridian of plus or minus 10 or more dioptres or is a lenticular lens) are eligible for part costs of the voucher being met;
- technical non-tolerance: people whose eye condition is altering progressively and who therefore need frequent changes of glasses or contact lenses, will need to pay only for the first pair of spectacles or contact lenses. (*SI 1989/396 r.8; SI 1989/392(S.46) r.8; SR 1989/114 r.8*).

B15.2.2.3.2.3. Voucher supplements. There are voucher supplements available for the following:

- clinically required prisms and tints;
- small frame need;
- multi-focal/vari-focal clinically required (HES only);
- contact lenses voucher for clinical reasons (HES only);
- those who because of facial characteristics need custom-made frame;
- single vision lenses and other lenses payable where a photochromic lens is prescribed for clinical reasons *(for all this see: HC(89)12; NHS 1986(GEN)17; HSS(GHS)1/89); and SI 1989/396; SI 1989/392(S.46); SR 1989/114).*

B15.2.3. War pensioners (30.3.) are able to benefit from voucher help, and help with the cost of sight-testing, under separate arrangements via the DSS War Pensions Branch at Norcross, Blackpool. This help is available only if the need is due to the condition for which the war pension is received.

B15.2.4. Repair/replacement. Children under 16 receive repair/replacement free of charge.

Adults are eligible for help with repair if they qualify for a voucher and can show that illness caused the damage or loss of the appliance. Circular guidance takes illness to include mental disorder, or any injury or disability requiring medical treatment or nursing *(SI 1989/396 r.16; SI 1989/392(S.46) r.16; SR 1989/114 r.16) (HC(89)12; NHS 1989(GEN)14; HSS(GHS)1/89).*

15.3.2.1.3. Home visits for sight-testing. Sometimes OOs or OMPs make a home visit to a person who is housebound; if the person does not qualify for a free health service test (Box 15.2.), the test will be charged for but not the visit *(SI 1990/1051; SI 1990/1048).*

It was recognised in a 1987 White Paper, that there is a lack of domiciliary sight-testing services, and that 'an extension of the services to the housebound is desirable' *(Promoting Better Health. HMSO, 1987 p. 34).*

15.3.2.2. Hospital eye service (HES) sight-tests are free of charge, and are carried out either by the HES itself, or by an OO or OMP on its behalf.

At the time of writing, it appears that waiting lists for HES sight-tests have grown, since the abolition (in April 1989) of 'universal' free health service sight-tests *(see eg Community Health News. Association of Community Health Councils. No. 49, December 1989 p. 1).*

Sometimes the HES carries out home sight tests, if the person is housebound and the GP requests such a test (see eg DH leaflet G11 1989 p. 15). These are free of charge.

15.3.2.3. Dispensing opticians. Registered dispensing opticians are qualified to make up and dispense, but not to sight-test.

If the dispensing optician is selling readymade spectacles, it is important that nothing is done, for example, by the receptionist selling the glasses 'which could conceivably be construed as conducting a sight test' *(Advice to Members. Ready-made reading spectacles. FODO (information sheet).*

15.3.2.4. Unregistered practitioners. Unregistered practitioners (spectacle shops) cannot conduct formal sight-tests, though informal self-testing by the purchaser (eg such as reading a sign) will clearly take place.

15.3.3. Dispensing of optical appliances

15.3.3.1. Ophthalmic optician (OO) and dispensing optician (DO) dispensing.

15.3.3.1.1. Spectacles and contact lenses. Both ophthalmic opticians and dispensing opticians can dispense spectacles and contact lenses (and by agreement participate in the health service voucher system of payment).

Ophthalmic medical practitioners do not usualy dispense, but often work with a dispensing optician in a medical eye centre.

15.3.3.1.2. Low vision aids. OOs and DOs sometimes specialise in low vision work, and therefore dispense low vison aids on free loan following HES referral, and on behalf of the HES (eg where there is no low vision clinic in the area) (*In Touch Handbook 1989 p. 149*).

15.3.3.1.3. Vouchers. A health service voucher system (15./Box 2.2.3.) exists to meet, or contribute towards, the cost of spectacles, and (since April 1988) contact lenses.

15.3.3.2. HES dispensing

15.3.3.2.1. HES direct dispensing. Circular guidance states that the HES can itself dispense spectacles and contact lenses (making use of voucher system of payment), or prescribe low vision aids on free loan.

It can dispense either inhouse, or via GOS practitioners who are under (sessional) contract to the DHA, HB or HSSB. Occasionally, a consultant might insist on inhouse dispensing for monitoring purposes.

People have the right to make use of HES dispensing facilities, since this allows them to take advantage of certain 'maximum charging' arrangements, available within the HES but not the GOS.

Circular guidance also states that easily accessible facilities should be available, for people who are blind, partially sighted, or who have travelling difficulties (*for all this see: HC(89)12, Appendix 6 para 7; NHS 1986(GEN)17,Memo para. 1; HSS(GHS)1/89 para. 8*).

15.3.3.2.2. HES prescription dispensed elsewhere. Once a prescription has been made out, people can take prescriptions to any dispensing optician, ophthalmic optician or unregistered practitioners. These last, however, cannot dispense a prescription if health service vouchers are involved.

15.3.3.2.3. Contact lenses. Circular guidance states that contact lenses are prescribable under HES on clinical grounds only (*HC(89)12; NHS 1986(GEN)17; HSS(GHS)1/89*). However, spectacle vouchers can be used to contribute toward contact lenses (*HC(89)12; NHS 1989(GEN)14; HSS(GHS)1/89*).

Contact lens solutions (cleansing, sterilising solutions) are an integral part of therapy, and initially they might be made available through the HES. Subsequently they are obtainable through GP prescription (*HC(89)12; NHS 1986(GEN)17; HSS(GHS)1/89*).

15.3.3.2.4. Low vision aids. Circular guidance states that low vision aids (eg handheld magnifiers, post-cataract temporary glasses, post-cataract temporary tinted glasses, recumbent spectacles, and ptosis props) are available on free loan from HES low vision clinics. (*HC(89)12; NHS 1986(GEN)17); HSS(GHS)1/89*).

15.3.3.3. Unregistered practitioners can make up prescriptions for spectacles (not contact lenses), and sell readymade spectacles and magnifiers. They cannot by law, however do this for children (under 16) or for blind or partially-sighted people (15.3.1.4.2.). They cannot dispense a prescription if health service vouchers are involved.

15.4. Registration for people with a visual impairment

SSD/SWD/HSSBs keep registers of people who are blind or partially sighted. Registration is not necessary in order to benefit from SSD/SWD/HSSB services, but, in practice, it can be helpful in alerting the SSD/SWD/HSSB to individual need (15.5.1.).

It is, however, required for various other statutory benefits (*Ford M., Heshel T. In Touch Handbook 1989. BSS, 1989 p. 45)*).

Certification of blindness or partial-sight by a hospital consultant is part of the registration process.

15.4.1. Certification by HES. Consultant ophthalmologists are responsible for the certification of people who are partially sighted or blind.

Referral for certification could be made by, for example, a consultant ophthalmologist, a general practitioner, a community health doctor, the SSD/SWD/HSSB (either direct or via the GP), ophthalmic optician (via the GP) or local voluntary organisation (via the social services and GP) (*Co-ord.Serv. for Visually Handicapped People. DH. 1989 p. 2*).

The certification form is then normally distributed to various people, including the SSD/SWD/HSSB, GP and an appropriate voluntary body. It is intended to act as a 'trigger' for various services.

15.4.2. Registration requirements: SSD/SWD/HSSBs

15.4.2.1. England and Wales. SSDs have the power to keep a register of people who are blind or partially sighted (*National Assistance Act 1948 s.29(4)(g)*).

15.4.2.2. Scotland and Northern Ireland. SWD/HSSBs have no duty to maintain a register, but Circular guidance stresses that such registers should nevertheless be kept, especially for people with a visual impairment (*eg see NHS 1986(PCS) 35/SWSG 8/1986; HSS(OS5A)4/78 (NI)*).

15.4.3. Importance of registration. SSD/SWD/HSSBs have the power to provide services, whether or not a person is registered, but registration is necessary to qualify for other financial benefits (*LAC 17/74; WOC (74)93; NHS 1986(PCS)35 /SWSG 8/1986; HSS (OS5A) 4/78*).

Voluntary bodies sometimes require registration as a criterion for provision of services (*In Touch Handbook. BSS, 1989 p. 27*).

15.4.4. Site of registration. In some areas, where there is no eye clinic locally accessible, home ophthalmic examinations are sometimes arranged – or perhaps a monthly registration clinic is held at a selected site within the area (*Shore P. Local Authority Social Rehabilitation Services to Visually Handicapped People. RNID, 1985 p. 57*).

15.4.5. Speed of registration. The registration process can be quick; but sometimes there are delays of up to several months (and even years) between the certification examination and the circulation of the certification form (*Shore P. Local Authority Social Rehabilitation Services to Visually Handicapped People. RNID, 1985 p. 56*).

In the light of this, Circular guidance states that the effective date of registration should be the same as certification, so that a person does not face delays in becoming eligible for certain statutory benefits (*LAC 17/74; Joint Circular HN(90)5,HN(FP)(90)1,LASSL(90)1; WOC(74)93; HSS(OS5A) 4/76 p. 4*).

Practice is likely to vary from area to area.

15.4.6. Distribution of certification form. The certification form is normally sent to at least some of the following people: community physician, director of social services, social services area office, specialist social services/social work team for visual impairment, a local voluntary organisation (which maintains a register on behalf of the local authority) and the GP (*DH. Co-ordinating Services for the Visually Handicapped. HMSO 1989 p. 3*).

Practice in this respect is likely to vary from area to area.

15.4.7. Collaboration and co-ordination in relation to registration. Circular guidance (England, 1990) stresses the need for co-operation and collaboration between services, and makes a number of recommendations drawn from a recent DH report (see Box 15.3).

Box 15.3: Registration of blindness and visual impairment: collaboration and co-operation to ensure good practice

Circular guidance (England, 1990) quotes recommendations from a report (*DH. Co-ordinating Services for Visually Handicapped People. HMSO, 1989*), including:

- it is essential to have a designated social services case manager of sufficient status to ensure effective operation of the services system by regular monitoring performance against objectives;
- in order to ensure effective co-ordination of assessment, referral, service provision and follow-up, the responsibility for co-ordination in individual cases should be assigned to a specified number of staff, preferably at first line management level;
- eye hospitals or large ophthalmic out-patients departments will have sufficient numbers of patients in need of advice and reassurance to justify a fulltime worker;
- a representative of the social services department should contact the client quickly after certification to discuss the perceived needs for services and, if appropriate, to carry out a comprehensive assessment;
- the first priority of local agencies should be the establishment of mechanisms for co-ordination at system level and case level (*Joint guidance: HN(90)5/HN(FP)(90)1/ LASSL(90)1*).

An SSI (England, 1988) report found that, within English SSDs, there was insufficient SSD contact with GPs and ophthalmologists. An example of good practice referred to a multi-disciplinary team including social worker, ophthamologist, orthoptist, community physician, paediatrician, psychologist and special needs teacher (*SSI. Wider Vision. DHSS, 1988 p. 24*).

15.5. Environmental equipment for people with a visual impairment

15.5.1. Referral to the SSD/SWD/HSSB is open: it can be by self, family, friends, or professionals.

For example, people with visual impairment are often referred to the SSD/SWD/ HSSB by a consultant ophthamologist, following certification of either blindness or partial sight.

This type of referral is often part of the official registration process and seems to form the main channel of referral of people with visual impairment to SSD/SWD/ HSSBs. Other, though less common, sources of referral might be GPs, health visitors, district nurses (*Shore P. Local Authority Social Rehabilitation Services to Visually Handicapped People. RNIB, 1985 pp. 55–6*).

A special form is the means of registration for the purpose of inclusion of an individual's name in the the SSD/SWD/HSSB register of people with disabilities. The form, and associated procedures, have been recently revised in England (*see eg joint Circular (England) HN(90)5/HN(FP)(90)1/LASSL(90)1*).

15.5.2. Residence. The client must, by law, be normally resident in the area of the SSD/SWD/HSSB (*CSDPA 1970 s.2(1); CSDP(NI)A 1978 s.2*), in order to receive services.

15.5.3. Assessment for environmental daily living equipment for people with visual impairment

15.5.3.1. Staff. SSD/SWD/HSSBs employ staff to supply social services (including daily living equipment) to blind or partially-sighted people. Such staff can include social workers, social work assistants, occupational therapists, technical officers, mobility officers, rehabilitation officers (combined technical and mobility trained staff) and home teachers of the blind (*SSI. Wider Vision. DHSS, 1988 p. 15*).

15.5.3.1.2. Organisation of staff. Staff might work as a specialised central team or be scattered as members of other special teams for elderly or physically disabled people (*SSI. Wider Vision. DHSS, 1988, p. 15*).

15.5.3.2. Visits following registration. Following registration, the person with visual impairment is sometimes visited by SSD/SWD/HSSB staff: or sometimes, for example, receives a letter stating that his or her name has been added to the SSD/SWD/HPSSB register of people with a visual impairment (*DH. Co-ordinating Services for Visually Handicapped People. HMSO 1989 p. 3*).

Voluntary bodies sometimes make visits to people following registration.

15.5.3.3. Type of assessment. The nature of SSD/SWD/HSSB assessment some-times varies due to different practices and staff availability. If specialist staff are not able to cover the whole of the SSD/SWD/HSSB, for example, then assessment from area to area, even within one authority, can be uneven. Sometimes, initial assesssments are carried out by non-specialist social workers or social work assistants (*Shore P. Local Authority Social Rehabilitation Services to Visually Handicap-ped People. RNIB, 1985 p. 60*).

15.5.3.4. Waiting times. In some areas, SSD/SWD/HSSBs 'prioritise' and categorise clients, depending on the urgency of need, as they sometimes do in the case of assessment for daily living equipment, in general (2.4.6.2.). Local written guidelines sometimes exist to clarify the operation of any priority system (see Box 15.4 for an example).

Alternatively, there might be a local policy, for example, to visit newly registered people within a certain time such as three to four weeks (*eg Midlands SSD Guidelines received 1989/1990*).

Box 15.4: Local priority system concerning environmental daily living equipment for people with visual impairment

B15.4.1. Priority categories. SSD/SWD/HSSBs sometimes categorise people with visual impairment, depending on urgency of need for an initial visit.
Example 1. Criteria used:

- person at risk.
- work ability.
- high motivation.
- supportive family.
- other disabilities.
  family role.
- isolation.
- age.
- home environment (suitability). Other home users. Care factor.
- time-case-held factor (*Midlands SSD guidelines received 1990*).

15.5.3.5. Assessment of need. SSD/SWD/HSSBs are likely to make a distinction between equipment which is essential or needed, and equipment which is desirable or beneficial. Clients are likely to be judged in need of equipment in the former case, and less likely in the latter case.

15.5.3.6. SSD/SWD/HSSB guidelines. SSD/SWD/HSSBs sometimes operate according to written guidelines and criteria on assessment and provision of equipment. The existence, form and content of such guidelines is likely to vary from area to area.

Guidelines and criteria are sometimes general or specific, or both (see Box 15.5 for examples).

Box 15.5: Local guidelines and criteria on assessment and provision of environmental daily living equipment for people with visual impairment. Examples:

B15.5.1. General guidelines
Example 1. The service is available to people:

- resident within the SSD area or placed outside it by the SSD;
- to people assessed to have significant visual impairment;
- irrespective of age or ability to pay;
- for personal use: not for business/employment use;
- equipment is issued on loan and to be returned;
- equipment is usually provided as part of a domiciliary rehabilitation programme (*Southwest England SSD (40) guidelines received 1989/1990*).

Example 2. Equipment is supplied following assessment of functional level, and suitability of each piece of equipment. Factors affecting choice of equipment include personal choice, functional needs, degree of residual vision etc (*London SSD (45) guidelines received 1989/1990*).

Example 3. A number of 'major items' are available on loan following assessment by a specialist officer. These include braillers, typewriters, cassette recorders, angle-poise lamps. The list is not exhaustive, and other requests for major items are considered at Unit of Management level. It is recommended that other smaller items be obtained from the RNIB (catalogue) at concessionary rates (*HSSB guidelines received 1989/1990*).

Example 4. Equipment (for people who are deaf and blind) such as a watch, which would be purchased anyway in the absence of disability, should not be supplied free of charge (*HSSB guidelines received 1989/1990*).

Example 5. Assessment should be from 'a technical viewpoint to ensure that the aid is appropriate to the degree of . . . sight loss'. Many of the items needed are so small and simple that a detailed, intensive assessment is not necessary (*HSSB guidelines received 1989/1990*).

Example 6. A department which runs its own resource centre notes: 'Blind or partially sighted people may purchase aids to daily living from the resource centre for the blind if they or their representative calls there. Standard practice is that callers are advised that any specialist equipment needs can be assessed by a welfare or mobility officer from the social work office covering their area and provided free if the assessing officer recommends it. In practice, over 40% of callers buy the equipment at the centre' (*SWD guidelines received 1989/1990*).

Example 7. A range of equipment is available if it will 'increase the individual's independence or enhance quality of life'. It is available, through assessment by social workers for the blind, and includes household, kitchen, leisure, mobility equipment. Also radio, lighting, talking/braille/moon books, library service (*SWD guidelines received 1989/1990*).

Example 8. 'Aids for visually handicapped people are supplied, in the main, by the local Institute for the Blind, but one-off-aids can be supplied direct by the Social Services Department where such supply is deemed necessary and practicable' (*Midlands SSD guidelines received 1989/1990*).

Example 9. Equipment available includes braillers, lighting, cassette players, writing aids, dressing aids: 'given on loan free of charge to people who are assessed as needing them' (*London SSD guidelines received 1989/1990*).

B15.5.2. Specific guidelines and criteria

B15.5.2.1. Communication equipment
Example 1. Braillers are not supplied copiously because of their cost and primary purpose of allowing communication between braille readers (*HSSB guidelines received 1989/1990*).

Example 2. Typewriter, cassette recorder:

- the user is partially sighted;
- the user satisfactorily completes a training course;
- automatically supplied to eligible school-leavers up to 12 months prior to leaving date (*London SSD (45) guidelines received 1989/1990*).

Example 3. Brailler, typewriter, cassette recorder:

- the user is registered blind;
- the user satisfactorily completes a training course;
- automatically supplied to eligible school-leavers up to 12 months prior to leaving date (*London SSD (45) guidelines received 1989/1990*).

Example 4. Telephone handsets. Assessment takes account of level of residual vision, degree of isolation, ability to use handset, registration with the SSD.
The department will provide:

- the handset;
- if necessary cover the cost of a new phone socket;
- if necessary cover the cost of a callout fee where there is a fault;
- maintain and replace the special handset.

The client is responsible for the:

- telephone line installation and connection charges;
- cost of telephone calls;
- negotiation with BT concerning cancellation of rental for previous handset.
The handset remains the property of the Council, and is to be returned when no longer in use (*Southwest England SSD (40) guidance received 1989/1990*).

B15.5.2.2. Mobility equipment.
Example 1. Symbol canes, guide canes, white stick, guide dogs etc. are provided if:

- user is registered visually handicapped;
- user has undergone/will undergo specific training in the use of equipment;
- the provision will reduce the user's dependence on the carer or relative (*London SSD (45) guidelines received 1989/1990*).

Example 2. Rail leading to a washing pole. The department will not supply this for a blind person since it is contrary to mobility training (*SWD (1) guidance received 1989/1990*).
Example 3. Run for guide dogs: not provided since the Guide Dogs for the Blind Association will carry out and finance this (*SWD (1) guidance received 1989/1990*).

B15.5.2.3. Household and kitchen aids may be essential to some people (eg housewives and people living alone), but not to others (eg elderly people who have a Home Help). Assessment should be made with this in mind (*HSSB guidelines received 1989/1990*).

B15.5.2.4. Recreational equipment is available to 'maintain interest in a hobby, or to initiate a new interest' in woodwork, craft, music, games (*HSSB guidelines received 1989/1990*).

15.5.4. Provision of environmental daily living equipment for people with visual impairment

15.5.4.1. SSD/SWD/HSSB provision. SSD/SWD/HSSBs provide environmental daily living equipment for people with a visual impairment, often on free loan, although they do have the power to charge.

15.5.4.2. SSD/SWD/HSSB as agent providing/selling voluntary organisation equipment. The SSD/SWD/HSSB sometimes acts as an agent for voluntary bodies, obtaining equipment at a reduced rate and supplying it on free loan or at a small charge to clients.

RNIB and Partially Sighted Society equipment might be supplied in this way, and sometimes the British Wireless Fund for the Blind scheme, for example, is run on such agency lines (*eg Northern Metropolitan District Council guidelines received 1989*).

15.5.5. Delivery and training. Equipment is usually delivered only after the client has been shown how to use it correctly. Special mobility training is required for some equipment (for example, a long cane). Clients can expect equipment to be installed (where necessary) by SSD/SWD/HSSB staff, or by the supplier.

15.5.6. Recall. Some equipment issued to people with visual impairment, is needed for life; where not, it is returnable and re-issued to another person, if it is not too worn.

15.5.7. Replacement. The SSD/SWD/HSSB normally replaces equipment as needed. Maintenance or repair of more complex and expensive equipment might also be undertaken by the supplier/manufacturer of equipment.

15.5.8. Resource centres act as both display and sales points for environmental equipment for visual impairment. They are generally funded by the SSD/SWD/ HSSB, joint-funded or independently funded; and range in size from major premises to a car boot. They display equipment ranging from small daily living aids to sophisticated low vision aids and computer technology.

Visitors are able to try out equipment before they privately purchase it or before it is supplied by the SSD/SWD/HSSB (for details see Box 15.6).

Box 15.6: Resource centres for visual impairment

An increasing number of voluntary organisations and local authorities now run resource centres for people with visual impairment. Centres include, for example, RNIB premises (London and Stirling), displaying RNIB equipment, computer technology, low vision aids, computer technology; as well as smaller voluntary organisation or local authority premises, which hold a small stock of equipment (*see eg In Touch Handbook. BSS, 1989 p. 43*)

B15.6.1. Resource centres – size and position. Resource centres sometimes have a large display; or, at the other extreme, for example, a local authority might have a cupboard containing a very small range of equipment. Display could be literally a car-boot, which, since visits to the home are of necessity involved, has its advantages. Resource centres sometimes have a mobile display van, and sometimes also hold a number of exhibitions during the year in other towns.

B15.6.2. Resource centres – type of equipment. Depending on the size and remit of the centre, three categories of equipment might be displayed: RNIB equipment, commercial equipment, low vision aids.

B15.6.2.1. RNIB, Partially Sighted Society equipment. Depending on the scale of the centre, it displays and acts as a sales point for more, or fewer, of the items contained in the RNIB catalogue, and for equipment (Box 15.1.3.) supplied by the Partially Sighted Society.

For people who are registered blind or partially-sighted, the price of RNIB equipment is reduced by about a third. Thus, people either buy their own equipment, or the SSD/SWD/HSSB sometimes loans the equipment free of charge if it has identified a need (15.2.3.1.).

The RNIB also operates tele-sales facilities.

B15.6.2.2. Small commercial equipment. Where smaller commercial aids are displayed, they are likely to be for demonstration purposes only. The person can then either send off for the item by mail order, or go to a high street chain, for example, to purchase it. Alternatively, the SWD/SSD/HSSB might supply the item on loan.

B15.6.2.3. Low vision, high technology equipment. Special low vision aids and high technology equipment, including magnifiers, closed circuit televisions, voice synthesizers, braille production equipment and laptop computers, might be displayed in larger centres.

Some low vision aids, such as handheld magnifiers, are available from low vision clinics within the HES: following demonstration at the resource centre people may be advised to talk to the consultant ophthalmologist about possible loan through the HES.

Box 15.7: Special voluntary body equipment schemes for people with visual impairment

B15.7.1. The British Wireless for the Blind Fund provides a radio for anybody over the age of eight who is registered blind.

The Fund does not issue radios to people who are registered partially sighted. The local SSD/SWD/HSSB sometimes acts as an agent for the Fund, keeping local stocks, distributing and maintaining the radios as appropriate (*Midlands SSD (21) guidance received 1989/1990*).

Batteries are sometimes issued locally by the SSD/SWD/HSSB as well as paid for. This was urged, for example, by Circular guidance (Northern Ireland, 1976) in the interests of uniformity of provision. It noted that the cost was low, and as such there should not be a limit on the number of batteries issued annually to an individual (*HSS(OS5A) 4/1976*).

Alternatively, the batteries are often paid for, either by the Fund, or by a local voluntary body (*Northern SSD Guidelines, received 1989/1990*).

B15.7.2. RNIB Talking Book Service is used widely: the machine is loaned for an annual subscription charge, paid either by the user, by a SSD/SWD/HSSB, or a local voluntary organisation.

The service is open to people who are registered blind, or to people who have their application supported by a professional such as a mobility officer, rehabilitiation officer, GP or consultant ophthalmologist (*In Touch Handbook 1989. BSS, 1989 p. 233*).

The scheme is sometimes administered by a local voluntary body or SSD/SWD/HSSB on behalf of the Service. In the latter case administration could, for example, be through the SSD/SWD/HSSB's library service (*eg Southwest England SSD (40) guidance received 1989/1990*).

B15.7.3. Talking newspapers and magazines are often produced by local voluntary groups. They are sometimes able to loan cassette recorders to clients (*eg Midlands SSD (21) guidance received 1989/1990*).

B15.7.4. Special individual help with equipment. Voluntary bodies sometimes help people obtain certain equipment by means of grants or fundraising. Such help is likely to be dependent on individual circumstances, and on the failure, by statutory services, to provide equipment.

Some SSD/SWD/HSSBs might, for example, administer trust funds for the benefit of people with visual impairment (*eg Southwest England SSD (40) guidance received 1989/1990*).

15.5.9. Voluntary bodies

15.5.9.1. Local agency agreements. Voluntary bodies sometimes co-operate with the local SSD/SWD/HSSB, formally providing services on its behalf, by agreement. This is sometimes referred to as an 'agency' agreement if there is a contract involved.

Otherwise, the voluntary body, functioning independently, nevertheless informally complements SSD/SWD/HSSB services (*see eg SSI. Wider Vision. DHSS, 1988, p. 32*).

The type of service provided by voluntary bodies is likely to vary but might include assessment for, and advice on, daily living equipment; and is increasingly likely to involve the use of a resource centre (15.5.8.).

15.5.9.2. RNIB and Partially Sighted Society equipment. The RNIB (which operates a telephone sales system), and the Partially Sighted Society (to a lesser extent), sell a wide range of daily living equipment (Box15.1.3.) at a discount to people with visual impairment. People sometimes wish to buy equipment direct from these organisations, rather than obtain it on free loan through the SSD/SWD/HSSB.

Resource centres (15.5.8.) often act both as display and sales points for this equipment.

15.5.9.3. Special voluntary body schemes. Voluntary bodies run both national and local schemes in relation to, for example, radios, talking books and newspapers, and sometimes provide financial help for equipment (depending on individual circumstances) in the form of a grant or through fundraising activities. For details see Box 15.7.

16 Environmental Controls

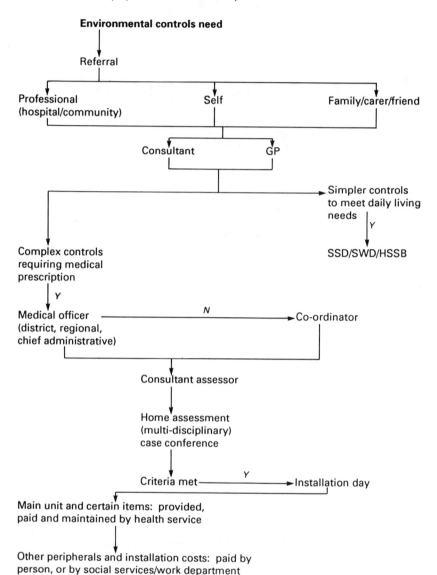

Environmental controls need

↓

Referral

Professional (hospital/community) — Self — Family/carer/friend

Consultant — GP

Simpler controls to meet daily living needs | Y

SSD/SWD/HSSB

Complex controls requiring medical prescription | Y

Medical officer (district, regional, chief administrative) — N → Co-ordinator

Consultant assessor

Home assessment (multi-disciplinary) case conference

Criteria met — Y → Installation day

Main unit and certain items: provided, paid and maintained by health service

Other peripherals and installation costs: paid by person, or by social services/work department

Introduction

Type of equipment. Environmental control systems enable people with severe disability to carry out various daily living tasks, which they would otherwise be unable to perform.

The systems, ranging from the simpler to the more complex, are of the selector type, operated, for example, by a variety of means such as limb extremity, eyebrow, or breathing control. The systems control a range of switches which are connected to equipment, such as television, telephone, door-entry system, alarm system, computer and curtain rail.

Provision of complex environmental control systems is made by medical prescription. The two most complex systems generally available are, in practice, assessed for, provided and maintained (on free loan) by health service (DHA/HB/HSSB) staff, although according to centrally produced criteria and guidelines. In England and Wales, administrative and financial responsibilities are also centrally located.

Referral and assessment procedures usually involve the referring GP or consultant, a special consultant assessor, a co-ordinator, various health professionals and the manufacturer/supplier of the equipment.

The main unit and some equipment (for example, the loudspeaking telephone, alarm and door lock) are provided free of charge; but installation charges and other peripheral equipment (such as television, radio, heater, printer and lighting) are the responsibility of the client. The SSD/SWD or HSSB (under social services functions) sometimes helps the client to meet these costs.

Provision of less complex environmental control systems. These systems are provided as daily living equipment by SSD/SWD and HSSBs (under social services functions). If an individual need has been identified, they are under a duty to make arrangements for the provision of such equipment. SSD/SWD/ HSSBs have the power to charge, but rarely make use of it.

(*Note:* Much of this chapter is based on the Department of Health (*DH, England*) *'Yellow book' (1989) (Arrangements for the provision of environmental control equipment through Department of Health (DH). 1989. Issued with Circular EL(89)P/180*).

Although the Welsh Health Common Services Authority (WHCSA, Wales) Pink book, Scottish Home and Health Department (SHHD, Scotland) guidance, and Department of Health and Social Services (DHSS, Northern Ireland) Blue book have not been updated at the time of writing, it is expected that they will follow the lead given by the DH in most respects).

16.1. Type of equipment

Environmental control equipment enables people with severe physical disabilities to carry out various daily living tasks, which they would otherwise be unable to perform. The technical complexity of such equipment varies, from simple modified controls to sophisticated 'selector' systems.

A selector system can be operated by a single residual action such as limb (including limb extremity) movement, eyebrow control, breathing (suck-blow). Selection of a number of switches is possible; each switch operates an appliance such as television, telephone, door-entry system, alarm call, curtains or computer.

16.1.1. Sophisticated controls. The number and type of appliances operated, depends on the system; the most sophisticated model generally available (the PSU6) is able to control, for example, an alarm, 2 door locks, television channel changer, curtain controls, tilt-bed control, a call system, three intercoms and various other on/off controls. It can also include communication equipment, which can store messages for display or printing (*DH Yellow Book p. 4*).

16.1.2. Simpler controls might operate just three functions; for example an alarm system, a door intercom and a door lock.

16.2. Legislative basis for provision

Legislation does not make direct reference to environmental control systems. However, central guidance does detail criteria and procedures for provision (see Note to this chapter).

16.2.1. Basis for medical prescription of environmental controls

16.2.1.1. Basis for medical prescription of environmental controls: England. Provision through DH arrangements is covered by the Secretary of State's duty to provide 'medical services' (*NHS Act 1977 s.3*).
   Provision (more rarely), at the discretion of a district health authority (DHA) (not through DH arrangements), is covered by the DHA duty to provide 'medical services' (*NHS Act 1977 s.3*).

16.2.1.2. Basis for medical prescription of environmental controls: Wales. Provision through Welsh Health Common Services Authority (WHCSA) arrangements is covered by the Secretary of State's duty to provide 'medical services' (*NHS Act 1977 s.3; see also eg SI 1985/996 for WHCSA*).
   Provision (rare) at the discretion of a DHA (not through WHCSA arrangements) is covered by the DHA duty to provide 'medical services' (*NHS Act 1977 s.3*).

16.2.1.3. Basis for medical prescription of environmental controls: Scotland. Provision by health boards (HBs) is covered by the HB duty to provide 'medical services' (*NHS (Scotland) Act 1978 s.36*).

16.2.1.4. Basis for medical prescription of environmental controls: Northern Ireland. Provision by health and social services boards (HSSBs) is covered by the HSSB duty to provide 'medical services' (*SI 1972/1265 HPSS(NI)O a.5*).

16.2.2. Provision of environmental controls as daily living equipment is covered by the SSD/SWD/HSSB duty (where an individual need is identified) to make arrangements for the 'provision of facilities for ... greater safety, comfort or convenience' (*CSDPA 1970 s.2(1)(e); CSDP(NI)A 1978 s.2(e)*).

Provision is also covered by both general welfare legislation (2.2.2.), and by legislation which places a duty on SSD/SWDs to make an assessment, in response to a request to do so by the disabled person or his/her carer (2.2.3.).

16.3. Organisation of selector environmental control (PSU6 and SEC1A) provision by medical prescription

16.3.1. England. The DH, for the present, retains central administrative and financial responsibility for the provision of selector environmental control systems by medical prescription. Guidance for DHAs, which undertake provision in practice, is produced centrally by the DH.

16.3.2. Wales. The position is much the same as for England, except that WHCSA (a special health authority) centrally administers and finances the provision of environmental controls and produces guidelines for DHAs.

16.3.3. Scotland. Health boards are responsible for prescription, arrangements and finance. However, guidance on provision is still produced centrally by the SHHD.

16.3.4. Northern Ireland. HSSBs have responsibility for provision and finance of environmental controls, although through central contract arrangements with the DHSS (NI), which also produces guidance for HSSBs.

16.3.5. Prescription other than according to central guidelines. Hospital consultants have the power (5.2.4.1.) to prescribe environmental control systems, other than according to central guidelines, if they believe that there is a medical need for such prescription.

Such prescription is also dependent on local DHA/HB/HSSB policy and decisions, on the use of resources (*Arrangements for the provision of environmental control equipment through Department of health (DH). 1989. p. 2*).

16.4. Referral, assessment, provision procedures for environmental controls

16.4.1. Simpler environmental control systems (provided as daily living equipment)

16.4.1.1. SSD/SWD and HSSB (under social services functions) provision. Simpler environmental controls are normally loaned by SSD/SWDs and by HSSBs (under social services functions) to meet a daily living need. Medical prescription is not necessary (*Arrangements for the provision of environmental control equipment through Department of Health (DH). DH, 1989, pp. 1, 2*).

Such controls are provided according to the same principles and procedures as other daily living equipment (2.). They are normally loaned free of charge, although the power to charge does exist (30.2.) (*Arrangements for the provision of environmental control equipment through department of health (DH). DH, 1989, p. 2*).

16.4.1.2. Health service consultant. In theory, simpler controls could be prescribed by a consultant, if he or she finds a medical need for such controls. Such prescription would depend upon the local decision of the DHA/HB/HSSB (*see eg Arrangements for the provision of environmental control equipment through Department of Health (DH). DH, 1989 p. 2*).

In practice, such prescription is rare, since such controls are normally deemed to be daily living equipment and therefore the responsibility of the SSD/SWD or HSSB (under social services functions).

16.4.2. Complex environmental control systems (supplied on medical prescription)

16.4.2.1. Provision of environmental controls through central guidelines and criteria

16.4.2.1.1. Type of environmental controls supplied on medical prescription. The two main types supplied in England are the SEC1A, and the more sophisticated PSU6 (*Arrangements for the provision of environmental control equipment through Department of Health (DH). DH, 1989 p. 3*).

In Scotland and Northern Ireland, the PSU6 is in theory available, but has not yet been prescribed widely: 'recycled' PSU3s are still issued.

16.4.2.1.2. GP or consultant referral. Initial referral is normally to the family doctor (GP), either self-referral (and family, friends) or referral through other professionals, such as health visitors, district nurses and occupational therapists.

Alternatively, a consultant might already be treating the person.

16.4.2.1.3. Referral to a medical officer or co-ordinator. If the GP or consultant feels that the person is eligible for provision on medical grounds, referral is then made to one of the following:

- regional medical officer (RMO, England);
- district medical officer (DMO, England);
- WHCSA administrator/co-ordinator (Wales);
- health board co-ordinator/administrator (Scotland);
- chief administrative medical officer (CAMO, Scotland, Northern Ireland).

Practice seems to vary as to whether an administrator/co-ordinator (16.4.2.1.7.1.) is contacted initially, or a medical officer. For example, in Wales a WHCSA administrator is contacted (and has ultimate responsibilty for provision); in Scotland a co-ordinator is contacted initially, the CAMO only becoming involved after assessment (*Verbal communication: Scottish Office, 1989*).

16.4.2.1.4. Referral to assessor. Referral is then made to a health service consultant acting as assessor, who makes a detailed assessment at the person's home to determine eligibility for medical prescription of an environmental control system.

16.4.2.1.5. Final decision. The medical officer or co-ordinator/administrator, depending on particular arrangements, has ultimate responsibility for the decision on supply.

16.4.2.1.6. Eligibility criteria for medical prescription. A number of centrally produced eligibility criteria are employed in assessment, and include reference to:

- degree of disability;
- potential independence afforded by provision;
- will to use the equipment.
  Details are given in Box 16.1.

16.4.2.1.7. Procedures for supply

16.4.2.1.7.1. Co-ordinator. If the eligibility criteria are satisfied, the RMO, DMO, WHCSA or CAMO delegates a 'co-ordinator' to arrange the supply of the equipment. Sometimes the co-ordinator is already involved by this stage (16.4.2.1.3.).

The co-ordinator is responsible for the ordering of equipment and for liaison with suppliers and with all agencies/authorities, in connection with the supply, installation, maintenance, modification and withdrawal of environmental control equipment. The co-ordinator is also the focal point for patients' queries (*Arrangements for the provision of environmental control equipment through Department of Health (DH). DH, p. 6*).

16.4.2.1.7.2. Case conference. A case conference will be held at the person's home with family/friends, the co-ordinator, the supplier's assessor (probably a therapist) and other health and social services professionals (*Arrangements for the provision of environmental control equipment through Department of Health (DH). DH, 1989 p. 7*).

16.4.2.1.7.3. Installation. On installation day, the co-ordinator, or the co-ordinator's representative, is present, as well as the supplier's engineer, a carpenter and an electrician (probably arranged by the SSD/SWD/HSSB) (*Arrangements for the provision of environmental control equipment through Department of Health (DH). DH, 1989 p. 8*).

In the past, installation charges for wiring, and other work carried out by electricians and joiners, has been paid for by the DH/WHCSA/HBs (England, Wales, Scotland). In the future, SSD/SWDs will have the discretion to help the individual meet these charges (*Arrangements for the provision of environmental control equipment through Department of Health (DH). DH, 1989 p. 11*).

In Northern Ireland, HSSBs (under social services functions) continue to have the discretion to help the individual with such charges (*Arrangements for the provision of environmental control equipment. DHSS (NI) 1985 para 6.2*).

16.4.2.1.7.4. Continuing responsibility. Once installation has taken place, the co-ordinator takes responsibility fo the equipment itself. Medical/clinical problems should be referred to the GP (*Arrangements for the provision of environmental control equipment through Department of Health (DH). DH, 1989 p. 8*).

16.4.2.1.8. Responsibility for costs of unit and peripheral equipment. Medical prescription includes provision of main controls (eg central unit, plinth, monitor), the 'bus cable', the decoding boxes, the interface boxes, a variety of switches. Also provided as integral to the system is a loudspeaking telephone (the LST9A) (though the installation of a socket is not included), a door lock and an alarm

---

Box 16.1: Eligibility criteria for supply on medical prescription of environmental controls

B16.1.1. General. General eligibility criteria for the supply of environmental controls on medical grounds include:

- the person is permanently so paralysed or so disabled by disease, injury or congenital defect that they are unable to carry out simple tasks such as ringing bells for attention or switching on lights.
- the person will be able to derive some continuing measure of independence, have the ability and will to use the apparatus and cannot be assisted so effectively by simpler or cheaper means (*Arrangements for the provision of environmental control equipment through department of health (DH). DH, 1989*).

B16.1.2. Provision in institutions. Although one of the aims of the equipment is to keep people out of institutions, nevertheless it may sometimes be supplied to people living in special homes, in a hospice, in a long-stay NHS hospital/ward (*Arrangements for the provision of environmental control equipment through Department of Health (DH). DH, 1989, pp. 5, 6*).

(*Note:* environmental controls are supplied to specific individuals: though in the past, for example, they have sometimes been supplied to young disabled units as assessment models.)

B16.1.3. Terminal illness. Environmental controls can be supplied to people with a deteriorating neurological condition (such as motor neurone disease), and where there is rapid deterioration the supply process can be speeded up (*Arrangements for the provision of environmental control equipment through Department of Health (DH). DH, 1989 p. 9*).

B16.1.4. PSU6 eligibility criteria. For the more sophisticated PSU6, 'extra' criteria for eligibility are used:

- it should be considered for those living at home – or in exceptional circumstances living in residential care – who have both the ability and the will to use this more sophisticated equipment and who require a communication facility because they are unable to communicate satisfactorily by any other means;
- where the appropriate statutory authority has provided, or proposed to provide, a computer for educational and/or employment purposes, provision of the PSU6 may also be considered;
- where appliances such as tilting beds and room curtains need to be controlled, and exceed the capability of simpler and cheaper equipment, the PSU6 may be considered. (The SEC1A is able to control beds and curtains but only at the expense of other outlets) (*Arrangements for the provision of environmental control equipment through Department of Health (DH). DH, 1989 p. 5*).

---

facility (eg flashing light, audio-alarm, facility for attachment to an existing warden or community alarm system) (*Arrangements for the provision of environmental control equipment through Department of Health (DH). DH, 1989*).

Peripheral equipment such as television, telephone, printer, heater, lighting cannot be provided under medical prescription. The SSD/SWD or HSSB (under social services functions) can help with these items, if the person is unable to afford them (*Arrangements for the provision of environmental control equipment through Department of Health (DH). DH, 1989 p. 11; Arrangements for the provision of environmental control equipment. DHSS (NI) 1985 para 7.1*).

16.4.2.1.9. Repair. Repair responsibility of the DH, WHCSA, the HB or HSSB extends to the main equipment and accessories supplied originally under medical prescription (*Arrangements for the provision of environmental control equipment through Department of Health (DH). DH, 1989 p. 10; Arrangements for the provision of environmental control equipment. DHSS (NI) 1985 para 8.1*).

Other (peripheral) equipment is the responsibility of the person, the person's representative or the SSD/SWD and HSSB (under social services functions) depending on the original supply source (*Arrangements for the provision of environmental control equipment through Department of Health (DH). DH, 1989 p. 10; Arrangements for the provision of environmental control equipment. DHSS (NI) 1985 para 8.4.*).

16.4.2.2. Provision of sophisticated controls other than through central guidelines and criteria.

16.4.2.2.1. Health service prescription. Consultants, using the wide prescription powers available to them, where there is a medical need, could prescribe the PSU6 or SEC1A without following central guidelines. This would depend on the local policies and resources of the DHA/HB/HSSB (*see eg Arrangements for the provision of environmental control equipment through Department of Health (DH). DH, 1989 p. 2*).

In practice, this is unlikely to happen very often. Such prescription might sometimes be necessary when a person fails to qualify for controls according to the criteria, laid down in central guidelines (see Box 16.1), but the consultant feels that there are, nevertheless, strong medical grounds for provision.

16.4.2.2.2. SSD/SWDs and HSSBs (under social services functions) have very wide powers (2.2.1.) to provide equipment for daily living; and do have the power to provide (or help with the provision of) both simple and sophisticated environmental control systems to meet daily living need.

In practice, such help with sophisticated systems (normally supplied on medical prescription) is rare, since such equipment is generally seen to meet a medical, not a daily living, need.

17 Equipment for the Management of Incontinence

Equipment for incontinence

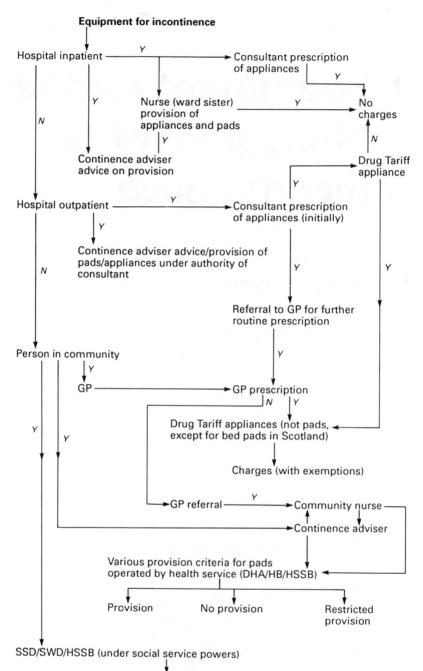

Introduction

Type of equipment. Equipment for the management of incontinence includes pads, pants, catheters, urinals, sheaths, enuresis alarms and special sheets. (It also includes less obvious equipment such as mobility equipment, commodes and chemical toilets and easily accessible WCs: all of which are discussed elsewhere.)

Responsibility for provision rests mainly with the health service:
- district health authorities (DHAs, England and Wales);
- health boards (HBs, Scotland);
- health and social services boards (HSSBs, Northern Ireland).

More rarely provision is made through social services (particularly to statutory residential homes):
- social services departments (SSDs, England and Wales);
- social work departments (SWDs, Scotland);
- HSSBs (Northern Ireland).

Referral, assessment, prescription. The problem of incontinence usually comes to light through the general practitioner (GP). The GP might treat the problem (in consultation with a community nurse), refer the patient to a hospital consultant or direct to a continence adviser (usually a specialist nurse).

GPs can prescribe a number of incontinence appliances to which prescription charges, and exemptions as appropriate, apply. Such prescription might be on the recommendation of the district nurse or continence adviser. GPs cannot prescribe incontinence pads, except for bed incontinence pads in Scotland.

Community nurses (and some continence advisers) have access to supplies of pads, pants and some bedding for the management of incontinence. Local policies and practice, in relation to the supply of these materials, vary from area to area.

Consultants and continence advisers sometimes respectively prescribe and supply appliances and pads initially; regular, subsequent supply is normally undertaken by the GP or community nurse, as appropriate.

There is evidence that the supply of incontinence pads and other materials to individuals in their own homes, or in residential and nursing accomodation, is inadequate.

17.1. Type of equipment

17.1.1. Equipment explicitly for management of incontinence includes body-worn pads and pants, pads for bed and chair, urinary catheters, drainage bags, penile sheaths, handheld urinals (male and female) enuresis alarms, mattress covers and drawsheets.

Enuresis alarms, both bed-based and bodyworn are usually used for children's bladder-training.

17.1.2. Equipment implicitly for management of incontinence: the above are examples of equipment 'obviously' connected with incontinence. Other relevant equipment includes mobility equipment, commodes, chemical toilets, easily accessible WCs, all of which are discussed elsewhere.

17.2. Legislative basis for the provision of equipment for the management of incontinence

Legislation does not explicitly mention equipment for the management of incontinence. Circular guidance does, however, and is quoted as appropriate below.

17.2.1. Basis: health service provision.

17.2.1.1. Basis: consultant provision is covered by the DHA/HB/HSSB duty to provide 'medical services' (*NHS Act 1977 s.3; NHS (Scotland) Act 1978 s.36; HPSS(NI)O 1972 a.5*).

17.2.1.2. Basis: continence adviser (usually a nurse) and community nurse provision of equipment/help/advice is covered by the DHA/HB/HSSB duty to provide 'nursing services' (*NHS Act 1977 s.3; NHS (Scotland) Act 1978 s.36; SI 1972/1265 HPSS(NI)O 1972 a.5*).

The provision of equipment for home nursing need is also covered by the DHA/HB/HSSB duty to provide facilities for the prevention of illness, the care of people who are ill, and the aftercare of people who have been ill (*NHS Act 1977, s.3; NHS (Scotland) Act 1978, s.37; SI 1972/1265 HPSS(NI)O a.7*).

17.2.1.3. Basis: GP provision is covered by the DHA (through FPC)/HB/HSSB duty to provide 'general medical services' (*NHS Act 1977 s.29; NHS (Scotland) Act 1978 s.19; SI 1972/1265 HPSS (NI)O Health and Personal Social Services (Northern Ireland) Order 1972 a.56*).

17.2.1.4. Basis: SSD/SWD or HSSB (under social services functions) provision is covered by powers to make arrangements for people to prevent illness, to care for them while they are ill, and to provide aftercare (*NHS Act 1977 Sched. 8 para 2(1)) and possibly under the Health Services and Public Health Act 1968 s.45(1); SI 1972/1265 HPSS(NI)O 1972 a.7*).

In Scotland, it is not clear on what such provision might be based, other than legislation covering general welfare duties (*Social Work (Scotland) Act 1968 s.12*).

17.3. Referral, assessment and prescription

17.3.1.General practitioners

17.3.1.1. Referral to the general practitioner (GP). The first step toward dealing with incontinence is normally through a GP, either by self-referral, referral from another professional, or the observation of the GP.

17.3.1.2. Difficulty in identification of the problem of incontinence. It seems that, for whatever reason (such as embarassment or unawareness of solutions), some people do not consult their GP and the problem remains concealed.

Two large scale surveys (1980,1984) suggested that the actual prevalence of both urinary and double incontinence is very much greater than the prevalence known to statutory or voluntary bodies (*Thomas TM et al. BMJ 1980 Vol. 281 pp. 1243–5;*

Thomas TM et al. Prevalence of faecal and double incontinence. Community Medicine: 1984;6, 216–220).).

Another survey (1986), of elderly people over 75 years of age, found that 50% of people with actual incontinence were not using personal aids to manage the condition (*McGrother C. et al. Provision of services for incontinent elderly people at home. Journal of Epidemiology and Community Health. 1986:40, 134-138*).

17.3.1.3. GP assessment and prescription. The management of incontinence is complex, and GPs have a difficult job, both in knowing when to refer a person to a hospital for a full assessment, and how to choose and fit the right items of equipment when they are themselves prescribing.

The selection of a specific item is sometimes left to the pharmacist (5.1.4.10.1.), or dispensing appliance centre (5.1.4.10.3.) when the GP is unsure of specification.

Thus, GPs might themselves:

- treat the problem (including appliance prescription);
- refer the person to a hospital consultant for a full assessment;
- refer the person to a continence adviser;
- refer the person to a community nurse for the provision of pads, and help with appliances prescribed by the GP.

17.3.1.4. Assessment of elderly people. Under the terms of the new GP contract (operative from 1st April, 1990), GPs have a duty to either visit people over the age of 75, or hold a surgery consultation with them, at least once a year.

The person's 'physical condition including continence' is one of the aspects which the GP must take into account (*SI 1974/160 Part 1, Sched 1 para 13B inserted by SI 1989/1897; SI 1974/506 (S.41) Part 1, Sched 1 para 10C inserted by SI 1989/1990 (S.139); SR&O 1973/421 Sched 1, para 8D inserted by SR 1989/454*).

17.3.1.5. GP prescription of Drug Tariff incontinence items

17.3.1.5.1. In England, Wales and Northern Ireland, GPs can prescribe items listed in the Drug Tariff (5.1.1./Box 5.1). These include drainable dribbling devices, catheters, incontinence belts, incontinence sheaths, incontinence sheath fixing strips and adhesives, leg bags, night drainage bags, suspensory systems, tubing and accessories, and urinal systems.

17.3.1.5.2. In Scotland, Drug Tariff items vary slightly from those in England and Northern Ireland, in that GPs can additionally prescribe bed (but not bodyworn) incontinence pads.

17.3.2. Community nurse referral, assessment and provision of incontinence equipment

17.3.2.1. Referral to and from community nurses. A district nurse (4.4.1.) and sometimes health visitor (4.4.1.), takes referrals from a GP, in order to meet a person's home nursing needs (including incontinence pads for example); or sometimes these community nurses initially identify the need and refer to the GP.

Circular guidance (Scotland, 1976) states the importance of referral by community nurses for medical diagnosis (*NHS 1976(GEN)11*).

17.3.2.2. District nurse remit. The district nurse (and sometimes health visitor) can advise the GP which Drug Tariff appliances need to be prescribed; can help a person use the appliances; and can supply incontinence pads, pants and bedding.

In the future it is expected that district nurses and health visitors will be able to prescribe certain incontinence appliances (currently GP prescribable) listed in a nurses' formulary (4.4.1.).

There is some evidence that nurses involved with incontinence appliances have difficulty in keeping up-to-date with new products (*see eg Carlisle D. Advancing incontinence care. Nursing Standard 1989:28;3, 40-41. McCorrigan J, Henderson A. Rationalising Incontinence Products in a fast changing market. Nursing Standard 1989:50;3,24-27*).

17.3.2.3. Circular guidance (England and Scotland) makes reference to the role of community nursing services (CNS) in the management of incontinence.

Incontinence pads, interliners/disposable linings, waterproof pants/ underclothing 'and other aids' have been mentioned as items which can be supplied by community nurses (*see eg HRC(74(16); NHS 1976(GEN)11*).

It has also been stated that community nurses are well placed to provide services and support to both people who are incontinent and to their family and carers, who also suffer considerable stress. This is particularly so when the nurse has 'sufficient awareness and knowledge of the importance of establishing the extent to which continence can be regained as well as the aids and facilities which are available to overcome the problems which are associated with incontinence' (*CNO(SNC)(77)1: issued for both England and Scotland*).

17.3.3. Consultant prescription. A consultant has the power (5.2.4.1.) to prescribe anything medically necessary. Prescription of items contained in the Drug Tariff, such as catheters, bags and urinals attract the normal prescription charge (at the time of writing) of £3.05 with the usual exemptions (Box 30.1.). Any other medically required items should be prescribed free of charge.

Specialist consultants involved with incontinence include urologists, gynaecologists, geriatricians and paediatricians, for example. They take referrals from the GP, or each other as appropriate.

17.3.3.1. Urodynamic clinic. Following GP referral, assessment might take place at a special urodynamic clinic, for example, at which a consultant and nurse are present, and sometimes a continence adviser.

Children are likely to be assessed by a paediatrician.

17.3.3.2. Transfer of prescription responsibility to GP. Drug Tariff items (Box 5.1.) might be prescribed initially at the hospital and while a person is regularly seen by a consultant. Thereafter a GP prescibes routinely, as appropriate.

17.3.3.3. Provision of incontinence pads. Pads might be supplied initially at the hospital clinic, but would normally be supplied thereafer by a community nurse.

In Scotland, bed pads can be formally prescribed by consultants (initially) and GPs (routinely) as a Drug Tariff item.

17.3.4. Continence advisers Continence advisers (often nurses) are the expert professionals on the management of incontinence. Their importance has been recognised recently by Circular guidance (England,1988) which advised the creation of DHA-wide incontinence services (*HN(88)26*).

17.3.4.1. Location. Continence advisers might work and be located in the following ways:

- attached to a health centre and taking many GP referrals (and sometimes operate open referral as well);
- community or hospital-based operating both doctor referral and varying degrees of open referral;
- at a hospital continence clinic working closely with a consultant (urologist).

Continence advisers increasingly take open referral from people themselves or from professionals other than doctors, as well as from doctors; especially since some people do not wish to discuss such problems with their GP. Publicity for open referral to continence advisers might be achieved, for example, by means of a local newspaper or radio item, or by a notice in GP surgeries.

17.3.4.2. Continence adviser provision of equipment. Continence advisers based at a hospital clinic can supply equipment (appliances and pads) at initial assessment, under the authority of the consultant. (Afterwards, GPs prescribe or community nurses provide, appliances and pads/pants respectively.)

In the community the continence adviser can request the GP to prescribe appliances, and either directly arrange the supply of pads/pants/bedding or refer to a community nurse for such supply.

17.3.4.2.1. Future prescribing powers. In the future, it is expected that continence advisers with suitable qualifications will be able to prescribe items (currently GP prescribed) from a nurses' formulary (*Report of the Advisory Group on Nurse Prescribing. DH 1989 p. 27*).

17.3.4.3. Home visits. The continence adviser sometimes makes home visits, especially to identify access and mobility problems for example.

17.3.4.4. Circular guidance (England, 1988) recommends to DHAs the 'provision of a district-wide incontinence service. Good practice would include a Continence Adviser acting as a focal point, provision for regular and adequate supply of incontinence aids and reasonable access to a urodynamic clinic. Authorities should identify a consultant and a physiotherapist to take a special interest in incontinence' (*HN(88)26*).

Circular guidance (England, 1988) also states that DHAs should develop ' plans for physically and sensorily disabled people and for people who are incontinent, including a statement of what is to be achieved, schedules for implementation and monitoring arrangements' (*Joint circular HC(88)43 LAC(88)14 FPN(88)457*).

17.3.5. SSD/SWD assessment for incontinence pads. SSD/SWDs sometimes supply incontinence pads to residential homes and occasionally to individuals in their own home. They might obtain advice from a continence adviser, who is sometimes (in England at least) joint-funded (by the SSD and DHA).

17.3.6. Assessment of children. Children are assessed by paediatricians, while health visitors, school nurses and district nurses might identify a problem and inform the child's GP.

17.4. Supply

17.4.1. Supply to hospital inpatients. As with other equipment, health service inpatients are entitled to any equipment medically necessary, free of charge.

Nevertheless, the supply to inpatients of incontinence equipment can be complex and is sometimes affected by the following factors:

- variable access to pads according to the type of ward involved;
- variable choice of pad throughout the hospital depending on hospital ordering policy;
- difficulty in maintaining previously (before hospital admission) established pad regime in hospital;
- difficulty in retention of personal equipment such as special commode or special urinal, given the nature of hospital cleaning and sterilisation procedures (*Verbal communication: ACA, 1989*).

17.4.2. Outpatient suppply. As already mentioned (17.3.3.2.), outpatients might have initially been prescribed or given some appliances and supplies (of pads) at a hospital clinic, but later supply is taken over either by the GP (prescription) or the community nurse (provision of incontinence pads and pants).

17.4.3. Community supply. As already mentioned above, GPs prescribe incontinence appliances (and in Scotland, bed pads) listed on the Drug Tariff. District nurses and sometimes health visitors and continence advisers supply incontinence pads, linings, pants etc.

For children the supply of pads and pants is sometimes the responsibility of the health visitor or school nurse.

Community mental handicap nurses (CMHNs) might sometimes be responsible for an individual regime of incontinence pads for a person with learning difficulties (mental handicap) in the community.

17.4.3.1. Supply of incontinence pads. The supply of incontinence pads in the community can be a complex matter. Complicating factors can include shortage of pads, non-provision of pads, delivery routines, pad disposal, supply to residential homes and supply to private nursing homes. For details of these see Box 17.1.

Box 17.1: Community supply of incontinence pads

B17.1.1. Delivery. District nurses (or sometimes health visitors) often arrange for the supply of incontinence pads to people living in the community. They might deliver the pads personally, or arrange for regular delivery, if an organised delivery system exists. Stocks may be delivered to health centres, from where they are distributed to individuals.

Computer systems might be used to manage the supply of incontinence pads (*Blannin J. Managing Supplies. Nursing Times 1987 April 15th p. 76*) and equipment store managers sometimes play a very active role in managing the supply of pads to individuals.

B17.1.1.1. Continuing assessment. The advantages of an efficient delivery service is sometimes offset by the consequent absence of continuing assessment by the district nurse on each weekly visit (*Verbal communication; ENB, 1989*). One solution to this

---

particular problem is for regular reassessment to take place at least every 3 months. Otherwise pads could be delivered to no end, and be used for wiping car windscreens, for example.

B17.1.2. Pad disposal

B17.1.2.1. Pad disposal. Collection services are organised by either the DHA/HB/HSSB or SSD/SWD, and sometimes jointly.

Services are likely to vary, existing in one area and not in another. They might be run in association with existing services for the collection of stoma bags or needles used for diabetes.

Where there are no collection services, people have to dispose of pads via normal rubbish collection. In theory this should not happen, and dustmen for example, have every right to refuse to handle faeces. (But there are no baby nappy collection services, for example, and nappies, also, are commonly disposed via normal rubbish collection).

B17.1.3. Shortage of pads and inefficient use of pads. Circular correspondence (England, 1987) recognises problems in the supply of pads and the effect on people's 'ability to live comfortably in the community' (*D(87)45*).

Discussion in the House of Lords (24th April, 1990) has highlighted the apparent inadequate provision of incontinence services and materials in England (*Hansard. House of Lords, 24th April, 1990 cols. 546–552*).

A 1986 survey, for example, found that, of elderly people (over 75) at home using health service incontinence aids, most did not use the aids successfully. This was chiefly because of restriction of supply and inefficient design or utilisation (*McGrother C. et al. Provision of services for incontinent elderly people at home. Journal of Epidemiology and Community Health. 1986:40, 134–138*).

B17.1.3.1. Rationing. DHA/HB/HSSB policy sometimes limits the number of pads/padding rolls, pants available to an individual per week/fortnight/month, or stops supply altogether (*eg Norton C. Nursing for Continence. Beaconsfield, 1986 p. 224; Holden G. What is the bottom line? Disability Now, March 1990 p. 9*). This could involve an upper limit of, for example:

- 4–5 pads a day;
- 100 pads a month;
- 30 sheets a month.

B17.1.3.2. Erratic delivery. Delivery services can be erratic, resulting sometimes in a lack of pads.

Supply problems can include, for example:

- inadequate supplies to distribution point;
- inaccessibility of the distribution point;
- lack of a home delivery service (*McGrother C. et al. Provision of services for incontinent elderly people at home. Journal of Epidemiology and Community Health. 1986:40, 134–138*).

B17.1.3.3. Budget. The relevant budget sometimes runs out before the end of the year, thus cutting or stopping altogether a supply of pads which might up to that point have been unrestricted.

B17.1.3.4. Professional assessment sometimes underestimates the quantity of pads needed, or fails to take into account a change in the incontinent person's condition.

B17.1.3.5. Restriction to certain categories. Some DHA/HB/HSSBs might impose certain restrictions, supplying, for example:

- only people with (other) disabilities and terminally ill people;
- terminally ill people only;
- people with continuous incontinence;
- no supplies to people needing under a certain quantity of pads per day.

The range of products available might also be restricted; or a waiting list operated for example.

B17.1.3.6. Ultimate DHA/HB/HSSB discretion. Legislation, Circular guidance and other government communications confirm that DHA/HB/HSSBs do not have a duty to supply incontinence pads, but do so at their discretion *(For legislation see 1.2.4.1.; HRC(74)16; D(87)45; DH Letter 22.5.89 to Ann Winterton, MP).*

Nevertheless, this discretion (rather than duty) is not necessarily common perception. For example, one detailed and exhaustive joint SSD/DHA document drawn up at local level states that incontinent clients are 'entitled to be supplied with certain incontinence materials without charge' *(London SSD (19) guidelines received 1989).*

B17.1.4. Supply of pads to residential homes. In theory, incontinence is not one of the conditions which residential homes are intended to cope with. Many residents are continent on admission to the home, but their condition deteriorates. The home may not see it is as their duty to supply pads for incontinence, as part of the integral services of the home.

B17.1.4.1. DHA/HB/HSSB powers. People in residential homes (public sector or private) are supposed to have the same rights to health and social services as anyone living in their own home (24.4.3.).

Indeed they are mentioned as one group of people at risk of incontinence in Circular guidance (England, Scotland 1977) *(CNO(SNC)(77)1).* Other Circular guidance (England, 1974) specifically mentions incontinence equipment such as 'incontinence pads, interliners, waterproof pants etc.', as suppliable by health authorities, to both individuals and residential homes *(HRC(74)16).*

B17.1.4.1.1. Discretionary use of power. DHA/HB/HSSBs have the power, used at their discretion, to supply pads.

A recent DH letter on incontinence materials states: 'health authorities are empowered to supply these and other nursing aids to people living in their own homes. They may also, at their discretion, provide a similar service for residents in local authority homes and in private and voluntary residential homes. The extent to which they exercise that discretion varies from place to place and is determined in the light of local needs and resources' *(DH POH(5)2143/141 22.5.89 Letter to Ann Winterton MP).*

B17.1.4.1.2. Practice. The discretion which DHA/HB/HSSBs have results in uneven practice. The position is confused. For example in England DHA policies are likely to vary, some supplying residential homes and others not. Financial pressures sometimes cause residential homes to be identified as a clear target for cuts in supply. Residential home owners then may supply pads, but charge for them *(eg Holden G. Disability Now, March 1990 p. 9).*

Where supply does not take place the resident or friends and relatives have to pay. The DH in 1987 recognised the level of the problem in a Letter to Regional General Managers requesting information on local policy *(D(87)45).*

B17.1.4.1.3. Examples of DHA (for example) restricted supply to residential homes could include the following practices:

- no supply;
- supply only to individuals regularly visited by district nurse;
- number of pads restricted;
- no bed pads;
- no supplies to children under 5;
- no supplies to children under 3;
- no supplies to children under 2.

B17.1.4.1.4. SSD/SWD provision. SSD/SWDs sometimes supply pads to their own residential homes.

The extent to which SSD/SWDs provide pads in practice is unknown.

B17.1.4.1.5. Private purchase. Where neither DHA/HB/HSSB or SSD/SWD provision takes place, residents (or their families) have to buy their own pads.

B17.1.5. SSD/SWD and HSSB (social services) powers and practice. Local SSD/SWD/ HSSB (social services) have the power (17.2.1.4.) to supply pads, and sometimes do so, usually to residential homes (4.1.).

B17.1.6. Supply to private nursing homes. According to Circular guidance, private nursing homes are expected to supply incontinence pads free of charge, as part of the home's integral services, although the extent to which they are prepared to supply different types of pad varies.

In practice, they might, for example, supply only standard bed pads, expecting the person to pay for any bodyworn pads or other types of pad. Some private nursing homes might charge extra for pads, anyway (*Hansard, House of Lords, April 24th 1990, cols. 545–552*).

Very occasionally, (and contrary to government policy), a DHA/HB/HSSB supplies incontinence pads to individual private nursing homes.

B17.1.6.1. Circular guidance (England, 1974). According to Circular guidance, DHAs do not have power to supply pads to private nursing homes. A 1974 English circular makes it quite clear concerning incontinence pads, that DHAs (then AHAs) 'should not therefore provide such services direct to patients in nursing homes' (*HRC(74)16*).

A recent DH letter stated that the reason for this non-provision to nursing homes is that the homes 'are under an obligation to provide continuous nursing care or treatment and generally fix their fees at a level which includes the costs of any nursing aids that may be needed' (*DH POH(5)2143/141 22.5.89 Letter to Ann Winterton MP*).

B17.1.6.2. Circular guidance (Scotland). Circular guidance (1989) makes it quite clear that on an individual basis, residents of private nursing homes should have access to health services just like anybody else. This access should be through their GP, and could therefore include bed incontinence pads, which are listed on the Drug Tariff (Scotland).

However, other pads, not prescribable through the GP, should be supplied by the home, as part of nursing services (*NHS 1989(GEN)39*).

B17.1.7. Supply to children by DHA/HB/HSSBs. Research in England, for example, has shown that children over seven are more likely to receive more DHA aids than those children under seven.

Further, children with severe incontinence might tend to receive proportionally fewer aids than with less severe incontinence, since they use more aids not generally provided by the statutory services. These aids include, for example, plastic/waterproof pants, (which in theory are available from DHAs) and extra toiletries and deodorants which are not provided by the DHA, unless exceptionally.

Supplies might be organised by health visitors, school nurses, or district nurses (*Parker G. Incontinence Services for the Disabled Child. Part 1: Provision of Aids and Equipment. Health Visitor 1984: 57, 44-*).

Restrictions in supply of incontinence pads to children might include for example:

- no supply;
- no supply to children under 2;
- no supply to children under 2.5;
- no supply to children under 3;
- no supply to children over 7;
- supply to children with spina bifida only.

17.4.3.2. Dispensing of prescription items. Dispensing of (Drug Tariff) equipment prescribed by GPs (or consultants) is undertaken either by a pharmacist (5.1.4.10.) who can offer more or less expertise in relation to incontinence appliances; or by a dispensing appliance centre which offers an expert dispensing and fitting service (5.1.4.10.).

17.4.4. Enuresis alarms are usually loaned to children for nocturnal bladder-training. The alarm is usually loaned for three months and its use monitored carefully. The alarm is either attached to the bed/bedding or is bodyworn.

A number of professionals loan such alarms; for example, school nurses, health visitors, GPs, paediatricians and psychologists.

Many parents buy the enuresis alarm themselves if they can afford it. Sometimes this is necessary, if there are waiting lists for the loan of the alarm.

17.4.5. Private purchase. Some people prefer to buy incontinence equipment privately anyway, while others may do so if, for example, they do not receive a sufficient supply of pads from the DHA/HB/HSSB. Items such as sanitary towels or baby diapers as substitutes are expensive. Private purchase has the drawback of little advice, mail order the additional drawback of lack of fitting or guarantee of performance (*Norton C. Nursing for Continence. Beaconsfield, 1986, p. 224*).

17.4.5.1. Highstreet availability. Opportunity for private purchase has improved recently, in that larger chemists are displaying and selling items, such as pads, urinals, (male and female) and mattress covers.

Although these tend to be found in the larger 'supermarket' type of chemist, where there is little informed advice available from specialist staff, nevertheless, responsible manufacturers do insert advice with the product. This advice might not only relate to the product itself, but suggest that the person should seek professional advice, if they have not already done so.

18 Equipment for Stoma Care

Introduction

Equipment for stoma care

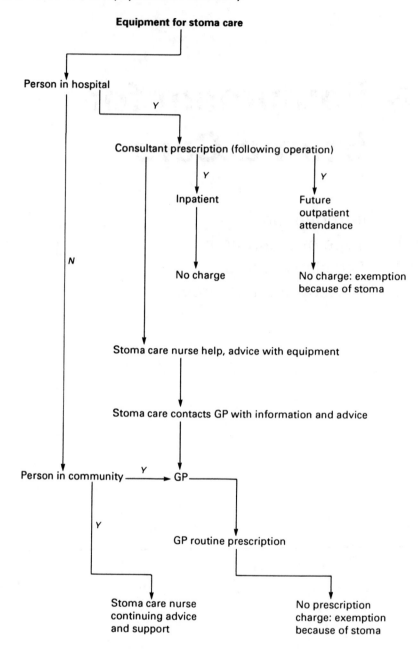

Person in hospital

Consultant prescription (following operation)

Y

Inpatient

No charge

Y

Future
outpatient
attendance

No charge: exemption
because of stoma

N

Stoma care nurse help, advice with equipment

Stoma care contacts GP with information and advice

Person in community — *Y* → GP

GP routine prescription

Y

Stoma care nurse
continuing advice
and support

No prescription
charge: exemption
because of stoma

Introduction

Type of equipment. Equipment for stoma care includes, for example, bags, belts, adhesives, filters and deodorants.

Responsibility for provision. The health service is responsible for provision of equipment:

- district health authorities and family practitioner committees (DHAs and FPCs, England and Wales);
- health boards (HBs, Scotland);
- health and social services boards (HSSBs, Northern Ireland).

Prescription and provision. The provision of stoma care equipment is normally initiated in hospital, following an operation; it is consultant prescribed, or supplied by a stoma care nurse under the authority of the consultant. Routine prescription of equipment is then usually taken over by a general practitioner (GP), perhaps with the advice of a stoma care nurse.

(Provision of stoma care appliances is generally straightforward as most equipment required is prescribable by GPs. In the future, it is expected that stoma care nurses will be able to prescribe certain items listed in a nurses' formulary.)

Regular review is undertaken by the hospital consultant, and advice and support (including advice on equipment use) given by the stoma care nurse.

18.1. Type of equipment

Examples of stoma care equipment are given in Box 18.1.

Box 18.1: Stoma care equipment includes:

- adhesive discs/rings/ pads/plasters;
- bag closures;
- bag covers;
- belts;
- colostomy bags;
- colostomy sets;
- deodorants;
- filters/bridges;
- flanges;
- ileostomy bags;
- ileostomy sets;
- irrigation/wash-out appliances;
- pressure plates/shield;
- skin protectors (wafers, blankets, foam pads, washers) (*as listed on the Drug Tariff, England and Wales, 1989*).

18.2. Legislative basis for provision

18.2.1. Basis: consulant prescription is covered by the DHA/HB/HSSB duty to provide 'medical services' (*NHS Act 1977 s.3; NHS (Scotland) Act 1978 s.36; SI 1972/1265 HPSS(NI)O a.5*).

18.2.2. Basis: GP prescription is covered by the DHA (through FPC) and HB/HSSB duty to provide 'general medical services' (*NHS Act s.29; NHS (Scotland) Act 1978 s.19; SI 1972/1265 HPSS(NI)O a.56*).

18.2.3. Basis: nurse recommendation, fitting, advice (and possible future prescription), are covered by the DHA/HB/HPSSB to provide 'nursing services' (*NHS Act 1977 s.3; NHS (Scotland) Act 1978 s.36; SI 1972/1265 HPSS(NI)O a.5*).

18.3. Prescription and provision of stoma care equipment

18.3.1. Hospital consultant prescription and provision. Stoma care equipment is initially supplied by the hospital following an operation. Consultants can prescribe whatever is listed on the Drug Tariff, and any other equipment which is medically necessary.

Consultants typically involved include general surgeons, urologists and gastro-enterologists; and medical consultant physicians, for example, when a person with a stoma is being treated for another problem.

18.3.2. General practitioners (GPs) regularly prescribe stoma care equipment (Box 18.1.), once a person with a stoma has been discharged from hospital.

18.3.3. Stoma care nurses sometimes supply hospital patients with the necessary equipment under the authority of the consultant. They usually counsel the patient both pre-and post-operatively and generally look after them for 3 or 4 days after the operation.

Stoma care nurses usually advise the person's GP on what to regularly prescribe once the person has returned home. Few GPs are experts in stoma care and the Drug Tariff is not necessarily self-explanatory (*see eg Elcoat, C. Stoma Care Nursing. Bailliere Tindall 1986 p. 191*).

It is expected that, in the future, stoma care nurses will be able to prescribe items from a nurses' formulary (*Report of the Advisory Group on Nurse Prescribing. DH 1989 p. 27*).

18.3.4. Dispensing and fitting. Routine dispensing is undertaken by pharmacists and sometimes by dispensing appliance centres.

18.3.4.1.Pharmacist dispensing and advice. Pharmacists dispense appliances and can give advice, especially where there is no stoma care nurse.

Depending on individual expertise, they can advise on diet, on equipment problems (eg out of date, ill-fitting), on the different types of equipment available and on skin problems; and refer people to a stoma care nurse, if they are not already in touch with one (*see eg Elcoat, C. Stoma Care Nursing. Bailliere Tindall 1986 p. 192*).

18.3.4.2. Dispensing appliance centres. There are a number of dispensing appliance centres (5.1.4.10.), run by private firms, which offer an expert dispensing and fitting service for Drug Tariff stoma care appliances, prescribed by doctors (5.1.4.10.).

18.3.5. Choice of equipment. A variety of appliances is available on the Drug Tariff, and people with a stoma are exempt from prescription charges. Manufacturers also exhibit their appliances, enabling people to see, and try out, what suits them best, as well as keep up with the latest developments. Such exhibitions of appliances typically take place within a hospital setting at a clinic, or at voluntary organisation meetings (for example, Ileostomy Association, whose magazine also carries advertisements for equipment).

18.3.6. Follow-up. Following hospital discharge, a person with a stoma normally attends a hospital clinic, for consultant assessment, at intervals, for example, at 6 weeks, 3 months, 6 months, 1 year. The stoma care nurse also holds his or her own clinics, and, where specific problems have arisen, can see a person by appointment at the hospital or by home visit.

The stoma care nurse keeps in contact with the person's GP, as necessary.

18.3.7. Charges. Drug Tariff (Box 18.1.) items, prescribed by a GP or consultant, attract a charge in theory, but people with a stoma are exempt from prescription charges (30.1./Box 30.1.1.6.).

18.3.8. Laryngectomy equipment. For laryngectomy, not all types of item are available on prescription; thus, for example, one type (Laryngofoam) of filter (piece of plastic with adhesive foam) is available, another type (Romet) available in a number of different colours, is not.

A consultant is able, where there is a medical need, to prescribe other items. For example, an ENT surgeon could prescribe suction machines or humidifiers.

People who have had a laryngectomy are exempt from prescription charges.

19 Equipment for Renal Dialysis

Renal dialysis equipment

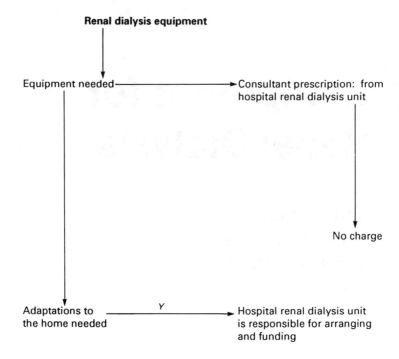

Equipment needed ⟶ Consultant prescription: from hospital renal dialysis unit

No charge

Adaptations to the home needed ⟶ Y ⟶ Hospital renal dialysis unit is responsible for arranging and funding

Introduction

Type of equipment. Equipment and adaptations needed for renal dialysis vary, depending on the type of dialysis being used, and can include the dialyser unit, catheter, bag, separate dialysing room, direct cold water supply and electrical generator for emergencies etc.

Responsibility for provision lies with the health service:

- district health authorities (DHAs, England and Wales);
- health boards (HBs, Scotland);
- health and social services boards (HSSBs, Northern Ireland);
- general practitioners (GPs).

Provision is made by hospital renal dialysis units, which are responsible for any equipment and home adaptations needed. Any prescription charges for accessories listed on the Drug Tariff are waived, since people utilising dialysis are exempt from prescription charges.

19.1. Type of equipment

There are now three main types of renal dialysis: haemodialysis (HD), intermittent peritoneal dialysis (IPD) and continous ambulatory peritoneal dialysis (CAPD).

19.1.1. HD: there are many different types of dialyser (separate from the kidney machine) through which blood passes and is cleaned. The kidney machine controls this operation by regulation of blood flow, pressure and rate of exchange.

19.1.2. IPD involves the pouring of the dialysate solution into the peritoneal cavity by means of a catheter; the solution attracts waste products from the bloodstream across the semi-permeable membrane wall of the peritoneum.

19.1.3. CAPD involves the pouring of dialysate solution into the abdomen via a catheter by holding a bag above the head; and the changing of the solution every five or six hours by letting it flow into the bag now held at a low level. After this the bag is changed for a new one, and the process repeated. This method of dialysis allows the person to walk about, although since infection is a risk, the changing of the bag must take place in clean surroundings (*information based on: Introduction to Dialysis. National Federation of Kidney Patients' Associations*).

19.1.4. Adaptations in the home, for HB and IPD may be required, including a separate waterproof floor treatment room (sometimes Portacabin), a direct cold water supply from the mains, an electrical generator for emergencies, sink, telephone, heating, alarm/bell and so on.

19.2. Legislative basis for provision

Health service provision of equipment for the management of renal dialysis lies in the DHA/HB/HSSB duty to provide 'medical services' (*NHS Act 1977 s.3; NHS (Scotland) Act 1978 s.36; SI 1972/1265 HPSS(NI)O a.5*).

19.3. Provision

Hospital renal dialysis units take responsibility for the provision of equipment adaptations required for renal dialysis.

19.3.1. Circular guidance (England, Scotland), for example, states that DHA/HBs are responsible for the following:

- adaptation of a patient's home;
- provision and maintenance of dialysis equipment;
- provision of necessary drugs, dressings, concentrates, etc.;
- cost of the electricity required to run the machines;
- cost of installation and rental of a telephone where one is not available;
- cost of maintaining the dialysis room at the desired temperature (*see eg HSC(IS)11; SHHD/DS(74)36*)).

19.3.2. Prescription charges. Any prescribable items (listed on the Drug Tariff) are free of charge, since dialysis patients 'have a permanent fistula requiring surgical dressing' (*HSC(IS)1*) (Box 30.1.1.6.).

19.3.3. Adaptations examples (*the following is based on English circular guidance, (HSC(IS)11*)).

19.3.3.1. Accommodation. Circular guidance states that this could involve adapting an existing room, providing an extension or transportable 'cabin' unit and/or (where there is no alternative) arranging re-housing through the local housing authority (*HSC(IS)11*).

19.3.3.2. Electricity. Circular guidance states that there is a responsibility to provide standby generators in case of power cuts, where the person cannot be taken back into hospital. The cost of running any machinery is met by the health authority/board (*HSC(IS)11*).

19.3.3.3. Heating. Circular guidance states that heating appliances are supplied, if necessary, and in any the case the cost of keeping the treatment room at a constant temperature (of at least 21 degrees C) is met (*HSC(IS)11*).

19.3.3.4. Electricity meter. Circular guidance states that electricity costs may be ascertained either by the installation of a separate meter, or by calculation (*HSC(IS)11*).

19.3.3.5. Water. Circular guidance states that the cold water supply should be direct from the mains, via a water softener, and sometimes through a filter to remove certain elements from the water.

The hot water can come from an existing domestic system (*HSC(IS)11*).

19.3.3.6. Flooring. Circular guidance states that flooring should be waterproof, and capable of supporting at least the water softener, dialysing fluid supply unit and the dialyser (with trolley). It must be level, with gaps between wall and floor filled in (*HSC(IS)11*).

19.3.3.7. Telephone. Circular guidance states that, where there is no telephone, the health authority has a responsbility to provide both the telephone installation and the rental costs (*HSC(IS)11*).

19.3.3.8. Sinks and draining board. Circular guidance states that a suitable sink and draining board is supplied and paid for by the health authority (*HSC(IS)11*).

19.3.4. Co-operation with other authorities. Circular guidance (England, Scotland) states that DHA/HBs need to co-operate with other authorities, housing and social services/work departments, in respect of dialysis patients at home (*HSC(IS)11; SHHD/DS(74)36*).

20 Equipment for People with Diabetes

Diabetes equipment

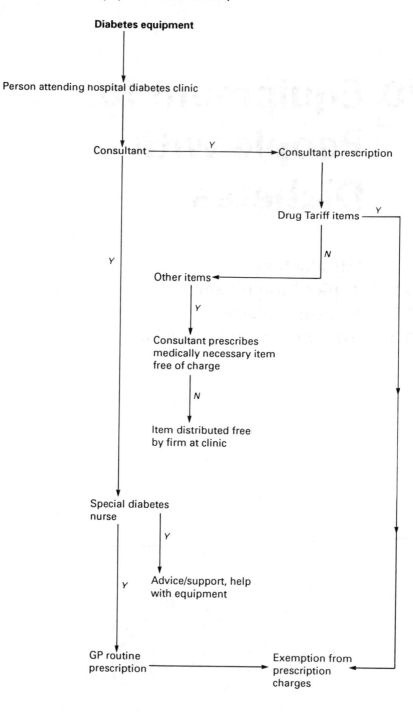

Person attending hospital diabetes clinic

Consultant —————Y————► Consultant prescription

Drug Tariff items —Y—

Other items ◄—— N

Y (Consultant) / Other items — Y

Consultant prescribes
medically necessary item
free of charge

N

Item distributed free
by firm at clinic

Special diabetes
nurse

Y

Advice/support, help
with equipment

Y

GP routine
prescription ——————► Exemption from
prescription
charges

Introduction

Type of equipment. Equipment for people who have diabetes, and who require insulin, includes syringes, syringe needles, lancets, blood-testing strips and blood testing machines.

Responsibility for provision lies with the health service:

- district health authorities and family practitioner committees (DHAs and FPCs, England and Wales);
- health boards (HBs, Scotland);
- health and social services boards (HSSBs, Northern Ireland).

Assessment, prescription and provision. Specialist diabetes consultants can prescribe equipment; otherwise routine supply is by general practitioner (GP) prescription. Some items, or particular makes/brands of item, are not prescribed; these are either available by private purchase or through free distribution (via the consultant) by manufacturers and suppliers at hospital diabetes clinics.

Specialist diabetes nurses provide much advice and support in the use of equipment for managing diabetes; in the future it is expected that they may be able to prescribe equipment for diabetes listed in a nurses' formulary.

20.1. Type of equipment

People with diabetes, and requiring insulin, need a variety of equipment. This includes:

- standard glass and plastic syringes;
- pre-set syringes for people with visual impairment;
- click/count syringes;
- standard needles;
- insulin cartridges (including for pen-type syringe);
- lancets (for taking blood samples);
- blood-testing strips;
- blood-testing machines;
- pen-type syringes;
- jet injectors;
- location trays;
- syringe magnifiers;
- strip guides;
- centre point funnel;
- syringe guide.

20.2. Legislative basis for provision

20.2.1. Basis: consultant prescription is covered by the DHA/HB/HSSB duty to provide 'medical services' (*NHS Act 1977 s.3; NHS (Scotland) Act 1978 s.36; SI 1972/1265 HPSS(NI)O a.5*).

20.2.2. Basis: GP prescription is covered by the DHA (through FPC) and HB/HSSB duty to provide 'general medical services' (*NHS Act s.29; NHS (Scotland) Act 1978 s.19; SI 1972/1265 HPSS(NI)O a.56*).

20.2.3. Basis: nurse recommendation, fitting, advice (and possible future prescription powers) is covered by the DHA/HB/HSSB duty to provide 'nursing services' (*NHS Act 1977 s.3; NHS (Scotland) Act 1978 s.36; SI 1972/1265 HPSS(NI)O a.5*).

20.3. Prescription and provision

20.3.1.GPs provide advice and prescribe equipment for diabetes listed on the Drug Tariff.

20.3.2. Hospital clinics. Apart from receiving services from their GP, people with diabetes might be under a hospital-based diabetes clinic, run by a specialist consultant. Care for children is likely to be handled in a paediatrics department.

20.3.3. Specialist diabetes nurses. In some areas there are now, attached to hospital clinics, specialist diabetes nurses, who extend the service out into the community. Sometimes such nurses are on call; she or he can, for example, talk a person through a crisis on the telephone.

The nurse may also contact GP practices, and help to increase awareness and improve services at a local level. Such improvements may include the establishment of a register, advice on equipment, advice on the screening of feet and eyes and so on (*eg MacKinnon M et al. Novel role for specialist nurses in managing diabetes in the community. BMJ 1989: 299, 552-554*).

In the future, it is expected that specialist diabetes nurses, appropriately qualified, may be able to prescribe some items, currently GP prescribed, from a nurses' formulary (*Report of the Advisory Group on Nurse Prescribing. DH 1989 p. 29*).

20.3.4. Items prescribed by GPs. A certain amount of equipment is available on prescription from GPs; it is listed on the Drug Tariff and includes: standard glass and plastic syringes (including pre-set syringes for use by blind people); click/count syringes; standard needles; insulin cartridges (including for pentype syringe); some lancets; some blood testing-strips.

People suffering from diabetes are exempt from prescription charges.

20.3.5. Items not prescribed by GPs but medically required. A consultant has the power (5.2.4.1.) to prescribe, free of charge, any other equipment medically needed.

20.3.6. Items not prescribed by GPs and not specially prescribed by a consultant are either distributed by firms (free of charge) to diabetes clinics, or are privately purchased.

Items in this category include pen-type syringes (eg Novopen) and needles for them, some lancets, some blood-testing strips, blood testing machines, jet injectors, location trays, syringe magnifiers, strip guides, centre point funnels, syringe guides (*Help received from: written communication, British Diabetic Association, 1989*).

21 Respiratory Equipment (nebuliser units, oxygen cylinders, oxygen concentrators)

Respiratory equipment need

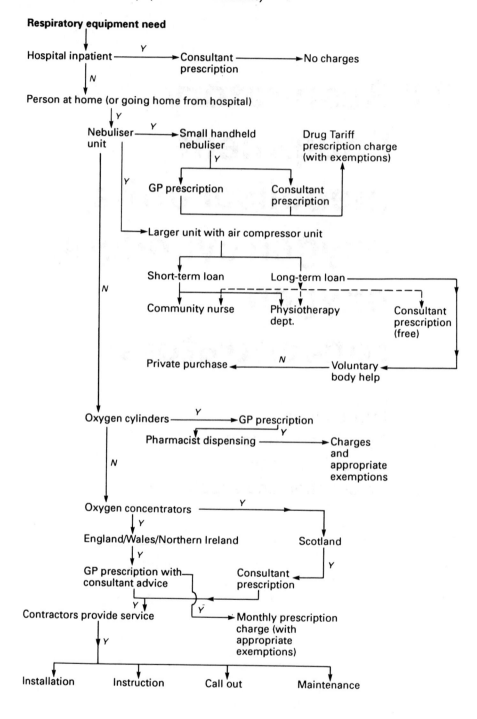

Introduction

Type of equipment. Nebuliser units range from small handheld appliances to large units, which are used with air compressor units. They are used to administer drugs in solution in the form of a fine 'spray', but are also sometimes used, without drugs, as humidifiers.

Respiratory equipment also includes both oxygen cylinders and oxygen concentrators, for intermittent and long term oxygen treatment respectively.

Responsibility for provision lies with the health services:

- district health authorities and family practitioner committees (DHAs and FPCs, England, Wales);
- health boards (HBs, Scotland);
- health and social services boards (HSSBs, Northern Ireland).

Prescription, provision, dispensing. Small nebuliser units are prescribed by GPs; larger units, for which there appears to be increasing demand, in terms of home use, are loaned (often short-term), free of charge, by community nursing services or physiotherapists. For longer term use, people may have to buy their own unit, or seek help from voluntary bodies. Drugs in solution, which the unit 'nebulises', are prescribed in the normal way by GPs (5.1.4.1.).

Oxygen cylinders are prescribed by general practitioners (GPs) for routine home use; pharmacists actually dispense the prescription (usually for two or three cylinders at a time). Standard prescription charges, with the usual exemptions, apply (Box 30.1.).

Oxygen concentrators are prescribed by GPs in England, Wales and Northern Ireland, though there should be close consultation with hospital respiratory consultants. In Scotland, hospital respiratory consultants prescribe oxygen concentrators; GPs are unable to. A monthly prescription charge, with exemptions, applies in England, Wales and Northern Ireland; there is no prescription charge in Scotland. Contracts for supply, maintenance, emergency callout etc are held by private contractors.

21.1. Type of equipment

21.1.1. Nebuliser units include both small handheld appliances and large units used in conjunction with air compression units (coming in one unit, or separately). Nebuliser units enable a drug (in solution) to be delivered in a fine spray or mist, thus ensuring better 'take-up' of the drug.

Sometimes nebuliser units are used as humidifiers; a saline solution (without a drug) is held in the unit.

21.1.2. Oxygen cylinders contain pressurised oxygen. They are supplied with either a mask or nasal cannulae. The cylinder is often used to supply oxygen alone, but is also used with a drug (in solution) filled 'nebuliser' between the cylinder and the mask.

21.1.3. Oxygen concentrators. Oxygen concentrators are electrically powered machines, which separate a high proportion of nitrogen and some other components from ordinary 'air' in order to deliver oxygen-enriched gases to patients (*Drug Tariff, Jan. 1989, Part 10, Appendix,p. 7*). As with oxygen cylinders, a mask or nasal cannulae can be used.

21.2. Legislative basis for provision

21.2.1. Basis: consultant prescription is covered by the DHA/HB/HSSB duty to provide 'medical services' (*NHS Act 1977 s.3, NHS Act (Scotland) 1978, s.36; SI 1972/1265 HPSS(NI)O 1972 a.5*).

21.2.2. Basis: GP prescription is covered by the DHA (through FPC)/HB/HSSB duty provide 'general medical services' (*NHS Act 1977 s.29; NHS (Scotland) Act 1978 s.19; SI 1972/1265 HPSS(NI)O 1972 a.56*).

21.2.3. Basis: community nursing service (CNS) loan (of nebuliser equipment) is covered by the DHA/HB/HSSB duty to provide 'nursing services' (*NHS Act 1977 s.3; NHS (Scotland) Act 1978 s.36; SI 1972/1265 a.5*).

It is also covered more specifically by the DHA/HB/HSSB duty entailing 'the prevention of illness, the care of persons suffering from illness' and the after-care of such people (*NHS 1977, s.3; NHS 1978, s.37; SI 1972/1265 HPSS(NI)O 1972, a.7*).

21.2.4. Basis: physiotherapist loan (of nebuliser equipment) is covered by the DHA/HB/HSSB duty to provide 'other services' (*NHS Act 1977 s.3; NHS (Scotland) Act 1978 s.36; SI 1972/1265 HPSS(NI)O 1972 a.5*).

21.3. Prescription and supply

21.3.1. Nebuliser unit assessment, prescription and supply

21.3.1.1. Small nebuliser units on prescription. GPs or consultants can prescribe small (handheld) nebuliser units which are listed on the Drug Tariff. Prescription charges and exemptions, as appropriate, apply (Box 30.1.).

21.3.1.2. Larger nebuliser units and air compression units, supplied separately or as one unit, are not listed on the Drug Tariff and are not prescribed by GPs.

Consultants have the power (5.2.4.1.) to prescribe such units if they are medically necessary; but, in practice, short-term loan tends to be made (free of charge) by either the community nursing services (CNS) or a hospital physiotherapy department.

Demand for these nebuliser units on home loan appears to be increasing (*Written communication: Welsh DHA CNS; Verbal communication: London DHA District physiotherapist; London DHA CNS manager*); and in such circumstances long-term loan of such equipment is unlikely to be financially viable for the DHA/HB/HSSB.

Longer term needs are therefore sometimes met by either private purchase, or by help from voluntary organisations, a list of which might be made available by the CNS or physiotherapy department.

21.3.2. Oxygen cylinder assessment and prescription

21.3.2.1. Criteria for provision. The Drug Tariff (England and Wales), for example, states that cylinders can be used in small amounts for intermittent therapy for hypoxaemia of short duration; recurring asthma is given as an example.

They can also be presribed for patients with advanced irreversible respiratory disorders to increase mobility and capacity for exercise and ease discomfort; in patients, for example, with chronic obstructive bronchitis, emphysema, widespread fibrosis and primary or thrombo-embolic pulmonary hypertension (*Drug Tariff Part 10 Appendix p. 1*).

21.3.2.2. Prescription. Oxygen cylinders are listed on the Drug Tariff (5.1.4.1.) and are prescribed by GPs (and consultants). Initial prescription is often made by the hospital consultant; thereafter regular prescription is by the GP. Prescription charges (together with exemptions from those charges) (Box 30.1.) apply; GPs usually prescribe in sets of 2 or 3 cylinders per prescription form.

Dispensing of prescriptions is carried out by pharmacists.

21.3.2.3. Delivery and collection of oxygen cylinders, should (the Drug Tariff (England and Wales) states) be undertaken by the patient's representative where he or she is willing, (and the pharmacist believes that he/she is able to transport the equipment and explain its use). Otherwise the pharmacist is responsible for delivery, erection, collection of cylinders and explanation of their use (*Drug Tariff (England and Wales) 1.89 Part 10 Appendix p. 4*).

21.3.3. Oxygen concentrator assessment and prescription

21.3.3.1. Criteria for provision. Oxygen concentrators are prescribed for people who need oxygen for 15 hours per day, or more, for a prolonged period of time (*Drug Tariff (England and Wales) Part 10 Appendix p. 5; NHS 1989(GEN)33; HSS(FPS) 6/89*).

21.3.3.2. Backup oxygen cylinders are prescribed with the concentrator, if the patient is at risk in case of concentrator breakdown (*Drug Tariff (England and Wales) 1.89 Part 10 Append. p. 7; NHS 1989(GEN)33; HSS(FPS) 6/89*).

21.3.3.3. Oxygen concentrator prescription

21.3.3.3.1. England, Wales, Northern Ireland. Oxygen concentrators are listed on the Drug Tariff and are prescribed by GPs. Prescription should take place in consultation with hospital respiratory consultants (*Drug Tariff (England and Wales) 1.89 Part 10, Appendix p.2; HSS(FPS) 6/89*).

21.3.3.3.2. Scotland. Oxygen concentrators are not listed on the Drug Tariff, in the same way as in the rest of the UK, and are not prescribed by GPs. They must be prescribed by hospital respiratory consultants (*NHS 1989(GEN)33*).

21.3.3.3.3. Prescription charges.

21.3.3.3.3.1. England, Wales and Northern Ireland. Prescription charges (and the relevant exemptions) (Box 30.1.) apply and are made on the basis of a standard charge per calendar month (*see eg HSS(FPS)6/89*).

21.3.3.3.3.2. Scotland. Prescription charges do not apply.

21.3.3.4. Supply contractors. Oxygen concentrators are supplied by private contractors. Contracts are put out to tender for three year periods by FPC groups (England and Wales), the Common Services Agency (Scotland), the Northern Ireland Central Services Agency (NICSA). Three contractors operate in England and Wales, one in Scotland, and one in Northern Ireland.

21.3.3.4.1 Supply service. The contractor is responsible for, for example, delivery, installation, maintenance, instruction in use, removal, and emergency callout, where necessary (*Drug Tariff (England and Wales) 1.89 Part 10 Append. p. 7; NHS 1989(GEN)33; HSS(FPS) 6/89*).

21.3.3.5. Electricity costs.

21.3.3.5.1. England, Wales and Northern Ireland. The supply contractor is responsible for the payment of electricity costs associated with use of the oxygen concentrator (*Drug Tariff (England and Wales) 1.89 Part 10 Append. p. 7; HSS(FPS) 6/89*).

21.3.3.5.2. Scotland. The contractor is responsible for arranging for the payment of electricity costs by the CSA (*NHS 1989 (GEN)33*).

22 Pain and other Treatment Equipment Loaned by Physiotherapists

22.1. Type of equipment

Cold packs, hot packs, heat pads, transcutaneous electrical nerve stimulators (TENS) (for pain treatment), flowtron equipment are used for treatment (for pain, or joint and muscle mobility) by physiotherapists, and sometimes loaned.

Flowtron can be used to treat, for example, peripheral oedema and fixed flexion contractures in people with rheumatoid arthritis or with severe haemophilia and consquent chronic haemophiliac arthropathy (*Allen, Anne L. Use of 'Flowtron' in Haemophiliac Patients and Others with Fixed Flexion Deformity Problems. Physiotherapy, November 1988, Vol. 74:11,581-2*).

22.2. Legislative basis for provision

Physiotherapist loan of such equipment is covered by the DHA/HB/HSSB duty to provide 'other services' (*NHS Act 1977 s.3; NHS (Scotland) Act s.36; SI 1972/1265 HPSS(NI)O 1972 a.5*).

22.3. Loan basis

Electrical equipment, such as TENS or Flowtron is usually loaned for short-term recovery or on a trial basis. If the equipment is needed for a longer period, a consultant might prescribe the item, but more usually the person would need to privately purchase the item or at least raise money from elsewhere.

It is recommended that the use of TENS equipment, for example, for pain relief at home, requires follow-up from a therapist in the form of continuing contact, especially when the person is initially experimenting with the machine (*see eg Bending, Jennifer. TENS in a Pain Clinic. Physiotherapy 1989:75;5,292-3*).

Questions of product liability in relation to the loan of TENS machines, Flowtron and heat pads, for example, have been drawn to the attention of physiotherapists (Box 31.1.).

23 Dental Equipment

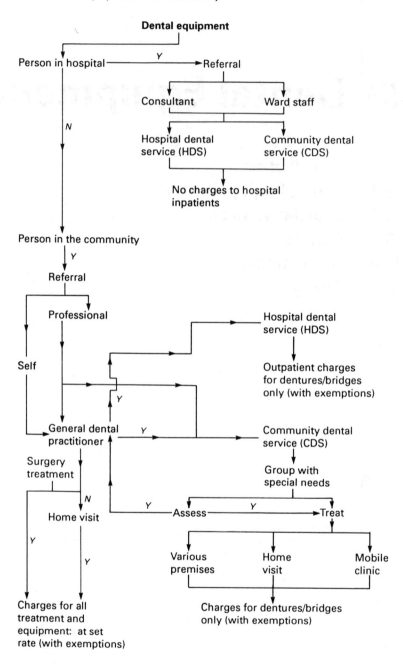

Dental equipment

Person in hospital ——— Y ———► Referral

Consultant   Ward staff

Hospital dental   Community dental
service (HDS)   service (CDS)

No charges to hospital
inpatients

N

Person in the community

Y

Referral

Professional   Hospital dental
                      service (HDS)

Self   Outpatient charges
                      for dentures/bridges
                      only (with exemptions)

Y

General dental   Y   Community dental
practitioner   service (CDS)

Surgery   Group with
treatment   special needs

N

Home visit   Y   Assess   Y   ►Treat

Y

Various   Home   Mobile
premises   visit   clinic

Y

Charges for all   Charges for dentures/bridges
treatment and   only (with exemptions)
equipment: at set
rate (with exemptions)

Introduction

Dental equipment includes, for example, dentures, braces, bridges and electric toothbrushes.

Responsibility for provision lies with the health service:
- district health authorities and family practitioner committees (DHAs and FPCs, England and Wales);
- health boards (HBs, Scotland);
- health and social services boards (HSSBs, Northern Ireland).

Provision. Dental services and equipment are available through the hospital dental service (HDS), community dental service (CDS) and general dental service (GDS).

Hospital dental service (HDS). The HDS provides specialist services to short-stay inpatients and outpatients. It sometimes provides routine care to long-stay inpatients.

All services and appliances supplied to hospital inpatients are free of charge. Hospital outpatients have to pay for dentures and bridges (unless exempt from such charges), but not for any other appliances which a consultant prescribes.

Community dental service (CDS). The CDS screens, assesses, and sometimes treats special groups of people who are disadvantaged and have special needs. These groups include, for example, some children, elderly people (in their own home and a residential home), people with physical disability and people with learning difficulties (a mental handicap).

The CDS is encouraged to refer people for treatment to the general dental service. However, it might carry out treatment, if access to GDS treatment is difficult. The CDS might also screen and treat people in long-stay health service accomodation.

CDS patients (except hospital inpatients) have to pay for dentures and bridges (unless exempt from such charges); but not for any other appliances supplied.

General dental service (GDS). The GDS consists of general dental practitioners (GDPs).

The GDP can make home visits, if access to the surgery is difficult for whatever reason, and can also make visits to individuals in residential and private nursing homes. Charges apply (except where exemption applies) for all appliances supplied through the GDS.

23.1. Type of equipment

Dental equipment can include, for example:

- dentures (from one or two teeth to complete denture set);
- braces;
- bridges (one or more artificial teeth cemented to sound teeth, beside a gap);
- crowns (artificial tooth fitted over the remains of a sound tooth);
- inlays and pinlays (large fillings in which gold or porcelain is made up to fit the whole tooth and then cemented in place);
- gold fillings (*NCC. You and Your Dentist. HMSO, 1987, p. 28*);
- electric toothbrushes;
- double-headed toothbrushes;
- self-pasting toothbrushes;
- long-handled toothbrushes;
- toothpaste tube winders/squeezers;
- toothbrush holders etc.

23.2. Legislative basis for provision of dental equipment

23.2.1. Basis for hospital and community dental services (HDS and CDS).

23.2.1.1. Basis for HDS and CDS: England and Wales. Provision is covered by the DHA duty to provide 'dental services' (*NHS Act 1977 s.3*).

23.2.1.2. Basis for HDS and CDS: Scotland and Northern Ireland. Provision is covered (by implication) by the duty of HBs and HSSBs to provide 'medical services' (*NHS (Scotland) Act 1978 (s.36); HPSS(NI)O 1972 a.5*).

23.2.1.3. Basis for school dental services. The DHA/HB/HSSB has a duty to provide regular dental inspection in schools 'to such extent as ... necessary to meet all reasonable requirements' (*NHS Act 1977 s.5 as amended by The Health and Medicines Act 1988 s.10; NHS (Scotland) Act 1978 as amended by Health and Medicines Act 1988 s.10; SI 1972/1265 HPSS(NI)O 1972 a. 9 as amended by SI 1988/2249 (NI 24) Health and Medicines (Northern Ireland) Order 1988 r.6*).

23.2.2. Basis for general dental services (GDS). Provision is covered by the DHA (through FPC)/HB/HSSB duty to provide 'general dental services' (*NHS Act 1977 s.15; NHS (Scotland) Act 1978, s.25; SI 1972/1265 HPSS(NI)O 1972 a.61*).

23.3. Referral

23.3.1. Referral to general dental practitioners (GDPs) is open, in that people choose their own dentist. Equally, other professionals such as the GP or CDS staff, for example, might make a referral.

GDPs are self-employed and are under contract to FPCs (England and Wales), HBs (Scotland) and HSSBs (Northern Ireland).

23.3.2. Referral to hospital dental service (HDS). GDPs might, in turn, refer a person either to another dentist or to specialist hospital services.

They are under a duty to do so, when they are unable to carry out the necessary treatment, but are aware that another GDP or hospital can (*SI 1973/1468 Sched 1; SI 1974/505 Sched 1; SR 1975/227 Sched 1*).

Specialist hospital dental services treat outpatients, and inpatients (including long-stay inpatients). Consultant dental surgeons and consultant orthodontists work within the service.

23.3.3. Referral to the community dental service (CDS).

23.3.3.1. Schoolchildren. The form of referral to the CDS varies. For example, school children may be routinely screened by the CDS (although the role of the CDS is changing in this respect) (23.4.3.2.).

23.3.3.2. Long-stay hospital inpatients. Long-stay hospital patients are sometimes treated by the CDS, in which case referral takes place within the hospital setting. There could be routine screening, or response to an individual need, identified by the person themselves, a nurse, hospital doctor or other professional.

23.3.3.3. People with physical disabilities. For people with physical disabilities (including elderly people) in the community, referral to the CDS might happen in various ways.

For example, health centre staff might 'screen' elderly people, with whom they come into contact, for dental need together with the fact of being mainly housebound. These two factors might indicate the necessity of CDS involvement (*Hogan J.I., A Domiciliary Dental Service to the Housebound from an Inner London Health Centre. Community Dental Health 1986: 3, 117–127*).

23.3.3.4. CDS remit. The CDS treats a number of different types of person; it is now increasingly seen as a safety net for special groups of people who are unable to gain access to normal general dental services (GDS). It might, for example, screen schoolchildren, screen and treat longstay health service inpatients; and treat elderly people, 'young adults' with physical disabilities and people with learning difficulties (a mental handicap).

The CDS is likely to be organised under a district (England/Wales) or area (at Board level in Scotland and Northern Ireland) dental officer. The CDS might screen and/or treat, at a variety of locations such as health centres, schools, people's own homes and residential homes.

23.4. Assessment and provision

23.4.1. Hospital and long-stay patients/residents

23.4.1.1. Hospital inpatient assessment and provision. Hospital inpatients receive treatment and equipment (including bridges and dentures free of charge (23.5.).

Short-stay inpatients are generally treated by the HDS; longstay inpatients by the HDS or CDS, depending on local arrangements.

Circular guidance (England, Wales, Scotland, 1989) draws attention to this possible variation (*PL/CDO(89)2 para 15; WHC(89)28; SHHD/DGM (1989)15)*); while a DHSS (NI) report has confirmed that the CDS is responsible for organising the care of long-stay inpatients (*HSS(CH)2/89 and Review of the Community Dental Services. DHSS (NI), 1987, p. 8*).

23.4.1.2. Denture care in longstay accomodation includes marking of dentures (to minimise the likelihood of loss) (*Dental Services for the Handicapped. SHHD 1984, p. 24*) and the provision of good facilities for the cleaning and safekeeping of dentures (HAS 1989 E.507). The provision of electric toothbrushes can greatly improve oral hygiene (*SHHD Dental Services for the Handicapped. HMSO 1984, p. 24*).

23.4.1.3. Access to dental care in private nursing homes. Legislation states that people in private nursing homes should retain access to their GDP (25.4.2.), so that they can either still visit (if physically able) their GDP, or be visited by him.

Payment for treatment and appliances supplied by a GDP should be on the same basis as if the person were in their own home.

23.4.2. Outpatient assessment and provision. Outpatients are treated by the hospital dental service (HDS). Treatment and appliances are free of charge except for bridges and dentures (23.5.).

23.4.3. Community assessment and provision. The GDS is responsible, in general, for treatment and equipment provision in the community; however, the CDS assesses and sometimes treats groups of people with special needs who do not have access to the GDS.

23.4.3.1. Home visits

23.4.3.1.1. General dental practitioners treat people with disabilities, and can make home visits where necessary. The GDP is under a duty to visit and treat a patient 'whose condition so requires at any place where that patient may be, which is not more than five miles from his surgery.' (*SI 1973/1468 Sched.1 s.4; SI 1974/505 (S.40) Sched.1 s.4; SI 1975/227 Sched.1 s.4*) Such visits are free of charge (*SI 1989/394, s.3; SI 1989/363(S.39) s.3; SR 1989/111 r.3*).

Some GDPs visit and treat people in residential homes.

23.4.3.1.2. Community dental service: home visits. The CDS makes home visits to both assess and treat. It sometimes operates a mobile surgery with special equipment such as hoists and wheelchair tipping equipment.

23.4.3.2. Children: assessment and provision. Central government has expressed the opinion that GDPs should provide services for the whole family, including schoolchildren (*see eg Promoting Better Health. HMSO, 1987 (p.27); SHARPEN. Scottish Health Service Planning Council. HMSO 1988 p.104; Primary Care Review. DHSS (NI), 1988 para 38*).

DHAs, HBs and HSSBs formerly had a duty to regularly (eg annually) provide for the dental inspection of schoolchildren. The duty now is to do so, only as far as is necessary to meet 'reasonable requirements' (23.2.1.3.). Circular guidance notes that this is in recognition of the fact that GDPs should provide care for the whole family (*PL/CDO(89)2; WHC(89)28; SHHD/DGM (1989)15; HSS(CH)2/89 and Review of the Community Dental Services. DHSS (NI), 1987)*).

23.4.3.2.1. CDS assessment and treatment. Some groups of children might still need special CDS attention. Circular guidance (England, Wales, Scotland) states, for example, that more frequent screening might be desirable in 'localities where levels of dental health and attendance are poor' (*PL/CDO(89)2; WHC(89)28; SHHD/DGM (1989)15*).

Circular guidance also states that where the CDS still does screen schoolchildren, it should if possible, not undertake treatment, but make a referral to a GDP (*PL/CDO(89)2; WHC(89)28; SHHD/DGM (1989)15; HSS(CH)2/89 and Review of the Community Dental Services. DHSS (NI), 1987, p. 4*).

Nevertheless, treatment (rather than referral to a GDP) might still be needed for children with special needs, and for children who live in isolated rural areas with no easy access to a GDP (*PL/CDO (89)2; WHC(89)28; SHHD/DGM(1989)15; HSS(CH)2/89 and Review of the Community Dental Services. DHSS (NI), 1987*).

23.4.4. Elderly people – assessment and provision. Circular guidance states that elderly people are one of the special groups requiring CDS assessment and treatment where GDS access cannot be arranged (*PL/CDO(89)2 para 14; WHC(89)28 para 10; SHHD/DGM (1989)15 paras 11; HSS(CH)2/89 and Review of the Community Dental Services. DHSS (NI), 1987, p. 7*).

It also states that the CDS should screen residential homes (*PL/CDO(89)2; WHC(89)28; SHHD/DGM(1989)15; HSS(CH)2/89 and Review of the Community Dental Services. DHSS (NI), 1987 p. 7*).

Treatment might be necessary, if residents have special needs, and access to a general dental practitioner is not possible (*PL/CDO(89)2; WHC(89)28; SHHD/DGM(1989)15; HSS(CH)2/89 and Review of the Community Dental Services. DHSS (NI), 1987 p. 7*), although older Circular guidance states that residents should not benefit from CDS priority group treatment (24.4.2.2.).

23.4.5. People with physical disabilities – assessment and provision. Circular guidance states that CDS assessment and treatment for this group is appropriate, where there is lack of access to premises (*PL/CDO(89)2; WHC(89)28; SHHD/DGM (1989)15; HSS(CH)2/89 and Review of the Community Dental Services. DHSS (NI), 1987*), or absence of suitable equipment for the treatment of people with physical disabilities (*HSS(CH)2/89 and Review of the Community Dental Services. DHSS (NI), 1987*) effectively bars them from the GDS.

A 1984 report (Scotland) stated that frequently 'the only service provided to the housebound and those resident in hostels is domiciliary visits by General Dental Practitioners. These domiciliary visits are often of an emergency nature and limited in scope' (*SHHD. Dental Services for the Handicapped. HMSO, 1984 p. 23*). Furthermore, even where GDPs do make domiciliary visits, lack of portable equipment might limit treatment.

23.4.6. Definition of dental fitness. Regulations define 'dental fitness' (for the purposes of the GDS) as 'such a reasonable standard of dental efficiency and oral health as is necessary to safeguard general health, and 'dentally fit' has a corresponding meaning' (*SI 1973/1468 s.2; SI 1974/505 (S.40) s.2; SR 1975/227 s.2*).

It has been pointed out that this definition has remained unchanged since 1948, but that its interpretation changes in response to 'changes in professional skill and knowledge and patient expectations' (*Weekly Hansard No.1442, 14-18 March 1988. Written answers: 10.3.88, col.345*).

23.5. Charges

23.5.1. Basic charges. Charges for dentures and bridges are no longer fixed, but are set at 75% of the fee payable to the dentist for the supply of the denture or bridge (*SI 1989/394; SI 1989/363 (S.39); SR 1989/111*). These charges apply to the HDS (outpatients only), the CDS, and the GDS.

23.5.2. Other items. Within the GDS items other than dentures and bridges are charged for on the same basis (75% of the cost).

The HDS and CDS makes no charges for items, clinically necessary, other than dentures or bridges (*SI 1989/394; SI 1989/363 (S.39); SR 1989/111*). Thus, a consultant sometimes prescribes (as medically necessary) electric toothbrushes, free of charge.

GDPs also sell ordinary equipment such as toothbrushes, toothpaste, dental floss; this may be at a cheap rate if it has been distributed by a firm to the dentist.

23.5.3. Exemption from charges. Exemptions apply to:

- under-18 year olds (birth certificate required);
- 18 year olds (under 19), and receiving full-time education (proof required);
- expectant mothers (doctor's signed certificate needed);
- mothers who have borne a child in the last 12 months (child's birth certificate required) (*SI 1989/394 s.5/Sched.2; SI 1989/363 (S.39) s.5 Sched 2; SR 1989/111*);
- a person receiving income support or family credit (or adult dependant, of the person receiving the benefit);
- a person whose requirements equal or exceed his income resources and whose capital resources fall below a certain level (or adult dependant of the person) (*SI 1989/394 r.7 and SI 1988/551 r.3); SI 1988/363(S.39) r.7 and 1988/546 (S.62) r.3; SR 1989/111 r.8 and SR 1989/348 r.3*).

Also specifically exempt, from charges for dentures and bridges, are people who have had operations affecting the mandible, the maxilla or the soft tissues of the mouth as part of treatment for invasive tumours (*SI 1989/394 r.2; SI 1989/363 (S.39); SR 1989/111 r.2*).

War pensioners (30.3.) can get a refund, if dentures or bridges, for example, are needed because of the disability for which they receive a war pension (*see eg DH leaflet: D11 NHS dental treatment*).

23.5.4. Partial exemption to charges is based on low income assessment (*SI 1989/394 r.7, SI 1988/551 r.5); (SI 1988/363(S.39) r.7, SI 1988/546(S.62) r.5); (1989/111 r.8, SR 1989/348 r.5*).

23.5.5. More expensive supply. If a person wants to have supplied or repaired any dental appliance (for example, gold inlays, pinlays or crowns) which is more expensive than the basic NHS type (and which is not clinically necessary), then extra charges are made (*SI 1989/394 r.8; SI 1989/363 r.8; SR 1989/111 r.9*).

23.5.6. Charges for repairs. There is no charge for the repair of dentures or bridges, unless the repair costs exceed basic health service costs, or are necessitated by an act or omission of the person (*1989/394 r.8; SI 1989/363 (S.39) r.8; SR 1989/111 r.9*).

23.5.7. Replacement charges for dentures and bridges are made, as if they were being supplied for the first time. The exception to this rule is if the person has lost the dentures, and claims, through the FPC/HB/HSSB, exemption from payment.

For a person, anyway exempt from payment, there are no charges for replacement, unless the need for replacement has been caused by an 'act or omission' of the person (*SI 1989/394 r.9 and NHS Act 1977 s.82; SI 1989/363(S.39) r.9, NHS (Scotland) Act 1978 s.74; SR 1989/111 r.10 and SI 1972/1265 HPSS(NI)O 1972 r.61, Schedule 15*).

23.5.8. Private treatment. Many dentists undertake private work, as well as health service work, and this can sometimes lead to confusion, when a person is unsure as to whether they are being treated privately or under the health service (*NCC. You and Your Dentist. HMSO, 1987, p. 14*).

24 Residential Home Equipment Provision

Equipment need in residential home

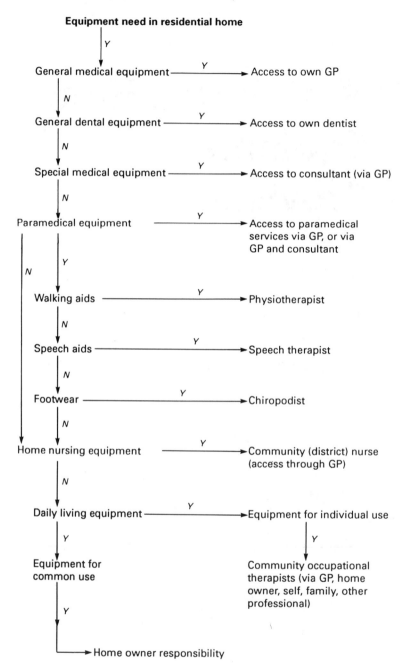

Introduction

Background. Legislation exists for the registration and inspection of private residential homes, by which means standards (including general equipment standards) are controlled by registering authorities:

- social services departments (SSDs, England and Wales);
- social work departments (SWDs, Scotland);
- health and social services boards (HSSBs, Northern Ireland).

Existing powers to inspect statutory residential homes are likely to be strengthened in the near future and brought into line with standards applied to the private sector.

Government guidance, and guidance recommended by government, details good practice concerning healthcare and other services which should be available in residential homes.

It is likely that, in the near future, SSD/SWD/HSSBs will become responsible for assessment of whether people in need require community care in their own home, or residential care with or without nursing.

Provision. Residents of both statutory (public sector) and private residential homes should (according to government guidance) retain the same access to all health and social services, as if they were in their own home.

Sometimes, where there are health or social services waiting lists, and priority categories are introduced to rationalise assessments, residents of homes might be given low priority. This is because they are already in care, and are seen to be at potentially lower risk than people living alone.

SSD/SWD/HSSBs normally expect to provide, for residents, daily living equipment, if it meets an individual need; the home owner is otherwise expected to provide furniture and equipment for common use. Where the SSD/SWD/HSSB is also the home owner, it provides both types of equipment (for common and individual use), but through different authorisation and financial procedures.

24.1. Type of equipment

This chapter covers the provision of equipment of all types (as discussed elsewhere in the book) for people in residential homes.

24.2. Type of home

There are three main types of residential home: statutory (SSD/SWD/HSSB), voluntary and private. For details, see Box 24.1.

Box 24.1: Types of residential home

B24.1.1. Statutory residential homes. Local SSD/SWD residential homes are known as Part III homes in England and Wales (referring to part 3 of the National Assistance Act 1948, Part IV homes in Scotland (referring to part 4 of the Social Work (Scotland) Act 1968). In Northern Ireland they are known as 'homes for persons in need'.

B24.1.2. Voluntary residential homes include homes for the elderly (for example, the 35 homes run by Methodist Homes for the Aged) (*Laing's Review of Private Healthcare 1988/89. Laing and Buisson, 1988, Vol.2 p. 29*).

Homes for young adults (16–64 years old) with physical disabilities might be run by SSD/SWD/HSSBs; or by voluntary organisations such as the Spastics Society, the Leonard Cheshire Foundation; the Shaftesbury Society; Sue Ryder; John Groom's Association (*Young Disabled Adult. Royal College of Physicians, 1986 p. 11*). Such homes might be dual registered, as both residential and private nursing home, depending on the severity of disability which residents have.

B24.1.3. Private (commercial) residential homes have increased greatly in number in the last few years.

Over the 18 years 1970–1988, the number of residential homes for elderly, chronically ill and physically handicapped people in the UK has risen in all three sectors. During that period local authority homes have risen from 2639 to about 3225; voluntary from 1259 to 1308; private sector homes from 1849 to 8277. For the last 10 years however, local authority provision has remained static (*Laing's Review of Private Healthcare 1988/89. Laing and Buisson, 1988, Vol.2 pp. 11–14*).

24.3. Basis for standards in residential accomodation

24.3.1. Legislation

24.3.1.1. Private residential homes. Legislation places general duties on SSD/SWD/HSSBs in relation to the registration and inspection of private (commercial or voluntary) residential homes (*Registered Homes Act 1984 and SI 1984/1345; Social Work (Scotland) Act 1968 s.6; SI 1972/1265 HPSS(NI)O 1972 a.50*).

Regulations (England/Wales) detail the necessary level of facilities and services, and include reference to equipment; the home owner has a duty to 'make such adaptations and provide such facilities as are necessary for residents who are physically handicapped' (*SI 1984/1345 r.10*).

24.3.1.2. Statutory/public sector residential homes. SSD/SWD/HSSBs have duties to make arrangements for residential accomodation where it is needed (*National Assistance Act 1948 s.21; Social Work (Scotland) Act 1968 s.12; SI 1972/1265 HPSS(NI)O 1972 a.15*).

The NHS and Community Care Bill (England/Wales, Scotland) proposes increased powers for inspection of these homes (*NHS and Community Care Bill 1989 cl. 43,47*), with the intention stated in government papers (applying UK wide), of achieving common standards in both private and public residential accomodation (*Caring for People. HMSO 1989 pp. 44, 81; DHSS(NI). People First, HMSO, 1990, p. 56*).

Similar legislation is expected for Northern Ireland.

24.3.2. Circular guidance and other guidance

24.3.2.1. Circular guidance (England and Wales) (intended for statutory residential homes) gives detailed guidance on provision of health care in residential homes for the elderly. This guidance is echoed by Circular guidance (Northern Ireland, 1978) (*Residential Homes for the Elderly. Arrangements for Health Care. A Memorandum of Guidance. DHSS, Welsh Office, 1977; HSS5(OS)3/78*); but there seems to be no exactly corresponding Scottish guidance.

24.3.2.2. Other Circular guidance has been issued relating more or less to residential homes: these are referred to as appropriate below.

24.3.2.3. 'Home Life', a 1984 book, details good practice in residential homes. It was intended that it apply to both statutory and private residential homes. It was endorsed by the Secretary of State for Social Services (England) and Secretary of State for Wales at the time: and received further government approval both in 1986 Circular guidance (LAC 1986(6), and in recent government papers (*Caring for People. HMSO, 1989 p. 45; DHSS(NI) People First. HMSO, 1990, p. 57*).

Although produced in an English and Welsh context, Home Life is probably used informally both in Scotland and Northern Ireland (*Home Life: a code of practice for residential care. Report of a Working Party sponsored by the Department of Health and Social Security and convened by the Centre for Policy on Ageing under the Chairmanship of Kina, Lady Avebury. Centre for Policy on Ageing, 1984*).

24.3.2.4. Forthcoming guidance. It is expected that government guidance, in relation to residential care, will soon be forthcoming, in the light of the NHS and Community Care Bill (2.2.4.).

Government papers state that such guidance will 'give a special emphasis to assessing the quality of care provided' as well as the residents' quality of life and physical conditions in the home (*Caring for People. HMSO, 1989, p. 45; DHSS(NI) People First. HMSO, 1990, p. 57*).

24.3.2.5. Assessment for entry into residential homes. In the past, there has been no formal system of assessment for state supported entry to private residential homes. The DSS has supported many people in these homes, in a rather indiscriminate manner (*Community Care: Agenda for Action. A Report to the Secretary of State for Social Services by Sir Roy Griffiths. HMSO 1988 p. v*).

As proposed by government papers, and the NHS and Community Care Bill (1989), this situation will change. SSD/SWD/HSSBs will be responsible for the assessment of people in need, to decide whether they should benefit from community care in their own home, or residential accommodation with or without nursing (*Caring for People HMSO 1989 pp. 18–19, 80; DHSS(NI) People First. HMSO, 1990, p. 26; NHS and Community Care Bill 1989 cl. 37, 42, 49, 50*).

Such assessment will include, in some cases, consideration of equipment and adaptations needs.

24.4. Equipment provision in residential homes

Much (though not all) of the detail below is drawn from the English/Welsh Regulations applying to private sector homes (24.3.1.1.); specific Circular guidance (England, Wales, Northern Ireland) applying to statutory homes

(24.3.2.); and 'Home Life' (applying to both statutory and private homes) (24.3.2.3.).

In general, all residents of both statutory and private residential homes should have access to medical, paramedical and daily living equipment for their individual needs, to the same extent as they would in their own home.

24.4.1. Medical equipment

24.4.1.1. English/Welsh regulations state that the private home owner has a duty to 'make arrangements, where necessary, for residents to receive medical services' *(SI 1984/1345 r.10(p))*. This refers to access to health service GPs, and the duty stands unless the resident requests that private arrangements be made instead.

24.4.1.2. Home Life and Circular guidance state that residents should have access to the family doctor of their choice (*Home Life: a code of practice for residential care. Report of a Working Party sponsored by the Department of Health and Social Security and convened by the Centre for Policy on Ageing under the Chairmanship of Kina, Lady Avebury. Centre for Policy on Ageing, 1984 p. 28; Residential Homes for the Elderly. Arrangements for Health Care. A Memorandum of Guidance. DHSS, Welsh Office, 1977 para 8; HSS5(OS)3/78 para 8*).

Circular guidance (England, 1988) emphasises that FPCs should ensure that people in residential homes receive adequate family practitioner services (*LAC(88)15*).

24.4.1.3. Thus, in practice, residents are able to benefit from Drug Tariff appliances prescribed by a GP (Box 5.1.), or from GP referral to specialist hospital services and equipment.

For example, a Scottish SWD's guidelines note that residents should be encouraged to keep their own GP, and that, where necessary, visits by geriatricians and other specialist doctors are possible by GP referral. The GP can also make the appropriate referral for permanent wheelchair provision (*local SWD Guide to Procedures for the Registration of Private and Voluntary Homes under the Social Work (Scotland) Act 1968. 1987*).

24.4.2. Dental appliances

24.4.2.1. Regulations (England and Wales) clearly state that the private home owner has a duty to 'make arrangements, where necessary, for residents to receive ... dental services' *(SI 1984/1345 r.10(p))*. This refers to access to health service general dental practitioners, and the duty stands unless the resident requests that private arrangements be made instead.

24.4.2.2. Circular guidance (England, Wales, Northern Ireland) states that residents should have at least annual mouth examinations, and, if a family dentist is not available, the community dental service can be consulted. However, it states that residents should not benefit from treatment 'under the 'priority' dental scheme or the school dental service' (*Residential Homes for the Elderly. Arrangements for Health Care. A Memorandum of Guidance. DHSS, Welsh Office, 1977 para 20; HSS5(OS)3/78) para 21*).

Other recent Circular guidance on the community dental service refers to the screening of residential homes (23.4.4.). It does not mention treatment in residential homes in particular, but states that any special needs group, with lack of access to a dentist, might need to be treated by the CDS (23.4.4.).

24.4.3. Home nursing equipment. Circular guidance (England, Wales, Northern Ireland) states that when residents require nursing care, they should normally be seen by a district nurse (*Residential Homes for the Elderly. Arrangements for Health Care. A Memorandum of Guidance. DHSS, Welsh Office, 1977 para 17; HSS5(OS)3/78 para 18*).

'Home Life' states that the 'rights of residents to have access to community nursing services does not in any way put at risk the registration of the home as a residential care home' (*Home Life: a code of practice for residential care. Report of a Working Party sponsored by the Department of Health and Social Security and convened by the Centre for Policy on Ageing under the Chairmanship of Kina, Lady Avebury. Centre for Policy on Ageing, 1984 p. 28*).

In practice, this means that residents should have access to home nursing equipment. Circular guidance (England, 1974,1987) states that DHAs have the same power to provide such equipment to residents, as to people in their own homes (*see eg HRC(74)16; D(87)45 (re: incontinence pads)*).

24.4.3.1. *Cover of residential homes by district nurses* is likely to vary. For example, if each resident retains his or her own GP, a number of district nurses might cover the home. If one GP, by arrangement, is responsible for all the residents, then one district nurse might similarly be reponsible for the whole home (*Eley M. Community Outlook. March 1989, pp .26–8*).

DHA/HB/HSSBs are normally expected to take responsibility for home nursing needs (through community nurses) in homes within their area, irrespective of the original home of the resident (*eg London SSD (19) guidelines 1989*).

24.4.4. Personal daily living equipment

24.4.4.1. *Individual, personal need.* Although the home might provide some daily living equipment for general use (see below), individual residents sometimes require equipment to meet an individual need.

Circular guidance (England, 1986) states that if the equipment is for an individual, then aids and equipment for use by that individual (eg walking aids and dressing aids) can be supplied by the SSD. Such supply should be on the same basis as supply to an individual in their own home (*LAC(86)6*).

24.4.4.1.1. Waiting lists. In practice, waiting lists, and decisions on priority (2.5.7.2.), can mean that people in residential homes are sometimes accorded low priority in relation to community OT assessment. This is because they are seen to already be in care, and therefore not at the same degree of risk as a person living alone in their own home, for example.

24.4.4.2. *Extent of SSD/SWD/HSSB responsibility.* The SSD/SWD/HSSB might take responsibility for residents placed outside its area (*SSD guidelines received 1989*).

SSD/SWD/HSSB internal guidelines sometimes state clearly that equipment is provided for individual use in private or voluntary residential homes, but not for common use (*Various SSD guidelines received 1989/1990*).

There might be a policy to not provide equipment for individuals in homes which are joint registered (residential and nursing) (*Midlands SSD (23) guidelines received 1989*); and occasionally a policy not to provide equipment at all to private residential homes (*SSD guidelines received 1989*).

24.4.5. Equipment for mobility

24.4.5.1. DHA/HB/HSSB physiotherapists sometimes visit homes either to treat individuals or to give advice to care staff. Walking aids might then be loaned for individual need.

The extent to which physiotherapists visit residential homes is likely to vary from area to area. Residents, of course, can also attend hospitals (as outpatients) or health centres to see physiotherapists (via GP referral).

24.4.5.2. Private physiotherapists might attend private residential homes, to treat individuals or to give exercise classes for example. Such physiotherapy might be integral to the home's services, or be charged to residents.

Equipment would normally have to be bought privately; or is sometimes hired out by the private physiotherapy service.

24.4.6. Chiropody equipment. Circular guidance (England,1974), for example, made it quite clear that the health service has the same power to provide chiropody services to people in residential homes as to people in their own homes.

In practice, with the shortage of NHS chiropodists, private practitioners might be used and charges made to the residents.

Circular guidance (England, Wales, Northern Ireland) states that important services such as toe-nail cutting can be taught to staff at the home (*Residential Homes for the Elderly. Arrangements for Health Care. A Memorandum of Guidance. DHSS, Welsh Office, 1977 para 21; HSS(OS)3/78 para 22*).

24.4.7. Equipment for people with visual disability. 'Home Life' states that there should be efficient lighting without glare, as well as colour contrasts, tactile clues (*Home Life: a code of practice for residential care. Report of a Working Party sponsored by the Department of Health and Social Security and convened by the Centre for Policy on Ageing under the Chairmanship of Kina, Lady Avebury. Centre for Policy on Ageing, 1984 p. 37*).

24.4.7.1. Detection by care staff. Circular guidance (England/Wales/Northern Ireland) recommends that care staff should identify deterioration of vision in residents; district nurses and health visitors can assist staff in this identification. The care staff should also ensure that spectacles are cleaned and worn properly, and make necessary arrangements if some adjustment is needed. Sight-testing should be provided for residents (*Residential Homes for the Elderly. Arrangements for Health Care. A Memorandum of Guidance. DHSS, Welsh Office, 1977 para 19,20; HSS(OS)3/78 para 19,20*).

Circular guidance (Scotland, 1982), to similar effect, states that attending staff should be alert to visual impairment. If the resident cannot visit an optician's premises, the resident's GP can request, if necessary, a visit by the hospital eye service. Failing this, a local optician might visit the home (15.3.2.1.3.) (*Joint

Circular NHS 1982(GEN)7,SWSG 1982/2 Care of the Eyesight and Hearing of Elderly and Disabled People).

24.4.7.2. In practice, residents (should) have access (like people in their own homes) to the health service for spectacles, contact lenses and low vision aids; and to SSD/SWD/HSSBs for environmental daily living equipment for visual impairment.

24.4.8. Equipment for people with hearing impairment

24.4.8.1. *Environmental equipment for people with hearing impairment.* 'Home Life' recommends that the home should provide equipment such as radio aids, door alarms and other electronic aids for people with hearing impairment, as well as services to ensure the fitting, use and repair of aids and equipment (*Home Life: a code of practice for residential care. Report of a Working Party sponsored by the Department of Health and Social Security and convened by the Centre for Policy on Ageing under the Chairmanship of Kina, Lady Avebury. Centre for Policy on Ageing, 1984 p. 37*).

Circular guidance (England/Wales/Northern Ireland) recommends that environmental equipment such as loop systems, television adaptors, amplified telephones need to be understood by both residents and staff. Such equipment might be chosen by the home following, for example, assessment by occupational therapists (*Residential Homes for the Elderly. Arrangements for Health Care. A Memorandum of Guidance. DHSS, Welsh Office, 1977 para 29,30; HSS(OS)3/78 para 28, 29*).

24.4.8.2. *Detection by care staff.* Circular guidance (England, Wales, Northern Ireland) recommends that care staff should identify deterioration of hearing in residents; district nurses and health visitors can assist staff in this identification. The care staff need to understand the use and limitation of hearing aids, identify the need for new batteries or repair and inform the resident's GP of problems (*Residential Homes for the Elderly. Arrangements for Health Care. A Memorandum of Guidance. DHSS, Welsh Office, 1977 para 19,20; HSS(OS)3/78 para 19,20*).

Circular guidance (Scotland, 1982) is to similar effect, urging attending staff to be watchful, and noting that the resident's GP can be contacted, and if necessary, a domiciliary visit (to the residential home) made by specialist hospital services (*Joint Circular NHS 1982(GEN)7,SWSG 1982/2 Care of the Eysight and Hearing of Elderly and Disabled People*).

24.4.8.3. In practice, residents (should) have access (like people in their own homes) to the health service for hearing aids; and to SSD/SWD/HSSBs for environmental daily living equipment for hearing impairment.

24.4.9. Incontinence equipment. In practice, equipment for the management of incontinence is of two types, environmental equipment and personal equipment. Equipment might not be needed at all; the problem might disappear with the re-establishment of a pattern of continence.

24.4.9.1. *Personal incontinence equipment.* Circular guidance (England, Wales, Northern Ireland) states that home staff should be aware of what items there are on the market so that the best choice for residents can be made (*Residential Homes* *for the Elderly. Arrangements for Health Care. A Memorandum of Guidance. DHSS, Welsh Office, 1977 para 24; HSS5(OS)3/78 para 25).*

The same guidance (England, Wales) also draws attention to the home responsibilities in terms of frequent changes of clothing, laundry equipment, pad disposal (*Residential Homes for the Elderly. Arrangements for Health Care. A Memorandum of Guidance. DHSS, Welsh Office, 1977 para 25*).

Many incontinence appliances are listed on the Drug Tariff (15.1.1./Box 5.1.), and so are available by GP prescription. In Scotland only, bed incontinence pads are prescribable by the GP.

The provision of incontinence pads in residential homes is a confusing area of provision, and is discussed elsewhere (Box 17.1.4.).

24.4.9.2. Environmental incontinence equipment. Circular guidance (England, Wales, Northern Ireland) notes the importance of type of clothing, the design and position of beds and chairs in relation to WCs, the adequate identification of WC doors (*Residential Homes for the Elderly. Arrangements for Health Care. A Memorandum of Guidance. DHSS, Welsh Office, 1977 para 23; HSS(OS)3/78 para 24*).

24.4.10. General equipment in the residential home

24.4.10.1. Equipment and adaptations in general.

24.4.10.1.1. Regulations (England, Wales) (for private homes) specify that the registered home owner must 'make such adaptations and provide such facilities as are necessary for residents who are physically handicapped' (*SI 1984/1345 r.10*).

24.4.10.1.2. 'Home Life' recommends that, for people with physical disabilities, residential homes should provide adapted or specially designed accomodation to compensate for disability, equipment 'to enable the disabled person to do things which he could not otherwise manage and also to ease the work of helpers'.

Assistance in the use of this equipment might also be needed (*Home Life: a code of practice for residential care. Report of a Working Party sponsored by the Department of Health and Social Security and convened by the Centre for Policy on Ageing under the Chairmanship of Kina, Lady Avebury. Centre for Policy on Ageing, 1984 p. 37*).

24.4.10.2. Other general equipment for residents. English/Welsh Regulations place a duty on the home owner to provide:

- 'adequate and suitable furniture, bedding, curtains, floor covering and, where necessary, equipment and screens in rooms occupied or used by residents';
- 'for the use of residents a sufficient number of water closets, and of wash-basins, baths and showers fitted with a hot and cold water supply, and any necessary sluicing facilities';
- 'adequate light, heating and ventilation in all parts of the home occupied or used by residents;'
- 'sufficient and suitable kitchen equipment, crockery and cutlery together with adequate facilities' (*SI 1984/1345 r.10*).

24.4.10.3. In statutory residential homes the SSD/SWD/HSSB provides both daily living equipment for individual need; and equipment for common use within the home. However, authorisation and budgetary procedures are different for the two types of equipment (2.5.7.).

24.4.11. Equipment in voluntary residential homes for people with severe disabilities. Special voluntary organisation residential homes for people with disabilities generally have more specialised equipment in the home anyway. Homes which are dual registered (both residential and nursing), have, as well, a stock of nursing equipment such as hoists, bathing systems, pressure relief mattresses.

In practice, statutory provision of equipment and services to these homes is highly variable, just as to any residential home (*Verbal communication: national voluntary organisation, 1989*).

24.4.11.1. Therapists employed by home. Therapists employed by voluntary bodies running such homes normally play an advisory role; they are likely to be too few in number to actively treat and rehabilitate themselves. Sometimes, however, they may have to do so if there is a low level of statutory service (*Verbal communication: national voluntary organisation, 1989*).

24.4.11.2. Extra equipment. Special voluntary homes for people with disabilities might make extra equipment provision for individuals where statutory provision fails to provide for specific individual need.

An organisation which runs a number of homes might have a central pool of equipment to fill gaps. However, where it is felt that statutory provision should take place, there might be reluctance to supply equipment from the organisation's own resources (*Verbal communication: national voluntary organisation 1989*).

24.4.11.3. Computer equipment. The younger residents of such homes might have educational or communication need for computer equipment; there is little statutory provision of such equipment, in such circumstances.

The organisation might hold a central pool of equipment which can be tried out on loan at a home, and then separately bought by the individual home (*Verbal communication: national voluntary organisation 1989*).

24.4.12. Training of home staff to understand needs including equipment needs. Circular guidance (England, Wales, Northern Ireland) recommends that there be training of care staff by health and social services staff.

This includes training in equipment need and use; for example 'care and management of elderly people who are mentally infirm, care of the dying, advice about incontinence, routine and simple foot care, instruction in remedial activities, dental, optical and aural care' (*Residential Homes for the Elderly. Arrangements for Health Care. A Memorandum of Guidance. DHSS, Welsh Office, 1977 para 33, HSS(OS)3/78 para 32*).

The training could be given by 'staff of the hospital departments of geriatric medicine and psychiatry, as well as members of primary health care teams, the area chiropodist . . .' (*Residential Homes for the Elderly. Arrangements for Health Care. A Memorandum of Guidance. DHSS, Welsh Office, 1977 para 34; HSS5(OS)3/78 para 32*).

'Home Life' states that, as well as actual provision of aids and appliances, 'Assistance may be necessary, for instance in the case of children and newly disabled people, to ensure that aids are used to the best advantage' (*Home Life: a code of practice for residential care. Report of a Working Party sponsored by the Department of Health and Social Security and convened by the Centre for Policy on Ageing under the Chairmanship of Kina, Lady Avebury. Centre for Policy on Ageing, 1984 p. 37*).

25 Private Nursing Home Equipment Provision

Equipment need in private nursing home

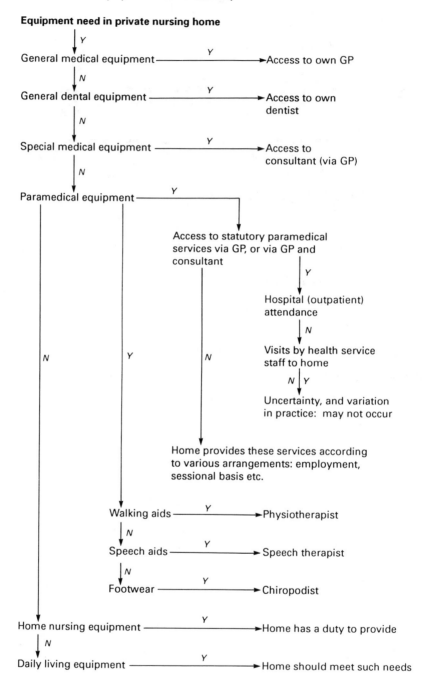

Y

General medical equipment ——————Y——————►Access to own GP

N

General dental equipment ——————Y——————►Access to own
dentist

N

Special medical equipment ——————Y——————►Access to
consultant (via GP)

N

Paramedical equipment ——————Y

Access to statutory paramedical
services via GP, or via GP and
consultant

Y

Hospital (outpatient)
attendance

N

Visits by health service
staff to home

N | Y

Uncertainty, and variation
in practice: may not occur

Home provides these services according
to various arrangements: employment,
sessional basis etc.

N   Y   N

Walking aids ——————Y——————►Physiotherapist

N

Speech aids ——————Y——————► Speech therapist

N

Footwear ——————Y——————► Chiropodist

Home nursing equipment ——————Y——————►Home has a duty to provide

N

Daily living equipment ——————Y——————► Home should meet such needs

Introduction

Registration and inspection of private nursing homes. Legislation exists for the registration and inspection of private nursing homes, by registering authorities:

- district health authorities (DHAs, England and Wales);
- health boards (HBs, Scotland);
- health and social services boards (HSSBs, Northern Ireland).

Registration and inspection can control standards (including equipment provision) in private nursing homes. Circular guidance, government recommended guidance, and local health service guidance also advises on the provision of services (including equipment) in private nursing homes.

New legislation (expected to come into force in 1991) is expected to make SSD/SWD/HSSBs ultimately responsible for deciding whether a person in need requires community care in their own home, or residential care with or without nursing.

Equipment provision. Private nursing homes are expected to provide all equipment, required for nursing purposes; whether it be general equipment (for example common lifting and bathing aids), or equipment for the needs of an individual resident (for example, bodyworn incontinence pads).

Residents of private nursing homes should also retain access to a general practitioner (GP) and general dental practitioner (GDP): their own, if possible. If necessary, the home owner must make arrangements to ensure that residents do have such access.

GP access. Access to the GP means that residents retain access to equipment as:

- prescribed by a GP (including wheelchairs);
- prescribed by a consultant (by means of GP referral);
- supplied (via GP or consultant referral) by other health service professionals such as physiotherapists, occupational therapists, speech therapists, chiropodists, for example.

Residents of private nursing homes can, by means of GP referral, attend hospital (as outpatients), or a health centre, to receive special services (including equipment) from these professionals; or, if necessary, they should be able to receive what amounts to a domiciliary visit to the private nursing home.

Variable practice. In practice there is some confusion, as some DHA/HB/HSSBs seem reluctant to allow staff, such as therapists, to enter private nursing homes, to provide services. Circular guidance (Scotland, 1989) attempts to clarify such confusion, by clearly stating that residents should retain full access to health services, on the condition that they are not nursing services and that referral for services is through the resident's GP.

Some private nursing homes (for example, voluntary homes for people with disabilities) sometimes provide therapy services as an integral part of the home's package of care.

There is some concern that residents sometimes have to pay extra for equipment which they should either be receiving as part of nursing services provided by the home; or which they are eligible to receive under the health service.

25.1. Type of equipment

This chapter looks at the provision of all types of equipment (as dealt with elswhere in the book) for residents of private nursing homes.

25.2. Basis for equipment provision in private nursing homes

25.2.1. Definition of nursing home. Legislation includes in its definition of nursing home: 'any premises used, or intended to be used, for the reception of, and the provision of nursing for, persons suffering from any sickness, injury or infirmity . . .' (*eg Registered Homes Act 1984 s.21; Nursing Homes Registration (Scotland) Act 1938 s.10*).

25.2.2. Basis for standards: registration and inspection

25.2.2.1. Legislation. Legislation places duties on DHA/HB/HSSBs concerning the registration and inspection of private nursing homes (*Registered Home Act 1984 and SI 1984/1578; 1938 Nursing Homes (Registration) Scotland Act and SI 1988/1861 (S.172) Nursing Homes Registration (Scotland) Regulations 1988; Nursing Homes and Nursing Agencies (Northern Ireland) Act 1971 and SR 1974/313*).

Regulations (England, Wales, Scotland) make specific reference to equipment and services (*SI 1984/1578; SI 1988/1861 (S.172)*). These are referred to, as appropriate, throughout the chapter.

25.2.2.2 Circular guidance has been issued with reference (in whole or in part) to equipment provision in private nursing homes. This is referred to, as appropriate, throughout the chapter.

25.2.2.3. Guidelines

25.2.2.3.1.

England and Wales. The National Association of Health Authorities (NAHA) for England and Wales has produced a 'Handbook on the Registration and Inspection of Nursing Homes' (1985). For DHAs, this was recommended by Circular guidance (England, Wales, 1984) as aiding the development of 'clear procedures for handling applications for registration and for use in monitoring homes once registered'. Its status, though, is that of advice; the contents are in no way binding (*HC(84)21; WHC(84)23 Health Services Management. Registration and Inspection of Private Nursing Homes and Mental Nursing Homes (including private hospitals)*).

Advice on equipment provision contained in the NAHA Handbook is referred to, as appropriate, throughout the chapter.

25.2.2.3.2. Scotland. Although the NAHA (25.2.2.3.1) handbook was produced for England and Wales, it has probably been used informally in Scotland.

However, the Scottish Home and Health Department (SHHD) has recently published its own 'Model Guidelines for the Registration and Inspection of

Nursing Homes for the Elderly' (*SHHD, 1989*). This gives advice both to health boards and home owners, includes advice on equipment provision, and is referred to, as appropriate, throughout this chapter.

25.2.2.3.3. Northern Ireland. Detailed central (DHSS (NI)) guidance on inspection and standards seems not to have been issued, but HSSBs produce their own guidelines which seem to be based, to some extent, on the NAHA Handbook (25.2.2.3.1).

25.3. Assessment for entry into private nursing home

Hitherto, no formal system for state supported entry to private nursing homes has existed. The DSS has supported many people in these homes, in a rather indiscriminate manner (*Community Care: Agenda for Action. A Report to the Secretary of State for Social Services by Sir Roy Griffiths. HMSO 1988, p. v*).

As proposed by government papers and the NHS and Community Care Bill (1989) (expected to come into force in 1991), this situation will change. These state that SSD/SWD/HSSBs should be responsible for the assessment of people in need, to decide whether they should benefit from community care in their own home; or residential accomodation with or without nursing (*Caring for People. HMSO 1989 p.18-19, 80; DHSS(NI) People First. HMSO, 1990, p. 26; NHS and Community Care Bill 1989 cl. 37, 42, 49, 50*).

Similar legislation for Northern Ireland is expected.

25.4. Equipment (and services relevant to equipment) in private nursing homes

Legislation and various guidelines refer to equipment provision within private nursing homes. The following information is based on a number of these references:

- legislation (regulations, England/Wales, Scotland) (25.2.2.1.);
- NAHA guidelines (recommended by Circular guidance (England, Wales) (HC(84)21); WHC(84)23 Health Services Management. Registration and Inspection of Private Nursing Homes and Mental Nursing Homes (including private hospitals)) (25.2.2.3.1.);
- SHHD guidelines (25.2.2.3.2.);
- HSSB guidelines (25.2.2.3.3.).

25.4.1. Medical equipment in private nursing homes

25.4.1.1. Medical equipment generally in the home. Regulations (England, Wales, Scotland) state that the home owner has a duty to 'provide and maintain adequate' (England/Wales) or 'provide ... to an adequate standard or level' (Scotland) medical and surgical equipment and treatment facilities (*SI 1984/1578 r.12; SI 1988/1861 (S.172)*).

25.4.1.2. General medical equipment (5.1.) (ie through the GP for individuals). Regulations (England, Wales, Scotland) state that the home owner has a duty to to 'make adequate arrangements ... where necessary' (England/Wales) or 'make ...

to an adequate standard or level . . . arrangements' (Scotland) for the provision of medical services (*SI 1984/1578 r.12; SI 1988/1861 (S.172) r.15*).

This means that residents should have access to their own GP.

This duty, on the home owner, stands, unless the resident wishes to arrange for such services outside the health service (*SI 1984/1578 r.12; SI 1988/1861 (S.172) r.15; Registration and Inspection of Nursing Homes. A Handbook for Health Authorities. NAHA, 1985 p. 68*).

Guidelines point out that the home owner should be familiar with the procedures for registration, with family doctors (GPs) and dentists (GDPs), of residents (*Registration and Inspection of Nursing Homes. A Handbook for Health Authorities. NAHA, 1985 p. 68; Registration and Inspection of Nursing Homes. A Code of Practice for Proprietors. Northern Health and Social Services Board, 1988, p. 22; Registration and Inspection of Nursing Homes. Guidelines. EHSSB, 1986 p. 9*).

25.4.1.3. Special medical equipment (5.2.) (ie through specialist health service consultants). As stated above, home owners have a duty to see that residents have access to their GP (unless the resident wishes for care from outside the health service).

In practice, this means that the GP can refer a person, in the normal way, to hospital consultants for special medical services (and equipment). The resident can attend a hospital, or if necessary, the consultant can make a 'domiciliary visit' to the nursing home.

25.4.2. Dental appliances in private nursing homes. The same position applies to dental equipment, as to general medical equipment.

Regulations (England, Wales, Scotland) state that the home owner has a duty to to 'make adequate arrangements . . . where necessary' (England/Wales) or 'make . . . to an adequate standard or level . . . arrangements' (Scotland) for the provision of dental services (*SI 1984/1578 r.12; SI 1988/1861 (S.172) r.15*).

This means that people should have access to the general dental practitioner (GDP), through whom they have access to dental appliances (23.) as needed; and to specialist treatment and appliances, by referral to the hospital dental service (23.).

This duty stands, unless the resident wishes to arrange for dental services outside the health service (*SI 1984/1578 r.12; SI 1988/1861 (S.172) r.15; Registration and Inspection of Nursing Homes. A Handbook for Health Authorities. NAHA, 1985 p. 68*).

25.4.3. Nursing equipment in private nursing homes

25.4.3.1. Nursing home duty to provide nursing services and equipment. Regulations state that the home owner has a duty to 'provide and maintain adequate' (England/Wales) or 'provide . . . to an adequate standard or level' (Scotland) nursing equipment and treatment facilities (*SI 1984/1578r.12; SI 1988/1861 (S.172) r. 15*).

In theory, this should apply to both nursing equipment for common use, and any nursing equipment needed for individuals. Circular guidance (England, Scotland) makes it quite clear that DHA/HBs should not provide nursing equipment to meet individual needs in private nursing homes (*see eg HRC(74)16*

(England); NHS 1989(GEN)39 (Scotland). This is because the charges of the home should include any necessary 'nursing services or equipment' *(eg HRC(74)16).*

For example, a DH letter (1989) to an MP states that the reason for DHA non-provision of incontinence pads to private nursing homes is because such homes 'are under an obligation to provide continuous nursing care or treatment and generally fix their fees at a level which includes the costs of any nursing aids that may be needed' *(DH Letter POH(5)2143/141 22.5.89 to Ann Winterton, MP).*

25.4.3.2. *Practice.* Some private nursing homes may charge the resident or his/her family extra for special items of nursing equipment, such as a special bed or special incontinence pads, not regarded as standard by the home *(Verbal communication: several private nursing homes, 1990).*

Nevertheless, a well equipped nursing home provides as part of its normal equipment stock, for example: hoists (bath and mobile), walking frames, rollators, sanichairs, respirators ('suckers'), chairlifts, easy chairs (with high seat), headsets and amplifiers, adjustable height beds, monkey poles, adapted cutlery and incontinence pads *(Verbal communication: Registered Nursing Home Association 1989).*

25.4.3.2.1. Financial considerations. However, it is thought that not all private nursing homes are equipped as well as they might be.

Some home owners claim that one reason for this is that the level of DSS payments has not kept pace with inflation *(Laing's Review of Private Health Care, 1988, Vol.2 p. 23),* thereby genuinely preventing home owners from providing the desired standards of service.

Another (common) view is that, in some cases, levels of service provided by the home simply do not justify the level of charges made to residents.

25.4.3.3. *Health service input in terms of nursing services.* DHA/HB/HSSBs generally do not provide nursing services to private nursing homes, given the duty of the home itself. Circular guidance (Scotland) recently summed up and made the following points:

- private nursing home care should be akin to that provided for health service long-stay patients;
- it is unlikely that the home will be able to provide specialist nursing (such as community psychiatric nursing or stoma care);
- health board nurses could be made available on a consultative basis to demonstrate techniques to nursing home staff;
- only exceptionally should health board nurses carry out such techniques regularly and routinely (ie for individual residents) *(NHS 1989(GEN)39).*

25.4.4. Paramedical services and equipment. The provision of health service physiotherapy, occupational therapy, speech therapy and chiropody services and equipment to individuals in private nursing homes seems to give rise, as Circular guidance (Scotland, 1989) points out, to misunderstanding.

25.4.4.1. *Duty of home owner to provide adequate professional staff.* Legislation places a duty on the home owner to provide adequate 'professional' staff, which could be taken to refer to paramedical staff.

25.4.4.2. Practice varies, from the home, which provides such services integrally; to the home, which provides them specially, at extra cost to the resident; to health service provision of such services or not, depending on local policies.

The whole subject is set out in Box 25.1.

Box 25.1: Paramedical services and equipment to private nursing homes

B25.1.1. Provision by private nursing homes of paramedical services: legislation, guidelines

B25.1.1.1. Regulations (England, Wales, Scotland) state that the home owner has a duty to provide adequate 'professional, technical, ancillary and other supporting staff' (*SI 1984/1478 r.12; SI 1988/1861 (S.172) r.15*). This could reasonably be interpreted as including paramedical staff, although the regulations do not provide a definition of 'professional staff'.

B25.1.1.2. Guidelines (various) recommend that paramedical staff may need to be employed by the home for the purpose of rehabilitation of residents (*Registration and Inspection of Nursing Homes. A Handbook for Health Authorities. NAHA, 1985 p. 68*); and the home owner should provide the services one way or another (*Registration and Inspection of Nursing Homes. A Handbook for Health Authorities. NAHA, 1985 p. 101); Model Guidelines for the Registration and Inspection of Nursing Homes for the Elderly. SHHD, 1989, p. 16; Registration and Inspection of Nursing Homes. A Code of Practice for Proprietors. Northern Health and Social Services Board, 1988, p. 22; Registration and Inspection of Nursing Homes. Guidelines. EHSSB, 1986 p. 29*). These guidelines do not however seem to state that the home owner has a duty to employ such paramedical staff.

B25.1.2. Provision by DHA/HB/HSSB

B25.1.2.1. Legislation and Circular guidance. There is nothing in health service legislation which prevents health service paramedical staff visiting and treating individual residents in private nursing homes.

B25.1.2.1.1. Scotland. Circular guidance (Scotland,1989) states that the SHHD believes that individual residents 'should be entitled to such NHS services as are recommended or prescribed by their GPs. The trigger of course for granting supplies and services must be the action of a GP in recommending or prescribing for a particular patient a service (eg physiotherapy) or supplies (eg incontinence aids). It would not be appropriate for a private nursing home to approach the health board directly in order to secure services or supplies for its patients' (*NHS 1989(GEN)39*).

B25.1.2.2. England. Circular guidance (England) discusses only chiropody services; in 1974, stating that the health service should not provide free chiropody services to private nursing homes (*HRC(74)16*), and in 1978, correcting this statement by clearly stating that health authorities have discretion to provide free chiropody services to priority groups (9.3.3.1.1.) (*HC(78)16*).

Other paramedical services, such as those involving physiotherapy, occupational therapy, speech therapy are not mentioned; although, on the basis of the guidance given concerning chiropody, it would be consistent for the same type of services (ie paramedical) to be available in the same way.

B25.1.3. Practice. In practice the position appears to be somewhat confused.

B25.1.3.1. Hospital treatment and equipment provision by paramedical services. No confusion seems to exist in this case at least. If a resident's GP refers a person for attendance at a hospital, the consultant may delegate rehabilitation to a paramedical department. In this case, treatment and equipment can be supplied, as necessary, to the resident as to any health service patient.

B25.1.3.2. Treatment and equipment provision in the home

B25.1.3.2.1. Provision by home of paramedical services and equipment

B25.1.3.2.1.1 Paramedical services integral to the home's services. A private nursing home sometimes offers paramedical services as integral to the package of care, which it is offering (especially voluntary organisation homes).

In this case, it might employ paramedical staff or bring them in on a sessional basis. Both general screening/treatment classes and individual treatment and equipment may be free of charge to the resident. Sometimes, individual treatment and equipment may be charged extra to the resident (and family).

Such services may be responsive only, or more regular and active (*g Independent Medical Care 1988: 7;3,p. 32*).

B25.1.3.2.1.2. Paramedical services not integral to the package of care. Alternatively, the home might not provide any paramedical services integral to the package of care. In this case it might rely, to some extent, on DHA/HB/HSSB help (see below), or simply bring in paramedical services on a private basis, charging the resident extra.

B25.1.3.2.2. Health service paramedical services in private nursing homes. Practice, concerning the availability of such services, seems to vary from area to area. A Parliamentary question earlier this year elicited government agreement that 'practice varies widely from place to place' as far as access to NHS 'ancillary' [paramedical?] care is concerned (*Hansard July 1989, p. 984*).

B25.1.3.2.2.1. DHA/HB/HSSB policy not to provide services to homes. Sometimes official DHA/HB/HSSB policy is that such services should not be provided, especially where there is the belief that health service staff cannot legally provide services on private nursing home premises (*Verbal communication: RHA policy maker, 1989*). (There appears, in fact, to be no legislative basis for such a belief).

Even where there is such a policy, some services (eg physiotherapists) may treat individuals in private nursing homes anyway, from humanitarian motives.

Awkward situations can arise where paramedical staff enter a private nursing home to treat a health service patient (see below) (ie in a health service bed within the home), but are not supposed to treat a DSS supported resident in the next bed.

B25.1.3.2.2.2. DHA/HB/HSSB policy to provide services to homes. Official DHA/HB/HSSB policy might be that services can be provided to individuals in private nursing homes.

Where this is the case, paramedical services are provided to needy residents in private nursing homes. Such services are likely to be subject to local priority criteria and home residents sometimes tend to be low priority; already in care they are pereceived to be at lower risk. Equipment loan to individual residents may be part of such services.

B25.1.3.2.2.3. DHA/HB/HSSB discretion. As with virtually all services, local policy and practice is determined by DHA/HB/HSSBs according to local circumstances and resources.

The problem is, that on the one hand, residents (often state supported) are in danger of losing their rights to NHS services; on the other, the potential demand for services, by private nursing home residents is enormous.

25.4.5. WCs, bathrooms. Regulations state that adequate or suitable wash basins, baths or showers supplying hot and cold water, and water closets and sluicing facilities must be provided (*SI 1984/1578 r.12; 1988/1861 (S. 172) r.15*). Guidelines include reference to:

- wide doors allowing wheelchairs access to WCs and wheelchair and hoist access to bathrooms;
- space by the bath allowing nurse-assisted bathing and use of hoist;

- toilets to allow wheelchair access, sideways transfer from wheelchair to toilet or nurse assistance;
- non-slip bathroom floors and non-slip bath bases;
- WC grab and wall rails, bath lifts and other bathroom aids, toilet seat raisers;
- in general, adequate provision of aids (fixed and mobile) for people with disabilities in WCs and bathrooms (*see variously in Registration and Inspection of Nursing Homes. A Handbook for Health Authorities. NAHA, 1985 p. 71; Model Guidelines for the Registration and Inspection of Nursing Homes for the Elderly. SHHD, 1989, p 11, 27; Registration and Inspection of Nursing Homes. Guidelines. EHSSB, 1986 p. 11; Northern HPSSB Code p. 10*).

25.4.6. Equipment for continence. Regulations state the home owner has a duty to provide nursing equipment (see above); nursing equipment is expected to include incontinence pads.

Guidelines recommend that incontinence pads should be provided by the nursing home (*Registration and Inspection of Nursing Homes. A Handbook for Health Authorities. NAHA, 1985 p. 103; Registration and Inspection of Nursing Homes. A Code of Practice for Proprietors. Northern Health and Social Services Board, 1988, p. 43*).

Circular guidance (England, Scotland) states that DHA/HBs should not be providing pads to individual residents in private nursing homes (Box 17.1.6.1.). In practice, the picture is confused, and Circular guidance (Scotland, 1989) has pointed out that in Scotland, residents can have bed incontinence pads prescribed by their GP (Box 17.1.6.2.).

The subject is discussed fully elsewhere (Box 17.1.6.).

25.4.7. Beds. Regulations (England/Wales, Scotland) state that the home owner has a duty to provide adequate furniture and bedding (*SI 1984/1578 r.12; SI 1988/1861 (S.171) r.15*).

Various guidelines recommend that people who require extensive nursing care, or who are elderly and spend a lot of time in bed should have variable height beds (*see eg Registration and Inspection of Nursing Homes. A Handbook for Health Authorities NAHA, 1985 p. 76, 103); Model Guidelines for the Registration and Inspection of Nursing Homes for the Elderly. SHHD, 1989, p. 10; Registration and Inspection of Nursing Homes. A Code of Practice for Proprietors. Northern Health and Social Services Board, 1988, p. 14, p. 43*).

SHHD guidelines include reference to beds and accessories, including the presence of a bedside nurse call system, bed type (hospital frame, divan, variable height), lockers, footstools, bed tables, bed (back) rests, bed footrests (*Model Guidelines for the Registration and Inspection of Nursing Homes for the Elderly, SHHD, 1989, p. 40*).

25.4.8. Heating. Regulations (England/Wales, Scotland) state that the home owner has a duty to provide adequate heating within the home (*SI 1984/1578 r.12; 1988/1861 (S.172) r.15*).

Guidelines recommend 21 degrees centigrade for bathrooms, toilet facilities, treatment rooms where people are likely to be undressed; 18 degrees centigrade in bedrooms, dayrooms, waiting rooms; 16 degrees centigrade in corridors, on staircases etc. Heating appliances should be adequately guarded

(*Registration and Inspection of Nursing Homes. A Handbook for Health Authorities NAHA, 1985 p. 72; Model Guidelines for the Registration and Inspection of Nursing Homes for the Elderly. SHDD, 1989, p. 10; Registration and Inspection of Nursing Homes. Guidelines. EHSSB, 1986 p. 11; Registration and Inspection of Nursing Homes. A Code of Practice for Proprietors. Northern Health and Social Services Board, 1988, p. 11*).

25.4.9. Lighting and colour contrast. Regulations (England/Wales, Scotland) state that the home owner has a duty to provide adequate lighting within the home (*SI 1984/1578 r.12; SI 1988/1861 (S.172) r.15*). Guidelines recommend that:

- rooms for daily living activities should have good natural light;
- every part of the home should have electric lighting sufficient for the use of that part;
- there should be individual bed lights;
- corridors and stairs should be well-lit;
- The special lighting needs of people with visual impairment should be considered (*referred to variously in Registration and Inspection of Nursing Homes. A Handbook for Health Authorities. NAHA, 1985 p. 73; Model Guidelines for the Registration and Inspection of Nursing Homes for the Elderly. SHHD, 1989, p. 10, 38, 40; Registration and Inspection of Nursing Homes. Guidelines. EHSSB, 1986 p. 12; Registration and Inspection of Nursing Homes. A Code of Practice for Proprietors. Northern Health and Social Services Board, 1988, p. 12*).

Colour contrast is helpful, but guidelines note that care must be taken over strong patterns in floor finishes and blocks of different colour. These can be mistaken for obstacles by people with visual impairment (*referred to variously in Registration and Inspection of Nursing Homes. A Handbook for Health Authorities. NAHA, 1985 p. 102; Registration and Inspection of Nursing Homes. A Code of Practice for Proprietors. Northern Health and Social Services Board, 1988, p. 42*).

25.4.10. Hoists. Guidelines recommend that hoists should be provided, as necessary, by the home owner, and that care must be taken that they are used correctly and safely (*Registration and Inspection of Nursing Homes. A Handbook for Health Authorities. NAHA, 1985 p. 103; NHSSB p. 43*).

25.4.11. Kitchen equipment. Regulations (England/Wales, Scotland) state that the home owner has a duty to provide adequate kitchen equipment, crockery and cutlery (*SI 1984/1578 r.12; SI 1988/1861 (S.171) r.15*).

25.4.12. Steps and stairs, ramps. Guidelines recommend that steps and stairs should have handrails and be safely constructed and carpeted. Ramps should be non-slip (*Registration and Inspection of Nursing Homes. A Handbook for Health Authorities. NAHA, 1985 p. 102; Registration and Inspection of Nursing Homes. A Code of Practice for Proprietors. Northern Health and Social Services Board, 1988, p. 42*).

25.4.13. Equipment for arthritis. Guidelines recommend that, for people with arthritis, a range of special aids might be required, and should be provided (*Registration and Inspection of Nursing Homes. A Handbook for Health Authorities.*

NAHA, 1985 p. 103; Registration and Inspection of Nursing Homes. A Code of Practice for Proprietors. Northern Health and Social Services Board, 1988, p. 43).

25.4.14. Equipment for children. Regulations state that the home owner has a duty to make adequate arrangements where appropriate, for play and education facilities for children (*SI 1984/1578 r.12; SI 1988/1861 (S.172) r.15*).

Guidelines recommend that children have a reasonable range of special equipment and toys (*Registration and Inspection of Nursing Homes. A Handbook for Health Authorities. NAHA, 1985 p. 104*). Children with a mental handicap might need specially designed furniture (eg simple, strong, cleanable) and play equipment including toys, books, pictures (*Registration and Inspection of Nursing Homes. A Code of Practice for Proprietors. Northern Health and Social Services Board, 1988, p. 54*)

Guidelines also recommend that children should be under the care of both a GP and a paediatrician. Links with social services or education departments should be established to enable the organisation of both play and education facilities. Speech therapy services may be required (*Registration and Inspection of Nursing Homes. A Handbook for Health Authorities. NAHA, 1985 p. 104*).

25.5. Health service patients in private nursing homes

Sometimes the health service arranges for a health service patient to be cared for in a private nursing home. The contract between the DHA/HB/HSSB and the home may vary.

25.5.1. Type of contract. Circular guidance (England, Scotland, 1981) states that such a contract may entail the private home providing an 'all inclusive' service; alternatively health service staff can enter the home and use its facilities, as part of their normal health service work (*HC(81)1, NHS 1981(GEN)30*).

25.5.2. Health service patient retains same rights. Circular guidance (England, Scotland, 1981) states that the health service patient in a private nursing home should receive, free of charge, the same services, as he or she would on health service premises. The services should be of the same standard, and the patient should not be pressed into extra payments for services not normally provided by the health service (*HC(81)1; NHS 1981(GEN)30*).

25.5.3. Confusion over services. Such arrangements can lead to questions over what facilities (and equipment) the home should be providing; and what health service staff should be bringing into the home.

26 Equipment for Children (medical, daily living, nursing)

Equipment for children (medical, nursing, daily living)

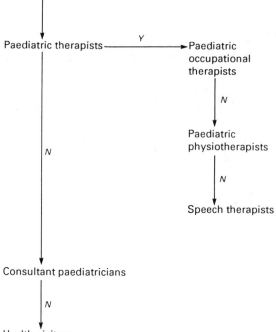

Introduction

This book describes services which, in the main, provide equipment for both adults and children. Children also benefit from special paediatric services. This chapter briefly indicates a few of these.

Basis of equipment provision for children. The legislative basis for children's services, involving equipment provision (other than education), is more or less the same as for adults; although:

- legislation and Circular guidance emphasises the importance of co-operation between statutory authorities in the case of young children;

- legislation places specific duties on authorities in relation to school-leavers; and
- legislation places duties on authorities in relation to school medical and dental inspection.

Special services and staff for children include:

- paediatric occupational therapists;
- paediatric physiotherapists;
- speech therapists (who anyway work a great deal with children);
- paediatric consultants;
- paediatric hospital nurses;
- paediatric district nurses;
- health visitors;
- multi-disciplinary teams;
- toy libraries;
- community child health services (mainly referral only);
- school health service (mainly referral only).

26.1. Type of equipment

Children with disabilities require all sorts of equipment and, as they grow and develop, frequent changes of equipment.

Equipment includes various beds, bedding, seating, desks, toilet equipment, bath equipment, standing and posture equipment, mobility equipment (including carriages, walking aids, car seats), developmental and play equipment. For details see Box 26.1.

Box 26.1: Type of equipment for children: example

B26.1.1. Beds, bedding: special beds, cots (with eg bed rails, cot sides, safety nets special mattresses, pillows).

B26.1.2. Seating: high chairs, sagbags/bean bags, tumbleform seating (foam seating with supports), ladderback chairs, chairs with various types of supports and restraints, special support seating systems for wheelchairs etc.

B26.1.3. Desks: various desks and tables including angled, adjustable angle sections, with cutouts, with support boxes attached.

B26.1.4. Toilet equipment: potties with backrest and pommel, musical potties, toilet training seats (fit within existing seat of WC to narrow aperture), various toilet support frames with supporting features (and seat), 'potty' chairs/commodes.

B26.1.5. Bath equipment: bath chairs, supports, frames, cushions, hammock type seats.

B26.1.6. Orthotic appliances: protective helmets, surgical appliances and footwear.

B26.1.7. Standing and posture equipment floor wedges, side-lying boards, prone boards, kneeling frames, standing frames, standing boxes.

B26.1.8. Mobility equipment: whelchairs including buggies, scooters, cycles (tricycles), go-karts, user-propelled trolleys, crawling equipment, toys for mobility.

B26.1.9. Walking aids: mobile frames (eg rollators, frame with suspended support seat), swivel walkers (eg lower limb orthosis with leg callipers supported on swivel foot base).

B26.1.10. Car seats and harnesses

B26.1.11. Developmental and play equipment: vestibular swings and suspension units, rocking equipment (eg boats, horses, hammocks), play structures and shapes (eg ball pools, large balls, foam playing shapes of all sizes, inflatable castles), playground equipment (swings, slides etc.), stimulating toys (hearing, vision, touch), response toys (eg respond to talk), electric toys with range of switch-types for operation (*DLF Information Service Handbook*).

B26.1.12. Eating and drinking equipment: special spoons, cutlery crockery, mugs and other such aids.

26.2. Legislative basis for children's equipment provision

The basis for provision of medical, nursing and daily living equipment is generally the same as provision for adults.

There is, however, special reference to school medical and dental inspection (which might identify equipment needs) (26.3.4.); and to co-operation between

SSD/SWD and HSSBs when children are about to leave school (26.3.2.2.) (this legislation is not yet in force in Northern Ireland).

The provision of equipment for children with special educational needs is discussed elsewhere (27.).

26.3. Co-operation between authorities

26.3.1. General co-operation.

26.3.1.1. England, Wales, Scotland. Health service legislation places a duty on DHA/SSD/LEAs (England and Wales) and HB/SWD/LEAs (Scotland) to co-operate, to promote health and welfare (England, Wales), or health (Scotland) (generally, not just with respect to children) (*NHS Act 1977 s.22; NHS (Scotland) Act 1978 s.13*).

26.3.1.2. Northern Ireland health and social services are integrated in the form of HSSBs; legislation places a duty on HSSBs, district councils (housing), education and library boards, and the Northern Ireland Housing Executive 'to co-operate with one another in order to secure and advance the health and social welfare of the people' (*SI 1972/1265 HPSS(NI)O 1972 a.67*).

26.3.2. Co-operation between authorities in relation to children

26.3.2.1. Circular guidance (education) emphasises the importance of co-operation between authorities in relation to children (*DES 22/89 para 80; SED Guidance Note SEN GENERAL/REC 2 para 8; DENI 1987/21 para 22*).

26.3.2.2. School-leavers. Recent 'disabled persons' legislation (not yet in force in Northern Ireland) requires a high a level of co-operation between education authorities (LEA/ELBs) and social services/work departments (SSD/SWD/HSSBs) concerning school leavers (*Disabled Persons (Services Consultation and Representation) Act 1986 s.5,6; (Disabled Persons (Services, Consultation and Representation) Act 1986 s.13; Disabled Persons (Northern Ireland) Act 1989 s.5,6: not yet in force*) (27.2.5.6.).

26.3.3. Under-fives. Education legislation (England, Wales, Northern Ireland) places a duty on DHA/HSSBs to inform LEAs (England/Wales,) and ELBs (Northern Ireland) of children under five who have special educational needs (*see eg Education Act 1981 s.10; SI 1986/594 (NI 3) Education and Libraries (Northern Ireland) Order 1986 r.36*).

Circular guidance (England, Scotland, Northern Ireland) emphasises the importance of co-operation between authorities in relation to children under 5 (*see eg LASSL (76)5; LASSL (78)1; DES 22/89; WOC 54/89; NHS 1982(GEN)38; DENI 1987/21*).

26.3.4. School medical and dental inspection. Legislation places a duty on DHA/HB/HSSBs to carry out, in schools maintained by LEA/ELBs:

- medical inspections, at 'appropriate intervals' (*NHS Act 1977 s.5; NHS (Scotland) Act 1978 s.39; SI 1972/1265 HPSS(NI)O 1972 a.9*);

- dental inspections, 'to meet all reasonable requirements' (*NHS Act 1977 s.5 as amended by the Health and Medicines Act 1988 s.10; NHS (Scotland) Act 1978 s.39 as amended by the Health and Medicines Act 1988 s.10; SI 1972/1265 HPSS(NI)O 1972 a.9 as amended by SI 1988/2249 (NI.24); Health and Medicines (Northern Ireland) Order 1988 r.6*).

26.4. Assessment, prescription, provision of equipment for children

26.4.1. Paediatric therapists. Whatever their base (eg hospital, school, health centre), paediatric physiotherapists, paediatric occupational therapists and speech therapists spend a lot of time, for example, in schools, nursery-schools, playgroups, toy libraries and children's own homes.

Independent special schools sometimes employ their own therapists.

26.4.1.1. Paediatric occupational therapist (daily living equipment)

26.4.1.1.1. Hospital occupational therapist department assessment and loan. Hospital paediatric OTs are the experts on assessment of daily living equipment for children.

They might not themselves loan a great deal of equipment, but they assess (often in schools, homes, playgroups) and make recommendations for the provision of all sorts of equipment such as bath aids, seating, wheelchairs, buggies, toilet equipment (including potties) and feeding aids.

The OT department might have some daily living equipment which can be loaned, perhaps on a short-term trial basis; but is likely to make recommendations to the SSD/SWD or in Northern Ireland, to community OTs within the HSSB. Simple equipment might be supplied by hospital OTs on behalf of the SSD/SWD or the HSSB community OTs (2.5.5.1.2.); or sometimes made (eg floor seating, wooden chairs) by OTs.

26.4.1.1.2. SSD/SWD/HSSB community OT assessment and loan. In England, Wales and Scotland, there is often a shortage of specialist paediatric OTs in the community; so DHA/HB OTs often undertake assessment and make recommendations on behalf of the SSD/SWD, which nevertheless arranges for provision (*SSD guidelines received 1989/1990; Verbal communication: paediatric OT, London DHA 1989*).

In Northern Ireland, specialist community paediatric OTs are sometimes placed in special schools, and in the community during school-holiday periods.

SSD/SWD/HSSB internal guidelines sometimes include reference to, and criteria for, the provision of daily living equipment for children. See Box 26.2, for examples. SSD/SWD/HSSB loan of daily living equipment to children follows, in general, the same procedures as to adults (2.) (see Box 26.2).

26.4.1.1.3. Part of multi-disciplinary team. Paediatric OTs might, for example, work within or without any multi-disciplinary team (26.4.7.) which exists within an area. For example, in one DHA, all four OTs might work within the team; in another DHA, one out of four.

26.4.1.2. Paediatric physiotherapist loan (mobility and other equipment for movement/activities). Paediatric physiotherapists are the experts on mobility

> **Box 26.2: SSD/SWD/HSSB guidelines and criteria on the provision of daily living equipment for children**
>
> **B26.2.1. General.** The SSD only provides equipment essential for disability: not equipment which a child of any given age would normally have (*SSD Midlands (1)*).
>
> **B26.2.2. Car seats.** Only provided for special needs, as parents normally buy such seats anyway (*Midlands SSD (1)*).
>
> **B26.2.3. Supportive furniture (standing frames, supine boards):** provision is considered.
>
> **B26.2.4. Feeding equipment**: considered only to meet special needs and not to provide normal type of equipment.
>
> **B26.2.5. Leisure equipment**: advice given, but leisure equipment not normally issued; referral should be made to toy libraries.

equipment for children. Depending on local arrangements, they might also be involved with the use of equipment such as mobile toys (to aid walking), prone boards, crawler boards, shapes, musical equipment, treatment balls, ladder-back ('Peto') chairs, standing boxes, wobble boxes and so on (*Hospital physiotherapy dept stock list*).

Some of this may be available for loan; otherwise it is for therapy and assessment purposes only.

Paediatric physiotherapists might be part of the hospital-based service (8.3.3.), or part of a community physiotherapy service (8.3.3.). They might be part of a multi-disciplinary team (26.4.7.).

26.4.1.3. Speech therapists anyway work with children a great deal; provision of equipment for speech replacement and assistance is discussed elsewhere (13.). They might be part of a multi-disciplinary team (26.4.7.).

26.4.2. General practitioners (GPs). GPs prescribe Drug Tariff appliances and wheelchairs for permanent use, as well as making referral to specialist hospital services and social services for other equipment (5.1.1./Box 5.1.). GPs have a key position in community health care (5.1.3.7.).

26.4.2.1. Special child GPs. The new GPs' contract (operative from April 1990) makes provision for what are called 'restricted service principal' GPs, who offer general medical services to special groups of people. One of the categories of service is 'child health surveillance'.

Such surveillance services include the monitoring of the health, well-being and physical, mental and social development of the child while under 5 years so as to identify any 'deviations from normal development' (*SI 1974/160 s.3A and Sched. 1A inserted by SI 1989/1897; SI 1974/506(S.41) s.4A and Sched.1 Part 1A inserted by SI 1989/1990 (S.139); SR&O 1973/421 s.3A and Sched. 1E inserted by SR 1989/454*).

In some areas, GPs hold 'well-child' clinics, undertaken by themselves or by a clinical medical officer (26.4.8.), on behalf of the GP.

26.4.3. General dental practitioners (GDPs) are discussed, in relation to children, elsewhere (23.4.3.2.).

26.4.4. Consultant paediatricians are involved to greater or lesser extent, and in consultation with other specialist consultants, with the provision of most of the medical (and some other) equipment discussed in this book.

The consultant paediatrician prescribes various items, such as wheelchairs (6.), orthotic appliances (10.), surgical footwear (9.), swivel walkers, protective helmets.

He or she also has the power (5.2.4.1.) to prescibe any other items clinically or medically necessary such as communication aids, for example (13.). This power, though practically constrained by resources, might be used where special children's equipment is needed and other specialist budgets (for example, physiotherapy, occupational therapy, speech therapy) are unable to supply the item. The pattern of consultant prescription of special items is likely to vary from area to area.

26.4.5. Consultant community paediatricians might participate in, or lead, the community child health services (26.4.8.), and work closely with GPs (*see eg Kirby J. Community paediatrics takes off. General Practitioner 1986; November, p. 43; Crouchman MR et al. A joint child health clinic in an inner London general practice. Practitioner 1986: 230;1417,667-672; NHS Handbook. NAHA, 1989, p. 119*).

26.4.6. Nurses and home nursing equipment

26.4.6.1. Paediatric clinical nurse specialists. These nurses work in hosptial paediatric units/departments and, under the (delegated) authority of consultants, recommend and loan home nursing equipment. The extent to which hospital paediatric units loan home nursing equipment (rather than the community nursing services) varies.

It is expected that, in the future, 'paediatric clinical nurse specialists' will be able to prescribe certain items, currently prescribed by GPs, from a nurses' formulary (*Report of the Advisory Group on Nurse Prescribing. DH, 1989, p. 28*).

26.4.6.2. Community nurses.

26.4.6.2.1. District nurses (4.4.1.1.) (part of the community nursing services), can loan home nursing equipment to children as well as adults – although hospital paediatric units might also undertake such loan (26.4.6.1.).

26.4.6.2.1.1. Paediatric district nurses are increasing in number: they tend to be attached to either hospital paediatric units or health centres (*Directory of Paediatric Community Nursing Services. 7th ed. RCN, 1989*). They loan home nursing equipment (4.), and, as district nurses, are one of the groups who are expected, in the future, to be able to prescribe certain items (currently prescribed by GPs) from a nurses' formulary (*Report of the Advisory Group on Nurse Prescribing. DH, 1989, p. 25*).

26.4.6.2. Health visitors (4.4.1.2.), depending on local arrangements, sometimes authorise the loan of home nursing equipment; otherwise they are well placed to identify problems (including equipment) and make referrals, to, for example, the district nurse, child assessment centre (26.4.7.1.) or GP.

Health visitors are nurses whose primary role has traditionally been concerned with infant and family health (though increasingly they also work with elderly people). They are often attached to GP practices (5.1.3.6.), and participate in child health clinics.

26.4.7. Multi-disciplinary teams (child assessment centres). The establishment of multi-disciplinary teams for assessment of, and provision for, children has been recommended by various Circular guidance (*see eg Joint circular HC(78)5 – LAC(78)2; NHS 1980(GEN)26; DENI 1987/21 para 22*).

The existence of these teams (and of community mental handicap teams for adults for example) is in contrast to the lack of such services for people with physical disabilities who are too old to benefit from special schools and paediatric health services (*see eg Beardshaw. V. Last on the List. 1988 p. 36; Bax M et al. Health care of physically handicapped young adults. British Medical Journal 1988: 296, 1153-1155*).

26.4.7.1. Name and definition of multi-disciplinary teams. A team might be known as, for example:

- child assessment centre (CAC);
- district handicap team (DHT);
- child development team (CDT);
- special needs team;
- early intervention team;
- district team for children with special needs.

The team might not have a name; efficiently co-operating professionals might not consider themselves to be a team; or there might not be a team or a high level of co-operation (*for all this, see eg Bax M, Whitmore K. District Handicap Teams. Structure, Functions and Relationships. A report to the DHSS. Community Paediatric Research Unit, Westminster Children's Hospital. 1985 pp. 25–8; Changing School Health Services. Primary Health Care Group. King's Fund Centre for Health Services Development. Section 1 p. 6; Social Services Year Book 1988/89. Longman, 1988*).

26.4.7.2. Location. The position can be confusing: the team might operate at a child assessment centre (CAC) which is:

- part of hospital premises;
- a separate unit in hospital grounds;
- a separate unit outside the hospital;
- based in 'community' premises (*Bax M, Whitmore K. District Handicap Teams. Structure, Functions and Relationships. A report to the DHSS. Community Paediatric Research Unit, Westminster Children's Hospital. 1985 p. 27*).

Alternatively, the team may not have a base as such, and see parents and children in a variety of different places.

26.4.7.3. Team composition. 'Core' membership of these teams can include: community health doctors, nurses, health visitors, psychologists, social workers, paediatricians, speech therapists, physiotherapists, occupational therapists and teachers. Many other professionals might also be involved (*Bax M, Whitmore K. District Handicap Teams. Structure, Functions and Relationships. A report to the DHSS. Community Paediatric Research Unit, Westminster Children's Hospital. 1985 p. 31*).

Community mental handicap nurses are sometimes part of the team.

26.4.7.4. Age range. The age limits of children seen by these teams vary greatly. Some teams only see children under five years; other teams see children up to 16, 18, and even over 20 years old (*Bax M, Whitmore K. District Handicap Teams. Structure, Functions and Relationships. A report to the DHSS. Community Paediatric Research Unit, Westminster Children's Hospital. 1985, p. 42*).

26.4.7.5. Referral/assessment. A child with a disability may be noticed either at birth by a consultant, later by a GP or health visitor, or later at school by a school doctor. The main sources of referral to the team are likely to be community health doctors, consultant paediatricians, GPs, neo-natal followup (including special baby care units), health visitors. GPs might refer through normal channels to a paediatrician rather than through a child assessment centre (*Bax M, Whitmore K. District Handicap Teams. Structure, Functions and Relationships. A report to the DHSS. Community Paediatric Research Unit, Westminster Children's Hospital. 1985 p. 41*).

Initial assessment at the centre is generally made by a paediatrician, together with other professionals. Subsequently, the members of the team are likely to visit special schools, nursery schools and sometimes secondary schools, and the child's home (*Bax M, Whitmore K. District Handicap Teams. Structure, Functions and Relationships. A report to the DHSS. Community Paediatric Research Unit, Westminster Children's Hospital. 1985 p. 52*).

26.4.7.6. Provision. Multi-disciplinary centres normally have a range of equipment for therapy and assessment purposes, and, possibly, some equipment for short-term loan. Therapists, or technicians with therapists, might make simple furniture. The centres are unlikely to be a major source of long-term equipment loan.

Instead, therapists are likely to make recommendations to the SSD/SWD and HSSB (under social services functions) for provision of daily living equipment (2.).

However, consultant paediatricians at the centres prescribe as normal; similarly a paediatric district nurse, connected with the centre, might authorise home nursing equipment, as normal.

A centre with a strong parents' group, for example, sometimes builds up a stock of loan equipment.

26.4.8. Community child health services. are the responsibility of the local DHA/HB/HSSB.

Child health clinics include amongst their functions general surveillance, referral in cases of acute or chronic medical conditions, advice to parents, health education and so on.

The exact organisation of community child health ervices varies; clinical work might be undertaken by consultant paediatricians, (senior) clinical medical officers ((S)CMOs). Health visitors and clinical medical officers (CMOs) often run the clinic; consultant paediatricians might hold regular or irregular sessions.

The importance for equipment provision of these services by (S)CMOs is mainly appropriate referral, although consultant paediatricians can prescribe equipment (26.4.4.).

26.4.9. School health service. The school health service is the responsibility of the local DHA/HB/HSSB. Consisting basically of doctor and nurse, the school doctor is usually a (S)CMO on a full-or part-time basis, or a GP employed on a sessional basis (*Review of the School Health Service Northern Ireland. DHSS 1989*).

Neither the (S)CMO nor nurse are traditionally prescribers of equipment: they undertake surveillance and make referrals as appropriate. Though normally empowered to prescribe Drug Tariff equipment, a GP acting as school doctor might instead refer a child to his or her own GP for treatment.

School nurses (who might be health visitors), however, are one of the groups who are expected, in the future, to be able to prescribe certain items, currently GP prescribed, from a nurses' formulary (*Report of the Advisory Group on Nurse Prescribing. DH 1989 p. 28*).

26.4.9.1. Independent schools health service. Independent schools (including voluntary special schools) might employ their own doctor and nurse for general screening purposes.

Independent schools, in general, may receive help from their local DHA/HB/ HSSB in running a school health service. A survey by the Independent Schools Information Service (ISIS) in 1988, for example, found that some 200 such schools had inspections provided by the DHA; whereas 431 made their own arrangements (*ISIS. NHS survey 1988*).

26.4.10. Special (rehabilitation) centres (29.). There are some special centres for children, combining both health and education services, designed for both longer or shorter periods of outpatient/day attender or inpatient/boarder child attendance.

Examples of this type include Chailey Heritage, consisting of independent school and NHS hospital, and the Cheney Centre for Children with Cerebral Palsy, which is an NHS unit with education authority provided teachers and classroom facilities.

Multi-disciplinary assessment is carried out and accessible rehabilitation engineering facilities might allow the making of 'one-off' solutions, where commercially available equipment is not suitable.

Post-discharge arrangements are various. One centre, for example, easily follows up children discharged in its own area by means of the local paediatric OT service. Otherwise, there might be annual medical reviews at the centre, or the parents might choose to make use of their own local services for continuing review.

Once the child has left schooling altogether, it is recognised, by specialist centres, that support services tend to diminish (26.4.12.).

26.4.10.1. Rehabilitation engineers, within a local hospital, special rehabilitation centre, or otherwise accessible, can make and adapt equipment, following participation in multi-disciplinary assessment, often with therapists.

There also a number of local panels consisting of engineers and other professionals, which act in a voluntary capacity under the name of REMAP (29.3.), and undertake to provide 'one-off' equipment solutions.

26.4.11. Toy libraries (*following points are based partly on information leaflets from National Toy Libraries Association, 1989*) are 'playgroups' for children with special needs: special toys are available for play at the centre, and for home loan. Scottish circular guidance has welcomed toy libraries (*NHS Circular 1976(GEN)42; NHS Circular 1978 (GEN) 60; SED 955/1976*). For details, see Box 26.3.

Box 26.3: Toy libraries

B26.3.1. Location. Toy libraries are found in a variety of places and forms: for example, hospital inpatient and outpatient departments, health clinics, playgroups, nursery and infants' schools, special units and schools, childrens' public libraries and mobile vans etc. The toy library can be part of a special group (for example, KIDS) which aims at child development, both within the group and at home, by means of Portage-type education (*Box 26.4., Example 8*).

B26.3.2. Running of toy libraries Toy libraries are organised and run by, for example, parents' groups by DHA/HB/HSSB/SSD/SWDs, by voluntary bodies, education authorities and public libraries.

26.3.3. Age range. Primarily for under-fives, the toy libraries may cater for children a good few years older. There is now a development toward 'leisure libraries', which are designed for older (teenage children).

B26.3.4. Staff often work on a voluntary basis and can range from 'unqualified' to retired physiotherapists, for example.
  Various professionals might make regular visits to the toy library: eg health visitors, occupational therapists, speech therapists, physiotherapists.

B26.3.5. Equipment loan. Toys are used and loaned by a library, though the range is quite often readily expanded to include equipment such as seating and wedges (for support and play). Sometimes the equipment is used, and loaned, to back up an organised education schedule, employing, for example, the Portage system of teaching (Box 26.4. Example 8).
  A loan, for example, allows a period of use before parents decide to actually buy a (expensive) toy; or allows use of toys, which are too expensive to buy.

26.4.12. Leaving school. Once a child has left schooling altogether, it is recognised that support services (health, paramedical, nursing) tend to diminish (*Written communication, specialist centre 1990. Bax M et al. Health care of physically handicapped young adults. BMJ 1988, Vol. 296, pp. 1153–5*).

Recent legislation introduces procedures for co-operation between statutory authorities (26.3.2.2.), but it is not primarily aimed at the health service.

26.4.13. Division of responsibility for provision. There is sometimes uncertainty as to which statutory service is responsible for which equipment. Generally speaking, DHA/HB/HSSBs are responsible for equipment required for an individual medical, nursing or paramedical (including mobility) need, SSD/SWD or HSSB (under social services functions) for daily living equipment, and LEA/ELBs for educational equipment.

Examples (both general and specific), given in Box 26.4, illustrate some of the possible complexities of provision.

Box 26.4: Examples of provision of equipment for children, illustrating possible complexity of provision

Example 1. Local general restrictions. Some SSDs (England), for example, might have specific policies which can be very generous or more restrictive (eg limiting a child to one piece of equipment at a time, or to a £50 maximum per item (*Verbal: paediatric OT (based on work at a special child assessment centre 1989)*).

Example 2. Continuing needs. Children's needs change as they grow and develop: this is not always understood by funding authorities (*Verbal communication: paediatric OT, 1989*).

Example 3. Prone boards, wedges, special seating The provision of these items sometimes falls between a DHA/HB (health) and a SSD/SWD (daily living). The DHA/HB might claim that such equipment is daily living in nature and therefore a SSD/SWD responsibility; the SSD/SWD could claim that they are a health responsibility.

Provision of such items might progress in an 'ad hoc' fashion, sometimes supplied by one authority, sometimes by another, sometimes by neither. When demand grows (for children with learning difficulties for example) and a 'policy' on certain equipment is required, problems might arise because of the financial implications of a firm policy.

A strong parents' group is sometimes invaluable in relation to supplementing statutory provision of this sort of equipment (*Verbal communication: OT, Welsh DHA, 1989*).

Example 4. Buggies. Hospital OTs or physiotherapists sometimes carry out minor adaptations to buggies which have been supplied by the local wheelchair service, although there are now some restrictions on prescription of buggies (Box 6.3.2.7.9.).

Such adaptatations can include the atttachment of a lap strap, a firm base or a firm back.

Example 5. Wheelchairs. The most likely person to fill in details of the prescription is the paediatric OT or paediatric physiotherapist. A range of wheelchairs is available from the DSA (Box 6.4.10.).

A survey (England, Wales, Scotland, 1987) found that some paediatric physiotherapists felt that wheelchair service wheelchairs and buggies were not satisfactory. Some reasons given were 'restricted range – not suitable for many conditions, lack of individuality, poor design, big gap between baby buggies and wheelchairs, poor finish, lack of adaptability, delays/slow service' (*Result of Questionnaire into the Provision and Funding of Equipment for Children with Special Needs. Association of Paediatric Chartered Physiotherapists 1987*).

A report (1986) on the wheelchair service (England) also found evidence that many children had unsuitable wheelchairs provided by the wheelchair service (*McColl I. Review of Artificial Limb and Appliance Centre Services. DHSS, 1986 Vol.1, p. 41*).

There is sometimes a system of wheelchair/buggy temporary loan run by a therapy department or child assessment centre (*see eg Result of Questionnaire into the Provision and Funding of Equipment for Children with Special Needs. Association of Paediatric Chartered Physiotherapists 1987*).

Example 6. Seating

E6.1. Seating. Therapists sometimes make wooden seating either for use at school (27.) [1] or at home. It may also be made by therapists, parents, hospital carpenters, a local DIY shop, REMAP (29.3.), a local rehabilitation engineering centre (29.2.). Alternatively, OTs and physiotherapists loan or recommend a variety of commercial seating.

E6.2. Special wheelchair seating. Therapists recommend (with medical authorisation) special seating such as moulded seats or matrix seating for use in buggies and wheelchairs; such special seating is available from the wheelchair service.

E6.3. Funding for seating at home may vary. In England, for example, some SSDs are prepared to supply very much more special seating than others.

It seems that funding for 'individually made wooden seating', for example, might be from any one of a number of sources: the SSD, the hospital therapy department budget, charities, parents, the DHA or joint funding (*Result of Questionnaire into the Provision and Funding of Equipment for Children with Special Needs. Association of Paediatric Chartered Physiotherapists 1987, p. 10*).

SSDs, for example, might supply bath and toilet seats adequately; but there is sometimes a problem in supply, if the child needs special, new chairs quite frequently as he or she grows. Sometimes a SSD store might stock one type of chair for children, which is not as suitable, for both the child and family, as other commercially available chairs, which are not in stock (*Written communication: specialist child centre 1990*).

Example 7. Standing frames and standing boxes. Some standing frames (including eg swivel walkers) are very specialised and may either be made by a rehabilitation engineering unit (29.2.), or supplied commercially. Consultant prescription is explicitly required for special items, such as swivel walkers.

Standing boxes are supplied and funded from a number of sources. Sometimes SSDs, for example, class standing frames as 'treatment' equipment and therefore the responsibility of the health service. They sometimes tend to provide such frames for young children, to meet social/play needs; but can be more reluctant to supply larger, more expensive frames for older children and adolescents (*Written communication: specialist child centre 1990*).

Example 8. Portage scheme. Equipment is sometimes used as part of programmes known as Portage, an educational routine for parents and children to follow over a certain period of time, in order to achieve a particular goal. Therapists sometimes undertake the organisation of a Portage scheme.

27 Equipment for Educational Need

Equipment for education

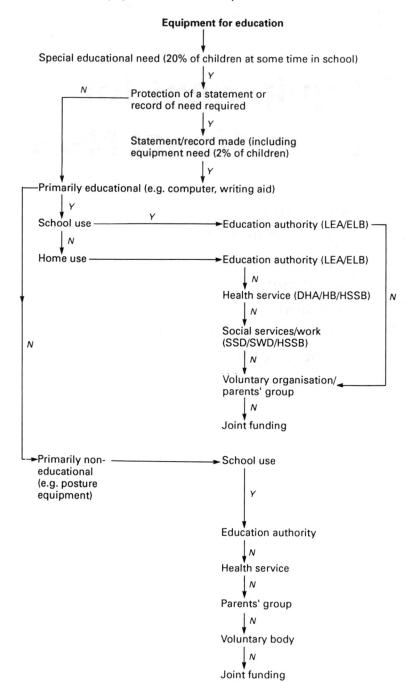

Introduction

Type of equipment. Equipment needed specially for education in schools can be divided into two main categories:

- equipment, which is clearly educational, such as electronic writing aids and computer aids;
- equipment, which is not obviously educational but necessary for the child to manage in school: equipment, such as special posture equipment, standing boxes, standing frames, special seating.

Responsibility for provision. There are various channels for provision of these two types of equipment, depending on various factors:

- education services:
  - local education authorities (LEAs, England, Wales and Scotland);
  - education and library boards (ELBs, Northern Ireland);
  - independent schools;
- health services:
  - district health authorities (DHAs, England and Wales);
  - health boards (HBs, Scotland);
  - health and social services boards (HSSBs, Northern Ireland);
  - wheelchair service;
- social services:
  - social services departments (SSDs, England and Wales);
  - social work departments (SWDs, Scotland);
  - health and social services boards (HSSBs, Northern Ireland).

LEA and ELB duties. LEAs and ELBs have a duty to meet the special educational (including equipment) needs of children, for whom they are responsible. This duty is three-fold and includes:

- general duties to all children at school (whether or not they have special educational needs);
- more specific duties to meet the needs of children with special educational needs (SEN);
- very specific duties to meet the needs of children, who have special educational needs and who also have a statement (England, Wales, Northern Ireland) or record (Scotland) of needs.

Provision. The provision of equipment for children in schools with SEN is relatively straightforward in some circumstances, but not in others. For certain types of equipment there are different possible avenues of provision, with variable practice from area to area.

Equipment defined as 'educational', is provided by LEA/ELBs, for use at school. For use at home, this is not always the case. The definition of 'educational', and the range of equipment embraced by the definition, can also vary considerably.

The LEA/ELB has a duty to provide any equipment, detailed in a statement or record of needs, and defined as educational.

Equipment defined as 'non-educational' is sometimes in practice supplied by:

- LEAs (England, Wales);
- LEA/ELBs (Scotland, Northern Ireland) (if supplied as, officially, 'educational' equipment);
- the health service (DHA/HB/HSSBs), including the wheelchair service;
- social services (SSD/SWD/HSSBs);
- charities;
- parents' groups;
- joint funding;
- private purchase.

The funding body depends on the sort of equipment involved, its perceived purpose, where it is needed (home or school) and local circumstances including policies, practice and resources available at any particular time.

For children with statements or records of needs, such equipment might be detailed on the statement or record as non-educational equipment, which the LEA (England, Wales) has the power and discretion, but not the duty, to provide.

Statements and records of needs. About 20% of children are thought to have special educational needs at some time during their education: a much smaller number (about 2%) have statements (England, Wales, Northern Ireland) or records (Scotland) of needs made.

Such statements/records are designed to 'protect' a child with very special needs, and ensure that adequate provision is made for the child.

Integration of children with SEN into ordinary schools. The integration of children into ordinary schools generally places greater strain on the resources of LEA/ELBs, since special resources (including equipment) become more widely scattered as a result of integration.

Status of school. The status of school affects responsibility for provision of equipment and premises adaptations. Independent special schools are normally expected to meet such needs out of fees received (from the LEA/ELB). Some categories of school might remain responsible for capital costs (including adaptations), while the LEA/ELB pays the running costs (including equipment).

27.1. Type of equipment

Equipment for school use is sometimes divided into (primarily) 'educational' and (primarily) 'non-educational' categories.

27.1.1. Educational equipment might typically include computers, a range of specialist access and control devices, electric typewriters, communication aids and adapted furniture (eg desks).

LEA/ELBs sometimes define educational equipment, as equipment which enables a child to follow a curriculum.

27.1.2. Non-educational equipment, classed as primarily non-educational, but needed in school, can include posture and mobility equipment, such as special seating, standing frames, standing boxes, special wheelchairs and scooters.

27.1.3. Definition affecting responsibility for provision. With respect to special educational needs, this division between 'educational' and 'non-educational' is sometimes used to identify division in responsibility for the provision of services (including equipment).

Both legislation (England, Wales) (*see eg Education Act 1981 s.7(2) as amended by the Education Reform Act 1988 Sched. 12 para 83*) and Circular guidance (England, Wales,) (see eg DES 22/89 para 63; WOC /89 para 63;) refer to the discretionary nature of non-educational provision by LEAs, as opposed to the mandatory nature of educational provision.

27.1.4. Common or individual equipment. There is a distinction between equipment provided for common use within the school, or for a particular individual. For example, sets of chairs and desks, as well as toilet aids, might be supplied generally for common use; but one special chair might be provided for individual use.

27.2. Legislative basis for provision of equipment

Legislation covering provision for children with special educational needs does not refer extensively to equipment, although it is mentioned in regulations (England, Wales, Northern Ireland).

Legislation does detail, however, procedures for provision, in general (ie not specifically equipment), for children with SEN; although this detail mainly concerns the small minority of children who have a statement or record of needs (27.2.2.), rather than the much larger number of children who have SEN, but do not have a statement or record of needs.

27.2.1. Definition of special educational need (SEN). It is thought that about 20% of children in school have SEN at some time, whereas only about 2% have statements or records of needs made (*see eg Hansard. House of Commons, 19th March 1990, col. 416*). Legislation defines SEN irrespective of whether a child has, or will need, a statement or record of needs.

A child has SEN, if he or she has learning difficulties, which require special educational provision. A learning difficulty is defined as:

- 'significantly greater difficulty in learning than the majority of children of his age'; or
- a disability which either prevents or hinders him from making use of educational facilities of a kind generally provided in schools . . . for children (also in Scotland, young persons) of his age; or
- he is under the age of five years and the above points apply (*Education Act 1981 s.1; Education (Scotland) Act 1981; SI 1986/594 (NI 3) Education and Libraries (Northern Ireland) Order 1986 a.33*).

27.2.2. Legislative basis for provision for SEN through a statement (England/ Wales/Northern Ireland) or record (Scotland) of needs

27.2.2.1. Basis: reference to equipment. Regulations (England/Wales, Northern Ireland) state that 'facilities and equipment' needed should be detailed in the statement/record of needs (*Education (Special Educational Needs) Regulations 1983; SI 1985/365 Education (Special Educational Needs) Regulations (Northern Ireland) 1986*).

27.2.2.2. Basis: provision through a statement of need: England, Wales, Northern Ireland. Legislation states that LEA/ELBs (England, Wales, Northern Ireland) have a duty to make a statement of needs, if assessment indicates that they need to determine the special educational provision for that child (*Education Act 1981 s.7; SI 1986/594 (NI 3) Education and Libraries (Northern Ireland) Order 1986 a.31*).

LEA/ELBs have a duty to make any educational provision which is contained in a statement (*Education Act 1981 s.7(2) as amended by the Education Reform Act 1988 Sched. 12 para 83; ; SI 1986/594 (NI 3) Education and Libraries (Northern Ireland) Order 1986 a.31*).

Circulars emphasise this duty (*see eg DES 22/1989 para 61; DENI 1987/21 para 16*).

27.2.2.3. Basis: provision through a record of needs: Scotland. In Scotland the LEA has a duty to make a record of needs, if it is established that a child has 'pronounced, specific or complex special educational needs which are such as to require continuing review' (*Education (Scotland) Act 1980 s.60 as amended by Education (Scotland) Act 1981 s.4*).

The LEA has a duty 'to ensure that the provision made by them under this Act for a recorded child or a recorded young person includes provision for his special educational needs' (*Education (Scotland) Act 1980 s.62 (as amended by Education (Scotland) Act 1981 s.4*).

27.2.3. Legislative basis for children with special educational needs, with or without a statement or record of needs. Legislation states that LEA/ELBs have a duty to meet the needs of children with special educational needs (*Education Act 1944 s.8(2) (as amended by Education Act 1981 s.2); Education (Scotland) Act 1980 s.1 (as amended by Education (Scotland) Act 1981 s.3); SI 1986/594 (NI3) Education and Libraries Board (Northern Ireland) Order 1986 a.6*).

Legislation does not detail procedures for meeting the needs of children, who have SEN but who do not have statements/records of needs, as it does for children who do have such statements or records (27.2.2.).

27.2.4. Legislative basis for general duties toward all children (with or without special educational needs). Legislation places general duties on LEA/ELBs to meet educational needs of all children, for whom they are responsible.

27.2.4.1. England/Wales, Northern Ireland. LEAs have a duty in England/Wales and Northern Ireland 'to secure that there there shall be available for their area sufficient schools . . . and the schools available for an area shall not be deemed to be sufficient unless they are sufficient in number, character and equipment to afford for all pupils opportunities for education offering such variety of instruction and training as may be desirable in view of their different ages, abilities, aptitudes...' (*Education Act 1944 s.8; SI 1986/594 (NI3) Education and Libraries (Northern Ireland) Order 1986 a.6*).

27.2.4.2. Scotland. In Scotland, LEAs have the duty 'to secure that there is made for their area adequate and sufficient provision of school education and further education' (*Education (Scotland) Act 1980 s.1*).

27.2.5. Legislative basis for duties and powers depending on age group. Variations are summarised below, and detailed in Box 27.1.

Box 27.1: Legislative basis of provision for different categories of child

B27.1.1. Under five years old. A DHA/HSSB, if it believes that a child has (or probably has) special educational needs, has a duty to inform the parent(s) of its belief and duty, discuss the matter with the parent(s), and then inform the LEA/ELB (*Education Act 1981 s.10; SI 1986/594 (NI.3) Education and Libraries (NI)Order 1986 a.36*).

Circular guidance (Scotland) states that health boards 'are in the best position to identify and initiate appropriate action in respect of a pre-school child whose physical or mental condition suggests a need for special educational arrangements...' (*NHS 1982(GEN)38*).

B27.1.2. Under-2 year olds. A LEA/ELB has the power to assess the needs of children under 2 years of age if it is thought that the child has SEN, which require assessment. The assessment can determine what educational provision needs to be made for the child.

The assessment is not obligatory (there is power to do so, not a duty) if dependent on the consent of the child's parent; but is, if dependent on parental request (*Education Act 1981 s.6; Education (Scotland) Act 1980 s.61(b) as amended by Education (Scotland) Act 1981; SI 1986/594 (NI.3) Education and Libraries NI (Order) 1986 a.30*).

The assessment can be requested by parents, and must be undertaken by the LEA or ELB unless they consider the request unreasonable (*Education Act 1981 s.9; Education (Scotland) Act 1980 s.61(6) as amended by the Education Act 1981; SI 1986/594 (NI.3) Education and Libraries (NI)Order 1986 s.30*).

For children under two, the making and keeping of a statement or record is discretionary, (*Education Act 1981 s.6; Education (Scotland) Act 1980 s.60(2) as amended by Education (Scotland) Act 1981; SI 1986/594 (NI.3) Education and Libraries (Order) 1986 a.30*).

B27.1.3. Between 2 and 5 years old

B27.1.3.1. England/Wales and Northern Ireland. The LEA or ELB has a duty to children over two years old to identify special educational needs, and, where it thinks that special educational provision is necessary, to make an assessment (*Education Act 1981, s.4; SI 1986/594 (NI.3) Education and Libraries (Order) 1986 r.29*). If special educational provision is needed the LEA/ELB has a duty to make a statement (*Education Act 1981 s.7; SI 1986/594 (NI.3) Education and Libraries (NI)Order 1986 a.31*).

B27.1.3.2. Scotland. In Scotland, the LEA has a duty to establish which 2-5 year olds have SEN (*Education (Scotland) Act 1980 s. 60(1) as amended 1981, 1989*); and has the duty to maintain a record of needs if necessary (*Education (Scotland) Act 1980 s.60(2) as amended by Education (Scotland) 1981 and by Self-Governing Schools etc (Scotland) Act 1989 s.72*).

B27.1.3.3. Requests for assessment can be made by parents: legislation states that the assessment must be carried out, unless the request is considered unreasonable (*see eg Education Act 1981 s.9; Education (Scotland) Act 1980 s.61(6) as amended by Education (Scotland) Act 1981; Education and Libraries (Northern Ireland) Order 1986 Sched 11, para 4*).

B27.1.3.4. Circular guidance. A DES circular notes that the LEA might give such children priority in admission to nursery schools and primary school nursery classes. Further, 'liaison between the school health services, social services, family doctor, health visitor, therapist, or any other specialists, the parent, any voluntary organisation involved, and the teacher is important' (*DES 22/89 para 80; WOC 54/89 para 80*).

B27.1.4. Between 5 and 16 years. LEA/ELBs have three different 'levels' of duty toward this age range: to all children (27.2.4.), to children with SEN (with or without a statement or record of needs) (27.2.3.), to children with a statement or record of needs (27.2.2.).

B27.1.4.1. Scope of assessment and statements/records. For 5-16 year-olds, the duty to identify SEN, assess (where appropriate), make and maintain statements or records of needs (where appropriate) applies to all children (*Education Act 1981 s.4; Education (Scotland) Act 1980 s.60(2) as amended by Education (Scotland) Act 1981; SI 1986/594 (NI.3) Education and Libraries (NI)Order 1986 a.29*).

B27.1.5. Between 16 and 19 years (England/Wales, Northern Ireland) and 16-18 year olds (Scotland)

B27.1.5.1. General duties

B27.1.5.1.1. Still at school. Although compulsory school age is 16 years, young people have a right to full-time education up to the age of 19. As such, general duties to provide facilities for 5-16 year olds apply also to pupils attending school up to that age (*Education Act 1944 s.8, s.41 as amended by the Education Reform Act 1988 s.120; Education (Scotland) Act 1980 s.1; SI 1986/594 (NI.3) Education and Libraries (Northern Ireland) Order 1981 a.6, a.27*).

B27.1.5.1.2. Further education. Where full-time education over the age of 16 is undertaken at college, for example, the LEA or ELB also has a duty to secure the provision of adequate facilities for futher education'(*Education Act 1944 s.41 as amended by Education Reform Act 1988 s.120; Education (Scotland) Act 1980 s.1; SI 1986/594 (NI.3) Education and Libraries (NI)Order 1986 a.27*).

B27.1.5.1.2.1. Legislation (England, Wales, Northern ireland) now stresses that in carrying out this duty the local education authority 'shall also have regard to the requirements of persons over compulsory school age who have learning difficulties'(*Education Act 1944 s.41 as amended by Education Reform Act 1988 s.120; Education Reform (Northern Ireland) Order 1989, a.100*).

Learning difficulty here is taken to include a person with 'a significantly greater difficulty in learning than the majority of persons of his age; or . . . disability which either prevents or hinders him from making use of facilities of a kind generally provided by the local education authority concerned in pursuance of their duty . . . for persons of this age' (*Education Act 1944 s.41 as amended by Education Reform Act 1988 s.120; Education Reform (Northern Ireland) Order 1989 a.100*).

B27.1.5.2. Statements and records for children or young persons 16-18/19 years old

B27.1.5.2.1. England/Wales, Northern Ireland. Statements cannot be made and maintained for 16-19 year olds in further education, but can for 16-19 year olds still at school (*Education Act 1981, s.4;SI 1986/594 (NI.3) Education and Libraries (NI)Order 1986 a.33*), to whom the procedures for children between 5 and 16 years old generally apply.

B27.1.5.2.2. Scotland. 16 to 18 year olds are referred to as young persons, and slightly different procedures for records of needs apply. For example, the young person (rather than parents) can appeal against decisions (Education (Scotland) Act 1980 s.63 as amended by Education (Scotland) Act 1981). Also, a young person can request the LEA to discontinue the record (*Education (Scotland) Act 1980 s.65C amended by Education (Scotland) Act 1981*).

Records cannot be made and maintained for 16-18 year olds in further education (*Education (Scotland) Act 1980 s.60(1) as amended by the Education (Scotland) Act 1981*).

B27.1.6. Leaving school. Recent legislation (England,Wales,Scotland, not yet in force in Northern Ireland) (*Disabled Persons (Services Consultation and Representation) Act 1986 s.5,6; Disabled Persons (Services Consultation and Representation) Act 1986 s.13; Disabled Persons (Northern Ireland) Act 1989 s.5,6 – not yet in force*) is designed (as Circular guidance states) to 'ensure a smooth transition for a disabled child between full-time education and adult life'. Closer co-operation between authorities is aimed at (LAC 88(2)).

B27.1.6.1. Establishment of disability. A summary of the provision is as follows: where a statement or record is made or maintained for a child after his/her birthday, the LEA must inform the SSD/SWD (as appropriate). The SSD/SWD then must assess whether the child is disabled (*Disabled Persons (Services Consultation and Representation) Act 1986 s.5,6; Disabled Persons (Services Consultation and Representation) Act 1986 s.13*).

B27.1.6.2. Date of leaving of full-time education. The LEA then, where a child is considered to be disabled, informs the SSD/SWD of the date on which the child is leaving full-time education.

In England and Wales, this information must be given at least 8 months before the leaving date, but not earlier than 12 months before that date. In Scotland, the information must be given not later than 6 months before the leaving date (*Disabled Persons (Services Consultation and Representation) Act 1986 s.5,6; Disabled Persons (Services Consultation and Representation) Act 1986 s.13*).

B27.1.6.2.1. Northern Ireland. Other current Northern Ireland legislation places a duty on ELBs to contact HSSBs when a child is about to leave school, if the child has special needs (*SI 1986/594 (NI 3) Education and Libraries (Northern Ireland) Order 1986 r.36*).

B27.1.6.3. SSD/SWD/HSSB provision concerning leaving date

B27.1.6.3.1. England/Wales, Northern Ireland. When the LEA has informed the SSD of the leaving date of the child, the latter then has a duty to carry out an assessment of need (*Disabled Persons (Services Consultation and Representation) Act 1986 s.5(5)*).

B27.1.6.3.1.1. Circular guidance (England), for example, lists the sequence of events:

- receipt by SSD of written notification from the LEA that a child who has been identified as disabled will be leaving full-time education;
- arrangements for SSD assessment;
- assessment in relation to the needs of the person in relation to statutory welfare services;
- information about other services eg health, employment, education should also be made available (*LAC 88(2)*).

B27.1.6.3.2. Scotland. Circular guidance (1988) (*see eg SW2/1988 – SED/1167*) explains that assessment is regarded as having already been carried out between the age of 14 and 15 years 3 months under duties in legislation (*Education (Scotland) Act 1980 s.65B as inserted by Education (Scotland) Act 1981*): and the SWD is ready to make provision, as necessary, for the school-leaver, when informed of the leaving date by the LEA (*Disabled Persons (Services Consultation and Representation) Act 1986 s.13*).

27.2.5.1. Under-five year olds. DHA/HSSBs (England, Wales, Northern Ireland) have a duty to contact the LEA, if they suspect that a child has special educational needs (*Education Act 1981 s.10; SI 1986/594(NI3) Education Libraries (Northern Ireland) Order 1986 a.26*).

The same duty does not seem to be stated in Scottish legislation, but Circular guidance (Scotland, 1982) recommends the same role for Health Boards (*NHS 1982(GEN)38*).

27.2.5.2. Under-two years old. LEA/ELBs have powers and duties to assess the needs of a child under two years old, if it is thought that the child has special educational needs (*Education Act 1981 s.6; Education (Scotland) Act 1980 s.61 (b) as amended by Education (Scotland) Act 1981 s.4; SI 1986/594 (NI.3) Education and Libraries (Northern Ireland) Order 1986 a.30*).

27.2.5.3. Between two and five years old. LEA/ELBs have a duty to assess children of this age with special educational needs, and to make a statement or record if necessary (*Education Act 1981 s.7; Education (Scotland) Act 1980 s.60(1) as amended by Education (Scotland) Act 1981; and by Self-Governing Schools, etc (Scotland) Act 1989 s. 72; SI 1986/594 (NI.3) Education and Libraries (Northern Ireland) Order 1986 a.31*).

27.2.5.4. Five to sixteen year olds. LEA/ELBs have general duties towards all children (27.2.4.), for whom they are responsible; duties toward children with special educational needs (27.2.3.); and duties toward children with statements or records of needs (27.2.2.).

27.2.5.5. 16-19 year olds. LEA/ELBs have general duties toward children or young persons in this age group whether at school or at further education college (*Education Act 1944 s.8, s.41 as amended by the Education Reform Act 1988 s.120; Education (Scotland) Act 1980 s.1; SI 1986/594 (NI.3) Education and Libraries (Northern Ireland) Order 1981 a.6, a.27*).

(English/Welsh legislation stresses that these duties should encompass children/young persons with learning difficulties (*Education Act 1944 s.41 as amended by the Education Reform Act 1988 s.120; Education Reform (Northern Ireland) Order 1989, a.100*).

Powers and duties as regards statements or records apply to this age range if the child is still at school, but not, if at further education college (*Education Act 1981 s.4; Education (Scotland) Act 1980 s.65C as amended by Education (Scotland) Act 1981; SI 1986/594 (NI.3) Education and Libraries (Northern Ireland) Order 1986 a.33*).

27.2.5.6. Leaving school.

27.2.5.6.1. England, Wales, Scotland. Legislation places a duty on LEAs and SSD/SWDs (as appropriate) to co-operate, when children/young persons with SEN are about to leave school, (*Disabled Persons (Services, Consultation, Representation) Act 1986*) in order to ensure that adequate provision is made for such people.

27.2.5.6.2. Northern Ireland. Similar Northern Ireland legislation, affecting ELBs and HSSBs, is not yet in force (*Disabled Persons (Northern Ireland) 1989 s.5,6 not yet in force*).

Other legislation, in force, does place a duty on the ELB to inform the HSSB if a school-leaver has 'physical, intellectual, emotional or social development' which requires 'further care, treatment or supervision' (*SI 1986/594 (NI.3) Education and Libraries (Northern Ireland) Order 1986 a.36*).

27.3. Assessment

27.3.1. Professionals involved in assessment

27.3.1.1. Legislation specifies that assessment (with a view to making a statement or record of needs) for SEN must include educational, medical and psychological advice (*Education Act 1981 s.4; Education (Scotland) Act 1980 s.61 as amended by Education Scotland) Act 1981; SI 1986/594 (NI3) Education and Libraries (Northern Ireland) Order 1986 Sched. 11 para 2*).

These professionals, who must contribute to the assessment (for example, head teacher, doctor, educational psychologist) also have the power (in law) to consult other professionals (*Education Act 1981 s.4; Education (Scotland) Act 1980 s.61 as amended by Education Scotland) Act 1981; SR 1985/365 r.4*).

In practice, therefore, as Circular guidance (England, Wales, 1989) states, the doctor (*designated by the DHA/HB/HSSB*) for example might call on other doctors, therapists, nurses etc (*DES 22/89 para 42; WOC 54/89 para 42*).

Also consulted, sometimes, are educational audiologists where they exist (14.3.3.3.).

27.3.1.2. Health professionals employed by, or placed in special schools. DHA/HB/HSSB paediatric therapists for example, might spend a lot of time in schools, working with children with SEN, whether or not they have statements or records of needs. They might be employed by special schools; placed, or work sessionally in the school.

27.3.2. Special micro technology centres. Sometimes, part of the assessment of SEN takes place with the help of an independent centre, specialising in micro-technology for communication (speaking and writing) in education.

For example, the ACE Centres (Oxford, Oldham) and the CALL Project (Edinburgh) (see Box 27.2 for details).

Box 27.2: Specialist centres (ACE and CAll project) for communication (speech and writing) aid assessment

B27.2.1. Aids to Communication in Education (ACE) Centres.

B27.2.1.1. Remit. The ACE Centre in Oxford and Northern ACE Centre in Oldham have a remit, covering England, Wales and Northern Ireland, and concern themselves 'with communication impaired children and young people in education, and the ways in which communication difficulties (both spoken and written) may be alleviated by the use of augmentative systems with a particular emphasis on microtechnology (*Information on the ACE Centre. ACE, 1989*).

B27.2.1.2. Referral is accepted from professionals or the parents of the child.

B27.2.1.3. Assessment. Once a referral has been accepted as appropriate, assessment can take more than more one form.

The child, together with teacher, parents and therapist can visit the centre, which itself has a team, including an occupational therapist, speech therapist, technical officer and technician.

Alternatively, the ACE team can visit the child at school, home or hospital. Thirdly, the ACE team may assess at an LEA's resource centre under the co-ordination of the LEA's microtechnology and special needs adviser (*Information on the ACE Centre. ACE, 1989*).

B27.2.1.4. Loan. It is recognised that sometimes an extensive trial loan period is needed before equipment can be finally recommended, particularly where purchase by a LEA or DHA may cost in the order of £2000-£3000. The ACE Centre is therefore trying to build up a stock of short-term loan equipment (*Information on the ACE Centre. ACE Centre, 1989*).

The ACE centre cannot loan equipment on a longterm basis, but it does now have a grant from the Nuffield Foundation to help about nine children a year with equipment. The children can use the equipment until it is no longer needed, when it is returned to the centre (*Information on the ACE Centre. ACE, 1989*).

B27.2.2. CALL project. The CALL project operates in Scotland and 'is open to anyone in Scotland who either has a communication, writing or drawing problem which impedes their learning . . . Age is of no importance'. Services provided are charged for, but these may be paid by a health board, SWD or education authority. The CALL team includes a speech therapist, psychologist, an electronic engineer and a specialist in educational computing and communication aids.

(At the time of writing assessments have ceased pending discussions with statutory bodies on funding for such assessments. However they are expected to resume sometime in 1990.) (*Communication aids for language and learning. CALL project, Edinburgh University; Verbal communication, CALL centre 1989*).

B27.2.2.1. Equipment loan. The trial loan of equipment is seen as part of assessment and the CALL project can sometimes loan its equipment on a short-term basis of up to one month. The CALL project states that its one month loan period can sometimes be extended (eg for a terminally ill person), but that it does not supplement school equipment shortfalls.

Because of its limited stocks, it cannot normally fill a time gap with an item of equipment, while fundraising or disussions with statutory bodies take place (*Communication aids for language and learning. CALL project, Edinburgh University; Verbal communication, CALL centre 1989*).

27.3.3. Assessment of under-fives. Circular guidance states the importance of early identification of a child's educational needs (*DES 22/89 para 80; WOC 54/89 para 80; SED 1087/1982Guidance Note – SEN General/Rec 2 para 7 and NHS 1982(GEN)38); DENI 1987/21 para 12*).

27.3.4. Statements/records of needs. Equipment provision for SEN is sometimes achieved through a statement or record of needs. Equally, it might be made without such a statement/record.

27.3.4.1. Special schools re: statements/records of needs. Children in special schools normally have a statement or record of needs.

Circular guidance (England, Wales), for example, notes: 'The Secretary of State would expect that children in special schools would normally be afforded the protection of a statement. . .' (*DES 22/89 para 31; WOC 54/89 para 31*).

27.3.4.2. Ordinary schools. In ordinary schools children may or may not require the protection of a statement.

Circular guidance (England, Wales) has stated that most children with special educational needs do not have statements (*DES 22/89 para 14; WOC 54/89 para 14*). Nevertheless, it goes on to state that LEAs and governors must reassure parents that such children's needs will be met: that LEAs will meet educational needs, and health authorities, medical, paramedical and nursing needs (*DES 22/89 para 16; WOC 54/89 para 16*).

27.3.4.3. Final decision on statement or record. Circular guidance (England, Wales, Northern Ireland) states that the responsibility for assessment, and the contents of a statement or record, ultimately rests with the LEA/ELB (*see eg DES 22/89 para 52; WOC 54/89 para 52; NI 1987/21 para 19*).

27.3.4.4. Necessary provision or practical provision contained in statement/record of needs. There is sometimes uncertainty whether a statement or record should contain what the child needs, or what can be provided, the two not always being the same.

Circular guidance (Northern Ireland, 1987) states that the ELB must make sure 'in consultation with other bodies as necessary, that the special provision they are considering for any case can be made available. It would be most unhelpful if parents were led to expect that their child would receive some particular provision which in the event cannot be made available.' (*DENI 1987/21 para 19*).

In practice, a report (*NAHA, 1988*) found that, sometimes, therapists, in giving advice to LEAs, 'are having to acknowledge their inability to meet the needs of children they assess. That is to say, the therapists now include in their report both the needs of the child and what can be provided within the resources available . . .' (*Health authorities concerns for children with special needs. A report on a survey of health authorities on the implementation of the Education Act 1981. NAHA, 1988 p. 8*).

A government committee report (1987) made the same finding (*Special Educational Needs: Implementation of the Education Act 1981. Third Report from the Education, Science and Arts Committee. HMSO, 1987, Vol.1 p. xv*).

27.3.4.5. Statement and record of needs procedures: length of time. It appears that statement and record-making procedures do not always function as well as they might.

For example, a report (England,1987) found that statement-making procedures were too long and complex, and that parents did not understand the language (*Special Educational Needs: Implementation of the Education Act 1981. Third Report from the Education, Science and Arts Committee. HMSO, 1987, Vol.1 p.xv*).

27.3.4.6. Specificity of statement/record.

27.3.4.6.1. Statement/record used generally to support recommendation of equipment. An existing statement/record (containing details of general need, but not of specific equipment) of needs might be used (if necessary) to generally support specific equipment requests by therapists, for example (*Verbal communication: paediatric occupational therapist, London DHA 1989*).

27.3.4.6.2. Equipment specified in the statement/record of needs. Circular guidance (England, Wales) states that sufficient detail should be included in a statement: 'Statements that fail to specify in detail what provision the particular child requires are of little use to parents and to the professionals who are to act upon them. Provision should be specified in terms of facilities and equipment, staffing arrangements . . .' (*DES 22/89 para 61; WOC 54/89 para 61*).

Sometimes a statement/record does not specify precise equipment types: less precision can enable equipment to be changed as the child develops, without the necessity for formal (time-consuming) review (*Verbal communication: special educational needs advisers, Northern Ireland 1988*).

27.3.4.7. Equipment needs included in statement or record

27.3.4.7.1. Regulations (England/Wales, Northern Ireland) state that a statement should contain details of a child's needs including 'facilities and equipment' (*Education (Special Educational Needs) Regulations 1983; Education (Special Educational Needs) Regulations (Northern Ireland) 1985*).

27.3.4.7.2. Circular guidance (England, Wales) gives examples of equipment which might be detailed in a statement or record:

- special equipment (eg physical aids, auditory aids, visual aids);
- specialist facilities (eg for incontinence, for medical examination, treatment and drug administration);
- special educational resources (eg specialist equipment for teaching children with physical or sensory disabilities, non-teaching aids);
- other specialist resources (eg nursing, social work, speech therapy, occupational therapy, physiotherapy, psychotherapy, audiology, orthoptics);
- physical environment (eg access and facilities for non-ambulant pupils, attention to lighting environment, acoustic environment, thermal environment, health care accomodation)' (*DES 22/89 Annex 1; WOC 54/89 Annex 1*).

27.3.4.7.3. Circular guidance (Scotland) states that 'the term 'facilities' is to be interpreted very widely, and is to include any additional resource input which a pupil may require to give him access to the curriculum'.

Examples given include radio microphone hearing aids (14.3.1.6.), electronic communication aids, soundproofing, braillers, and provision of auxiliary and nursing staff' (*SED 1087/1982 Annex 2 Guidance Note REC 1 para 12*).

27.3.4.8. Statement/record inclusion of both Educational and Non-Educational Provision. A statement/record often includes details of both educational and non-educational needs.

27.3.4.8.1. LEA/ELB duty to meet educational needs. Legislation states that an LEA or ELB has a duty to meet SEN as specified in a statement/record (*Education Act 1981 Act s. 7(2) as amended by Education Reform Act 1988 Sched. 12 para 83; Education (Scotland) Act 1980 (as amended by Education (Scotland) Act 1981 s. 62(3); SI 1986/594 (NI.3) Education and Libraries (Northern Ireland) Order 1986 a.31*).

27.3.4.8.2. Discretion to meet non-educational needs. A statement or record sometimes also contain details of non-educational provision, which other authorities (eg health) may provide, or which the LEAs (England, Wales) have the power, but not the duty, to provide.

Legislation (England, 1988) emphasises that LEAs have the power to provide for non-educational, as well as educational needs detailed in a statement: 'the authority may arrange that any non-educational provision specified in the statement is made for him in such manner as they consider appropriate...' (*Education Act 1981 s.7 as amended by 1988 Act Sched 12 para 83*). Circular guidance (England, Wales, 1989) states that such power on the part of the LEA does not remove any DHA/SSD responsibility (*DES 22/89 para 63; WOC 54/89 para 63*). Similar legislation does not exist for Scotland and Northern Ireland.

27.3.5. Definition of equipment as primarily educational or non-educational. There is sometimes uncertainty over whether certain types of equipment are primarily educational or non-educational.

Equipment which seems to fall into a grey area can include: speech aids, special desks, special chairs, postural equipment (including standing boxes/tables), wheelchairs/cycles (other than those provided by the wheelchair service), radio microphone hearing aids (14.3.1.6.).

Such definitions can affect speed and channel (eg education or health) of provision; especially if financial pressures on authorities aggravate the situation.

27.3.5.1. Example of confusion over definition of 'educational' and 'non-educational'. Recent events in the English law courts have highlighted possible uncertainty over the status of, for example, speech therapy.

(Although the cases have involved questions of intensive speech therapy, speech aids are covered by implication (as potentially part of speech therapy services)).

The latest 1989 judgement (1989 R v Lancashire County Council ex parte CM (a minor), 10.3.89), somewhat inconsistent with an earlier 1986 judgement (1986 R. v Oxfordshire County Council ex parte A.G.W.), ruled that, depending on individual circumstances, speech therapy can be primarily educational in nature.

However, the judge ruled that provision for a child, who had never been able to speak from genetic or social cause, for example, was indeed educational (*Daily Telegraph reporting LJ Bacombe 3.4.89*).

Circular guidance (England, Wales, 1989) has drawn attention to these court cases (*DES 22/89 para 63; WOC 54/89 para 63*).

27.4. Provision of equipment

27.4.1. Provision in special schools for children with SEN

27.4.1.1. Special school stock of equipment. Special schools are likely to have a stock of equipment, built up from a general LEA/ELB equipment budget (if LEA/ELB run); or their own resources (if independent).

Such 'stock' daily living equipment in a special school could include adapted cutlery, adapted toilets, special toilet seats, Parker baths, bath lifts, adapted chairs, hoists, adjustable height beds (residential schools), ramps and lifts, tables adjusted for height, adapted sinks etc. (*Written communication: national voluntary organisation 1989*).

27.4.1.2. Special school: single budget. Special schools are likely to have special equipment budgets for SEN, covering both educational and non-educational equipment. This can make provision of (eg therapist) recommended 'non-educational' equipment much easier in a special school than in an ordinary school, where there might not be a well-defined channel of provision (*Verbal communication: paediatric OTs; Result of Questionnaire into the Provision and Funding of Equipment for Children with Special Needs. Association of Paediatric Chartered Physiotherapists. 1987*).

27.4.2. Ordinary school provision of equipment

27.4.2.1. Provision for special educational needs without a statement/record (in an ordinary school). Circular guidance (England, Wales, Northern Ireland) states that many children have special educational needs but that only a small number of these children need a statement. In particular, statements are not required where an ordinary school is making provision anyway from its own resources (*DES 22/89 para 31; WOC 54/89 para 31; DENI 1987/21 para 6*).

27.4.2.2. Financial arrangements for provision in ordinary schools. Ordinary schools sometimes fund special equipment and adaptations from their own budget, or from a central LEA/ELB budget, depending on local arrangement (*eg* see DES 22/89 para 12; WOC 54/89 para 12; written communication: LEAs 1990).

In certain types of school, where running costs but not capital costs are met by the LEA/ELB, adaptations remain the responsibility of the school governors or managers.

27.4.2.3. Resource transfer from special to ordinary schools. Special schools have generally built up a 'stock' of various general equipment for children with special educational needs (27.4.1.1.); while access arrangements and adaptations are part of the building.

Similarly special schools 'have generally been provided with high quality health services'. However, in some districts, 'there seem to be difficulties reorienting health services away from a focus on special schools towards the needs of individual children in mainstream schools' (*Changing School Health Services. King's Fund 1988. Part 1, p. 6*).

The provision of equipment in ordinary schools generally requires greater resources as specialist equipment is no longer 'pooled' in one place but dispersed, and as teachers have to be taught to understand the child and the use of the equipment (*see eg Ait-Hocine N. A case for occupational therapy: integrating children with mental and physical handicap into mainstream education. British Journal of Occupational Therapy 1990 53(1) pp. 19–23; Verbal communication: paediatric OT, London DHA 1989*).

27.4.2.3.1. Various channels of provision for 'non-educational' equipment in ordinary schools

27.4.2.3.1.1. LEA/ELB provision of 'non-educational' equipment. Some LEA/ELBs are likely to devote more resources to equipment which could be seen as primarily 'non-educational' (27.3.5.) than others. For example, some might provide equipment such as standing boxes, standing frames, special desks (to improve posture), electronic speech aids: others might not, or at least, not to the same extent.

27.4.2.3.1.2. Various sources for provision of non-educational equipment. A therapist, for example, might need then to try four or five different sources when recommending equipment for a child in an ordinary school. Possible sources can include – LEA/ELB (central budget);

- school budget;
- hospital aids and appliances budget (consultant prescription, for example);
- physiotherapy budget;
- occupational therapy budget (*Result of Questionnaire into the Provision and Funding of Equipment for Children with Special Needs. Association of Paediatric Chartered Physiotherapists. 1987 p. 10*);
- parents' groups;
- voluntary organisations;
- personal fundraising.

27.4.3. Funding of 'educational' equipment (in ordinary or special schools). Equipment defined as primarily educational generally includes a large range of computers together with special controls, electric typewriters, communication aids or adapted furniture, for example.

The LEA/ELB normally funds such equipment, unless it is to be provided in an independent school (27.4.7.ox 3.4.).

27.4.4. Equipment for common use, or for individual use. Equipment detailed in a statement/record of needs is always in relation to individual need. Alternatively, through other channels, equipment might be provided for common use (for example, a set of special chairs or desks).

It might be then that there are more individual requests (eg for one special desk) in an ordinary school, than in a special school (where a set of desks already exists).

27.4.5. Equipment for individual medical, nursing or paramedical needs is supplied as normal through the health (and wheelchair service): for example, wheelchairs/wheelchair seating, footwear, splints, callipers, environmental control systems (on medical prescription), walking frames, hearing aids, spectacles/ low vision aids etc.

27.4.6. Independent schools (including special voluntary schools) normally arrange and fund equipment and adaptations from their own resources. Where a child attends by LEA/ELB arrangement, fees paid to the school are taken to cover such needs.

If a child has very special equipment needs, beyond the provision which the school would normally expect to make, LEA/ELBs sometimes give extra help (*Written communication: LEAs 1990; Written communication: national voluntary organisation 1989*).

27.4.7. Type of school. Responsibilities and arrangements for provision of equipment and adaptations vary depending on the status of school and pupil. For details of different types of school, see Box 27.3.

Box 27.3: Provision by different type of school

The LEA or ELB duty to provide what (including equipment and adaptations) is specified in a statement or record varies depending on what type of school is involved, and whether or not the child is attending the school by LEA/ELB arrangement.

B27.3.1. England and Wales

B27.3.1.1. LEA schools ('county schools'). LEAs provide equipment for education in state schools, ordinary or special. These have been set up under the Education Act 1944 by LEAs and are both financed and controlled by the LEA (*Statham J* et al. *Education Fact File. Hodder and Stoughton, 1989*). Thus LEA responsibility includes both capital (eg adaptations to structure) and running costs.

The school may have its own resources allocated to provide for special needs, or draw on resources held centrally by the LEA.

B27.3.1.2. Grant-maintained schools. The new grant-maintained schools introduced by the Education Reform Act 1988 can opt out from LEA finance and control, and instead receive central government funding.

However, when a school decides to opt out in this way, proposals must be submitted to the Secretary of State for Education. These proposals must include a description of arrangements to be made for 'the provision to be made at the school for pupils who have special educational needs' (*Education Reform Act 1988 s.62(7)(f)*).

Circular guidance (1988) states: 'LEAs will continue to have certain responsibilities for the welfare of pupils at grant-maintained schools . . . include . . . the duties given to LEAs under the Education Act 1981 and, in particular, the duty to secure that appropriate provision is made for pupils who have special educationl needs, with or without statements' (*DES 10/88 Part K.*).

B27.3.1.3. *Voluntary schools.* There are two main types of voluntary school.

B27.3.1.3.1. Voluntary aided schools (usually church) established by bodies such as the Church of England, or the Roman Catholic Church. The voluntary body provides the premises and is responsible for external repairs and maintenance with assistance from an LEA grant (*Statham J* et al. *Education Fact File. Hodder and Stoughton, 1989*). The LEA is responsible for running costs, including internal repairs and classroom equipment provision.

B27.3.1.3.2. Voluntary controlled school premises are almost all provided by the Church of England. The LEA otherwise more or less controls the school (*Statham J* et al. *Education Fact File. Hodder and Stoughton, 1989*), meeting all costs, and therefore authorising both equipment and premises adaptations.

B27.3.2. Scotland. In Scotland, schools are, in the main, either public (ie LEA maintained) or independent (church-run or otherwise).

B27.3.3. Northern Ireland. Schools in Northern Ireland are divided into three main types: controlled, voluntary (maintained) and voluntary grammar (*Statham J* et al. *Education Fact File. Hodder and Stoughton, 1989*).

B27.3.3.1. *Controlled schools* are managed by ELBs through boards of governors. Both capital expenditure and running costs are met by the ELB (*Statham J* et al. *Education Fact File. Hodder and Stoughton, 1989*): and therefore ELB responsibility includes both equipment and premises adaptations for children with special educational needs (*Verbal communication: Special Educational Needs Advisers, Northern Ireland 1988*).

B27.3.3.2. *Voluntary maintained schools* are managed by boards of governors. The DENI contributes towards capital expenditure, and the ELB meets all running costs (*Statham J* et al. *Education Fact File. Hodder and Stoughton, 1989*). The ELB is therefore responsible for equipment provision for special educational needs: premises adaptations might be, to some extent, the responsibilty of the governors of the school.

B27.3.3.3. *Voluntary grammar schools* are managed by boards of governors. The Department of Education Northern Ireland (DENI) contributes toward capital expend-iture and meets most running costs. Recommended premises adaptations and equipment provided are the responsibility of the governors, although the DENI may then contribute (*Verbal communication: special educational needs advisers, Northern Ireland 1988*).

B27.3.4. Independent schools in general. Independent (non-maintained) schools are outside the maintained education system, and as such charge fees. Some may be run by charities.

Such independent schools belonging to charities have assisted places to greater or lesser extent. Thus, an LEA pays a fee to the school to cover the needs of a pupil including equipment needs. The school, though, rather than the LEA, is ultimately responsible for the provision of equipment and premises adaptations.

27.5. Conditions of equipment provision

27.5.1. Loan. Equipment for specific individual children is normally supplied on loan, for as long as the child needs it or is attending school. The equipment is then returned to the LEA/ELB for re-use.

Exceptions to this rule are sometimes made, for example, if:

- equipment is so specialised for an individual that no other child is likely to use it (eg custom-made magnifier lens);
- equipment is too worn to re-use;
- equipment has become outdated;
- the child/young person is going into further or higher education; the LEA/ELB sometimes allows him or her to retain the equipment for that period;
- the equipment was originally supplied through voluntary effort (eg voluntary organisation or fundraising) for the individual rather than the school or LEA/ELB).

27.5.2. Duplication and use at home. Some LEA/ELBs do not allow equipment to be used at home; others do allow this, if it is thought to be useful. Some might duplicate items (eg typewriters or wheelchairs) if transportation is difficult or inadvisable: others would expect such duplication to be funded from alternative sources. Thus, in some areas, voluntary funding for equipment at home is sought, in order to achieve duplication.

For example, one joint local authority policy document (England) states that:

- daily living equipment should be provided by the LEA/ELB at school, while the same item could then be provided at home by the SSD, if necessary; – treatment equipment (eg standing frames) should be supplied by the DHA at both home and school;
- educational equipment such as typewriters should be provided by the LEA at school, and perhaps by voluntary funding at home (*London SSD (19) guidelines received 1989*).

27.6. Examples of equipment provision for educational need are given in Box 27.4.

Box 27.4: Examples of equipment provision in relation to school/education

B27.4.1. Postural equipment, seating. Some LEA/ELBs provide postural equipment such as seating, standing boxes, special desks, regarding such equipment as necessary for education. Other LEA/ELBs do not supply such equipment (especially in ordinary schools): provision through other statutory services, parents, fundraising, or voluntary bodies is then necessary.

Individually made wooden seating, for example, for school use is funded by various sources: a 1987 survey (England) identified, for example, school, LEA, DHA, joint funding, individual OT/physiotherapy budgets. Similarly, commercially available seating might be supplied in the same way (*Result of Questionnaire into the Provision and Funding of Equipment for Children with Special Needs. Association of Paediatric Chartered Physiotherapists. 1987*).

B27.4.1.2. Wheelchairs

B27.4.1.2.1. Wheelchair service. Certain wheelchairs and and buggies are provided (on free loan) by the wheelchair service to meet medical needs of children.

B27.4.1.2.2. Other sources of provision. Where other wheelchairs or buggies are needed in school, the funding might come from outside: for example, charities, golf clubs, fundraising events or parents (*Result of Questionnaire into the Provision and Funding of Equipment for Children with Special Needs. Association of Paediatric Chartered Physiotherapists. 1987*).

Some LEA/ELBs might, for example, supply their own wheelchairs (*Written communication: LEA 1990*), to either meet needs not met by the wheelchair service, or because of transportation difficulties.

Equally, some wheelchair service centres supply a second wheelchair for school use; but in some cases might not do so, instead placing responsibility for transport on the LEA (6./B3.2.7.2.) (*Verbal communication: DSA regional manager, 1989*).

Special schools sometimes have a stock of their own user controlled indoor/outdoor electric wheelchairs; but in some areas at least, major problems can be faced by LEA/ELBs, especially with the integration of children with special needs in ordinary schools (*London SSD (19) guidelines received 1989*).

B27.4.1.3. Cycles. The wheelchair service is no longer supplying cycles or tricycles extra to a wheelchair, on social grounds (ie to aid playground mobility. Medical or clinical grounds are required to justify provision (6./B3.2.7.8.).

B27.4.1.4. Adaptations to school premises are sometimes required, for example in order to make possible the integration into an ordinary school of a child (or several children) with special educational needs.

Clearly, there are instances where to 're-build a school around one child' is not financially practicable. Thus although the LEA is under a duty to secure ordinary school education for a child, this duty is subject amongst other conditions, to 'the efficient use of resources' (*see eg Education Act 1981 s.2; SI 1986/594 (NI.3) Education and Libraries (Order) 1986 s.32*).

On the other hand, however, the adaptation can be viewed as good use of resources weighed both against the high fees involved in, for example, five years' attendance at a special school; and against the possibility of other children requiring the same adaptation in the future.

Depending on the type of school, the responsibility for deciding on and arranging an adaptation rests with the LEA/ELB or the governors/managers; depending on which of these has responsibility for the capital costs of the premises.

B27.4.1.5. Small items such as pencil grips, dycem mats or angled desk tops are sometimes supplied to the LEA/ELB for children by DHA/HB/HSSB therapists at little or no charge (*Verbal communication: paediatric OTs 1989*).

Statement/records might or might not mention such minor items under equipment needs (*Written communication: ELB special needs adviser, 1988*).

28 Equipment for Employment

Equipment/adaptations need for retention of, or entry into, employment

Referral

Professional   Self/employer   Family/friend

DRO   DAS team or BPRO (Northern Ireland)

Equipment/adaptation need primarily for employment

Y

Need not normally encountered by employer

Y

Need on employer's premises

N

Need at home ——— Y ———▶ Person is outworker

Y | N

Person is self-employed

Y

Equipment need ———▶ No cost limits, so long as criteria are met

Equipment on loan to person, to be returned when no longer needed

N

Adaptation of premises/equipment need

Y

Application by employer ———▶ Maximum of £6000

Employment services (ES, DED) pay some or all of this depending on various factors

Adaptation is employer's property

Employer is expected to keep the person for as long as possible, and replace him or her, if necessary, with somebody with a similar need

Introduction

Type of equipment. There is no precise definition of equipment and adaptations supplied for employment use, other than that the individual need should relate primarily to employment.

Responsibility for the provision of equipment and adaptations to enable people with disabilities to retain or enter employment, rests with the:

- Employment Service (ES, England, Wales, Scotland);
- Department of Economic Development (DED, Northern Ireland).
 The ES and DED have powers, rather than duties, to make such provision.

Provision. Both equipment loaned free of charge to employees, and grants (for the adaptation of equipment or premises) made to employers, are for the purpose of allowing a disabled person to retain or enter employment.

 In order to benefit from the equipment loan scheme, the disabled person must be registered with the ES or DED. Such registration is, however, not necessary in the case of grants given to employers for adaptations.

 Eligibility criteria require that the equipment or adaptation be primarily for employment purposes, and that the need is not one which an employer is normally expected to meet.

Maintenance and repair. Equipment maintenance, repair and replacement is the responsibility of the ES or DED; the employer is responsible for any adaptations which have been carried out to premises or equipment.

28.1. Type of equipment and adaptations

No precise definition of equipment and adaptations for employment exists, other than that they meet what is primarily an individual employment need.

 Employment Service (ES) leaflets give examples of the sort of equipment and adaptations which can be supplied to meet individual employment needs. These are listed in Box 28.1. It should be stressed that they are only examples.

Box 28.1: Examples of equipment, and adaptations to premises and equipment, for employment (taken from Employment Service leaflets)

It should be stressed that the following are only examples:

B28.1.1. Equipment for employment includes:
 for people with visual impairment:
 – special computer equipment;
 – closed circuit television systems (CCTVs);
 – large print output devices;
 – tape recorders;
 – pocket memos;
 – talking calculators;
 – telephone switchboards with touch indicators/audio output;

- braille measuring devices;
- measuring equipment, with audio output;
- for people with hearing impairment:
  - amplifiers;
  - loudspeaking telephone aids;
  - communicating terminals and computers;
  - adaptations to switchboards;
- for people with various physical disabilities:
  - electrically powered wheelchairs with riser seats;
  - wheelchairs with stand-up and kerb-mounting facilities;
  - electronic writing systems;
  - special computer equipment and software packages;
  - special telephones;
  - page turners;
  - special chairs;
  - stools;
  - workbenches and tools (*Employment Service leaflet EPWD9*).

B28.2.2. Adaptations to equipment and premises include:

- wheelchair ramps;
- wheelchair lifts;
- hoists;
- stairlifts;
- adapted lavatories (including wide doors and grab rails);
- alarm systems with flashing lights;
- extra lighting;
- modified machinery (eg conversion of controls from foot to hand);
- adapted switchboards (eg for blind people);
- modified computer systems with braille or talking terminals (*Employment Service leaflet EPWD10*).

28.2. Legislative basis for provision

28.2.1. Special aids to employment scheme (SAE). The ES (England, Wales, Scotland) and DED (Northern Ireland) have powers to provide equipment to help people who are registered with them as disabled to obtain or keep employment. Equipment is not mentioned specifically, but is covered by the word 'facilities' (*Disabled Persons (Employment) Act 1944; s.15(1); Disabled Persons (Employment) (Northern Ireland) Act 1945, s.15*) (see Box 28.2 for details).

28.2.2. Adaptations to premises and equipment grants (APE, England, Wales, Scotland). The Employment Service has a duty to make various arrangements to help people select, train for and obtain employment; and to help employers obtain suitable employees. As part of these arrangements, it has the power to make grants or loans to employers (*Employment and Training Act 1973*) (see Box 28.2).

28.2.3. Capital grants to employers for adaptations to premises and equipment (CGEAPE, Northern Ireland). The DED has the power to make payments to help employers to retain employees or take on new employees (*Employment Subsidies Act 1978*) (see Box 28.2 for details).

Box 28.2: Legislative basis for provision, by employment services, of equipment and adaptations to premises and equipment

B28.2.1. Basis for special aids to employment (SAE) scheme and also for SPS, PRS, BoA schemes):
'Facilities may be provided as specified in this section for enabling persons registered as handicapped by disablement, who by reason of the nature or severity of their disablement are unlikely either at any time or until after the lapse of a prolonged period to be able otherwise to obtain employment, or to undertake work on their own account (whether because employment or such work would not be available to them or because they would be unlikely to be able to compete therein on terms comparable as respects earnings and security with those enjoyed by persons engaged therein who are not subject to disablement), to obtain employment or to undertake such work under special conditions, and for the training of such persons for the employment or work in question' (*Disabled Persons (Employment) Act 1944 s.15(1); Disabled Persons (Employment) (Northern Ireland) Act 1945 s.15*).

B28.2.1.1. Definition of disability re: registration for help under SAE, SPS, PRS, BoA schemes:
'In this Act the expression 'disabled person' means a person who, on account of injury, disease, or congenital deformity, is substantially handicapped in obtaining or keeping employment, or in undertaking work on his own account, of a kind which apart from that injury, disease or deformity would be suited to his age, experience and qualifications; and the expression 'disablement', in relation to any person, shall be construed accordingly'.
'For the purposes of the definitions contained in the preceding subsection, the expression 'disease' shall be construed as including a physical or mental condition arising from imperfect development of any organ' (*Disabled Persons (Employment) Act 1944 s.1; Disabled Persons (Employment) (Northern Ireland) Act 1945 s.1*).

B28.2.2. Adaptations to premises and equipment scheme

B28.2.2.1. APE: England, Wales, Scotland. 'The Secretary of State shall make such arrangements as he considers necessary for the purpose of assisting persons to select, train for, obtain and retain employment suitable for their age and capacities and to obtain suitable employees (including partners and business associates)'.
Included is the 'provision for the making of payments by the Secretary of State, by way of grant or loan or otherwise, to persons who promote facilities in pursuance of the arrangements, to persons who use these facilities and to other persons specified in or determined under the arrangements' (*Employment and Training Act 1973 s.2 amended by Employment Act 1988 s.25*).

B28.2.2.2. Capital grants to employers for adaptations to premises and adaptations (Northern Ireland). 'The Secretary of State may, if in his opinion unemployment in Great Britain continues at a high level and with Treasury approval, set up schemes for making payments to employers which will enable them to retain persons in employment who would or might otherwise become unemployed, to take on new employees, and generally to maintain or enlarge their labour force'.
'In Northern Ireland the Department of Manpower Services may, if in its opinion unemployment in Northern Ireland continues at a high level, with the approval of the Department of Finance set up schemes for making such payments to employers as are referred to' above (*Employment Subsidies Act 1978 s.1*). (*Note:* the responsible department is the Department of Economic Development (DED)).

28.2.4. Personal reader service (PRS) (see below). Employment Service and DED provision has the same legislative basis as the SAE scheme (28.2.1.).

28.2.5. Sheltered placement scheme (SPS) (see below). Employment Service and DED provision has the same legislative basis as the SAE scheme (28.2.1.).

28.2.6. Business on account scheme (BoA) (see below). Employment Service and DED provision has the same legislative basis as the SAE scheme (28.2.1.).

28.3. Referral

28.3.1. Referral for special aids to employment scheme

28.3.1.1. Referral to disablement resettlement officers (DROs) based at job centres is open: self-referral, representatives (eg voluntary organisation), employer (current or future), professionals (such as GPs, consultants, therapists, teachers, social workers).

28.3.1.2. Referral to DAS teams or the BPRO (Northern Ireland). The DRO refers, if appropriate, a person with a disability to the local disablement advisory service (DAS) team, or blind person's resettlement officer (Northern Ireland), who, in turn, can assess for equipment and adaptations.

· Equally, referral (self or otherwise) is sometimes made direct to the DAS team, or to the BPRO (Northern Ireland).

28.3.2. Application for adaptations to premises and equipment scheme (APE, England, Wales, Scotland); capital grants to employers for adaptations to premises and equipment scheme (CGEAPE, Northern Ireland). Application must be made formally by the employer (current or future), since a grant for an adaptation is made to the employer, rather than the employee.

28.3.3. Registration of disability is necessary in order to receive help in the form of the SAE, SPS, PRS or BoA schemes (*Disabled Persons (Employment) Act 1944 s.15(1); Disabled Persons (Employment) (Northern Ireland) 1945 s.15*).

It is not a statutory requirement, in the case of the APE or CGEAPE schemes, that the employee be registered.

28.3.3.1. Definition of disability for the purposes of help under Employment Service or DED schemes is given in Box 28.2.

28.3.3.2. Registration practice. The insistence on registration of disability, in the case of the ES/DED, is in contrast to SSD/SWD/HSSB practice in relation to daily living equipment (2.3.2.).

The registration schemes, operated by employment and social services, respectively, are quite separate and should not be confused with each other.

28.4. Assessment

28.4.1. Services and professionals involved

28.4.1.1. Disablement advisory service (DAS, England, Wales, Scotland). Where there are special equipment or adaptation needs, referral is made either via the DRO, or directly, to a disablement advisory service (DAS) team.

There are 68 DAS teams based in area offices in England, Wales and Scotland.

28.4.1.2. Blind persons' resettlement officers (BPROs).

28.4.1.2.1. Blind persons' resettlement officer (BPRO, Northern Ireland). In Northern Ireland, a single BPRO acts as 'one-person' equivalent to the DAS team for equipment assessment and provision.

28.4.1.2.2. BPROs, England, Wales, Scotland. BPROs have traditionally worked within DAS teams; their name has now been changed in some areas in recognition of the various disabilities which they have to understand. Their new title is 'disablement adviser' (DA) (28.4.1.3.).

There are other areas, however, in which the title of BPRO is retained in recognition of the continuance of a specialist service for people with visual impairment (the majority of people benefiting under the SAE scheme, for example, are people with visual impairment).

28.4.1.3. Disablement adviser (DA, England, Wales, Scotland). This is a new title, introduced in some areas, for an officer formerly known as a BPRO.

DAs undertake assessment for equipment and where necessary call in additional technical advice.

28.4.1.4. Technical consultants (TCs, England, Wales, Scotland). Technical support is given to DAS teams by technical consultants (TCs) who, based in pairs in nine regions, are called on by DAS team area offices, as necessary.

Technical consultants generally have an engineering background, although increasingly they are also familiar with computer technology.

(Technical consultants were formerly known as blind persons' technical officers (BPTOs).)

28.4.1.5. Blind persons' technical officers (BPTOs, England, Wales, Scotland) are now called 'technical consultants' (TCs) (28.4.1.4.).

28.4.1.6. RNIB employment officers (England, Wales). A number of RNIB employment officers cover England and Wales, providing expert advice on computer technology and a technical support service.

In some areas they might, in practice, play the role of specialist consultants to the DAS team.

28.4.2. Other assessment sources. The DAS team, or BPRO in Northern Ireland, sometimes seeks advice from other sources.

Contacts are sometimes formed with, for example, occupational therapists, local hospitals audiology departments, equipment manufacturers or local voluntary organisations. Such contacts are usually informal and vary from area to area.

28.4.3. Assessment criteria

28.4.3.1. Employment need. Assessment by the DAS team (or BPRO and Grants to Employers Branch, Northern Ireland) must establish that any equipment or adaptation need is primarily for the purpose of employment. Thus, daily living or health needs will not be met by the Employment Service or DED.

By way of illustration three examples are listed in Box 28.3 (it should be stressed that they are only possible examples).

Box 28.3: Examples to illustrate 'employment need' in relation to equipment

Example 1. A person, who does not qualify for wheelchair provision (by the the wheelchair service) at home is unlikely (though every case is considered on its merits) to be provided with a wheelchair at work.

However, there are exceptional cases. For example, a person, who at home uses crutches rather than a wheelchair might be entitled to a wheelchair at work provided by the ES/DED if the work required a high level of mobility.

Example 2. A stand-up wheelchair (used for drawing board work, for example) is an example of equipment which cannot be supplied by the wheelchair service, but which can be supplied by the ES or DED for employment purposes.

Example 3. Face-worn optical appliances (ie spectacles) are normally considered to be the responsibility of the health service rather than the Employment Service or the DED.

28.4.3.2. Exceptional need re: employer. The equipment or adaptation required should not be something that the employer could reasonably be expected to supply in any case, irrespective of whether the employee concerned was disabled. Unless the need is exceptional in this respect, and results from disability, the DAS team or BPRO (Northern Ireland) will not approve the application.

28.4.3.3. Eligibility: place of work, employment status

28.4.3.3.1. SAE scheme. The SAE scheme applies to employees working either on an employer's premises, or as an outworker in their own home. In the latter case, the person's home (or part used for employment) is regarded as an extension of the employer's premises.

Alternatively, a self-employed person (as both employee and employer) can also apply for help under this scheme.

28.4.3.3.2. APE and CGEAPE schemes. The APE and CGEAPE schemes, for adaptations to premises and equipment, require application through the employer (or somebody who is self-employed).

Opportunities afforded by computers for home self-employment are increasing and a self-employed disabled person is eligible to apply for help under these schemes.

(*Note:* housing legislation also gives housing authorities powers to help with adaptations which will make the home suitable for employment purposes (3.6.2.)).

Adaptation grants cannot normally be made to help employers meet access, sanitary and parking facilities needs, where the provision of new premises or newly converted premises is covered by the Chronically Sick and Disabled Persons' Acts.

28.4.3.4. Assessment procedure of closed circuit television systems. A special procedure exists for partially sighted people if a closed circuit television (CCTV) magnification system is needed. This involves referral to, and assessment at, a special health service low vision clinic (15.3.1.5.2.). The order of events may be in reverse; the low vision clinic identifies an employment need in the first place, and refers the person to the DAS team or BPRO for possible provision, at work, of a CCTV magnification system.

Special low vision clinics carrying out such assessments are located at, for example, Moorfields Hospital (London), Royal Eye Hospital (Birmingham), Royal Eye Hospital (Manchester), Radcliffe Infirmary (Oxford), Glasgow Infirmary (*In Touch Handbook. BSS 1989. p. 82*).

28.4.3.5. Assessment for business on own account scheme. Under this scheme, now rarely used, a grant can be made to cover capital expenses to set up a business. Fairly strict assessment criteria operate, and the viability of the business must be demonstrated.

28.4.3.6. Ordinary or special equipment. Equipment loaned through the SAE scheme (or adapted under the APE, CGEAPE schemes) can be 'ordinary' equipment, not necessarily designed for disability. Computers, for example, fall into this category of ordinary equipment.

28.4.3.7. Personal reader service (PRS) scheme. The aim of the scheme is to help:

- supplement reading aid a person may already be getting from colleagues, friends, relatives;
- people who are starting a new job and need help;
- people who might otherwise lose their job;
- people returning to a different job;
- people whose career development is being restricted (*Employment Service: EPWD 8 leaflet*).

An RNIB employment officer normally fills in the application form, which is also signed by both employer and employee (England, Wales, Scotland).

28.5. Provision

28.5.1. Conditions of equipment loan or carrying out of adaptations to premises and equipment

28.5.1.1. SAE scheme: loan of equipment. Equipment supplied is on loan: it is returnable to the Employment Service or DED when it is no longer required.

28.5.1.2. SAE or CGEAPE scheme adaptations. Adaptations carried out to premises and equipment are the 'property' of the employer. However, the employer is expected to keep the employee (for whose benefit the adaptation was carried out) in the job for as long as possible. If the employee has to give up the job, the employer is then expected to employ somebody else with a similar need (*EPWD10, DPL 16(NI)*).

28.5.2. Equipment and adaptations through sheltered placement scheme (SPS).
The ES and DED organise and fund this scheme which allows people with disabilities to work, even though they may be 'less productive' than a person without such disabilities.

Sponsoring organisations include voluntary bodies, local authorities, banks, high street shops, small businesses, multi-national companies (*Written communication: Employment Service, 1990*). The employer pays salary only for work actually done by the employee; the ES or DED pays the rest, to bring the salary up to the full amount.

Special equipment or adaptations for sheltered placement schemes are available under the SAE or APE/CGEAPE schemes; or sometimes the sponsoring organisation might organise such provision.

28.5.3. Equipment and adaptations through employment rehabilitation services. Employment rehabilitation centres (employment rehabilitation units, Northern Ireland) assess and help rehabilitate people using the expertise of a multi-disciplinary team.

They make some equipment in their own workshops to meet special needs; otherwise equipment and adaptations can be obtained via the SAE or APE/CGEAPE schemes.

Between 1985 and 1990, the number of SPS jobs has risen from 1050 to over 6000 (*Written communication: Employment Service, 1990*).

28.5.4. Equipment and adaptations on training schemes, job introduction schemes. Equipment and adaptation needs on any government training schemes or job introduction schemes can be met through the SAE or APE/CGEAPE schemes.

26.6. Training in the use of equipment

Training in the use of equipment might be required, and, if possible, more complex equipment is used for a trial period, or at least tried out a few times before formal loan is made.

The increasing complexity of (computer) equipment necessitates special training, and this might be carried out by, for example, a member of a DAS team or by a technical consultant. Alternatively, such training might be part of the package of provision made by the equipment supplier or manufacturer.

28.7. Follow-up

DAS teams and the BPRO (Northern Ireland) follow up provision by means of telephone calls and selected visits.

28.8. Repair and maintenance.
The DAS team or BPRO is responsible for arranging the repair and replacement of equipment: it is Employment Service or DED property.

Any adaptation to premises or equipment is the responsibility of the employer.

28.9. Finances

28.9.1. SAE finance. Under the SAE scheme there is, in theory, no limit to provision so long as the equipment meets an employment need. Sums spent on one individual can sometimes run into many thousands of pounds. Nevertheless, a local area DAS team (or Northern Ireland BPRO) cannot authorise equipment which costs more than a specified amount, and central authorisation must be given above that amount.

28.9.2. APE/CGEAPE finance. Unlike the SAE scheme, for which no limits are set, a limit is set on grants given towards adaptations of premises or equipment schemes.

At the time of writing, it is limited to a maximum (depending on various conditions) of £6000, and is normally paid retrospectively. An application needs to be accompanied by three estimates of the work required.

The ES or DED might contribute differing proportions of the total cost, as shown by the following possible examples:

- 100%: where a new employee is to benefit (perhaps the first disabled employee an employer has had);
- 75%: where an old employee, of value to the employer, is to benefit;
- 50%: where an adaptation to premises will benefit the employer considerably; for example, a ramp into a shop. In such a case customers will benefit by the adaptation as well as the employee.

28.9.3. Personal reader service finance. The grant, to allow use of a personal reader, is fixed at an hourly rate for up to fifteen hours a week. The duration of a grant is usually two years, after which it is renewable. It is paid, without regard to the salary of the person receiving the service, for the first two years. Thereafter, salary is taken into account (*Employment Service leaflet EPWD8*).

29 Specialist services

118 Pentonville Road, London N1 9JN Tel 071-833 2307 Fax 071 837 2917

Physical Management of Multiple Handicaps

A Professional's Guide, 2nd ed

Beverly A Fraser, MA, PT, formerly with Wayne County Intermediate School District, Wayne, Michigan, Robert N Hensinger, MD, Professor of Surgery, Department of Orthopedic Surgery, University Hospital, Ann Arbor, Michigan, & Judith A Phelps, OTR, Wayne County Intermediate School District, Wayne, Michigan, with contributions by Dean S Louis, MD, Lawrence W Schneider, PhD, Glenda Atkinson, PT, Judy C Arkwright, MA, CCC-SLP, Carol Topper, OTR, CO, & Steven R Taylor, CO

1990 ISBN 1-55766-047-6 336 pages hb £26.50

The authors of this expanded and updated text use a multidisciplinary approach to supply the background and guidance needed in helping to improve the physical well-being and educational development of persons with multiple handicaps. Experienced physical therapists, occupational therapists, orthopedic surgeons, orthotists, and a research scientist and speech/language therapist detail the use of various techniques. Subjects covered include orthopedics, physical and occupational therapy, specialized seating, orthotics, transportation safety, and adapted devices for function and communication.

The book is organised into five sections, with numerous illustrations to assist helpers in evaluating, managing, and monitoring every individual they serve. Completely updated and providing an abundance of innovative data, this resource offers expanded sections on wheelchair safety, therapeutic positioning, feeding, hygiene, and adaptive devices, including computer assisted instruction.

Augmentative and Alternative Communication Systems for Persons with Moderate and Severe Disabilities

Diane Baumgart, PhD, Associate Professor, Department of Counseling and Special Education, University of Idaho, Jeanne Johnson, PhD, Assistant Professor, Department of Speech and Hearing, Washington State University, and Edwin Helmstetter, PhD, Assistant Professor, Department of Counseling and Psychology, Washington State University

1990 ISBN 1 55766 049 2 224 pages paper £17.50

This practical book is a guide to designing a communication system and evaluating its success.

Health Care for Students with Disabilities

An Illustrated Medical Guide for the Classroom.

J Carolyn Graff, RN, MS, Children's Rehabilitation Unit, University of Kansas Medical Center, Marilyn Mulligan Ault, PhD, Department of Special Education, University of Kansas, Doug Guess, EdD, Department of Special Education, University of Kansas, Marianne Taylor, RN, MS, Children's Development and Rehabilitation Unit, The Oregon Health Sciences University, and Barbara Thompson, PhD, Department of Special Education, University of Kansas

1990 ISBN 1-55766-037-9 282 pages, 90 illus hb £18.95

How do you ensure a child's safety during a seizure? What should you do to guarantee the dignity of a student with a colostomy? How can you monitor a child with diabetes?

This practical guidebook - evaluated for accuracy and practicality by 15 teachers and nurses - answers these important questions and more.

Introduction

This book describes the equipment scene, in separate chapters, according to generally recognised classifications, based on equipment type and source of provision. The various chapters refer frequently to links already operating, or which should be operating, locally between different agencies involved in provision – particularly the links between hospital and community services. Special reference is made in this chapter to a number of facilities which operate over a wider geographical area than 'local' and/or which offer services of an above average nature.

29.1. Specialist rehabilitation services

29.1.1. Examples of services. There are a number of units for spinal injury and for the young disabled (16-64 years) offering both long-stay facilities and short-term stays (including both rehabilitation and respite stays).

There are other units, not for long-stay purposes which offer highly concentrated rehabilitation and assessment. One such well-known unit is Mary Marlborough Lodge in Oxford, which assess inpatients (for fortnight periods) from all over the country and (local) outpatients.

In Edinburgh, this type of service has been developed on a larger scale; the Edinburgh Rehabilitation Medicine Service extends to two hospitals, a community physiotherapy clinic, a wheelchair and driving assessment centre and a GP supervised community rehabilitation service (*Roy CW* et al. *Work of a rehabilitation medicine service. BMJ 1988: 297, 601-604*).

An independent hospital, the Royal Hospital Home, Putney, for example, offers both long-stay and shorter stay rehabilitation facilities for people with severe disabilities.

Centres such as Chailey Heritage (independent school and NHS hospital) and the Cheney Centre for Children with Cerebral Palsy (NHS unit with education authority support) represent centres which offer combined health and education services to children with disabilities.

29.1.2. Pattern of service. All such units/hospitals generally have a high staff/patient ratio, which gives time and scope for a patient's equipment needs to be thoroughly assessed within his or her total assessment for rehabilitation purposes. When hospital discharge arrangements are being made the patient's local services are contacted to try and ensure appropriate and prompt provision, where necessary, of equipment and adaptations.

Sometimes, even when such specialist rehabilitation units are involved, local services and support are inadequate following hospital discharge (*Beardshaw V. Last on the List. 1988 p. 36*).

The distribution of specialist rehabilitation services (including rehabilitation engineering services) is uneven, leading, in turn, to their uneven provision (*Beardshaw V. Last on the List. Community Services for People with Physical Disabilities. King's Fund Institute, 1988, p. 34*).

29.2. Rehabilitation engineering

Rehabilitation engineering units (REUs) are sometimes part of a rehabilitation unit (as described above), or separate but easily accessible. Such a unit might also be known as a medical physics department.

Rehabilitation engineering is relevant to the long-term needs of people with disabilities; the engineer works with a multi-disciplinary team including, for example, doctors, therapists and nurses. Rehabilitation engineers make and adapt a wide range of equipment including special seating, mobility equipment, postural equipment, daily living equipment and communication aids etc.

Engineers also collaborate with the wheelchair service (6.4.2.) (often in relation to special seating) and communication aids centres (13.3.3.).

29.3. REMAP

REMAP is a voluntary organisation which harnesses the skills of (rehabilitation) engineers to one-off equipment solutions where neither statutory nor commercial channels are able to meet the need. All sorts of equipment are made or adapted.

The panels include, besides engineers, people with technical skills such as carpenters, machinists, DIYers, as well as occupational therapists, physiotherapists, doctors, district nurses and social workers.

Referrals are mainly initiated by occupational therapists, but also by other professionals, people with disabilities and voluntary organisations.

Charges are not made to the client; occasionally the SSD or SWD might be asked to contribute to cost of materials; waste and scrap materials are often used. REMAP members undertake work voluntarily.

29.4. Disabled living centres are discussed elsewhere (2.4.2.2.)

29.5. Communication aids centres
are discussed elsewhere (13.3.3.)

30 Charges for Equipment

Introduction

Charges in general (medical equipment and daily living equipment)

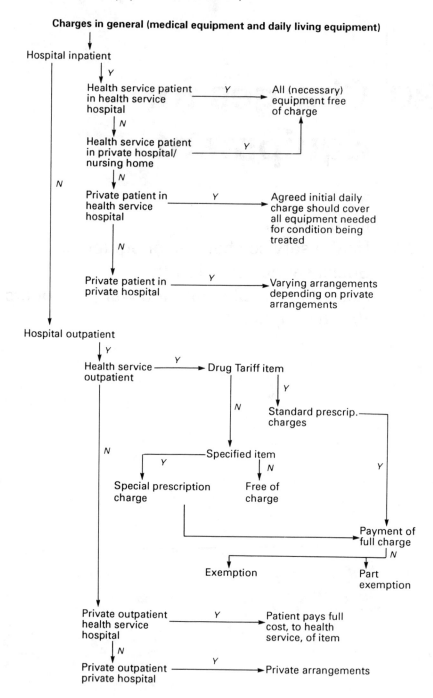

Charges in general (continued)

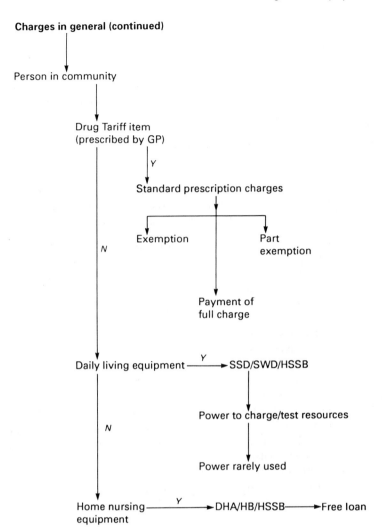

Person in community

Drug Tariff item
(prescribed by GP)

Y

Standard prescription charges

Exemption

N

Part
exemption

Payment of
full charge

Daily living equipment —— *Y* —→ SSD/SWD/HSSB

Power to charge/test resources

N

Power rarely used

Home nursing —— *Y* —→ DHA/HB/HSSB ——→ Free loan
equipment

Introduction

The system of charges outlined in this chapter relates to the supply of various health and daily living equipment, in general.

Charges for specific types of equipment, such as dental appliances, optical appliances and home adaptations, are dealt with elsewhere, as appropriate.

Equipment for people with disabilities is subject to VAT exemption; this is summarised in this chapter.

A note on special arrangements, in general, for war pensioners is also included.

Health service. Certain charges are made under health service provision. The general principle, however, is that, where no charge is specified in legislation, provision is free of charge. With this in mind, the following applies:

- hospital (health service) inpatients: equipment (clinically necessary) is provided free of charge;
- hospital (health service) outpatients: charges apply to any equipment provided, which is either listed in the Drug Tariff, or which is a 'specified appliance' – otherwise there is no charge (for clinically necessary equipment);
- GP patients: GPs prescribe only items listed in the Drug Tariff. These items attract prescription charges;
- health service patients attending a private hospital (or private nursing home): the same arrangements apply as if they were attending a health service hospital (as inpatient or outpatient);
- private inpatients in a health service hospital: this category of patient should have any equipment costs included in the agreed fixed daily charge; they should not normally be charged extra if the equipment is needed as part of the originally agreed treatment;
- private outpatients in a health service hospital should pay the full cost (to the health service) of any equipment provided;
- private patients attending a private hospital: various arrangements are likely to apply.

Health service prescription charges are sometimes waived, in part or in full, depending on what degree of exemption, if any, patients qualify for. This depends on factors such as age, medical condition and financial circumstances.

Social services charges. SSD/SWDs and HSSBs (under social services functions) have powers to make charges in return for services provided. The level of such charges is also discretionary, and charges can only be made if it is judged that the client can reasonably afford to meet such charges.

In relation to equipment, the power to charge is infrequently used. Tests of resources are made more frequently in relation to home adaptations, when the SSD/SWD/HSSB assesses what assistance it can give (additional to an housing authority grant, for example).

30.1. Health service charges for equipment

30.1.1. Equipment free of charge by default. Despite the somewhat complex legislation concerned with charges for certain equipment, the overall position is simple: where there is no charge specified, the equipment is, by default, free of charge (*NHS Act 1977 s.1; NHS(Scotland) Act 1978, s.1; SI 1972/1265 HPSS(NI)O 1972, a.98*).

30.1.2. Hospital charges for equipment

30.1.2.1. Health service inpatient. A health service inpatient, in a health service hospital, will receive any equipment needed free of charge.

This is stated clearly (England, Wales, Scotland) in legislation (*NHS Act 1977, Sched.12; NHS (Scotland) Act, Sched. 11; SI 1972/1265 (HPSS(NI)O 1972 a.98*).

30.1.2.1.1. Inpatient leaving hospital. For an inpatient leaving hospital the position as to payment may be different; even if the assessment for an appliance is made while a person is still an inpatient, a charge can be made if it is supplied and fitted when the person is no longer an inpatient. In effect, the status of the patient is then that of outpatient (30.1.2.2.) when the equipment is provided.

Any such possible charge only applies to items which attract a charge: Drug Tariff items or certain specified items (fabric supports and wigs).

30.1.2.2. Hospital outpatient. An outpatient has, subject to exemptions (Box 30.1.), to pay a prescription charge, either for items included in the Drug Tariff (Box 5.1.), or for 'specified items' (30.1.2.2.2.).

30.1.2.2.1. Drug Tariff items. The Drug Tariff is a list of drugs and appliances, which doctors can prescribe and which attract prescription charges.

The basis for the Drug Tariff lies in legislation. It includes a list of approved appliances, specifications for appliances and 'the prices on the basis of which the payment for drugs and appliances ordinarily supplied is to be calculated' (*SI 1974/160 r.28; SI 1974/506(S.41) r.32; SR&O 1973/421 a.40*).

At the time of writing the prescription charge for a Drug Tariff item is £3.05 (*SI 1989/419 as amended; SI 1989/326 (S.36); SI 1973/419 and SR&O 1973/419 as amended*).

There is a system of exemption or part exemption from payment for Drug Tariff items (Box 30.1.).

30.1.2.2.2. Specified appliances are prescribed by consultants and attract charges when prescribed for outpatients (rather than inpatients). Certain appliances which are not Drug Tariff items, supplied to outpatients, and prescribed by consultants, attract charges. These appliances are named and the charge is specified.

The specified items (and the charge at time of writing) are:

- surgical brassiere (£12.00);
- abdominal or spinal support (£16.00);
- wigs (stock modacrylic: £24.00, partial human hair: £62.00, full bespoke human hair: £97.00).
(*SI 1989/419 as amended; SR&O 1989/326 (S.36) as amended; SR&O 173/419 as amended*).

There is a system of exemption or part-exemption from charges for these specified items (*see Box 30.1 for details*).

Box 30.1: Exemptions from prescription charges for Drug Tariff equipment and specified appliances

B30.1.1. Exemptions for Drug Tariff and specified appliances. The following groups of people are exempt or partially exempt from prescription charges for Drug Tariff appliances (Box 5.1.) and specified appliances (30.1.2.2.2.).

B30.1.1.1. Inpatients do not pay any charges if the appliance is supplied while the person is in hospital (30.1.2.1.).

B30.1.1.2. Children and full-time education. People under 16 years of age or under 19 and in full-time education (*NHS Act 1977, Sched. 12,s.1 and SI 1989/419 r.5,6; NHS (Scotland) Act 1978, Sched.11 para 1 and SI 1989/326(S.36) r.7; SR&O 1973/419 r.10, r.15 amended by SR 1988/79 r.2*).

B30.1.1.3. Accepted disablement. People with an exemption certificate (from the Secretary of State, ie: War Pensioners Welfare Branch, DSS) for an 'accepted disablement' (30.3.). This covers, for example, war pensioners (30.3.) in relation to the injury which has caused the disability and placed them in the category of 'war pensioners' (*SI 1989/419, r.6; SI 1989/326 (S.36) r.7; SR&O 1973/419 r.10, r.15*).

B30.1.1.4. Over retirement age (does not apply, as exemption criterion, to wigs and fabric supports). Men who are 65 years old or over, and women of 60 years of age or over (*SI 1989/419, r.6; SI 1989/326 r.7); (SR&O 1973/419 r.15*).

B30.1.1.5. Expectant mother, recent mother status (does not apply, as exemption criterion, to wigs and fabric supports). A woman who has a certificate from an FPC, HB or the NICSA which states that she is expecting a baby, or has given birth to a child within the last 12 months (*SI 1989/419,r.6; SI 1989/326, r.7; SR&O 1973/419 r.15*).

B30.1.1.6. Certain medical conditions do not apply, as exemption criteria, to wigs and fabric supports. A person with an exemption certificate issued (by an FPC/HB/NICSA) for one (or more) of the following conditions:

- permanent fistula (including caecostomy, colostomy, laryngostomy or ileostomy) which requires continuous surgical dressing or appliance;
- one of the following:
  - forms of hydro-adrenalism (including Addison's disease) for which specific substitution therapy is essential;
  - diabetes insipidus and other forms of hypo-pituitarism;
  - diabetes mellitus (except where treatment is by diet alone);
  - hypoparathyroidism;
  - myasthenia gravis;
  - myxoedema;
  - epilepsy which requires regular anti-convulsive therapy;
  - 'continuing physical disability which prevents the patient from leaving his residence without the help of another person' (*SI 1989/419, r.6 as amended; SI 1989/326 (S.36) r.7 as amended; SR&O 1973/419 r.15 as amended*).

B30.1.1.7. Free prescription based on income. A person who receives income support or family credit, or a member of the same family (ie the dependant partner) of the person who receives either of these two benefits, is entitled to free appliances on prescription.

Also eligible for free prescription are people whose 'requirements are greater than their resources' (*SI 1989/419, r.3, r.4, r.5 and SI 1988/551 r.3,r.4; SI 1989/326 (S.36) r.3,r.4 and SI 1988/546, r.3,r.4; SR&O 1973/419, r.10, r.15; and SR 1989/348 r.3, r.4*).

B30.1.1.8. Part help with prescriptions

B30.1.1.8.1. Pre-payment certificates (apply only to Drug Tariff items including elastic hosiery/tights). Pre-payment certificates are supplied by a family practitioner committee (FPC), health board (HB) or the Northern Ireland Central Services Agency (NICSA).

Pre-payment certificates can be applied for by people not eligible for free prescriptions, but who wish to reduce heavy prescription costs by buying a 'season ticket'. At the time of writing, this certificate costs £5.80 for 4 months and £3.50 for 12 months (*SI 1989/419 r.8 as amended; SI 1989/326 (S.36) r.8 as amended; SR&O 1973/419 r.6 as amended*).

B30.1.1.8.2. Part 'remission' (applies only to hospital supply of fabric supports and wigs). If, after various calculations, a person does not qualify for full exemption from prescription charges for specified appliances, they may nevertheless still be eligible for part-exemption from prescription charges.

However, such part-exemption only applies to wigs, fabric supports and surgical brassieres (*SI 1988/551 r.5; SI 1988/546 (S.62) r.5; SR 1989/348 r.5*).

30.1.3. GP patient. GPs can prescribe Drug Tariff items (Box 5.1.). The prescription charge, currently £3.05, is subject to fairly frequent rises.

A system of exemption and part-exemption applies to such prescription (Box 30.1.).

30.1.4. Charges for optical appliances are discussed elswhere (Box 15.2.).

30.1.5. Charges for dental appliances are discussed elsewhere (23.5.).

30.1.6. Appliance replacement and repair

30.1.6.1. Defective appliance. No charge can be made to either inpatients, outpatients, or GP patients if the replacement or repair is necessary because there is something wrong with the appliance 'as supplied' (*NHS Act 1977, Sched.12; NHS (Scotland) Act 1978, Sched.11; by implication SI 1972/1265 HPSS(NI)O 1972 Sched.15*).

30.1.6.2. Repair and replacement of equipment. In theory, a charge can be made for repair and replacement of an appliance (even one not normally attracting charges), if the need has arisen because of an 'act' or omission of the person (*NHS Act 1977,s.82; NHS (Scotland) Act 1978,s.74; SI 1972/1265 HPSS(NI)O Sched. 15*).

However, replacement of an appliance, which normally attracts an initial prescription charge, attracts a charge in case of replacement, unless the defect was present at the outset.

30.1.7. Health service patient in a private hospital or private nursing home. Circular guidance (England, Scotland, 1981) states that, where a health service patient is treated by the DHA/HB/HSSB in a private hospital or nursing home, he or she retains the same entitlements to equipment as if attending, as in-or outpatient, a health service hospital.

The Circular guidance states that the DHA/HB/HSSB must be sure that the facilities are appropriate for health service patients (*eg HC(81)1; NHS 1981(GEN)30*), and it is important that patients are not persuaded to pay for additional amenities which they do not need. At the same time there 'should be no disparity between the clinical care and services provided to NHS patients and the hospital or nursing home's own private patients' (*HC(81)1; NHS 1981(GEN)30*).

Other guidance (DH/WO, SHHD) states that the private hospital needs to be aware of health service procedures for the provision of, and charging for, appliances (*MHM 50 NWTRHA p. 21; MHM 50 SHHD p. 18*).

30.1.8. Private patient in a health service hospital. Legislation states that health service hospitals can provide accomodation and services (including equipment) for private patients (*NHS Act 1977 and NHS (Scotland) 1978 as amended by the Health and Medicines Act 1988; SI 1972/1265 HPSS(NI)O 1972 as amended by SI 1988/2249 (NI.24) Health and Medicines (Northern Ireland) Order 1988*).

Such provision can be made as long as services to health service patients do not significantly suffer as a result of this private provision.

30.1.8.1. Private inpatients

30.1.8.1.1. Equipment covered by fixed daily charge. Guidance (*DH/SHHD/ DHSS(NI)*) states that equipment (including implants) required during the course of treatment should be covered by the agreed fixed daily charge, and 'supplementary charges must not be made for implants, aids and appliances'.

This is so, 'even if an appliance has been fitted after discharge', provided it was prescribed when the person was a private inpatient, and was prescribed as part of the treatment for the medical condition which gave rise to admission (*Management of Private Practice in Health Service Hospitals in England and Wales. DHSS 1986 para 84; Management of Private Practice in Health Service Hospitals in Scotland. SHHD 1987 para 97; Management of Private Practice in Health Service Hospitals in Northern Ireland para 81*).

30.1.8.1.2. Undertaking to pay. Guidance (DH/SHHD/DHSS(NI)) states that, at the outset of treatment and residence, the patient has to give an undertaking to pay the estimated costs of the hospital accomodation and treatment.

The patient should also be warned that a higher charge will be made if the stay is longer than anticipated (*Management of Private Practice in Health Service Hospitals in England and Wales. DHSS 1986 para 51,54; Management of Private Practice in Health Service Hospitals in Scotland. SHHD 1987 para 66,67; Management of Private Practice in Health Service Hospitals in Northern Ireland para 49,53*).

30.1.8.2. Private outpatients

30.1.8.2.1. Whole cost of equipment. Guidelines (DH/SHHD/DHSS(NI)) state that private outpatients should be charged for appliances supplied to them. Charges should include the cost to the health service of the item, together with associated overheads, which include, for example, measuring, ordering, and fitting procedures. The patient should be made aware, at the outset, of the amount involved and give a written undertaking to pay.

Similar arrangements exist where the hospital makes its own appliances (*Management of Private Practice in Health Service Hospitals in England and Wales. DHSS 1986 para 84; Management of Private Practice in Health Service Hospitals in Scotland. SHHD 1987 para 97; Management of Private Practice in Health Service Hospitals in Northern Ireland. DHSS(NI) para 81*).

30.1.8.2.2. Examples. Guidance (DH/SHHD/DHSS(NI)) states that hearing aids are not included in such charges. Examples given, of chargeable items, include: surgical footwear, limb callipers, crutches, walking sticks, frames, spinal and abdominal supports, appliances for the head and neck and elastic hosiery

(*Management of Private Practice in Health Service Hospitals in England and Wales. DHSS 1986 para 84; Management of Private Practice in Health Service Hospitals in Scotland. SHHD 1987 para 97; Management of Private Practice in Health Service Hospitals in Northern Ireland. DHSS(NI), para 81*).

30.1.8.2.3. Referral to private contractor for supply. Guidance (DH/SHHD/ DHSS(NI)) states that private outpatients can be referred direct to a private contractor because of their personal preference for a contractor who does not attend the hospital; because the appliance is one the health service would not normally supply; or because the provision of the appliance would interfere with services to non-private patients at the hospital.

The private patient, in this case, meets the whole cost according to private arrangements made with the contractor (*Management of Private Practice in Health Service Hospitals in England and Wales. DHSS 1986 para 103-105; Management of Private Practice in Health Service Hospitals in Scotland. SHHD 1987 para 112-114; Management of Private Practice in Health Service Hospitals in Northern Ireland. DHSS(NI), para 100–102*).

30.1.8.3. Change of status from private to NHS patient. Guidance (DH/SHHD/ DHSS(NI)) states that it is possible for both private in-and outpatients to change their status from private to health service patient during treatment; this could be desirable if a more serious medical condition is identified, and, for example, an unforeseen need for expensive equipment arises.

A private outpatient can change from one visit to the next (not on the same visit); a private inpatient during the course of his or her stay in hospital (*Management of Private Practice in Health Service Hospitals in England and Wales. DHSS 1986 para 22-27; Management of Private Practice in Health Service Hospitals in Scotland. SHHD 1987 para 54-56; Management of Private Practice in Health Service Hospitals in Northern Ireland. DHSS(NI), para 22-27*).

30.1.9. Private patient in a private hospital. Private hospitals mostly carry out acute, elective surgery and generally do not take on people with rehabilitation needs involving protracted care and the provision of equipment.

30.1.9.1. Equipment supplied as part of treatment. Many patients treated in private hospitals ('commercial' or 'voluntary') are treated under various health insurance schemes. These tend not to cover the provision of equipment. There seems to be an absence of rules concerning such provision, but equipment routinely needed as a direct result of surgery might be supplied as part of the insurance 'package' (*Verbal communication: private hospital group, 1989*).

Stoma care equipment, for example, might be supplied during the hospital stay and on discharge. Subsequent to this the person is likely to return to the care of the GP and a NHS hospital-based stoma care nurse (*Verbal communication: private hospital, 1989*).

30.1.9.2. Equipment supplied with additional charges. However, a patient requiring, for example, special feeding aids (eg cutlery) during the inpatient recovery period might have to pay for this equipment (*Verbal communication private hospital, 1989*).

30.1.9.3. Equipment on deposit loan. Where an inpatient, on discharge, requires the loan of a walking aid, for example, for a determined recovery period, a deposit might be payable to the hospital (*Verbal communication: private hospital, 1989*).

30.1.9.4. Miscellaneous provision. It is possible, in cases of special need, where the patient cannot afford to buy the necessary equipment, that a voluntary body might help. Such voluntary aid, in a private (commercial) hospital setting, is an area of uncertainty though, and would depend very much on individual and local circumstances.

30.1.10 War pensioners treated in NHS hospital. Guidance (DH, informally applying to Northern Ireland, SHHD) states that war pensioners attending a health service hospital for treatment (including the supply of a medical or surgical appliance) for an 'accepted disablement' (see above) are eligible to receive priority treatment. However, should the treatment not be for the accepted disablement, then they will receive no preferential treatment (*eg MHM 50 NWTRHA p. 1, MHM 50 SHHD p. 17*).

It has sometimes proved necessary to remind hospitals of this provision. Thus Circular guidance (Scotland, 1973) states that priority treatment (for their accepted disablement) should be given to both war pensioner in-and outpatients (*SHM 20/1973*).

30.1.10.1. Priority treatment subject to other priority patients. However, such priority treatment is available subject to the needs of emergency and other urgent cases, which take precedence (*HB6 Booklet. DH, 1990*).

30.2. Social services/work charges

SSD/SWDs and HSSBs (under social services functions) have the power to make charges for services provided, including those involving equipment and home adaptations (*HASSASSA 1983 s.17; Social Work (Scotland) Act 1968 s.87 as amended by HASSASSA 1983 s.18; SI 1972/1265 HPSS(NI)O a.15,98, Sched.15*).

Legislation (England, Wales, Scotland) states that charges can be made to an extent which is considered reasonable. However, charges cannot be made if 'a person satisfies the authority providing the service that his means are insufficient for it to be reasonably practicable for him to pay for the service the amount he would otherwise be obliged to pay for it' (*HASSASSA 1983 s.17; Social Work (Scotland) Act s.87 as amended by HASSASSA Act 1983 s.18*).

30.3. Accepted disablement and war pensioners

30.3.1. Accepted disablement. Throughout the book various references are made to special arrangements which are made for war pensioners. These services are available when they are needed as a result of the condition for which the person receives a pension. The condition is known as the 'accepted disablement', which is war, or service, related.

30.3.2. Accepted disablement groups. In fact, the term 'war pensioners' covers a number of groups of pensioners with accepted disablements, other than 'mainstream' army, navy, air force ex-servicemen (*see eg SI 1983/883. Naval, Military and Air Forces etc (Disablement and Death) Service Pensions Order 1983*).

These groups include, for example, injured (1939-1946) civilians (*SI 1983/686 Personal Injuries (Civilians) Scheme 1983*), Polish forces (*SI 1964/2007 Pensions (Polish*

Forces) Scheme 1964), mercantile marine (*SI 1964/2058 War Pensions (Mercantile Marine) Scheme 1964*), naval auxiliary personnel (*SI 1964/1985 War Pensions (Naval Auxiliary Personnel) Scheme 1964*), Indian and Chinese seamen (*SR & O 1944/1083 War Pensions (Indian seamen, etc) Scheme 1944 and SR & O 1944/1186 War Pensions (Chinese seamen, etc) Scheme 1944*, coastguards (*SR & O 1944/500 War Pensions (coastguards) Scheme 1944*).

30.4. VAT exemption applies to the various types of equipment and adaptations. These are given in Box 30.2.

Box 30.2: Equipment exempt from VAT

Included are:
B30.2.1. Items prescribed by doctors and dentists, and dispensed by pharmacists (*VAT Act 1983 Schedule 5 Group 14*).

B30.2.2. Equipment supplied (or repaired or maintained) to a disabled person for domestic or personal use, or supplied to a charity which will make the equipment available to disabled people for the same purpose (also includes services, parts, accessories necessary for installation; and includes hiring and letting of such goods):
- medical or surgical appliances designed solely for the relief of a severe abnormality or severe injury;
- electrically or mechanically adjustable beds designed for invalids;
- commode chairs, commode stools, devices incorporating a bidet jet and warm air drier and frames or other devices for sitting over or rising from a sanitary appliance;
- chair lifts or stair lifts designed for use in connection with invalid wheelchairs;
- hoists and lifters for use by invalids;
- motor vehicles designed or substantially and permanently adapted for the carriage of a person in a wheelchair or on a stretcher and of no more than five other persons;
- equipment and appliances not included above, designed solely for use by a disabled person;
- parts and accessories designed solely for use in or with goods described above (*VAT Act 1983 Schedule 5 Group 14*).

Not included are:
- hearing aids (except hearing aids designed for the auditory training of deaf children), dentures, spectacles and contact lenses.

Included are:
- clothing, footwear, wigs;
- invalid wheelchairs and invalid carriages other than mechanically propelled vehicles intended or adapted for road use;
- renal haemodialysis units, oxygen concentrators, artificial respirators and other similar apparatus (*VAT Act 1983 Schedule 5 Group 14*).

B30.2.2.1. Definition of 'designed for people with disabilities'. The question as to whether an item is designed solely for use by a disabled person has been considered by the VAT Tribunal, and concerned forty hospital bed tables:
'We are of opinion, however, that the particular value of the table to the chronically disabled is by no means sufficient to enable us to infer that the table was solely designed for them, and an inspection of the table produced by the appellants confirms our view. We asked ourselves: does the appearance and method of operation of this table suggest to us, using the words with their ordinary and natural meaning, that it was designed 'solely for use' by a chronically disabled person? We can only say that the table struck us as eminently practicable and convenient for all sorts of hospital patients and was not designed with a particular class in mind' (*from British Value Added Tax Reporter, CCH Editions*).

B30.2.3. Adaptations. Supply to a disabled person of services of adapting goods (and supply, maintenance, repair of goods in connection with such adaptation) to suit his condition (or to a charity for the same purpose of provision, by sale or otherwise) (*VAT Act 1983 Schedule 5 Group 14*).

B30.2.4. Access. Supply to a disabled person (or to a charity) of a service of constructing ramps or widening doorways or passages for the purpose of facilitating his entry to or movement within his private residence.

This includes goods supplied in connection with such supply (*VAT Act 1983 Schedule 5 Group 14*).

B30.2.5. Supply to a disabled person of a service providing, extending or adapting a bathroom, washroom or lavatory in his private residence where such provision, extension or adaptation is necessary by reason of his condition (or such supply by a charity in a residential home).

This includes goods supplied in connection with such supply (*VAT Act 1983 Schedule 5 Group 14*).

B30.2.6. Hiring of a motor vehicle for a period of not less than three years to a disabled person in receipt of a mobility allowance or supplement where the lessor's business consists predominantly of the provision of such motor vehicles to disabled people (*VAT Act 1983 Schedule 5 Group 14*).

B30.2.7. Supply to a disabled person of services necessarily performed in the installation of a lift for the purpose of facilitating his movement between floors within his private residence (or such supply by a charity providing permanent or temporary residence or a day centre for disabled people).

This includes the supply, maintenance or repair of goods in connection with such installation (*VAT Act 1983 Schedule 5 Group 14*).

B30.2.8. Alarm system. Supply to a disabled person for domestic or personal use, or to a charity (providing for disabled people by sale or otherwise, equipment for such use), of an alarm system to be operated by the disabled peson, to enable him or her to alert directly a specified person or control centre.

This includes the supply of services, by a control centre, in connection with the receiving of, and response to, alarm calls (*VAT Act 1983 Schedule 5 Group 14*).

B30.2.9. Supply to charities (such as the RNIB) of equipment for people who are blind:
- magnetic tape specially adapted for the recording and reproduction of speech for the blind or severely disabled, and supply of various equipment in connection with such tape;
- wireless receiving sets (if being loaned free to blind people);
- apparatus solely for the making and reproduction of a sound recording on a magnetic tape permanently contained in a cassette (if being loaned free to blind people) (*VAT Act 1983 Schedule 5, Group 7*).

31 Product Liability

Introduction.

Since the coming into force of the Consumer Protection Act 1987 a great deal of concern over product liability in relation to equipment has existed.

31.1. The Consumer Protection Act 1987 places liability for 'damage ... caused wholly or partly by a defect in a product' on:
- the producer of the product;
- anyone who places his/her name or trade mark on the product thus holding him/herself out as the producer of the product;
- 'any person who has imported the product into a member State from a place outside the member States in order, in the course of any business of his, to supply it to another' (*Consumer Protection Act 1987 s. 2*).
- any supplier of the defective product who cannot identify, within 'a reasonable period', the person who supplied the product to him or her (*Consumer Protection Act 1987 s.2*).

31.2. Circular guidance

31.2.1. Identification of producer or supplier. Circular guidance (England, 1988) states that a health authority could become liable if a defective product causes injury or damage and the health authority cannot identify either the producer of the product or the authority's supplier (*HN(88)3*).

31.2.2. Record keeping. Circular guidance (England, 1988) states that records, containing the following type of detail should be kept:
- serial and batch number;
- date of issue of the product for patient use;
- proof that instructions/warnings, in relation to the use, maintenance, storage, expiry dates etc, have been followed (*HN(88)3*).

31.2.2.1. Limits to record keeping. Circular guidance (England, 1988) states that there is a practical limit to the amount of record keeping possible (*HN(88)3*).

Circular guidance (Scotland, 1988) goes a little further, stating that both health boards (HBs) and the Common Services Agency (CSA) 'should consider carefully, before instituting new procedures which are not otherwise required, whether the cost of keeping extra records is worthwhile in the light of the likelihood and size of a successful claim for damages' (*SHHD/DGM (1988)20*).

31.2.3. Health service as producer. The health service makes, as well as supplies, products, and Circular guidance (England, 1988) states that all products made should conform to any relevant standards; and that components used in the product should also be traceable to their original supplier. Records should be kept to ensure that the following of such procedures is demonstrable (*HN(88)3*).

31.2.4. Examples of professional advice given

31.2.4.1. Medical equipment. The Journal of the Medical Defence Union has stated in relation to product liability, for example: 'Many examples will spring to mind in hospital practice. There are occasions in general practice when equipment is used in treatment or loaned to patients. It is essential that such equipment is properly maintained and that records are kept to show that this has been done' (*Saunders MT. Product Liability. Journal of the Medical Defence Union Summer 1989 p. 38*).

31.2.4.2. Paramedical (physiotherapy) equipment. Professional advice has been given by the CSP in its journal on a number of different types of equipment (*Consumer Protection Act 1987. Implications for Physiotherapists. Physiotherapy 1988:74;4,175-176; Consumer Protection Act 1987 – Update. Physiotherapy 1988:74;530*). Examples of this advice are given in Box 31.1.

Box 31.1: Examples of advice given by physiotherapists, in relation to product liability

Example 1. Crutches and walking sticks should be checked for wear or stress and discarded if they appear unsafe. The manufacturer could deny liability if attempts have been made to mend such equipment. The items should be clearly (indelibly) labelled with the manufacturer's name, date of purchase and the department name (ie physiotherapy department) (*Consumer Protection Act 1987. Implications for Physiotherapists. Physiotherapy 1988:74;4,175-176; Consumer Protection Act 1987 – Update. Physiotherapy 1988:74;530*).

Example 2. Ferrules must be checked, but may fall into the category to which practical record-keeping limitations apply. For small items, a record of the batch number may be sufficient (*Consumer Protection Act 1987. Implications for Physiotherapists. Physiotherapy 1988:74;4,175-176*).

Example 3. Collars and corsets are often supplied at the request of a doctor; and, in such circumstances, the physiotherapist is acting as a supplier. Extra care should be taken to keep records of such transactions (*Consumer Protection Act 1987. Implications for Physiotherapists. Physiotherapy 1988:74;4,175-176*).

Example 4. Artificial limbs should not be tampered with; instead, the patient should be referred back to the limb centre (*Consumer Protection Act 1987. Implications for Physiotherapists. Physiotherapy 1988:74;4,175-176*).

Example 5. Custom-made equipment from, for example, hospital workshops or REMAP (29.3.) engineers must also be appropriately labelled. Equipment which has been adapted needs to be carefully checked to make sure that it is still safe, and adequate instructions need to be given to the user (*Consumer Protection Act 1987. Implications for Physiotherapists. Physiotherapy 1988:74;4,175-176*).

Example 6. Electrical equipment such as TENS machines, Flowtron or heat pads, for example, should be clearly labelled with the name of the manufacturer and the date of purchase. A record or register should also be kept, including the name of the manufacturer and the date of purchase. Equipment should be obtained from a reputable supplier, and physiotherapists should be aware which manufacturers are still producing, and which firms have been taken over (*Consumer Protection Act 1987. Implications for Physiotherapists. Physiotherapy 1988:74;4,175-176*).

Example 7. Equipment for use at home. Full instructions should be given to the user, especially when the equipment is for use at home (*Consumer Protection Act 1987. Implications for Physiotherapists. Physiotherapy 1988:74;4,175-176*)

Appendix 1

Central Assessment Criteria for Daily Living Equipment

A1.1. General guidance

Legislation contains reference to 'additional facilities for … greater safety, comfort and convenience' (*CSDPA 1970 s. 2(1)(e); CSDP(NI)A 1978 s.2(e)*). Circular guidance (Scotland, 1976) gives a list of examples of equipment meeting such criteria (2.1.2.).

A1.2. Specific central guidance

A1.2.1. Telephones. Legislation specifically mentions telephones and equipment to use the telephone. The Association of Municipal Corporations (now AMA) and County Councils Association (now ACC) (England/Wales) produced guidance in the early 1970s; there is similar Circular guidance for Scotland and Northern Ireland.

A1.2.1.1. England/Wales. AMA/ACC guidance lists the following criteria.
People who would qualify would firstly 'live alone, or are frequently left alone, or live with a person who are not in a position or cannot be relied on to be able either to deal with an emergency or to maintain necessary outside contacts'.

Secondly, they 'have a prima facie need to be able to get in touch with a doctor, ancillary medical worker or helper; and are in danger or at risk unless provided with a telephone'.

Thirdly, they 'are either unable to leave the house in normal weather without the help of another person or have seriously restricted mobility; and in the view of the authority need a telephone to avoid isolation'.

Of these three sets of criteria, the first and either the second or third 'should be satisfied in full and there should be no family friend and neighbours available, willing and able to help'.

A1.2.1.1.1. Discretion. The guidance points out that 'it is wholly open to authorities to adopt any criteria they wish' (*ACC/AMA Circular March 1971. Chronically Sick and Disabled Persons Act 1970: Provision of telephones as amended by ACC/AMA letter 20.4.72. Chronically Sick and Disabled Persons Act 1970: Provision of telephones*).

A1.2.1.2. Scotland. Circular guidance (Scotland, 1972) contains suggested minimum criteria, 'entitling the applicant to such assistance towards the provision or retention of a telephone as he may require. Either the medical or non-medical criteria should be satisfied in full, and in either case there should be no family, friends or neighbours generally available and willing and able to help'.

A1.2.1.2.1. Medical criteria are met when the person 'has a prima facie need to get in touch with his doctor quickly and is in danger if left alone unless provided with a telephone; and lives alone or, if not, is regularly and frequently left alone.

In the case of medical need it will occasionally be necessary for authorities to consider applications from husband and wife living together; in such cases regard should be had to the medical condition of both partners and the extent to which the less handicapped partner is able, without a telephone, to maintain contact with their doctor'.

A1.2.1.2.2. Non-medical criteria are met when the applicant 'lives alone; and is able to indicate at least one person willing to be in touch by telephone and, in the view of the authority, needs a telephone to avoid isolation; and is unable in normal weather to leave the house without the help of another person'.

A1.2.1.2.3. Discretion. 'The amount of assistance to be given in any particular case will depend on the circumstances of the applicant, and is entirely at the discretion of the local authority. In some cases a grant towards the installation charge may be needed, while in other cases it may be necessary to provide continuing assistance towards the rental of the telephone' (*SWSG SW7/1972 Telephones for Severely Disabled Persons Living Alone*).

A1.2.1.3. Northern Ireland Circular guidance (1978) widened the criteria, already being operated by HSSBs in relation to a scheme set up in 1973, for help with telephone.

A1.2.1.3.1. 'Help with the cost of installing and/or renting a telephone should be provided for people who meet the following minimum criteria:
i. live alone, or are frequently left alone, or live with a person or persons who are not in a position or cannot be relied on to be able to deal with an emergency or to maintain necessary outside contacts.
ii. Are in danger or at risk unless provided with a telephone to enable them to get in touch when necessary with a doctor, community nurse or social worker.
iii. In the view of the Board need a telephone to avoid isolation which would otherwise result either from seriously restricted mobility or from being unable to leave the house in normal weather without the help of another person.'

A1.2.1.3.2. Criteria i and either ii or iii should be satisfied in full and there should be no family friends or neighbours available, willing and able to help.

A1.2.1.3.3. Nearest telephone. In considering whether criteria ii or iii are satisfied, account should also be taken of the location and availability of the nearest telephone.

A1.2.1.3.4. Discretion. It is pointed out that the 'help given will continue to be at the discretion of the Board, taking the form of a grant towards the installation charge or assistance with the rental. No help can be given with the cost of calls' (*HSS(OS5A) 5/78. Telephones for the Handicapped and Elderly*).

A1.2.2. Television. Legislation mentions television in particular (*CSDPA 1970 s.2(1)(b); CDSDP(NI)A 1978 s.2(b) (2.2.1.2.)*).
    It appears that in England/Wales and Scotland, no specific government guidance has been issued on help with televisions.

A1.2.2.1. Northern Ireland Circular guidance (1979) states that:

- 'Boards are required to make arrangements to provide or to help in providing television for any person' (under the Chronically Sick and Disabled Persons (Northern Ireland) Act 178 'where they are satisfied that television is necessary to meet the needs of that person' (*HSS(PH)5/79 para 1*);
- the person has to be housebound and living alone or confined to a room within the household necessitating the provision of a television set in that room;

- help is not dependent upon the means of the applicant.
  The guidance states, in relation to the licence:
- 'where an applicant who is eligible for help under the scheme does not have a television the Board should provide and maintain a set and meet the cost of the licence fee';
- 'if an eligible applicant already owns or rents a set the Board should meet the cost of either a monochrome or colour licence when the fee becomes due for payment';
- in certain circumstances the licence fee may not be paid, ie where the television is provided to a person not living alone but who is 'confined to a room within the household necessitating the provision of a television set in that room'; (*HSS(PH)5/79*).
- 'colour television should not be provided unless the Board is unable to make satisfactory arrangements to obtain a monochrome set' (*HSS(PH)5/79 Help with Television*).

A1.2.3. Radio. Radio is mentioned specifically in legislation (*CSDPA 1970 s.2(1)(b); CSDP(NI)A 1978 s.2(b)*).

Circular guidance (Northern Ireland, 1976) states that HSSBs supplying batteries for people with radio sets issued by the British Wireless Fund for the Blind should do so free of charge. This was recommended in the interests of uniformity between the HSSBs, and because of the small cost involved (*DHSS HSS(OS5A)4/76*).

Appendix 2

Examples of Local Authority (SSD/SWD/HSSB) Assessment and Provision Criteria for Daily Living Equipment

A2.1. General guidelines

General criteria applying to the provision of all daily living equipment may be made by the SSD/SWD/HSSB.

Example 1. Criteria for equipment:
   'The applicant must be registered or registerable as Physically Handicapped. The applicant must require an aid to promote their functioning as an independent person and to enhance the quality of their lives, in the context of the family and community. It must be established that the aid is technically suitable for the client's condition' (*HSSB guidance, received 1989*).

Example 2. Information for professional staff: daily living equipment is available for any 'person with a disability who, with appropriate assistance, can be helped to achieve, increase or maintain independence at home' (*SWD guidelines received 1989*).

Example 3. Equipment and appliances can be supplied 'if handicap is permanent with little hope of improvement and if equipment is required to overcome disability to assist the client to help himself or the people or caring for him/her' (*London SSD guidelines received 1989*).
Example 4.

- purpose of providing equipment or adaptations is to increase or maintain functional independence of people with permanent and substantial disabilities. The level of provision will be dependent on the needs in relation to the client's disability and technical feasibility;
- where the SSD is solely involved in supporting those works that are essential to overcome the client's disability, there may be other work considered desirable by the client which would not be provided through Social Services. The client may need to obtain advice and alternative funding for such work;
- the planning of the equipment or adaptation should take into account the client's current and long term needs;
- consideration of the role and needs of the carer will be of equal importance in that:
   a. the provision will improve the quality of care given to clients; and
   b. it will alleviate physical demands experienced by the carer.
- age should not itself be a barrier for the provision of adaptations. Careful consideration of circumstances will be essential, eg it would be unrealistic and bad practice to embark on a major adaptation which the clients will not be able to use;
- ethnic and cultural aspects of the household must be considered. It may be necessary to consult with appropriate race advisers.
- in some circumstances, alternative housing, rather than adaptations, may be the only viable solution. Equipment or adaptations should not be considered to overcome social or economic problems. (*London SSD (45) guidelines 1989*).

Example 5. The main concern should be that all the activities which the patient has to perform can be done with absolute safety:

- ask patient to demonstrate how they attempt tasks which they say they cannot do;

- teach patient alternative methods not using gadgets, eg straining vegetables, wringing dishcloths etc;
- teach patient how to use appropriate aid for activity and if more than one aid available, see which is most suitable;
- allow patient to have aid on trial and if possible check in 2 weeks that they are using it properly;
- only supply aid permanently if it is really essential, and the patient will make proper use of it;
- payment for aids – whilst no patient should be denied a necessary aid, payment for the smaller, less expensive aids can be psychologically advantageous.

In summary, aids should be a last resort rather than be issued indiscriminately (*SWD (1) guidelines 1990*).

A2.2. Specific guidelines on assessment for particular equipment

A2.2.1. Telephones. SSD/SWD/HSSB guidelines often seem to follow the criteria issued centrally (A1). Some quote the central guidelines; others modify them. Various arrangements and tests of resources are used to determine financial assistance with telephone rentals.

Example 1. The client's life must be deemed to be critically at risk, and ready access to a telephone essential to call a doctor in an emergency. Assistance is limited to installation only; rental charges are the responsibility of the client (*Midlands SSD (3) 1990*).

Example 2 (exceptionally detailed guidelines). A distinction is made between chronically sick and disabled.

a) Chronically sick

- the applicant must live alone (excludes accommodation which has warden or alarm facilities or is adjacent to a family residence)

OR

- must be left alone for a substantial period of time (guidance would a half-time job, ie 6 hours per day, 3 days per week)
- must live with a person who, because of their physical disability or mental understanding, cannot be relied upon to deal with an emergency (would include a child aged under 11, a mentally handicapped person, an elderly mentally infirm person living with the person who is chronically sick

OR

- must because of his/her physical ability or mental understanding, be unable to be left by the carer during an emergency

AND

- must suffer from an illness which the general practitioner has certified would be a life threatening risk if, in an emergency, help could not be be summoned immediately;

b) People with disabilities

- must live alone (excludes accommodation which has warden or alarm facilities, or is adjacent to a family residence)

AND

- must have a limited neighbourhood or family support network (excludes people receiving three or more such support visits each week)

AND

- must be unable to leave the house in normal weather conditions (being unable to leave the house in icy conditions is insufficient)

AND

- must need a telephone to help carry out the normal functions of daily living (for instance to contact a chemist or the butcher). 'Life threatening risk' includes, for example, conditions such as severe asthma, epilepsy, severe neurological disease or spinal injury, severe heart failure or other cardiac conditions, stroke, diabetes (*Midlands SSD (23) 1989*).

Example 3. Options for SSD help (based on 'local discretion' within 'broad criteria') include:

- meet the rental charge
- pay for installation charge
- pay for both installation and rental
- part contribution to installation and rental
- pay for extension provision or installation charge
- get BT to install as a matter of priority even where the SSD is not actually financially aiding the client (*Southwest England SSD (26) 1989*).

A2.2.2. Telephone adaptations. 'Telephone adaptations such as adapted phones, handsets, extension bells, additional phone sets can be provided to users with disability'. They may be provided for 'severely handicapped users of any age group' or to the 'elderly or hard of hearing'.

Installation and possibly rental of the adaptation will be paid for by the SSD if it is already paying the installation and rental of the telephone itself. If this is not the case, then only the installation is paid. (British Telecom installs free an extension bell for elderly people with impaired hearing) (*London SSD guidelines received 1989*).

A2.2.3. Television
Example 1. 'The Borough supplies 20″ colour TVs with teletext remote control and colour TV licence. No charge is made for this service but it is subject to the applicant's income and savings, the financial criteria being linked to Income Support and disability allowance'.

In certain circumstances TV licences may be paid on clients' own TV sets.

'Applications will normally be accepted from those who are housebound and unable to participate regularly in recreational activities and entertainments outside the home . . .' (*London Borough public information booklet 1989*).
Example 2. Criteria for provision: there 'is no television set in the same household, or no reasonable access to a television in the same household . . . and the applicant cannot reasonably afford to pay the costs (and it is unreasonable to expect the other members of the household to do so) . . .' (*London SSD guidance received 1989*).

Example 3. Necessary criteria are:

- client is registered or listed by SSD as 'permanently and substantially handicapped'
- client lives alone
- client is permanently housebound
- client will benefit from television set.

If all these conditions are met, the SSD pays for both television and licence (or just licence, if there is already a television) (*London borough SSD (10)*).

Example 4. Assistance with television depends on the person being substantially or permanently handicapped, alone for most of the day, and able to benefit from a television. The first licence is paid by the SSD (at the black and white rate only): help and degree of help with subsequent licence fees depends on a test of resources (*London borough (18) 1990*).

Example 5. (applies also to radios). Client must be registered or registerable and must:

- live alone and be unable in normal weather to leave the house without the assistance of another person
- if living with others in a home where and/or television facilities are available be confined to a room in the house (eg bedfast) so that such facilities are not accessible
- live with others who do not have and are unable to provide these facilities, and be unable in normal weather to leave the house without the assistance of another person
- live with others, be unable in normal weather to leave the house without the assistance of another person, and be left alone for lengthy periods during the day
- television or radio facilities must be considered necessary to the needs of the individual to avoid the effect of isolation and loneliness (*Northeast England SSD (25) 1989*).

Example 6. TV licences

- must be permanent resident;
- must not be in receipt of TV licence under any other concessionary scheme;
- must not be in receipt of a bus pass under any of the current concessionary schemes. Clearly, anyone with a bus pass is able to leave the house, and the TV scheme is designed for housebound people;
- must not be a holder of a Disabled Persons' Parking Badge;
- must be over retirement age;
- must live alone, ie no other person permanently sharing the home;
- must be totally housebound, ie can only leave the home infrequently and then only with considerable assistance (*SWD (1) guidelines 1990*).

A2.2.4. Radios. (issue of radios to blind people is discussed elsewhere in this book (15.5.9.3.).

Example 1. Radios are often available free of charge. They may be available where the 'provision of a set is reasonably necessary to avoid the effects of isolation. Eg the client is housebound and unable to participate regularly in recreational

activities and entertainments outside the home' . . . and 'there is no radio set in the same household, or no reasonable access to a television in the same household . . .' (*London Borough's guidance*).
Example 2. See Example 5 above (A.2.3.).

A2.2.5. Seating. Special seating for use with wheelchairs is available through the local wheelchair service (6.4.4.4.). Other seating, however, is supplied, variably by the SSD/SWD/HSSB.
Example 1. Chairs:

- if existing chair gives correct support, but is merely too low, chair raising sleeves/carpentry work should be carried out;
- if the existing chair does not give required support and cannot be made suitable by raising the height and the client may be eligible for help from Social Services;
- specialised chairs for severely handicapped clients may be supplied by Social Services;
- sometimes special funding is sought for unusual/very expensive chairs from charities (*London SSD (24) guidance received 1989*).

Example 2. High chairs. 'A high chair should only be supplied when every effort has been made to raise or otherwise adapt the client's existing chair. Chairs should only be supplied when it is harmful, painful or very difficult for the client to rise to the standing position' (*Scottish SWD guidance received 1989*).
Example 3. Chairs should not be supplied simply to provide furniture. Alteration to existing chairs should be the first consideration. A chair should only be supplied if the client is at risk without it:

- self-lift chairs are only recommended if high seat chairs are not suitable because of stress on joints. Electric self-lift chairs can be considered if the client is totally unable to initiate the rising movement;
- recliner chairs are issued exceptionally if the client needs to alter position frequently;
- chair raising platforms, but not raising blocks, should be considered if the client's existing chair is suitable in every respect but height;
- pressure relief cushions are not normally issued by the SSD: they are supplied mainly by the Wheelchair Service in conjunction with a person's wheelchair.

Ideally, assessment should take place at a DLC, a stock chair supplied if possible, or, if necessary, a special order placed (*SSD guidelines received 1989*).
Example 4. High seat chairs should be assessed for, if possible, only by OTs. The client or carer must be at severe risk (eg heart condition, severe muscular weakness) or the client has severe postural problems and normal seating would be counter-productive or dangerous (*North of England SSD (15) 1990*).
Example 5. Chairs are only issued if an existing chair cannot be raised (*South of England SSD (16) 1990*).
Example 6. A riser recliner armchair is only issued if it helps a person retain independence, and other types of chair have been considered and found unsuitable (*Midlands SSD (3) 1990*).
Example 7. Special chairs are only supplied if provision significiantly reduces the risk of institutional care (*Midlands SSD (23) 1989*).
Example 8. Reclining chairs are not provided (*Northern Ireland questionnaire 1988*).

Example 9. Reclining chairs are supplied for short-term use and for people who are terminally ill (*Northern Ireland questionnaire 1988*).

Example 10. Geriatric chairs and electric self-rise chairs

- in general not supplied, except for geriatric chairs in stock which have been gifted, or exceptionally (*SWD questionnaire 1988*).

Example 11. Chair raisers

- user has difficulty or is unable to transfer on/off existing chair safely;
- provision of this equipment would ensure greater independence in transfers (*London SSD (45) guidelines 1989*).

Example 12. High chair

- conditions as in Example 10, above, met;
- chair raisers have been tried/considered but are unsuitable due to either the type of chair or the client's needs;
- the client's existing chair is unsuitable due to the client's postural needs (*London SSD (45) guidelines 1989*).

Example 13. Footrests
- client's medical condition will be aggravated by not having legs raised: eg swelling of legs (*London SSD (45) guidelines 1989*).

Example 14. Electric recliner chairs

- the conditions for provision of footrests and high chairs are met;
- the client uses the chair to sleep in, rather than going to bed (*London SSD (45) guidelines 1989*).

A2.2.6. Footstools
Example 1. A SWD's guidance states that footstools are 'not normally supplied by the Department as they are usually required for health reasons such as oedamatous legs'.
Example 2. Medical consent must be sought before supplying leg rests.

A2.2.7. Toilet aids
Example 1. Raised toilet seat

- user is unable to transfer safely on/off the toilet, even with the help of a grab rail (*London SSD (45) guidelines 1989*).

Example 2. Toilet frame:technical staff state that it is not possible to fit a grab rail to the wall due to the construction of the property;

- there is no wall adjacent to the toilet;
- the user has a weakness/paralysis affecting the side of the body adjacent to the wall (*London SSD (45) guidelines 1989*).

A2.2.8. Commodes
Example 1

- user is unable to reach their usual toilet facilities and an adaptation to the property is not considered feasible.

A2.2.9. Chemical toilets

Example 1. A London borough's guidance states that the SSD can supply chemical toilets to: 'Clients who are not able to reach a toilet at any time. Clients living alone or who are frequently left alone for long periods. Clients unable to empty a commode due to a degree of disability or that of elderly/disabled relatives with whom they are living'.

Example 2. The first bottle of fluid is supplied with the commode. Thereafter the client is expected to purchase the fluid from eg camping shops (*Midlands SSD (1), received 2.90*).

Example 3. Chemical commodes are only issued if the client has no access to a WC night and day because of disability, and the client lives alone and there is nobody to empty an ordinary commode or the carer is so incapacitated as to be unable to empty a commode (*London borough SSD (17) 1990*).

Example 4. Chemical commodes/toilets are only provided if the existing WC is inaccessible; if nobody can empty a commode on a daily basis; if there is a named person to take responsibility for cleaning and maintenance; the client will supply the chemical fluid.

Example 5.

- user is unable to reach their usual toilet facilities and an adaptation to the property is not considered feasible;
- user is living alone and dependent upon Home Care Service/District Nurse/ relative to empty the bucket. (*London SSD (45) guidelines 1989*).

A2.2.10. Bathroom equipment

Example 1. Bath mats cannot be supplied alone since they are a normal household item. They can be issued as part of a set (eg including rail, board, seat).

Bath aids are contra-indicated in the case of people who have had a hip replacement (*Midlands SSD, received 1990*).

Example 2. Bath aids can be provided if there is a permanent medical need to use a bath or shower (eg colostomy, skin conditions) or where there the client is at risk in using a bath or shower. Bath mats are not supplied as a single item.

Example 3. Mangar bath lifts can only be issued for independence purposes where there are:

- permanent medical needs: (eg psoriasis, severe arthritis, incontinence, skin care, heart conditions, cystic fibrosis);
- social needs: (longterm independence/privacy for a younger disabled person, to avoid necessity of supervision and lifting);
- temporary needs: (terminally ill clients);
- elderly: assessment can only take place after all other solutions have been tried, and where independence will result and/or eliminate the need for a paid carer, or the carer's health is at risk).

Example 4. Mangar bath aids can only be supplied where a significant increase in independence can be achieved and where the criterion for supply will be disability rather than age (*Midlands SSD (23) 1989*).

Example 5. Autolifts and Mangar bath aids

- removal of the bathroom/WC wall can be considered for space for an autolift
- Autolift is first choice if there is a carer to assist
- if an Autolift is not possible, but a medical condition precludes a shower, medical support for Mangar is necessary
- Manger can be considered for a young handicapped person (ie 12 or over) wanting privacy and independence where shower is inappropriate, and the person cannot wind an Autolift
- Mangar is particularly useful for temporary use in terminal cases or to allow bathing to continue while alterations are being processed
- Mangar or autolift not supplied for use by district nurse
- before the ordering of an Autolift, the client must try one in a day centre or in the home of another client
- Mangar bath lifts are only considered as a last resort when bath aids, Autolift an showers are unsuitable (*Northeast England SSD (25) 1989*).

Example 6. Bath aids and rails.
Never order bath aids before checking that they fit the bath and demonstrating them to the client (*Northeast England SSD (25) 1989*).

Example 7. Specialised bathing equipment

- Portable (eg dipper seat, mangar, messerlie):
  - other simpler pieces of equipment have been considered/tried first, eg bath board and seat, but found to be unsuitable due to the degree of the user's functional loss;
  - the carer is unable to lift the equipment in/out of the bath.
- Fixed (eg autolift).
  - conditions (above) for portable equipment are met;
  - the floor is of suitable structure to have equipment fixed to it;
  - there is suitable space available (*London SSD (45) guidelines 1989*).

Example 8. Bath board and seat

- user is unable to transfer safely into the bath, either with a bath rail or with the carer's help;
- provision will enable the client to become independent in bathing;
- a padded bath board (rather than a wooden type) will only be issued to those with sensory deficit in lower limbs (*London SSD (45) guidelines 1989*).

Example 9. Shower chairs

- SSD has adapted the user's bathroom to provide showering facilities (*London SSD (45) guidelines 1989*).

Example 10. Shower attachment/long handled sponge

- user is unable to reach their feet or back using normal washing methods;
- non-fixed shower attachments are not thermostatically controlled – so are not issued to anyone with sensation loss or appearing to be confused (*London SSD (45) guidelines 1989*).

A2.2.11. Beds
Example 1. The SSD does not normally provide beds, but might occasionally isssue a special bed to enable a client to remain independent (*Midlands SSD (1), received 2.90*).

Example 2. Beds to increase independence

- eg a specifically designed bed, usually electric, which helps stand the client or sit the client without any effort being made by the client;
- all other lifting equipment has been tried/considered, but is not suitable due to the degree of the user's functional loss;
- the provision of such equipment would enable the client to remain in their own home, even with assistance of carer or other agency (*London SSD (45) guidelines 1989*).

A2.2.12. Adjustable bed tables

Example 1. Normally only supplied for people who are terminally ill or bedbound; or for people with very severe disability who cannot use a suitable alternative as a table (*Midlands SSD (1) rec. 2.90*).

Example 2. Cantilever tables are only provided if the client is bedbound or chairbound or if the client is unable to sit at the table for meals (*Southwest England SSD (20) 1990*).

Example 3. Cantilever tables are only for therapeutic use eg feeding or writing practice, but not for the client's or carer's convenience.

Example 4. Over bed/chair table.

- user is bed/chairbound and unable to to eat from a dining table, or balance a tray on their lap (*London SSD (45) guidelines 1989*).

A2.2.13. Bed raisers

Example 1. Bed raisers can only be supplied to raise the height of the whole bed (as opposed to one end only) (*South of England SSD (16) 1990*).

Example 2. Blocks or tubes fitted to the castors or legs of the bed.

- client has considerable difficulty transferring safely on and off the bed, even with the assistance of a carer;
- client is a wheelchair user and the height of the wheelchair differs from the height of the bed, thus making tranfer more difficult; (*London SSD (45) guidelines 1989*).

A2.2.14. Bed equipment

Example 1. Cot sides are supplied by the SSD when used as a restraint for people with learning difficulties; and by the DHA for other needs (*North of England SSD (15) 1990*).

Example 2. Beds are supplied by the SSD as an aid to independence; and by the DHA when there is a nursing or care need in connection with a district nurse (*North of England SSD (15) 1990*).

Example 3. Cot sides

- for a hospital bed they are health service responsibility;
- the Department may provide them for a standard bed (*SWD (1) guidelines 1990*).

Example 4. Fracture boards

- bed raisers have been fitted but there is still a problem;
- the client has a particular medical condition in which a firmer bed is required.

Example 5. Cot sides

- the client has a weakness of the body which inhibits the normal turning process;
- the client has a tendency to wander during the night thus putting self or carer at risk (*London SSD (45) guidelines 1989*).

Example 6. Rope ladders

- client is unable to pull himself into a sitting position from a lying position due to weakness of the trunk.

Example 7. Monkey pole

- client is unable to pull himself into a sitting position from a lying position;
- client has weakness/paralysis in one arm (*London SSD (45) guidelines 1989*).

A2.2.15. Hoists

Example 1. Hoists are only issued if the main user is the client or carer (as opposed to the district nurse) (*London borough SSD (17) 1990*).

Example 2. Hoists (manual, electric, free-standing, fixed) and electric beds can be supplied to clients by the SSD if they encourage independence or if the predominant user will be the carer rather than the district nurse (*London borough SSD (10) 1990*).

Example 3. Mobile hoists

- client is confined to a wheelchair or bed and has severely limited function in arms and legs, making transfers a problem;
- provision will increase the client's independence in transfers;
- provision will support the carer by reducing physical exertion of transferring client (*London SSD (45) guidelines 1989*).

Example 4. Fixed overhead hoists

- conditions for mobile hoists (in example 3 above) are met;
- mobile hoists, monkey poles and other similar lifting equipment have been considered/tried and are inappropriate due to the degree of the client's functional loss, the capacity of the carer, or the lack of space in the home;
- provision is dependent on structural feasibility; (*London SSD (45) guidelines 1989*).

Example 5. Slings

- normally mesh slings are used;
- clients who are susceptible to sores or who have sensation loss will be eligible for a sheepskin lined sling;
- those who sit on the sling during the day or lie on it at night will also be eligible for a sheepskin lined sling;
- a maximum of two slings will be issued to each client using the hoist (*London SSD (45) guidelines 1989*).

A2.2.16. Wheelchairs. SSD/SWDs may have a small pool of wheelchairs for temporary loan, though this would be the exception rather than the rule. A

Scottish SWD notes for instance: 'Provision and maintenance of wheelchairs are not the responsibility of the Department'(*SWD guidance received 1989/1990*).

In Northern Ireland, HSSB wheelchairs on temporary loan would normally be the responsibility of the community nursing department (rather than the social services side of the Board).

For a full discussion, see Chapter 6.

A2.2.17. Walking aids

Example 1. Wooden walking sticks are no longer issued because they are not adjustable.

Example 2. Walking sticks: only aluminium adjustable walking sticks can be issued (*Midlands SSD (23) 1990*).

Example 3. Rollators are only issued if no other standard walking frame is suitable and if outdoor mobility will be significantly increased by the rollator (*Southwest England SSD (20) 1990*).

A2.2.18. Dressing and grooming equipment

Example 1. Includes sock/tights aid, long-handled shoehorn, dressing stick, long handled brush/comb etc.

- user is unable or has great difficulty coping with a particular aspect of the dressing or grooming procedure;
- provision of equipment would greatly reduce the need for carer/district nurse/care attendant to assist with dressing (*London SSD (45) guidelines 1989*).

A2.2.19. Leisure equipment: Leisure equipment is usually not provided by the SSD/SWD/HSSB. Local guidelines sometimes state that such equipment is low priority and is unlikely to be provided.

Example 1. A SWD's guidance states: 'The Department would give advice on leisure aids eg gardening tools but would not normally supply them. These may be kept in stock for loan on trial. The Department would adapt tools or other leisure equipment where possible.'

Example 2. Low priority equipment includes items which improve the quality of life but are not essential, eg long handled gardening equipment, some items for people with hearing or visual impairment, sporting, hobbies and recreational items (*Southwest England SSD (13) 1990*).

Example 3. Subject to availability within stock, remedial toys, gardening and leisure equipment is available on loan (*London SSD (24) 1989*).

Example 4. Knitting and sewing aids are available. Gardening and other leisure equipment is available depending on individual circumstances (*Northern Ireland questionnaire 1988*).

Example 5.

- give advice on leisure aids, eg gardening tools but encourage clients to purchase their own equipment. The facility to lend equipment still remains;
- would adapt tools and other aids to leisure. (*SWD (1) guidelines 1990*).

A2.2.20. Reading and writing aids

Example 1. Such equipment 'eg magnifying glasses, book rests, are the responsibility of the Department only where they are needed because of the

client's primary disability rather than poor eyesight.' (*SWD guidelines received 1989*).
Example 2. The LEA is responsible for the provision of reading and writing aids (*London SSD (18) 1990*).

A2.2.21. Eating and drinking equipment
Example 1.

- user has specific difficulty using generally available cutlery or crockery due to specific aspects of their disability;
- provision will significantly increase the user's independence in eating/drinking (*London SSD (45) guidelines 1989*).

Example 2. Special drink maker: 'hot shot'

- user is chairbound and therefore unable to get to the kitchen unaided.

A2.2.22. Cooking equipment
Example 1. Includes tin openers, non-slip matting, adapted knives, bottle openers, tap turners etc.

- user is the person carrying out the main role of cook in the household;
- provision of equipment would significantly reduce the need for other services;
- own methods of using utensils have been considered/tried, but are unsuccessful due to the user's degree of functional loss;
- simplest piece of equipment is tried as first option. Eg for a person with loss of one hand, a one-handed tin opener is tried before considering an electric tin opener;
- specific piece of equipment chosen (eg there are at least 6 different jar openers available) should be the joint decision of the assessor and the user (*London SSD (45) guidelines 1989*).

A2.2.23. Kitchen equipment
Example 1. Perching stools are only issued if a client makes regular use of the kitchen facilities, has a low standing tolerance and no other suitable stool (*South of England SSD (16) 1990*).
Example 2. Trolleys should not be issued as walking aids, nor if the kitchen can be used for eating purposes. The client must be capable of using the kitchen facilities on a regular basis (*South of England SSD (16) guidance received 1990*).
Example 3. Trolleys should be issued after careful assessment and to promote independence by enabling the tranportation of food or other commodities. Trolleys should never be used as an alternative to a walking frame because they are not safe (*London borough SSD (17) guidance received 1990*).
Example 4. Trolleys are only provided if the kitchen is unsuitable for eating in due to limited space, poor layout or inadequate heating – and the client is regularly able to prepare a full meal using the kitchen facilities (*Southwest England SSD (20) guidance received 1990*).
Example 5. Kitchen chairs and stools are only issued if the client needs to make regular, full use of the kitchen; if the client has low standing tolerance; if there is no other suitable chair or stoool (*Southwest England SSD (20) guidance received 1990*).

Example 6. Small unadapted kitchen aids will not be supplied if they can be purchased locally (*Midlands SSD (23) guidance received 1989*).
Example 7. Trolleys.

- user is dependent on the use of walking equipment, and is therefore unable to carry food or drink from the kitchen to the eating area (*London SSD (45) guidelines received 1989*).

A2.2.24. Household equipment
Example 1. Cookers, washing machines are normal household items and would only exceptionally be provided (*Midlands SSD (3) guidance received 1990*).
Example 2. Cookers, washing machines. Cookers cannot be provided by the SSD as they are a normal household item. They may sometimes be included within a grant (housing authority) for kitchen alterations.

Washing machines can exceptionally be provided together with the cost of the plumbing (*SSD guidelines received 1989*).
Example 3. Split-level cookers are not provided.
Example 4. Split-level cookers are not provided, but are sometimes included within a discretionary grant for kitchen adaptation (*SWD OT questionnaire 1988*).

A2.2.25. Fireguards/Cooker guards
A SWD's guidance states: 'The Department would supply a fireguard/cooker guard to an adult where safety is an issue, eg epilepsy, ataxia . . . only supply . . . for a child beyond the age when these would be essential for all children'.
Example 2. Fireguards. Would give advice but not normally supply (*SWD (1) guidelines 1990*).

A2.2.26. Shopping aids
Example 1. Shopping trolleys can only be provided if the client is living alone or with others who are unable to assist; is unable to manage any shopping at present; can use the trolley safely on their own (*Southwest England SSD (20)*).

A2.2.27. Cars
Example 1. Adaptations to cars such as hoists are not normally considered: the client is expected to meet such expenditure from Mobility Allowance (*Midlands SSD (3) 1990*).
Example 2. Car seat harnesses can supplied for use at home only if a person has seating problems (*Northern Ireland questionnaire 1988*).
Example 3. Car seats and harnesses.

- provision of these for a disabled child would be a departmental responsibility as long as they would not normally be necessary for a child of that age or when a special seat or harness is required;
- a special harness for a severely handicapped adult may be provided if a standard seat belt is inadequate (SWD (1) guidelines 1990).

Example 4. Adaptations to cars. These are not funded (SWD (1) guidelines 1990).

A2.2.28. Unusual equipment.
Requests for unusual equipment should not automatically be given a negative response as in the past . . . (*Northeast England SSD (25) 1989*).

Appendix 3

Examples of local authority (SSD/SWD/HSSB) assessment criteria for home adaptations

A3.1. General guidelines
Example 1
Independence. The 'purpose of providing adaptations is to increase or maintain functional independence of people with permanent and substantial disabilities. The level of provision will be dependent on the needs in relation to the client's disability and technical feasibility' (*Occupational therapists' criteria for the provision of adaptations in the homes of people with disabilities. London Boroughs Occupational Therapy Managers Group. 1988*).

Future needs. 'The planning of the adaptation should take into account the client's current and long term needs' (*Occupational therapists' criteria for the provision of adaptations in the homes of people with disabilities. London Boroughs Occupational Therapy Managers Group. 1988*).

Carer consideration. 'Consideration of the role and needs of the carer will be of equal importance in that: a) the provision will improve the quality of care given to the client, and b) it will alleviate the physical demands experienced by the carer' (*Occupational therapists' criteria for the provision of adaptations in the homes of people with disabilities. London Boroughs Occupational Therapy Managers Group. 1988*).

Age and prognosis. 'Age and/or prognosis should not be itself be a barrier to the provision of adaptations. Careful consideration of the circumstances will be essential, eg it would be unrealistic and bad practice to embark on a major adaptation which the client will not be able to use' (*Occupational therapists' criteria for the provision of adaptations in the homes of people with disabilities. London Boroughs Occupational Therapy Managers Group. 1988*).

Ethnic origin and culture. 'Equal opportunities: ethnic and cultural aspects of the household must be considered. It may be necessary to consult with appropriate race advisers' (*Occupational therapists' criteria for the provision of adaptations in the homes of people with disabilities. London Boroughs Occupational Therapy Managers Group. 1988*).

Example 2. Medical condition but no functional deficit. OTs can assess for functional disability: medical advice should be sought if there is a medical condition with no apparent functional disability (*London SSD guidelines received 1989/1990*).

Example 3. Level of provision. Facilities provided will be the minimum required to meet the needs of the disabled person (*Midlands SSD (3) guidelines 1990*).

Example 4. Future use. The adaptations should provide at least 5 years use, and be the most economical solution (*London SSD guidelines (24) 1989*).

Example 5. An adaptation should be a longterm solution to a problem. The client must be eligible for registration as a person with a disability. Assessment must take into account:

- diagnosis, prognosis and long term implications of diagnosis;
- family-size, acceptance of disability;
- property – structural limitations;
- client's ability to carry out activities should be assessed by means of a functional assessment whenever possible;
- confirmation of the client's diagnosis and prognosis should be sought via GP or consultant together with their opinion as to the need for the work;
- a standard assessment form should be completed by the OT and a copy to the client (*SSD guidelines received 1990*).

A3.2. Specific guidelines

A3.2.1. Intercom and door unlock systems
Example 1. Provision can be made if: 'client is bedbound or has severely restricted mobility and is unable to reach the front door; client is living above or below the ground floor and there is no lift access' (*Occupational therapists' criteria for the provision of adaptations in the homes of people with disabilities. London Boroughs Occupational Therapy Managers Group. 1988*).

Example 2. Door entry systems are not installed purely as a means of extra security (*Midlands SSD (1) guidelines received 1990*).

Example 3. The user should be physically and mentally able to use the equipment. If not, they may be more vulnerable than with an ordinary lock.

The user should be housebound and unable to reach an outside door because of their disability. This would include people who are chairbound, who have assistance getting up/going to bed, and those who live on the 1st or 2nd floor and who cannot manage stairs.

The user should be either living alone or be left alone for long periods and receiving regular visitors, or be living with someone who is equally unable to answer the door.

For people who are hard of hearing, it is possible to amplify the speech slightly, and to install a louder bell elsewhere in the house, but this is not a suitable provision for people with severe learning difficulties (*London SSD (24) guidelines received 1989*).

Example 4. The client is chair or bed, bound, or has severely restricted mobility and is unable to reach the front door. The client is living alone and dependent on services coming in, eg home help, meals on wheels, district nursing etc. The client is at risk (*London SSD (45) guidelines received 1989*).

Example 5. Can be recommended when the client has severely restricted mobility, severe pain, is bed-bound and unable to reach the front door in an acceptable time. If the client can reach the door, slowly but surely, an intercom only is supplied to inform the caller.

A3.2.2. Alarm systems.
Community alarm systems may be telephone or radio-operated, alerting mobile wardens, for example, or a central computer which identifies friends, relatives who can respond immediately.

Example 1. Criteria for provision of a 'Lifeline' alarm system are as follows:

- meet criteria for telephone provision;
- elderly or elderly disabled (persons of pensionable age);
- living alone, or frequently left alone for significant periods, or sharing a home exclusively with other elderly people who have severe medical or mobility problems as defined below (at 5.);
- registered or eligible for registration as physically handicapped;
- at risk due to severe physical or medical condition the effects of which would mean that they would be unable to reach or use an ordinary telephone in an emergency;
- willing to have an emergency communication system;
- able to understand the purpose of the system and be physically capable of using it (*HSSB guidelines received 1989*).

Example 2. The department will consider the provision of an alarm system if the client does not qualify for help in the form of a DSS community care grant.

SSD criteria are similar to those listed in Example 1 above. (*South of England* SSD, *(16) guidelines received 1990*).

Example 3. Criteria are:

- the client must live on their own or be on their own most of the day;
- be at risk of falling because of frailty, age or disability – or for any other reason need help in an emergency and be unable to use a phone;
- have 2 relatives/friends/neighbours living close who are prepared to respond day and night to an emergency;
- have a telephone or be in a position to obtain one;
- be mentally alert and physically capable of pressing the button on the transmitter, in an emergency. The system is not suitable for a confused person (*Midlands SSD (3) guidelines received 1990*).

A3.2.3. Ramps and rails

Example 1. Ramps. Criteria for non-self propelling wheelchair users: 'Where the client is able to walk short distances and negotiate steps with the assistance of a helper, a ramp may not necessarily be provided. However, frequency of use will be taken into account.

Criteria for self-propelling wheelchair users: 'Where the client is a fulltime wheelchair user and it is feasible, provision will be made' (*Occupational therapists' criteria for the provision of adaptations in the homes of people with disabilities. London Boroughs Occupational Therapy Managers Group. 1988*).

Example 2. For self-propelling wheelchair users, only one ramp access will normally be constructed. For non-self propelling wheelchair users, where the client can walk a few steps and receive carer assistance, ramps may not be provided.

Location, structure, gradient, surface, kerbing, permission of other shared access users must all be considered (*South of England SSD (16) guidelines received 1990*).

Example 3. Ramps and rails

- on door steps are only considered unless there are exceptional circumstances (eg essential access to back garden).

Ramps are not installed if the client is able to walk up and down the steps (*Northeast England (25) guidelines received 1989*).

Example 4. Temporary and permanent ramps

- temporary wooden ramp may be provided when the use is for temporary measures only, or if there are technical problems which prohibit installation of a concrete ramp;
- permanent ramps may be provided if the person is dependent on the use of a wheelchair for outdoor mobility, and is likely to use the ramp for a long period of time. Also if the property is generally considered to be suitable for wheelchair use;
- in some circumstances ramp provision may be contra-indicated, depending on the nature of the physical disability;

- particular care must be taken concerning structure and location of the ramp to ensure its safe use, not only by the person with the disability but also by other members of the public (*London SSD (45) guidelines received 1989*).

Example 5. Ramps and rails

- rails and/or a ramp would only be considered for back and front entrances if there was no reasonable access from the front to the back and the client needed to get out at the back, eg to hang out washing;
- ramped access could normally be provided to the house if a person would qualify for a wheelchair from the Health Services;
- there would be reluctance to pay for the removal of a concrete ramp; preferably the house should be allocated to a disabled tenant (*SWD (1) guidelines rec. 1990*).

A3.2.4. Heating
Example 1. Northern Ireland. HSSBs often recommend a change of heating with various possible options, rather than central heating specifically. It is the NIHE which makes the final decision on installation of central heating specifically, as opposed to some other form of suitable heating. The criteria it employs are generally mobility criteria. Specific medical and paramedical advice is of course followed.

Sometimes the NIHE improves its own stock anyway by the installation of central heating (*Verbal communication: NIHE, 1988*).
Example 2. Full central heating systems must be recommended firmly by a doctor. Part central heating is only considered if it is for an extension to the property which has been recommended by an OT.

Otherwise, alternative heating units might be considered (*SSD guidelines received 1989*).
Example 3. Heating can only be recommended in rooms used by the client. The client must have:

- physical inability to cope with present system (eg coal carrying);
- a specific medical condition which affects body temperature;
- have a severe medical condition which can be made worse by uneven room temperatures;
- conditions which may create danger for the client or other people even after the provision of safety equipment by the family (eg severe learning difficulty, sensory impairment, hyper-activity).

Example 4. Applications for the provision of heating are only considered if the client cannot cope with the existing system due to functional impairment as a result of disability. Requests based on the grounds of minimum temperature need due to disability or medical condition must be referred to the Community Physician (*Midlands SSD (3) guidance received 1990*).
Example 5. Central heating: there must be strong medical grounds supporting an application (*London SSD (24) guidance received 1989*).
Example 6. Change in the type of heating or appliance is possible if:

- the client lives alone or is left alone all day and is so handicapped as to be unable to deal with the present form of heating (usually solid fuel type) and there are no neighbours or voluntary helpers available;

- it is impossible to alter the controls (usually the gas fire) to make them accessible;
- if the change in the type of heating would lead to significant savings for the SSD eg avoiding the need of a daily home help firelighting service;
- in exceptional circumstances the consultant confirms the need is essential for medical reasons (usually clients suffering from chest conditions) (*Northeast England SSD (25) guidelines received 1989*).

Example 7. Additional heating

- the client must have a medical condition that requires a constant room temperature;
- additional heating should only be considered for the room used by the client;
- the client is at risk operating heating facilities;
- unable to operate existing heating facilities and has no one capable of operating the facilities for them (*Midlands SSD (23) guidelines received 1989*).

Example 8. Fires and central heating. The department:

- will not provide alternative direct heating sources;
- would provide adapted handles for gas fires;
- would not replace gas fires where the controls are inaccessible;
- would not move gas or electric meters unless all alternatives have been investigated;
- would not replace a coal fire where it cannot be managed by a client. There are alternatives such as electric fires;
- it is not the responsibility of the department to install central heating;
- repositioning central heating controls would be done in exceptional cases, but not in new-built or newly modernised houses (*SWD (1) guidelines received 1990*).

A3.2.5. Home lifts and stair lifts

Example 1. Criteria for the provision of a stair or home lift are:
1. the disabled person should have a substantial handicap which is of a permanent or lasting nature and which inhibits to such an extent that it is virtually impossible for him to negotiate stairs or travel a reasonable distance to a bathroom or other needed facility unaided;
2. the age and prognosis of the disabled person should be such that special adaptation of the house and/or installation of a stair vertical lift would be of distinct benefit for the foreseeable future;
3. other alternatives have been explored and rejected with reasons stated, eg a. rearranging of existing rooms in dwelling b. alternative adaptations c. rehousing (*HSSB guidelines received 1989*).

Example 2. Stairlifts are not supplied to people with poor balance, degenerative conditions, uncontrollable epilepsy, vertigo, reduced mental capacity (*SSD Midlands (1) guidelines received 1989/1990*).

Example 3. Stairlift contra-indications include fast deteriorating conditions, progressive conditions which may affect transfer; poor sitting/standing balance; severe epilepsy; confusion or spatial orientation problems; anxiety unresolved after trial use (*South of England SSD (16) guidelines received 1990*).

Example 4. Through floor lifts can be provided where:

- a stairlift is not suitable;
- the carer needs to accompany the client;
- or where there is an essential need for access to more than two floors (*South of England SSD (16) guidelines received 1990*).

Example 5. Short-rise/step lifts. Internal: where there is insufficient space to safely install a ramp. External: where there is insufficient space to provide a permanent ramp at the main access to the property (*South of England SSD (16) guidance received 1990*).

Example 6. Stairlifts are not normally considered when there are two downstairs rooms, one of which can reasonably be converted into a bedroom with reasonable access to adequate washing and toilet facilities (*Midlands SSD (3) guidance received 1990*).

Example 7. Stairlifts

1. Client unable to climb stairs because of severe handicap. Client's health 'at risk'. Reasons identified by OT confirmed by GP or consultant in written report.

    a) Client's facilities for toileting/bathing/sleeping all upstairs.

    b) Client, as above, sleeps downstairs, WC/bathing facilities upstairs.

    c) Client as above, sleeps upstairs, no available space downstairs for sleeping (bath/WC) up or down (essential medical need for bathing must be identified).

2. a) Severely M.H./P.H. Disabled Child Recommendation from GP or consultant – stating reasons for support.

    b) Disabled child 'at risk': if sleeping downstairs. Carers unable to carry child upstairs to bedroom/bathroom/WC. Recommendation from GP or consultant stating reasons for support.

3. Clients with recognised 'deteriorating' conditions (stairlift may be temporary 2/3 year solution). Independence and longterm prognosis will always be taken into consideration. Recommendation from GP or consultant stating reasons for support.

In all cases clients/carers and families views must be considered alongside recommendations from GP/consultant and nurses (*Midlands SSD (21) guidelines received 1990*).

Example 8. Through floor lifts

Same as for stairlifts in Example 7 above, but in addition:

1. where stairlift is likely to be a very short term solution – because the client's condition is known to be likely to deteriorate rapidly;
2. when it is anticipated that the client will shortly become wheelchair bound and is incapable of transferring with ease and safety;
3. where there is no possibility of fitting a stairlift on a particular staircase and a through lift is a safer and more reasonable adaptation (*Midlands SSD (21) guidance received 1990*).

Example 9. Seated stairlifts. Client is unable to to climb stairs due to:

- physical limitations, eg severe physical impairment; OR
- medical limitations, eg risk to health due to severe heart/respiratory problems AND
- the toilet, bathroom and bedroom are all upstairs and are suitable or adaptable;

OR

- the client sleeps downstairs and the WC etc are upstairs where it is not feasible to provide ground floor WC facilities;
OR
- the client sleeps upstairs, WC etc are on the ground floor and there is no space for sleeping downstairs and it is not feasible to adapt;
OR
- the client is at risk if sleeping on a separate floor to the carers (*Midlands SSD (23) guidelines received 1989*).

Example 10. Vertical/shaft lift. Criteria are as for stairlifts in Example 9 above, but also:

- client is incapable of transferring with ease and safety;
- there is no possibility of fitting a stairlift. (*Midlands SSD (23) guidelines received 1989*).

A3.2.6. Ground floor facilities
Example 1. Ground floor facilities can only be provided if all other solutions have been tried and found unsuitable.

A3.2.6.1. Ground floor WC
Example 1. Only considered if the client is sleeping downstairs and a lift is not a reasonable alternative (*Midlands SSD (1) guidelines received 1990*).
Example 2. Access to adequate toilet facilities for the majority of the day would be considered a basic need (*Midlands SSD (3) guidelines received 1990*).
Example 3. Downstairs toilets are frequently requested by clients because they consider that a toilet downstairs would save them climbing stairs too often, a difficult activity. The installation of a toilet is usually only a short term answer. In due course such a client will almost inevitably find that climbing the stairs to go to bed also becomes difficult and then requests a stairlift. The client should be offered a commode or chemical toilet to assist in the short term, and consideration given to the installation of a stairlift either immediately or when the medical condition deteriorates and warrants such an installation (*Northeast England SSD (25) guidance received 1989*).
Example 4. Criteria for additional downstairs WC where there are upstairs bathroom facilities
1. Severely disabled client permanently living/sleeping downstairs and unable to use upstairs facilities.
2. Severely disabled client – downstairs during daytime. Medical necessity identified for downstairs WC. Has a stairlift been considered? Is this impractical? Please state clearly if both stairlift and downstairs WC are essential.
3. Clients with learning difficulties, where toileting is a severe problem. Medical recommendation and paediatric OT support necessary (when relevant). In all cases GP support requested to state clearly the medical need (*Midlands SSD (21) guidance received 1990*).
Example 5. Ground floor WC/bathroom and bedroom

- client has a condition that is likely to lead to wheelchair use;
- client's existing facilities are not suited to their needs or are inaccessible;

- client's home facilities are not suitable for wheelchair use upstairs and/or a lift cannot be accomodated;
- installation of a lift is not appropriate as a longterm solution;
- ground floor bedroom should be considered where there is no other room available for conversion (*Midlands SSD (23) guidelines received 1989*).

Example 6. Groundfloor WC, where there are upstairs bathroom facilities
- the client is permanently living/sleeping downstairs and is unable to use upstairs facilities;
  OR
- the client is downstairs during the day time and there is a medical need for a downstairs WC;
  AND
- the installation of a stairlift is impracticable;
- the client has deteriorating condition – independence and longterm usage should be taken into account (*Midlands SSD (23) guidelines received 1989*).

A3.2.6.2. Ground floor bathroom
Example 1. Can be considered only if existing facilities are inaccessible even with adaptations (*Midlands SSD (1) guidance received 1989/1990*).
Example 2. Criteria for downstairs bedroom and toilet/bathroom facilities.
1. Client returning home after hospital treatment following trauma causing severe permanent disablement.
2. Client with deteriorating condition where it is apparent to the OT that the client will become wheelchair bound.
3. Severely disabled young person/child.

A3.2.6.3. Ground floor bedroom
Example 1. Considered if lift installation is inappropriate, and there is not an available room downstairs for use as a bedroom (*Midlands SSD (1) guidance received 1989/1990*).

A3.2.7. Special WCs
Example 1. WC providing flushing, warm washing and drying functions from one operation, combining the functions of a WC and bidet together with drying facility

- client is unable to maintain proper hygiene after toileting, due to degree of their functional loss;
- provision would give the client an appreciable degree of independence in toileting (*London SSD (45) guidelines 1989*).

Example 2. Dryad Medic-loo and Clos-o-mats

- provision of these is dependent on OT assessment in consultation with appropriate Senior OT (*SWD (1) guidelines received 1990*).

A3.2.8. Personal care facilities
Example 1. Washing and toilet extensions are only recommended if the existing facilities are not accessible and cannot be suitably adapted; if the client is completely unable to negotiate the stairs or has extreme difficulty with future deterioration expected; if the installation of a lift is technically impracticable.

Example 2. Special baths can only be recommended when supported by a GP and both bath equipment and shower provision have been rejected as solutions (*South of England (16) guidance received 1990*).

Example 3. Showers are considered if bath equipment is no solution, and clients are unable to wash down because of disability. Consideration of disadvantage of shower to the carer must be considered. Elderly people should be encouraged to wash down as a safer alternative to showering. Many elderly people dislike showers, so a willingness to use one must be demonstrated.

Overbath showers may be considered if they assist the carer or can be used by other members of the family. The client must demonstrate the ability to transfer but to then be unable to wash.

Level access showers should be provided if the client is a wheelchair user or likely to become one. The client must demonstrate that he or she is unable to otherwise transfer either with equipment or with the help of a carer.

Example 4. Showers

Present bathing must be looked at including bath transfer, height of rim of bath, client's abilities, possible aid by adjustable bath seat, bath rail, tap rail, bath step, bath design etc. Mechanical alternatives include:

- Autolift (floor fixed bath hoist) if sufficient space beside bath;
- Mangar bath lift (in bath lift) if insufficient space beside bath for autolift, and is dependent on client's ability to transfer and family's ability to lift the equipment in and out of the bath;
- electric overhead hoists, suitable for clients with progressive conditions. Requires floor space for wheelchair only;
- mobile hoists, not generally suitable for family homes; a large amount of space required.

Overhead showers: only fitted in special circumstances, ie when a private landlord refuses to allow the removal of the bath (*Northeast England SSD (25) guidance received 1989*).

Example 5. Floor drainage shower

- client is unable to use their existing facilities;
- carer is unable to assist client to use existing facilities;
- client/carer is unable to bath using standard bathing equipment or Mangar, Aquajack, Autolifts etc (*Midlands SSD (23) guidelines received 1989*).

Example 6. Level access shower

- all other bathing equipment has been considered/tried by the client, and is inappropriate due to the degree of functional loss. Clients must try all feasible options first;
- the user is likely to become, or already is, a wheelchair user;
- the provision will enable the client to remain independent in personal care;
- the user is unable to transfer safely into the bath, even with equipment or the carer's help (*London SSD (45) guidelines received 1989*).

Example 7. Combined toilet/shower unit

- client meets the criteria for an additional toilet, and for a shower, but the limitations of the accomodation and/or family considerations preclude the provision of each as a separate facility (*London SSD (45) guidelines 1989*).

Example 8. Showers

- would not reinstate a bath for a new tenant of a house where the Department had installed a shower unless the new tenant cannot use a shower;
- showers will be installed in upstairs bathroom only after the possibilities of rehousing and alternative provision such as autolifts have been fully investigated, and then only an overbath shower will be considered;
- will not install a shower cabinet unless it is suitable for a wheelchair user eg Chiltern Cabinet;
- maximum use must be made of 'special offers' of shower installation where the type of shower is appropriate for the purpose (*SWD (1) guidelines received 1990*).

Example 9. Showers. Bathing equipment should be tried out first. Bathing attendants/nursing auxiliary help should be considered first.

Over-bath showers are generally not installed (because person can therefore negotiate bath edge and probably use other bathing equipment safely). However, they may be considered for certain conditions, eg renal dialysis, colostomy, ileostomy, incontinence, skin problems. The medical advantages of the shower as opposed to a bath should be considered: eg showers may be contra-indicated for people with a tracheotomy or laryngectomy. Cardiac and chest conditions can also be aggravated by the force and direction of the water from a shower (*Midlands SSD (1) received 1990*).

A3.2.9. Fixed (usually ceiling, wall or gantry fixed) (electric) track hoists
Example 1. Only considered where a manual hoist is inadequate for the client or carer to look after the client in the long term (*Midlands SSD (3) guidance received 1990*).
Example 2. Fixed overhead hoist

- client is confined to a wheelchair or bed and has severely limited function in arms and legs, making transfers a problem;
- provision will increase the client's independence in transfers;
- provision will support the carer by reducing the physical exertion of transferring a client;
- mobile hoists, monkey poles and other similar lifting equipment have been considered/tried and are inappropriate due to the degree of clients' functional loss, the capacity of the carer, or the lack of space in the home – provision is dependent on structural feasibility;
- room layout: it may be preferable to provide hoists in 2 rooms instead of continuous tracking between rooms, for example from bed to toilet;
- safe use of the hoist requires correct positioning of client and sling; adequate fastening of the sling; appropriate sequencing of ascent/descent/transverse controls etc. Where the client lives alone, or will use the hoist alone, the presence of symptoms impairing the judgement needed for safe use of the hoist may preclude the issue of a hoist (*London SSD (45) guidelines received 1989*).

A3.2.10. Extra room/space
Example 1. Extra bedroom. It is not normally the responsibility of the SSD to provide an extra bedroom if a family purchase or is allocated a property with insufficient bedroom space for the number of people in the family. In certain circumstances expenditure can be justified:

- if a severely handicapped child has to share a bedroom with a sibling of the same sex because there is no alternative room, and that handicapped child by reason of his/her disability causes night disturbance, an extra bedroom may be considered. Consultant and if possible paediatric OT assessment and information is required;
- elderly, handicapped people living with a family; where these people, because of increasing handicap/frailty, have to sleep downstairs thus reducing family living space;
- alternatives: stairlift, relocation of family space to vacated bedroom (*Northeast England SSD (25) guidelines received 1989*).

Example 2. Bedroom extension. An extension in the form of a bedroom is only considered if a lift is not feasible and there is only one reception room on the ground floor with more than one person living in the accomodation; if two reception rooms have not been converted into one (allowing possible reconversion); if a disabled child has to share a bedroom and creates disturbance (GP support is required); independence for a wheelchair user can be encouraged by the provision of a bedroom with washing and toileting facilities; if the size of the household (including the client) makes it unreasonable to use a second reception room as a bedroom.

Example 3. Additional room/space

- client has to share a bedroom with others because there is no alternative and this disturbs the other person;
- client needs constant attention from carer during the night;
- client's medical condition has deteriorated to warrant permanent wheelchair use;
- there are no alternative rooms to use;
- alternatives to adaptation should be considered as an option when accomodating extended families (*Midlands SSD (23) guidance received 1989*).

A3.2.11. Kitchens
Example 1. Kitchen enlargement is only considered if the client is dependent on a wheelchair or large mobility aid, and is the predominant user of the kitchen (*Midlands SSD (1) guidance received 1989/1990*).
Example 2. Kitchen enlargement can only be considered if the client prepares and cooks food for himself (if alone) or the family. Permanent wheelchair users (if not main user of kitchen) should have access to running water and one suitable working surface to allow a hot drink to be prepared (*South of England SSD (16) guidelines received 1990*).

A3.2.12. Household adaptations
Example 1. Immersion heaters. The provision of immersion heaters is not normally made by the SSD, but may be so if a change of heating is involved (*Northeast England SSD (25) guidelines received 1989*).
Example 2. Immersion heaters. It is not normally the responsibility of the department; however, in exceptional cases involving severe disability and financial need, help will be given (*SWD (1) guidelines received 1990*).
Example 3. Extractor fans/opening windows. Clients with respiratory problems often consider that extractor fans or small opening windows will solve their

breathing difficulties. A better solution would be to refer them to their GP for a medical solution (*Northeast England SSD (25) guidelines received 1989*).

Example 4. Windows. It is not normally the responsibility of the department to replace windows (*SWD (1) guidelines received 1990*).

Example 5. Power points

- before considering an electric socket all available aids should be tried first including extension lead. If none of these are suitable, the department would raise a socket;
- in exceptional circumstances will provide additional power points for specific purpose, eg installation of environmental controls (*SWD (1) guidelines received 1990*).

Example 6. Insulation. It is not the responsibility of the dept to insulate houses (*SWD (1) guidelines received 1990*).

A3.2.13. Safety equipment

Example 1. Safety features such as safety glass, fencing, locks will only be provided where the requirement is above that normally required (*Midlands SSD (3) guidelines received 1990*).

Example 2. Fencing can only be considered when the client cannot be safely contained in the garden, and where the client's vulnerability is due to a medical condition and not a 'normal development' (aging), and where existing fencing is inadequate (*Midlands SSD (1) guidelines received 1989/1990; South of England SSD (16) guidance received 1990*).

Example 3. Fences for children. Before agreeing to the provision of a fence around a garden, the following should be considered:

- do the parents wish to keep the child secure in the garden unable to socialise with other children for their own peace of mind?
- would behaviour modification be more appropriate?
- would it be dangerous to play with the other children in the area?

Example 4. Fencing

- would fence a garden to keep in a hyperactive child;
- would not fence a garden to keep out other children or dogs;
- would not fence a garden where the mother has no quick access to the child who is in it and where this could put the child in danger;
- would not repair or maintain a fence; this is the responsiblity of the property owner, with the exception of fences erected by the SWD (*SWD (1) guidelines received 1990*).

Example 5. Gates

- would fit a gate for a hyperactive child's safety;
- would consider fitting a gate for a physically and/or mentally handicapped childs'safety but only where this would not be considered a necessity for any child of the same age, ie in exceptional cirumstances;
- would not put up a gate to save cars or batricars from vandalism;
- would consider installing a gate at an internal stair for the safety of a confused elderly person.

A3.2.14. Garages, sheds

Example 1. Garages/car ports. The SSD does not assist with garages nor with devices to open garage doors. It is not considered essential that a car be kept in a garage.

Car ports are only considered where the client has extreme difficulty transferring from wheelchair to car and the client is in employment and requires to use the car daily, whatever the weather (*Northeast England SSD (25) guidelines received 1989*).

Example 2. Storage facilities for outdoor electric wheelchairs. Policy has been that the Wheelchair Service provides a shed after six months if necessary, and the SSD provides the concrete base and socket outlet. This may eligible for housing authority grant aid in private property (*Northeast England SSD (25) guidance received 1989*).

Example 3. Sheds. Sheds with a power supply for battery charging for a powered wheelchair can only be recommended if facilities are inadequate or unsafe within existing accomodation. They should only be recommended for wheelchairs rather than 'vehicles' (eg Batricars); and when other outside accomodation is unavailable (eg porch, garage or other outbuilding).

A3.2.15. Paths

Example 1. Garden paths. Access to the garden is not normally considered essential, but alterations to garden paths are not to be recommended except where gardening is the main leisure activity.

The need to hang washing out of doors is a matter for the OT's judgement as essential or beneficial (*Northeast England SSD (25) guidance received 1989*).

Example 2. Paved areas

- would consider paving an area as a drying green for a wheelchair-bound person;
- would not normally pave an area for storing a battery-operated wheelchair or provide any shelter for the same unless all other possibilities had been investigated. These chairs are not standard issue and their maintenance and shelter are normally the owner's responsibility;
- would only provide a run-in for a car if a disabled passenger or driver is unable to get from the door of the house to the pavement or where the disabled driver is at risk from passing traffic when transferring from wheelchair to car or is unable to transfer on the street for any other valid reason;
- would pave small areas for children using lobster-pot walkers, chailey trolleys and Carters crawlers;
- would not replace a garden with paving to save a client effort. This would be seen as something a voluntary agency might do (*Guidelines received 1989/1990*).

Example 3. Paths

- would consider relaying the path if the path surface is unsuitable or too narrow for the requirements of a disabled person;
- would see the work as the responsiblity of the property owner if the path requires maintenance or re-laying for general use (*Guidelines received 1989/1990*).

Appendix 4

Directory of equipment suppliers

BEDS

Adjustamatic Beds Ltd, Sphire House, White Street, Great Dunmow, Essex, CM6 1DB. tel: (0371) 5633

Aidserve Ltd, Unit 106, Bradley Hall Trading Estate, Bradley Lane, Standish, Wigan, WN6 0XQ. tel: (0257) 425538

Airsprung Ltd, Canal Road Ind. Est., Trowbridge, Wiltshire, BA14 8RQ.tel (0225) 754411

Altonaids Mobility, Park Road, Gateshead, NE8 3HL. Tel: (091) 4773733/4773683

Amilake Ltd, Haslemere Industrial Estate, 20 Ravensbury Terrace, London SW18 4SB. Tel:(081) 947 7771/7191

Anatomia Ltd, 21 Hampstead Road, Euston Centre, London NW1 3JA. tel: (071) 387 5700

Aremco, Grove House, Lenham, Kent, ME17 2PX. tel: (0622) 85802

Arnold Designs Ltd,London Road, Chalford, Stroud, Glos, GL6 8NR tel: (0453)882310

Arwin Products & Co, 11 Irwell House, East Philip Street, Salford, Greater Manchester, ME3 7LE. tel: (061) 832 2789 & (061) 832 1407

ASM Medicare, Picow Farm Industrial Estate, Runcorn, Cheshire WA7 4UG. tel: (09285) 74301/2/3

Astric Medical Ltd, Astric House, Lewes Road, Brighton, E Sussex, BN2 3LG. tel: (0273) 608319

Axminster Electronics Ltd, Milwey Industrial Estate, Milwey Rise, Axminster, Devon, EX13 5HU. tel: (0297) 32360

The Black Shop, 24 New Cavendish St, London W1M 7LH. tel: (071) 935 9120/9148

Bay Jacobsen (UK) Ltd, Auriema House, 442 Bath Road, Slough, SL1 6BB. tel: (06286) 4049

Bedboards, 33 Daniel Street, Bath BA2 6ND. tel: (0225) 63905

Boots the Chemists Ltd, City Gate, Toll House Hill, Nottingham NG2 3AA. tel: (0602) 418522. *Enquiries should be made at local branches*

JH Bounds Ltd, Stethos House, 68 Sackville Street, Manchester, Gt Manchester, M1 3WJ. tel: (061) 236 7331−4

Bowmans, 69 Fore Street, Hertford, Herts, SG14 1AL. tel: (0992) 583504

Brevet Hospital Products, Unit 1/3, Waymills, Whitchurch, Shropshire SY13 1QN. tel: (0948) 4487

Camp Ltd, Northgage House, Staple Gardens, Winchester, Hampshire S023 8ST. tel: (0962) 55248

Capital Projects (Leasing) Ltd, 71 Kenilworth Road, Coventry CV4 7AF. tel: (0203) 419471/413815

Carters (J&A) Ltd, Alfred Street, Westbury, Wiltshire, BA13 3DZ. tel: (0373) 822203

Cefndy Enterprises, Cefndy Road, Rhyl, Clwyd, LLl8 2HG. tel: (0745) 343877

Central Medical Equipment, 7 Ascot Park Estate, Lenton Street, Sandiacre, Nottingham, NG10 5DL. tel: (0602) 390949

Centromed Ltd, Brookfield Industrial Estate, Leacon Road, Ashford Kent, TN23 2TU. tel: (0233) 628018

Chester−Care Ltd, 16 Englands Lane, London, NW3 4TG. tel: (071) 586 2166 or (071) 722 3430

Chiltern Medical Developments Ltd, Chiltern House, Wedgewood Road, Bicester, Oxon OX6 7UL. tel: (0869) 246470

Community Health Supplies Co, 16 Dinsdale Gardens, New Barnet, Herts. tel: (081) 440 4931

Connevans Ltd, 54 Albert Road North, Reigate, Surrey, RH2 9YR. tel: (0737) 247571

Contenta Surgical Co, Unit G3, Marabout Trading Estate, Dorchester, Dorset, DT1 1SN. tel: (0305) 66001

Cooper & Sons Ltd, Wormley, Godalming, Surrey, GU8 5SY. tel: (042 879) 2251

Crownhythe Commercial Services Ltd, 1 Fford Brenig, Bryn−y−Baal, Mold, Clwyd CH7 6NJ. tel: (0352) 56688

Cuneiform, The Old Post Office, Weasenham Road, Great Massingham, Norfolk, PE32 2EY. tel: (048 524) 309

Daniels Healthcare, Head Office, 130 Western Road, Tring, Hertfordshire HP23 4BU. tel: (0442) 826881

Days Medical Aids Ltd, Litchard Industrial Estate, Bridgend, Mid−Glamorgan, CF31 2AL. tel: (0656) 57495/60150

Doherty Medical, Charlton Road, London, N9 8HS. tel: (081) 804 1244

Dunlopillo UK, Retail Division, Pannal, Harrogate, North Yorkshire HG3 1JL. tel: (0423) 872411

NH Eastwood & Sons Ltd, 118 East Barnet Road, Barnet, Herts, EN4 8RE. tel: (081) 441 9641

Edgeley Textiles Ltd, Vale Road, Heaton Mersey, Stockport SK4 3DX. tel: (061) 431 8886

Egerton Hospital Equipment Ltd, Tower Hill, Horsham West Sussex, RH13 7JT. tel: (0403) 53800

Enterprise Engineering, 157 Ermine Way, Arrington, Royston, Herts, SG8 0AU. tel: (0223) 207281

Peter Evans Associates, Golf Course Road, North Road, Bath, BA2 6JG. tel: (0225) 63626/63922

Feeder Products Ltd., PO Box 481, Blackmore, Ingatestone, Essex CM4 0NA. tel: (0277) 821224

Ferris Appliances Ltd, 150C Shore Road, Greenisland, Carrickfergus, Co. Antrim BT38 8TT. tel: (0232) 860618

Fullers Medcial Products, 43 Earl Street, Hastings, East Sussex, TN34 1SG. tel: (0424) 426094

Furniture Productions (Knightsbridge) Ltd, Domestic Range, 191 Thornton Road, Bradford, West Yorkshire, BD1 2JT. tel: (0274) 731442

FW Equipment Co Ltd, Hanworth Road, Low Moor, Bradford, West Yorkshire, BD12 0SG. tel: (0274) 601121

Gallops Hospital Equipment, Finmere Road, Eastbourne, East Sussex BN21 8QG tel: (0323) 646681

Ganmill Ltd, 38/40 Market Street, Bridgewater, Somerset, TA6 3EP. Tel (0278) 423037

Gimson−Tendercare, 62 Boston Road, Beaumont Leys, Leicester LE4 1AZ. tel (0533) 366779

Golden Plan Ltd, 14 Golden Square, London, W1R 3AG. tel (071) 439 1066/(071) 434 2066 24hr answering service

Griffin Products Ltd, Holland Way, Blandford, Dorset, DT11 7SU. tel: (0258) 56601

Headingley Scientific Services, 45 Westcombe Avenue, Leeds, West Yorkshire, LS8 2BS. tel: (0532) 664222

Health & Comfort Ltd, PO Box 15, Westbury, Wiltshire, BA13 4LS. Tel: (0373) 822394

Helping Hands Shop, 114 Queens Road, Leicester LE2 3AD. tel: (0533) 708821

Henleys Medical Supplies Ltd, Brownfields, Welwyn Garden City, Herts AL7 1AN. tel: (0707) 33164. *Wholesaler Only*

High Seat Ltd, Carlton Mills, Victoria Road, Dewsbury WF13 2AB. tel: (0924) 464809

Home Nursing Supplies Ltd, Headquarters Road, West Wilts Trading Estate, Westbury, Wilts, BA13 4JR.tel: (0373) 822313

Homecraft Supplies Ltd, Low Moor Estate, Kirkby–in–Ashfield, Notts NG17 7JZ. tel: (0623) 754 047

Hoskins Ltd, Upper Trinity Street, Birmingham, B9 4EQ. tel: (021) 773 1144

Hospital Aids Ltd, 9 Staveley Way, Brixworth, Northampton NN6 9EU. tel: (0604) 881650

Hospital Metalcraft Ltd, Blandford Heights, Blandford Forum, Dorset DT11 7TE. tel: (0258) 51338

Hygicare Ltd, 1 Macon Court, Macon Way, Crewe, Cheshire CW1 1EA.tel: (0270) 580061

Hyman Polyfreem Ltd., 12 Holton Road, Holton Trading Park, Poole, Dorset BH16 6LQ. tel: (0202) 625501 *Sell to trade only, but supply list of retailers.*

Innovention Products Ltd, The Business Centre, Colne Way, Watford, Herts, WD2 4ND. tel: (0923) 245050/9

Interform Contract Furniture, 9 West Hampstead Mews, London NW6 3BB. tel: (071) 328 2340

Keymet Co, Keymet Works, Sylvan Grove, London, SE15 1PE. tel: (071) 639 6644

Keep Able Ltd, Fleming Close, Park Farm, Wellingborough, Northants NN8 3BR. tel: (0933) 679426

Kencan Ltd, Unit 9, Wolfe Close, Parkgate Ind. Est., Knutsford, WAl6 8XJ. tel: (0565) 53991

Kirton Designs Ltd, Bungay Road, Hempnall, Norwich, Norfolk, NR15 2NG. tel: (050 842) 8411

Krausz–Harari Ltd, 87 Ravensdale Road, London N16 6TH. tel: (081) 800 7000

Langham Products, Unit 26, Bennettsfield Trading Est, Wincanton, Somerset BA9 9DT. tel: (0963) 33869

Lattoflex UK Ltd, 46 Station Road, Worthing, W Sussex, BN11 12JP tel: (0903) 207442

Lewis Woolf Griptight Ltd, 144 Oakfield Road, Selly Oak, Birmingham B29 7EE. tel: (021) 414 1122

Limericks Linens Ltd, Limericks House 117 Victoria Avenue, Southend–on–Sea, Essex, SS2 6EL, tel: (0702) 34386

Llewellyn Health Care Services, Regents House, 1 Regents Road, City, Liverpool L3 7BX. tel: (051) 236 5311

Mackworth Medical Products Ltd, Morgan Street Works, Llambradach, Caerphilly, Mid Glamorgan CF8 3QT. tel: (0222) 861281

Marcon Bed Elevators, P.O. Box 31, Dorking, Surrey, RH5 5SU. tel: (030 679) 382

Masterpeace Products Ltd, Tormen House, Booth Hill Works, Booth Hill Lane, Oldham, OL1 2PH tel: (061) 624 2041

Medimail, JL Owen Ltd, FREEPOST, Manchester, ME4 8BP. tel: (061) 236 0896

Medipost Ltd, Unit 1, St Johns Estate, Elder Road, Lees, Oldham, Lancs. OL4 3DZ. tel: (061) 678 0233

Melco Products Ltd, Melco House, Market Street, Tottington, Bury, BL8 3LL tel: (020 488)4127

Metra West Co, Unit 4c,Lightpill Trading Estate, 117 Bath Road, Stroud, Glos, GL5 3LL tel: (04536) 72400

Mobilia, Drake House, 18 Creekside, London SE8 3DZ. tel:(081) 692 7141 ext 202. *No. to contact for all enquiries (081) 892 1850*

Molnlycke Ltd, Hospital Products Division, Southfields Road, Dunstable, Beds LKU6 3EJ. tel: (0582) 600211

Morleys Contracts Ltd, Arkwright Road, Bicester, Oxon, OX6 7UU. tel: (0869) 320320 *(supply to contract holders only)*

Morpeths Contracts Ltd, Morpeth House, Spring Garden Lane, Newcastle–upon–Tyne NE4 5TD. tel: (091) 2327051

MW Plastic Protection, 180 High Street, Pensnett, Dudley DY5 4JG. tel: (0384) 261060

Horatio Myer & Co Ltd, Contracts Division, Windover Road, Huntingdon, Cambs, PE18 7EF. tel: (0480) 52111

National Bed Federation, 251 Brompton Road, London SW3 2EZ. tel: (071) 589 4888

Neckease, 5 Firs Walk, Woodford Green, Essex. IG8 0TD. tel:(081) 504 0839

Nesbit Evans, J And Co. Ltd., Woden Road West, Wednesbury, West Midlands, WS10 7BL. tel: (021) 556 1511

Nicholas Laboratories Ltd, 225 Bath Road, Slough, Berks, SL1 4AU. tel: (0753) 23971 ext. 156

Northern Blankets Ltd, Vine Mill, Royton, Oldham, Lancs. OL2 5LN. tel: (061) 652 1211

Nottingham Rehab Ltd, 17 Ludlow Hill Road, West Bridgford, Nottingham, NG2 6HD. tel: (0602) 234251

Ollerton Hall Decorating Service, Ollerton, Knutsford, Cheshire. WA16 8SF. tel (0565) 50222

Pentonville (Rubber Products) Ltd, 50 Pentonville Road, London, N1 9HF. tel: (071) 837 0283

Pira Ltd, 10 Hoxton Square, London N1 6NU. tel: (071) 739 7865

Platt & Hill Ltd, Belgrave Mill, Keswick Avenue, Oldham, Lancs OL8 2JP. tel: (061) 626 4638

Posthaste, 9 Weston Road, Gloucester, GL1 5AE. tel: (0452) 502176

PRA Plastics (& Delvelopments) Ltd., 21a Kingsland High Street, Dalston, London, E8 2JS. tel: (071) 254 9753

IN Rankin Sales Ltd., 63 Marlborough Place, London NW8 0PT. tel: (071) 286 0251

Relyon Ltd., PO Box 1, Wellington, Somerset, TA21 8NN tel: (082 347) 7501

Remploy Ltd (Medical Products Div) & Head Office, 415 Edgware Road, Cricklewood, London NW2 6LR. tel: (081) 452 8020

Renray Group Ltd., Road Five, Winsford Industrial Estate, Winsford, Cheshire, CW7 3RB tel: (0606) 593456

Roma Medical Aids Ltd, Llandow Industrial Estate, Cowbridge, South Glamorgan, CF7 7PB. tel: (04463) 4519

WS Rothband & Co Ltd, 21 Elizabeth Street, Manchester M8 8WT. tel: (061) 834 1303

Safe–Tie, 15 Meadow Close, High Wycombe, Bucks HP11 1RG. tel: (0494) 31887/21438 *Contact : Mr Pearce*

Sander & Kay Ltd, Pall Mall Building, 124-8 Barlby Road, London, Wl0 6BU. tel: (081) 969 3553

Sanitary Appliances Ltd, 3 Sandiford Road, Kimpton Industrial Estate, Sutton, Surrey, SM3 9RN. tel: (081) 641 0310

Sars Bags Ltd, 37 Paisley Road, Renfrew, Renfrewshire, PA4 8LG tel: (041) 886 7893

Shackletons (Carlinghow) Ltd, 501 Brandford Road, Batley, West Yorkshire WF17 8LN. tel: (0924) 474430

Shaw Manufacturing Ltd, Portland Road, Kingston-upon-Thames, Surrey, KT1 2RG. tel: (081) 541 4471

Showeray Enterprises, Ashleigh House, Station Road, Baildon, Bradford BD17 6SE. tel: (0274) 588574-evening telephone (0274)594246/588574

WESTON & ROSS LTD

H E A L T H   C A R E   S U P P L I E S

Nursing & Residential Homes and Head Office

Weston & Ross Ltd, 20/22 Dalston Gardens, Stanmore
Middlesex HA7 1DA

Incontinence appliances, residential home provision, private nursing home provision, medical equipment provision and private purchase.

Mail Order Division

Healthiness, Weston & Ross, Freepost (RCC1828), Horsham,
West Sussex RH13 5ZA

Daily living equipment, home nursing equipment, mobility equipment, incontinence appliances, medical equipment provision and private purchase.

Retail Showroom

Weston & Ross Care Centre, 120 Church Road, Hove
East Sussex BN3 2EA

Daily living equipment, home nursing equipment, mobility equipment, incontinence appliances, medical equipment provision and private purchase.

JM Sidebottom Ltd, 525 York Road, Leeds, West Yorkshire, LS9 6TA tel: (0532) 491449

Sidhil, Boothtown, Halifax, West Yorkshire, HX3 6NT. tel: (0422) 63447

Silentnight PLC, PO Box 9, Barnoldswick, Colne, Lancs. tel: (0282) 813051

Simcare, Eschmann Bros & Walsh Ltd, Personal Products Division, Peter Road, Lancing, West Sussex BN15 8TJ. tel: (0903) 761122

Simpla Plastics Ltd, Phoenix Estate, Caerphilly Road, Cardiff, Mid-Glamorgan, CF4 4XG. tel: (0222) 621000

Skandi-Form UK, 36 Dashwood Avenue, High Wycombe, HP12 3DX. tel: (0494) 24222

Slumberland Medicare, Hallam Field Road, Ilkeston, Derbyshire DE7 4BQ. tel: (0602) 440359

SML Healthcare Ltd, Bath Place, High Street, Barnet, Herts EN5 5XE tel: (081) 440 6522

Sommelier Ltd, 33 Park Street, Bristol BS1 5JG. tel: (0272) 298940

Southern Sanitary Specialists, Cerdic House, West Portway, Andover, Hants SP10 3LF. tel: (0264) 24131/52534

James Spencer & Co Ltd, Moor Road Works, Moor Road, Headingley, Leeds, West Yorkshire LS6 4BH. tel: (0532) 785837/741850

Spenco Medical UK Ltd, Burrell Road, Haywards Heath, West Sussex RH16 1TW. tel: (0444) 415171

Stryker UK Ltd, Unit 5, Waldo Road, Bromley BR1 2QX. tel: (081) 290 6135

Sunrise Medical Ltd, Fens Pool Avenue, Brierley Hill, West Midlands, DY5 1QA. tel: (0384) 480480

Teemee Ltd, Unit 2, Greenwood Court, Ramridge Road, Luton, Bedfordshire, LU2 0TN. tel: (0582) 27015

Theraposture Ltd, 4 The Downsland, Warminster, Wiltshire, BA12 0BD. tel: (0985) 213440

Thompson Renovation Services, 60a. New Lane, Burscough, Ormskirk, Lancs. L40 0SX. tel: (0704) 893794

Thorpe Mill Ltd, West House, Cottingley Road, Allerton, Bradford, West Yorkshire, BD15 9LH. tel: (0274) 542433

Toy & Furniture Workshop, Church Hill, Totland Bay, Isle of Wight, PO39 0ET. tel: (0983) 752596

Tullos Furniture Products, 132 Wellington Road, West Tullos Industrial Estate, Aberdeen AB9 1LQ tel: (0224) 873366

Charles Turner & Co Ltd, Hospital Products Division, Bentinck Street, Bolton, Lancs BL1 4QD. tel: (0204) 46226

Universal Hospital Supplies, 313 Chase Road, Southgate, London N14 6JB. tel: (081) 882 6444/5/6/7

Vernon & Co (Pulp Products) Ltd, Slater Street, Bolton, Lancs. BL1 2HP. tel: (0204) 29494 *Supply to hospitals only*

WAVES, Corscombe, Nr Dorchester, Dorset, DT2 0NU. tel: (093 589) 248

AJ Way and Co. Ltd, Riverlock House, Spring Gardens, High Wycombe, Buck, HP13 7AG. tel: (0494) 27507

Wessex Medical Equipment Co Ltd., Budds Lane, Romsey, Hants, S051 0HA. tel: (0794) 830303

WM Supplies (UK) Ltd, Park Mill, Royton, Oldham, Lancs OL2 6PZ.tel: (061) 624 5641

Wundarest Products, Chester House, Windsor End, Beaconsfield, Bucks HP9i 2JJ. tel: (049 46) 71257

Zimmer Ltd, Dunbeath Road, Elgin Industrial Estate, Swindon, Wilts SN2 6EA. tel: (0793) 481441

CHAIRS AND CHAIR ACCESSORIES

Aidserve Ltd, Unit 106, Bradley Hall Trading Estate, Bradley Lane, Standish, Wigan, WN6 0XQ. tel: (0257) 425538

Akron Therapy Products Ltd, 1 Farthing Road, Ipswich, IP1 5AP.tel: (0473) 49544

Altonaids Mobility, Park Road, Gateshead NE8 3HL. tel: (091) 4773733

Alvescot International Ltd, Alvescot House, Oxford, OX8 2QJ tel: (0993) 842898

Anatomia Ltd, 21 Hampstead Road, Euston Centre, London NW1 3JA. tel: (071) 387 5700

Aremco, Grove House, Lenham, Kent, ME17 2PX. tel: (0622) 858502

Asgo Ltd, 22b Hawthorne Road, Lottbridge Drove, Eastbourne, East Sussex Bn23 6PZ. tel: (0323) 38228

F Ashton Ltd, 16 Groton Road, London, SW18 4EP. tel: (081) 874 4245

ASM Medicare, Picow Farm Ind. Est, Runcorn, Cheshire WA7 4UG. tel: (09285) 74301/2/3

B Line Industries, Kingston Works, 460 Beverley Road, Hull, HU5 1NF. tel: (0482) 42296/442223

Jane Bertram Products, The Gorse House, Grimston, Melton Mowbray, Leics. LE14 3BZ. tel: (0664) 812751

Boots the Chemist Ltd, City Gate, Toll House Hill, Nottingham NG2 3AA. tel: (0602) 418522*Enquiries should be made at local branches*

Carter (J&A) Ltd, Aintree Avenue, White Horse Business Park, North Bradley, Trowbridge, Wilts, BA14 0XA. tel: (0225) 751901

B Cartwright & Son Ltd, MendySt, High Wycombe, Bucks HP11 2EU tel: (0494) 26780

Cefndy Enterprises, Cefndy Road, Rhyl, Clwyd, LL18 2HG. tel: (0745) 343877

Celebrity Furniture Ltd, Wimsey Way, Alfreton Trading Estate, Somercotes, Derbyshire DE55 4QE. tel: (0773) 604607

Central Medical Equipment, 7 Ascot Park Estate, Lenton St, Sandiacre, Nottingham, NG10 5Dl. tel: (0602) 390949

Chairwarm Ltd, Pomona Dock, Manchester M15 4LY tel: (061 848) 8016

Chester-Care Ltd, 16 Englands Lane, London, NW3 4TG. tel (071) 586 2166 or (071) 722 3430

J. Cinnamon Ltd, Firmback Works, 43 Andrews Road, Cambridge Heath, London E8 4RN. tel: (071) 254 1262

Clinical Engineering Consultants Ltd, Unit D8, Barwell Trading Estate, Chessington, Surrey, KT9 2NY. tel (01) 974 1439

Commercial Services Northern, Unit 9T, Askern Ind Est, Doncaster DN6 0DD. tel: (0302) 700022/700053.*Supply mainly to nursing and residential homes.*

Cuneiform, The Old Post Office, Weasenham Road, Great Massingham, Norfolk, PE32 2EY. tel: (048 524) 309

Daniels Healthcare, Head Office, 130 Western Road, Tring, Herts HP23 4BU. tel: (0442) 826881

Days Medical Aids Ltd, Litchard Ind. Est, Bridgend, Mid-Glamorgan, CF31 2AL. tel: (0656) 57495/60150

Doherty Medical, Charlton Road, London, N9 8HS. tel: (081) 804 1244

Dynamic Seating Products, Head Office, Oakleigh, High Street, Bream, Lydney, Glos. Tel: (0594) 562271 *Northern Office* (0565) 3574

Ercol Furniture Ltd, Ercol Buildings, London Rd, High Wycombe, Bucks HP13 7AE. tel: (0494) 21261

Everaids Ltd, 38 Clifton Rd, Cambridge, CB1 4ZT. tel: (0223) 243336

Ferris Appliances Ltd, Unit 23a. Crawfordsburn Road Ind Est. Newtonards, Co. Down, Northern Ireland tel: (0247) 818938

Forwood Designs Ltd, The Mews, Mitcheldean, Glos G117 0SL. tel: (0594) 542181

Furniture Productions (Bradford) Ltd, Contract Range, 191 Thornton Road, Bradford BD1 2JT. tel: (0274) 731442

Gallops Hospital Equipment, Finmere Road, Eastbourne, E. Sussex BN21 8QG. tel: (0323) 646681

RJ Gemmell & Associates, 42 Methil St, Scotstoun, Glasgow G14 0AN. tel: (041) 954 9473

Gimson-Tendercare, 62 Boston Road, Beaumont Leys, Leicester LE4 1AZ. tel: (0533) 366779

Godfrey Syrett Ltd, Eagle Works, Killingworth Township, Newcastle Upon Tyne, Tyne & Wear, NE12 0RJ tel: (091) 2681010

Goodearl-Risboro Ltd, PO Box 2, Princes Risborough, Bucks, HP17 9DP. tel (084 44) 3311

Health & Comford Ltd, PO Box 15, Westbury, Wilts, BA13 4LS. tel: (0373) 822394

Helping Hand Co (Ledbury) Ltd, Unit 9L Bromyard Trading Estate, Ledbury, Herts HR8 1NS. tel: (0531) 5678

Hemco (UK) Ltd, Unit 17 Llandow Ind Est, Cowbridge, South Glamorgan CF7 7PB tel: (04463) 3393/3394

High Seat Ltd, Carlton Mills, Victoria Road, Dewsbury WF13 2AB tel: (0924) 464809

M Hogarth & Sons, Princes St, Corbridge, Northumberland NE45 5AE. tel: (0434) 712134

Home Supplies (Wessex) Ltd, South Stour Avenue, Eastmead Estate, Ashford, Kent TN23 1RS. tel: (0233) 26099

Homecraft Supplies Ltd, Low Moor Estate, Kirby-in-Ashfield, Notts, NG17 7JZ tel: (0623) 754 047

Hospital Metalcraft Ltd, Blandford Heights, Blandford Forum, Dorset, DT11 7TE. tel: (0258) 51338

Howmedica (UK) Ltd, 622 Western Avenue, Park Royal, London W3 0TF. tel: (081) 992 8044

Huntleigh Technology Plc, Healthcare Division, 310-312 Dallow Road, Luton LU1 1SS. tel (0582) 413104

Hyman Polyfreem Ltd., 12 Holton Road, Holton Trading Park, Poole, Dorset BH16 6LQ. tel: (0202) 625501 *Sell to trade only, but supply list of retailers*

Independence, 52 Exeter Road, Exmouth, Devon, EX8 1PY. tel: (0395 268555

Innovention Products Ltd, The Business Centre, Colne Way, Watford, Herts, WD2 4ND. tel: (0923) 245050/9

Interform Contract Furniture, 9 West Hampstead Mews, London NW6 3BB. tel: (071) 328 2340

Jenaro Ltd., Atlas Mill No.. 4, Mornington Road, Bolton, Lancs, BL1 4EP. tel: (0204) 496122

Joncare Ltd, 7 Ashville Trading Estate, Nuffield Way, Abingdon, Oxon OX14 1RL tel: (0234) 28120/35600

Kirton Designs Ltd, Bungay Road, Hempnall, Norwich, Norfolk, NR15 2NG. tel: (050 842) 8411

Krausz-Harari Ltd., 87 Ravensdale Road, London N16 6TH. tel: (081) 800 7000

The Lacy Hulbert Co, 66 Midhurst Road, Lavant, Chichester, West Sussex, PO18 0DA. tel (0243) 527399

Langham Products, Unit 26, Bennettsfield Trading Estate, Wincanton, Somerset BA9 9DT. tel: (0963) 33869

James Leckey Design, Design House, Kilwee Ind Est., Dunmurry, Northern Ireland BT17 0HD. tel: (0232) 602277

Limericks Linens Ltd, Limericks House, 117 Victoria Avenue, Southend-on-Sea, Essex, SS2 6EL. tel (0702) 343486

Llewellyn Health Care Services, Regent House, 1 Regent Road, City, Liverpool L3 7BX. tel: (051) 236 5311

Macnish Recliners, Little Grove, Grove Lane, Orchard Leigh, Chesham, Bucks HP5 3QL. tel: (0494) 773120

Masterpeace Products Ltd, Tormen House, Booth Hill Works, Booth Hill Lane, Oldham, OL1 2PH. tel: (061) 624 2041

May Corporation (Europe) Ltd., 17a. Luton Road, Harpenden, Herts AL5 2UA. tel: (0582) 461155

G McLoughlin & Co Ltd, Victoria Works, Oldham Road, Rochdale, Lancs, OL11 1DG. tel: (0706) 49911

Medeci Rehab Ltd, Research Unit, Warley Hospital, Brentwood, Essex CM14 5HQ. tel: (0277) 212637

Medesign Ltd, Unit 7, Clock Tower Works, Railway St, Southport, PR8 5BB. tel (074) 42373

Meditech Developments Ltd, Lenton Business Centre, Lenton Boulevard, Nottingham NG7 2BY. tel (0602) 784194

Mobilia, Drake House, 18 Creekside, London SE8 3DZ. tel: (081) 692 7141 ext. 210 *(general enquiries)*or (081) 892 1850 *(technical enquiries)*..

Monarch Marketing Ltd, Ind. Est., Unit 1, Llanwrtyd Wells, Powys. tel: (059) 13 577

National Back Pain Association, 31-33 Park Road, Teddington, Middlesex TW11 0AB. tel: (01) 977 5474

J Nesbit Evans & Co Ltd, Woden Road West, Wednesbury, West Midlands WS10 7BL. tel: (021) 556 1511

Ness Furniture Ltd, Croxdal, Durham, Co Durham DH6 5HT. tel: (0388) 816109

Neutex, Enterprise House, Distillery Lane, Dundalk, Co Louth, Ireland. tel: (042) 39060

Nicholas Laboratories Ltd, 225 Bath Road, Slough, Berks, SL1 4AU tel: (0753) 23971 Ext 156

Nottingham Rehad Ltd, 17 Ludlow Hill Road, West Bridgford, Nottingham, NG2 6HD. (0602) 234251

Nursing Home Furnishers Ltd., Brown Avenue, Gelderd Road, Leeds LS11 0DS. tel: (0532) 712279

Ortho-Kinetics (UK) Ltd, Unit 4, Planetary Road Ind Est, Wednesfield, Wolverhampton WV13 3XA. tel: (0902) 866166

Richard Orton Ltd, 1325 High Road, Whetstone, London N20 9HR. tel (081) 446 4407/8

Oxylitre Ltd, Morton House, Skerton Road, Old Trafford, Manchester, M16 0WL. tel: (061) 872 6322

Palatine Products, Poole, Whickham View, Newcastle upon Tyne, Tyne & Wear, NE15 6UN. tel: (091) 2280505

Paraglide Ltd., 2 Churwell Avenue, Heaton Mersey, Stockport SK4 3QE. tel: (061) 432 7315

Parker Care Ltd, P O Box 22, Frogmoor, High Wycombe, Bucks, HP13 5DJ. tel: (0494) 21144

Parker Knoll Furniture Ltd, The Courtyard, PO Box 22, Frogmoor, High Wycombe HP13 5DJ. tel: (0494) 21144

Pelvic Support Chairs, Oaklands, New Mill Lane, Eversley, Basingstoke, Hants RG27 0RA. tel: (0734) 732365

Portopaedic Products, Willowmead, Shutlanehead, Newcastle-under-Lyme ST5 4DS. tel: (0782) 680633

Positive Posture, 120 Church Lane, London N2 0TB. tel: (081) 883 7828

Posture Research, Semersdon Manor, North Tamerton, Holsworthy, Devon, EX22 6RL. tel: (040 927) 370

Powell Seat Co Ltd, 70 Lodge Lane, Derby DE1 3HB. tel: (0332) 47757

PRA Plastics (& Developments) Ltd, 21a Kingsland High St, Dalston, London, E8 2JS. tel: (071) 254 9753

Primo Furniture Ltd, Baird Road, Enfield, Middlesex EN1 1SJ. tel: (081) 804 3434

Putnams, 333 Goswell Road, The Angel, Islington, London, EC1 7JT. tel: (071) 278 932'52

Recliners Unlimited, 20 Cowbridge Road, Pontyclun, Mid Glam, CF7 9EE. tel: (0443) 229119

John Reed & Son Ltd, 141 Regent St, Kettering, Northants, NN16 8QH. tel: (0536) 510584/83742

Relaxator Ltd, Island Farm Avenue, West Molesey, Surrey, KT8 0UH. tel: (01) 941 2555

Remploy Ltd (Medical Products Div) & Head Office, 415 Edgware Road, Cricklewood, London NW2 6LR. tel: (081) 452 8020.

Renray Group Ltd, Road Five, Winsford Ind Est, Winsford, Cheshire, CW7 3RB. tel (0606) 593456

ER Richards Thermal Screens, 29 Penycae Road, Port Talbot, West Glamorgan SA13 2EP. tel: (0639) 882524

Rifton & Community Playthings, Robertsbridge, East Sussex, TN32 5DR. tel: (0580) 880626

Roma Medical Aids Ltd, Llandow Ind Est, Cowbridge, South Glamorgan, CF7 7PB. tel: (044 63) 4519

Rompa (Flexus Plastics Ltd), PO Box 5, Wheatbridge Road, Chesterfield S40 2AE. tel (0246) 211777

Safe-Tie, 15 Meadow Close, High Wycombe, Bucks HP11 1RG. tel: (0494) 31887/21438. Contact: Mr Pearce.

Scan-Sit Ltd, Unit 4, 111 Mortlake Road, Kew, Richmond, Surrey TW9 4AB. tel: (01) 392 1896

Scoliosis Association UK, 380/384 Harrow Road, LKondon W9 2HU. tel: (071) 289 5652

Self-Lift Chair Co, Mahler House, 130 Worcester Road, Droitwich Spa, Worcester. tel: (0905) 778116

Shackletons (Carlinghow) Ltd, 501 Bradford Road, Bratley WF17 7LN. tel: (0924) 474430

Skandi-Form UK, 36 Dashwood Avenue, High Wycombe, HP12 3DX. tel: (0494) 24222

JC & MP Smith Ltd, Spring Gardens, High Wycombe, Bucks HP13 7AB. tel: (0494) 30255

JS Smith - High Wycombe, 36 Dashwood Avenue, High Wycombe, HP12 3DX. tel: (0494) 24222

SML Healthcare Ltd, Bath Place, High Street, Barnet, Herts EN5 5XE. tel (081) 440 6522

James Spencer & Co Ltd, Moor Road Works, Moor Road, Headingley, Leeds LS6 4BH. tel (0532) 785837/741850

Spinal Publications (UK), PO Box 275, West Byfleet, Surrey KT14 6ET. tel: (09323) 47166

Hugh Steeper Ltd, 237-239 Roehampton Lane, London SW15 4LB. tel (081) 788 8165

Stoneyford Design Ltd, The Coach House, Unit 6, Matfen Hall, Matfen, Northumberland NE20 0RH. tel: (06616) 444

Stowaway Furniture & Design Co Ltd, 44/46 Bunyan Road, Kempson, Beds. MK42 8HL. tel: (0234) 854993

R Taylor & Son (Orthopaedic) Ltd, Compton Works, 49 Woodwards Road, Pleck, Walsall, WS2 9RN. tel: (0922) 27601

Teal Furniture Ltd, Wycombe Road, Stokenchurch, Bucks, HP14 3RR. tel: (024 026) 30077

Texquisite, 97 Parkmore, Craigavon, N. Ireland BT64 2AF. tel: (0762) 338580

Theraposture Ltd, 4 The Downlands, Warminster, Wilts. BA12 0BD. tel: (0985) 213440

Toys for the Handicapped, 76 Barracks Road, Sandy Lane Ind Est, Stourport-on-Severn, Worcs., DY13 9QB. tel: (0299) 827820

Tullos Furniture Products, 132 Wellington Road, West Tullos Ind Est., Aberdeen AB9 1LQ. tel: (0224) 873366

Twickenham Trading Co, 16 Ailsa Avenue, Twickenham, Middlesex TW1 1NG. tel: (081) 891 2028

Tyler International, Meeting House Lane, Baldock, Herts. SG7 5BP. tel: (0462) 895800

AJ Way & Co Ltd, Riverlock House, Spring Gardens Road, High Wycombe, Bucks, HP13 7AG, tel: (0494) 27507

Welland Medical Supplies, Unit 12 Centre House, Wimbledon St, Leicester LE1 1SN tel: (0533) 516912

Wundarest Products, Chester House, Windsor End, Beaconsfield, Bucks, HP9 2JJ. tel: (049 46) 71257

CHILDREN'S AIDS

Amilake Ltd, Haslemere Ind Est, 20 Ravesbury Terrace, Wandsworth, London SW18 4SB. tel: (081) 947 7771/7191

Aremco, Grove House, Lenham, Kent, ME17 2PX. tel: (0622) 858502

EJ Arnold & Son Ltd, Parkside Lane, Dewsbury Road, Leeds LS11 5TD. tel: (0532) 772112

W & F Barrett Ltd, 22 Emery Road, Bristol, Avon, BS4 5PH. tel: (0272) 779016/774070

Beard Bros Ltd (Bushey), Rossway Drive, Little Bushey Lane, Bushey, Herts WD2 3RY. tel: (081) 950 2306

Bencraft Ltd, The Avenue, Rubery, Rednal, Birmingham B45 9AP. tel: (021) 453 1055/6/7

Booster Electric Vehicles Ltd, Bank Street, Brighouse, West Yorkshire HD6 1BD. tel: (0484) 722599

Bradford Activity Toys, 103 Dockfield Road, Shipley, W Yorkshire, BD17 7AR. tel: (0274) 594173 / 596030

Britax-Excelsior Ltd, 1 Churchill Way West, Portway Ind Est, Andover, Hants SP10 3UW. tel: (0264) 333343

Broadway (Mobility), Unit 9, The Arches, Sherwood Road, South Harrow, Middlesex HA2 8AU. tel: (081) 423 0641

Buss Mobility Designs Ltd, 102 Ashford Road, Bearsted, Maidstone, Kent, ME14 4LX. tel: (0622) 37012

Camp Ltd, Northgate House, Staple Gardens, Winchester SO23 8ST. tel: (0962) 55248

Carters (J&A) Ltd, Aintree Avenue, White Horse, Business Park, North Bradley, Trowbridge, Wilts BA14 0XA. tel: (0225) 751901

Chailey Heritage, Rehab Engineering Unit, Chailey Heritage Hospital and School, North Chailey, Lewes, East Sussex, BN8 4EF. tel: (082 572) 2112 ext. 210

Child Accident Prevention Trust, 28 Portland Place, London WIN 4DE. tel: (071) 636 2545

Cindico Nursery Products Ltd, Station Road, Long Buckby, Northampton, NN6 7PF. tel: (0327) 842662

Clinical Engineering Consultants Ltd, Unit D8, Barwell Trading Estate, Chessington, Surrey, KT9 2NY. tel: (01) 974 1439

Combat Tricycle Co Ltd, Unit 44, Telford Industrial Centre, Stafford Park 4, Telford TF3 3BA. tel: (0952) 290279

Cooper & Sons Ltd, Wormley, Godalming, Surrey GU8 5SY. tel: (042 879) 2251

Crelling Harnesses for the Disabled, 12-12 The Crescent, Cleveleys, Lancs, FY5 3LJ. tel: (0253) 852298 / 821780

Davies, Theo M, Argoed, Glyn Ceeirog, Llangollen, Clywd, LL20 7HN. tel: (069 172) 218

Days Medical Aids Ltd, Litchard Ind Est, Bridgend, Mid-Glamorgan, CF31 2AL. tel: (0656) 57495/60150

Department of Transport (Road Safety Officer), 2 Marsham Street, London SW1P 3EB. tel: (071) 212 4431

Disablement Services Authority (DSA), 14 Russell Square, London WC1B 5EP. tel:(071) 636 6811

Electric Mobility Corporation, Sea King Road, Lynx Trading Estate, Yeovil, Somerset, BA20 2NZ. tel: (0935) 22156

Ellis Son & Paramore Ltd, Spring Street Works, Sheffield S3 8Pb. tel:(0742) 738921

Engments Ltd, Chequers Road, West Meadows Ind Est, Derby DE2 6EN. tel: (0332) 44579

Everaids Ltd, 38 Clifton Road, Cambridge, CB1 4ZT. tel: (0223) 243336

Everest & Jennings Ltd., Princewood Road, Corby, Northants NN17 2DX. tel: (0536) 67661

FDTS Ltd, Highfields Works, West Byfleet Corner, West Byfleet, Surrey, KT14 6LP. tel: (093 23) 42043

Fortress Mobility Ltd, Building 31, Pensnet Trading Estate, Kingswinford, W. Midlands DY6 7PU. tel: (0384) 294876

Fortune Works, 34 Garscadden Road, Old Drumchapel, Glasgow G15. tel: (041) 944 4383

Forwood Designs Ltd, The Mews, Mitcheldean, Glos Gl17 OSL. tel: (0594) 542181

Galt, James & Co Ltd, Brookfield Road, Cheadle, Cheshire SK8 2PN. tel: (061) 428 8511

Gimson-Tendercare, 62 Boston Road, Beaumont Leys, Leicester LE4 1AZ. tel: (0533) 366779

GPSP Ltd, PO Box 25, Portishead, Bristol BS20 9NJ. tel: (0272) 842322

RC Hayes (Leicester) Ltd, 12a Wood Street, Earl Shilton, Leicester, LE9 7ND. tel: (0455) 46027

Hestair Hope Ltd, St Philip's Drive, Royton, Oldham, Lancs, OL2 6AG. tel: (061) 633 6611

Hestair Maclaren Ltd, Station Works, Long Buckby, Northampton NN6 7PF. tel: (0327) 842662

Hunt International Ltd, Unit 3, Gillmoss Ind Est, Liverpool L11) tel: (051) 547 3640

Huntercraft, Ramsan Stable, Priestlands Lane, Sherborne, Dorset DT9 4EY. tel: (0935) 812288

Innovention Products Ltd, The Business Centre, Colne Way, Watford, Herts, WD2 4ND. tel: (0923) 245050/9

Jenx Ltd, 74 Hoyland Road, Sheffield S3 8AB. tel: (0742) 756312

Joncare Ltd, 7 Ashville Trading Estate, Nuffield Way, Abingdon, Oxon OX14 1RL. tel: (0235) 28120/35600

Keep Able Ltd, Fleming Close, Park Farm, Wellingborough, Northants NN8 3UF. tel: (0933) 679426

R Kellie & Son Ltd, Rutherford Road, Dryburgh Ind Est, Dundee, Scotland, DD2 3XF. tel: (0382) 816722

Kirton Designs Ltd, Bungay Road, Hempnall, Norwich, Norfolk, NR15 2NG. tel: (050 842) 8411

James Leckey Design, Design House, Kilwee Ind Est, Dunmurry, Northern Ireland BT17 0HD. tel: (0232) 602277

Llewellyn Health Care Services, Regent House, 1 Regent Road, City, Liverpool L3 7BX. tel: (051) 236 5311

Medway Itec, Information Technology Centre, Upbury Manor Centre, Marlborough Road, Gillingham, Kent ME7 5HT. tel: (0634) 281234

Mobility Advice & Vehicle Information Service, Department of Transport, TRRL, Old Wokingham Road, Crowthorne, Berks RG11 6AU. tel: (0344) 770456

Mobility Aids Centre, 88D South Street, Stanground, Peterborough, Cambs, PE2 8Ez. tel: (0733) 44930

Molnlycke Ltd, Hospital Products Division, Southfields Road, Dunstable, Beds, LU6 3EJ. tel: (0582) 600211. *Accept quantity orders only*

Neill & Bennett, 7 Wyngate Road, Cheadle Hulme, Cheadle, Cheshire SK8 6ER. tel: (061) 485 3149

Newton Products -Spastics Society, Meadway Works, Garretts Green Lane, Birmingham, B33 0SQ. tel: (021) 783 6081/2/3

Nomeq, 23-24 Thornhill Road, North Moons Moat, Redditch, Worcs B98 9ND. tel: (0527) 64222

Nottingham Rehab Ltd, 17 Ludlow Hill Road, West Bridgford, Nottingham, NG2 6HD. tel: (0602) 234251

Otho-Kinetics (UK) Ltd, Unit 4, Planetary Road Ind Est, Wednesfield, Wolverhampton WV13 3XA. tel: (0902) 866166

Paraid, Weston Lane, Birmingham B11 3RS. tel: (021) 706 6744

WR Pashley Ltd, Masons Road, Stratford-upon-Avon CV37 9NL. tel: (0789) 292263

John Paxton Flexi Products Ltd, Unit 14, Stockton Close, Minworth Industrial Park, Sutton Coldfield B76 8DH. tel: (021) 351 3572

Petrena Products, 12 The Halcroft, Syston, Leicester LE7 8LD. tel: (0533) 605966

Poirier (UK) Ltd, 17 St George's Ind Est, Frimley Road, Camberley, Surrey GU15 2QW. tel: (0276) 28562/3

Prince & Fletcher Ltd, Bonding House, 26 Blackfriars Street, Manchester, Gt Manchester. tel: (061) 834 5573

Quest 88 Ltd, 2 Turnberry Close, Perton, via Wolverhampton WV6 7PE. tel: (0902) 755906

Rainbow Rehab, PO Box 546, Bournemouth BH8 8YD. tel: (0202) 32651

Remploy Ltd *Medical Products Div,*Russ Street, Broad Plain, Bristol BS2 OHJ. tel: (0272) 277512 *Wheelchair div.,* 11 Nunnery Drive, Sheffield S2 1TA. tel: (0742) 757631

Renray Group Ltd, Road Five, Winsford Ind Est, Winsford, Cheshire CW7 3RB. tel: (0602) 593456

Rifton & Community Playthings, Robertsbridge, East Sussex, TN32 5DR. tel: (0580) 880626

Roma Medical Aids Ltd, Llandow Ind Est, Cowbridge, South Glamorgan, CF7 7PB. tel: (044 63) 4519

Rompa (Flexus Plastics Ltd), PO Box 5, Wheatbridge Road, Chesterfield, Derbyshire S40 @AE. tel: (0246) 211777

Samson Products (Dorset) Ltd., 239 Alder Road, Parkstone, Dorset BH12 4AP. tel: (0202) 734171

Scottish National Insitution for the War Blinded, Linburn, Wilkieston, Kirknewton, Midlothian, EH27 8DU. tel: (031) 333 1369/1334

Silver Cross Ltd, Otley Road, Guisley, Leeds LS20 8LP. tel: (0943) 76177

Gerald Simmonds Wheelchairs Stoke Mandeville, 9 March Place, Gatehouse Way, Aylesbury, HP19 3UG. tel: (0296) 436557

G & S Smirthwaite, Unit 11, Rydon Industrial Estate, Newton Road, Newton Abbot, Devon TQ12 3RX. tel: (0627) 2690 or (0626) 56973

SML Healcare Ltd, Unit 4, The Sphere Ind Est, Campfield Road, St Albans. tel: (0727) 46046

Snugli UK, 43 Richmond Road, Lincoln LN1 1LQ. tel: (0522) 544917. *Available by mail order.*

Speedwell Enterprises, Northampton Avenue, Slough, Berks, SL1 3BP. tel: (0753) 72249

Hugh Steeper Ltd, 237-239 Roehampton Lane, London SW15 4LB. tel: (081) 788 8165

Suffolk Playworks, Box Farm, Allwood Green, Rickinghall, Suffolk IP22 1LU. tel: (03598) 8844

Sunrise Medical Ltd, Fens Pool Avenue, Brierley Hill, West Midlands DY5 1QA. tel: (0384) 480480

T & S Motion and Sport, Head Office, Potter Lane, Wellow, Via Newark, Notts NG22 0EB. tel: (0623) 835362

R Taylor & Son (Orthopaedic) Ltd, Compton Works, 49 Woodwrds Road, Plech, Walsall, WS2 9RN. tel: (0922) 27601

Toy Furniture Workshop, Church Hill. Totland Bay, Isle of White, PO39 0ET. tel: (0983) 752596

Toys for the Handicapped, 76 Barracks Road, Sandy Lane Ind Est, Stourport-on-Severn, Worcs, DY13 9QB. tel: (0299) 827820

Triaid Manufacturing Co Ltd, 32 Welbeck Road, Darnley Ind Est, Glasgow G53 7SD. tel: (041 881) 2273/4

Uniscan Ltd, 12 Samson House, Arterial Road, Basildon, Essex SS15 6DR. tel: (0268) 419228

University of Salford, The Secretary, Department of Orthopaedic Mechanics, Salford M5 4WT. tel: (061) 736 5843 ext 7402

Vessa Ltd, Paper Mill Lane, Alton, Hants, GU34 2PY. tel: (0420) 83294

Victor and Sally Wilkins, Penrallt, Pantyderi, Boncath, Nr Cardigan SA37 0JB. tel: (023 974) 390

JP Wilson (Surgical Appliances) Ltd, 26 Elswick East Terrace, Newcastle upon Tyne NE4 7LJ. tel: (091) 2736341

WRK (Marketing), Ashfield House, School Road, St Johns Fen End, Wisbech, Cambs. tel: (0945) 880014

CHILDREN'S EQUIPMENT

Altonaids Mobility, Park Road, Gateshead NE8 3HL. tel: (091) 4773733

Aremco, Grove House, Lenham, Kent, ME17 2PX. tel: (0622) 858502

EJ Arnold & Son Ltd, Parkside Lane, Dewsbury Road, Leeds LS11 5Td. tel: (0532) 772112

ASM Medicare, Picow Farm Industrial Estate, Runcorn, Cheshire WA 7 4UG. tel: (09285) 74301/2/3

Atkinson Engineering, Marsh House Mill, Brussels Road, Darwen, Lancs. tel: (0254) 773524

Ayrton-Graham (Contracts) Ltd, 10 North Drive, Wallasey, Merseyside L45 0LZ. tel: (051) 639 5848

Bakaware Ltd, Cecil Street, Birmingham, West Midlands, B19 2SY. tel: (021) 359 3552

Banwell Packaging Ltd, Niagra Works, Jubilee Road, Weston Super Mare, Avon. tel: (0934) 628217

Bettacare Ltd, Welbeck House, Cliftonville, Dorking, Surrey, RH4 2JF. tel: (0306) 888 299

Bickiepegs Ltd, Unit 5, Blackburn Industrial Estate, Woodburn Road, Blackburn, Aberdeen AB5 0TZ. tel: (0224) 790626

Bitteswell Employment Alliance Ltd, Unit 1, Arches Industrial Estate, Spon End, Coventry, CV1 3JQ. tel: (0203) 74817

Boots the Chemists Ltd, City Gate, Toll House Hill, Nottingham NG2 3AA. tel: (0602) 418522. *Enquiries should be made at local branches.*

Camp Ltd-Northgate House, Stable Gardens, Winchester SO23 8ST. tel: (0962) 55248 -or-DH Seating Division, Portfield Industrial Estate, Nevil Shute Road, Portsmouth, Hampshire PO3 5RL. tel: (0705) 697411

CB Gifts Ltd, 6 Portland Place, Stevenston, Ayrshire, Scotland KA20 3NN. tel: (0294) 602823

Central Medical Equipment, 7 Ascot Park Estate, Lenton Street, Sandiacre, Nottingham. NG10 5DL. tel: (0602) 390949

Chailey Heritage, Rehab Engineering Unit, Chailey Heritage Hospital and School, North Chailey, Lewes, East Sussex, BN8 4EF. tel: (082 572) 2112 ext. 210

Chiltern Medical Developments Ltd, Chiltern House, Wedgewood Road, Bicester, Oxon OX6 7UL. tel: (0869) 246470

Cindico Nursery Products Ltd, Station Road, Long Buckby, Northampton, NN6 7PF. tel: (0327) 842662

Clinical Engineering Consultants Ltd, Unit D8, Barwell Trading Estate, Chessington, Surrey, KT9 2NY. tel: (01) 974 1439

Computer Aids, The Fox Covert, Picton Gorse, Chester CH2 4HB. tel: (0244) 300363

Cooper & Sons Ltd, Wormley. Godalming, Surrey GU8 5SY. tel: (042 879) 2251

Crelling Harnesses for the Disabled, 11-12 The Crescent, Cleveleys, Lancs, FY5 3LJ. tel: (0253) 852298 / 821780

Days Medical Aids Ltd, Litchard Industrial Estate, Bridgend, Mid-Glamorgan, CF31 2AL. tel: (0656) 57495/60150

Easi Care Ltd, Mullions, Lymington Road, Milford-on-Sea, Hampshire SO41 0QN. tel: (0590) 43839

Ellis Son & Paramore Ltd, Spring Street Works, Sheffield S3 8PB. tel: (0742) 738921

Engments Ltd, Chequers Road, West Meadows Industrial Estate, Derby, DE2 6EN. tel: (0332) 44579

Everest & Jennings Ltd., Princewood Road, Corby, Northants NN17 2DX. tel: (0536) 67661

Fortune Works, 34 Garscadden Road, Old Drumchapel, Glasgow G15. tel: (041) 944 4383

Forwood Designs Ltd, The Mews, Mitcheldean, Glos GL17 OSL. tel: (0594) 542181

W Freeman & Co Ltd, Suba-Seal Works, Staincross, Barnsley S75 6DH. tel: (0226) 284081

FW Equipment Co Ltd, Hanworth Road, Low Moor, Bradford BD12 0SG. tel: (0274) 601121

Gallops Hospital Equipment, Finmere Road, Eastbourne BN21 8QG. tel: (0323) 646681

A W Gegory & Co Ltd, Glynde House, Glynde Street, London SE4 1RY. tel: (081) 690 3437

Haberman Feeders -c/o Mrs M. Haberman, 44 Watford Road, Radlett, Herts WD7 8LR. tel: (0923) 853544

Hago Products Ltd, Shripney Road, Bognor Regis, PO22 9NH. tel: (0243) 863131. *Wholesale supplier only*

RC Hayes (Leicester) Ltd, 12a Wood Street, Earl Shilton, Leicester, LE9 7ND. tel: (0455) 46027

Headingley Scientific Sevices, 45 Westcombe Avenue, Leeds LS8 2BS. tel: (0532) 66422

Heinz Baby Club, Vinces Road, Diss, Norfolk IP22 3HH. tel: (0379) 651981

Hestair Hope Ltd, St Philip's Drive, Royton, Oldham, Lancs, OL2 6AG. tel: (061) 633 6611

M Hogarth & Sons, Princess Street, Corbridge, Northumberland NE45 5AE. tel: (0434) 712134

Homecraft Supplies Ltd, Low Moor Estate, Kirkby-in-Ashfield NG17 7JZ. tel: (0623) 754 047

Hospital Management & Supplies Ltd, Selinas Lane, Dagenham, Essex RM 8 1QD. tel: (01) 593 7511

Huntercraft, Ramsam Stable, Priestlands Lane, Sherborne, Dorset, DT9 4EY. tel: (0935) 812288

Independent Living Centre, 9 Caldecote Gardens, Bushey Heath, Herts WD2 3RA. tel: (01) 950 6635

Innovention Products Ltd, The Business Centre, Colne Way, Watford, Herts, WD2 4ND. tel: (0923) 245050/9

Jackel International Ltd, Dudley Lane, Cramlington, Northumberland, NE23 7RH. tel: (091) 250 1864. *Products retailed by chemists and supermarkets*

Jenx Ltd, 74 Hoyland Road, Sheffield S3 8AB. tel: (0742) 756312

Joncare Ltd, 7 Ashville Trading Estate, Nuffield Way, Abingdon, Oxon OX14 1RL. tel: (0235) 28120/35600

Keep Able Ltd, Fleming Close, Park Farm, Wellingborough, Northants NN8 3UF. tel: (0933) 679426

Kidd-Proof Products Ltd, Design House, 9 Centre Way, Claverings Industrial Estate, Montague Road, Edmonton, London N9 0AJ. tel: (081) 807 4552

Kirton Designs Ltd, Bungay Road, Hempnall, Norwich, Norfolk, NR15 2NG. tel: (050 842) 8411

James Leckey Design, Design House, Kilwee Industrial Estate, Dunmurry, Northern Ireland BT17 0HD. tel: (0232) 602277

Lewis Woolf Griptight Ltd, 144 Oakfield Road, Seely Oak, Birmingham B29 7EE. tel: (021) 414 1122

Llewellyn Health Care Services, Regent House, 1 Regent Road, City, Liverpool L3 7BX. tel: (051) 236 5311

Mackworth Medical Products Ltd, Morgan Street Works, Llambradach, Caerphilly, Mid Glamorgan CF8 3QT. tel: (0222) 861281

Masterpeace Products Ltd, Tormen House, Booth Hill Works, Booth Hill Lane, Oldham, OL1 2PH. tel: (061) 624 2041

Mobil Aids (Wales) Ltd, 144 Woodville Road, Cathays, Cardiff CF2 4NW. tel: (0222) 32242

Molnlycke Ltd, Hospital Products Division, Southfields Road, Dunstable, Beds Lu6 3EJ. tel: (0582) 600211

Mothercare Plc, Cherry Tree Road, Watford, Herts, WD2 5SH. tel: (0923) 33577. *Customer enquiries only* (0923) 31616

Mulberry Furniture, 1 Mulberry Close, Chingford, London E4 8BS. tel: (081) 529 8306/524 2263

Horatio Myer & Co Ltd, Contracts Division, Windover Road, Huntingdon, Cambs, PE18 7EF. tel: (0480) 52111

Neckease, 5 Firs Walk, Woodfield Green, Essex IG8 OTD. tel: (081) 504 0839

J Nesbit Evans & Co Ltd, Woden Road West, Wednesbury WS10 7BL. tel: (021) 556 1511

Newton Products -Spastics Society, Meadway Works, Garretts Green Lane, Birmingham, B33 0SQ. tel: (021) 783 6081/2/3

Nicholls & Clarke Ltd, 3/10 Shoreditch High Street, London E1 6PE. tel: (071) 247 5432

Nottingham Rehab Ltd, 17 Ludlow Hill Road, West Bridgford, Nottingham, NG2 6HD. tel: (0602) 234251

Ortho-Kinetics (UK) Ltd, Unit 4, Planetary Road Industrial Estate, Wednesfield, Wolverhampton WV13 3XA. tel: (0902) 866166

Pressalit Ltd, 25 Grove Promenade. Ilkley LS29 8AF. tel: (0943) 607651

Prince & Fletcher Ltd, Bonding House, 26 Blackfriars Street, Manchester. tel: (061) 834 5573

Proctors Nets, High Street, Brentford, Middlesex TW8 8JX. tel: (081) 560 0331

Radford Orthopaedic Co Ltd, Rebecca House, Rebecca Street, Westgate, Bradford BD1 2RX. tel: (0274) 723729

Rainbow Rehab. PO Box 546, Bournemouth BH8 8YD. tel: (0202) 32651

Rehab Products, 9/10 Standard Way, Fareham Industrial Park. Fareham, Hants PO16 8XB. tel: (0329) 286628

Remploy Ltd (Medical Products Div), Russ Street, Broad Plain, Bristol BS2 OHJ. tel: (0272) 277512

Rialto, The Old School house, Raydon, Hadleigh, Suffolk, IP7 5LH. tel: (0473) 311211

Sylvia Rice, 120 St. Stephens Avenue, London W12 8JD. tel: (01) 749 3841

Rifton & Community Playthings, Robertsbridge, East Sussex, TN32 5DR. tel: (0580) 880626

Roma Medical Aids Ltd, Llandow Industrial Estate, Cowbridge, South Glamorgan, CF7 7PB. tel: (044 63) 4519

Rompa (Flexus Plastics Ltd), PO Box 5, Wheatbridge Road, Chesterfield, Derbyshire S40 2AF. tel: (0246) 211777

Scan-Sit Ltd., Unit 4, 111 Mortlake Road, Kew, Richmond, Surrey TW9 4AB. tel: (01) 392 1896

Sherwood Industries, Sherwood Village Settlement, Southwell Road West, Rainworth, Nr. Mansfield,

Notts NG21 0HW. tel: (0623) 792151. *Sell to contract holders only.*

Sidhil Care, Boothtown, Halifax HX3 6NT. tel: (0422) 363447

G & S Smithwaite, Unit 11, Rydon Industrial Estate, Newton Road, Newton Abbot, Devon TQ12 3RX. tel: (0627) 2690 or (0626) 56973

SML Healthcare Ltd, Bath Place, High Street, Barnet, Herts EN5 5XE. tel: (081) 440 6522

Spastics Society - Fitzroy Square, Equipment Resource Room, 16 Fitzroy Square, London W1P 5HQ. tel: (071) 387 9571

Starters, Division of Slater & Frith Ltd, Lurista House, Stalham Road, Wroxham, Norwich NR12 8DV. tel: (0603) 784202

Hugh Steeper Ltd, 237-239 Roehampton Lane, London SW15 4LB. tel: (081) 788 8165

Stowaway Furniture and Design Co Ltd, 44/46 Bunyan Road, Kempson. Bedfordshire MK42 8HL. tel: (0234) 854993

Swim Shop, 52/58 Albert Road, Luton, Beds LU1 3PR. tel: (0582) 416545

R Taylor & Son (Orthopaedic) Ltd, Compton Works, 49 Woodwards Road, Pleck, Walsall, WS2 9RN. tel: (0922) 27601

Thinking Little Ltd, 11 Lonsdale Road, London NW6 6RA. tel: (071) 328 1666

Thistle-Binby Products Ltd, Office and Showroom, Beswick Street, Manchester M4 7HS. tel: (061) 273 5756

Toys & Furniture Workshop, Church Hill, Totland Bay, Isle of Wight PO39 0ET. tel: (0983) 752596

Toys for the Handicapped, 76 Barracks Road, Sandy Lane Industrial Estate, Stourport-on-Severn, Worcs., DY13 9QB. tel: (0299) 827820

Triaid Manufacturing Co Ltd, 32 Welbeck Road, Darnley Industrial Estate, Glasgow G53 7SD. tel: (041 881) 2273/4

Trylon Ltd, Thrift Street, Wollaston, Northants NN9 7QJ. tel: (0933) 664275

Unit Installations, Unit 26, Yates Brothers, Lime Lane, Pelsall, Walsall. tel: (0922) 413538

Vernon & Co (Pulp Products) Ltd, Slater Street, Bolton, Lancs BL1 2HP. tel: (0204) 29494. *Supply to hospitals only*

WAVES, Corscombe, Nr Dorchester, Dorset, DT2 0NU. tel: (093 589) 248

JP Wilson (Surgical Appliances) Ltd, 26 Elswick East Terrace, Newcastle upon Tyne NE4 7LJ. tel: (091) 273 6341

CLOTHING

Able-Lable Department, Steepleprint Ltd, Earls Barton, Northampton, NN6 0YZ. tel: (0604) 810781

Action Brief Company Ltd, 13-15 Mavor Close, Woodstock, Oxon, OX7 1YL. tel: (0993) 811450 or 084 421-6814

Aldrex Ltd., Department C, Newnham, Gloucester, Glos., GL14 1AG. tel: (0594) 516306

Andre de Brett, Brett House, P.O. Box 11, Keighley, BD20 6AZ. tel: (01) 998 6565

Aremco, Grove House, Lenham, Kent, ME17 2PX. tel: (0622) 858502

Arjay Associates (Handi-Aids), 82 Wordsworth Court, Middlefield, Hatfield, Hertfordshire, AL10 0EF. tel: (07072) 74210

E.J. Arnold & Son Ltd., Parkside Lane, Dewsbury Road, Leeds, LS11 5TD. tel: (0532) 772112

Artimaze Ltd (Dept. C88) 6 Lechmere Road, London, NW2 5BU. tel: (081) 459 7053

Artimaze Ltd., 118 Wood Lane, London, NW9 7LX. tel: (081) 205 5545

Arwin Products & Co., No.11 Irwell House, East Philip Street, Salford, Gt. Manchester M3 7LE. tel: (061 832) 2789 or (061 835) 1407

Association for Research into Restricted Growth, 18 Cliff Road, Great Haywood, Staffordshire, ST18 0SZ

Association for Spina Bifida & Hydrocephalus, 22 Upper Woburn Place, London WC1H 0EP. tel: (071) 388 1382 or 388 1385

Barber & Nicholls Ltd., Tytex Dept., Moatway, Barwell, Leicester, LE9 8EY. tel: (0455) 44181

BCS Products, Old Woods Trading Estate, Torquay, Devon, TQ2 7AU. tel: (0803) 62772

Beakbane Ltd., PO Box 10, Stourport Road, Kidderminster, Worcs., DY11 7QT. tel: (0562) 820561

Beard Bros. Ltd., Unit 2, The Crystal Centre, Elmgrove Rd, Harrow, HA1 2HS. tel: (081) 861 4070

Beaver of Bolton Ltd., Gilnow Mill, Spa Road, Bolton, BL1 4LF. tel: (0204) 386824

A.D. & D.J. Belle, 15 Martins Drive, Ferndown, Dorset, BH22 9SG. tel: (0202) 873249

Bennett Safetywear Ltd., Mersey Road,Crosby, Liverpool, Merseyside, L23 3AF. tel: (051) 924 3996 Alternative tel: 924 3997

Berbette, 50 Cambridge Road, New Malden, Surrey, KT3 3QL. tel: (081) 949 5691 Alt. tel No: (081) 949 6912

Chistina Berry, 3 Waggon Mews, Southgate. London, N14 5HY. tel: (01) 886 7633

Big Mans Shop, George Deakin & Sons Ltd, PO Box 3, Fore Street, Redruth, Cornwall, TR15 2DQ. tel: (0209) 216868/216222

Birkett & Phillips, 1 Mill Buildings, Lea Bridge, Matlock, Derbyshire DE4 5AG. tel: (0629) 534331

Boots Co. plc., Medical Merchandise Dept., City Gate, Toll House Hill, Nottingham, Notts., NG2 3AA. tel. (0602) 418522 *Enquiries should be made at local branches.*

Bradley's, 83-85 Knightsbridge, London, SW1X 7RB. tel: (071) 235 2902

George Brettle & Co., Meadow Lane, Alfreton, DE5 7EZ. tel: (0773) 520400 *Showroom:* 10 St George St, off Conduit St, London, W1R 9DF, tel: (071) 629 8560

Buckley Lamb Ltd., Eastfield Side, Sutton-in-Ashfield, Notts., NG17 4JW. tel: (0623) 550350

Butterick and Fashion Marketing, Butterick and Vogue, New Lane, Havant, Hants., PO9 2ND. tel: (0705) 486221

Buyona (Health and Bodycare), PO Box 13, Unit 5, Lealand Way, Boston, Lincs, PE21 7SW. tel: (0205) 62742

D Byford & Co., Ltd., PO Box 10, Nottingham Road, Somercotes, Derbyshire, DE55 4SF. tel: (0773) 607433

Camp Ltd (North Division), Strodex House, Nottingham Road, London Eaton, Nottingham, NG10 1JW. tel: (0602) 732203

Can-Can, 188 Grays Inn Road, London, WC1X 8EW. tel: (071) 833 3531

Carr & Westley Ltd., Bourne Mill, Hadlow, Tonbridge, Kent, TN11 0EU. tel: (0732) 850280

Carters (J&A) Ltd., Aintree Ave, White Horse Business Park, North Bradley, Trowbridge, Wiltshire BA14 0XA. tel: (0225) 715901.

Chailey Heritage, Rehab Engineering Unit, Chailey Heritage Hospital & Sch. North Chailey, Lewis, E. Sussex. BN8 4EF. tel: (082 572) 2112 ext. 99

Chalkleys (Kettering) Ltd., 7/8 Silver Street, Kettering, Northants. NN16 0BN. tel: (0536) 513959

Chester-Care Ltd., 16 Englands Lane, London NW3 4TG. tel: (071) 586 2166 or (071) 722 3430

Child Growth Foundation, 2 Mayfield Avenue, London, W4 1PW. tel: (081) 994 7625

Christi-Anna, White Cottages, Lodge, Nr. Wrexham, Clwyd, Wales. tel: (0978) 752534

Chums Ltd., Caddick Road, Knowsley Industrial Park, South Prescot, Merseyside, L34 4AB. tel: (051) 548 8088

(Cloth Kits) Lewes Design Workshop Ltd., 24 High St., Lewes E. Sussex, BN7 2LB. tel: (0273) 477111

Colostomy Welfare Group, Fourth Floor, 38/39 Eccleston Sq.,London SW1V 1PB. tel: (071) 828 5175

Comfortably Yours, 53 Dale Street, Manchester, M60 6ES. tel: (061) 236 9911

Comfy Products, Providence Place, Bridlington, YO15 2QW. tel: (0262) 676417

Conoley & Johnson, 99-103 Hamlet Court Road, Westcliff-on-Sea, Essex, SS0 7ES. tel: (0702) 334188/9.

Contact Direct Ltd., 30 Western Road, Hove, East Sussex, BN3 1AF. tel: (0273) 770467

Cotton On 29 North Clifton St., Lytham, Lancs., FY8 5HW. tel: (0253) 736611

C & H Coverdale, Boundary Road, Mountsorrel, Loughborough, Leics, LE12 7ER. tel: (0533) 302334

Damart, Bowling Green Mills, Lime Street, Bingley, W. Yorkshire, BD16 4BH. tel: (0274) 568211

Days Medical Aids Ltd., Litchard Industrial Estate, Bridgend, M. Glam, CF31 2AL. tel: (0656) 57495 Alt. tel no: (0656)60150

Delia Marketing Ltd., 24 Craven Park Road, London NW10, 4AB. tel: (081) 965 8707

Dollycare (Cosby) Ltd, 13 Elm Tree Road, Cosby, Leics. LE9 5SR. tel: (0533) 773013/(0533) 477727 *24hr Mail Order.*

Rita Eaton MA, Mastectomy Designs, Rita Eaton MA, 12 Brancaster Close, Leicester, LE4 0LA. tel: (0533) 352247

Elderwise Ltd., 29 Villa Road, Bingley, West Yorkshire, BD16 4EU. tel: (0274) 565976

Evans, Head Office, 60/62 Margaret Street, London, W1 7JF. tel: (071) 636 8040

Exchange, National Eczema Society, Tavistock House North, Tavistock Sq., London, WC1H 9SR. tel: (071) 388 4097

Exquisite Form Ltd, 30 Market Place, Oxford Circus, London, W1N 8DL. tel: (071) 580 9265

Fashion Extra, Family Album, Devonshire Street, Ardwich, Manchester, M60 6EL. tel: (061) 273 7171

Charles Fellows Supplies Ltd., Dawley Trading Estate, Kings Winford, W. Midlands, DY6 7BH. tel: (0384) 273204

Forget-me-Not, 168 Commercial Road, London, E1 2JY. tel: (071) 790 6454

JA Freeman Manufacturing, 22 Broadlands Drive, Walderslade, Chatham, Kent, ME5 8HJ. tel: (0634) 65597

Functional Clothing Ltd., Causeway Avenue, Wilderspool Causeway, Warrington, WA4 6QQ. tel: (0925) 53111

Ganmill Ltd., 38/40 Market Street, Bridgwater, Somerset, TA6 3EP. tel: (0278) 423037

Gimson-Tendercare, 62 Boston Road, Beaumont Leys, Leicester, Leics., LE4 1AZ. tel: (0533) 366779

Greenham Trading Ltd., Head Office, 671 London Road, Isleworth, TW7 4EX. tel: (081) 560 1244

Hartington House, PO Box. 167, 53 Dale Street, Manchester, M60 6ES. tel: (061) 228 1199

Roy Harwood, 6B Imperial Chambers, 62 Dale Street, Liverpool, Merseyside. L2 5SX. tel: (051) 236 3977

Health & Comfort Ltd., PO Box 15, Westbury, Wilts, BA13 4LS. tel: (0373) 822394

Helly-Hanson (UK) Ltd., College Street, Kempston, Bedford, Beds., MK42 8NA. tel: (0234) 41431

Helping Hand Company (Ledbury) Ltd., Unit L9, Bromyard Rd Ind. Trading Estate, Ledbury, Herefordshire. HR8 1NS. tel: (0531) 5678

Helping Hands Shop, 114 Queens Road, Leicester, LE2 3FL. tel: (0533) 881200 ext: 149

Henleys Medical Supplies Ltd., Brownfields, Welwyn Garden City, Hertfordshire, AL7 1AN. tel: (0707) 333164

High & Mighty, Head Office, The Old School House, High Street, Hungerford, Berkshire, RG17 0NS. tel: (0488) 84913

Eric Hill ltd., High Street, Bramley, Guildford, Surrey, GU5 0HQ. tel: (0483) 898222

Holborn Surgical Instrument Co Ltd., Dolphin Works, Margate Road, Broadstairs, Kent CT10 2QQ. tel: (0843) 61418

SR Holbrook Ltd (Brinmark), Jackson Road, Coventry, CV6 4LY. tel: (0203) 667576

Home Nursing Supplies Ltd., Headquarters Road, West Wilts Trading Estate, Westbury, Wilts., BA13 4JR. tel: (0373) 822313

Homecraft Supplies Ltd., Low Moor Estate, Kirkby-in-Ashfield, Notts, NG17 7JZ. tel: (0623) 754047

Hospital Aids Ltd., 9 Staveley Way, Brixworth, Northampton, Northants., NN6 9EU. tel: (0604) 881650

Husky Ltd., 115 Bury Street, Stowmarket, Suffolk, IP14 1HE. tel: (0449) 674471

Ileostomy Association (Mansfield), Amblehurst House, Black Scotch Lane, Mansfield, Notts. NG18 4PF.

Independent Living Centre, 9 Caldecote Gardens, Bushey Heath, Hertfordshire, WD2 3RA. tel: (081) 950 6635

J & J Cash Ltd., Torrington Avenue, Coventry, West Midlands, CV4 9UZ. tel: (0203) 466466

Janine Fashions, 43 Oakleys Road, Long Eaton, Nottingham, NG10 1FQ; tel: (0602) 7385669

Jean Jerrard Fashions, Designer House, Lime Street, Bingley, W. Yorkshire, BD16 4SY. tel: (0274) 561211

A. Katz Ltd., 156 Seven Sisters Road, Finsbury Park, London, N7 7PL tel: (071) 272 3263/8013

S A Kenner Ltd., 146 High Street North, East Ham, London, E6 2HT. tel: (081) 472 1078

Kenton Fashions Ltd., 2 Hans Road, Knightsbridge, London, SW3. tel: (071) 589 9293 and: 1021 Whitgift Centre, Croydon, London CR0 1UU, tel: (081) 681 1153

A.H. Kidman Ltd., 141-143 Castle Road, Bedford, Beds., tel: (0234) 54090

Knit Kits, 2 Mount Pleasant, Guildford, Surrey GU2 5HZ. tel: (0483) 33052

Llewellyn Health Care Services, Regent House, 1 Regent Road, City, Liverpool, Merseyside, L3 7BX. tel: (051) 236 5311

Long Tall Sally, Mail Order Dept., 13 Chapel Place, Tunbridge Wells, Kent, TN1 1YQ. tel: (0892) 46878

Maja, 13 Courtleigh Bridge Lane, London, NW11 tel: (081) 458 6236

Diana Martin Ltd., (Dept. X), 678-682 High Street, Tottenham, London, N17 0AZ. tel: (081) 808 5473

Mastectomy Association, 26 Harrison Street, off Grays Inn Road, King's Cross, London, WC1H 8JG. tel: (071) 837 0908.

Maubri Fashions, Unit 13b, Springfield Commercial Centre, Farsley, Leeds, LS28 5LY. tel: (0532) 553274

Medimail Ltd., JL Owen Ltd, FREEPOST, Manchester, M4 8BP. tel: (061) 236 0896

Medipost Ltd., Unit 1, St. Johns Estate, Elder Road, Lees, Oldham, Lancs, OL4 3DZ.tel: (061) 678 0233

Medmek Ltd., PO Box 18, Romsey, Hampshire, S05 9ZX. tel: (0794) 8556

Mirella, 7 Old Westhall Close, Warlingham, Surrey, CR3 9HR. tel: (088 32) 4843

Molnlyke Ltd., Hospital Products Div., SSouthfields Rd, Dunstable, Beds. LU6 3EJ. tel: (0582) 600211

Mothercare Plc., Cherry Tree Road, Watford, Herts., WD2 5SH. tel: (0923) 33577 *Customer enquiries on:* (0923) 31616

Mountain Equipment Ltd., Leech Street, Stalybridge, Cheshire, SK15 1SD. tel: (061) 338 8793

MW Plastic Protection, 180 High Street, Pesnett, Dudley, West Midlands, DY5 4JG. tel: (0384) 261060

Nealbourne Ltd., PO Box 10, Nealbourne House, Pitt Street, Keighley, W. Yorkshire, BD21 4PP. tel: (0535) 667535

Neutex, 97 Partmore, Craigavon, Co. Armagh, BY64 2AF Northern Ireland. tel: (0762) 338580

Next (Retail) Ltd., Defford Road, Endoby, Leicestershire, LE9 5AT. tel: (0533) 866411

Nicholas Laboratories Ltd., Head Office, 225 Bath Road, Slough, Berks., SL1 4AU. tel: (0753) 23971

Kanga-Kylie Advisory Service, *Mail order address:* FREEPOST, Slough, SL1 4BX. tel: 0753 23971

Nicholl Knitwear, Piper Close, Corbridge, Northumberland. tel: (043 471) 2283.

Nottingham Rehab Ltd., 17 Ludlow Hill Road, West Bridgford, Nottingham, Notts., NG2 6HD. tel (0602) 234251 *Mail Order Div:* PO Box 96, Nottingham NG2 6HE

Noyna (J Birtwistle), 222 Stretford Road, Urmston, Manchester, Gt. Manchester, M31 1NB. tel: (061) 748 2724

One of Gillies, Llantnthyd, Cowbridge, S. Glamorgan, CF7 7UB. tel: (044 68) 357

Oxendale & Co. Ltd., Galleau House, PO Box 150, Dale Street, Manchester, Gt. Manchester, M1 8JL. tel: (061) 236 9911

Pantherella plc, Midland Hosiery Mills, Hallaton Street, Leicester, Leics., LE2 8QY. tel: (0535) 831111

Pegasus Airwave Ltd., Pegasus House, Kingscroft Court, Havant, Hants, PO9 1LS. tel: (0705) 451444

Perfectos - Douglas Fraser & Sons (MFG) Ltd., Frockheim, Angus, DD11 4TU, Scotland. tel: (024 12) 341

Playtex, 36 Chertsey Road, Woking, Surrey, GU21 5BB. tel: (048 62) 21121

Plus, Littlewoods Organisation, J M Centre, Old Hall Street, Liverpool, Merseyside, L70 1AB. tel: (051) 235 3037

Polyotter Ltd., 25 Cambray Place, Cheltenham, Glos,50 1JN. tel: (0242) 39230

Raynaud's Association Trust, 112 Crewe Road, Alsager, Cheshire, ST7 2JA. tel: (0270) 875167

Redimed Ltd., PO Box 51, Princes Risborough, Bucks, HP17 9BT. tel (084 44) 4242

Brenda Redmile, 32 Cherry Tree Avenue, Leicester Forest East, Leicestershire, LE3 3HN

Remploy Ltd., Medcial Products Division, 415 Edgware Road, Cricklewood, London, NW2 6LR. tel: (081) 452 8020

Research Trust for Metabolic Diseases in Children, 53 Beam Street, Nantwich, Cheshire, CW5 5NF. tel: (0270) 629782

Richer of London Ltd, The Royal Mills, Station Rd, Steeton, Keighley, BD20 6RA. *Shop at:* 206 Kilburn High Rd, London NW6 tel: (071) 624 3393

Rifton & Community Playthings, Robertsbridge, E. Sussex, TN32 5DR. tel: (0580) 880626

Rompa (Flexus Plastics Ltd), PO Box 5, Wheatbridge Road, Chesterfield, Derbyshire, S40 2AE. tel: (0246) 211777

W. S. Rothband & Co Ltd, 21 Elizabeth St, Manchester, M8 8WT. tel: (061) 834 1303

Royal National Institute for the Blind, 224 Great Portland St, London, W1N 6AA. tel: (071) 388 1266

Salt & Sons Ltd., Saltair House, Lord Street, Nechells, Birmingham B7 4DS. tel: (021) 359 5123

Sander & Kay Ltd., Pall Mall Buildings, 124/8 Barlby Road, London, W10 6BU. tel: (081) 969 3553/4498

Scanmark, 43/44 Debden Road, Newport, Essex, CB11 3RU. tel: (0799) 41081

Scoliosis Association (UK), 380-384 Harrow Road, London, W9 2HU. tel: (071) 289 5652

Scott-Nicol, John Ltd., Old Station Close, Shepshed, Loughborough, Leics., LE12 9AT. tel: (0509) 502261

Scottish Knitwear & Fashions Ltd., PO Box 40, 84 Crasswell Street, Portsmouth, Hants., PO1 1HU. tel: (0705) 821925

Security Vision Nameplates Ltd., 8 Telford Court, 9 South Avenue, Clydebank Business Park, Clydebank, G81 2NR. tel: (041) 941 3016/041 941-2239

Selectus Ltd., Biddulph, Stoke on Trent, Staffs., ST8 7RH. tel: (0782) 522316

Secton Group of Companies, Tubiton House, Medlock Street, Oldham, Lancs, OL1 3HS. tel: (061) 652 2222

Shackletons (Carlinghow) Ltd., 501 Bradford Rd., Batley, W. Yorkshire, WF17 8LN. tel: (0924) 474430

Simplantex Eastbourne Ltd., Willowfield Road, Eastbourne, E. Sussex BN22 8AR tel: (0323) 410470

W.A. Smith & Co. Ltd., 550 High Road, Ilford, Essex, IG3 8EB. tel: (081) 597 1116

Spencer (Banbury) Ltd., Spencer House, Britannia Road, Banbury, Oxon. OX16 8DP. tel (0295) 57301

James Spencer & Co., Ltgd., Moor Road Works, Moor Rd, Headingley, Leeds, LS6 4BH. tel: (0532) 785837/741850

Spenco Medical (UK) Ltd., Burrell Road, Haywards Heath, W. Sussex, RH16 1TW. tel: (0444) 415171

Spirella Company of G.B. Ltd., Bridge Road, Letchworth, Herts., SG6 4ET. tel: (046) 2686161

Stanfield, Brian Co Ltd., 127 Hassall Road, Winterley, Sandbach, Cheshire, CW11 0RT. tel: (0270) 765325

Hugh Steeper (Roehampton) Ltd., 237-239 Roehampton Lane, London, SW15 4LB. tel (081) 788 8165

Tall Girls Shop Ltd., 17 Woodstock Street, London, W1 tel: (071) 499 8748

Tamar Neckwear Ltd., 21-22 Tudor Grove, Hackney, London, E9 7SM. tel: (081) 985 4771

Taylor & Cross Ltd., Dept C, 31-33 Stamford New Road, Altrincham, Cheshire, WA14 1EB. tel: (061) 928 1130

R.Taylor & Son (Orthopaedic) Ltd., Compton Works, 49 Woodwards Road, Pleck, Walsall, WS2 9RN. tel: (0922) 27601

Terrapin Aqua Products International (Middie Foord), 19 Maple Way, Earl Shilton, Leicester, Leics., LE9 7HW. tel: (0455) 46505

Thackraycare, 45-47 Great George Street, Leeds, W. Yorkshire, LS1 3Bb. tel: (0532) 430028

Three Jay & Co., 9 The Precinct, High road, Broxbourne, Herts., EN10 7HY. tel. (0992) 442974/463947

Top to Toe, 3 Alderney Road, Croftlands, Dewsbury, W. Yorks. tel: (0924) 464304

Torplay, PO Box 235, Ringwood, Hants, BH24 2SW. tel: (0425) 475952

Totectors Ltd., Totector House, Rushden, Northants, NN10 9SW. tel: (0933) 59311

Tremorvah Industries, Rentoul Works, Threemilestone Ind. Estate, Truro, Cornwall, TR4 9LD. tel: (0872) 40036

Turner, Charles & Co Ltd., Hospital Products Division, Bentinck Street, Bolton, Lancs, BL1 4QG. tel: (0204) 46226

Tutor Safety Products., Bridge Street, Sturminster Newton, Dorset, DT10 1BZ. tel: (0258) 72921 or 73181

Urostomy Association, Mrs. A. Cooke, Buckland, Beaumont Park, Danbury, Essex, CM3 4DE. tel: (024 541) 4294

Vessa Ltd., Paper Mill Lane, Alton, Hants., GU34 2PY. tel: (0420) 83294

Vollers, 112 Kingston Road, Portsmouth, Hants., PO2 7PB. tel: (0705) 660740

W M Supplies (UK) Ltd., Park Mill, Royton, Oldham, Lancs., OL2 6PZ. tel: (061) 624 5641

Warm n Dry, 138 Lancaster Road, Enfield, Middx., EN2 0JR. tel: (081) 366 4978

Watkins & Cole Ltd., 6 Highfield Road, Felixstowe, Suffolk, 1P11 7BR.

Whitfords (Bury) Ltd., Woodhill Works, Brandlesholme Road, Bury, Lancs., BL8 1BG. tel: (061) 705 2200

Joan Wiles (of London) Ltd., 14 Market Street, Malton, N. Yorkshire, Y017 0LY. tel. (0623) 600232

JD Williams & Co. Ltd., 53 Dale Street, Manchester, Gt. Manchester, M60 6ES. tel: (061) 236 3764

U Williams & Co. ltd., Head Office, 23/25 Wyche Grove, South Croydon, Surrey, CR2 6EX. tel (01) 688 8308

Ambrose Wilson plc, PO Box 123, Ambron House, 7 Dale Street, Manchester, Gt. Manchester, M60 1UH. tel: (061) 236 9911

Wizzywear Ltd., 218 Barnsole Road, Gillingham, Kent, ME7 4JB tel: (0634) 55606

Womens Royal Voluntary Service, 234-244 Stockwell Road, London, SW9 9SP. tel: (071) 733 3388

Zimmer Ltd, Dunbeath Road, Elgin Industrial Estate, Swindon, Wiltshire, SN2 6EA. tel: (0793) 481441

COMMUNICATION EQUIPMENT

Connevans Ltd, 54 Albert Road North, Reigate, Surrey, RH2 9YR. tel: (0737) 247571

Council for the Advancement of Communication with Deaf People, Pelaw House, School of Education, University of Durham, Durham DH1 1TA. tel: (091) 374 3607

Cray Modular Products Ltd, 1 Brooklands Road, Weybridge, Surrey KT13 0RU. tel: (09323) 52644

Cubex Radio Link Ltd, 324 Grays Inn Road, London, WC1X 8DH. tel: (071) 837 6127

Datamed Ltd, 39 Thorburn Road, Edinburgh, Scotland, EH13 0BH. tel: (031) 441 3185

Dayston Ltd, 34-36 Maddox Street, Regent Street, London WIR 9D. Tel: (071) 629 3246

Department of Trade & Industry, Radiocommunications Division, Licensing Section Room 712, Waterloo Bridge House, Waterloo Road, London SE1 8UA. tel: (071) 215 2316

Deron, Unit 3, Point Pleasant Ind Est, Walls End, Newcastle Upon Tyne NE28 6HA. tel: (091) 263 2981

RW Dixon & Co, The Old Auction Rooms, Beacon Road, Crowborough, Sussex, TN6 1AS. tel: (0892) 654397

Easiaids Ltd, 48 Mill Green Road, Mitcham, Surrey, CR4 4HY. tel: (01) 648 4186

Electronic Aids for the Blind, Brian Payne, 28 Crofton Ave, Orpington, Kent BR6 8DU. tel: (0689) 55651

Elfin Systems Ltd, Llanthony Road Trading Estate, Gloucester, GL1 1SB. tel: (0452) 411533

Engineering & Design Plastics, 84 High Street, Cherry Hinton, Cambridge CB1 4HZ. tel: (0223) 249431

Engments Ltd, Chequers Road, West Meadows Industrial Estate, Derby, DE2 6EN. tel: (0332) 44579

FKI-Metmac Ltd., c/o Breckland Distribution, The Old Manor House, Worthing, Norfolk NR20 5HR. tel: (0362) 81620

Foundation for Communication for the Disabled, Foundation House, Church Street West, Woking, Surrey GU21 1DJ. tel: (04862) 27844/27848

Fresnel Precision Optics, 7 Hunstead Lane, Brooke, Norwich NR15 1JP

Friends for the Young Deaf, East Court Mansion, Council Offices, College Lane, East Grinstead, Sussex RH19 3LT. Tel: (0342) 323444

Gent Ltd, Temple Road, Leicester, Leics, LE5 4JF. tel: (0533) 490000/490400

MA Gethen, 173 Old Bath Road, Cheltenham, Glos, GL53 7DW. tel: (0242) 516560

Hand Loom Centre, 38 Dalewood Road, Petts Wood, Kent. tel: (0689) 22908

Hayden Laboratories Ltd, Hayden House, Chiltern Hill, Chalfond St Peters, Bucks, SL9 9UG. tel: (0753) 888447 *Contact: Mr John Willet*

Hearing Dogs for the Deaf, Training Centre, London Road (A.40), Lewknor, Oxon OX9 5RY. tel: (0844) 53898

Hearing Research Trust, 330-332 Grays Inn Road, London WC1X 8EE. tel: (071) 833 1733

Hestair Hope Ltd, St Philip's Drive, Royton, Oldham, Lancs, OL2 6AG. tel: (061) 633 6611

Highfield Centre, 26 Allensbank Road, Heath, Cardiff, S. Glamorgan. tel: (0222) 750315

Highgate Optical Co, 55 Campfield Road, St. Albans, Herts AL1 5HU. tel: (0727) 64584

Hitman Holsters, 22a. Cornmarket, Thame, Oxon OX9 3EP. tel: (084421) 7053

Homecraft Supplies Ltd, Low Moor Estate, Kirkby-in-Ashfield, Notts. NG17 7JZ. tel: (0623) 754 047

Icom Design Ltd, Long Leys Road, Lincoln, LN1 1EH. tel (0522) 512276

Insight Electronic Products Ltd, Unit 6, The Old Granary, The Street, Chichester, West Sussex PO18 0ES. tel: (0243) 771748

International Society for Augmentative and Alternative Communication (ISAAC), c/o Radar, 25 Mortimer Street, London W1N 8AB. tel: (071) 637 5400

Iris Fund for Prevention of Blindness, York House, Ground Floor, 199 Westminster Bridge Road, London SE1 7UT, tel: (071) 928 7743/928 7919

IVA Engineering Co Ltd, Winchfield Lodge, Winchfield, Hartley Wintney, Hants. tel: (025 126)

Jedcom Speech & Hearing Ltd, Ash House, Moxon Street, Barnet, Herts EN5 5TY. tel: (081) 441 0041

R Jefcoate, Willowbrook, Swanbourne Road, Mursley, Milton Keynes, Bucks, MK17 0JA. tel: (029 672) 533 *up to 7pm*

Jessop-Ralph Ltd, Unit 6a, 3 Long Street, London, E2 8HJ. tel (071) 739 3232

Joncare Ltd, 7 Ashville Trading Estate, Nuffield Way, Abingdon, Oxon OX14 1RL. tel: (0235) 28120/35600

Keeler Ltd, Clewer Hill Road, Windsor, Berks, SL4 4AA. tel: (0753) 857177

GH Kilby Services, 4 The Causeway, Teddington, Middlesex, TW11 0HE. tel: (081) 943 3077 *Contact Mr Graham Sims*

Geoffrey King Enterprises, 5 Monmouth Square, Olivers Battery Road North, Winchester, Hants S022 4HY. tel: (0962) 60851

Learning Developments Aids, Duke Street, Wisbech, Cambs. PE13 2AE tel: (0945) 63441

Liberator Ltd, Whitegates, Swinstead, Lincs. NG33 4PA. tel: (047 684) 391

Lic Ltd, 129 Groveley Road, Sunbury-on-Thames, Middlesex, TW16 7JZ. tel: (01) 751 1141

Limpet Tapes Ltd, Bond House, 9a George Street, Huntington, Cambs PE18 6BD. tel: (0480) 59461

Linco Acoustics Ltd, PO Box 258, Sheffield, S8 0AS. tel: (0742) 350835

Llewellyn Health Care Services, Regent House, 1 Regent Road, City, Liverpool L3 7BX. tel: (051) 236 5311

London Music Shop Ltd, 157-159 Ewell Road, Surbiton, Surrey, KT6 6AW. tel: (01) 390 5685

LVA Marketing Ltd, 18 Regent Street, Nottingham, NG1 5BQ tel: (0602) 474011

Magiboards Ltd, Stafford Park 12, Telford, Shropshire TF3 3BJ. tel: (0952) 292111

Makaton Vocabulary Development Project, Mrs M Walker MSc LCST, 31 Firwood Drive, Camberley, Surrey GU15 3QD. tel (0276) 61390

Malt Keyboard Ltd, 262 Woodstock Road, Oxford, OX2 7NW. tel: (0865) 510043

MAR Design Services, 7 Elmscroft Gardens, Potters Bar, Herts, EN6 2JP. tel: (0707) 58543

Marconi Hillend Enterprise, AF18 Taxi Way, Hillend Industrial Estate, Dunfermline, Fife, KY11 5JE. tel: (0383) 823008

Edward Marcus Ltd, 5 Ludgate House, 107-110 Fleet St, London EC4A 2AB. tel: (071) 353 3554

Marker Board Supplies Ltd, Keg Services, Twyford Road, Rotherwas Industgrial Estate, Hereford, HR2 6JR. tel: (0432) 276062

Mayfield Designs (Fife) Ltd, Mayfield House, Collinburgh, Fife KY9 1LX. tel: (033334)588

Mr. M. Mclachlan, 39 Westerton Ave, Busby, Glasgow. G76 8JS

Meridian Metier Ltd, Unit l, Lammas Courtyard, Weldon North Ind Est, Corby NN17 1FZ. tel: (0536) 205145

Metropolitan Soc for the Blind, Duke House (4th Floor), 6-12 Tabard St, London SE1 4JT. tel: (071) 403 6184/6571

Minim Electronics Ltd, Lent Rise Road, Burnham, Slough SLl 7NY. tel: (062 86) 63724

Mobilia, Drake House, 18 Creekside, London SE8 3DZ. tel: (081) 692 7141 ext. 210,*(general enquiries);*(081) 892 1850*(technical enquiries)*

Moorhouse Technology Ltd, 30 New Road, Moortown, Ringwood BH24 3AU. tel: (0425) 472983

Musisca Ltd, 27 Fire Street, Topsham, via Exeter, Devon, EX3 0HD. tel: (0392) 875855

National Association of Deafened People - c/o Hon. Membership Secretary, 103 Heath Road, Widnes, Cheshire WA8 7NU

National Association of Laryngectomee Clubs, 39 Eccleston Sq, London, SW1V 1PB. tel: (01) 834 2857

National Deaf Blind & Rubella Assoc (SENSE), 311 Grays Inn Rd, London WC1X 8PT. tel: (071) 278 1000

National Deaf Blind League, 18 Rainbow Court, Paston Ridings, Peterborough, Cambs PE4 6UP. tel: (0733) 73511

National Deaf Children's Society, 45 Hereford Road, London, W2 5AH. tel: (071) 229 9272

New Horizon Woodcrafts, c/o West Denton First School, Hillhead Road, West Denton, Newcastle upon Tyne, NE5 1DN. tel: (091) 2644711

Newtech, Unit 7 William's Industrial Park, New Milton, Hants BH25 6RJ. tel: (0425) 620210

Niagara Manufacturing Ltd, Colomendy Industrial Estate, Rhyl Road, Denbigh, North Wales, LL16 5TS. tel: (074 571) 3666

Nicholls & Clarke Ltd, 3/10 Shoreditch High Street, London, E1 6PE. tel: (071) 247 5432

Nottingham Rehab Ltd, 17 Ludlow Hill Road, West Bridgford, Nottingham, NG2 6HD. tel: (0602) 234251

OEM Office & Electronic Machines plc, 140/154 Borough High Street, London, SE1 1LH tel: (071) 407 3191

Open University, Faculty of Technology, Milton Keynes MK7 6AA. tel: (0908) 653356 *(contact D B Jones)*

Optical Information Council, Temple Chambers, Temple Avenue, London, EC4Y 0DT. tel: (071) 353 3556

Orley Co Ltd, 6 Moorhead, Cowgate, Newcastle upon Tyne, NE5 3 AP. tel (091) 2713451

Outdoor Life Centre (Watford) Ltd, 473 Cockfosters Road, Hadley Wood, Hertfordshire EN4 0HJ. tel: (081) 441 6050

Partially Sighted Society, Queens Road, Doncaster, South Yorkshire, DN1 2NX tel: (0302) 68998

Pathway Communications, Berrows House, Bath Street, Hereford HR1 2HF. tel: (0432) 273311

Pelltech Ltd, Station Lane, Witney, Oxon, OX8 6YS. tel: (0993) 76451/2

Perforag Ltd, Greaves Way, Leighton Buzzard, Beds LU7 8UD. tel: (0525) 376743

Philips Service, 604 Purley Way, Waddon, Croydon, Surrey, CR9 4DR. tel: (081) 686 0505

Pay Matters (Active), 68 Churchway, London NW1 1LT. tel (071) 387 9592

Portland Training College for the Disabled, Nottingham Road, Mansfield, Notts. NG18 4Tj. tel: (0623) 792141/2

Positive Posture, 120 Church Lane, London N2 0TB. tel: (081) 883 7828

Possum
Sales Dept. - Possum Controls Ltd, Middlegreen Trading Estate, Middlegreen Road, Langley, Berks SL3 6DF. tel: (0753) 79234
Repairs & Service - Possum Controls Ltd, Unit 8 Farmbrough Close, Aylesbury Vale Industrial Park, Stocklake, Aylesbury HP20 1DQ. tel: (0296) 81591
The Possum Trust 14 Greenvale Avenue, Timsbury, Bath BA3 1HP tel: (0761) 71184

Prototype System Developments, Rushford, Glebe Close, Moulsford, Oxon OX10 9JA. tel (0491) 651587

Puretone Ltd, 10 Henley Business Park, Trident Close, Medway City Estate, Rochester ME2 4ER. tel: (0634) 719427

Pyser Ltd, Fircroft Way, Edenbridge, Kent TN8 6HA. tel: (0732) 864111

Quest Educational Designs Ltd, 1 Prince Alfred Street, Gosport, Hants, PO12 1QH. tel: (0705) 581179

RAT (Manufacturing) Ltd, 17 - 18 Great Sutton Street, London EC1V 0DN. tel (071) 251 2437

Rayner Optical Co Ltd, 17 Lorna Road, Hove, East Sussex, BN3 3EP. tel (0273) 778331/2/3

Remedian Instrucments Ltd, 3 Over Links Drive, Poole, Dorset, BH14 9QU. tel: (0202) 708404

Remploy Ltd (Spennymoor), Merrington Lane Trading Estate, Spennymoor, Co. Durham DL16 7EY. tel: (0388) 814511

Robotronic (UK) Ltd, Lait International House, Horsecroft Road, The Pinnacles, Harlow, Essex CM19 5SX. tel: (0279) 29511

Rompa (Flexus Plastics Ltd), PO Box 5, Wheatbridge Road, Chesterfield, Derbyshire S40 2AE. tel (0246) 211777

Royal Association for Disability & Rehabilitation, 25 Mortimer Street, London W1N 8AB. tel (071) 637 5400

Royal Association in Aid of Deaf People, 27 Old Oak Road, Acton, London, W3 7HN. tel (081) 743 6187

Royal National Institute for the Blind
Head Office: 224 Great Portland Street, London, W1N 6AA. tel: (071) 388 1266
Production & Distribution Centre, RNIB, Bakewell Road, Orton Southgate, Peterborough PE2 0XU. tel (0733) 370 777

Royal National Institute for the Deaf, 105 Gower Street, London, WC1E 6AH. tel: (071) 387 8033

Sarabec Ltd, Unit 15C, High Force Road, Riverside Park Industrial Estate, Middlesborough, Cleveland TS2 1RH. tel: (0642) 247789

SB Systems, 1st Floor, Unit 2D, Jefferson Way, Thame Ind. Estate, Thame, Oxfordshire, OX9 3UJ. tel: (084 421) 5681

SCI Instruments Ltd, 39 Hinton Way Great Shelford, Cambridgeshire, CB2 5AX. tel: (0223) 845282

Sensory Systems Ltd, Unit 10, Cameron House, 12 Castlehaven Road, London NW1 8QU. tel: (071) 485 4485

Sequal, Welfare and Administration Office, Ddol Hir, Glyn Ceiriog, Llangollen, Clwyd, LL20 7NP. tel: (0691) 72331

Sight & Sound Technology Ltd, Qantel House, Anglia Way, Moulton Park, Northampton, NN3 1BD. tel: (0604) 790969

Sonovision UK Ltd, 96 Brent Street, Hendon, London, NW4 2HH. tel: (081) 202 9741

Sound and Communications Industries Federation, 4b High Street, Burnham, Slough SL1 7JH. tel: (062 86) 67633

Sparks Fire Protection Ltd, ''Cornubia'',Groeswen Lane, Port Talbot, West Glamorgan SA13 2LA. tel: (0639) 885837

Special Needs Co Ltd, 66 Settrington Road, London SW6 3BA. tel: (071) 736 8110

Specialist Optical Sources Ltd, 57 Dukes Wood Drive, Gerrards Cross, Bucks SL 9 7LJ. tel: (0753) 888411

Spicers Ltd, Sawston, Cambridge, CB2 4JG. tel: (0223) 834555

Hugh Steeper Ltd, 237-238 Roehampton Lane, London, SW15 4LB. tel: (081) 788 8165

Summit, 74 Wheeleys Road, Edgbaston, Birmingham B15 2LN. tel: (021) 440 8078

Sun Alliance Insurance Group, Rickford House, 12 Rickford Hill, Aylesbury, Bucks HP20 2RX. tel: (0296) 24688

Tally Ho Lighting Co, Unit 31, The Cam Centre, 45 Wilbury Way, Hitchin, Herts SG4 0TW. tel: (0462) 38336

H Tanner & Co Ltd., 23/24 Barnack Trading Centre, Novers Hill, Bristol BS3 5QE. tel: (0272) 661751/667303

Taskmaster Ltd, Morris Road, Leicester, LE2 6BR. tel: (0533) 704286

Techno-Vision Systems Ltd, 4 Hazelwood Road, Northampton, NN1 1LN. tel: (0604) 239363

Thackraycare, 45-47 Great George St, Leeds LS1 3BB. tel (0532) 430028

Thousand & One Lamps Ltd, 4 Barmeston Road, London, SE6 3BN. tel: (081) 698 7238

Richard Toft, Technical Consultants, West Street, Lenham, Kent, ME17 2EP. tel (0622) 858995

Toucan Communication Aids Ltd, Unit 21, Third Avenue, Crewe Gates Industrial Estate, Crewe CW1 1XU. tel (0270) 588039

Toys for the Handicapped, 76 Barracks Road, Sandy Lane Industrial Estate, Stourport-on-Seven, Worcs., DY13 9QB. tel: (0299) 827820

Traditional Toys, 6 The Bullring, Llantrisant, Mid Glamorgan CF6 8BR. tel: (0443) 229015

Triumph Communications Ltd, Nathanael House, 21-23 High Street, Bassingham, Lincolnshire LN5 9'JZ. tel: (0522) 858115

Universal Aids Ltd, 8/14 Wellington Road South, Stockport, Cheshire, SK44 1AA. tel: (061) 480 9228

Vanpoulles Ltd, 1 Old Lodge Lane, Purley, Surrey, CRF2 4DG. tel (081) 668 6266

Visionaid Systems, The Old School, Ruddington, Nottingham, NG11 6HH. tel (0602) 847879

Vocal - c/o Mrs. E. Grey, Director, 336 Brixton Road, London, SW9 7AA. tel (071) 274 4029

Edward Watts & David Woods, 14 Chelmsford Road, Shenfield, Essex, CM15 8RQ. tel: (0277) 212978

WAVES, Corscombe, Nr. Dorchester, Dorset, DT2 0NU. tel: (093 589) 248

PC Werth Ltd, Audiology House, 45 Nightingale Lane, London, SW12 8SP. tel: (081) 675 5151

Winslow Press, Telford Road, Bicester, Oxon OX6 0TS. tel: (0869) 244733

COMMUNICATION EQUIPMENT A: WRITING, SPEECH AND HEARING EQUIPMENT

A & M Hearing Ltd, Faraday Road, Crawley, Sussex RH10 2LS. tel: (0293) 540471

ACE (Aids to Communication in Education), Ormerod School, Waynflete Road, Headington, OX3 8DD. tel: (0865) 63508

Action for Dysphasic Adults, Northcote House, 37a Royal Street, London, SE1 7LL tel: (071) 261 9572

AFASIC, 347 Central Markets, Smithfield, London EC1A 9NH. tel (071) 236 3632

L & R Albon, 58 Purbeck Road, Hornchurch, Essex, RM11 1NA. tel: (040 24) 43169

Alphavision Ltd, Seymore House, Copyground Lane, High Wycombe, Bucks, HP12 3HE. tel: (0494) 30555

Ancilaid Ltd, 128 Southdown Road, Harpenden, Herts AL5 1PU. tel:(05827) 2306

Aremco, Grove House, Lenham, Kent, ME17 2PX tel: (0622) 858502

Assoc. for Education & Welfare of the Visually Handicapped, c/o Dept of Special Education, Birmingham University, PO Box 363, Birmingham. tel (021) 414 3344 ex. 4799 *Contact: Mrs Juliet Stone*

Assoc of Bland & Partially Sighted Teachers & Students (ABAPSTAS) - c/o Ms Caroline Kelly, B.M. Box 6727, London WC1N 3XX.

Assoc. of Visually Handicapped Office Workers - c/o Mrs. K Shelley, Flat 5, 43 Avenue Gardens, London W3 1HB. tel (081) 992 9921*(after 6pm)*.

Audiometric Instruments Ltd, Albion Street, Driffield, North Humberside, Y025 7QB. tel: (0377) 42397

Auralaide Ltd, 2 London Road, Southampton, S01 2AF.tel: (0703) 220300/630300

B & H Designs, 2 Pepys Way, Baldock, Hertfordshire SG7 5AB. tel: (0464) 893039

Back Shop, 24 New Cavendish Street, London W1M 7LH. tel: (071) 935 9120/9148

Beaumont Products, The Spastic Society, Cockshutts Lane, Oughtibridge, Sheffield, Yorkshire, S30 BFX. tel: (0742) 862764

Birmingham Optical Group Ltd, 583 Moseley Road, Birmingham, W Midlands B12 9BW. tel: (021) 449 2222

Blissymbolics Communication Resource Centre UK, South Glamorgan Institute of Higher Education, Thomas House, Cyncoed Centre, Cyncoed Road, Cardiff CF2 6XD. tel (0222) 7577826

Breakthrough Trust c/o Charles W Gillett Centre, Selly Oak Colleges, Bristol Road, Birmingham, B29 6LE. tel: (021) 472 6447 *(voice only)* or (021) 471 1001 *(deaf communication terminal only)*.Brigstowe Products, 3 Rockhave Gardens, St. Minver, Wadebridge, Cornwall PL27 6PJ. tel: (020 886) 2811

British Association of the Hard of Hearing, 7-11 Armstrong Road, London W3 7JL. tel (081) 743 1110/1353 Vistel:(081) 743 1492

British Centre for Deafened People, 19 Hartfield Road, Eastbourne, East Sussex BN21 2AR. tel: (0323) 638230

British Deaf Association, 38 Victoria Place, Carlisle, Cumbria, CA1 1HU. tel: (0228) 48844 *(Vistel)* or 79:BKU044*(telecom Gold)*or (022) 848 844*(Prestel)*.

British Dyslexia Association - c/o Mrs Jennifer Smith, 98 London Road, Reading, RG1 5AU. tel: (0734) 668271/2

British Tinnitus Association, c/o RNID, 105 Gower Street, London, WC1E 6AH. tel: (071) 387 8033

Cambridge Adaptive Communication, 24 Fulbrooke Road, Cambridge, CB3 9EE. tel (0223) 312194

FJ Campion Ltd, PO Box 18, Hampton, Middlesex, TW12 2UD. tel (081) 979 2351

Canon UK Ltd, Canon House, Manor Road, Wallington, Surrey, SM6 0AJ. tel: (081) 773 3173

Carters (J&A) Ltd, Alfred Street, Westbury, Wiltshire, BA13 3DZ. tel: (0373) 822203 *New address from 1.6.89:* Aintree Avenue, White Horse Business Park, North Bradley, Trowbridge, Wiltshire BA14 0XA. tel: (0225) 715901

Central Medical Equipment, 7 Ascot Park Estate, Lenton Street, Sandiacre, Nottingham, NG10 5DL. tel: (0602) 390949

Chailey Heritage, Rehab Engineering Unit, Chailey Heritage Hospital and School, North Chailey, Lewes, E. Sussex. BN8 4EF. tel: (082 572) 2112 ext.210

Chattanooga UK Ltd, Unit 1 & 2, Goods Road, Belper, Derbyshire DE5 1UU. tel: (077382) 6993/4

Chest Heart & Stroke Association, Tavistock House North, Tavistock Square, London, WC1H 9JE. tel: (071) 387 3012

Chester-Care Ltd, 16 Englands Lane, London, NW3 4TG. tel: (071) 586 2166 or (071) 722 3430

Toby Churchill Ltd, 20 Panton Street, Cambridge, Cambs, CB2 1HP. tel: (0223) 316117

City College St Albans, Newman Library, 29 Hatfield Road, St Albans, AL1 3RJ tel: (727) 60423

City Lit, Centre for the Deaf, Keeley House, Keeley Street, London WC2B 4BA.

Clarke & Smith Manufacturing Co Ltd, Melbourne House, Melbourne Road, Wallington, Surrey, SM6 8SD. tel: (081) 669 4411

Clinical Engineering Consultants Ltd, Unit D8, Barwell Trading Estate, Chessington, Surrey, KT9 2NY. tel: (01) 974 1439

College of Speech Therapists, Harold Poster House, 6 Lechmere Road, London, NW2 5BU. tel: (081) 459 8521

Combined Optical Industries Ltd, 200 Bath Road, Slough, Berks, SL1 4DW. tel: (0753) 75011

Communication Aids Centres

Mrs H Robinson, Communication Advice Centre, Mustrave Park Hospital, Stockmans Lane, Belfast. tel: (0232) 669501

Ms Jayne Easton, Communication Aids Cente, Speech Therapy Dept, Frenchay Hospital, Bristol BS16 1LE tel: (0272) 701212 ext. 2151

Mrs C Ellis, Communication Aids Centre, Rookwood Hospita, Fairwater Road, Llandaff, Cardiff CF5 2YN. tel: (0222) 566281 ext. 51

Scottish Centre of Technology for the Communication Impaired, Victoria Infirmary, Longside Road, Glasgow G42 9TY. tel: (041) 649 4545 ext 5579/5580

London - *Adults:* Communication Aids Centre, Charing Cross Hospital, Fulham Place Road, London W6 8RF. tel (081) 846 1057. *Children:* Ms Nicola Joffeff, Communication Aids Centre, The Wolfson Centre, Mecklenburgh Square, London WC1N 2AP. tel: (071) 837 7618 ext.9

Communication Aids Centre, Castle Farm Road, Newcastle Upon Tyne NE3 1PH. tel: (091) 2840480

Communication Aids Centre, Sandwell Health Authority, Boulton Road, West Bromwich B70 6NNtel: (021) 553 0908

In Touch Bulletin, British Broadcasting Corporation, Broadcasting House, Portland Place, London WA1A 1AA, tel: (071) 580 4468

International Society for Augmentative & Alternative Communication, Artificial Language Laboratory, Michigan State University, 405 Computer Centre, East Lansing, 48824 1042 U.S.A. tel: (517) 353 0870

Library Association, 7 Ridgmount Street, London WC1E 7AE. tel: (071) 636 7543

Library Services Trust, c/o Library Association, 7 Ridgmount Street, London, WClE 7AE. tel: (071) 636 7543

National Association for Deaf/Blind Rubella Handicapped, 311 Grays Inn Road, London, WC1X 8PT, tel: (071) 278 1005

National Council for Special Education, 1 Wood Street, Stratford upon Avon CV37 6JE tel: (0789) 5332

National Deaf Children's Society, 45 Hereford Road, London, W2 5AH. tel: (071) 229 9272

New Beacon, Royal National Institute for the Blind, 338-346 Goswell Road, London, EC1V 7JE, tel: (071) 837 9921

Newcastle Upon Tyne Polytechnic, Handicapped Persons Research Unit, Sanford Road, Newcastle Upon Tyne, NE1 8ST. tel: (091) 2326002

Northamptonshire County Council, Social Services Dept, County Hall, Northampton, NN1 1DN, tel: (0604) 256515/6/7

Partially Sighted Society, Queens Road, Doncaster, S. Yorkshire DN1 2HX. tel: (0302) 68998

Robert Hale, Clerkenwell House, 45-47 Clerkenwell Green, London, EC1R 0HT. tel: (071) 251 2661

Royal Association for Disability & Rehabilitation, 25 Mortimer St., London W1N 8AB. tel: (071) 637 5400

Royal National Institute for the Blind (Peterborough), Production and Distribution Centre, Bakewell Road, Orton Southgate, Peterborough PE2 0XU. tel (0733) 370 777

Royal National Institute for the Deaf, 105 Gower Street, London WC1E 6AH. tel: (071) 387 8033

Sensory Information Systems, Unit 10, Cameron House, 12 Castlehaven Road, London NW1 8QU, tel: (071) 485 4485

COMMUNICATION EQUIPMENT B: TELEPHONES, ALARMS, INTERCOMS, INCLUDING REMOTE CONTROL APPARATUS

Adam Leisure Ltd, Adam House, Ripon Way, Harrogate, North Yorkshire HG1 2AU tel: (0423) 501151

Aid-Call Plc, Head Office, Moreton House, Moreton Hampstead, Devonshire TQ13 8NF. tel: (0647) 40804. *London Office:*(071) 352 2822

Air Call Communications Ltd, Systems Sales Division, Queensborough House, Friars Walk, Dunstable, Bedfordshire LU6 3JA. tel: (0582) 699666

AJW Trading (Opalake Ltd), 42 Alderney Road, Slade Green, Erith, Kent DA8 2JD tel: (0322) 334426

Alcatel Terryphone, Station Approach, London Road, Bicester, Oxon OX6 7BZ. tel: (0869) 244661

Aldridge Securiphone Ltd, Silica House, 30-34 Eagle Wharf Road, London, N1 7EB. tel: (071) 251 4791

Ancilaid Ltd, 128 Southdown Road, Harpenden, Herts AL5 1PU. tel: (05827) 2306

ANT Telecommunications Ltd, 17 Liverpool Road, Slough, Berkshire SL1 4QZ. tel: (0753) 820242

Aremco, Grove House, Lenham, Kent ME17 2PX. tel: (0622) 858502

EJ Arnold & Son Ltd, Parkside Lane, Dewsbury Road, Leeds, LS11 5TD. tel: (0532) 772112

Asthma Society, and Friends of the Asthama Research Council, 300 Upper Street, London N1 2XX tel: (071) 226 2260

Audio Communications, 2 The Street, Shipton Moyne, Tetbury, Glos., GL8 8PN. tel (0666) 88331

Auralaide Ltd, 2 London Road, Southampton, SO1 2AF. tel: (0703) 220300/630300

Austin Taylor Electrial Ltd, Bethesda, Bangor, North Wales, LL57 3BX. tel: (0248) 600561

Auto Control Systems Ltd, Units 44-45 Bookham Industrial Park, Church Road, Bookham, Surrey KT23 3EU tel: (0372) 59536/7/8

Autophon (UK) Ltd., Cypress Drive, St. Mellons, Cardiff CF3 0EG. tel (0222) 777800

Baldwin Boxall Communications Ltd, Doubleby House, Crowborough Hill, Crowborough, E Sussex, TGN6 2HB. tel: (0892) 664422

Janet Bancroft, Victoria Garage Workshop, New Road Side, Horsforth, Leeds, LS18 4DR. tel: (0532) 585332

Bell Johnson & Green Ltd, Tuley Street, Manchester, M11 2DY. tel: (061) 223 9144

AP Besson, St Joseph's Close, Hove, East Sussex BN3 7EZ. tel: (0273) 722651

Bit 32 Ltd, Century Buildings, Brunswick Business Park, Liverpool, Merseyside L3 4BJ. tel: (051) 227-3232

Bleepers, Freepost, Barnet, Herts, EN4 0BR. tel: (081) 936 9100

Blindminder Ltd, 7 Oakdene Road, Peasmarsh, Guildford, Surrey GU3 1ND. tel: (0483) 63326

Breakthrough Trust, c/o Charles W Gillett Centre, Selly Oak Colleges, Bristrol Road, Birmingham, B29 6LE tel: (021) 472 6447*(voice only);*(021) 471 1001 *(deaf communication terminal only).*

Brilliant Computing, Box 142, Bradford, BD3 0JN. tel: (0274) 632223

Britannia Delta Communications Ltd, Telecom House, 22 London Road, Hazel Grove, Stockport, Cheshire SK7 4AH. tel (061) 477 1233

Britannia Monitoring Services Ltd, Security House, Florence Road, Maidstone, Kent, ME16 8EP. tel: (0622) 672864

Britannia Security Systems, 30 London Street, Chertsey Surrey KT16 8AA. tel: (0932) 564977

British Telecom
See local telephone directory under ''British Telecom'' for details of sales offices and some services.

British Telecom Action for Disabled Customers, British Telecom Centre, Newgate Street, London, EC1A 7AJ. tel: (071) 356 4915

British Telecom Materials Department (MP6323), Queens Drive House, Dudmore Road, Swindon SN3 1AH. tel: (0793) 484201

British Telecom Mobile Communications, Sales Desk, Mobile House, Euston Square, London NW1 2DN. tel: (071) 388 4222

British Telecom Paging Service, Peter Hurst, FREEPOST BS3333, Bristol BS1 4YP. tel: (0800) 222 666

British Telecom Voicebank - tel: (0800) 222 666, or write to: Andrew Barton, Voicebank, FREEPOST BS333, Bristol BS1 4YP.

Budd Radio & Electrical Ltd, 70 Milton Road, Hampton TW12 2LJ. tel: (01) 979 1419/4430

Burgess Micro Switch Co Ltd, Dukesway, Team Valley Trading Estate, Gateshead, Tyne & Wear, NE11 0UB. tel (091) 4877171

C & E Computing Services Ltd, 9 Elizabeth Close, Barnet, Herts EN5 4DP tel. (081) 440 1936

C Com Internation Ltd, 396 Kenton Road, Harrow, Middlexsex, HA3 9DH. tel: (081) 907 8713

Call-Saver CRV Electronics Ltd, Telephone Systems, 3 Caledonian Road, London, N1 9DX. tel: (071) 278 5187

Cass Electronics Ltd, Delta Way, Thorpe Industrial Estate, Egham, Surrey, TW20 8RN. tel: (0784) 36266

Castleham Industries, Collett Close, St. Leonards-on-Sea, East Sussex, TN38 9QS. tel: (0424) 53629

Chester-Care Ltd, 16 Englands Lane, London, NW3 4TG. tel: (071) 586 2166 or (071) 722 3430

Toby Churchill Ltd, 20 Panton Street, Cambridge CB2 1HP tel: (0223) 316117

L Clark, Bridgeview, Rothienorman, Inverurie, Aberdeenshire, Scotland AB5 8UH. tel (065181) 428

Ralph Clarke, 12 Glebe Drive, Countesthorpe, Leicester, LE8 3QR. tel: (0533) 778809

Clos-O-Mat GB Ltd, 55 Waverley Road, Sale, Cheshire M33 1AY. tel: (061) 905 1399

Closed Door Security Systems, 14 Limetrees Gdns, Gateshead, Tyne and Wear, NE9 5BE. tel: (091) 478 1398

Control Universal Ltd, 137 Ditton Walk, Cambridge, CB5 8QF. tel:(0223) 244447

Cotag International Ltd, Mercers Row, Cambridge, CB5 9'EX. tel: (0223) 321535

Cray Modular Products Ltd, 1 Brooklands Road, Weybridge, Surrey KT13 0RU. tel: (09323) 52644

CTS Security Ltd, Southgates Corner, Wisbech Road, Kings Lynn, Norfolk, PE30 5JH. tel: (0553) 765429

Custodian Central Station, 245 Whitehorse Road, Croydon, Surrey CR0 2HQ. tel: (081) 689 6633

Davis Security Communications Ltd, Davis House, Barrow Road, Sheffied S9 1JQ. tel (0742) 431577

Department of Health, 13-16 Russell Square, London WC1B 5EP. tel: (071) 636 6811 ext. 3166

Department of Trade and Industry, Radiocommunications Division, Licensing Section Room 712, Waterloo Bridge House, Waterloo Road, London SE1 8UA. tel: (071) 215 2316

Deron, Unit 3, Point Pleasant Industrial Estate, Walls End, Newcastle Upon Tyne NE28 6HA. tel: (091) 263 2981

Dialatron Ltd, 2 Kingfisher House, North Wood Park, Gatwick Road, Crawley, West Sussex RH10 2XN. tel (0293) 565100

Diktron Ltd, 5 Highgate Square, Birmingham, West Midlands, B12 0DR. tel: (021) 440 1321

Draft Designs, 2a. Unit L, The Maltings, Station Road, Sawbridgeworth, Herts CM21 9JX tel: (0279) 726163

Eagle International, Unit 5, Royal London Estate, 29-35 North Acton Road, London, NW10 6PE. tel: (081) 965 3222

Easiaids Ltd, 48 Mill Green Road, Mitcham, Surrey, CR4 4HY. tel: (081) 648 4186

Elfin Systems Ltd, Llanthony Road Trading Estate, Llanthony Road, Gloucestershire GL1 1SB. tel: (0452) 411533

Enterprise Engineering, 157 Ermine Way, Arrington, Royston, Herts, SG8 0AU. tel: (0223) 207281

EPC Ltd, Friggle Street, Frome, Somerset BA11 5LH. tel: (0373) 62542

Eteq Ltd, Units B & C, Lamnas Courtyard, Lamnas Road, Weldon Industrial Estate North, Northants NN17 1EZ. tel: (0535) 68041

Ferranti Business Communications Ltd, St Marys Road, Moston, Manchester M10 0BE. tel: (061) 682 4000

Gas Alert Ltd, Cory Technology Group, George House, 121 High Street, Henley in Arden, Warwickshire B95 5AU. tel: (05642) 4454/5

Geemarc Ltd, Unit 5, Swallow Court, Swallow Field Welwyn Garden City, Herts AL7 1SB tel: (0707) 372372

Gould Electronics, Ann-Jar, Chapel Square, Troon, Camborne, Cornwall TR14 9EA. tel: (0209) 717014

GPT, Whindbank, Newton Aycliffe, Co Durham DL5 6GA. tel: (0325) 300720

GPT Reliance Ltd, Turnells Mill Lane, Wellingborough, Northamptonshire NN8 2RB. tel: (0933) 225000

Hadley Sales Services, 112 Gilbert Road, Smethwick, Warley, West Midlands, B66 4PZ. tel: (021) 558 3585

Hartana Ltd, Larchwind, Wilton Lane, Jordans, Beaconsfield, Bucks HP9 2RF. tel: (024 07) 3266

Headingley Scientific Services, 45 Westcombe Avenue, Leeds, LS8 2BS. tel (0582) 664222

Heinz Baby Club, Vinces Road, Diss, Norfolk IP22 3HH. tel: (0379) 651981

Help the Aged, Community Alarms Dept., 16-18 St James' Walk, London EC1R 0BE. tel (071) 253 0253

Hertfordshire Association for the Disabled, The Woodside Centre, The Commons, Welwyn Garden City, Herts AL 74DD. tel: (0707) 324581

Home Automation Ltd, Pindar Road, Hoddesdon, Herts, EN11 0ET. tel: (0992) 460355

Homecraft Supplies Ltd, Low Moor Estate, Kirkby-in-Ashfield, Notts NG17 7JZ. tel: (0623) 754 047

Homelink Telecom Ltd, Unit 24C & D Perivale Industrial Park, Horsenden Lane South, Perivale, Greenford, Middlesex UB6 7RJ. tel: (081) 991 1133

Icom Design Ltd, Long Leys Road, Lincoln, LN1 1EH. tel: (0522) 512276

Identiplugs, 39 Whitehouse Enterprise Centre, Whitehouse Road, Newcastle upon Tyne NE15 6EP. tel: (091) 228 0068

Intertan UK Ltd., Ms Amanda Taylor, Tandy Centre, Leamore Lane, Walsall WS2 7PS. tel: (0922) 710000

R Jefcoate, Willowbrook, Swanbourne Road, Mursley, Milton Keynes, Bucks, MK17 0JA. tel: (029 672) 533 up to 7pm

John Bell and Croyden, 54 Wigmore Street, London W1H 0AU. tel: (071) 935 5555 or 0527 575422

Ken Ketteridge, 10 Walpole Road, Cambridge CB1 3TJ. tel: (0223) 247326

Kiddi-Proof Products Ltd, Design House, 9 Centre Way, Claverings Industrial Estate, Montague Road, Edmonton, London N9 0AJ. tel: (081) 807 4552

KRS Electronics Ltd, Dynamic Works, Saltaire Road, Shipley, W. Yorkshire, BD18 3HN. tel: (0274) 584115

Kwik-Link, 62 Kenilworth Road, Edgware, Middlesex, HA8 8XD. tel: (081) 958 5476

C Lord, 61 Forknell Avenue, Wyken, Coventry, W Midlands, CV2 3EN. tel: (0203) 444332/72191

LVA Marketing Ltd, 18 Regent Street, Nottingham, NG1 5BQ. tel: (0602) 474011

MAR Design Services, 7 Elmscroft Gardens, Potters Bar, Herts, EN6 2JP. tel: (0707) 58543

Matthews Office Furniture Ltd, PO Box 70, Reginald Road, St. Helens, Merseyside WA9 4JE. tel: (0744) 813671

Medic-Alert Foundation, 17 Bridge Wharf, 156 Caledonian Road, London N1 9RD. tel: (071) 833 3034

Meridian Metier Ltd, Unit 1, Lammas Courtyard, Weldon North Industrial Estate, Corby, Northants NN17 1FZ. tel: (0536) 205145

Modern Vitalcall Ltd, Fringe Meadow Road, North Moons Moat, Redditch, Worcestershire B98 9NS. tel (0527) 67607

Harry Moss International Ltd, 2 Enfield Industrial Estate, Redditch, Worcestershire B97 6BH. tel: (0527) 584584

Mothercare Plc, Cherry Tree Road, Watford, Herts, WD2 5SH. tel (0923) 33577 *Customer enquiries:* (09923) 31616

Multitone Communciation Systems Ltd, 12 Underwood Street, London, N1 7JT tel: (071) 253 7611

Newington Electronics, 93 Newington Road, Edinburgh EH9 1QW. tel: (031) 667 4218

Newtech, Unit 7 William's Industrial Park, New Milton, Hants BH25 6RJ. tel: (0425) 620210

Newton Products - Spastics Society, Medway Works, Garretts Green Lane, Birmingham, B33 0SQ. tel: (021) 783 6081/2/3

Nottingham Rehad Ltd, 17 Ludlow Hill Road, West Bridgford, Nottingham, NG2 6HD. tel: (0602) 234251

Partially Sighted Society, Queens Road, Doncaster, South Yorkshire, DN1 2NX. tel: (0302) 68998

Personal Communications Plc, Cornwallis House, Howard Chase, Basildon, Essex SS14 3BB. tel: (0268) 555883

Philips Consumer Electroncs, P O Box 298, City House, 420-430 London Road, Croydon, Surrey CR9 3QR. tel: (081) 689 2166

Pifco Salton Carmen, Failsworth, Manchester, Greater Manchester M35 0HS. tel: (061) 681 8321

Possum Controls Ltd, Sales Dept, Middlegreen Trading Estate, Middlegreen Road, Langley, Berks SL3 6DF. tel: (0753) 79234

Power-Tech (UK) Ltd, Unit 8c, Ford Airfield Industrial Estate, Yapton, Arundel, West Sussex, BN18 0HY. tel:(0903) 713227

Quest Educational Designs Ltd, 1 Prince Alfred Street, Gosport, Hants, PO12 1QH. tel: (0705) 581179

Raytel Security Systems Ltd., Raytel House, Brook Road, Rayleigh, Essex SS6 7XH. tel: (0268) 775656

Retell, Crescent House, Darby Crescent, Sunbury on Thames, Middlesex TW16 5LB. tel: (0932) 785594

Ridley Electronics Ltd, 206 Wightman Road, Hornsey, London, N8 0BU. tel: (081) 340 9501

Ripul Ltd, Bumpers Way, Chippenham, Wiltshire SN14 6LF. tel: (0249) 443511

Rocom Ltd, Thorpe Arch Trading Estate, Wetherby, West Yorkshire LS23 7BJ. tel: (0937) 845840

Ross Consumer Electronics Plc, Silver Road, White City Industrial Park, London W12 7SG. tel: (081) 740 5252

Royal National Institute for the Blind
224 Great Portland Street, London, W1N 6AA tel (071) 388 1266
Production and Distribution Centre, Bakewell Road, Orton Southgate, Peterborough PE2 0XU. tel: (0733) 370 777

Royal National Institute for the Deaf, 105 Gower Street, London, WC1E 6AH. tel: (071) 387 8033

Safe & Sound Personal Protection Ltd, Finance House, Wilberforce Road, London NW9 6BB. tel (081) 202 7986

Sarabec Ltd, Unit 15C, High Force Road, Riverside Park Industrial Estate, Middlesborough, Cleveland TS2 1RH. tel (0642) 247789

Scantronic Ltd, Unit 24C, Perivale Industrial Park, Greenford, Middx UB6 7RJ. tel (081) 997 9472

Seager Wedo (UK) Ltd, 5-25 Scrutton Street, London EC2A 4HJ. tel: (071) 739 6856

Security Alert Ltd, Pug House, 2 Waterlow Road, Reigate, Surrey RH2 7EX. tel (0737) 248148

Senflow UK Ltd, 1a. Norton Hill Drive, Wyken, Coventry, West Midlands, CV2 3BH. tel: (0203) 621096

Sequal, Welfare and Administration Office, Ddol Hir, Glyn Ceiriog, Llangollen, Clwyd, LL20 7NP. tel: (0691) 72331

Sharma Design Consultants, 35 Crouch Hill Court, Lower Halstow, Kent ME9 7EJ. tel: (0795) 842968

Shorrock, Community Care Division, Unit 10 Barrsford Close, Wingate Industrial Estate, Westhorighton, Bolton, Lancs BL5 3XH. tel: (0942) 811717

Sparks Fire Protection Ltd, 'Cornubia' Groeswen Lane, Port Talbot, West Glamorgan SA13 2LA. tel: (0639) 885837

Spicers Ltd, Sawston, Cambridge, CB2 4JG. tel: (0223) 834555

Status Electronics Ltd, Video & Audio Door Entry Systems, 42B Chigwell Lane, Loughton, Essex, IG10 3NZ. tel: (081) 502 0136/0421

Hugh Steeper (Roehampton) Ltd, 237-239 Roehampton Lane, London, SW15 4LB. tel: (081) 788 8165

Stentofon Communications Ltd, 3 Baird Close, Maxwell Way, Crawley, West Sussex RH10 2XE. tel: (0293) 545911

Summit, 74 Wheeleys Road, Edgbaston, Birmingham B15 2LN. tel: (021) 440 8078

Surrey Voluntary Association for the Blind, Rentwood, School Lane, Fetcham, Surrey, KT22 9JX. tel: (0372) 377701

Suzy Lamplugh Alarms, Bill Grayson Ltd, 213 Two Trees Lane, Haughton Green, Denton, Lancs M34 1QL. tel: (061) 336 8158 (2pm-6pm

Swift Communications Ltd, PO Box 142, Hardwick, Cambridge CB3 7QH. tel (0954) 210607

Switchkraft Products Ltd, Glan Eldon House, Bighton Road, Medstead, Alton, Hampshire GU34 5NA. tel: (0420) 64067

Sycotek Electronics Ltd, 16 Shakespeare Business Centre, Hathaway Close, Eastleigh, Hants S05 4SR. tel: (0703) 629262

Synaptics Ltd, PO Box 3, Stow on the Wold, Cheltenham GL54 1LW. tel: (0451) 31476

Tackfield Ltd, Unit 38, Sapcote Trading Centre, Dudden Hill Lane, London NW10 2QE. tel (081) 451 5003

Talman Ltd, 21 Grays Corner, Ley Street, Ilford, Essex, IG2 7RQ. tel: (081) 554 5579

H Tanner & Co Ltd, 23/24 Barnack Trading Centre, Novers Hill, Bristol BS3 5QE. tel: (0272) 661751/667303

Tape Recording Service for the Blind, 48 Fairfax Road, Farnborough, Hampshire GU14 8JP. tel: (0252) 547943

Tele-Nova, 111 Endwell Road, Brockley, London SE4 2LY. tel: (081) 692 9816

Telecare Communications Ltd, 19 Lee Bank House, Holloway Head, Birmingham B1 1HP. tel: (021) 643 9600

Telecom Gold, Dialcom, 60-68 St Thomas' Street, London SE1 3QU. tel: (071) 403 6777

Tools for Living, Middlewood, 45 Croft Road, Broad Haven, Haverfordwest, Dyfed, SA62 3HY. tel (0437) 781 472

Tunstall
Tunstall Healthcare, Fountain House, Cleeve Road, Leatherhead, Surrey KT22 7NU. tel: (0372) 373163
Tunstall Lifeline Ltd, Glenwood, 92 Nore Road, Portishead, Bristol, Avon BS20 8EN. tel: (0272) 842319
Tunstall Telecom Ltd, Whitley Lodge, Whitley Bridge, Yorkshire DN14 0JT. tel: (0977) 661234

UML Ltd, PO Box No 115, Wood Street, Port Sunlight, Wirral, Merseyside L62 4ZL. tel (051 644) 8555

Universal Aids Ltd, 8/14 Wellington Road South, Stockport, Cheshire, SK4 1AA. tel: (061) 480 9228

Volumatic Ltd, Taurus House, Endemere Road, Coventry, W Midlands, CV6 5PY. tel: (0203) 684217

Walsh Fonadek Ltd, 243 Beckenham Road, Beckenham, Kent BR3 4TS. tel (081) 778 7061 ext. 11

WAVES, Corscombe, Nr Dorchester, Dorset, DT2 0NU. tel: (093 589) 248

Ways and Means, FREEPOST, Nottingham NG2 1BR. tel: (0602) 234251

Welwyn Tool Co Ltd, 4 South Mundells, Welwyn Garden City, Hertfordshire, AL7 1EH. tel: (0707) 331111

PC Werth Ltd, Audiology House, 45 Nightingale Lane, London, SW12 8SP. tel (081) 675 5151

Wolsey Electronics Ltd, Gellihirion Industrial Estate, Pontypridd, Mid-Glam, CF37 5SX. tel: (044 385) 3111

Wychwood Communications Ltd, PO Box 389, Great Missenden, Bucks HP16 0HF. tel: (02406) 3294

Zettler UK, Zettler House, Pinner Road, Northwood, Middlesex HA6 1DL. tel: (09274) 26155

EATING AND DRINKING EQUIPMENT

Anglia Vale Medical Ltd, Unit 6, Lancaster Way Business Centre, Ely, Cambridgeshire CB6 3NW. tel: (0353) 666195

Antiference Ltd, Bel Product Division, Bicester Road, Aylesbury, Bucks, HP19 3BJ. tel: (0296) 82511 *Manufacturer only.*

Anything Left Handed Ltd, 65 Beak Street, London, W1R 3LF. tel: (071) 437 3910

Aremco, Grove House, Lenham, Kent, ME17 2PX. tel: (0622) 858502

Arterial Medical Services Ltd, Arterial House, 313 Chase Road, Southgate, London N14 6JH. tel: (081) 882 44434

Arwin Products & Co, 11 Irwell House, East Philip Street, Salford M3 7LE. tel: (061) 832 2789 & (061) 835 1407

ASM Medicare, Picow Farm Ind Estate, Runcorn, Cheshire WA7 4UG. tel: (0928) 574301/2/3.

BCS Products, Old Woods Trading Estate, Torquay, Devon TQ2 7AU. tel: (0803) 612772

Beacon Developments Ltd, 105 Station Road, Ashwell, Baldock, Herts, SG7 5LT. tel: (046 274) 2214

Boots the Chemists Ltd, City Gate, Toll House Hill, Nottingham NG2 3AA. tel: (0602) 418522. *Enquiries should be made at local branches*

BXL Plastics Ltd, Foams Business, Croydon Division, Mitcham Road, Croydon, Surrey CR9 3AL tel: (081) 684 3622

CB Gifts Ltd, 6 Portland Place, Stevenston, Ayrshire, Scotland, KA20 3NN. tel: (0294) 602823

Chailey Heritage, Rehab Engineering Unit, Chailey Heritage Hospital & School, North Chailey, Lewes, East Sussex, BN8 4EF. tel: (082 572) 2112 ext. 210

Chester-Bowes Ltd, PO Box 19, Earby, Colne, Lancashire, England BB8 6JU. tel: (0282) 844000 *dZ: (0282) 844092*

Chester-care Ltd, 16 Englands Lane, London, NW3 4TG. tel: (071) 586 2166 or (071) 722 3430

Days Medical Aids Ltd, Litchard Ind Estate, Bridgend, Mid-Glamorgan, CF31 2AL. tel: (0656) 657495/660150

Deeko plc, Garman Road, London, N17 0UG. tel: (081) 808 5871

DRG Hospital Supplies Healthcare Division, 1-3 Dixon Road, Brislington, Bristol B54 5QY. tel: (0272) 716111

Easiaids Ltd, 48 Mill Green Road, Mitcham, Surrey, CR4 4HY. tel: (081) 648 4186

Elamor Kitchens, 36 Rose Hill, Sutton, Surrey, SM1 3EU. tel: (081) 641 3020

First Technicare Ltd, 20 Abercorn Place, London NW8 9XP. tel: (081) 609 8761. *Bulk suppliers to NHS*

W Freeman & Co Ltd, Suba-Sea Works, Staincross, Barnsley, South Yorkshire, S75 6DH. tel: (0226) 284081

Gimson-Tendercare, 62 Boston Road, Beaumont Leys, Leicester LE4 1AZ. tel: (0533) 366779

Goldene Designs Ltd, 7c Moss Lane, Whitefield, Manchester,M25 7QE. tel: (061) 796 9367

AW Gregory & Co. Ltd, Glynde House, Glynde Street, London, SE4 1RY. tel: (081) 690 3437

Guildbeck Ltd, 5 Mill Close, Great Bardfield, Braintree, Essex CM7 4RJ. tel: (0371) 810645

Harfield Components Ltd, Hammond Avenue, Whitehill Industrial Estate, Stockport, Cheshire, Sk4 1PQ. tel: (061) 477 5678

Health and Comfort, P.O. Box 15, Westbury, Wiltshire BA13 4LS. (0373) 822394

Helping Hands Shop, 114 Queens Road, Leicester LE2 3LF (0533) 708821

Henleys Medical Supplies Ltd, Brownsfields, Welwyn Garden City, Herts AL7 1AN. tel: (0707) 333164 Wholesaler only.

Hestair Hope Ltd, St Philip's Drive, Royton, Oldham, Lancs, OL2 6AG. tel: (061) 633 6611

SR Holbrook Ltd, Jackson Road, Coventry, CV6 4LY. tel: (0203) 667 576

Home Nursing Supplies Ltd, Headquarters Road, West Wilts Trading Estate, Westbury, Wilts, BA13 4JR. tel: (0373) 822313

Homecraft Supplies Ltd, Low Moor Estate, Kirkby-in-Ashfield, Notts NG17 7JZ. tel: (0623) 757955*Mail order*(0623) 754047*(sales)*

Independent Living Centre, 9 Caldecote Gardens, Bushey Heath, Herts WD2 3RA. tel: (081) 950 6635

Keep Able Ltd, Fleming Close, Park Farm, Wellingborough, Northants NN8 3UF. tel: (0933) 679426 NB. *Agents for Maddak Inc USA*

Lap-Mate Ltd, 8 Fore Street, St. Ives, Cornwall, TR26 1SD tel: (0736) 797199

Lefthanded by Post, Duntish Court, Buckland Newton, Dorchester, DT2 7DE. tel: (03005) 291

Llewellyn-SML Health Care Services, Regent House 1 Regent Riad, City, Liverpool L3 7BX. tel: (051) 236 5311

Medical Rehab Ltd, Research Unit, Warley Hospital, Brentwood, Essex CM14 5HQ. tel:(0277) 212637

Medical and Surgical Supply Ltd, 21 Frobisher Gardens, Guildford, GU1 2NT. tel: (0483) 64385

Medimail, JL Owen Ltd, 13 Blossom Street, Manchester, M4 5AF. tel: (061) 236 0896

Medipost Ltd, Unit 1, St. Johns Estate, Elder Road, Lees, Oldham, Lancs. OL4 3SDZ. tel: (061) 678 0233

Michaelis Engineering, 68 Argyle Road, Southampton S02 0BQ. tel: (0703) 639771

Minnow Plastics, Unit B2, Connaught Business Centre, Malham Road, London SE23.1AG tel: (081) 291 6749

Molnlycke Ltd, Southfields Road, Dunstable, Beds, LU6 3EJ. tel: (0582) 600211 *fax: (0582) 600899. Accept quantity orders only*

Newton Products - Spastics Society, Meadway Works, Garretts Green Lane, Birmingham, B33 0SQ. tel:(021) 783 6081/2/3 *(021) 783 5723*

Nottingham Rehab Ltd, 17 Ludlow Hill Road, West Bridgford, NG2 6HB. tel (0602) 452345

Frank Odell Ltd, 70 High Street, Teddington, Middlesex, TW11 8JD. tel: (081) 977 8158/1007

Orthopaedic Systems, Units G22/33 Oldgate, St Michael's Industrial Estate, Widness, Cheshire, WA8 8TL. tel: (051) 420 3250

Oxford Orthopaedic Engineering Centre, Nuffield Orthopaedic Centre, Oxford OX3 7LD. tel: (0865) 64811 ext. 514.*Contact - Mr M Evans*

Poly Form Medical, Unit 27A, Morelands Trading Estate, Bristol Road, Gloucester GL1 5RZ. tel: (0452) 507144

Quest Educational Designs Ltd, 1 Prince Alfred Street, Gosport, Hants, PO12 1QH. tel: (0705) 581179

Renray Group Ltd, Road Five, Winsford Industrial Estate, Winsford, Cheshire, CW7 3RB. tel: (0606) 593456

Salter Housewares Ltd, 211 Vale Road,Tonbridge, Kent TN9 1SU. tel: (0732) 354828

Smith & Nephew Chiromed, Green Pond Road, London, E17 6EN. tel: (081) 531 4100

Smith & Nephew Medical Ltd, P O Box 81, 101 Hessle Road, Hull, HU3 2BN. tel: (0482) 25181

James Spencer & Co Ltd, Moor Road Works, Moor Road, Headingley, Lees, LS6 4BH. tel: (0532) 785837/741850

Hugh Steeper Ltd, 237-239 Roehampton Lane, London SW15 4LB. tel: (081) 788 8165 *fax: (081) 788 0137*

Tamworth Plastics, Appollo, Lichfield Road Industrial Estate, Tamworth, Staffordshire, B79 7TA. tel: (0827) 68383/4/5

Taskmaster Ltd, Morris Road, Leicester, LE2 6BR. tel (0533) 704286

Temp-Rite International Ltd, Ashford House, Church Road, Middlesex TW15 2TQ. tel: (0784) 243983/6

Tremorvah Industries, Rentoul Works, Three Milestone Industrial Estate, Truro, Cornwall, TR4 9LD. tel: (0872) 40036

Charles Turner & Co Ltd, Hospital Products Division, Bentinck Street, Bolton, Lancs BL1 4QG. tel: (0204) 46226

WAVES, Corscombe, Nr Dorchester, Dorset, DT2 0NU. tel: (093 589) 248

Ways and Means, Freepost, Nottingham NG2 1BR. tel: (0602) 23451

Webs, Business Enterprise Centre, Eldon Street, South Shields, Tyne and Wear NE33 5JE. tel: (091) 455 4300 Ext 207 *fax: (091) 455 1847*

WM Supplies (UK) Ltd, Park Mill, Royton, Oldham, Lancs OL2 6PZ. tel: (061) 624 5641

Yeates Catering Equipment, Victoria House, Victoria Road, Portslade, Brighton, East Sussex BN4 1XZ. tel (0273) 411776

ELECTRIC WHEELCHAIRS

All Handling (Movability) Ltd, 492 Kingston Road, Raynes Park, London, SW20 8DX. tel: (081) 542 2217

Altonaids Mobility, Park Road, Gateshead, Tyne and Wear, NE8 3HL. tel: (091) 4773733/4773683

Aremco, Grove House, Lenham, Kent, ME17 2PX. tel: (0622) 858502

Arun Mobility Services, 29 Parkside Avenue, Littlehampton, West Sussex. BN17 6BG. tel: (0903) 721973

Auto Leisure (UK) Ltd, Unit 15, Hooe Farm, Tye Lane, Walberton, Arundel, West Sussex. BN18 0LU. tel: (024368) 4127

Banstead Mobility Centre, Park Road, Banstead, Surrey SM7 3EE. tel: (0737) 351674/356222

W & F Barfrett Ltd, 22 Emery Road, Bristol, Avon, BS4 5PH. tel: (0272) 779016/774070

Batricar Ltd, Tanlaw Park, East Street, Chard, Somerset, TA20 1EP. (0460) 67681/8

FWO Bauch Ltd., 14 Gunnels Wood Industrial Estate, Gunnels Wood Road, Stevenage, Herts, SG1 2BH. tel: (0438) 359090

Beard Bros Ltd., Unit 2, The Crystal Centre, Elmgrove Road, Harrow, Middx. HA1 2HS. Tel: (081) 861) 4070

Bencraft Ltd, The Avenue, Rubery, Rednal, Birmingham, W. Midlands B45 9AP. tel: (021) 453 1055/6/7

Booster Electric Vehicles Ltd, Bank Street, Brighouse, West Yorkshire HD6 1BD. tel: (0484) 722599

Breckland Rova Ltd., Southgate Avenue, Mildenhall, Suffolk, IP28 7AT. tel: (0638) 713533

British Association of Wheelchair Distributors: *Secretary-* D R Smytheman, Grove Cottage, Packwood Road, Lapworth, Solihull B94 6AS. tel: (0564) 773843. *Telephone enquiries from professionals only, and during office hours only.*

British Surgical Trades Association, Secretary, Centre Point, 103 New Oxford Street, London, WC1A 1DU. tel: (071) 240 5904

Buckingham Engineering Co, River Gate, West Street, Buckingham MK18 1HP. tel: (0280) 816808

Carters (J&A) Ltd, Alfred Street, Westbury, Wiltshire, BA13 3DZ. tel (0373) 822203

Chairpower Products Plc, Avondale, Freshford, Bath BA3 6BX. tel: (022122) 3755

Curtis Instrucments (UK) Ltd, 51 Grafton Street, Northampton, NN1 2NT. tel: (0604) 29755

Disabled Drivers Insurance Bureau, 292 Hale Lane, Edgware, Middlesex, HA8 8HP. tel: (081) 958 3135

Disablement Services Authority (DSA), 14 Russell Square, London WC1B 5EP. tel: (071) 636 6811

Electric & Manual Chairs Ltd, 43 Teville Road, Worthing, West Sussex, BN11 1UX. tel: (0903) 821515

Electric Mobility Corporation, Sea King Road, Lynx Trading Estate, Yeovil, Somerset, BA20 2NZ. tel: (0935) 22156

Eurotech marine Products Ltd., 4 West Halkin St, Belgrave Square, London, SW1 tel: (071) 235 8273

Everest & Jennings Ltd., Princewood Road, Corby, Northants NN17 2DX. tel: (0536) 67661

MJ Fish & Co, 3 Rivers Way Business Village, Navigation Way, Ashton-on-Ribble, Preston, Lancs PR2 2YT. tel. (0772) 724442

Hemco (UK) Ltd, Unit 17, Llandow Industrial Estate, Cowbridge, South Glamorgan CF7 7PB. tel: (04463) 3393/3394

Independence, 52 Exeter Road, Exmouth, Devon, EX8 1PY (0395) 268555

Joncare Ltd, 7 Ashville Trading Estate, Nuffield Way, Abingdon, Oxon OX14 1RL. tel: (0235) 28120/35600

Kensington Traders Ltd, Unit 11, Mulberry Business Centre, Quebec Way, London SE16 1AA. tel: (071) 232 1746

Malden Electronics Ltd, Malden House, 579 Kingston Road, Raynes Park, London, SW20 8SD. tel: (081) 543 0077

Melrotree Ltd, Huttons Buildings, 146 West Street, Sheffield, S1 4ES. tel: (0742) 739370

Mobility 2000 (Telford) Ltd, Telford Industrial Centre,Stafford Park Four, Telford, Shropshire, TF3 3BA. tel: (0952) 290180

Mobility Informational Service, National Mobility Centre, Unit 2a. Atcham Estate, Shrewsbury, SY4 4UG. tel: (074 377) 489

Mobuggies-Cuffley, 14 Warwick Avenue, Cuffley, Potters Bar, Herts, EN6 4RS. tel: (0707) 872870

Motability, Gate House, West Gate, The High, Harlow, CM20 1HR. tel: (0279) 635666

Neill & Bennett, 7 Wyngate Road, Cheadle Hulme, Cheadle, Cheshire, SK8 6ER. tel: (061) 485 3149

Newton Products - Spastic Society, Meadway Works, Garretts Green Lane, Birmingham, B33 0SQ, tel (021) 783 6081/2/3

RF Nicholls Ltd, Soothouse Spring, Valley Road Industrial Estate, St. Albans, Herts, AL3 6PF. tel: (0727) 34255

NV Distributors Ltd, 2 Southdown Industrial Estate, Southdown Road, Harpenden, Herts AL5 1PW. tel: (0582) 461518

Oldham Crompton Batteries Ltd, Stephenson Street, Newport, Gwent NP9 0XJ. tel: (0633) 277673

Ortho-Kinetics (UK) Ltd, Unit 4, Planetary Road Industrial Estate, Wednesfield, Wolverhampton WV13 3XA. tel: (0902) 866166

Poirier (UK) Ltd, 17 St. George's Industrial Estate, Frimley Road, Camberley, Surrey GU15 2QW. tel: (0276) 28562/3

Raymar, P O Box 16, Fairview Estate, Reading Road, Henley-on-Thames, Oxon, RG9 lLL. tel: (0491) 578446

Remploy Ltd (Wheelchair Div), 11 Nunnery Drive, Sheffield S2 1TA. tel: (0742) 757631

Ridley Electronics Ltd, 206 Wightman Road, Hornsey, London, N8 0BU. tel: (081) 340 9501

Ross Auto Engineering Ltd (Wallasey) 2-3 Westfield Road, Wallasey, Merseyside L44 7HX

Samson Products (Dorset) Ltd., 239 Alder Road, parkstone, DXorset BH12 4AP. tel: (0202) 734171

Shopmobility, St. Nicholas Centre, Stanford Street, Nottingham NHG1 6AE. tel: (0602) 584486

SML Healthcare Ltd, Bath Place, High Street, Barnet, Herts EN5 5XE. tel: (081) 440 6522

Sun Alliance Insurance Group, Rickford House, 12 Rickford Hill, Aylesbury, Bucks HP20 2RX. tel: (0296) 24688

Sunrise Medical Ltd, Fens Pool Avenue, Brierley Hill, West Midlands DY5 1QA. tel: (0384) 480480

SVO Ltd, Lottage Road, Aldbourne, Nr. Marlborough, Wiltshire, SN8 2EB. tel (0789) 40001

CN Unwin Ltd, Lufton, Yeovil, Somerset, BA22 8SZ. tel: (0935) 75359

Vessa Ltd, Paper Mill Lane, Alton, Hants, GU34 2PY. tel: (0420) 83294

David Wenman (Associates)Ltd, 9 Guild Street, Stratford-upon-Avon, Warwickshire, CV37 6RE.tel:(0789)69400

Worktown Yarrow Young Ltd, 327 Station Road, Harrow, Middlesex, HA1 2XN. tel: (081) 863 5577

FOOTWEAR

3M UK plc, PO Box 1, Bracknell, Berks. RG12 1JU. tel: (0344) 58536

Abbott FE & Co., 10 Morningtons, Harlow, Essex, CM19 4QH. tel: (0279) 27062

Adams & Jones Ltd., White Cottage Courtyard, Magdalene Street, Glastonbury, Somerset, BA6 9EH. tel: (0458) 34356

Allen & Caswell Ltd., Regent Works, Cornwall Road, Kettering, Northants NN16 8PR. tel: (0536) 512804

Aremco, Grove House, Lenham, Kent, ME17 2PX. tel: (0622) 858502

Association for Chartered Physiotherapists with Special Interest in Elderly People, c/o L M Smythe, Physio-Department, West Norwich Hospital, Bowthorpe Road, Norwich, Norwich, NR2 3TU. tel: (0603) 28377

Atlas Traders, 26 Watford Way, Hendon Central, London NW4 3AD. tel. (081) 202 8924

Austenal Ltd, 4 Crystal Way, Harrow, Middx. HA1 2HG tel: (081) 863 9044

Avalon Shoe Materials, 40 High Street, Street, Somerset BA16 0YA. tel: (0458& 43131

Barkers Shoes (Sales) Ltd., Earls Barton, Northampton NN6 0NU. tel: (0604) 810387

Beaver of Bolton Ltd., Gilnow Mill, Sap Road, Bolton, BL1 4LF. tel. (0204) 386824

Jane Bertram Products, Dognests, Grimston, Melton Mowbray, Leics., LE14 3BZ. tel: (0664) 821751

Big Mans Shop, George Deakin & Sons Ltd., PO Box 3, Fore Street, Redruth, Cornwall, TR15 2DQ. tel: (0209) 216868/216222

Blackmans, 44 Cheshire St, London E2 6EH. tel: (071) 739 3902

Boots the Chemists Ltd., City Gate, Toll House Hill, Nottingham NGH2 3AA. tel: (0602) 4158522. *(enquiries should be made at local branches.)*

Bopy, 64 Great Bushey Drive, Totteridge, London N20 8QL. tel: (081) 446 4251

Brevitt Shoes Ltd., St. Georges St., Northampton NN1 2TN. tel: (0604) 27921

British Footwear Manufacturers Federation, Royalty House, 72 Dean St., LondonW1V 5HB. tel: (071) 437 5573

British Shoe Corporation Ltd., Sunningdale Road, Leicester LE3 1UR. tel: (0533) 320202

British Surgical Trades Association, 1 Webbs Court, Buckhurst Ave, Sevenoaks, Kent, TN13 1LZ. tel: (0732) 458868

Brooks (UK) Ltd., Brooks House, Unit 8, Hambridge Lane Industrial Estate, Newbury, Berks. R614 5TU. tel: (0635) 35235

JE Brown, 39 Kings Road, New Oscott, Sutton Coldfield, West Midlands, Tel: (021) 354 1449

BTR Silvertown Ltd., Footwear Sales Dept, Horninglow Road, Burton on Trent, Staffs DE13 0SN. tel: (0283) 510510/510052

Tony Burt, Somerset Orthopaedic Shoes, Merry Gardens, High Ham, Langport, Somerset, TA10 9DB. tel: (0458) 250309

Bury Boot and Shoe Co. Ltd., Woodhill Works, Brandlesholme Road, Bury, Lancs., BL8 1BG. tel: (061) 705 2200

BXL Plastics Ltd., ERP Division, 675 Mitcham Rd, Croydon, Surrey, CR9 3AL. tel: (081) 684 3622

D Byford & Co. Ltd., PO Box 10, Nottingham Road, Somercotes, Derbyshire DE55 4SF. tel: (0773) 607433

Camp Ltd. (Southern Div), Northgate Hse, Staple Gardens, Winchester S023 8ST. tel: (0962) 55248

Carita House, Stapeley, Nantwich, Cheshire CW5 7LJ. tel: (0270) 627722

Castle (Orthopaedic) Footwear Ltd., Unit 5, The Landing, 151 Oldham Road, Rochdale, Lancs, OL16 5QT. tel: (0706) 45567

Joseph Cheaney & Sons Ltd., Rushton Road, Desborough, Northants, NN14 2RZ. tel. (0536) 760383

Chester-Care Ltd, 16 Englands Lane, London NW3 4TG. tel: (071) 586 2166 or (071) 722 3430

Society of Chiropodists, 53 Welbeck Street, London W1M 7HE. tel: (071) 486 3381

Church & Co (Footwear) Ltd., St. James, Northampton. tel: (0604) 51251

Clarks Shoes Ltd., 40 High Street, Street, Somerset, BA16 0YA. tel: (0458) 43131

Clifford James, High St, Ripley, Woking, Surrey GU23 6AF

PR Cooper (Footline) Ltd., Sycamore Works, Tilton-on-the-Hill, Leicester, Leics, LE7 9LG. tel: (053 754) 263

Cosyfeet, 179 Ashton Drive, Ashton, Bristol, BS3 2PU. tel: (0272) 637590

Alfred Cox (Orthopaedic) Ltd., 108 Whitechapel Road, London El IJD. tel: (071) 247 1178

Crisfactors, 67 Foxholes Hills, Exmouth, Devon, EX8 2DH. tel: (039 52) 75832

Crispins Shoes Ltd., 28-30 Chiltern Street, London W1M 1PF. tel: (071) 486 8924- *and* - Royal Exchange, off St. Annes Square, Manchester M2 7DB. tel: (061) 833 0022

Crockett & Jones Ltd., Perry Street, Northampton NN1 4NH. tel: (0604) 31515

Culmknits, 38 Eastlands, Hemyock, Devon, EX15 3QP

Cumbria Orthopaedic Ltd., Floor 6, Shaddon Mill, Shaddongate,Carlisle, Cumbia, CA2 5TY tel: (0228) 29774 - *and* - 25 Chaucer Industrial Park, Watery Lane, Kensing, Sevenoaks, Kent. (0732) 63407

Damart, Bowling Green Mills, Lime Street, Bingley, W. Yorkshire, BD16 4BH. tel: (0274) 568211

Davies & Co., Durban Road, Kettering, Northants, NN16 0JW. tel: (0536) 513456

Days Medical Aids Ltd., Litchard Ind Est, Bridgend, M. Glamorgan, CF31 2AL. tel: (0656) 57495/60150

DB Shoes Ltd., Inchester Road, Rushden, Northants, NN10 9XF. tel: (0933) 59217

Design Studio, Longwater Ind. Est, Dereham Road, Norwich, Norfolk, NR5 0TL. tel: (0603) 742003

Devcon, Brunel Close, Park Farm, Wellingborough, Northants, NN8 3QX. tel: (0933) 675299

Devon, Exeter Orthotic Services, 59 Wonford Road, Exeter, Devon. EX2 4UF. tel: (0392) 433062

RJ Draper & Co. Ltd., Glastonbury, Somerset, BA6 8YA. tel: (0458) 31420

John Drew (London) Ltd., 433 Uxbridge Road, Ealing, London W5 3NT. tel: (081) 992 0381 - *or* - *(for orders only)* - Lake Lane, Barnham, Bognor Regis, West Sussex, PO22 0EG. tel: (0243) 553043

Dubarry Shoemakers International Ltd., Galway House, Astonfields House, Astonfields Road, Staffs, ST16 3UF. tel: (0785) 22313

Ducker & Son Ltd., 6 The Turl, Oxford. Tel: (0865) 242461

Dudley Surgical Appliances Ltd., Horseley Heath, Tipton, W. Midlands, DY4 7AA. tel: (021) 557 4204/7192

Dunkelmen & Sons Ltd., Head Office, The Manor House, GoldStreet, Desborough, Kettering, Northants. NN14 2PF. tel. (0536) 760760 *London Office:* 15 Jermyn Street, Piccadilly Circus, London SW1Y 6LT. tel. (071) 734 7340

Dunlop Footwear Ltd., Burlington House, Crosby Road North, Liverpool L22 0LG. tel: (051) 920 4163

Easicare, Unit 11, Wintonlea, Monument Way West, Woking, Surrey, GU21 5EN. tel: (04862) 63237

Easirider Co., Dolphin House, 188 Kettering Road, Northampton, Northants., NN1 4BH. tel: (0604) 30426

Equity Shoes Ltd., 42 Western Road, Leicester, Leics, LE3 0GQ. tel: (0533) 549313

Field & Trek Plc, 3 Waters Way, Brentwood, Essex, CM15 9TB. tel: (0277) 233122

Foot Shop Ltd., 5 The Tanyard, Leigh Road, Street, Somerset, BA16 0HR. tel: (0458) 47275

Footjoys, 23 Farm Drive, Shirley,Croydon, Surrey, CR0 8HX. tel: (01) 777 7541

Freeman Tonkin, 34 Chiltern Street, LondonW1 tel: (071) 487 3487

W Freeman & Co. Ltd., Suba-Sea Works, Staincross, Barnsley S75 6DH. tel: (0226) 284081

Gates Rubber Co Ltd., Edinburgh Road, Heathhall, Dumfries D61 1QA. tel: (0387) 53111

Gilbert & Mellish Ltd., 496-503 Bristol Road, Birmingham B29 6AU. tel: (021) 471 3055

Golden Footprints Ltd (Birkenstock), Upper Sapey, Worcester, Worcs., WR6 6XT. tel: (088 67) 274

Greenham Trading Ltd., Head Office, 671 London Road, Isleworth, Middx, TW7 4EX. tel: (081) 560 1244

Grenson Shoes, Queen Street, Rushden, Northants, NN10 0AB. tel: (0933) 58734

R Griggs & Co., Cobbs Lane, Wollaston, Northants, NN9 7SW. tel: (0933) 665381

Ken Hall Ltd., 39 Regent Street, Kettering, Northants, NN16 8BR. tel: (0536) 516674

Hammerpett Products Ltd., 1 Horn Lane, Stony Straftford, Bucks, MK11 1LB. tel: (0908) 562815

Frank Harvey & Co., 21 Violet Hill Road, Stowmarket, Suffolk, IP14 1NE. tel: (0449) 612646/613187

HATRA (Hosiery & Associated Trades Research Association), 7 Gregory Boulevard, Nottingham, NH7 6LD. tel: (0602) 623311

GT Hawkins Ltd., Overstone Road, Northampton, NN1 3JJ. tel: (0604) 32293

Health & Comfort Ltd., PO Box 15, Westbury, Wilts, BA13 4LS. tel: (0373) 822394

Health Education Authority, Hamilton House, Mabledon Place, London WC1H 9TV. tel: (071) 631 0930

Helping Hands Shop, 114 Queens Road, Leicester, LE2 3FL. tel: (0533) 881200 ext: 149

Henleys Medical Supplies Ltd., Brownfields, Welwyn Garden City, Herts. AL7 1AN. tel. (0707) 333164

High and Mighty, Head Office, The Old School House, High Street, Hungerford, Berks RG17 0NS. tel: (0488) 84913

Muriel Hitchcock, 47 Tarrant Street, Arundel, Sussex, BN18 9DJ. tel: (0903) 883982

SR Holbrook Ltd (Brinmark), Jackson Road, Coventry, CV6 4LY. tel:(0203) 667576

Edward Holmes Ltd, Drayton Road, Norwich, Norfolk, NR3 2DB. tel: (0603) 787222

Homecraft Supplies Ltd., Low Moor Estate, Kirkby-in-Ashfield, Notts, NG17 7JZ. tel: (0623) 754047

Howard & Hallam, Elmdale Works, Devonshire Road, Leicester, Leics., LE4 0AT. tel: (0533) 532112

Hucky Ltd, 115 Bury Street, Stowmarket, Suffolk IP14 1HE. tel: (0449) 674471

Ideal Footwear, Paul Herniman, PO Cottage, Chilgrove, Chichester, W. Sussex. PO18 9HU. tel: (024 359) 305

Insteps, 11 Market Place, Glastonbury, Somerset, BA6 9DD tel: (0458) 33280

Intershoe Ltd., 76 High Street, Stockton-on-Tees, Cleveland, TS18 1AF. tel: (0642) 677222

Jane Saunders & Manning, 1070-72 London Road, Thornton Heath, Surrey, CR4 7ND. tel: (081) 684 2584

Jen Shoes Ltd., Contract Services Division, Castlefields, Newport Road, Stafford ST16 1BQ. tel: (0785) 211311

John Florence Ltd., Orthotic Workshop, The Chailey Heritage, North Common, Lewes, E. Sussex, BN8 4EN. tel: (082 572) 2063

K Shoes, PO Box 31, Kendal, Cumbria, LA9 7BT. tel: (0539) 24343

Keep Able Ltd, Fleming Close, Park Farm, Wellingborough, Northants NN8 3UF. tel: (0933) 679426

Kettering Surgical Flotwear Ltd., 73 Overstone Road, Northampton NN1 3JW. tel: (0604) 22886

Kinway (UK) Ltd, Unit 7, 55-57 Park Royal Road, London NW10 7JP. tel: (081) 961 4410

Lace-N-Lock Co, Downalong, Bushey Heath, Herts., WD2 1HZ. tel: (081) 487 3487

Littlejohn Associates, Apney Downs Farm, Stow Road, Cirencester, Glos, GL7 5EU. tel: (0285) 659789

Llewellyn-SML. Health Care Services, Regent House, 1 Regent Road, City, Liverpool L3 7BX. tel: (051) 236 5311

Loake Bros (Sales) Ltd, Wood Street, Kettering, Northants, NN16 9SN. tel: (0536) 512801

Lotus Group, Freeman Street, Stafford, Staffs, ST16 3JA. tel: (0785) 223200

LSB Orthopaedics Ltd., 203/4 Melchett Road, Kings Norton, Birmingham B30 3HU. tel: (021) 458 2425/(021) 451 3016. *London Office:* 63 Fortress Road, Kentish Town, London, NW5 1AO. tel: (071) 485 8855

Made-To-Last, 77 Raglan Road, Leeds, LS2 9DZ. tel: (0532) 426079

Magnus of Northampton, 2 High Street, Harpole, Northampton NN7 4DH. tel: (0604) 831271

Medesign Ltd, Unit 7, Clock Tower Works, Railway Street, Southport PR8 5BB tel: (0704) 42373

Medipost Ltd., Unit 1, St. Johns Estate, Elder Road, Lees, Oldham, Lancs. OL4 3DZ. tel: (061) 678 0233

Meditech Developments Ltd, Unit 1, Crocus Place, Crocus Street, Nottingham NG2 3DE. tel: (0602) 863263

Minehead Shoe Co-operative Ltd, 1 North Road, Minehead, Somerset, TA24 5QW. tel: (0643) 705591

MML, 9 Sibford road, Hook Norton, Oxon, OX15 5LA. tel: (0608) 737504

Myron Medical Products Ltd., Chester House, Windsor End, Beaconsfield, Bucks, HP9 2JJ. tel: (049 46) 71257

Needletrade International, 351A Whitehouse Road, Croydon, Surrey, CRO 2PR. tel. (081) 684 9629

New Balance Athletic Shoes (UK) Ltd., Unit 16, Chesford Grange, Woolston, Warrington, Cheshire, WA1 4RQ. tel: (0925) 821182

Nicholl Knitwear, Piper Close, Corbridge, Northumberland. tel: (043) 471 2283

Nil Simile Shoes, 308 St. Saviours Road, Leicester, Leics, LE5 4HR. tel: (0533) 734985

Nobelpharma UK Ltd, 4 Crystal Way, Harrow, Middlesex, HA1 2HG. tel: (081) 863 9044

Nottingham Rehab Ltd., 17 Ludlow Hill Road, West Bridgford, Nottingham NG2 6HD. tel: (0602) 234251. *Mail order:* PO Box 96, Nottingham, NG2 6HE.

Nursing Care Products Ltd., Ryburn Mills, Hanson Lane, Halifax HX1 4SD. tel: (0422) 343243

Orthopaedic Footwear Ltd (James Taylor & Son), 4 Paddington St, Marylebone High St., London W1M 3LA. tel: (071) 935 4149

Orthopaedic Systems, Unit G22, 23 Oldgate, St. Michael's Ind. Estate, Widnes, Cheshire, WA8 8TL. tel: (051) 420 3250

W. Paton ltd., PO Box 6, Johnstone, Renfrewshire, PA5 8SW. tel: (0505) 21633

Plus 50, Lodge road, Kingswood, Bristol, BS15 1JX. tel (0272) 353637

Poole, H.W. & Sons Ltd., Crispin House, New York Road, Leeds LS2 7PG. tel: (0532) 433 045

Portland Shoes, Gateway Street, Leicester LE2 7DL. tel: (0533) 556112

Pryor & Howard Ltd., 39 Willow Lane, Mitcham, Surrey,CR4 4US. tel: (081) 648 1177

Punch Sales Ltd., Lower Farm Road, Moulton Park, Northampton, NN3 1XF. tel: (0604) 46426

Reddimade, Unit 22m Thornhill Road, North Moons Moat Ind. Est., Redditch, Worcs, B98 9ND.

Reedcrafts, 49 Turner Road, Long Eaton, Derby, NG10 3GP. tel: (0602) 721138

Remploy Ltd (Medical Products Division), 415 Edgware Road, London NW2 6LR. tel: (081) 452 8020

Rud Chains Ltd., 1-3 Belmont Road, Whitstable, Kent CT5 1QJ. tel: (0227) 276611

SATRA Footwear Technology Centre, Satra House, Rockingham Road, Kettering, Northants, NN16 9JH. tel: (0536) 410000

T Savva Ltd., 37 Chiltern Street, LondonW1M 1HJ. tel: (071) 935 2329

Scholl (UK) Ltd, 182-204 St John Street, London EC1P 1DH.tel: (071) 253 2030 - *or (for orders)* - (071) 253 3636

Sedgemoor Shoes Ltd., River Lane, Dunwear, Bridgewater, Somerset, TA7 0AA. tel. (0278) 427662

Shoe & Leather News, 100 Avenue Road, London NW3 3TP. tel: (071) 935 6611

Society of Shoe Fitters, The Anchorage, 28 Admirals Walk, Hingham, Norwich, Norfolk, NR9 4JL. tel: (0953) 851171

Shoecare Ltd., 33 St. Mary's Street, Preston, Lancs. PR1 5LN. tel. (0772) 703366

Skerry Shoes Ltd., 58-64 Suffolk Street, Ballymena, Co. Antrim, BT43 7DB. N. Ireland. tel: (0266) 652591

Skinsmiths, Upper Crossway, Newton St. Margarets, Hereford, HR2 0QY. tel: (098) 123620

Small & Tall Shoe Shop, 71 York Street, London, WlH 2BJ. tel: (071) 723 5321

Snowchains Ltd., Bourne Ind. Est, Borough Green, Nr. Sevenoaks, Kent, TN15 8DG. tel: (0732) 884408

Sole Mates, Mrs. Cross, 46 Gordon Road, Chingford, London E4 6BU. tel: (081) 524 2423

Soma (UK) Ltd., 3-7 Moss Street, Liverpool L6 1EY. tel: (051) 207 3539

Sorbothane, Golden Hill Lane, Leyland, Preston, Lancs PR5 1UB. tel. ()0772) 421434

Spearhead Marketing Ltd., 8 Mandervell Road, Oadby, Leicester, LE2 5LQ. tel: (0533) 710551

James Spencer & Co. Ltd., Moor Road Works, Moor Road, Headingley, Leeds LS6 4BH. tel: (0532) 785837/741850

Spenco Medical (UK) Ltd, Burrell Road, Haywards Heath, W. Sussex, RH16 1TW. tel: (0444) 415171

Stanfield, Brian Co. Ltd., 127 Hassall Road, Winterley, Sandbach, Cheshire, CW11 0RT. tel: (0270) 765325

Start-rite Shoes Ltd., Crome Road, Norwich, Norfolk, NR3 4RD. tel: (0603) 423841

Stockport Odd Feet Association, 32 Mallard Crescent, Poynton, Cheshire, SK12 1HT

R Taylor & Son (Orthopaedic) Ltd., Compton Works, 49 Woodwards Road, Pleck, Walsall, WS2 9RN. tel: (0922) 27601

Tecnic Shoe Co Ltd., Bedford Road, Rushden, Northants, NN10 0ND. tel: (0933) 53073/4

TUF GB Britton, Lodge Road, Kingswood, Bristol, BL15 1JB. tel: (0272) 352777

Tuskers Footwear, Barwell, Leics, LE9 86R. tel: (0455) 44101

Van-Dal Shoes Ltd., Dibden Road, Norwich, Norfolk, NR3 4RR. tel (0603) 426341

Warm 'N Dry, 138 Lancaster Road, Enfield Middx. EN2 0JR. tel: (01) 366 4978

Chris Webber, 28 Reedham Close, London N17 9PT. tel: (01) 808 0778

John White, Lime Street, Rushden, Northants, NN10 9DY. tel: (0933) 410333

J D. Williams & Co. Ltd., 53 Dale Street, Manchester M60 6ES. tel: (061) 236 3764

John Wood & Son Ltd., Linton, Old Cleeve, Minehead, Somerset, TA24 6HT. tel: (0984) 40291

HOISTS AND LIFTING EQUIPMENT

Aidserve Ltd, Unit 106, Bradley Hall Trading Estate, Bradley Lane, Standish, Wigan, WN6 0XQ. tel: (0257) 425538

AMP Engineers Ltd, Unit 2b, Portland Ind Est, Hitchin Road, Arlesey, Beds.SG15 6SG. tel: (0462) 730443/730789

AMP Services, 34a, Vale Road, Portslade, Brighton, E Sussex BN41 1GG. tel: (0273) 418918

Anglia Mobility Enterprises Ltd, 9 North Videw, Barney, Fakenham, Norfolk NR21 0NE. tel: (0328) 878938 (Contact: Mr J Worsnop)

Aremco, Grove House, Lenham, Kent ME17 2PX. tel: (0622) 858502

Arjo Mecanaids Ltd, St. Catherine Street, Gloucester, GL1 2SL. tel: (0452) 500200

Asgo Ltd, 22b Hawthorne Road, Lottbridge Drive, Eastbourne, East Sussex BN23 6PZ. tel: (0323) 38228

Atlantic Medical Ltd, Winchmore Hill, 12-15 Fetter Lane, London EC4A 1BR. tel: (071) 583 9481

Baronmead International Ltd, Bank Building, 39 Elmer Road, Middleton-on-Sea, West Sussex, PO22 6DZ. tel: (0243) 586692

Bell Johnson & Green Ltd, Tuley Street, Manchester, Mll 2DY tel: (061) 223 9144

Bencraft Ltd, The Avenue, Rubery, Rednal, Birmingham, West Midlands, B45 9AP. tel: (021) 453 1055/6/7

Boots the Chemist Ltd, City Gate, Toll House Hill, Nottingham NG2 3AA tel: (0602) 418522.Enquires should be made at local branches.

Bright Home Products, Unit 7, Lancaster Road, Caraby Ind Est, Bridlington Y015 3QY. tel: (0262) 606376

Britannia Lift Ltd, New Road, Sheerness, Kent ME12 1NB. tel: (0795) 664581

British Elevators Ltd, Unit 2, 64 Gloucester Road, Croydon, Surrey CR0 UDB. tel: (081) 689 6629

Brooks Stairlifts Ltd, Westminster Ind Est, Station Road, North Hykeham, Lincoln, LN6 3QY. tel: (0522) 500288

J Burton & Co Ltd, Clarendon Street, Haworth, Keighley BD22 8PU. tel: (0535) 42314

Carters (J&A) Ltd, Aintree Avenue, White Horse Business Park, North Bradley, Trowbridge, Wilts. BA14 0XA. tel: (0225) 751901

Chailey Heritage, Rehab Engineering Unit, Chailey Heritage Hospital and School, North Chailey, Lewes, East Sussex, BN8 4EF. tel: (082 572) 2112 ext. 210

Chattanooga UK Ltd, Unit 1 & 2, Goods Road, Belper, Derbyshire DE5 1UU. tel: (077382) 6993/4

Chester-care Ltd, 16 Englands Lane, London NW3 4TG. tel: (071) 586 2166 or (071) 722 3430

Chiltern Medical Developments Ltd, Chiltern House, Wedgewood Road, Bicester, Oxon OX6 7UL tel: (0869) 246470

JS Clayton & Co. Ltd, Morewood Estate, London Road, Sevenoaks, Kent TN13 2UH. tel: (0732) 460588

Contracts Direct - Lift Dv, PO.Box 1, Rexmore Way, Liverpool L15 0HZ. tel: (051 34) 4396

Days Medical Aids Ltd, Litchard Ind Est, Bridgend, Mid-Glamorgan, CF31 2AL. tel: (0656) 657495/660150

Doherty Medical, Doherty House, 278 Alma Road, Enfield, Middlesex EN3 7BH tel: (081) 804 1244

Ellis Son & Paramore Ltd, Spring Street Works, Sheffield S3 8PB.tel: (0742) 738921

Evans Lifts Ltd, 51 Handforth Road, Clapham Road, London SW9 0LP. tel: (071) 735 6692

Express Lift Co Ltd, Box 19, Abbey Works, Weedon Road, Northampton NN5 5BT. tel: (0604) 51221/8

Frazer Safety Products, Hebburn, Tyne & Wear NE31 1BD. tel (091) 428 0242

FW Equipment Co Ltd, Hanworth Road, Low Moor, Bradford BD12 0SG tel: (0274) 601121

Gimson-Tendercare, 62 Boston Road, Beaumont Leys, Leicester LED4 1AZ. tel: (0533) 366779

Gough & Co (Handley) Ltd, Clough Street, Hanley, Stoke-on-Trent, ST1 4AP. tel (0782) 208708

Grorud Bison Bede Ltd, Castleside Ind Est, Consett, Co Durham, DH8 8JB tel: (0207) 590149/508308

Haltract Ltd, 119/123 Sandycombe Road, Richmond, Surrey, TW9 2ER. tel (081) 940 3322

Hammond & Champness Ltd, Gnome House, Blackhorse Lane, London E17 6DT. tel (081) 527 5522

Holborn Surgical Instrument Co Ltd, Dolphin Works, Margate Road, Broadstairs, Kent, CT10 2QQ. tel: (0843) 61418

Mrs. Christina Hollick, Top of the Hill,Shantock Lane, Bovingdon, Herts HP3 0NG. tel: (0442) 832264

Homecraft Supplies Ltd, Low Moor Estate, Kirby-in-Ashfield, Notts, NG17 7JZ. tel: (0623) 754 047

Hoskins Ltd, Upper Trinity Street, Birmingham B9 4EQ. tel (021) 766 7404

Hospital Aids Ltd, 9 Staveley Way, Brixworth, Northampton, NN6 9EU tel: (0604) 881650

Hospital Metalcraft Ltd, Blandford Heights, Blandford Forum,Dorset, DT11 7TE. tel: (0258) 51338

Hymo-Lift Ltd, Scaldwell Road, Brixworth, Northampton NN6 9EN. tel: (0604) 880724

Independence, 52 Exeter Road, Exmouth, Devon EX8 1PY. tel: (0395) 268555

Kone Lifts Ltd, 168-170 Wellington Road South, Hounslow, Middlesex, TW4 5JN. tel: (081) 570 7799

Langham Products, Unit 26, Bennettsfield Trading Estate, Wincanton, Somerset BA9 9DT. tel: (0963) 33869

Leggat Lifts, Unit 5, Coatbridge Workshops, Coatbank Way, Coatbridge ML5 3AG. tel: (0236) 31012

The Lift & Hoist Co Ltd, 1 Queens Row, Southwark, London SE17 2PX 2PX. tel: (071) 703 8383

Llewellyn-SML Health Care Services, Regent House, 1 Regent Road, City, Liverpool L3 7BX. tel: (051) 236 5311

Mangar Aids Ltd, Presteigne Ind Est, Presteigne, Powys LD8 2UF. tel: (0544) 267674

Manor Lifts Ltd, 22a Sefton Street, Litherland, Liverpool L21 7LB tel: (051) 949 0515

Medesign Ltd, Unit 7, Clock Tower Works, Railway St, Southport, PR8 5BB. tel: (0704) 42373

Robert Mudd, 2 Down View, Chippenham, Wilts. SN14 0QP. tel (024 975) 222 (ask for Mrs Labouchere)

National Association of Lift Makers, Leicester House, 8 Leicester Street, London WC2H 7BN. tel: (071) 437 0678

Nomeq, 23/24 Thornhill Road, North Moons Moat, Redditch, Worcs. B98 9ND. tel: (0527) 64222

Nottingham Rehab Ltd, 17 Ludlow Hill Road, West Bridgford, Nottingham, NG2 6HD. tel: (0602) 234251

Oakland Elevators Ltd, Mandervell Road, Oadby, Leicester LE2 5LL tel: (0533) 720800

Otis Handling, Abbey Lane, Leicester, LE4 5QX. tel: (0533) 665353

Paraid, Weston Lane, Birmingham B11 3RS. tel: (021) 706 6744

Parker Bath Developments Ltd, Queensway, Stem Lane Ind Est, New Milton, Hants, BH25 5NN. tel: (0425) 617598

T Parry Ltd, Hendy, High Street, Bangor on Dee, Wrexham LL13 0AU tel (0978) 780430

FJ Payne Manufacturing Ltd, Stanton Harcourt Road, Eynsham, Oxford OX8 1JT. tel: (0865) 881881

Pear Associates Ltd, Iroko House, Bridge Street, Derby, DE1 3LB. tel: (0332) 291851

Pickerings Ltd, Globe Elevator Works, PO Box 19, Stockton-on-Tees, Cleveland TS20 2AD. tel: (0642) 607161

Porn & Dunwoody Lifts Ltd, Union Works, Bear Gardens, London SE1 9EB. tel (071) 261 1162

Power Lifts Ltd, Hadley Works, Caxton Way, Holywell Ind Est, Watford WD1 8TJ. tel (0923) 227724

Power-Tech (UK) Ltd, Unit 8c, Ford Airfield Ind Est, yapton, Arundel, West Sussex, BN18 0HY. tel: (0903) 713227

Project and Design Ltd, 72 Jay Avenue, Teeside Ind.Est., Thornaby, Stockton-on-Tees TS17 9LZ. tel: (0642) 750707

Ratcliff Ltd, Bessemer Road, Welwyn Garden City, Herts. AL7 1ET. tel: (0707) 325571

Renray Group ltd, Road Five, Winsford Ind Est, Winsford, Cheshire CW7 3RB. tel: (0606) 593456

Revolutionary Fire Escapes Ltd, Churchill House, Cavendish Road, London SW12 0PG, tel: (071) 673 4534

RJS Trading Ltd, Doric House, Charlbury, Oxford OX7 3BR. tel: (0608) 810189

Samson Products (Dorset) Ltd., 239 Alder Road, Parkstone, Dorset BH12 4AP. tel: (0202) 734171

Schindler Lifts UK Ltd, Sunningend Works, Lansdown Ind Est, Gloucester Road, Cheltenham GL51 8PS tel: (0242) 232091

Scottish National Institution for the War Blinded, Linburn, Wilkieston, Kirknewton, Midlothian, EH27 8DU tel (031) 333 1369/1334

Smiths Leisure Services, 10 Hall Drive, Morecambe, Lancs, LA4 6SX. tel: (0524) 66510

Somerquip, 138 Berrow Road, Burnham-on-Sea, Somerset. tel: (0278) 780777

James Spencer & Co Ltd, Moor Road Works, Moor Road, Headingley, Leeds LS6 4BH. tel: (0532) 785837/741850

Spenco Medical UK Ltd, Burrell Road, Haywards Heath, West Sussex. RH16 1TW. tel: (0444) 415171

Stannah Stairlifts Ltd, Watt Close, East Portway, Andover, Hants, SP10 3SD. tel: (0264) 64311

Sterling Finance, St. George House, 40 Great George Street, Leeds, Ls1 3DL. tel: (0532) 431426

Sunrise Medical Ltd, Fens Pool Avenue, Brierley Hill, West Midlands, DY5 1QA. tel: (0384) 480480

Suntrap Systems Ltd, 105 Argent Centre, 60 Frederick Street, Birmingham B1 3HS. tel: (021) 236 2642

Tanks and Drums Ltd, Victoria Street, Pontycymmer, Bridgend, Mid Glamorgan CF32 8LR. tel: (0656) 870415

Terry Lifts Ltd, Unit 6, Wolfe Close, Parkgate Ind Est, Knutsford, Cheshire WA16 8XJ. tel (0565) 3211/50377

Toplift UK Ltd, Head Office, Rustat House, 61 Clifton Road, Cambridge CB1 4GY. tel: (0223) 243122

Unit Installations, Horseley Fields Trading Estate, Horseley Fields, WolverhamptonWVl 3BZ. tel: (0902) 351041 (Contact Mr A Jones).

CN Unwin Ltd, Lufton, Yeovil, Somerset BA22 8SZ.tel: (0935) 75359

Velmore Ltd, 55 Swandene, Pagham, West Sussex, England, PO21 4UR. tel: (0243) 267424

Wards Mobility Services Ltd, Ware Works, Bells Yew Green, Tunbridge Wells, TN3 9BD. tel: (089 275) 686

Wessex Medical Equipment Co Ltd, Budds Lane, Romsey, Hants, S051 0HA. tel: (0794) 830303

Young - Arch'd & Son Ltd, 37 Constitution Street, Edinburgh, Scotland, EH6 7BG tel: (031) 554 0591

HOUSEHOLD EQUIPMENT

3M UK plc, Head Office, 3M House, PO Box 1, Bracknell, Berks. RG12 1JU. tel: (0344) 426726

Abru Henderson Ltd, Pennygillam Ind Est, Launceston, Cornwall PL15 7ED. tel: (0566) 6611

Aidserve Ltd, Unit 106, Bradley Hall Trading Estate, Bradley Lane, Standish, Wigan, WN6 0XQ. tel: (0257) 425538

Aladdin International Corporation, Polychrome Estate, Sandown Rd, Watford WD2 4XP. tel: (0923) 247776

G & S Allgood Ltd, Carterville House, 297 Euston Road, London NW1 3AQ. tel: (071) 387 9951

Anything Left Handed Ltd, 65 Beak St, London W1R 3LDF tel: (071) 437 3910

Aquafilm Ltd, Unit 229, Arctic Trading Estate, Droitwich Road, Hartlebury, Worcs DY10 4EU. tel: (0299) 251335

Aremco, Grove House, Lenham, Kent. ME17 2PX. tel: (0622) 858502

ASM Medicare, Picow Farm Ind Est, Runcorn, Cheshire WA7 4UG.tel: (09285) 74301/2/3

Beam, Central Vacuum Systems, St. Martin's Gate, Worcester WR1 2DU (0905) 611042

Beldray Ltd, PO Box 20, Mount Pleasant, Bilston, W Midlands, WV14 7NF. tel: (0902) 353500

Bissell Appliances Ltd, 2 Jubilee Avenue, Highams Park Ind Est, Highams Park, London E4 9HN. tel: (081) 531 7241

Black & Decker Ltd, 75 Rushey Green, Catford SE6 tel: (081) 698 9933

Bodman Agencies, 96 Harborne Road, Warley, West Midlands, B68 9JH. tel: (021) 429 3272

Bonny Products Ltd, Unit 5, Telford Road, Basingstoke, Hants RG21 2YU. tel: (0256) 475466

Boots the Chemists Ltd, City Gate, Toll House Hill, Nottingham NG2 3AA. tel: (0602) 418522 Enquiries should be made at local branches.

Ray Branch & Co. Ltd., 29/31 Lower Loveday St, Birmingham, B19 3SE.tel (021) 359 8125-8

M Brennan & Co, 35 Upper Library St, Belfast, Northern Ireland BT1 2JH. tel: (0232) 325576

Budgie Office Products Ltd, Birch Close, Eastbourne, E. Sussex. BN23 6PE. tel: (0323) 648471

Burco Maxol, Rose Grove, Burnley, Lancs. BB12 6AL. tel: (0282) 27241

Carters (J&A) Ltd, Aintree Avenue, White Horse Business Park, North Bradley, Trowbridge, Wilts BA14 0XA.

Cash Clip Ltd, 99 Satchell Lane, Hamble, Hants, S03 58L. tel: (0703) 453692

Cee Vee Engineering Ltd, Cooden Sea Road, Bexhill-on-Sea, East Sussex, TN39 4SL. tel: (042 43) 5566

Central Medcial Equipment Ltd, 7 Ascot Park Estate, Lenton St, Sandiacre, Nottingham NG10 5DL. tel: (0602) 390949

Chester-care Ltd, 16 Englands Lane, London NW3 4TG. tel: (081) 586 2166 or (081) 722 3430

CMT Wells Kelo Ltd, Progress Works, Kingsland, Holyhead, Anglesey, Gwynedd. (0407) 2391/5

Cowley Components Ltd, Masons Road, Stratford-Upon-Avon, Warwickshire CV57 9NR. tel: (0789) 69687

Creda Ltd, Creda Works, PO Box 5, Blythe Bridge, Stoke-on-Trent, ST11 9LJ. tel: (0782) 388388

Criterion Electric Ltd, Criterion House, Penfold Works, Imperial Way, Watford, Herts WD2 4YY. tel: (0923) 227227

Croydex Co Ltd, Central Way, Walworth Ind. Est, Andover, Hants SP10 5AW. tel: (0264) 65881

D & K Manufacturing, Unit 2, Holly Hall Road Ind. Est, Holly Hall Road, Dudley, W Midlands tel: (0384) 54311

Damart, Bowling Green Mills, Lime St, Bingley, W Yorkshire BD16 3ZD. tel: (0274) 568211

Dauphin International Ltd, Peter St, Blackburn, Lancs BB1 5LH. tel: (0254) 52220

Days Medical Aids Ltd, Litchard Ind Est, Bridgend, Mid-Glamorgan, CF31 2AL. tel: (0656) 657495/660150

Dennison Equipment Co (Midlands) Ltd, Abbey Works, Bleachfield St, Alcester, Warwickshire B49 5BE. tel: (0789) 763811

Denroy International Ltd, 11 Berkley St, London W1X 6BU tel: (071) 495 6737

Derby Health Care, Trent Lane, Castle Donington, Derby DE7 2PW. tel: (0332) 850011

Drove Precision Engineering, Hargreaves Road, Highfield Ind. Est, Eastbourne, East Sussex BN23 6QL. tel: (0323) 507701

Ellis Son & Paramore Ltd, Spring Street Works, Sheffield S3 8PB. tel: (0742) 738921

Elna Sewing Machines GB Ltd, Queens House, 180/182 Tottenham Court Road, London W1P 9LE. tel: (071) 323 1187

Enak Ltd, Redkiln Way, Horsham, West Sussex, RH13 5Qh. tel: (0403) 65544

Engments Ltd, Chequers Rd, West Meadows Ind Est, Derby, DE2 6EN. tel: (0332) 44579

Fast Systems Ltd, 54 Friday St, Henley-on-Thames, Oxon, RG9 1AH. tel: (0491) 572374

H Fereday & Sons Ltd, Shaftesbury Works, 45 Holloway Road, London N7 8JT. tel: (071) 607 5601

Four Wheels Trolleys, 221 Bow Road, London E3 2SJ tel: (081) 980 5047

W Freeman & Co Ltd, Suba-Seal Works, Staincross, Barnsley S75 6DH. tel: (0226) 284081

M Gilbert (Greenford) Ltd, 1109/15 Greenford Road, Greenford, Middlesex, UB6 0EH. tel: (081) 864 6566 *Do not supply to public - retail list available.*

Goblin Ltd, Cross Green Approach, Leeds LS9 0SX. tel: (0532) 488994

Goldene Designs Ltd, 7c Moss Lane, Whitefield, Manchester, M25 7QE. tel: (061) 796 9367

Golding, Stanley Ltd. 29 Charlton Church Lane, Charlton, London SE7 7AG. tel: (081) 853 0238

Greenbank Project Co-operatives, Edwards Lane, Speke, Liverpool, L24 9HG. tel (051) 486 3525

GT (Boston) Industrial Services Ltd, Cowbridge, Boston, Lincs PE22 7DJ. tel: (0205) 357053

DH Haden Ltd, Mount Road, Burntwood, Walsall WS7 0AW. tel: (05436) 75222

Hago Products Ltd, Durban Rd, Bognor Regis, West Sussex, PO22 9QT. tel: (0243) 863131 *Wholesale supplier only*

Handicart Ltd, Winnall Manor Road, Winchester S023 8LJ. tel: (0962) 840844

Harp Products, Riverside House, Carnwath Road, London SW6 3HS. tel: (071) 736 7511

Hartbeam Ltd, 14 Norman Way, Over, Cambridge CB4 5QE. tel (0954) 30308

Hawkins Handcrafts Ltd, Fore St, Kentisbeare, Cullompton, Devon. tel: (08846) 309

Health & Comfort Ltd, PO Box 15, Westbury, Wilts BA13 4LS. tel: (0373) 822394

Heatrae Sadia Heating Ltd, Hurrican Way, Norwich, Norfolk NR6 6EA. tel: (0603) 424144 *Do not supply direct to the public*

Heinz Baby Club, Vinces Road, Diss, Norfolk IP22 3HH. tel: (0379) 651981

The Helping Hand Company (Ledbury) Ltd, Unit 9L, Bromyard Road Trading Estate, Ledbury, Herefordshire HR8 1NS. tel: (0531) 5678

Helping Hands Shop, 114 Queens Road, Leicester LE2 3LF. tel: (0533) 708821

Hestair Hope Ltd, St. Philip's Drive, Royton, Oldham, Lancs, OL2 6AG. tel: (061) 633 6611

Hills Industries Ltd, Pontygwindy Ind Est, Caerphilly, Mid-Glamorgan CF8 3HU. tel: (0222) 883951

Home Nursing Supplies Ltd, Headquarters Road, West Wilts Trading Estate, Westbury, Wilts, BA13 4JR. tel: (0373) 822313

Homecraft Supplies Ltd, Low Moor Estate, Kirkby-in-Ashfield, Notts NG17 7JZ. tel: (0623) 757955

Hoover plc, Dragonparc, Abercanaid, Merthyr Tydfil, Mid-Glamorgan, CF48 1PQ. tel: (0685) 721000

Hozelock-ASL Ltd, Haddenham, Aylesbury, Bucks, HP17 8JD. tel: (0844) 291881

Jani-Jack Ltd, Coat Road, Martock, Somerset, TA12 6EY. tel: (0935) 825500

Joncare Ltd, 7 Ashville Trading Estate, Nuffield Way, Abingdon, Oxon. OX14 1RL. tel: (0235) 28120/35600

Keep Able Ltd, Fleming Close, Park Farm, Wellingborough, Northants NN8 3UF. tel: (0933) 679426

Kiddi-Proof Products Ltd, Design House, 9 Centre Way, Claverings Ind Est, Montague Road, Edmonton, London N9 0AJ. tel: (081) 807 4552

King Cole Tube Bending Co Ltd, 40 Buckland Road, Pen Mill Trading Estate, Yeovil, Somerset BA21 5EJ. tel: (0935) 26141/2

Lakeland Plastics, Alexandra Buildings, Windermere, Cumbria, LA23 1BQ. tel: (096 62) 2255/7

Lefthanded by Post, Duntish Court, Buckland Newton, Dorchester, Dorset DT2 7DE. tel: (03005) 291

Lefties, The Left Handed Co., PO Box 52, South DO, Manchester M20 8PJ. tel: (061) 445 0159

Leifheit International (UK) Ltd, 4 Eastman Road, Acton Park, London W3 7QS. tel: (081) 749 7211

Lesway, 3 Clarendon Terrace, Maida Vale, London W9 1BZ. tel: (071) 289 7197

William Levene Ltd, 167 Imperial Drive, Harrow, Middlesex HA2 7JP. tel: (081) 868 4355

Lever Industrial Ltd, PO Box 208, Lever House, St James Road, Kingston-upon-Thames, Surrey KT1 2BB. tel: (081) 541 5577

Lion Sheltered Workshop, Unit 4c, Lion Works, Pool Rd, Newtown, Powys SY16 3AG. tel: (0743) 790128

Llewellyn-SML Health Care Services, Regent House, 1 Regent Road, City, Liverpool L3 7BX. tel: (051) 236 5311

M Margolis Ltd, 63-65 New Oxford St, London WC1A 1DG. tel: (071) 240 5057

Marsden Weighing Machine Group Ltd, 388 Harrow Road, London W9 2HU. tel (071) 289 1066

Martek Ltd, PO Box 20, Redruth, Cornwall, TR15 2UF. tel (0209) 219911

Medeci Rehab Ltd, Research Unit, Warley Hospital, Brentwood, Essex CM14 5HQ. tel: (0277) 212637

Medipost Ltd, Unit 1, St. Johns Estate, Elder Road, Lees, Oldham, Lancs. OL4 3DZ. tel: (061) 678 0233

Meditech Developments Ltd, Unit 1 Crocus Place, Crocus St, Nottingham NG2 3DE. tel: (0602) 863263

David Mellor, 4 Sloane Square, London SW1 8EE. tel: (071) 730 4259

Miele Co Ltd, Fairacres, Marcham Road, Abingdon, Oxon, OX14 1TW. tel: (0235) 554455 *Do not supply direct to public*

Mobilia, Unit B32 Barwell Business Estate, Leatherhead Road, Chessington, Surrey. KT9 2NY. tel: (081) 397 1166

Mothercare Plc, Cherry Tree Road, Watford, Herts, WD2 5SH. tel: (0923) 33577 *Customer enquiries on (0923) 31616*

Newton Products - Spastics Society, Meadway Works, Garretts Green Lane, Birmingham, B33 0SQ. tel: (021) 783 6081/2/3

Nord International Marketing Co Inc. Ltd., 47A. Joseph Wilson Ind. Estate, Millstrood Road, Whitstable, Kent CT5 3PS. tel: (0227) 770701

Nottingham Rehab Ltd, 17 Ludlow Hill Road, West Bridgford, Nottingham, NG2 6HD. tel: (0602) 234251

Orbit Enterprises Ltd, Head Office, 77 Oxford St, London W1R 1RB. tel: (071) 434 0101

Parr, F Ltd, 115-121 Sherlock St, Birmingham B5 6PW. tel: (021) 622 3553

Pentonville (Rubber Products) Ltd, 50 Pentonville Road, London N1 9HF. tel: (071) 837 0283

Philips Electronics, PO Box 298, City House, 420-430 London Road, Croydon, Surrey CR9 3QR. tel: (081) 689 2166

Pifco Salton Carmen, Failsworth, Manchester M35 0HS. tel: (061) 681 8321

Porvair Ltd, Medical Products, Estuary Rd, King's Lynn, Norfolk PE30 2HS. tel: (0553) 761111

Precision Engineering Co (Reading) Ltd, Meadow Rd, Reading, Berks RG1 8LB. tel: (0734) 599444

Probus Housewares PLC, Watling St, Tamworth, Staffs, B77 1EZ. tel (0827) 288588

PZ Products Ltd, Unit 4, Thorpe Close, Banbury, Oxon, OX16 9DA. tel: (0295) 263888

Redring Electric Ltd, Redring Works, Peterborough, Cambs, PE2 9JJ. tel: (0733) 313213

Renray Group Ltd, Road Five, Winsford Ind Est, Winsford, Cheshire, CW7 3RB. tel: (0606) 593456

Riders Ltd, Fulledge Works, Holmes St, Burnley BB11 3BG. tel: (0282) 59592/3

Roma Medical Aids Ltd, Llandow Ind Est, Cowbridge, South Glamorgan, CF7 7PB. tel: (044 63) 4519

Ronco Sales Organisation, 89 East End Road, Finchley, London N2 0SR. tel: (081) 883 9753

Royal National Institute for the Blind (Peterborough), Production and Distribution Centre, Bakewell Road, Orton, Peterborough PE2 OXU. tel: (0733) 370 777

Russell Hobbs Tower Ltd, Bridgnorth Road, Wombourne, Wolverhampton WV5 8AQ. tel: (0902) 324123

Salter Housewares Ltd, 211 Vale Road, Tonbridge, Kent TN9 1SU. tel: (0732) 354828

SDL Ltd, Coleman Road, Leicester, LE5 4LE. tel: (0533) 769471

Servis Group Ltd, Darlaston Road, Kings Hill, Wednesbury, West Midlands WS10 7TE. tel: (021) 526 3199

Shopeasy Design Ltd, Releath Water Farm, Helston, Cornwall, TR13 0HD. tel: (0209) 831761

Silleck Mouldings Ltd, Eaglescliffe Ind Est, Stockton-on-Tees, Cleveland TS16 0PN. tel (0642) 790555

Gerald Simonds Healthcare Stoke Mandeville, 9 March Place, Gatehouse Way, Aylesbury, Bucks. HP19 3UG. tel: (0296) 436557

Sitting Pretty Products Ltd, The Business Centre, Colne Way, Watford, Herts WD2 8FP. tel. (0923) 245050

Smit & Co Ltd, 99 Walnut Tree Close, Guildford, Surrey GU1 4UQ. tel: (0483) 33113

James Spencer & Co Ltd, Moor Road Works, Moor Road, Headingley, Leeds LS6 4BH. tel: (0532) 785837/741850

Sparson Products, Sweetpool Lane, West Hagley, Stourbridge, WorcesterDY8 2XD. tel: (0562) 886439

Steeper Hugh Ltd, 237-239 Roehampton Lane, London SW15 4LB. tel: (081) 788 8165

Stewart Plastics Plc, Purley Way, Croydon CR9 4HS. tel: (081) 686 2231

R Taylor & Son (Orthopaedic) Ltd, Compton Works, 49 Woodwards Road, Pleck, Walsall, WS2 9RN. tel: (0922) 27601

Tefal UK Ltd, 11-49 Station Road, Langley, Slough, Berks, SL3 8DR. tel: (0753) 44100.*Details of retailers only from this address.*

Mike & Hilary Temple, 1 Morland Avenue, Dartford, Kent DA1 3BW. tel: (0322) 22287

Unico Components Ltd, 101 Walnut Tree Close, Guildford, Surrey, GU1 4UQ. tel: (0483) 577545

Unit Installations, Horseley Fields Trading Estate, Horseley Fields, Wolverhampton, WV1 3BZ. tel: (0902) 351041.*(Contact Mr A Jones.)*

Vale Mill (Rochdale) Ltd, John St, Rochdale OL16 1HR. tel: (0706) 353535

Vax Appliances Ltd, Quillgold House, Kingswood Road, Hampton Lovett, Droitwich, Worcs WR9 0QH. tel: (0905) 795959

Visual Merchandising Ltd, 35 Whitton Dene, Hounslow, Middlesex TW3 2JW. tel: (081) 898 9933

Vitopan Ltd, Causeway Mill, Express Trading Estate, Stonehill Road, Farnworth, Bolton BL4 9TP. tel: (0204) 78315

A & G Walden Brothers Ltd, 34 Wimbledon Avenue, Brandon Ind Est, Brandon, Suffolk IP27 0NZ. tel: (0842) 811776

Walley Ltd, 728 London Road, West Thurrock, Grays, Essex. RM16 1LU. tel: (0708) 862862

WAVES, Corscombe, Nr. Dorchester, Dorset, DT2 0NU. tel: (093 589) 248

J & CR Wood, 303 Hull Rd, Anlaby Common, Hull, North Humberside, HU4 7RZ. tel: (0482) 51915

Woodfit Ltd, Kem Mill, Whittle-le-Woods, Chorley, Lancs, PR6 7EA. tel: (025 72) 66421

HOUSEHOLD FITTINGS

3M UK plc, Head Office, 3M House, PO Box 1, Bracknell, Berks. RG12 1JU tel: (0344) 426726

Access Control Equipment Supplies Ltd, PO Box 90, Rickmansworth, Herts, WD3 4PN. tel: (081) 953 6724

Acme Flooring Ltd, St. Peters Road, Huntingdon, Cambs, PE18 7DN. tel: (0480) 52101

W Adams & Sons Ltd, Marketing & Sales, 5/6 Credenda Rd, Bromford Rd Ind Est, West Bromwich B70 7JE (021) 544 8092

AJW Trading (Opalake Ltd), 42 Alderney Road, Slade Green, Erith, Kent. DA8 2JD. tel: (0322) 334426

Akzent International (Rushcrown Ltd), c/o 66 Prettygate Road, Colchester, Essex C03 4Ed. tel: (0206) 561710/760666

Aldridge Securiphone Ltd, Silica House, 30-34 Eagle Wharf Road, London N1 7EB. tel: (071) 251 4791

G & S Allgood Ltd,Carterville House, 297 Euston Road, London NW1 3AQ. tel: (071) 387 9951

Allmand-Smith Ltd, Regency Mill, Chester Road, Macclesfield, Cheshire. tel: (0625) 613311/23085

Alternative Plans Contracts, 9 Hester Road, Battersea, London SW11 5AN. tel: (071) 228 6460

Altro Floors, Works Road, Letchworth, Herts SG6 1NW. tel: (0462) 480480

Ansador Ltd, Southampton House, 192-206 York Road, London SW11 3RX. tel: (071) 228 7777

APV Vent-Axia Ltd, Fleming Way, Crawley, West Sussex RH10 2NN. tel (0293) 26062

Aremco, Grove House, Lenham, Kent, ME17 2PX. tel: (0622) 858502

Armitage Shanks Ltd, Armitage, Rugeley, Staffs., WS15 4BT. tel: (0543) 490253

Auto Control Systems Ltd, Units 44-45 Bookham Industrial Park, Church Road, Bookham, Surrey KT23 3EU. tel: (0372) 59536/7/8

Automatic Door Suppliers Association, 411 Limpsfield Road, The Green, Warlingham, Surrey. CR3 9HA. tel: (0883) 624961

Ayrton-Graham (Contracts) Ltd, 10 North Drive, Wallasey, Merseyside L45 0LZ. tel: (051) 639 5848

B & R Electrical Products Ltd, Temple Fields, Harlow, Essex CM20 2BG. tel: (0279) 641800

Barber Wilsons & Co. Ltd., Crawley Road, Westbury Avenue, Wood Green, London N22 6AH. tel: (081) 888 3461/2041

Barking-Grone Ltd, 1 River Road, Barking, Essex, IH11 0HD. tel: (081) 594 7292

Bath Services International Ltd, 27 Frith Street, London W1V 5TR. tel: (071) 437 8238/8713

Belco Manufacturing Co Ltd, Hovefields Avenue, Nore Ind Est, Burnt Mills, Basildon, Essex SS13 1EB. tel: (0268) 728577

Benchcraft of Birmingham, 145-150 Brighton Road, Birmingham B12 8QB tel: (021) 449 2647

Berglen Group, Masons House, Kingsbury Road, London NW9 9NQ. tel: (081) 204 3434

Berry Magicoal Ltd, Cotmanhay Road, Ilkeston, Derbyshire DE7 8LP. tel: (0602) 325933 *Do not supply direct*

Besam Ltd, Washington House, Brooklands Close, Sunbury-on-Thames, Middlesex TW16 7EQ. tel: (0932) 765888

Beta Naco Ltd, Stourbridge Road, Bridgnorth, Shopshire WV15 5RB. tel: (0746) 761921

Bi-Design, 49 The Lawns, Sompting, Lancing, West Sussex BN15 0DT. tel: None Given.

Howard Bird & Co. ltd, Manor Works, 168 Worcester Road, Bromsgrove, Worcs B61 7AX. tel: (0527) 72832

BJP Window Controls, Unit 11, Springvale Industrial Park, Bilston, West Midlands. tel: (0902) 409461

Blackburn London Ltd, Unit 2, Tylong Way, Off Beddington Farm Road, Croydon, Surrey CR0 4XX. tel: (081) 689 6890

Bonar & Flotex Ltd, High Holborn Road, Ripley, Derby DE5 3NT. tel: (0773) 744121

Simon Boosey, The Tun House, Whitwell, Hitchin, Herts, SG4 8AG. tel: (043 887) 563

Boots the Chemists Ltd, City Gate, Toll House Hill, Nottingham, NG2 3AA. tel: (0602) 418522 *Enquiries should be made at local branches.*

Border Craft Workshops, The Breese House, Dorstone, Herts, HR3 6AS. tel: (0981) 550251

Boulton Fabrications Ltd, Ladywell Works,Etruria Road, Hanley, Stoke-on-Trent ST1 5RR. tel: (0782) 262902

Ray Branch & Co Ltd, 29/31 Lower Loveday Street, Birmingham, B19 3SE. tel: (021) 359 8125-8

Briman Contracts Ltd, 83 Clarendon Gardens, Wembley, Middlesex HA9 7LD. tel: (081) 908 0102

Broen Valves Ltd, Bishopsgate Works, 68 Lower City Road, Tividale, Oldbury, Warley, West Midlands B69 2HF. tel. (021) 552 4616

Mr Buck, 102 Chatsworth Road, Stratford, London E15 1RD. tel: (081) 555 2281

Burley Appliances Ltd, Pillings Road, Oakham, Leics LE15 6QF. tel: (0572) 55220

Caldwell Hardware (UK) Ltd, Berrington Road, Sydenham Ind Est, Leamington Spa CV31 1NB. tel: (0926) 451767

Call-Saver CRV Electronics Ltd, Telephone Systems, 3 Caledonian Road, London N1 9DX. tel: (071) 278 5187

Camping Gaz Ltd, Optimus Division, Holcot Lane, Sywell, Northants NN6 0BE. tel: (0604) 790303

Caradon Mira Ltd, Cromwell Road, Cheltenham, Gloucester GL52 5EP

Caradon Twyfords Ltd, Lawton Road, Alsager, Stoke-on-Trent ST7 2DF. tel: (0270) 879777'

Care Design, Moorgate, Ormskirk, Lancs L39 4RX. tel: (0695) 579061

Caretaker Communications Ltd, 47 Ealing Road, Wembley, Middx. HA0 4BA. tel: (081) 900 0708

Carron Stainless Products Ltd, PO Box 30, Carron, Falkirk, Stirling, FK2 8DW. tel: (0324) 38321

CDS Services Ltd, 20 Breckhill Road, Woodthorpe, Nottingham, NG8 4GP. tel: (0602) 670485

Chester-care Ltd, 16 Englands Lane, London NW3 4TG. tel: (071) 586 2166 or (071) 722 3430

Christopher Safety Products Ltd, Unit 1, Epsom Downs Metro Centre, Waterfield, Tadworth, Surrey KT20 5EZ. tel: (07373) 60512

Cimex Ltd, Matador Division, Millfield Road,Faversham, Kent (0795) 533220

LT Clark Ltd, Fresh Wharf, Highbridge Road, Barking, Essex, IG11 7BQ. tel: (081) 594 5666/7/8

Clos-O-Mat GB Ltd, 55 Waverley Road, Sale, Cheshire M33 1AY. tel: (061) 905 1399

Closed Door Security Systems, 14 Limetrees Gardens, Gateshead, Tyne and Wear NE9 5BE. tel: (091) 478 1398

Colorroll Crossley, PO Box 24, Mill Street, Kidderminster, Worcs. DY11 6UZ. tel: (0562) 829998

Construction Specialties UK Ltd, Conspec House, Springfield Road, Chesham, Bucks HP5 1PW. tel: (0494) 784844

Control Universal Ltd, 137 Ditton Walk, Cambridge, CB5 8QF. tel: (0223) 244447

Cope & Timmins Ltd, Angel Road Works, Edmonton, London N18 3AY. tel: (081) 803 6481 Sales: (081) 803 3333

Crabtree Electrical Industries Ltd, Head Office, Lincoln Works, Walsall WS1 2DN. tel: (0922) 721202

Croydex Co Ltd, Central Way, Walworth Ind Est, Andover Hants SP10 5AW. tel: (0264) 65881

CTS Security Ltd, Southgates Corner, Wisbech Road, Kings Lynn, Norfolk PE30 5JH. tel: (0553) 765429

Cumbria Furniture, Cumbria House, Blackdyke Road, Kingstown Ind Est, Carlisle, Cumbria CA3 0PJ. tel: (0228) 38688

Davell Ltd., Wheatsheaf Wharf, Lower Hythe Street, Dartford, Kent DA1 1BN. tel: (0322) 72223

Davis Security Communications Ltd, Davis House, Barrow Road, Sheffield S9 1JQ. tel: (0742) 431577

Dawneasy Ltd, 58 Templar Road, North Yate, Bristol BS127 5TG. tel: (0454) 316569

Devcon, Brunel Close, Park Farm, Wellingborough, Northants NN8 3QX. tel: (0933) 675299

Dimplex Heating Ltd, Millbrook, Southampton, SO9 2DP. tel: (0703) 777117

Domestic Storage Systems Ltd, Penallta Ind Est, Ystrad Mynach, Mid Glamorgan CF8 7QZ. tel: (0443) 814831

Door Dwell Ltd, 16 Feeder Road, St. Philips, Bristol, BS2 0SB. tel: (0272) 710960

Dor-O-Matic Ltd, Berrington Road, Sydenham Ind. Est., Leamington Spa, CV31 1NB. tel: (0926) 334231

Dorma Door Controls Ltd, Dorma Trading Park, Staffa Road, Leyton, London E10 7QX. tel: (081) 558 8411

Double A Records, 224 Mansfield Road,Worksop, Notts. S80 3DP. tel: (0909) 473067

Drad Architectural hardware, North Bridge Place, Frog Island, Leics. LE3 5DP. tel: (0533) 538844

Duraflex Products Ltd, Duraflex House, Tewkesbury Road, Cheltenham, Glos, GL51 9PP tel: (0242) 580868

ER Dyer (UK) Ltd, 4a. High Street, Fareham, Hants PO16 7AN. tel (0329) 285451

Eagle International, Unit 5, Royal London Estate, 29-35 North Acton Road, London NW10 6PE. tel: (081) 965 3222

Easiaids, 51a. St. Annes Avenue, Middlewich, Cheshire. tel: (060684) 4641

Easiaids Ltd, 48 Mill Green Road, Mitcham, Surrey, CR4 4HY. tel: (01) 648 4186

Electrak International Ltd, No. 1 Ind Est, Medomsley Road, Consett, Co. Durham DH8 6SX. tel (0207) 503400/1. *do not supply direct*

Edllard Sliding Door Gears Ltd, Works Road, Letchworth Garden City, Herts, SG6 1NN tel: (0462) 678421

Entryphone Co Ltd, 23 Granville Road, London SW18 5SD. tel: (081) 870 8635

Fairway Kitchens,741/743 Garrett Lane, Wimbledon, London SW17 0PD. tel: (01) 879 1373

Ferodo Ltd, Flooring Products Division, Griffiths Crossing, Caernarfon, Gwynedd, LL55 1TR. tel: (0286) 76401

Finnish Valve Co Ltd., 279-291 Balham High Road, London SW17 7BA. tel: (081) 767 4521

Fixatrad Ltd, 763 Harrow Road, London NW10 5NY tel: (081) 969 3232

Focal Displays Ltd, 12 Wandle Way, Mitcham, Surrey, CR4 4NB. tel: (081) 640 6821

Formtex Platstics Ltd, Harlequin Avenue, Great West Road, Brentford, Middx. TW8 9EW. tel (081) 568 6791-5

Forwood Designs Ltd, The Mews, Mitcheldean, Glos, GL17 0SL. tel: (0594) 542181

Foster Beard Plc, Oxygate Lane, Cricklewood, London NW2 7JN. Sales & Enquiries tel: (081) 452 3399

Franke, UK Sales, Suite 15b, Manchester Int Office Centre, Styal Road, Manchester M33 5WB. tel: (061) 436 6280

Geemarc Ltd, Unit 5, Swallow Court, Swallow Field, Wellwyn Garden City, Herts AL7 1SB. tel: (0707) 372372

Gibbons, James Format Ltd, Colliery Road, Wolverhampton WV1 2QW. tel: (0902) 58585

Gidgee Gadgets, 52 Radway Close, Church Hill, Redditch, Worcs. B98 8RZ. tel: (0527) 63754

Gradus Ltd, Park Green, Macclesfield, Cheshire SK11 7NE tel: (0625) 28922

Gratnells Ltd, 258 Church Road, London E10 7JQ. tel. (081) 556 9021

A & J Gummers Ltd., 16 Pentos Drive, Formans Road, Birmingham B11 3AT. tel: (021) 778 2241

DH Haden Ltd, Mount Road, Burntwood, Walsall, West Midlands WS7 0AW. tel: (05436) 75222

James Halstead Ltd, Radcliffe New Road, Whitefield, Manchester, M25 7NR. tel: (061) 766 3781

R. Hamilton & Co. Ltd., Unit G, Quarry Ind Est., Mere, Warminster BA12 6LA. tel: (0747) 860088

Harrison Thompson & Co Ltd., Yeoman House, Whitehall Estate, Whitehall Road, Leeds. LS12 5JB. tel: (0532) 795854

Heatrae Sadia Heating Ltd., Hurricane Way, Norwich, Norfolk NR6 6EA. tel. (0603) 424144 *(do not supply direct to the public)*

Heckmondwike Fibre Bonded Ltd., PO Box 7, Wellington Mills, Liversedge, West Yorkshire WF15 7XA. tel: (0924) 406161

Heinz Baby Club, Vinces Road, Diss, Norfolk IP22 3HH. tel: (0379) 651981

Helping Hands Shop, 114 Queens Road, Leicester LE2 3LF. tel: (0533) 708821

Henderson Door Systems, Tangent Works, Harold Hill, Romford, Essex RM3 8UL. tel: (040 23) 45555/40101

Henderson Security Electronics Ltd, Unit 4, Tannery Road Ind Est, Gomm Road, High Wycombe, Bucks, HP13 7EQ. tel: (0494) 450211

Herga Electric Ltd, Northern Way, Bury St Edmunds, Suffolk IP32 6NN. tel: (0284) 701422

Hestair Hope Ltd, St. Philip's Drive, Royton, Oldham, Lancs. OL2 6AG. tel: (061) 633 6611

Hewi (UK) Ltd, Scimitar Close, Gillingham Business Park, Gillingham, Kent ME8 0RN. Tel: (0634) 377688

Hillaldam Coburn Ltd., Unit 27 Barwell Business Park, Leatherhead Road, Chessington, Surrey KT9 2NY. tel: (01) 397 5151

ED Hinchcliffe & Sons Ltd, Pennington Close, Albion Road, West Bromwich, West Midlands B70 8BA. tel: (021) 553 5561

HLS Ltd, Clayfields Ind Est, Tickhill Road, Balby, Doncaster, DN4 8QG. tel (0302) 855991

Home Automation Ltd, Bumpers Way, Chippenham, Wilts SN14 6LF. tel: (0249) 443515

Homecraft Supplies Ltd, Low Moor Estate, Kirkby-in-Ashfield, Notts NG17 7JZ. tel (0623) 757955 for mail order, (0623) 754047 for sales.

Hozelock-ASL Ltd, Haddenham, Aylesbury, Bucks, HP17 8JD. tel (0844) 291881

Huntley & Sparks Ltd, Sterling House, Crewkerne, Somerset TA188 8LL. tel: (0460) 72222

Ideal Standard Ltd, PO Box 60 National Avenue, Kingston-upon-Hull, HU5 4JE tel: (0482) 46461

Indentiplugs, 39 Whitehouse Enterprise Centre, Whitehouse road, Newcastle Upon Tyne. NE15 6EP. tel (091) 228 0068

IMP Industrial Maintenance Products, Guardian Works, 88 Foxberry Road, London SE4 2SH. tel: (081) 469 2066

Industrial Devices Ltd, Architectural Ironmongery Division, 309 West End Lane, London NW6 1RG tel: (071) 431 1118

Industrial Supplies Ltd, Martin Court, Sellerswood Drive, Bulwell, Nottingham NG6 8US. tel: (0602) 272681

Ingersoll Locks Ltd, Wood Street, Willenhall, West Midlands WV13 1LA. tel: (0902) 366911

Intertan UK Ltd, Ms Amanda Taylor, Tandy Centre, Leamore Lane, Walsall WS2 7PS. tel: (0922) 710000

Jalite UK Ltd, 21 The Seax Centre, Southfields Ind. Park, Basildon, Essex, SS15 6SL. tel: (0268) 417946

Jaymart Rubber & Plastics Ltd, Woodlands Trading Estate, Eden Vale road, Westbury, Wilts, BA13 3QS. tel: (0373) 864926

Jebron Ltd, Bright St, Wednesbury, West Midlands, WS10 9HY. tel: (021) 526 2212

Johnson Wax Ltd, Frimley Green, Camberley, Surrey, GU16 5AJ. tel: (0276) 63456

Keep Able Ltd, Fleming Close, Park Farm, Wellingborough, Northants NN8 3UF. tel: (0933) 679426 *(Agents for Maddak)*Kiddi-Proof Products Ltd, Design House, 9 Centre Way, Claverings Ind Est, Montague Road, Edmonton, London N9 0AJ. tel: (01) 807 4552

King Door Products Ltd, Hammond Avenue, Whitehall Ind Est, Reddish, Stockport, Cheshire SK4 1PQ. tel: (061) 429 0990

Klassic Fittings, Linden House, Croughton, Nr. Brackley, Northants NN13 5LT. tel: (0869) 810152

KRS. Electronics Ltd, Dynamic Works, Saltaire Road, Shipley BD18 3HN. tel: (0274) 584115

Lamacrest Ltd, Crown Works, Cold Bath Road, harrogate HG2 0NR. tel: (0423) 66656

Landywood Group Ltd, Holly Lane, Great Wyrley, Walsall WS6 6AN. tel: (0922) 416600

W Langley & Co Ltd, 14-24 Magdalen Street, London SE1 2EW. tel: (071) 407 6271/4

RJ Lendrum Ltd, Stourbridge Road Ind Est, Faraday Drive, Bridgnorth, Shropshire WV15 5BA. tel: (0746) 767272

Llewellyn-SML Health Care Services, Regent House, 1 Regent Road, City, Liverpool L3 7BX. tel: (051) 236 5311

Macwood (London) Ltd., 169 Station Road, Chingford, London E4 6AG. tel: (081) 524 4128/9

MAR Design Services, 7 Elmscroft Gardens, Potters Bar, Herts, EN6 2JP. tel: (0707) 58543

Marley Floors Ltd, Dickley Lane, Lenham, Maidstone, Kent ME17 2DE. tel: (0622) 858877

Albert Marston & Co. Ltd., Wellington Works, Planetary Road, Willenhall, West Midlands WV13 3ST. tel: (0902) 305511

Mastiff Electronic Systems Ltd, Little Mead, Cranleigh, Surrey GU6 8ND. tel: (0483) 272097

MDH Ltd, Walworth Road, Andover, Hants SP10 5AA tel (0264) 62111

Medeci Rehab Ltd, Reasearch Unit, Warley Hospital, Brentwood, Essex. CM14 5HQ. tel: (0277) 212637

Medipost Ltd, Unit 1 St. Johns Estate, Elder Road, Lees, Oldham, Lancs OL4 3DZ. tel: (061) 678 0233

Meditech Developments Ltd, Unit 1, Crocus Place, Crocus Street, Nottingham NG2 3DE. tel: (0602) 863263

Meynell Valves Ltd, Shaw Road, Bushbury, Wolverhampton WV10 9LB. tel: (0902) 28621

MK Electric Ltd, Edmonton, London N9 0PB. tel: (01) 803 3355

George A Moore & Co Ltd, Thorp Arch Trading Estate, Wetherby, West Yorkshire LS23 7DD tel: (0937) 842394

Mothercare Plc, Cherry Tree Road, Watford Herts, WD2 5SH. tel.(0923) 33577 *customer enquiries on (0923) 31616*

Multi-Alarm Systems GB Ltd, Unit 16B. Barton Hill Trading Estate, Barton Hill, Bristol BS5 9TF. tel. (0272) 555301

Nac Electrical Component Manufacturers, Earlywood Rise, Coronation Road, South Ascot, Berks, SL5 9LH tel: (0990) 872296

Nairnflair Ltd, Woodside Road, Glenrothes, Fife, KY7 4AF. tel: (0592) 759666

Newman Tonks Engineering Ltd, Bescot Crescent, Walsall WS1 4NF. tel: (0922) 38101

Newman Tonks Hardware Ltd, Moorsom Street, Birmingham B6 4NT. tel: (021) 359 4751

WH Newson & Sons Ltd, 61 Pimlico Road, London SW1W 8NF. tel: (071) 730 6262/8

Newton Products - Spastic Society, Meadway Works, Garretts Green Lane, Birmingham, B33 0QS. tel. (021) 783 6081/2/3

Nicholls & Clarke Ltd, 3/10 Shoreditch High Street, London E1 6PE. tel. (071) 247 5432

Nottingham Rehab Ltd, 17 Ludlow Hill Road, West Bridgforfd, Nottingham, NG2 6HD. tel: (0602) 452345

Nufins Ltd, Brunswick Ind Est, Newcastle-upon-Tyne, NE13 7BA. tel: (091) 2364126

Nuway Manufacturing Co Ltd, Endurance Works, Coalport, Telford, Salop TF8 7HX. tel: (0952) 680400

Ollerton hall Decorating Service, Ollerton, Knutsford, Cheshire WA16 8SF. tel: (0565) 50222

Ousey & Marris, Greenfield Business Park, Bagillt Road, Holywell, Clwyd CH8 7HN. tel. (0352) 712156

Panavista Plc, Fircroft Way, Edenbridge, Kent TN8 6EL. tel. (0732) 865371

Parker Anderson, Mullions, Lymington Road, Milford-on-Sea, Hants S04 10QN. tel: (0590) 43839

Josiah Parkes & Sons Ltd, Union Works, Gower Street, Willenhall, West Midlands WV13 1JX. tel: (0902) 366931

Parr, F Ltd, Merse Road, North Moons Moat, Redditch, Worcs. B98 9PL. tel: (0527) 585777

Partially Sighted Society, Queens Road, Doncaster DN1 2NX. tel: (0302) 368998

Paul Fabrications, Town End Road, Draycott, Derbyshire DE7 3PT. tel: (033 17) 3021

Pegler Ltd, (Head Office), Belmont Works, St. Catherine's Avenue, Doncaster DN4 8DF tel: (0302) 368581

Pilkingtons Tiles Ltd, PO Box 4, Clifton Junction, Manchester, M27 2LP. tel: (061) 794 2024

Pinescan Windows (UK) Ltd, Unit 12 Cobnar Wood Close, Sheepbridge Trading Estate, Chesterfield Derbyshire S41 9RQ. tel: (0246) 260712

PJP Trading Ltd, 151 Dixon Hill Road, North Mimms, Hatfield, Herts AL9 7JE. tel: (0707) 266726/273573

Plastic Extruders Ltd, Russell Gardens, Wickford, Essex, SS11 8DN. tel: (0268) 735231

Daniel Platt and Sons Ltd, Brownhils Tileries, Tunstall, Stoke-on-Trent, Staffs, ST6 4NY tel: (0782) 577187

Poggenpohl Group UK Ltd, 368 Silbury Boulevard, Second Floor, Milton Keynes MK13 9DN. tel: (0908) 606886

Possum Controls Ltd, Sales Dept., Middlegreen Road, Langley, Berks SL3 6DF. tel: (0753) 79234 *repairs and service also at this address.*

PRA Aids for the Handicapped Ltd, Bayford Mews, Bayford Street, London E8 3SF. tel: (081) 985 3570

Priory Furniture Ltd, P.O. Box 15, Saxon Works, Medlock Street, Droylsden, Manchester M35 7BT. tel: (061) 370 5151

Probity Trading International, 34 Grasmere Road, Ashford, Kent TN24 9BE. tel: (0233) 625146 or London No. (071) 402 6486

Racal-Guardall (Scotland) Ltd, Lochend Ind Est, Edinburgh EH2 8PL. tel: (031) 333 2900

Raytel Security Systems Ltd., Raytel House Brook Road, Rayleigh, Essex SS6 7XH. tel: (0268) 775656

Reduced Swing Doors Ltd, 21 St. Mary's Road, Sindlesham, Wokingham, Berks Rg11 5DA. tel: (0734) 792021/794586

Regisgold Enterprises Ltd, Beare House, Broadclyst, Exeter, Devon EX5 3JX. tel: (0392) 881124

Relcross Ltd, Washington Road, West Wilts Trading Estate, Westbury, Wilts, BA13 4JP. tel: (0373) 822849

Ridley Electronics Ltd, 66a Capworth Street, Leyton, London E10 7HA. tel: (081) 558 7112

Ripul Ltd, Bumpers Way, Chippenham, Wilts SN14 6LF. tel: (0249) 443511

Rolac Ltd, Unit 16, Enterprise Centre 2, Chester Street, Stockport, SK3 0BR. tel: (061) 429 8477

Roscho Ltd, 62-66 York Street, London W1H 1DA. tel: (071) 723 9161 *(contact Mr D Ryan)*

Royal Association for Disability & Rehabilitation, 25 Mortimer Street, London W1N 8AB. tel: (071) 637 5400

As Royston Ltd, Camwal Road, Starbeck, Harrogate HG1 4PT. tel: (0423) 889771

RS Components Ltd, PO Box 99, Corby, Northants NN17 9RS. tel: (0536) 201234

SAV United Kingdom Ltd, Scandia House, Armfield Close, Molesey, Surrey KT8 0JS. tel: (081) 941 4153

Saville Stainless Ltd, PO Box 74, Altrincham, Cheshire, WA14 3RP. tel: (0565) 830156

Sealmaster Ltd, Pampisford, Cambridge, Cambs, CB2 4HG. tel: (0223) 832851

Security Vision Nameplates Ltd, 8 Telford Court, 9 South Avenue, Clydebank Business Park, Clydebank G81 2NR. tel: (041) 94

Sentrymatic Britannia Ltd, Unit 5, Oxgate Centre, Oxgate Lane, London NW2 7JE. tel: (081) 208 2311

SGB Architectural (Ironmongery) Ltd, Five Ways, Finchfield Lane, Merry Hill, Wolverhampton WV3 8EE. tel: (0902) 764551

Shavrin Levatap Co Ltd, 32 Waterside, King's Langley, Hertfordshire WD4 8HH. tel: (09277) 67678

Sign Systems Ltd, Head Office, Latham Close, Bredbury Industrail Park, Stockport, Cheshire SK6 2SD. tel: (061) 494 6125

Silent Gliss Ltd, Star Lane, Margate, Kent, CT9 4EF. tel: (0843) 63571

Silverplan Ltd Hastings Work Conway Road, London N15 3BE tel: (081) 802 6071

W & G Sissons Ltd, Calver Mill, Calver Bridge, Sheffield S30 1XA. tel: (0433) 30791

Sitting Pretty Products Ltd, The Business Centre, Colne Way, Watford WD2 8FP. tel: (0923) 245050

Smiths Industries Environmental Controls Ltd, Waterloo Road, Cricklewood, London NW2 7UR. tel: (081) 450 8944

Snaidero UK Ltd, London House, 42 Upper Richmond Road West, London SW14 8DD. tel: (081) 878 9595/6

Len Softley & Co Ltd, Baring Road, St James, Northampton NN5 7BA. tel: (0604) 5562/2

Sommer Allibert UK Ltd, Container Division, Berry Hill Ind Est, Droitwich, Worcs, WR9 9AB. tel: (0905) 795796

Sparks Fire Protection Ltd, 'Cornubia', Groeswen Lane, Port Talbot, West Glamorgan SA13 2LA. tel: (0639) 885837

SRS Wholesale Ltd, 121 Dawes Road, Fulham, London SW6 7DU. tel: (071) 386 7211

Stanley Magic-Door, 802 Oxford Avenue, Slough Trading Estate, Slough, Berks, SL1 4LN. tel: (0753) 32437/8

Status Electronics Ltd, Video & Audio Door Entry Systems, 42B Chigwell Lane, Loughton, Essex, IG10 3NZ. tel: (01) 502 0136/0421

Hugh Steeper Ltd, 237-239 Roehampton Lane, London SW15 4LB. tel: (01) 788 8165

Sterdy Telephones Ltd, Plumpton Road, Hoddesdon, Herts EN11 0ET. tel: (0992) 469603

Stocksigns Ltd, Ormside Way, Holmethorpe Ind Est, Redhill, Surrey, RH1 2LG. tel: (0737) 764764

JAS Strutton & Son Ltd, Slough Lane, Ardleigh, Colchester CO7 7RU. tel: (0206) 230553/230886

Superswitch Electric Appliances Ltd, Houldsworth Street, Reddish, Stockport, Cheshire, SK 6BZ. tel: (061) 431 4885/4543 *(orders)*

JW Swain (Plastics) Ltd, Inva-dex, Byron Street, Buxton Derbyshire SH17 6LY. tel: (0298) 22365

Swift Communications Ltd, PO Box 142, Hardwick, Cambridge CB3 7QH. tel: (0954) 210607

Symphony Group PLC, Gelderd Lane, Leeds LS12 6AL. tel: (0532) 792521

Tappers Ltd, UK Division, 34-35 Hatton Garden, London EC1 8DX. tel: (071) 831 6156

Techno-Vision Systems Ltd, 4 Hazelwood Road, Northampton, NN1 1LN. tel: (0604) 239363

Telefusion Communications Ltd, Unit 9, Wingates Industrial Park, Westhoughton, Lancs BL5 3XH. tel: (0942) 814343

Telequip Communications & Security Systems Ltd, 92 Filton Road, Horfield, Bristol BS7 0PD. tel: (0272) 236523

Tenby Electrical Accessories, 17-21 Warstone Lane, Birmingham B18 6JG. tel: (021) 200 1999

Therm-A-Stor Ltd, Orton Southgate, Peterborough PE2 0SF. tel: (0733) 236333

Thielmann (UK) Ltd, 177 Milton Park, Abingdon, Oxon OX14 4SE. tel: (0235) 83 4845

Da Thomas (London) Ltd, 124-126 Denmark Hill, London SE5 8RX. tel: (01) 733 2101

Threshold Floorings Ltd, Vorda Works, Highworth, Swindon, Wilts SN6 7AJ. tel: (0793) 764301

Titan Tapes Ltd, Whitefield Road, Bredbury, Stockport, Cheshire SH6 2QR. tel: (061) 494 1344

TR Powermate UK Ltd, Unit 21, Edward Street Ind Est, Darlington, Co Durham. tel: (0325) 284012/3

Tretford Carpets Ltd, Lynn Lane, Shenstone, Lichfield, Staffs, WS14 0DU. tel: (0543) 480577

Tretol Ltd, 88 Bestovell Road, Slough, Berks SL2 4SZ. tel: (0753) 24164

Tunstall Telecom Ltd, Whitley Lodge, Whitley Bridge DN14 0JT. tel: (0977) 661234

TVJ Ltd, Claverhouse, Dundee DD§ 9RD. tel: (0382) 507020

Two R Signs Services Ltd, Unit 3C Moss Road, Withiam, Essex, CM8 3UQ. tel: (0376) 518851

Universal Aids Ltd, 8/14 Wellington Road South, Stockport, Cheshire SK4 1AA. tel: (061) 480 9228

Valor Gas, Wood Lane, Erdington, Birmingham B24 9QP. tel: (021) 373 8111

Vitopan Ltd, Causeway Mill, Express Trading Estate, Stonehill Road, Farnworth, Bolton BL4 9TP. tel: (0204) 78315

Wadsworth Security Products Ltd, Unit 1 Epsom Downs Metro Centre, Waterfield, Tadworth, Surrey KT20 5EZ. tel: (07373) 60512

Wandsworth Electrical Ltd, Albert Drive, Sheerwater, Woking, Surrey, GU21 5SE. tel: (048 62) 27521

Waverlink Electronics Ltd, 4 Hazelwood Road, Northampton, NN1 1LN. tel: (0604) 230758

WAVES, Corscombe, Nr Dorchester, Dorset, DT2 0NU. tel: (093 589) 248

Weatherbar Sills Ltd, Unit 1, Union Estate, Union Road, Macclesfield, Cheshire SK11 7BP. tel: (0625) 611324

Wessex Medical Equipment Co Ltd, Budds Lane, Romsey, Hants, SO51 0HA. tel: (0794) 830303

Weston Hyde Products Ltd, Vallis Road, Frome, Somerset, BA11 3EQ. tel: (0373) 63271

Woodfit Ltd, Lem Mill, Whittle-le-Woods, Chorley, lancs, PR6 7EA. tel: (025 72) 66421

Yale Security Products Ltd, Wood Street, Willenhall, West Midlands, WV13 1LA. tel: (0902) 366911

Zeyko Ltd, 8 Maryland Road, Tongwell, Milton Keynes, Bucks MK15 8HF. tel: (0908) 615535

LEISURE ACTIVITY EQUIPMENT

Agility Sports Products Ltd, 112 Banstead Road, Carshalton Beeches, Surrey SM5 3NH. tel: (081) 642 7683 or (01) 642 8948

Anders Design Ltd, 185 Great Tattenhams, Tattenham Corner, Epsom Downs, Surrey KT18 5RA.

Anything Left Handed Ltd, 65 Beak St, London W1R 3LF. tel: (071) 437 3910

Aremco, Grove House, Lenham, Kent, ME17 2PX. tel: (0622) 858502

EJ Arnold & Son Ltd, Parkside Lane, Dewsbury Road, Lees, LS11 5TD. tel: (0532) 772112

Arts Council, Arts & Disability Officer, Dr. Linda Moss, 105 Piccadilly, London W1V 0AU. tel: (071) 629 9495 ext 299

Artsline, 5 Crowndale Road, London NW1 1TU. tel: (071) 388 2227

Atlas Caravan Co Ltd, Wykeland Ind Est, Wiltshire Road, Hull HU4 6PH. tel: (0482) 562101

Bags of Books, 7 South St, Lewes, Sussex BN7 2BT. tel (0273) 479320

Barton Crafts, Barton Lodge, The Avenue, Radlett, herts WD7 7FQ. tel: (0923) 856011

Bedford Sewing and Knitting Machines Ltd, Head Office, Murdock Road, Manton Ind Est, Bedford MK41 7LE tel: (0234) 217096

HC Bexfield Ltd., Mundial House, Kiveton Park Station, Sheffield S31 8NP. tel: (0909) 772866

Birmingham Tapes for the Handicapped Association, 20 Middleton Hall Rd, Kings Norton, Birmingham B30 1BY tel (021) 459 4874

Bogod Machine Co Ltd, 50/52 Great Sutton St, London EC1V 0DJ tel: (071) 253 1198

Boots the Chemist Ltd, City Gate, Toll House Hill, Nottingham NG2 3AA. tel: (0602) 418522 *enquiries should be made at local branches*

Muriel Braddick Foundation, 14 Teign St, Teignmouth Devon. tel (062 67) 6214

Bradford Activity Toys, 103 Dockfield Road, Shipley BD17 7AR. tel (0274) 594173/596030

Bradshaw Engineering, 88 South Road, Portishead, Bristol BS20 9DY. tel (0272) 84807

British Association of Art Therapists, 11A Richmond Road, Brighton, Sussex BN2 3RL. tel: (0273) 685852 *for urgent enquiries only*

British Association of Drama Therapists, PO Box 98, Kirkbymoorside, York YO6 6EX.

British Association of the Hard of Hearing, 7-11 Armstrong Road, London W3 7JL. tel: (081) 743 1110/1353 or *vistel:* (081) 743 1492

British Jigsaw Puzzle Library, 8 Heath Terrace, Leamington Spa CV32 5LY. tel: (0926) 311874

British Wireless for the Blind Fund, 226 Great Portland St, London W1N 6AN. tel (071) 388 1266

Calibre, Aylesbury, Bucks, HP22 5XQ. tel: (0296) 432339 or (0296) 81211

Carefree Holidays Ltd, 64 Florence Road, Northampton NN1 4NA. tel: (0604) 34301/30382

Carousel, 2 St. George's Place, Brighton BN1 4GB. tel: (0273) 570840

Carter & Parker Ltd, Gordon Mills, Guiseley, Leeds LS20 9PD. tel: (0943) 72264

Chailey Heritage, Rehab Eng Unit, North Chailey, Lewes, BN8 4EF. tel: (082 572) 2112 ext 210

Charitylink, c/o Retail Travel Ltd, Priestgate House, Peterborough PE1 1JX. tel: (0733) 558313 *(bookings)* or (0733) 555225*(office)*

Chattanooga UK Ltd, Unit 1 & 2, Goods Road, Belper, Derbyshire DE5 1UU. tel (077382) 6993/4

Chester-care Ltd, 16 Englands Lane, London NW3 4TG. tel: (071) 722 3430

Chivers Library Services Ltgd, 93-100 Locksbrook Road, Bath, Avon BA1 3HB. tel: (0225) 335336

Chivers Press Publishers, Windsor Bridge Road, Bath, Avon, BA2 3AX. tel: (0225) 335336

CI Caravans Ltd, The Oaks, Fordham Road, Newmarket, Suffolk CB8 7AL. tel: (0638) 663251

Clarke & Smith Manufacturing Co Ltd, Melbourne House, Melbourne Road, Wallington, Surrey, SM6 8SD. tel: (081) 669 4411

Conquest, The Society for Art for Physically Handicapped People, c/o Mrs U Hulme, 3 Beverley Close, East Ewell, Surrey. tel: (01) 393 6102

Correspondence Care & Support Group, 14 Windsor Terrace, East Herrington, Sunderland, Tyne and Wear SR3 3SF *Contact: Lisa Rowe*

Countrywide Computers, Victoria House, 1 High St. Wilburton, Cambs. CB6 3RB. tel: (0353) 740323

Cover to Cover Cassettes Ltd, PO Box 112, Marlborough, Wiltshire SN8 3UG. tel: (0264) 89227

Crafts Council, 1 Oxendon St, London SW1Y 4AT. tel: (071) 930 4811

Crypt Foundation, Forum Work Space, Stirling Road, Chichester, West Sussex PO19 2EN. tel: (0243) 786064

Derbyshire Maid Ltd, Mansfield Road, Chesterfield S44 5SD. tel: (0246) 853040

Deron, Unit 3, Point Pleasant Ind Est, Walls End, Newcastle Upon Tyne NE28 6HA. tel: (091) 263 2981

Dingle Hill Products, Mid Cowden, Comrie, Perthshire, PH6 2HU. tel (0764) 70667

Disabled Drivers Association, Ashwellthorpe Hall, Ashwellthorpe, Norwich NR16 1EX. tel: (050 841) 449

Disabled Drivers Motor Club, Cottingham Way, Thrapston, Northants NN14 4PL. tel: (08012) 4724

Disabled Motorists Federation, National Mobility Centre, Unit 2A, Atcham Estate, Upton Magna, Shrewsbury SY4 4UG.tel: (074 375) 889

Disabled Photographers Society, 151 Sandy Lane South, Wallington, Surrey SM6 9NP tel: (081) 647 3179

Disdate, 56 Devizes Avenue, Bedford MK41 8QT. tel: (0234) 40643

Docklands Canal Boat Trust, St. John's Centre, Albert Road, London E16 2JY

Dogs for the Disabled, Frances Hay, Brook House, 1 Lower Ladyes Hills, Kenilworth, Warwickshire CV8 2GN.tel: (0926) 59726

Draft Designs, 2a. Unit L, The Maltings, Station Road, Sawbridgeworth, Herts CM21 9JX. tel: (0279) 726163

Dryad, PO Box 38, Northgates, Leicester, LE1 9BU. tel: (0533) 510405

Duke of Edinburgh's Award, Advisor for the Handicapped, 5 Prince of Wales Terrace, Kensington, London W8 5PG. tel: (071) 937 5205

Dunlicraft Ltd, Pullman Road, Wigston, Leicester, LE8 2DY. tel: (0533) 811040

Elna Sewing Machines GB Ltd, Queens House, 180/182 Tottenham Court Road, London W1P 9LE tel: (071) 323 1187

Eloquent Reels, Alhampton, Castle Cary, Somerset, BA4 6PZ, tel: (074 968) 593

Engments Ltd, Chequers Road, West Meadows Ind Est, Derby, DE2 6EN. tel: (0332) 44579

Everaids Ltd, 38 Clifton Road, Cambridge, CB1 4ZT. tel: (0223) 243336

Exchange Value Video Club, Nacton, Ipswich, IP10 0JZ. tel: (0473) 717088

Fast Systems Ltd, 54 Friday St, Henley-on-Thames, Oxon, RG9 1AH. tel: (0491) 572374

Federation of British Tape Recordists:*Membership Sec:*Richard Porter, 30 Belgrave Court, Sloane Walk, Croydon CR0 7NW. tel: (081) 777 0357. *Contest Sec:* Robin Bester, 193 Ashdown Crescent, Waltham Cross, Herts EN8 0RL

Federation to Promote Horticulture for Disabled People, 9 Miles Close, Yapton, Arundel, West Sussex, BN18 0TB. tel: (0903) 724014

Feminist Audio Books, 52-54 Featherstone St, London EC1Y 8RT. tel: (071) 251 2908

Firemain Services, 27 Lorton Close, Gravesend, Kent DA12 4EX. tel: (0474) 533493

MJ Fish & Co, 3 Rivers Way Business Village, Navigation Way, Ashton-on-Ribble, Preston, Lancs. PR2 2YT. tel: (0772) 724442

Frame Knitting Ltd, P.O Box 21, Oakham, Leics, LE15 6XB. tel: (0572) 724187

Friends by Post, 6 Bollin Court, Macclesfield Road, Wilmslow, CheshireSK9 2AP. tel: (0625) 527044

Fulham Pottery Ltd., 8/10 Ingate Place, London SW8 3NS. tel: (071) 720 0050

Galt, James & Co. Ltd., Brookfield Road, Cheadle, Cheshire, SK8 2PN. tel: (061) 428 8511

Gardens for the Disabled Trust, c/o Hon Sec. Mrs. S. Van Laun, Old House Farm, Peasmarsh, Nr. Rye, E.Sussex TN31 6YD

Gillmore Travel Services, Gillmour House, Blennerhasset, Carlisle, Cumbria CA5 3RE. tel: (0965) 21553

Girl Guides Association, 17-19 Buckingham Palace Road, London SW1 WOPT. tel: (071) 834 6242

Good Book Guide Service, 91 Gt. Russel St, London WCIB 3PS. tel: (071) 580 8466

Goodlad & Goodlad, 147 Commercial St, Lerwick, Shetland. tel (0595) 3797

Graeae Theatre Co, 25 Bayham Road, Camden Town, London NW1 0EY. tel: (071) 383 7492

Great Elm Services, Great Elm, Frome, Somerset, BA11 3NZ. tel: (0373) 812275

Great London Assoc for Disabled People, 336 Brixton Road, London SW9 7AA. tel: (071) 274 0107

Hagger Electronics, Spirella Building, Bridge Road, Letchworth, SG6 4ET. tel (0462) 677331/670349

Handicapped Adventure Playground Assoc, Fulham Palace, Bishops Avenue, London SW6 6EA. tel: (071) 731 1435

Handicapped Aid Trust - c/o Mrs. J Marshall, 21 Malden Hill, New Malden, Surrey KT3 4DS. tel: (071) 900 2151

Handidate, The Wellington Crentre, 52 Chevallier St, Ipswich, Suffolk IP1 2PB tel: (0473) 226950

Handigolf Foundation, Launton Road, Stratton Audley, Oxfordshire OX6 9BW

Handihols, 12 Ormonde Avenue, Rochford, Essex, SS4 1QW. tel: (0702) 548257

M Hartnoll, Little Bray House, Brayford, Barnstaple EX32 7QG. tel: (059 88) 295

Helping Hands Shop, 114 Queens Road, Leicester LE2 3LF. tel: (0533) 708821

Hestair Hope Ltd, St. Philip's Drive, Royton, Oldham, Lancs, OL2 6AG. tel: (061) 633 6611

Holiday Care Service, 2 Old Bank Chambers, Station Road, Horley, Surrey, RH6 9HW. tel: (0293) 774535

Homecraft Supplies Ltd, Low Moor Estate, Kirkby-in-Ashfirld, Notts NG17 7JZ. tel: (0623) 754 047

Horticultural Therapy, Goulds Ground, Vallis Way, Frome, Somerset, BA11 3DW. tel: (0373) 64782

Hospice Arts, c/o Forbes Trust, 9 Artillery Lane, London E1 7LP

Hospital Arts, Christine Bull, The Arts Centre, St. Mary's Hospital, Hathersage Road, Manchester M13 0JH. tel: (061) 276 1234 ext. 6350

Hymo-Lift Ltd, Scaldwell Road, Brixworth, Northampton NN6 9EN. tel: (0604) 880724

In Court Sports Ltd, 26 Laurel Park, St. Arvans, Chepstow, Gwent NP6 6ED. tel (02912) 711841 *contact: Ken Nicholls*

Innovention Products Ltd, The Business Centre, Colne Way, Watford, Herts, WD2 4ND. tel: (0923) 245050/9

Intertan UK Ltd, Ms Amanda Taylor, Tandy Centre, Leamore Lane, Walsall WS2 7PS. tel: (0922) 710000

Intervac, 6 Siddals Lane, Allestree, Derby DE3 2DY. tel: (0332) 558931

John Jaques & Son Ltd, 361 Whitehorse Road, Thornton Heath, Surrey.tel: (081) 684 4242

Joncare Ltd, 7 Ashville Trading Estate, Nuffield Way, Abingdon, Oxon OX14 1RL. tel: (0235) 28120/35600

JW Products, 14 Willow Green, Agar Nook, Coalville, Leics LE6 3SZ. tel: (0530) 38300

Keep Able Ltd, Fleming Close, Park Farm, Wellingborough, Northants NN8 3UF. tel: (0933) 679426 *(Agents for MADDAK)*

Key Products Ltd., 4C Hempstead Road Ind Est, Holt, Norfolk, NR25 6ES. tel: (0263) 713294

Kids-Link, Lynmar Marketing, Yew Tree Close, Little Budworth, Cheshire CW6 9BT. tel: (082 921) 574

Knitterella Ltd, 52 Warnford Court, Throgmorton St, London EC2N 2AY

EJ & IM Law, 9 Pinfold St, Rugby, Warwickshire, CV21 2JD. tel: (0788) 61764

Lefthanded by Post, Duntish Court, Buckland Newton, Dorchester, Dorset DT2 7DE tel: (03005) 291

Lefties, The Left Handed Co., P.O Box 52, South DO, Manchester M20 8PJ. tel (061) 445 0159

Llewellyn-SML Health Care Services, Regent House, 1 Regent Road, City, Liverpool L3 7BX. tel: (051) 236 5311

London Disability Arts Forum, The Diorama, 14 Peto Place, London NW1 4DT. tel: (071) 935 5588

AM (PG) Marrs Ltd, 3rd Floor, Altay House, 869 High Road, North Finchley, London N12 8QA. tel: (081) 446 9620

Medipost Ltd, Unit 1, St Johns Estate, Elder Road, Lees, Oldham, Lancs. OL4 3DZ. tel: (061) 678 0233

Metropolitan Sports & Social Club for the Visually Handicapped, 29 Gilda Court, Watford Way, London NW7 2QN. tel: (081) 203 1286

Mobilia, Unit B32 Barwell Business Estate, Leatherhead Rd, Chessington, Surrey KT9 2NY. tel: (081) 974 1430

Moorhouse Technology Ltd, 30 New Rd, Moortown, Ringwood, Hants BH24 3AU tel: (042 54) 72983

Mouth & Foot Painting Artists, 9 Inverness Place, London W2 3JF. tel: (071) 229 4491

Music Advisory Service, Disabled Living Foundation, 380-384 Harrow Road, London W9 2HU tel: (071) 289 6111

National Federation of Gateway Clubs, Mencap Centre, 117-123 Golden Lane, London EC1Y 0RT. tel: (071) 253 9433

National Library for the Blind, Cromwell Rd, Bredbury, Stockport, Cheshire, SK6 2SG. tel (061) 494 0217

National Listening Library, 12 Lant St., London SE1 1QH. tel: (071) 407 9417

National Playing Fields Association, Information Officer, 25 Ovington Square, London SW3 1LQ. tel: 584 6445

National Subtitling Library for Deaf People, Victoria Mill, 3rd Floor, Compstall Mill Estates, Andrew St, Stockport SK6 5HN. tel: (061) 449 9650(*Voice & Minicom 5*)

National TV Licence Records Office, Barton House, Bond St, Bristol BS98 1TL. tel: (0272) 48021

New Home Sewing Machine Co. Ltd., Cromwell Road, Bredbury, Stockport, Cheshire SK6 2SH. tel: (061) 430 6011

ES Nicholson, 4 Louville Avenue, Withernsea, North Humberside HU19 2PB. tel: (0964) 612115

Nottingham Rehab Ltd, 17 Ludlow Hill Road, West Bridgford, Nottingham, NGH2 6HD. tel: (0602) 23451

Outsiders Club, P. O. Box 4ZB, London W1A 4ZB. tel: (071) 499 0900

Partially Sighted Society, Queens Road, Doncaster, DN1 2NX. tel: (0302) 368998

Path Productions, 38a Duncan Terrace, London N1 8AL. tel: (071) 359 7866

Pet Mate Ltd, Crane House, Gould Road, Twickenham, Middlesex, TW2 6RS. tel (081) 898 7393

Peta Scissorcraft Ltd, PO Box 990, Brentwood, Essex CM15 8LJ. tel: (0277) 220 495

Pfaff (Britain) Ltd, Pfaff House, East St, Leeds LS9 8EH. tel: (0532) 450645

Phobics Society, 4 Cheltenham Road, Chortlon-cum-Hardy, Manchester M21 1QN tel: (061) 881 1937

Physically Handicapped & Able Bodied (PHAB), Tavistock House North, Tavistock Square, London WC1H 9HX. tel: (071) 388 1963

Pioneer Westward Travel, 17 Victoria Road, St. Budeaux, Plymouth, Devon PL5 1RW. tel: (0752) 368987

Polka Childrens Theatre, 240 The Broadway, Wimbledon, London SW19 1SB. tel: (081) 542 4258*contact: Naomi Adler (081) 543 0363*

Polyotter Ltd, 25 Cambray Place, Cheltenham, Gloucester, GL50 1JN. tel: (0242) 39230

Potters Mates, Cust Hall, Toppesfield, Halstead, Essex C09 4EB. tel: (0787) 237 704

Pottycrafts Ltd, Campbell Rd, Stoke-on-trent, Staffs ST4 4ET. tel: (0782) 272444

Quest Educational Designs Ltd, 1 Prince Alfred St, Gosport, Hants, PO12 1QH. tel: (0705) 581179

Quickstep Ltd, Chichester Road, Ponswood, Hastings, East Sussex Tn34 1YS. tel: (0424) 434202

R & N Engineering, Beckley Hill Works, Lower Higham, Rochester ME3 7HX. tel: (042 482) 3654

Radion Society of Great Britian, Lambda House, Cranbourne Road, Potters Bar, Herts, EN6 3JE. tel: (0707) 59015

REMAP, Technical Equipment for Disabled People, 25 Mortimer St, London W1N 8AB. tel: (071) 637 5400 ext 357

Rompa (Flexus Plastics Ltd), PO Box 5, Wheatbridge Road, Chesterfield, Derbyshire S40 2AE. tel: (0246) 211777

Ross Consumer Electronics Plc, Silver Road, White City Industrial Park, London W12 7SG. tel: (081) 740 5252

WS Rothband & Co Ltd, Albion Mill, Helmshore Road, Helmshore, Rossendale, Lancs BB4 4JR. tel: (0706) 830086

Royal Association for Disability & Rehabilitation, 25 Mortimer St, London W1N 8AB. tel: (071) 637 5400

Royal National Institute for the Blind (RNIB): *(Peterborough)*- Production & Distribution Centre, Bakewell Rd, Orton, Peterborough PE2 0XU. tel (0733) 370 777

Moon Branch, Holmesdale Rd, Reigate, Surrey RH2 0BA. tel: (07372) 46333

Talking Book Service,Mount Pleasant, Alperton, Wembley, Middlesex HA0 1RR. tel: (081) 903 6666

Customer Services Dept, Braille House, 338-346 Goswell Road, London EC1V 7JE. tel; (071) 837 9921 or (01) 278 9611

Scout Association, Gilwell Park, Chingford, London E4 7QW. tel: (081) 524 5246

Scribblers, PO Box 68, Horley, Surrey RH6 8YG.

SDL Ltd, Coleman Rd, Leicester, LE5 4LE. tel: (0533) 769471

Sesame Institute (UK) 27 Blackfriars Road, London SE1 8NY. tel: (071) 633 9690

Shape London 1 Thorpe Close, London W10 5XL. tel: (081) 960 9245 *Director: Chris Davies*

Sight & Sound Technology Ltd, Qantel House, Anglia Way, Moulton Park, Northampton, NN3 1WD. tel: (0604) 790969

Sitty Pretty Products Ltd, The Business Centre, Colne Way, Watford, Herts WD2 8FP. tel: (0923) 53282/50705

John T Slade, 170 Cambridge Rd, Seven Kings, Ilford, Essex IG3 8NA. tel: (081) 599 4256

Soft Toy Workshop, Rosemarycott, Five Ashes, Mayfield, East Sussex TN20 6JD. tel: (082 585) 562

Sony UK Ltd, Customer Relations Dept, Pipers Way, Thatcham, Newbury RG13 4LZ. tel: (0635) 69500

Soundings Ltd, Essell House, 48 Roxburgh Terrace, Whitley Bay NE26 1DS. tel: (091) 253 4155

Hugh Steeper Ltd, 237-239 Roehampton Lane, London SW15 4LB. tel: (081) 788 8165

Stephens Ltd, Unit 6, Greets Green Ind Est, West Bromwich B70 9EW. tel: (021) 557 1272

Swim Shop, 52/58 Albert Road, Luton, Beds LU1 3PR. tel: (0582) 416545

Take-A-Guide Ltd, 11 Uxbridge St, London W8 7TQ. tel: (071) 221 5475

Talking Books Library, 12 Lant St, London SE1 1QH. tel: (071) 407 9417

Talking Newspaper Assoc of the UK, 90 High Street, Heathfield, E. Sussex. TN21 8JD. tel: (043 52) 6102

Talktapes, 13 Croftdown Road, London NW5 1EL. tel: (071) 485 9981

Tape Recording Service for the Blind, 48 Fairfax Road, Farnborough, Hampshire GU14 8JP tel: (0252) 547943 547943

Taskmaster Ltd, Morris Road, Leicester, LE2 6BR. tel: (0533) 704286

Toulan 2000 Ltd, Unit 2, Richard Street Ind Centre, Portwood, Stockport SK1 2AX. tel: (061) 480 1271

Toys for the Handicapped, 76 Barracks Road, Sandy Lane Industrial Estate, Stourport-on-Severn, Worcs, DY13 9QB. tel: (0299) 827820

Visionaid Systems, The Old School, The Gree, Ruddington, Nottingham, NG11 6HH. tel: (0602) 847879

JGH Walker, Colgrims Mede, Aviary Road, Pyrford, Woking, Surrey GU22 8TH. tel: (093 23) 41557

WAVES, Corscombe, Nr. Dorchester, Dorset, DT2 0NU. tel: (093 589) 248

Wider Horizons, 'Westbrook', Back Lane, Malvern, Worcs, WR14 2HJ.

Winslow Press, Telford Road, Bicester, Oxon OX6 0TS. tel: (0869) 244733

Wireless for the Bedridden, 81b Corbets Tey Rd, Upminster, Essex, RM14 2AJ. tel (040 22) 50051

Woodfit Ltd, Kem Mill, Whittle-le-Woods, Chorley, Lancs, PR6 7EA. tel: (025 72) 66421

Worldwide Tapetalk - c/o Sec: Mr Charles Towers, 35 The Gardens, West Harrow, Middlesex, HA1 4HE. tel: (081) 863 0706

MANUAL WHEELCHAIRS

All Handling (Movability) Ltd, 492 Kingston Road, Raynes Park, London, SW20 8DX. tel: (081) 542 2217

Aremco, Grove House, Lenham, Kent, ME17 2PX. tel: (0622) 858502

W & F Barrett Ltd, 22 Emery Road, Bristol, Avon, BS4 5PH. tel: (0272) 779016/774070

Beard Bros Ltd
Unit 2, The Crystal Centre, Elmgrove Road, Harrow, Middx. HA1 2HS. tel: (081) 861 4070
Rossway Drive, Little Bushey Lane, Bushey, Hertfordshire WD2 3RY. tel: (081) 950 2306

Alfred Bekker, The Green, Langtoft, Nr. Driffield, North Humberside YO25 0TF. tel: (0377) 87276

Bencraft Ltd, The Avenue, Rubery, Rednall, Birmingham, West Midlands B45 9AP. tel: (021) 453 1055/6/7

Boots the Chemists Ltd, City Gate, Toll House Hill, Nottingham NG2 3AA. tel: (0602) 418522. *Enquiries should be made at local branches*

British Association of Wheelchair Distributors - Secretary: D R Smytheman, Grove Cottage, Packwood Road, Lapworth, Solihull B94 6AS. tel: (0564) 773843. *Telephone enquiries from professionals only, and during office hours only*

British Castors Ltd, Golds Green Works, Bagnall Street, Hill Top, West Bromwich, West Midlands, B70 0UA. tel: (021) 556 7221

Bromakin Wheelchairs, Unit 1, Falcon Street, Loughborough, Leicester, LE11 1EH. tel: (0509) 217569

Buckingham Engineering Co, River Gate, West Street, Buckingham MK18 1HP. tel: (0280) 816808

Buss Mobility Designs Ltd, 102 Ashford Road, Bearsted, Maidstone, Kent ME14 4LX. tel: (0622) 37012

Camp Ltd, Northgate House, Staple Gardens, Winchester, Hampshire, SO23 8ST. tel: (0962) 55248

Car Chair Ltd, Station Road Industrial Estate, hailsham, East Sussex BN27 2ES. tel: (0323) 840283

Carters (J&A) Ltd, Alfred Street, Westbury, Wiltshire, BA13 3DZ. tel: (0373) 822203

Chailey Heritage, Rehab Engineering Unit, Chailey Heritage Hospital and School, North Chailey, Lewes, East Sussex, BN8 4EF. tel: (082 572) 2112 ext. 210

Chester-Care Ltd, 16 Englands Lane, London, NW3 4TG. tel: (071) 586 2166 or (071) 722 3430

Colson Castors (Europe) Ltd, Hingley Road, Halesowen, West Midlands B63 2RR. tel: (0384) 893535

Comfy Products, 29 Havelock Crescent, Bridlington, East Yorkshire, YO16 4JH. tel: (0262) 676417/400062

Community Health Supplies Co, 16 Dinsdale Gardens, New Barnet, Herts. tel: (081) 440 4931

Cory (Pharmacy) Ltd, 166-168 High Road, East Finchley, London, N2 9AS. tel: (081) 444 7464

Crelling Harnesses for the Disabled, 11-12 The Crescent, Cleveleys, Lancs, FY5 3LJ. tel: (0253) 852298/821780

Days Medical Aids Ltd, Litchard Industrial Estate, Bridgend, Mid-Glamorgan, CF31 2AL. tel: (0656) 57495/60150

Disablement Services Authority (DSA), 14 Russell Square, London WC1B 5EP. tel: (071) 636 6811

Econa Appliances Ltd, Units 15-20, Coleshill Industrial Estate, Station Road, Coleshill, Birmingham B46 1JR. tel: (0675) 64460

Electric & Manual Chairs Ltd, 43 Teville Road, Worthing, West Sussex, BN11 1UX. tel: (0903) 821515

Everest & Jennings Ltd., Princewood Road, Corby, Northants NN17 2DX. tel: (0536) 67661

Expanded Metal Co Ltd, Oakwood, Unit 1, 205 Old Oak, Common Lane, London W3 7DX. tel: (081) 743 1000

Greenbank Project Co-Operatives, Edwards Lane, Speke, Liverpool, L24 9HG. tel: (051) 486 3525

Hancock & Lane Ltd, Frome Manor, Bishops Frome, Worcester WR6 5BB. tel: (08853) 429 *Head Office:* (0788) 540094

Hatrick Industries Ltd, 12 Canonbury, Shrewsbury, Salop, SY3 7AH. tel: (0743) 850151

The Helping Hand Company (Ledbury) Ltd, Unit 9L, Bromyard Road Trading Estate, Ledbury, Hertfordshire HR8 1NS. tel: (0531) 5678

Hestair Maclaren Ltd, Station Works, Long Buckby, Northampton NN6 7PF. tel: (0327) 842662

CF Hewerdine Ltd, Devels Lane, Thorpe Lea, Egham, Surrey, TW20 8HF. tel: (0784) 451258/9

Homecraft Supplies Ltd, Low Moor Estate, Kirkby-in-Ashfield, Notts NG17 7JZ. tel: (0623) 754 047

Innovention Products Ltd, The Business Centrem, Colne Way, Watford, Herts, WD2 4ND. tel: (0923) 245050/9

J & S Services for the Disabled, Unit 11, Riverside Industrial Estate, Littlehampton, BN17 5DF. tel: (0903) 723141

Joncare Ltd, 7 Ashville Trading Estate, Nuffield Way, Abingdon, Oxon OX14 1RL. tel: (0235) 28120/35600

K C Mobility Services, Unit 4A, Victoria Mills, Bradford Road, Batley, West Yorkshire WF17 8LN. tel: (0924) 442386

Langham Products, Unit 26, Bennettsfield Trading Estate, Wincanton, Somerset BA9 9DT. tel: (0963) 33869

Lieuse Technology Ltd, 6 Hornton Place, London W8 4LZ. tel: (071) 938 1762

Llewellyn Health Care Services, Regent House, 1 Regent Road, City, Liverpool L3 7BX. tel:(051) 236 5311

Mangar Aids Ltd, Presteigne Industrial Estate, Presteigne, Powys. tel: (0544) 267674

Masterpeace Products Ltd, Tormen House, Booth Hill Works, Booth Hill Lane, Oldham, OL1 2 PH. tel: (061) 624 2041

May-Isle Co Ltd, 64 East March Street, Kirkcaldy, Fife, KY1 2DP. tel: (0592) 55533

G McLoughlin & Co Ltd, Victoria Works, Oldham Road, Rochdale, Lancs, OL11 1DF. tel (0706) 49911

Medipost Ltd, Unit 1, St. Johns Estate, Elder road, Lees, Oldham, Lancs. OL4 3DZ. tel: (061) 678 0233

Meditch Developments Ltd, Lenton Business Centre, Lenton Boulevard, Nottingham NG7 2BY. tel: (0602) 784194

Mobilia, Drake House, 18 Creekside, London SE8 3DZ. tel. (081) 692 7141 ext 210. *for general enquires* (081) 892 1850 *(for technical enquiries)*

Mobility Aids Centre, 88D South Street, Stanground, Peterborough, Cambs, PE2 8EZ. tel: (0733) 44930

Mobility Engineering Design, 114 Norbury Hill, London, SW16 3RT. tel: (01) 764 6023

Mobility Information Service, National Mobility Centre, Unit 2a Atcham Estate, Shrewsbury, SY4 4UG . tel: (074 377) 489

Molnlycke Ltd, Hospital Products Division, Southfields Road, Dunstable, Beds, LU6 3EJ. tel: (0582) 600211

Nesbit Evans, J And Co. Ltd., Woden Road West, Wednesbury WS10 7BL. tel: (021) 556 1511

Newton Products - Spastics Society, Meadway Works, Garretts Green Lane, Birmingham, B33 0SQ. tel: (021) 783 6081/2/3

Nicholls & Clarke Ltd, 3/10 Shoreditch High Street, London, E1 6PE. tel: (071) 247 5432

RF Nicholls Ltd, Soothouse Spring, Valley Road Industrial Estate, St. Albans, Herts, AL3 6PF. tel: (0727) 34255

Nottingham Rehab Ltd, 17 Ludlow Hill Road, West Bridgford, Nottingham, NG2 6HD. tel: (0602) 23451

Nursing Care Products Ltd, Ryburn Mill, Hanson Lane, Halifax, HX1 4SD. tel: (0422) 343243

Ortho-Kinetics (UK) Ltd, Unit 4, Planetary Road Industrial Estate, Wednesfield, Wolverhampton WV13 3XA. tel: (0902) 866166

Paraglide Ltd, 2 Churwell Avenue, Heaton Mersey, Stockport, Cheshire SK4 3QE. tel: (061) 432 7315

Paraid, Weston Lane, Birmingham, West Midlands, B11 3RS. tel: (021) 6744

Parris & Greening, 105 Church Road, Hove, East Sussex BN3 2AF. tel: (0273) 732216-7

PcP Grating Ltd, Steetley Industrial Estate, Bean Road, Coseley, Bilston, West Midlands WV14 9EE. tel: (09073) 75824

Poirier (UK) Ltd, 17 St. George's Industrial Estate, Frimley Road, Camberley, Surrey GU15 2QW. tel: (0276) 28562/3

Progressive Productions Ltd., Clarke Street, Ashton-Under-Lyne, Lancashire OL7 0LJ. tel: (061) 330 6721/2/3/4

Proudline Associates Ltd, 16 Smithbarn, Horsham, W Sussex, RH13 6EB. tel (0403) 41123

Rainbow Rehab, PO Box 546, Bournemouth BH8 8YD. tel: (0202) 32651

Remploy Ltd (Wheelchair Div), 11 Nunnery Drive, Sheffield S2 1TA. tel: (0742) 757631

Rolac Ltd, Unit 16, Enterprise Centre 2, Chester Street, Stockport, SK3 0BR. tel: (061) 429 8477

Roma Medical Aids Ltd, Llandow Industrial Estate, Cowbridge, South Glamorgan, CF7 7PB. tel: (044 63) 4519

Ross Auto Engineering Ltd (Southport), 27 Banastre Road, Southport, Lancs PR8 5AS. tel: (0704) 35757

Samson Products (Dorset) Ltd., 239 Alder Road, Parkstone, Dorset BH12 4AP. tel: (0202) 734171

SEM Canterbury, South Essex Motors (Basildon) Ltd., Swinborne Road, Burnt Mills Industrial Estate, Basildon, Essex, SS13 1EF. tel: (0268) 727603

Shackletons (Carlinghow) Ltd., 501 Bradford Road, Batley, West Yorkshire WF17 8LN. tel (0924) 474430

Simcross Services, 4 Holywell Road, Watford, Herts, WD1 8HU. tel: (0923) 228664/248167

Gerald Simonds Wheelchairs Stoke Mandeville, 9 March Place, Gatehouse Way, Aylesbury, HP19 3UG. tel: (0296) 436557

HC Slingsby plc. 89/95/97 Kingsway, London, WC2B 6SB. tel: (071) 405 2551

SML Healthcare Ltd, Bath Place, High Street, Barnet Herts EN5 5XE. tel: (081) 440 6522

James Spencer & Co Ltd, Moor Road Works, Moor Road, Headingley, Leeds, West Yorkshire LS6 4BH. tel: (0532) 785837/741850

SSL Patient-Care, Standard House, Banks Lane, Bexley Heath, Kent, DA6 7BH. tel: (081) 301 1666

Hugh Steeper (Roehampton) Ltd, 237-239 Roehampton Lane, London, SW15 4LB. tel: (081) 788 8165

Sunrise Medical Ltd, Fens Pool Avenue, Brierley Hill, West Midlands DY5 1QA. tel: (0384) 480480

T and S Motion and Sport, Head Office, Potter Lane, Wellow, Via Newark, Notts, NG22 0EB. tel: (0623) 835362

Third Dimension, Callingwood House, 134 Abbots Road, Hanham Green, Bristol, Avon BS15 3NS. tel: (0272) 672519

Toys for the Handicapped, 76 Barracks Road, Sandy Lane Industrial Estate, Stourport-on-Severn, Worcs., DY13 9QB tel: (0299) 827820

Typrod Ltd, Lydney Industrial Estate, Harbour Road, Lydney, Glos, GL15 4EP. tel: (0594) 42186

Unit Installations, Unit 26, Yates Brothers, Lime Lane, Pelsall, Walsall. tel: (0543) 370383

University of Salford - The Secretary, Department of Orthopaedic Mechanics, Salford, Greater Manchester, M5 4WT. tel: (061) 736 5843 ext. 7402

CN Unwin Ltd., Lufton, Yeovil, Somerset, BA22 8SZ. tel: (0935) 75359

Vessa Ltd, Paper Mill Lane, Alton, Hants, GU34 2PY. tel: (0420) 83294

Vitamol Ltd, Ryecroft Street, Ashton under Lyne, Thameside tel: (061) 330 1681

A & G Walden Brothers Ltd, 34 Wimbledon Avenue, Brandon Industrial Estate, Brandon, Suffolk IP27 0NZ. tel: (0842) 811776

U Williams & Co Ltd., 23/25 Wyche Grove, South Croydon, Surrey, CR2 6EX. tel: (081) 688 2030 Alt. tel: (081) 688 8308

OFFICE FURNITURE AND EQUIPMENT

Acco Europe Ltd, Halesowen Industrial Park, Hereward Rise, Halesowen, West Midlands B62 8AN. Tel: (021) 550 8883

Advance Seating Designs, Unit 7, Everitt Rd, London NW10 6PL. tel: (081) 961 4515

Altonaids Mobility, Park Rd, Gateshead, Tyne & Wear, NE8 3HL. tel: (091) 477 3733

Antocks Lairn Ltd, Lancaster Rd, Cressex, High Wycombe, Bucks., HO12 3HZ. tel: (0494) 465 454

Aremco, Grove House, Lenham, Kent, ME17 2PX. tel: (0622) 858502

Assoc. of Visually Handicapped Office Workers -c/o Sec: Mrs K Shelley, Flat 5, 43 Avenue Gardens, London W3 1HB. tel: (081) 992 9921 *(after 6pm)*

Ayrton-Graham (Contracts) Ltd, 10 North Drive, Wallasaey, Merseyside L45 OLZ. tel: (051) 639 5848

The Back Shop, 24 New Cavendish St, London W1M 7LH. tel: (071) 935 9120/9148

The Back Store, 330 King St., Hammersmith, London W6 0RR. tel: (081) 741 5022

LP Bradburn Ltd, 272 Upper St, London N1 2UQ. tel: (071) 359 9251

British Olivetti Ltd, 1st Avenue, Bletchley, Milton Keynes, Bucks MK1 1RL. tel: (0908) 374900

British Thornton Ltd, PO Box 3, Wythenshawe, Manchester, M22 4SS. tel: (061) 998 1311

Brocks Office Supplies, Avad House, Belvue Rd, Northolt Ind Est, Northolt, Middx UBS 5HY. tel: (081) 842 4141

Budgie Office Products Ltd, Birch Close, Eastbourne, East Sussex, BN23 6PE. tel: (0323) 648471

Caplan Office Furniture Ltd, Head Office, Asher House, Ripley, Derbyshire DE5 3RE. tel: (0733) 570700 *London Showroom: (071) 388 9616*

Carlton Brookes Ltd, New Rd, Dudley, West Midlands DY2 8JQ. tel: (0384) 231211/213782

Copiers Direct, 63-67 Main St, Mursley, Milton Keynes, Bucks Mk17 ORT. tel: (0296 72) 323

Copygraphic, CG House, Chiswick Park, Bollo Lane, London W4 5UW. tel: (081) 747 1573

Dauphin International Ltd, Peter St, Blackburn, Lancs BB1 5LH. tel: (0254) 52220

Disabled Graduates Careers Information Service, Hereward College for Further Education, Bramton Crescent, Tile Hill, Coventry CV4 9SW. tel: (0203) 694302

DN Computer Services Plc, Truedata House, Green Lane, Heywood, Manchester OL10 2DY. tel: (0706) 67567; London (081) 368 1221

Dudley Stationery Ltd, Crown Close, Osswick Lane, Bow, London E3 2JT. tel: (01) 980 7199

Dynamic Seating Products, Head Office, Oakleigh, High St, Bream Nr Lydney, Glos. tel: (0594) 562271; Northern Office: (0565) 3574

Eldon Industries (UK) Ltd, Unit 1, Clifton Rd, Shefford, Beds SG17 5AB. tel: (0462) 814914

Elite Manufacturing Co Ltd, Elite Works, Station Rd, Manningtree, Essex CO11 1DZ. tel: (0206) 392171

Employment Service, Special Needs Programmes, Rockingham House, 123 West St, Sheffield SS1 4ER. tel: (0742) 739190

Energy Facilities Management Ltd, Pendlebury Ind Est, Manchester M27 1FJ. tel: (061) 793 9333

ESA Mcintosh, Mitchelston Drive, Kirkaldy KY1 3LX, Scotland. tel: (0592) 52551

Evertaut Seating, Cross St, Darwen, Lncs BB 2PW. tel: (0254) 704922 *London Showroom: (071) 288 6202*

Expandex Ltd, Hitchin St, Biggleswade, Beds SG18 8BS. tel: (0767) 312700

Facit Furniture Systems, 3-5 Delaware Drive, Tongwell, Milton Keynes MK15 8HG. tel: (0908) 617272

Forwood Designs Ltd, The Mews, Mitcheldean, Glos GL17 OSL. tel: (0594) 542181

Gordon Russell Plc, 44/46 Eagle St., London WC1R 4AP. tel: (071) 831 0031

Hago Products Ltd, Durnban Rd, Bognot Regis, West Sussex, PO22 9QT. tel: (0243) 863131 *N.B. wholesale supplier only*

Hille Executive Furniture & Seating Ltd, Hamlet Green, Haverhill, Suffolk CB9 8QL. tel (0440) 702537

Joncare Ltd, 7 Ashville Trading Estate, Nuffield Way, Abingdon, Oxon OX14 1RL. tel: (0235) 28120/35600

King Cole Tube Bending Co Ltd, 40 Buckland Rd, Pen Mill Trading Estate, Yeovil, Somerset BA21 5EJ. tel: (0935) 26141/2

Lacelink Ltd, 13 Pinehurst, Sevenoaks, Kent TN14 5AQ. tel: (0732) 63221

Llewellyn-SNL Health Care Services, Regent House, 1 Regent Rd, City, Liverpool L3 7BX. tel: (051) 236 5311

Malt Business Products Ltd, 12 Kings Meadow, Ferry Hinksey Rd, Oxford ODP. tel: (0865) 793969

M Margolis Ltd, 63-65 New Oxford St, London WC1A 1DG. tel (071) 240 5057

Martela plc, Rooksley, Milton Keynes, Bucks, MK13 8PD. tel: (0908) 227418 *London Showroom: (071) 288 6043*

Masterpeace Products Ltd, Tormen House, Booth Hill Works, Booth Hill Lane, Olham, Ol1 2PH. tel: (061) 624 2041

Matthews Office Furniture Ltd, PO Box 70, Reginald Rd, St Helens WA 9 4JE. tel: (0744) 813671

Meditech Developments Ltd, Unit 1 Crocus Place, Crocus St, Nottingham NG2 3DE. tel: (0602) 863263

Herman Miller Ltd, 149 Tottenham Court Rd, London W1P OJA. tel: (071) 388 7331 or (081) 759 7777

Mobilia, Unit B32 Barwell Business Estate, Leatherhead Rd, Chessington, Surrey KT9 2NY. tel: (081) 397 1166

Morleys Contracts Ltd, Arkwright Rd, Bicester, Oxon, OX6 7UU. tel: (0869) 320320 *(contracts holders only)*

M Myers & Son Plc, PO Box 16, Vicarage St, Oldbury, Warley, West Midlands B68 8HF. tel: (021) 552 3322

National Association of Deafened People -c/o Hon. Membership Secretary, Geoffrey T. Brown, 103 Heath Rd, Widnes, Cheshire WA8 7NU.

Nesor Products Ltd, Claremont Hall, Pentonville Rd, London N1 9HR. tel: (071) 278 7401

Ness Furniture Ltd, Croxdale, Durham, Co Durham DH6 5HT. tel: (0388) 816109

Newton Products -Spastics Society, Meadway Works, Garretts Green Lane, Birmingham, B33 OSQ. tel: (021) 6081/2/3

Nobo Visual Aids Ltd, Alder Close, Compton Ind Est, Eastbourne, East Sussex BN23 6QB. tel: (0323) 641521

Nomeq, 23/24 Thornhill Rd, North Moons Moat, Redditch, Worcs B98 9ND. tel: (0527) 64222

Outset, Drake House, 18 Creekside, London SE8 3D2. tel: (081) 692 7141

Panilet Tables, Brick St, Braggs Lane, Old Market, Bristol BS2 0EA. tel: (0272) 554559

Paramount Laker, Laker House, 34 Pitlake, Croydon CRO 3RY. tel: (081) 688 8301

Pelvic Support Chairs, Oaklands, New Mill Lane, Eversley, Hants RG27 0RA. tel: (0734) 732365

Prince Moran Ltd, Greenfield Works, Cranberry Lane, Darwen, Lanc, BB3 2HL. tel: (0254) 775216

Rathbone Society, First Floor, Princess House, 105-107 Princess St, Manchester M1 6DD. tel: (061) 236 5358

Reading Chair & Desks Ltd, Basingstoke Rd, Riseley, Berks RG7 1QF. tel: (0734) 884646

Remploy Ltd, (Medical Products Div), Russ St, Broad Plain, Bristol BS2 OHJ. tel: (0272) 277512

Rifton & Community Playthings, Robertsbridge, East Sussex, TN32 5DR. tel: (0580) 880626

Rompa (Flexus Plastics Ltd), PO Box 5,Wheatbridge Rd, Chesterfield, Derbyshire S40 2AE. tel: (0246) 211777

Ronco Sales Organisation, 89 East End Rd, Finchley, London N2 0SR. tel: (081) 883 9753

Rotadex Systems Ltd, 35 Fortnum Close, Kitts Green, Birmingham B33 0JL. tel: (021) 783 7411/4

Royal National Institute for the Blind, 224 Great Portland St, London W1N 6AA. tel: (071) 388 1266

Royal Sovereign Graphics, Unit 6&7 St. Georges Ind Est, White Hart Lane, Wood Green, London N22 5QL. tel: (081) 888 8822

Gordon Russell plc, 44-46 Eagle St, London WC1R 4AP. tel: (01) 831 0031

Scan-Sit Ltd., Unit 4, 111 Mortlake Rd, Kew, Richmond, Surrey TW9 4AB. tel: (081) 392 1896

Seager Wedo (UK) Ltd, 5-25 Scrutton St, London EC2A 4HJ. tel: (071) 739 6856

James Spencer & Co Ltd, Moor Rd Works, Moor Rd, Headingley, Leeds LS6 4BH. tel: (0532) 785837/741850

Spicers Ltd, Sawston, Cambridge, CB2 4JG. tel:)0223) 834555

Stowaway Furniture Design Co Ltd, 44/46 Bunyan Rd, Kempston, Beds MK42 8HL. tel: (0234) 854993

Tansad Ltd, Lodge Causeway, Fishponds, Bristol, Avon, BS16 3JU. tel: (0272) 657386

R Taylor & Son (Orthopaedic) Ltd, Compton Works, 49 Woodwards Rd, Pleck, Walsall, WS2 9RN

Thousand & One Lamps Ltd, 4 Barmeston Rd, London SE6 3BN. tel: (081) 698 7238

Townsend Associates Ltd, Dutch Yard, 177A Wandsworth High St, London SW18 4LE. tel: (081) 871 2566

Tullos Furniture Products, 132 Wellington Rd, West Tullos Ind Est, Aberdeen AB9 1LQ. tel: (0224) 873366

William Vere Ltd, Chapel Lane, Sands, High Wycombe, Bucks HP12 4BG. tel: (0494) 22361

Vickers plc, Dartford, Kent DA1 1NY. tel: (0322 23477)

A & G Walden Brothers Ltd, 34 Wimbledon Avenue, Brandon Ind Est, Brandon, Suffolk 1P27 ONZ. tel: (0842) 811776

Westra Office Equipment Ltd, The Green, Southall, Middlesex UB2 4DE. tel: (081) 843 1122

Chas White Son Ltd, 2-18 Curtain Rd, London ECSA 3 NE. tel: (071) 247 4388

PERSONAL CARE

Adam Rouilly (London) Ltd, Crown Quay Lane, Sittingbourne, Kent ME10 3JG. tel: (0795) 71378

Addis Ltd, Ware Road, Hertford, Herts SG13 7HL. tel: (0992) 584221

ADM Product Services Ltd, Anchor House, Thornhill Road, Dewsbury, West Yorkshire WF12 9QE. tel: (0924) 457122

Aidserve Ltd, Unit 106, Bradley Hall Trading Estate, Bradley Lane, Standish, Wigan WN6 0XQ. tel: (0257) 425538

AKW Medi-Care, Orchard Croft, Stock Green, Redditch B96 6SZ. tel: (0386) 792785

G & S Allgood Ltd, Carterville House, 297 Euston Road, London NW1 3AQ. tel: (071) 387 9951

Allia UK Ltd, Whieldon Road, Stoke on Trent, Staffordshire ST4 4HN. tel: (0782) 49191

Amilake Ltd, Haslemere Industrial Estate, 20 Ravensbury Terrace, Wandsworth, London SW18 4SB. tel: (081) 947 7771

Anything Left Handed Ltd, 65 Beak St., London W1R 3LF. tel (071) 437 3910

Aqualisa Products Ltd, 6 The Flyer's Way, Westerham, Kent TN16 1DE. tel (0959) 63240

Aremco, Grove House, Lenham, Kent, ME17 2PX. tel: (0622) 858502

Arjo Mecanaids Ltd, St. Catherine Street, Gloucester, GL1 2SL. tel: (0452) 500200

Armitage Shanks Ltd, Armitage, Rugeley, Staffs., WS15 3BT. tel: (0543) 490253

Associated Metal Works Ltd, 30 St. Andrews Square, Glasgow, Scotland S1 5PJ. tel: (041) 552 2004/5/6

ASM Medicare, Picow Farm Industrial Estate, Runcorn, Cheshire, WA7 4UG. tel: (09285) 74301

Autumn Mobility Ltd, PO Box 18, Oldham, Lancashire, OL8 1XS. tel: (061) 627 5492

Avery (W&T) Ltd, Smethwick, Warley, West Midlands, B66 2LP. tel (021) 558 1112/2161

Ayelco, Drayton House, Stede Quarter, Biddenden, Kent, TN27 8JQ. tel: (0580) 291931

B Line Industries, Beverley Road, Hull, North Humberside, HU1 1NF. tel: (0482) 42296

Bar Knight Precision Engineers Ltd, 5th Floor, Elliot Place, Clydeway Industrial Centre, Glasgow G3 8EP. tel: (0412) 216649

Barking-Grohe Ltd, 1 River Road, Barking, Essex IG11 0HD. tel: (081) 594 8898

Bath Services International Ltd, 27 Frith Street, London, W1V5TR. tel: (071) 437 8238/8713

Bell Johnson & Green Ltd, Tuley Street, Manchester, M11 2DY. tel: (061) 223 9144

Birch Products Ltd, 37 Homewood Avenue, Cuffley, Potters Bar, Herts EN6 4QQ. tel (0707) 873075

Boots the Chemist Ltd, City Gate, Toll House Hill, Nottingham, NG2 3AA. tel: (0602) 418522. *Enquiries should be made at local branches.*

Bower Products Ltd, Unit 31, Abbey Industrial Estate, Woodside End, Wembley, Middx. HA0 1ZD. tel: (081) 903 0983

Boyco Products, Brook Road, Cheadle, Cheshire, SK8 1PQ. tel: (061) 428 7077

S Brannan & Sons Ltd, Cleator Moor, Cumbria, CA25 5QE. tel: (0946) 810413

Braun Electric (UK) Ltd, Dolphin Estate, Windmill Road, Sunbury on Thames, Middlesex TW16 7EJ. tel: (0932) 785611

Brausch & Co. (UK) Ltd, The Gate Centre, Great West Road, Brentford, Middlesex TW8 9DD tel: (081) 847 4455

British Red Crtoss Society - London, 9 Grosvenor Crescent, London SW1X 7EJ. tel: (071) 235 5454

Caradon Mira Ltd, Cromwell Road, Cheltenham, Gloucester GL52 5EP. tel: (0242) 221221

Caradon Twyfords Ltd, Lawton Road, Alsager, Stoke-on-Trent, Staffordshire tel: (0270) 879777

Carron Steelyne Ltd, PO Box 37, Carron, Falkirk, FK2 8DW. tel: (0324) 38313

Carters (J&A) Ltd, Alfred Street, Westbury, Wiltshire, BA13 3DZ. tel: (0373) 822203

Cee-Jay, Unit 5 & 12, Birchanger Industrial Estate, Stansted Road, Bishop's Stortford, Hertfordshire CM23 2TH. tel: (0279) 755768/9

Cefndy Enterprises, Cefndy Road, Rhyl, Clwyd, LL18 2HG. tel: (0745) 343877

Cel Products Ltd, Glen Street Works, Glen Street, Hebburn, Tyne & Wear, NE31 1NE. tel: (091) 4835818

Chailey Heritage, Rehab Engineering Unit, Chailey Heritage Hospital and School, North Chailey, Lewes, East Sussex, BN8 4EF. tel: (082 572) 2112 ext. 210

Chelsea Artisan Plc, Unit 7, The Ember Centre, Lyon Road, Hersham, Surrey, KT12 3PU tel: (0932) 231000

Chester-Care Ltd, 16 Englands Lane, London, NW3 4TG. tel: (071) 586 2166 or (071) 722 3430

Chiltern Medical Developments Ltd, Chiltgern House, Wedgewood Road, Bicester, Oxon OX6 7UL. tel: (0869) 246470

Clos-O-Mat GB Ltd, 55 Waverley Road, Sale, Cheshire M33 1AY. tel: (061) 905 1399

Croydex Co Ltd, Central Way, Andover, Hants, SP10 5AW. tel: (0264) 65881

Daniels Healthcare, Head Office, 130 Western Road, Tring, Hertfordshire HP23 4BU. tel: (0422) 826881

Davis & Tamplin, Westhampnett Private Nursing Home, 17 Roman Way, Fishbourne, Chichester, West Sussex PO19 3QN. tel: (0243) 788885/782986

Days Medical Aids Ltd, Litchard Industrial Estate, Bridgend, Mid-Glamorgan, CF31 2AL. tel: (0656) 57495/60150

Dentene, 37 Knowsley Street, Bury, Lancashire BL9 0ST tel: (061) 761 2671

DMSS Ltd, Unit 7, Cyfartha Industrial Estate, Merphry Tydsyl, Mid Glamorgan, South Wales, tel: (0685) 722 605

Dolphin Showers Ltd, Bromwich Road, Worcester, Worcs, WR2 4BD. tel: (0905) 422487/428000

Easi Care Marketing Ltd, Mullions, Lymington Road, Milford-on-Sea, Hampshire S041 0QN. tel: (0590) 43839

EKS (Sales) Ltd, 315-317 Ballards Lane, North Finchley, London N12 8LY. tel: (081) 446 8297

Gordon Ellis & Co, Trent Lane, Castle Donington, Derby, DE7 2PW. tel: (0332) 810504

Fancy Metal Goods Ltd, Famego Works, 12 Commercial Street, Birmingham B1 2RS. tel: (021) 643 7399

H Fereday & Sons Ltd, Shaftesbury Works, 45 Holloway Road, London, N7 8JT. tel: (071) 607 5601

FFWD London Ltd, 14a. Newburgh Street, London W1V 4LF. tel: (071) 439 0091

Fittleworth Medical Ltd, Mallows, Limbourne Lane, Fittleworth, West Sussex RH20 1HR. tel: (079 882) 449

Fixatrad Ltd, 763 Harrow Road, London, NW10 5NY. tel: (081) 969 3232

Fordham Bathrooms & Kitchens Ltd, Fordham House, Dudley Road, Wolverhampton, West Midlands, WV2 4DS. tel: (0902) 59123

W Freeman & Co Ltd, Suba-Seal Works, Staincross, Barnsley, South Yorkshire, S75 6DH. tel: (0226) 284081

FC Frost Ltd, Bankside Works, Benfield Way, Braintree, Essex. CM7 6YS. tel: (0376) 29111

Gainsborough Electrial Ltd, Fifers Lane, Norwich, NR6 6XB. tel: (0603) 787171

Gallops Hospital Equipment, Finmere Road, Eastbourne, East Sussex BN21 8QG. tel: (0323) 646681

Gibbons, James Format Ltd, Colliery Road, Wolverhampton, West Midlands, WV1 2QW. tel: (0902) 58585

AW Gregory & Co Ltd, Glynde House, Glynde Street, London, SE4 1RY. tel: (081) 690 3437

A & J Gummers Ltd., 16 Pentos Drive, Formans Road, Birmingham B11 2AT. tel: (021) 778 2241

Hampshire Medical Developments Ltd, Appollo House, 34 Church Road, Romsey, Hants, SO51 8EY,tel: (0794) 523455

Harrison Thompson & Co. Ltd, Yeoman House, Whitehall Estate, Whitehall Road, Leeds LS12 5JB. tel: (0532) 795854

Haviland Bathrooms Ltd, 228-230 High Road, Wood Green, London N22 4HH. tel: (081) 888 4262

Health & Comfort Ltd, PO Box 15, Westbury, Wiltshire, BA13 4LS. tel (0373) 822394

Heatons Bathrooms Ltd, Denby Way, Euroway Industrial Est., Hellaby, Rotherham S66 8HR. tel: (0709) 549551

Heatrae Sadia Heating Ltd, Hurricane Way, Norwich NR6 6EA. tel: (0603) 144/424244

Helping Hands Shop, 114 Queens Road, Leicester LE2 3AD. tel: (0533) 708821

Hemco (UK) Ltd, Unit 17, Llandow Industrial Estate, Cowbridge, South Glamorgan CF7 7PB. tel: (04463) 3393/3394

Heron Plastics Ltd, Rue des Pres Trading Estate, St. Saviour, Jersey, Channel Islands. tel: (0534) 72183

Hestair Hope Ltd, St Philip's Drive, Royton, Oldham, Lancs. OL2 6AG. tel: (061) 633 6611

Hewi (UK) Ltd, Scimitar Close, Gillingham Business Park, Gillingham, Kent.ME8 0RN. tel: (0634) 377688.

Hitchdesk Co., 13 Riverbank, Shoreham-by-Sea, West Sussex BN4 5YH. tel: (0273) 4544833

SSR Holbrook Ltd, Jackson Road, Coventry, CV6 4LY. tel (0203) 667 576

Home Mobility Services, 12 Vernon Drive, Chapletown, Sheffield, Yorks, S30 4XY. tel:(0742) 460578

Home Nursing Supplies Ltd., Headquarters Road, West Wilts Trading Estate, Westbury, Wilts, BA13 4JR. tel: (0373) 822313

Home Supplies (Wessex) Ltd, South Stour Avenue, Eastmead Estate, Ashford, Kent. TN23 RS (0233) 626099

Homecraft Supplies Ltd, Low Moor Estate, Kirkby-in-Ashfield, Notts NG17 7JZ. tel: (0623) 754 047

Ideal Standar Ltd, P O Box 60, National Avenue, Kingston-upon-Hull, HU5 4JE. tel (0482) 46461

Industrial Cleaning Papers Ltd, Manchester House, Church Way, Church Stretton, Shropshire, SY6 6DJ. tel: (0694) 723601

Innovention Products Ltd, The Business Centre, Colne Way, Watford, Herts, WD2 4ND. tel: (0923) 245050

J & J Products Ashford Ltd, 609 Spur Road, North Feltham Trading Estate, Feltham, Middlesex, TW14 0SL tel: (081) 890 5080 Alt. tel: (081) 890 5086

Jackson Medical Aids, Old Mill, P°ool Road, Newtown, Powys, SY16 1DW. tel: (0686) 27172

Keep Able Ltd, Fleming Close, Park Farm, Wellingborough, Northants, NN8 3BR. tel: (0933) 679426

AH Kidman Ltd, 141-143 Castle Road, Bedford, Beds. tel: (0234) 54090

Kimberly-Clerk Ltd, Simplicity Product Advisory Service, Larkfield, Maidstone, Kent ME20 7PS. tel: (0622) 717700

Krausz-Harari Ltd., 87 Ravensdale Road, London N16 6TH. tel: (081) 800 7000

Langham Products, Unit 26, Bennettsfield Trading Estate, Wincanton, Somerset BA9 9DT. tel (0963) 33869

EJ & IM Law, 9 Pinfold Street, Rugby, Warwickshire, CV21 2JD. tel: (0788) 61764

Llewellyn Health Care Services, Regent House, 1 Regvent Road, City, Liverpool L3 7BX. tel (051) 236 5311

Mangar Aids Ltd, Presteigne Industrial Estate, Presteigne, Powys. tel: (0544) 267674

Marc Appliances, Clybank Road, Copnor, Portsmouth, Hants, PO3 5NH. tel: (0705) 696731

Marsden Weighing Machine Group Ltd, 388 Harrow Road, London, W9 2HU tel: (071) 289 1066

Albert Marston & Co Ltd, Wellington Works, Planetary Road, Willenhall WV13 3ST. tel: (0902) 305511

Matthews Simons Partnership, (Dental Medical and Surgical Ltd,) 28 Ashworth Mansions, Elgin Ave, London W9 1JP. tel: (01) 286 8961/266 3783

G McLoughlin & Co Ltd, Victoria Works, Oldham Road, Rochdale, Lancs OL11 1DF tel: (0706) 49911

MDH Ltd, Walworth Road, Andover, Hants, SP10 5AA. tel: (0264) 62111

Medeci Rehab Ltd, Research Unit, Warley Hospital, Brentwood, Essex CM14 5HQ. tel: (0277) 212637

Medic-Bath Ltd, PO Box 12, Ashfield Works, Hulme Hall Lane, Manchesterm M10 8AB. tel: (061) 205 7495

Medipost Ltd, Unit 1, St. Johns Estate, Elder Road, Lees, Oldham, Lancs. OL4 3DZ. tel (061) 678 0233

Meditech Developments Ltd, Lenton Business Centre, Lenton Boulevard, Nottingham NG7 2BY. tel: (0602) 784194

Meridian Metier Ltd, Unit 1, Lammas Courtyard, Weldon North Industrial Estate, Corby, Northants NN17 1FZ. tel: (0536) 205145

Metlex Industries Ltd, Metlex House, 29 Vicarage Road, Croydon, Surrey, CR9 3BQ. tel: (081) 688 113

Meynell Valves Ltd, Shaw Road, Bushbury, Wolverhampton, W Midlands, WV10 9LB. tel: (0902) 28621

Midequip Services, 199 Upperdale Road, Derby, Derbyshire DE3 8BS. tel: (0332) 767981

Mothercare Plc, Cherry Tree Road, Watford, Herts, WD2 5SH. tel: (0923) 33577. *Customer enquiries on (0923) 31616*

Mountway Ltd, Dan-y-Bont Mill, Gilwern, Abergavenny, Gwent, NP7 0DD. tel: (0873) 831678 Alt. tel: (0873) 831195

Myco (UK), 31 Malpas Drive, Pinner, Middlesex HA5 1DQ. tel: (081) 868 2430

Myson Ryders Ltd, Victoria Works, Nelson Street, Bolton, Lancs, BL3 2DW. tel. (0204) 382017

Nicholls & Clarke Ltd, 3/10 Shoreditch High Street, London, E1 6PE. tel: (071) 247 5432

Nordic Saunas Ltd, Fairview Estate, Holland Road, Oxted Surrey, RH8 9BZ. tel: (0833) 716111

Norton Engineering Alloys Company Ltd, Norton Grove Industrial Estate, Norton, Malton, Yorkshire YO17 9HQ. tel: (0653) 695721

Nottingham Rehab Ltd, 17 Ludlow Hill Road, West Bridgford, Nottingham, NG2 6HD. tel: (0602) 234251

Ortho-Med Ltd, 5 Loaning Road, Edinburgh, EH7 6JE. tel: 652 1603

Paperchase Products Ltd, 213 Tottenham Court Road, London W1. tel: (071) 580 8496/631 0088

Parker Anderson, Mullions, Lymington Road, Milford-on-Sea, Hampshire, SO4 10QN. tel: (0590) 43839

Parker Bath Developments Ltd, Queensway, Stem Lane Industrial Estate, New Milton, Hants, BH25 5NN. tel: (0425) 617598

FJ Payne Manufacturing Ltd, Stanton Harcourt Road, Eynsham, Oxford, Oxon, OX8 1JT. tel: (0865) 881881

Pharmagen Ltd, Church Road, Perry Barr, Birmingham B42 2LD. tel: (021) 356 0478

PJP Trading Ltd, 151 Dixons Hill Road, North Mymms, Hatfield, Hertfordshire AL9 7JE. tel: (07072) 66726/73573

Power-Tech (UK) Ltd, Unit 8c, Ford Airfield Industrial Estate, Yapton, Arundel, West Sussex BN18 0HY. tel: (0903) 713227

Precision Engineering Co (Reading) Ltd, Meadow Road, Reading, Berks RG1 8LB. tel: (0734) 599444

Pressalit Ltd, 25 Grove Promenade, Ilkley, West Yorkshire LS29 8AF. tel: (0943) 607651

Quoteforce Ltd, The Old Post Office, Bucks Hill, Chipperfield, Hertfordshire, WD4 9AT. tel: (09277) 63588

Redring Electric Ltd, Redring Works, Peterborough, Cambs, PE2 9JJ. tel: (0733) 313213

Remploy Ltd (Medical Products Div), 415 Edgware Road, Cricklewood, London NW2 6LR. tel: (081) 452 8020.

Renray Group Ltd, Road Five, Winsford Industrial Estate, Winsford, Cheshire, CW7 3RB. tel: (0606) 593456)

Rentokil Ltd, (Sanitact Service), Felcourt, East Grinstead, West Sussex RH19 2JY. tel: (0342) 833022

Ri-Med Medical Appliances, 82 Whitby Crescent, Woodthorpe, Nottingham, NG5 4LZ. tel: (0602) 266647

Roma Medical Aids Ltd, Llandow Industrial Estate, Cowbridge, South Glamorgan, CF7 7PB. tel: (04463) 4519

Rompa (Flexus Plastics Ltd), PO Box 5, Wheatbridge Road, Chesterfield, Derbyshire S40 2AE. tel: (0246) 211777

WS Rothband & Co Ltd, 21 Elizabeth Street, Manchester, Greater Manchester, M8 8WT. tel: (061) 834 1303

Royal National Institute for the Blind, 224 Great Portland Street, London, W1N 6AA. tel: (071) 388 1266

Sanitary Appliances Ltd, 3 Sandiford Road, Kimpton Industrial Estate, Sutton, Surrey, SM3 9RN. tel: (081) 641 0310

Santric Ltd, Hawksworth, Swindon, Wilts, SN2 1DZ. tel: (0793) 36756

Saville Stainless Ltd, PO Box 74, Altrincham, Cheshire, WA14 3RP. tel: (0565) 830156

Seca Ltd, Seca House, 40 Barn Street, Digbeth, Birmingham, B5 5QB. tel: (021) 6439349

Shackletons (Carlinghow) Ltd, 501 Bradford Road, Batley, West Yorkshire Wf17 8LN. tel: (0924) 474430

Shires Ltd, Guiseley, Leeds, West Yorkshire, LS20 8AP. tel: (0943) 870055

SIA Aids & Services Ltd, Newpoint House, 76 St James's Lane, London N10 3DF. tel: (081) 444 2121

Gerald Simonds Wheelchairs Stoke Mandeville, 9 March Place, Gatehouse Way, Aylesbury, HP19 3UG. tel: (0296) 436557

SML Healthcare Ltd, Bath Place, High Street, Barnet, Herts EN5 5XE. tel: (081) 440 6522

Southern Sanitary Specialists, Cerdic House, West Portway, Andover, Hants SP10 3LF. tel: (0264) 24131/52534

James Spencer & Co Ltd, Moor Road Works, Moor Road, Headingley, Leeds, West Yorkshire LS6 4BH. tel (0532) 785837/741850

Su-Med International (UK) Ltd, 11 Beaumont Business Centre, Beaumont Close, Banbury, Oxon OX16 7TN. tel: (0295) 270499

JW Swain (Plastics) Ltd, Byron Street, Buxton, Derbyshire SK17 6LY. tel: (0298) 2365

Taskmaster Ltd, Morris Road, Leicester, LE2 6BR. tel: (0533) 704286

R Taylor & Son (Orthopaedic) Ltd, Compton Works, 49 Woodwards Road, Pleck, Walsall, WS2 9RN. tel: (0922) 27601

Tefal UK Ltd, 11–49 Station Road, Langley, Slough, Berks, SL3 8DR. tel: (0753) 44100 *(Details of retailers only from this address)*

DA Thomas (London) Ltd, 124–126 Denmark Hill, London SE5 8RX. tel: (071) 733 2101

Titan Tapes Ltd, Whitefield Road, Bredbury, Stockport, Cheshire SK6 2QR. tel: (061) 494 1344

Toys for the Handicapped, 76 Barracks Road, Sandy Lane Industrial Estate, Stourport-on-Severn, Worcs., DY13 9QB. tel: (0299) 827820

Triton PLc, Triton House, Weddington Industrial Estate, Nuneaton, Warwickshire CV10 0AG. tel: (0203) 344441

Trojan Plastics Ltd, Bracknell Works, Bradford Road, Huddersfield HD2 1DT. tel: (0484) 535724

Truflow Brassware Ltd, 102 Lichfield Street, Tamworth, Staffs B79 7QB. tel: (0827) 62621 and works (0827) 283827

Unit Installations, Unit 26, Yates Brothers, Lime Lane, Pelsall, Walsall. tel: (0543) 370383

Victor Hoists Ltd, High Acres, Hartford Bridge, Hartford, Norwich, Cheshire, CW8 1PP. tel: (0606) 74959

CA Wallgate & Co Ltd, Crow Lane, Wilton, Salisbury, Wiltshire SP2 0HB. tel: (0722) 743505

Wandsworth Electrical Ltd, Albert Drive, Sheerwater, Woking, Surrey, GU21 5SE. tel: (048 62) 27521

Warren Hooker UK Ltd, Unit 20 Chalwyn Industrial Estate, St Clements Road, Parkstone, Poole, Dorset BH15 3PF. tel: (0202) 721707/574655

Watershed, 575/577 London Road, Westcliffe-on-Sea, Essex SS0 9PQ. tel: (0702) 348568

WAVES, Corscombe, Nr Dorchester, Dorset, DT2 0NU. tel: (093 589) 248

Wessex Medical Equipment Co Ltd, Budds Lane, Romsey, Hants, SO51 0HA. tel: (0794) 522022

Worldwide Dryer Group, Durkan House, 155 East Barnet Road, New Barnet, Herts EN4 8QZ. tel: (081) 441 5675

GH Zeal Ltd, Lombard Road, Merton, London SW19 3UU. tel: (01) 542 2283

PERSONAL TOILET

Aidserve Ltd, Unit 106, Bradley Hall Trading Estate, Bradley Lane, Standish, Wigan WN6 0XQ. tel: (0257) 425538

Allia UK Ltd, Whieldon Road, Stoke on Trent, Staffordshire, ST4 4HN. tel: (0782) 49191

Alphabet Site Services Ltd, St Leonards, Ringwood, Hants, BH24 2RY

Amilake Ltd, Haslemere Industrial Estate, 20 Ravensbury Terrace, Wandsworth, London SW18 4SB. tel: (081) 947 7771

GEC Anderson Ltd, 89 Herkomer Road, Bushey, Hertfordshire, WD2 3LS. tel: (081) 950 1826

Anglia Vale Medical Ltd, Unit 7 Studlands Business Centre, Exning Road, Newmarket, Suffolk CB8 7EA. tel: (0638) 665140

Arema, Grove House, Lenham, Kent, ME17 2PX. tel: (0622) 858502

Armitage Shanks Ltd, Armitage, Rugeley, Staffs., WS15 4BT. tel: (0543) 490253

ASM Medicare, Picow Farm Industrial Estate, Runcorn, Cheshire, WA7 4UG. tel: (09285) 74301

Associated Metal Works Ltd, 30 St Andrews Square, Glasgow, Scotland, S1 5PJ. tel (041) 552 2004/5/6

Autumn Mobility Ltd, PO Box 18, Oldham, Lancashire, OL8 1XS. tel: (061) 627 5492 or (061) 652 5492. *Answerphone tel:* (061) 652 8996

B Line Industries, Kingston Works, 460 Beverley Road, Hull, HU5 1NF. tel: (0482) 42296/442223

Bencraft Ltd, The Avenue, Rubery, Rednal, Birmingham, W Midlands B45 9AP. Tel: (021) 453 1055/6/7

Blindcraft Dundee, 59 Magdalen Yard Road, Dundee, Tayside, DD1 4LJ. tel: (0382) 644433

Boots the Chemists Ltd, City Gate, Toll House Hill, Nottingham NG2 3AA. tel: (0602) 418522 *Enquiries should be made at local branches*

Boyco Products, Brook Road, Cheadle, Cheshire, SK8 1PQ. tel: (061) 428 7077

Brausch & Co (UK) Ltd, The Gate Centre, Great West Road, Brentford, Middlesex TW8 9DD. (081) 847 4455

Cabinmill Ltd, Newport Road, Market Drayton, Shropshire. Tel: (0630) 57288

Cannon Hygiene Ltd, Middlegate, White Lund, Morecambe, Lancs, LA3 3BJ. tel: (0524) 60894

Caradon Twyfords Ltd, Lawton Road, Alsager, Stoke-on-Trent, Staffordshire. tel: (0270) 879777

Carters (J&A) Ltd, Alfred Street, Westbury, Wiltshire, BA13 3DZ. tel: (0373) 822203

B Cartwright & Son Ltd, Mendy Street, High Wycombe, Bucks HP11 2EU. tel: (0494) 26780

Carter-Sport Services Ltd, Windsor House, Ansty Garage, Ansty, Coventry, West Midlands CV7 9JA. tel: (0203) 612569

CC Products Ltd, 152 Markham Road, Charminster, Bournemouth, Dorset BH9 1JE. tel: (0202) 522260

Cefndy Enterprises, Cefndy Road, Rhyl, Clwyd, LL18 2HG. tel: (0745) 343877

Cel Products Ltd, Glen Street Works, Glen Street, Hebburn, Tyne & Wear, NE31 1NE. tel: (091) 4835818

Chailey Heritage, Rehab Eng. Unit, Chailey Heritage Hospital & School, North Chailey, Lewes, E. Sussex, BN8 4EF. tel: (082 572) 2112 ext 210.

Chester-Care Ltd, 16 Englands Lane, London, NW3 4TG. tel: (071) 586 2166 or (071) 722 3430

Chiltern Medical Developments Ltd, Chiltern House, Wedgwood Road, Bicester, Oxon OX6 7UL. tel: (0869) 246470

Claudgen Ltd, Fulton Road, Wembley, Middlesex, HA9 0DF. tel: (081) 902 3682

Clos-O-Mat GB Ltd, 55 Waverley Road, Sale, Cheshire M33 1AY tel: (061) 905 1399

Cooper & Sons Ltd, Wormley, Godalming, Surrey, GU8 5SY. tel: (042 879) 2251

Cory (Pharmacy) Ltd, 166-168 High Road, East Finchley, London, N2 9AS. tel: (01) 444 7464

Crown Safegard (UK), Ashcroft House, Cobham, Surrey, KT11 2DN. tel: (0932) 67084

Days Medical Aids Ltd, Litchard Industrial Estate, Bridgend, Mid-Glamorga, CF31 2AL. tel: (0656) 57495/60150

Drainage Systems, Cray Avenue, Orpington, Kent BR5 3RQ. tel: (0689) 31311

Econa Appliances Ltd, Units 15-20, Coleshill Industrial Estate, Station Road, Coleshill, Birmingham B46 1JR. tel: (0675) 64460

Edincare Ltd, Unit 2, Tudor Enterprise Park, Tudor Road, Harrow, Mddx. HA3 5JQ. tel (081) 861 2700

Ellis, Gordon & Co., Trent Lane, Castle Donington, Derby, DE7 2PW. tel: (0332) 810504

Elsan Ltd, Buxted, Uckfield, East Sussex, TN22 4LW. tel: (082 581) 3291

Fixatrad Ltd, 763 Harrow Road, London, NW10 5NY. tel (01) 969 3232

Fordham Bathrooms & Kitchens Ltd, Fordham House, Dudley Road, Wolverhampton, West Midlands, WV2 4DS. tel (0902) 59123)

W Freeman & Co Ltd, Suba-Sea Works, Staincross, Barnsley, South Yorkshire, S75 6DH. tel: (0226) 284081

FC Frost Ltd, Bankside Works, Benfield Way, Braintree, Essex, CM7 6YS. tel: (0376) 29111

Gallops Hospital Equipment, Finmere Road, Eastbourne, East Sussex BN21 8QG. tel: (0323) 646681

Ganmill Ltd, 38/40 Market Street, Bridgewater, Somerset, TA6 3EP. tel: (0278) 423037

Goodearl-Risboro Ltd., PO Box 2, Princes Risborough, Bucks, HP17 9DP. tel (084 44) 3311

A W Gregory & Co Ltd, Glynde House, Glynde Street, London, SE4 1RY. tel: (081) 690 3437

A & J Gummers Ltd., 16 Pentos Drive, Formans Road, Birmingham B11 3AT. tel: (021) 778 2241

Harrison Thompson & Co Ltd., Yeoman House, Whitehall Estate, Whitehall Road, Lereds LS12 5JB. tel: (0532) 795854

Hartana Developments Ltd (Hassa Div), 21 Kingsland High Street, Dalston, London E8 2JS. tel: (071) 254 9084

Health & Comfort Ltd, PO Box 15, Westbury, Wiltshire, BA13 4LS. tel: (0373) 822394

The Helping Hand Company (Ledbury) Ltd, Unit 9L, Bromyard Road Trading Estate, Ledbury, Hertfordshire HR8 1NS. tel: (0531) 5678

Herga Electric Ltd, Northern Way, Bury-St-Edmunds, Suffolk, IP32 6NN. tel: (0284) 701422

Hewi (UK) Ltd, Scimitar Close, Gillingham Business Park, Gillingham, Kent, ME8 0RN. tel: (0634) 377688

SR Holbrook Ltd, Jackson Road, Coventry, CV6 4LY. tel: (0203) 667 576

Home Nursing Supplies Ltd, Headquarters Road, West Wilts Trading Estate, Westbury, Wilts, BA13 4JR tel: (0373) 822313

Homecraft Supplies Ltd, Low Moor Estate, Kirby-in-Ashfield, Notts NG17 7JZ. tel: (0623) 754 047

Hoskins Ltd, Upper Trinity Street, Birmingham B9 4EQ. tel tel: (021) 773 1144

Hughes & Hughes Ltd, Elms Industrial Estate, Church Road, Harold Woods, Romford, Essex, RM3 0HR. tel: (040 23) 49017

Ideal Standard Ltd, PO Box 60, National Avenue, Kingston-upon-Hull, HU5 4JE. tel: (0482) 46461

Industrial Cleaning Papers Ltd, Manchester House, Church Way, Church Stretton, Shropshire, SY6 6DJ. tel (0694) 723601

Innovention Products Ltd, The Business Centre, Colne Way, Watford, Herts, WD2 4ND. tel: (0923) 245050

Joncare Ltd, 7 Ashville Trading Estate, Nuffield Way, Abingdon, OX14 1RL. tel: (0235) 28120/35600

Keep Able Ltd, Fleming Close, Park Farm, Wellingborough, Northants NN8 3BR. tel: (0933) 679426

Landsmans Ltd, Buckden, Huntingdon, Cambridgeshire PE18 9UJ. tel: (0480) 81287

Leyland Medical Ltd, 15 Colweston Crescent, London E8. tel: (071) 254 6571

Llewellyn Health Care Services, Regent House, 1 Regent Road, City, Liverpool L3 7BX. tel: (051) 236 5311

Albert Marston & Co Ltd, Wellington Works, Planetary Road, Willenhall, W Midlands, WV13 3ST. tel: (0902) 305511

Masterpeace Products Ltd, Tormen House, Booth Hill Works, Booth Hill Lane, Oldham, OL1 2PH tel: (061) 624 2041

G McLoughlin & Co Ltd, Victoria Works, Oldham Road, Rochdale, Lancs, OL11 1DF. tel: (0706) 49911

Medeci Rehab Ltd, Research Unit, Warley Hospital, Brentwood, Essex CM14 5HQ. tel: (0277) 212637

Medic-Bath Ltd, PO Box 12, Ashfield Works, Hulme Hall Lane, Manchester, M10 8AB. tel: (061) 7495

Medical Resupply UK Ltgd, Homewoodgate House, Novington Lane, East Chitgtington, Lewes, East Sussex BN7 3AU. tel: (0273) 890303

Medimail, JL Owen Ltd, FREEPOST, Manchester, M4 8BP. tel: (061) 236 0896

Metlex Industries Ltd, Metlex House, 29 Vicarage Road, Croydon, Surrey, CR9 3BQ. tel: (081) 688 1133

Midequip Services, 199 Upperdale Road, Derby, Derbyshire DE3 8BS. tel: (0332) 767981

Myson Ryders Ltd, Victoria Works, Nelson Street, Bolton, Lancs, BL3 2DW. tel: (0204) 382017

Nesbit Evans, J And Co Ltd, Woden Road West, Wednesbury, West Midlands, WS10 7BL. tel: (021) 556 1511

Nicholls & Clarke Ltd, 3/10 Shoreditch High Street, London,E1 6PE. tel (071) 247 5432

Norton Engineering Alloys Company Ltd, Norton Grove Industrial Estate, Norton, Malton, Yorkshire Y017 9HQ. tel: (0653) 695721

Nottingham Rehab Ltd, 17 Ludlow Hill Road, West Bridgford, Nottingham, NG2 6HD. tel: (0602) 234251

Ortho-Med Ltd, 5 Loaning Road, Edinburgh, EH7 6JE. tel: (031) 652 1603

P & H Enterprises Ltd, FREEPOST, 15 South Lane, New Malden, Surrey, KT3 5BR. tel: (081) 942 9094

Palindon Ltd, 1 High Street, Wargrave, Berkshire, RG10 8JQ. tel: (073 522) 3327

Parker Anderson, Mullions, Lymington Road, Milford-on-Sea, Hampshire, S04 10QN. tel: (0590) 43839

Parker Bath Developments Ltd, Queensway, Stem Lane Industrial Estate, New Milton, Hants, BH25 5NN tel: (0425) 617598

Park House (Distributors) Ltd., Blackburn Road, Birstall, Bateley, West Yorkshire, WF17 9PL. tel: (0924) 441881

Permapure Commercial Ltd, Unit 5, 44 Southside, Clapham Common, London SW4 9BU. tel: (071) 627 5427

Pilot Hire Ltd, Wimpey Estate, Lancaster Road, Southall, Middlesex UB1 1NR. tel: (081) 574 3882

PJP Trading Ltd, 151 Dixons Hill Road, North Mymms, Hatfield, Hertfordshire AL9 7JE. tel: (07072) 66726/73573

Portasilo Ltd, Huntington, York, YO3 9PR. tel: (0904) 624872

Powell Sea Co Ltd, 70 Lodge Lane, Derby, Derbyshire, DE1 3HB. tel: (0322) 47757

Pressalit Ltd, 25 Grove Promenade, Ilkley, West Yorkshire LS29 8AF. tel: (0943) 607651

Prudence Distribution, Nath House, Whitemore, Congleton, Cheshire, CW12 3NE. tel: (0782) 511552

Pryor & Howard Ltd, 39 Willow Lane, Mitcham, Surrey, CR4 4US. tel: (081) 648 1177

Remploy Ltd (Medical Products Div) & Head Office, 415 Edgware Road, Cricklewood, London NW2 6LR. tel (081) 452 8020

Renray Group Ltd, Road Five, Winsford Industrial Estate, Winsford, Cheshire, CW7 3RB. tel: (0606) 593456

Rentaloo Ltd, Denaport House, 57 Guildford Street, Luton, Beds W1 2NL. tel: (0582) 402 610

Rentokil Ltd, (Sanitact Service), Felcourt, East Grinstead, West Sussex RH19 2JY. tel (0342) 833022

Roma Medical Aids Ltd, Llandow Industrial Estate, Cowbridge, South Glamorgan, CF7 7PB. tel: (044 63) 4519

WS Rothband & Co Ltd, 21 Elizabeth Street, Manchester, Greater Manchester, M8 8WT. tel: (061) 834 1303

Royal Association for Disability & Rehabilitation, 25 Mortimer Street, London W1N 8AB. (071) 637 5400

Saniflo Ltd, Howard House, The Runway, Off Station Approach, South Ruislip, Middlesex HA4 6SE. tel: (081) 842 0033

Sanitary Appliances Ltd, 3 Sandiford Road, Kimpton Industrial Estate, Sutton, Surrey, SM3 9RN. tel (081) 641 0310

Santic Ltd, Hawksworth, Swindon, Wilts, SN2 1DZ. tel: (0793) 36756

Saville Stainless Ltd, P O Box 74, Altrincham, Cheshire, WA14 3RP. tel: (0565) 830156

William G Search Ltd, Whitehall Road, Lees, W Yorkshire, LS12 6EP. tel: (0532) 639081

Self-Lift Chair Co, Mahler House, 130 Worcester Road, Droitwich Spa, Worcester. tel: (0905) 778116

Shackletons (Carlinghow) Ltd, 501 Bradford Road, Batley, West Yorkshire WF17 8LN. tel: (0924) 474430

Shires Ltd, Guisley, Leeds LS20 8AP. tel: (0943) 870055

Sidhil, Boothtown, Halifax, Yorkshire HX3 6NT. tel: (0422) 63447

Simcare, Eschmann Bros & Walsh Ltd, Personal Products Division, Peter Road, Lancing, West Sussex BN15 8TJ. tel: (0903) 761122

W & G Sissons Ltd, Calver Mill, Calver Bridge, Sheffield S30 1XA. tel: (0433) 30791

SML Healthcare Ltd, Bath Place, High Street, Barnet, Herts EN5 5XE. tel (081) 440 6522

Southalls Hygiene Services, Alum Rock Road, Birmingham, B8 3DZ. Tel: (021) 327 4750

Southern Mobile Ltd, 53 School Lane, Bushey, Herts WD2 1BY. tel: (081) 950 5051

Southern Sanitary Specialists, Cerdic House, West Portway, Andover, Hants SP10 3LF. tel: (0264) 24131/52534

James Spencer & Co Ltd, Moor Road Works, Moor Road, Headingley, Leeds, LS6 4BH. tel: (0532) 78537/41850

Hugh Steeper (Roehampton) Ltd, 237-239 Roehampton Lane, London, SW15 4LB. tel: (081) 788 8165

Street Equipment Ltd, Unit 4, Goldhawk Industrial Estate, 2A. Brackenbury Road, London, W6 0BA. tel: (081) 749 3906

JW Swain (Plastics) Ltd, Byron Street, Buxton, Derbyshire SK17 6LY. tel: (0298) 2365

Talley Group Ltd, 47 Theobald Street, Borehamwood, Herts, WD6 4RT. tel: (081) 953 7171

Taw Manufacturing Co Ltd, Campsbourne Works, High Street, Hornsey, London, N8 7PP. tel (081) 340 6293

Thackraycare, 45-47 Great George St, Leeds LS1 3BB. tel: (0532) 430028

DA Thomas (London) Ltd, 124-126 Denmark Hill, London SE5 8RX. tel (081) 733 2101

Throne Designs Ltd, Unit 4, 25 The Avenue, Cirencester, Glos., GL7 1EE. tel: (0793) 771321

Tweedy of Burnley Ltd, Peel Mill, Gannow Lane, Burnley, Lancs, BB12 6JL. tel: (0282) 27921

Unit Installations, Unit 26, Yates Brothers, Lime Lane, Pelsall, Walsall. tel: (0543) 370383

TC Vere Ltd, St. Christopher House, 325-327 Cricket Inn Road, Sheffield S2 5AV. tel: (0742) 728 005/6

Vernon & Co. (Pulp Products) Ltd, Slater Street, Bolton, Lancs BL1 2HP. tel: (0204) 29494. *Supply to Hospitals Only.*

Vessa Ltd, Paper Mill Lane, Alton, Hants, GU34 2PY. tel (0420) 83294

Wandsworth Electrical Ltd, Albert Drive, Sheerwater, Woking, Surrey, GU21 5SE. tel: (048 62) 27521

Warne-Franklin, P O Box 138, Cressex Industrial Estate, High Sycombe, Bucks, HP12 3NB. tel: (0494) 3261

Warren Hooker UK. Ltd., Unit 20 Chalwyn Industrial Estate, St. Clements Road, Parkstone, Poole, Dorset, BH15 3PF. tel: (0202) 721707/574655

AJ Way and Co Ltd, Riverlock House, Spring Gardens Road, High Sycombe, Bucks, HP13 7AG. tel: (0494) 27507

Zimmer Ltd, Dunbeath Road, Elgin Industrial Estate, Swindon, Wilts SN2 6EA. tel: (0793) 481441

PRESSURE RELIEF

3M Health Care, 3M United Kingdom plc, 1 Morley Street, Loughborough, Leicestershire, LE11 1EP. tel: (0509) 611611

Anglia Vale Medical Ltd, Unit 7, Studlands Business Centre, Exning Road, Newmarket, Suffolk CB8 7EA tel: (0638) 665140

Antler Plc, Plastics Division, Western Way, Exeter, Devon EX1 2AA. Tel (0392) 51002

Aremco, Grove House, Lenham, Kent ME17 2PX. tel: (0622) 858502

Arjo Mecanaids Ltd, St. Catherine Street, Gloucester, GL1 2SL. tel: (0452) 500200

Arterial Medical Services Ltd, Arterial House, 313 Chase Road, Southgate, London, N14 6JH. tel: (081) 882 4434

Astec Environmental Systems Ltd, 31 Lynx Crescent, Weston-Super-Mare, Avon BS24 9DJ.tel: (0934) 418685

Bay Jacobsen (UK) Ltd, Auriema House, 442 Bath Road, Slough, SL1 6BB. tel: (06286) 4049

Anthony Bayles (Medical) Ltd, Prospect Road, Alresford, Hampshire SO24 9QF. tel: (096 273) 3289/3025

Jane Bertram Products, The Gorse House, Grimston, Melton Mowbray, Leics, LE14 3BZ. tel: (0644) 812751

Boots the Chemist Ltd, City Gate, Toll House Hill, Nottingham NG2 3AA. tel: (0602) 418522 *Enquiries should be made at local branches*

British Astec (Medical), Eagle Works, Eagle Lane, Great Bridge, Tipton, West Midlands DY4 7AZ. tel: (021) 520 7201

Camp Ltd, Northgate House, Staple Gardens, Winchester, Hampshire, SO23 8ST. tel (0962) 55248

Carters (J&A) Ltd, Alfred Street, Westbury, Wiltshire, BA13 3DZ tel: (0373) 822203

Chester-Care Ltd, 16 Englands Lane, London NW3 4TG. tel: (081) 722 3430

Chiltern Medical Developments Ltd, Chiltern House, Wedgewood Road, Bicester, Oxon OX6 7UL. tel: (0869) 246470

Comfy Products, 29 Havelock Crescent, Bridlington, East Yorkshire, YO16 4JH. tel: (0262) 676417/400062

Coventry Motor and Sundries Co Ltd., Spon End, Coventry CV1 3GY. tel: (0203)20363

Cumbria Orthopaedic Ltd, Floor 6, Shaddon Mill, Shaddongate, Carlisle, Cumbria CA2 5TY. tel: (0228) 29774

Robert Davenport and Co Ltd, Ravenscliffe Mills, Calverley, Pudsey, West Yorkshire, LS28 5RY. tel: (0274) 612541

Days Medical Aids Ltd, Litchard Industrial Estate, Bridgend, Mid-Glamorgan, CF31 2AL tel: (0656) 57495/60150

Easirider Co Ltd, Dolphin House, 188 Kettering Road, Northampton, Northants NN1 4BH. tel: (0604) 30833/30426

Egerton Hospital Equipment Ltd, Tower Hill, Horsham, West Sussex, RH13 7JT. tel: (0403) 53800

Engments Ltd, Chequers Road, West Meadows Industrial Estate, Derby, DE2 6EN. tel: (0332) 44579

Everest & Jennings Ltd., Princewood Road, Corby, Northants NN17 2DX. Tel: (0536) 67661

First Technicare Ltd, 20 Abercorn Place, London NW8 9 XP. tel: (071) 609 8761 *Bulk suppliers to NHS*

W Freeman & Co Ltd, Suba-Seal Works, Staincross, Barnsley, South Yorkshire, S75 6DH. tel: (0226) 284081

E & R Garrould Ltd, 7 Hardwicks Way, London, SW18 4AN. tel: (071) 262 2675

Gimson-Tendercare, 62 Boston Road, Beaumont Leys, Leicester LE4 1AZ. tel: (0533) 366779

Gosling Medical Supplies Ltd, Unit 4, Brindley Road, Gorse Lane Industrial Estate, Clacton-on-Sea, Essex CO15 4XP. tel (0255) 424484

AW Gregory & Co Ltd, Glynde House, Glynde Street, London, SE4 1RY. tel: (081) 690 3437

Hawksley & Son Ltd, Marlborough Road, Lancing, West Sussex BM15 8TN tel: (0903) 752815

Health & Comfort Ltd, PO Box 15, Westbury, Wiltshire, BA13 4LS. tel: (0373) 822394

The Helping Hand Company (Ledbury) Ltd, Unit 9L, Bromyard Road Trading Estate, Ledbury, Hertfordshire HR8 1NS. tel: (0531) 5678

Henleys Medical Supplies Ltd, Brownfields, Welwyn Garden City, Herts AL7 1AN. tel: (0707) 333164

SR Holbrook Ltd, Jackson Road, Coventry, CV6 4LY. tel: (0203) 667 576

Home Nursing Supplies Ltd, Headquarters Road, West Wilts Trading Estate, Westbury, Wilts, BA13 4JR. tel: (0373) 822313

Homecraft Supplies Ltd, Low Moor Estate, Kirkby-in-Ashfield, Notts NG17 7JZ. tel: (0623) 754 047

Huntleigh Technology Plc, Healthcare Division, 310-312 Dallow Road, Luton, Bedfordshire LU1 1SS. tel: (0582) 413104/459000

Independence, 52 Exeter Road, Exmouth, Devon EX8 1PY. tel: (0395) 268555

Joncare Ltd, 7 Ashville Trading Estate, Nuffield Way, Abingdon, Oxon OX14 1RL. tel: (0235) 28120/35600

Keep Able Ltd, Fleming Close, Park Farm, Wellingborough, Northants NN8 3BR. tel: (0933) 679426

R Kellie & Son Ltd, Rutherford Road, Dryburgh Industrial Estate, Dundee, Scotland, DD2 3XF. tel: (0382) 816722

Kennick Medical, 3 King Edward Road, Oldfield Park, Bath, Avon. BA2 3PB. tel: (0225) 707786

Leyland Medical International Ltd, 15 Colvestone Crescent, Dalston, London, E8 2LN. tel: (071) 254 6571

Llewellyn Health Care Services, Regent House, 1 Regent Road, City, Liverpool L3 7BX. tel: (051) 236 5311

M & F Systems, 35/37 Grosvenor Road, Aldershot, Hants, GU11 3DP. tel: (0252) 29551

Macarthy Medical Ltd, Selinas Lane, Dagenham, Essex. Tel: (081) 593 7511

Maynard Projects, 72 The Lane, Hauxton, Cambridgeshire, CB2 5HP. tel: (0223) 871645

Medical Support Systems, 23 Argyle Way, Ely Distribution Centre, Cardiff CF5 5NJ. tel (0222) 595425

Medipost Ltd, Unit 1, St Johns Estate, Elder Road, Lees, Oldham, Lancs OL4 3DZ tel: (061) 678 0233

Mediscus Products Ltd, 10 Westminster Road, Wareham, Dorset, BH20 4SP. tel: (092 95) 6311

Meditech Developments Ltd, Lenton Buysiness Centre, Lenton Boulevard, Nottingham NG7 2BY. tel: (0602) 784194

Nesbit Evans, J And Co Ltd, Woden Road West, Wednesbury, West Wednesbury, West Midlands WS10 7BL. tel: (021) 556 1511

Nottingham Rehab Ltd, 17 Ludlow Hill Road, West Bridgford, Nottingham, NG2 6HD. tel: (0602) 234251

Jonathan Oak Ltd, The Old Bakery, Basingstoke Road, Spencers Wood, Reading RG7 1AA tel: (0734) 883643

Paraglide Ltd, 2 Churwell Avenue, Heaton Mersey, Stockport, Cheshire SK4 3QE. tel: (061) 432 7315

Park House (Distributors) Ltd, Blackburn Road, Birstall, Batley, West Yorkshire WF17 9PL. tel: (0924) 441881

Peacocks (Surgical & Medical Equipment) Ltd, Hobson Ind. Estate, Burnopfield, Newcastle NE16 6EA. tel: (0207) 71160

Pegasus Airwave Ltd, Pegasus House, Kingscroft Court, Havant, Hants PO9 1LS. tel: (0705) 451444

Power-Tech (UK) Ltd, Unit 8c, Ford Airfield Industrial Estate, Yapton, Arundel, West Sussex, BN18 0HY. tel: (0903) 713227

Raymar, P O Box 16 Fairview Estate, Reading Road, Henley-on-Thames, Oxon. RG9 1LL. tel: (0491) 578446

Reylon Ltd, Wellington, Somerset, TA21 8NN. tel: (082 347) 7501

Remploy Ltd (Medical Products Div) & Head Office, 415 Edgware Road, Cricklewood, London2 6LR. tel: (081) 452 8020

Renray Group Ltd, Road Five, Winsford Industrial Estate, Winsford, Cheshire, CW7 3RB. tel: (0606) 593456

Richardson (Liverpool) Ltd, Howe Street, Liverpool, L20 8NG. tel: (051) 922 6511

Roma Medical Aids Ltd, Llandow Industrial Estate, Cowbridge, South Glamorgan, CF7 7PB. tel: (044 63) 4519

WS Rothband & Co Ltd, 21 Elizaabeth Street, Manchester, Greater Manchester, M8 8WT. tel: (061) 834 1303

Scanmark, 43/44 Debden Road, Newport, Essex, CB11 3RU. tel: (0799) 41081

Seton Healthcare Group, Tubiton House, Medlock Street, Oldham OL1 3HS. tel: (061) 652 2222

Shackletons (Carlinghow) Ltd, 501 Bradford Road, Batley, West Yorkshire WF17 8LN. tel: (0924) 474430

Shelley Textiles Ltd, Barncliffe Mills, Shelley, Huddersfield, West Yorkshire, HD8 8LU. tel: (0484) 604336

Sidhil, Boothtown, Halifax, West Yorkshire, HX3 6NT. tel: (0422) 63447

Gerald Simonds Healthcare Stoke Mandeville, 9 March Place, Gatehouse Way, Aylesbury, Buckinghamshire HP19 3UG. tel (0296)436557

Slumberland Medicare, Hallam Field Road, Ilkestone, Derbyshire DE7 4BQ. tel: (0602) 440359

SML Healthcare Ltd, Bath Place, High Street, Barnet, Herts EN5 5XE. tel (081) 440 6522

James Spencer & Co Ltd, Moor Road Works, Moor Road, Headingley, Leeds, West Yorkshire LS6 4BH. tel:(0532) 785837/741850

Spenco Medical UK Ltd, Burrell Road, Haywards Heath, West Sussex RH16 1TW. tel: (0444) 415171

SSI Medical Services Ltd, Finch Close, Lenton Industrial Estate, Nottingham, NG7 2NN. tel: (0602) 866433

SSL Patient-Care, Standard House, Banks Lane, Bexley Heath, Kent, DA6 7BH. tel: (081) 301 1666

Hugh Steeper (Roehampton) Ltd, 237-239 Roehampton Lane, London, SW15 4LB. tel: (081) 788 8165

Su-Med International (UK) Ltd, 11 Beaumont Business Centre, Beaumont Close, Banbury, Oxon, OX16 7TN. tel: (0295) 270499

Sunrise Medical Ltd, Fens Pool Avenue, Brierley Hill, West Midlands, DY5 1QA. tel: (0384) 48080

Surgicon Ltd, Wakefield Road, Brighouse, West Yorkshire, HD6 1QL. tel:(0484) 712147

T and S Motion and Sport, Head Office, Potter Lane, Wellow, Via Newark, Notts NG22 0EB. tel: (0623) 835362

Talley Group Ltd, 47 Theobald Street, Borehamwood, Hertfordshire WD6 4RT. tel: (081) 953 7171

Tescan Ltd, Carn Tannery, Wilson Way, Redruth, Cornwall. TR15 3RX. tel: (0209) 214101

Thackraycare, 45-47 Great George St, Leeds LS1 3BB. tel: (0532) 430028

Ultra Laboratories Ltd, Tribune Drive, Sittingbourne, Kent ME10 2PG. tel (0795) 70953

Universal Hospital Supplies, 313 Chase Road, Southgate, London, N14 6JB. tel: (081) 882 6444/5/6/7

University of Salford, The Secretary, Department of Orthopaedic Mechanics, Salford, Greater Manchester, M5 4WT. tel: (061) 736 5843 ext 7402

Wards Mobility Services Ltd, Ware Works, Bells Yew Green, Tunbridge Wells, TN3 9BD. tel: (089 275) 686

Waterbed Rest, 33 Elm Walk, Radlett, Herts WD7 8DP. tel: (0923) 854331

WAVES, Corscombe, Nr. Dorchester, Dorset, DT2 ONU. tel: (093 589) 248

Zimmer Ltd, Dunbeath Road, Elgin Industrial Estate, Swindon, Wilts SN2 6EA tel: (0793) 481441

TRANSPORT

AA Insurance Services, PO Box 2AA, Newcastle-upon-Tyne, NE99 2AA. tel: (091) 261 2345 ext. 8937/89513/89530

AA St John Alert, Coppenhagen Court, New Street, Basingstoke, RG21 1DT. tel: (0256) 842121

Adaptacar, Cookscross, South Molton, North Devon, EX36 4AW. tel:(076 95) 2785

Advanced Vehicle Builders, Upper Mantle Close, Clay Cross, Derbyshire S45 9NU. tel: (0246) 250022

Aid Vehicle Supplies, Hockley Industrial Centre, Hooley Lane, PO Box 26, Redhill RH1 6JF. tel: (0737) 770032

Alder Valley South Ltd, Wheels Within Wheels, Private Hire Department, Halimote Road, Aldershot, Hants. GU11 3EG. tel: (0252) 27181 ext. 261

Ambucare, Private Ambulance, Ambulance Station, 7 Toll House Road, Cannington, Nr. Bridgwater, Somerset TA5 2NW. tel: (0278) 653129

Amicable Insurance Consultants, 40 The Broadway, Crawley, W. Sussex, RH10 1HG. tel: (0293) 561233

AMK, The Springs, Conford, Liphook, Hampshire GU30 7QN. tel: (042877) 256 or (042877) 675

Ken Anderton, 44 Penny Lane, Haydock, Merseyside WA11 0QS. tel: (0942) 720738

Apex Doors Ltd, Crown Lane, Horwich, Bolton, BL6 5HP. tel: (0204) 68151

Aremco, Grove House, Lenham, Kent, ME17 2PX. tel: (0622) 858502

Ashley Healthcare Ltd, 71 Allesley Street, Birmingham, B6 4ND. tel: (021) 333 3362

Atlas Conversions Ltd, 75 Alverstone Road, Milton, Portsmouth, PO4 8TG. tel: (0705) 756265

Austin Rover, Mobility Sales Department, Austin Rover Group, PO Box 395, Longbridge, Birmingham B31 2TB. tel: (021) 475 2101

Auto Safety Centres, Trafford House, Chester Road, Stretford, Manchester M32 2ORS. tel: (061) 872 5321

Autochair, Millford Lane, Bakewell, Derbyshire DE4 1DX. tel: (0629) 813493

Autohome Ltd, 202/204, Kettering Road, Northampton, Northants. NN1 4HE. tel: (0604) 28730

Automobile & Industrial Developments Ltd, Queensdale Works, Queensthrope Road, Sydenham, London SE26 4JP. tel: (081) 698 3451

Automobile Association, Head Office, Fanum House, Basingstoke, Hants., RG21 2EA. tel: (0256) 20123

Avialift Products Ltd, Southend Airport, Southend on Sea, Essex SS2 67P. tel: (0702) 348691

Banstead Mobility Centre, Park Road, Banstead, Surrey SM7 3EE. tel: (0737) 351674/356222

Barker Fresson (London) Ltd, The McLaren Building, 35 Dale End, Birmingham B4 7NS. tel: (021) 2331631

Barras Garages Ltd, Walker's Island Garage, Greenway Road, Runcorn WA7 5AW. tel: (09285) 63434

Bay Jacobsen (UK) Ltd, Auriema House, 442 Bath Road, Slough, SL1 6BB. tel: (06286) 4049

Beacon Associates Ltd, 65a. Sheen Lane, London SW14. tel: (081) 878 7060

Alred Bekker, The Green, Langtoft, Nr. Driffield, North Humberside Y025 OTF. tel: (0377) 87276

Berks Bucks Bus Company Ltd, Bus Station, The Wharf, Newbury, Berks. RG14 5AS. tel: (0635) 40743

Birch Products Ltd, 37 Homewood Avenue, Cuffley, Potters Bar, Herts. EB6 4QQ. tel: (0707) 873075

Brig-Ayd Controls, Warrengate, Tewin, Welwyn, Herts, AL6 0JD. tel: (043 871) 4206 *(Contact: Mr Briggs)*

Britax-Excelsior Ltd, 1 Churchill Way West, Andover, Hants SP10 3UW. tel: (09264) 333343

British Nursing Association, Head Office, North Place, 82 Great North Road, Hatfield, Herts. AL9 5BL. tel: (070 72) 63544

British Red Cross Society - London, 3 Grosvenor Crescent, London SW1X 7EJ. tel: (071) 235 3241

British Safety Council Sales Ltd, National Safety Centre, Chancellors Road, London W6 9RS. tel: (081) 748 7480/1231

Broadway (Mobility), Unit 9 The Arches, Sherwood Road, South Harrow, Middlesex HA 8 AU. tel: (081) 423 0641

Brotherwood Automobility Ltd, Station Garage, Yetminster, Sherborne, Dorset DT9 6LH. tel: (0935) 872603

S Burvill & Son, Primrose Road, Hersham, Walton-on-Thames, Surrey, KT12 5JD. tel: (0932) 221124/227454

Buss Mobility Designs Ltd, 102 Ashford Road, Bearsted, Maidstone, Kent, ME14 4LX. tel: (0622) 37012

C-Baq Ltd, 47 Brunswick Centre, London WC1 1AF. tel: (081) 203 6325

Cabs Ltd, 15 Hales Industrial Park, Rowleys Green Lane, Rowleys Green, Coventry CV6 6AN tel: (0203) 689670

Car Chair Ltd, Station Road Industrial Estate, Hailsham, East Sussex BN27 2ES. tel: (60323) 840283

Carbodies Ltd, Holyhead Road, Coventry CV5 8JJ. tel: (0203) 595001

Cardale Doors Ltd, Buckingham Road Industrial Estate, Brackley, Northants NN13 5EA. tel: (0280) 703022

Carmobility, Littlemead House, Blue Ball Works, Colaton Raleigh, Sidmouth, Devon EX10 OLB. tel: (0393) 68830

Carrychair, 6 Hilton Drive, Prestwich, Manchester, M25 8NN. tel: (061) 737 7121

Catnic Components Ltd, Garador Division, PO Box 8, CaERPHILLY, Mid Glamorgan, CF8 2WJ. tel: (0222) 885955

Chailey Heritage, Rehab Engineering Unit, Chailey Heritage Hospital and School, North Chailey, Lewes, East Sussex, BN8 4EF. tel: (082 572) 2112 ext. 210

Chester-Care Ltd, 16 Englands Lane, London NW3 4TG. tel: (071) 586 2166

City Vehicle Engineering Ltd, Hackworth Industrial Park, Shildon, County Durham DL4 1HF. tel: (0388) 775115

Cleveland Spastics Work & Welfare Centre, Acklam Road, Middlesbrough, Cleveland, TS5 4EG. tel: (0642) 818854

Coachwork Walker Ltd, Norfolk Street, Colne, Lancs BB8 9JW. tel: (0282) 866724

Coldstream Cycles, The Lees Stables, Coldstream, Berwickshire TN12 4NN. tel: (0890) 2709 or 3167

Combined Optical Industries Ltd, 200 Bath Road, Slough, Berks, SL1 4DW. tel: (0753) 75011

Complete Mobility Ltd, 56 Walton Way, Shaw, Newbury, Berks RG13 2LJ. tel: (0635) 580247

Consumer Insurance Services, 2 Osborns Court, High Street South, Olney, Bucks. MK46 4AB. tel: (0234) 713535

Continental Caravan Conversions, Parkengue, Kernick Industrial Estate, Penry, Cornwall TR10 9EP. tel: (0326) 77474

Corbeau Equipe Ltd, Invyhouse Industrial Area, Hastings TN35 4NN. tel (0434) 435480

Corbridge Fabrication Ltd, Bourne Works, Collingbourne Ducis, Nr. Marlborough, Wilts. SN8 3EH. tel: (026485) 813

Cowal Mobility Aids Ltd, 32 New Pond Road, Holmer Green, High Wycombe, Bucks, HP15 6SU. tel: (0494) 714400

Crelling Harnesses for the Disabled, 11-12 The Crescent, Cleveleys, Lancs. FY5 3LJ. tel: (0253) 852298/821780

WB Cunliffe & Son (Coachbuilders) Ltd, Unit G2, Europa Trading Estate, Stoneclough Road, Radcliffe, Manchester M26 9HE. tel: (0204) 73308

Davis Garages, St. Johns Hill, Sevenoaks, Kent, TN13 3NY. tel: (0732) 455174

Department of Social Security (N9), Block 3, Government Buildings, Warbeck Hill Road, Blackpool FY2 0YF.

Department of Trade and Industry, Radiocommunications Division, Licensing Section Room 712, Waterloo Bridge House, Waterloo Road, London SE1 8UA. tel: (071) 215 2316

Department of Transport Head Office, 2 Marsham Street, London SW1P 3EB. tel: (071) 212 4431

Derby Disabled Driving Centre, Kingsway Hospital, Kingsway, Derby, DE3 3LZ. tel: (0332) 371929

Devon Conversions (CP) Ltd, Vulcan Works, Water Lane, Exeter, Devon EX2 8BY. tel: (0392) 211611

Disabled Driving Training Centre, BSM Specialist Services Ltd, 81-87 Hartfield Road, Wimbledon, London SW19 3TJ. tel: (081) 540 8262

Disabled Drivers Association, 18 Creekside, London SE8 3DZ. tel:(081) 692 7141 or registered office, Ashwellthorpe, Norwich NR16 1EX. tel: (050 841) 449

Disabled Drivers Insurance Bureau, 292 Hale Lane, Edgware, Middlesex, HA8 8NP. tel: (081) 958 3135

Disabled Drivers Motor Club, Cottingham Way, Thrapston, Northants NN14 4PL. tel: (08012) 4724

Disabled Motorists Federation, National Mobility Centre, Unit 2A, Atcham Estate, Upton Magna, Shrewsbury, Shropshire, SY4 4UG. tel: (074 375) 889

Dodds Garage, Automobile Engineers, Moorfield Industrial Estate, High Street, Yeadon, Leeds LS19 7BN tel: (0532) 502835

Dormobile Ltd, Tile Kiln Lane, Folkestone, Kent, CT19 4PD. tel: (0303) 276321

Driver & Vehicle Licensing Centre, Drivers Medical Branch, Swansea SA99 1TU. tel: (0792) 304000

Easi-Lift Ltd, Unit 5, St. Georges Industrial Estate, Frimley Road, Camberley, Surrey,GU15 2QW. tel: (0276) 21175

Easirider Co Ltd, Dolphin House, 188 Kettering Road, Northampton NN1 4BH. tel: (0604) 30833/30426

Easyreach, 1 Innisfree Close, Harrogate HG2 8PL. tel: (0423) 883811

Elap Engineering Ltd, 43 King Street, Accrington, Lancs BB5 1QE. tel: (0254) 871599

Electric Mobility Corporation, Sea King Road, Lynx Trading Estate, Yeovil, Somerset BA20 2NZ. tel: (0935) 22156

Electric Vehicle Association, Aberdeen House, Headley Road, Grayshott, Hindhead, Surrey GU26 6LA. tel: (042 873) 5536

Electricars Ltd, Carlyon Road Industrial Estate, Atherstone, Warwks CV9 lLQ. tel: (0827) 716889

Ellard Sliding Door Gears Ltd, Works Road, Letchworth Garden City, Herts, SG6 1NN tel: (0462) 678421

Europ Assistance Ltd, 252 High Street, Croydon, Surrey CRO 1NF. tel: (081) 680 1234

Evans Halshaw (Bristol), Victoria House, Temple Gate, Bristol BS1 6PR. tel: (0272) 294222

Expec-Roper UK, Mechanical & Development Engineers, Garveston, Norwich, Norfolk NR9 4QT. tel: (0362) 850205

Farnley House Enterprises, 32 Farnley Road, London SE25 6NX. tel: (081) 653 1782

FDTS Ltd, Highfields Works, West Byfleet Corner, West Byfleet, Surrey, KT14 6LP. tel: (093 23) 42043

Feenyh & Johnson Ltd, Alperton Lane, Wembley, Middlesex HA0 1JJ. tel: (081) 998 4458

MJ Fish & Co, 3 Rivers Way Business Village, Navigation Way, Ashton-on-Ribble, Preston, Lancs. PR2 2YT. tel: (0772) 724442

Ford Personal Import Export Ltd. (fao: Brian Wright), 8 Balderton St., London W1Y 2BN. tel: (071) 493 4070

P & J Fretwell Ltd, A Mediquip Healthcare Co., Linwell House, 153 Bennett Street, Ardwick, Manchester M13 5BW. tel (061) 274 3711

Gibbs Hartley Cooper Ltd, Chartist Tower, Dock Street, Newport, Dock Street, Newport, Gwent, NP9 1DW. tel: (0633) 250222 *London Office:*(071) 247 5433

Gillmore Travel Services, Gillmour House, Blennerhasset, Carlisle, Cumbria CA5 3RE. tel: (0965) 21553

Gowrings Mobility International, The Old Barn, 18-21 Church Gate, Thatcham, Berks, RG13 4PH tel: (0635) 71502

GP Special Projects Ltd, 69 West Hill, Portishead, Bristol BS20 9LG. tel: (0272) 842322

Grayston Engineering Ltd., 41 Stonecot Hill, Sutton, Surrey SM3 9HH. tel: (081) 641 4053

Greater London Association for Disbaled People, 336 Brixton Road, London SW9 7AA. tel: (071) 274 0107

Greenbank Project Co-Operatives, Edwards Lane, Speke, Liverpool, L24 9HG tel: (051) 486 3525

Guidosimplex UK, PO Box 57, Stirling, Scotland FK7 7YH. tel: (0786) 61900

Helping Hands Shop,114 Queens Road, Leicester LE2 3AD. tel: (0533) 708821

PC Henderson Ltd, Tangent Works, Harold Hill, Romford, Essex RM3 8UL. tel: (040 23) 45555/40101

Henerson Mobile, Henderson Doors Ltd, Ashton Road, Harold Hill, Romford, Essex, RM3 8UL. tel: (04023) 81466

Hertfordshire Association for the Disabled, The Woodside Centre, The Commons, Welwyn Garden City, Herts, AL7 4DD. tel: (0707) 324581

Hertz, 4th & 5th Floors, Radnor House, 1272 London Road, London SW16 4XW. tel: (081) 679 1777/679 1799

CF Hewerdine Ltd, Devels Lane, Thorpe Lea, Egham, Surrey, TW20 8HF. tel: (0784) 451258/9

DG Hodge & Son Ltd, Feathers Lane, Hythe End, Wraysbury, Staines, Middlesex TW19 5AN. tel: (078 481) 3580

Hollingbourne Hire, 38 Culpeper House, Hollingbourne, Kent, ME17 1UE. tel: (062 780) 308

VB Hughes & Son Ltd, 44 Littleton Road, Ashford, Middlesex. tel: (0784) 243370/244997

Indespension Ltd, Belmont Road, Bolton, BL1 7AQ. tel: (0204) 58434

Interbility Ltd, 5 Badminton Close, Bragbury End, Stevenage, Herts SG2 8SR. tel: (0438) 813365

Intercounty (East Coast) Private Ambulance Service Ltd, 22a, Church Street, Harwich, Essex CO12 3DS. tel: (0255) 553152

Interstyl, Park Farm, Compton Verney, Warwick, CV35 9HJ. tel: (0926) 640241

Invatravel, 66 Knob Hall Lane, Southport, PR9 9QS. tel: (0704) 231081

Joint Committee on Mobility for the Disabled - c/o Tim Shapley (Hon Sec), 9 Moss Close, Pinner, Middlesex, HA5 3AY. tel: (081) 866 7884

K C Mobility Services, Unit 4A, Victoria Mills, Bradford Road, Batley, West Yorkshire WF17 8LN. Tel: (0924) 442386

Kemfab, Keith Evans Motors, Unit 21, Arches Industrial Estate, Spon End, Coventry CV1 3JQ. tel: (0203) 714193

Kenning Car & Van Rental, 477/479 Green Lanes, Palmers Green, London N13 4BS. tel: (081) 882 3576

Mr Harry King, 16 Newbridge Road, Tiptree, Essex CO5 0HS. tel: (0621) 819016

King Door Products Ltd, Hammond Avenue, Whitehall Industrial Estate, Reddish, Stockport, Cheshire SK4 1PQ. tel: (061) 429 0990

Bernard J Knibbs Insurance Ltd, 66 Boutport Street, Barnstaple, North Eveon EX31 1HG. tel: (0271) 45005

Krausz-Harari Ltd, 87 Ravensdale Road, London N16 6TH. tel: (081) 800 700

Leisure Vehicles, Brook Cottage, Stainsby, Nr Heath, Chesterfield, Derbyshire S44 5NR. tel: (0246) 851454

Lest We Forget Association - c/o Hon Transport Officer, 14 Alric Avenue, New Malden, Surrey, KT3 4JN. tel: (081) 942 5131

London Country Bus (NW) Ltd, Coaching Office, St Albans Road, Garston, Herts WD2 6NN. tel: (0923) 662113

London Garage Doors Ltd, 320 West Barnes Lane, Motspur Park, New Malden, Surrey KT3 6NB. tel: (081) 942 3186/(081) 949 6608

London Regional Transport, Unit for Disabled Passengers, 55 Broadway, London SW1H 0BD. tel: (071) 227 3176/3299

London Taxis International Ltd, 15 Cornwath Road, Fulham, London SW6 3HP. tel: (071) 731 1341

Gerard Mann, 15 Charles Henry Street, Birmingham B12 0SN. tel: (021) 622 3031

Tony Mason Ltd, Great Central Way, Woodford Halse, Daventry, Northants, NN11 6PZ. tel: (0327) 61771

Maund McLeonards & Co Ltd, CTS Department, 16 Romsey Road, Eastleigh, Hants, SO4 4YP. tel: (0703) 620007

Meditech Developments Ltd, 1 Crocus Place, Crocus Street, Nottingham. tel: (0602) 863263 or 784194

Mellor Coachcraft, Miall Street, Rochdale, Lancs OL11 1BU. tel: (0706) 860610

Metair Aircraft Equipment Ltd, The Air Station, West Malling, Kent, ME19 6PP. tel: (0732) 848555

Metro Products (Accessories & Leisure) Ltd, Eastman House, 98-102 Station Road East, Oxted, Surrey RH8 0AY. tel: (0883) 717644

CG Miller & Son, 4 Seuchie Bank, Russell Road Industrial Estate, Edinburgh, EH11 2NW. tel: (031) 337 8533

Donald Miller & Sons Ltd, Spring Street Garage, Bridgehouse, West Yorks HD6 1BB. tel: (0484) 712222

Millers Coaches, 18 Cambridge Road, Foxton, Cambs, CB2 6SH. tel: (0223) 870220

Millers Coaches, 18 Cambridge Road, Foxton, Cambs, CB2 6SH. tel: (0223) 870220

Minibus Options Ltd, PO Box 4, Macclesfield, Cheshire SK10 5EW. tel: (0625) 75859

Mobile Access Services, PO Box 213, Winslow, Buckingham, Bucks, MK18 1NX. tel: (029 671) 3169

Mobility Advice & Vehicle Information Service, Department of Transport, TRRL, Old Wokingham Road, Crowthorne, Berks RG11 6AU. tel: (0344) 770456

Mobility Engineering Design, 114 Norbury Hill, London SW16 3RT. tel: (081) 764 6023

Mobility Information Service, National Mobility Centre, Unit 2a Atcham Estate, Shrewsbury, SY4 4UG. tel: (0743) 75889

Mobility Trust, 4 Hughes Mews, 143a Chatham Road, London Sw11 6HJ. tel: (071) 924 3597 or (081) 672 9170 *(weekends/evenings)*

Moorhouse Technology Ltd, 30 New Road, Moortown, Ringwood, Hants, BH2 3AU. tel: (042 54) 72983

Motability, Gate House, West Gate, The High, Harlow, CM20 1HR. tel: (0279) 635666

Motor Services Manchester Ltd, Royal Works, Canal Side, Edge Lane, Stretford, Manchester M32 8HS. tel: (061) 865 6922

National Advisory Unit for Community Transport, Keymer Street, Beswick, Manchester, M11 3FY. tel: (061) 273 6038

National Beakdown Recovery Club, PO Box 300, Leeds, LS99 2LZ. tel: (0532) 393606

Natural Power Systems Ltd, 40 Sanderstead Road, Croydon, Surrey, CR2 0PA. tel: (081) 688 5572

Neatwork, Bespoke Technology, The Lees Stables, Coldstream, Scotland TD12 4NN. tel: (0890) 2709 or 3167

Neill & Bennett, 7 Wyngate Road, Cheadle Hulme, Cheadle, Cheshire SK8 6ER: (061) 485 3149

Nissan UK Ltd, Nissan House, Worthing, Sussex, BN13 3HD. tel: (0903) 68561

Oatia Vehicle Conversions, Unit 1b, Quarry Wood Industrial Estate, Aylesford, Maidstone ME20 7TQ. tel: (0622) 882122

Optare, Crossgates Carriageworks, Manston Lane, Leeds LS15 8SU. tel: (0532) 645182

Brian Page Controls, 18 Pooley Green Road, Egham, Surrey, TW20 8AF. tel: (0784) 35850

T Parry (Car Hoists), 1 Church Avenue, Bangor-Is-y-Coed, Wrexham, Clwyd LL13 0AF.

WR Pashley Ltd, Masons Road, Stratford-upon-Avon, Warwks CV37 9NL. tel: (0789) 292263

WH Perry Ltd, Mike Bowkett, 51-55 High Street, Edgware, Middlesex, HA8 7DZ. tel: (081) 952 2353

Pilcher-Greene Ltd, Consort Way, Burgess Hill, West Sussex RH15 9NA. tel: (04446) 5707/8/9

Pioneer Seating, 18 Thorburn Road, Northampton NN3 3DA. tel: (0604) 411659

PMT Ltd., 33 Woodhouse Street, Stoke-on-Trent, Staffs ST4 1EQ. tel: (0782) 744744

Power Lifts Ltd, Hadley Works, Caxton Way, Holywell Industrial Estate, Watford WD1 8TJ. tel: (0923) 227724

Poynting Conversions, Faraday Road, Churchfields Industrial Estate, Salisbury, Wilts, SP2 7NR. tel: (0722) 336048

The Private Ambulance Co Ltd & Junesco Ambulance Services, (rear of) 48 Horn Lane, Acton, London W3 6NP. tel: (081) 992 9988

Quickstep Ltd, Chichester Road, Ponswood, Hastings, East Sussex TN34 1YS. tel: (0424) 434202

RAC Motoring Services Ltd, RAC House, Lansdowne Road, Croydon, Surrey, CR9 2JA. tel: (081) 686 2525 ext 2462

Ratcliff Tail Lifts Ltd, Bessemer Road, Welwyn Garden City, Herts, AL7 1ET. tel: (0707) 325571

Reeve Burgess Ltd, Bridge Street, Pilsley, Chesterfield, Derbyshire S45 8HF. tel: (0773) 872292

Remploy Ltd (Wheelchair Div), 11 Nunnery Drive, Sheffield S2 1TA. tel: (0742) 757631

Renault UK Ltd, Western Avenue, London W3 0RZ. tel: (081) 992 3481/5544

Reselco Engineering Ltd, Kew Bridge Pump Station, Green Dragon House, Brentford, Middlesex TW8 0EN. tel: (01) 847 4509

Restall Bros Ltd, No. 1 Factory, Anne Road, Smethwick, Warley, West Midlands, B66 2NZ. tel: (021) 558 4761

Richards & Shaw (Trim) Ltd., Units 3-6, Lodge Forge Trading Estate, Cradley Road, Cradley Heath, Warley, West Midlands B64 7RW. tel: (0384) 633800

Ridley Electronics Ltd, 206 Wightman Road, Hornsey, London N8 0BU. tel: (081) 340 9501

Rifton & Community Playthings, Robertsbridge, East Sussex, TN32 5DR. tel: (0580) 880626

Robin Hood Vehicle Builders Ltd., 7 Crompton Way, Segensworth Industrial Estate West, Fareham, Hants PO15 5SP. tel: (04895) 82211

Rolac Ltd, Unit 16, Enterprise Centre 2, Chester Street, Stockport, SK3 0BR. tel: (061) 429 8477

Rompa (Flexus Plastics Ltd), PO Box 5, Wheatbridge Road, Chesterfield, Derbyshire S40 2AE. tel: (0246) 211777

Ross & Bonnyman Ltd, Unit 10, Hyatt Trading Estate, Stevenage, Herts. tel: (0438) 728551

Ross Auto Engineering Ltd (Southport), 27 Banastre Road, Southport, Lancs PR8 5AS. tel: (0704) 35757

Royal Association For Disability & Rehabilitation, 25 Mortimer Street, London W1N 8AB. tel: (071) 637 5400

Royal British Legion, Taxi Drivers Training School, Brixton Estate, 1-3 Brixton Road, London SW9 6DE. tel: (071) 735 8423

Royal National Institute for the Blind (Peterborough), Production & Distrivution Centre, Bakewell Road, Orton Southgate, Peterborough PE2 0XU. tel: (0733) 370 777

Saab Great Britain Ltd, Saab House, Globe Park, Marlow, Bucks SL7 1LY. tel: (062 84) 6977

Saginaw Steering Gear Sales Office, PO Box 4, High Street North, Dunstable, Beds LU6 1BQ. tel: (0582) 666971

Salvador Caetano UK Ltd, Mill Lane, Heather, Nr Ibstock, Leics LE6 1QE. tel: (0530) 63333

Securon Amersham Ltd, Winchmore Hill, Amersham, Bucks, HP7 0NZ. tel: (0494) 434455

SEM Canterbury, South Essex Motors (Basildon) Ltd, Swinborne Road, Burnt Mills Industrial Estate, Basildon, Essex, SS13 1EF. tel: (0268) 727603

Servicecall Systems Ltd, Millford Lane, Bakewell, Derbyshire DE4 1DX. tel: (0629) 812422

Slave-Dor Ltd, Control House, 9 Station Road, Radlett, Herts. WD7 8JY. tel: (092 76) 3866

Snowchains Euro-Products, West Kingsdown Industrial Estate, London Road, Kingsdown, Sevenoaks, Kent TN15 6EL. tel: (047 485) 3221

Sochulbus, White House Garage, Ashford Ltd, Kingston Road, Ashford, Middlesex TW15 3SE. tel: (0784) 243264

Special Vehicle Designs Ltd, Revenstone Rd Industrial Estate, Coalville, Leice LE6 2NB. tel: (0530) 510880

Speedograph Ltd, Seats Division, 104 Rollestone Rd Industrial Estate, Coalville, Leics LE6 2NB. tel: (0530) 510880

Speedograph Ltd, Seats Division, 104 Rolleston Drive, Arnold, Nottingham, NG5 7JR. tel: (0602) 264235

Speedworld Ltd, 22 Clifron Gardens, London N15 6AP. tel: (081) 800 6912

Spruce Howlett & Co Ltd, Trowse, Norwich, Norfolk, NR14 8SY. tel: (0603) 615100 contact: Richard Moakes

Steedrive Ltd, Queens Avenue, Hurdfield Industrial Estate, Macclesfield, Cheshire SK10 2BN. tel: (0625) 616752

Steering Developments Ltd, Unit 3, Eastman Way, Hemel Hempstead, Herts, HP2 7HF. tel: (0442) 212918

Stormont Vehicle Hire Ltd, Otford Road, Sevenoaks, Kent TN14 5EG. tel: (0732) 458000

Stylex Motor Products Ltd, Boby Industrial Estate, Bury St Edmunds, Suffolk, IP33 3PL. tel: (0284) 701666

Sunstar Travel Worldwide Ltd, Unit 13, Gateway Estates, Hythe Road, London NW10 6RJ. tel: (081) 969 0363

Rod Surrage Appeal Fund, 1 Johnston Green, Guildford, Surrey GU2 6XS. tel: 0483) 233640

SVO Ltd, Lottage Road, Aldbourne, Nr Marlborough, Wiltshire SN8 2EB. tel: (0672) 40001

SWS Motor Bodies, Unit 9, Hartford House, Newport Road/Weston Street, Bolton, Lancs. tel: (0204) 395660

Taylor Lightfoot Transport Consultancy, John Taylor, 27 Windsor Road, Levenshulme, Manchester M19 2FA. tel: (061) 225 3141

TGA Electric Leisure, Bells Lane, Glemsford, Sudbury, Suffolk CO10 1QA. tel: (0787) 280820

Topper Cases Ltd, St Peters Hill, Huntingdon, Cambs, PE18 7ET. tel: (0840) 57251

William Towns Ltd, Park Farm, Compton Verney, Warwks CV35 9HJ. tel: (0926) 640241

Transport Seating Ltd, 179 New Town Row, Birmingham B6 4QZ. tel: (021) 359 2155/7617

Tremorvah Industries, Rentoul Works, Three Milestone Industrial Estate, Truro, Cornwall, TR4 9LD. tel: (0872) 40036

Triscope, 63 Esmond Road, London W4 1JE. tel: (081) 994 9294

Tyser (UK) Ltd, Acorn House, Great Oak, Basildon, Essex, SS14 1AL. tel: (0268) 284361

CN Unwin Ltd, Lufton, Yeovil, Somerset, BA22 8SZ. tel: (0935) 75359

Vauxhall Motability Programme, PO Box 159, Dunstable, Beds LU5 5TE. tel: (0852) 472472

Vauxhall Motors Ltd, PO Box 3, No 3, Luton LU2 0SY. tel: (058242) 6584/6525

Virtex Ltd, 457-463 Caledonian Road, London N7 9BB. tel: (071) 609 0011

Volvo Concessionaires Ltd, Special Vehicles Dept, Parkway, Globe Park, Marlow SL7 1YQ. tel: (062 84) 77977

Wadham Stringer Coachbuilders Ltd, Hambledon Road, Waterlooville, Portsmouth PO7 7UA. tel: (0705) 258211

Wales Disabled Drivers Assessment Centre, 18 Plasnewydd, Whitchurch, Cardiff. tel: (0222) 615276

Wards Mobility Services Ltd, Ware Works, Bells Yew Green, Tunbridge Wells, TN3 9BD. tel: (089 275) 686

Whitacres Stoke on Trent Ltd, Clough Street, Hanley, Stoke on Trent, Staffs ST1 4BA. tel: (0782) 281365

Martin Williams, Pantygollen, Whitland, Dyfed, Wales SA34 0RR. tel: (0994) 240566

Winton Marketing, Winton House, Common Hill, Medstead, Hants GU34 5LZ. tel: (0420) 63770

Wood & Picket of London, Queensbury Road, Wembley, Middlesex HA0 1PG. tel: (081) 998 2127

Wrights of Wishaw Ltd, 10 Netherdale Road, Netherton Industrial Estate, Wishaw, Lanarkshire ML2 0ER. tel: (0698) 355577

WRK (Marketing), Ashfield House, School Road, St Johns Fen End, Wisbech, Cambs. tel: (0945) 880014

Women Royal Voluntary Service Escort Service, 233-244 Stockwell Road, London SW9 9SP. tel: (071) 733 338

Zell-Em Ltd, 210 Watson Road, Blackpool, Lancs, FY4 3EF. tel: (0253) 45287

Zemco Ltd, 509 Walsgrave Road, Coventry CV2 4AG. tel: (0203) 441428

WALKING AIDS

Alarmagrip, Forge House, Wish Street, Rye, East Sussex TN31 7DA. tel: TN31 7DA. tel: (0797) 224330

Aremco, Grove House, Lenham, Kent, ME17 2PX. tel: (0622) 858502

ASM Medicare, Picow Farm Industrial Estate, Runcorn, Cheshire WA7 4UG. tel: (09285) 74301/2/3

Atlantech Medical, The Forge, High Street, Cromer, Stevenage, Hertfordshire SG2 7QA. tel: (043 886)628/9

Banwell Ltd, 115 Lentons Lane, Coventry, West Midlands, CV2 1NY. tel: (0203) 610257

Beacon Developments Ltd, 105 Station Road, Ashwell, Baldock, Hertfordshire, SG7 5LT. tel: (046 274) 2214

Boots the Chemist Ltd, City Gate, Toll House Hill, Nottingham NG2 3AA tel: (0602) 418522 *enquires should be made at local branches*

Camp Ltd, Northgate House, Staple Gardens, Winchester, Hampshire, S023 8ST. tel: (0962) 55248

Caray Associates, Castlewood, Chute Forest, Andover, Hampshire SP11 9DG. tel: (026470) 659

Carters (J&A) Ltd, Alfred Street, Westbury, Wilshire, BA13 3DZ. tel: (0373) 822203

Central Medical Equipment, 7 Ascot Park Estate, Lenton Street, Sandiacre, Nottingham, NG10 5DL. tel: (0602) 390949

Chattanooga UK Ltd, Unit 1 & 2, Goods Road, Belper, Derbyshire DE5 1UU. tel: (07382) 6993/4

Chester-Care Ltd, 16, Englands Lane, London, NW3 4TG. tel: (071) 586 2166 or (071) 722 3430

Collinson, AJ Ltd, Castle Trading Estate, Porchester, Hants, PO16 9SF. tel: (0705) 379392

Cooper & Sons Ltd, Wormley, Godalming, Surrey, GU8 5SY. tel: (042 879) 2251

Davies, Theo M, Argoed, Glyn Ceiriog, Llangollen, Clwyd, LL20 7HN. tel: (069 172) 218

Days Medical Aids Ltd, Litchard Industrial Estate, Bridgend, Mid-Glamorgan, CF31 2AL tel (056) 57495/60150

Design Marketing Ltd, London House, London Street, Andover, Hampshire SP10 2QX. tel: (0264) 58036

Drove Precision Engineering, Hargreaves Road, Highfield Industrial Estate, Eastbourne, East Sussex BN23 6QL. tel: (0323) 507701

Ellis Son & Paramore Ltd, Spring Street Works, Sheffield, South Yorkshire, S3 8PB. tel: (0742) 738921

ESLA, Freepost, London SW16 2BR. tel: none given.

Flipstick International Ltd., Cobham Road, Pershore, Worcestershire WR10 2EY. tel: (0386) 554836

T Fox and Co Ltd, Head Office, 118 London Wall, London EC2Y 5JA. tel: (071) 606 4720

W Freeman & Co Ltd, Suba-Seal Works, Staincross, Barnsley, South Yorkshire, S75 6DH. tel: (0226) 284081

Goldene Designs Ltd, 7c Moss Lane, Whitefield, Manchester, M25 7QE. tel: (061) 796 9367

Health & Comfort Ltd, PO Box 15, Westbury, Wiltshire, BA13 4LS tel: (0373) 822394

The Helping Hand Company (Ledbury) Ltd, Unit 9L, Bromyard Road Trading Estate, Ledbury, Hertfordshire HR8 1NS. tel: (0531) 5678

Hestair Maclaren Ltd, Station Works, Long Buckby, Northampton NN6 7PF. tel (0327) 842662

Homecraft Supplies Ltd, Low Moor Estate, Kirkby-in-Ashfield, Notts NG17 7JZ. tel: (0623) 754 047

Independent Living Centre, 9 Caldecote Gardens, Bushey Heath, Herts WD2 3RA. tel: (081) 950 6635

Jasper Products, PO Box 22, Stratford-upon-Avon, Warwickshire. tel: (0203) 687235 *(office)*, (0789) 67086 *(home-Mr Skelcher)*

Jenx Ltd, 74 Hoyland Road, Sheffield, South Yorkshire, S3 8AB. tel: (0742) 756312

Joncare Ltd, 7 Ashville Trading Estate, Nuffield Way, Abingdon, Oxon OX14 1RL. tel: (0235) 28120/35600

Lanfold Healthcare Ltd, Unit 18, Vanguard Way, Vanguards Industrial Estate, Shoeburyness, Essex SS3 9QY. tel: (0702) 297388

Llewellyn Health Care Services, Regent House, 1 Regent Road, City, Liverpool L3 7BX. tel: (051) 236 5311

Magnacraft, Slipway Building, Penton Hook, Staines Road, Chertsey, Surrey, KT16 8PP. tel: (0932) 568888

Martek Ltd, PO Box 20, Redruth, Cornwall, TR15 2UF. tel: (0209) 219911

Midlands Engineering Tools Co., PO Box 163, Breaston, Derbyshire DE7 3UN. tel: (03317) 2510

Nomeq, 23/24 Thornhill Road, North Moons Moat, Redditch, Worcestershire, B98 9ND. tel: (0527) 64222

Nottingham Rehab Ltd, 17 Ludlow Hill Road, West Bridgford, Nottingham, NG2 6HD. tel: (0602) 23451

Numas Ltd, Unit 1B, New Street Industrial Estate, Stradbroke, Suffolk IP21 5JG. tel: (037984) 8208

Ortho-Med Ltd, 5 Loaning Road, Edinburgh, EH7 6JE. tel: (031) 652 1603

Paraid, Weston Lane, Birmingham, West Midlands, B11 3RS. Tel: (021) 706 3936

Poole Flexlink, Timberland House, 46 Horncastle Road, Woodhall Spa, Lincolnshire, LN10 6UZ. tel: (0526) 52809

Prince & Fletcher Ltd, Bonding House, 26 Blackfriars Street, Manchester, Gt. Manchester, tel: (061) 834 5573

Proudline Associates Ltd, 16 Smithbarn, Horsham, W Sussex, RH13 6EB. tel: (0403) 41123

Pryor & Howard Ltd, 39 Willow Lane, Mitcham, Surrey, CR4 4US. tel: (081) 648 1177

Rainbow Rehab, PO Box 546, Bournemouth BH8 8YD tel: (0202) 32651

John Reid & Sons (Strucsteel) Ltd., Strucsteel Works, Mill Road, Christchurch, Dorset BH23 2LT. tel: (0202) 483333

Renray Group Ltd, Road Five, Winsford Industrial Estate, Winsord, Cheshire CW7 3RB. tel: (0606) 593456

Remploy Ltd (Medical Products Div) & Head Office, 415 Edgware Road, Cricklewood, London NW2 6LR. tel: (081) 452 8020

Rifton & Community Playthings, Robertsbridge, East Sussex, TN32 5DR. tel: (0580) 880626

Ringwood Precision Engineering, The Close, Ringwood, Hants, BH24 1LA. tel: (042 54) 6296

Bob Rogers, 60 Delph Common Road, Aughton, Ormskirk, Lancs L39 5DW. tel: (0695) 423081

Roma Medical Aids Ltd, Llandow Industrial Estate, Cowbridge, South Glamorgan, CF7 7PB. tel: (044 63) 4519

Royal National Institute for the Blind, 224 Great Portland Street, London, W1N 6AA. tel (071) 388 1266

Salford University - The Secretary, Department of Orthopaedic Mechanics, Salford, Greater Manchester, M5 4WT. tel: (061) 736 5843 ext 7402

Gerald Simonds Wheelchairs Stoke Mandeville, 9 March Place, Gatehouse Way, Aylesbury, HP19 3UG. tel: (0296) 436557

SML Healthcare Ltd, Bath Place, High Street, Barnet, Herts EN5 5XE. tel: (081) 440 6522

James Spencer & Co Ltd, Moor Road Works, Moor Road, Headingley, Leeds, West Yorkshire LS6 4BH. tel: (0532) 785837/741850

Spiro Engineering Ltd, Henson Way, Telford Way Industrial Estate, Northants, NN16 8UU. tel: (0536) 512122

Sunrise Medical Ltd, Fens Pool Avenue, Brierley Hill, West Midlands DY5 1QA. tel: (0384) 263191

Swaine Adeney Brigg & Sons Ltd, 185 Piccadilly, London, W1V 0HA. tel: (071) 734 4277

T & S Motion and Sport, Head Office, Potter Lane, Wellow, Via Newark, Notts NG22 0EB. tel: (0623) 835362

R Taylor & Son. (Orthopaedic) Ltd, Compton Works, 49 Woodwards Road, Pleck, Walsall, WS2 9RN. tel: (0922) 27601

Theramed Ltd, Unit 11, Carlton Park Industrial Estate, Ronald Lane, Saxmundham, Suffolk, P17 2NL. tel: (0493) 751291

Toy & Furniture Workshop, Church Hill, Totland Bay, Isle of Wight, PO39 0ET. tel: (0983) 752596

Uniscan Ltd, 12 Samson House, Arterial Road, Basildon, Essex SS15 6DR. tel: (0268) 419288

WAVES, Corscombe, Nr Dorchester, Dorset, DT2 0NU. tel: (093) 589) 248

Index

Index of Advertisers